The History of the Book in the Middle East

The History of the Book in the East
Series Editor: Peter Kornicki

Titles in the Series:

The History of the Book in East Asia
Cynthia Brokaw and Peter Kornicki

The History of the Book in South Asia
Francesca Orsini

The History of the Book in the Middle East
Geoffrey Roper

The History of the Book in the Middle East

Edited by

Geoffrey Roper

University of Cambridge, UK

Routledge
Taylor & Francis Group
LONDON AND NEW YORK

First published in paperback 2024

First published 2013 by Ashgate Publishing

Published 2016 by Routledge
4 Park Square, Milton Park, Abingdon, Oxon OX14 4RN

and by Routledge
605 Third Avenue, New York, NY 10158

Routledge is an imprint of the Taylor & Francis Group, an informa business

British Library Cataloguing in Publication Data
The history of the book in the Middle East. – (The history
of the book in the East)
1. Books–Middle East–History. 2. Printing–Middle
East–History.
I. Series II. Roper, Geoffrey.
002'.0956-dc23

The Library of Congress has cataloged the printed edition as follows: 2012948368

ISBN: 978-1-4094-3310-1 (hbk)
ISBN: 978-1-03-291828-0 (pbk)
ISBN: 978-1-315-23918-7 (ebk)

DOI: 10.4324/9781315239187

Contents

Acknowledgements ix
Series Preface xiii
Introduction xv

PART I GENERAL AND INTRODUCTORY

1 Michael W. Albin (1985), 'Islamic Book History: Parameters of a Discipline', *International Association of Orientalist Librarians Bulletin*, **26–27**, pp. 13–16. 3
2 Franz Rosenthal (1995), '"Of Making Many Books There Is No End": The Classical Muslim View', G.N. Atiyeh (ed.), *The Book in the Islamic World: The Written Word and Communication in the Middle East*, Albany: State University of New York Press [for] the Library of Congress, pp. 33–55. 7

PART II MANUSCRIPTS

3 Malachi Beit-Arié (2009), 'The Script and Book Craft in the Hebrew Medieval Codex', Piet van Boxel and Sabine Arndt (eds), *Crossing Borders: Hebrew Manuscripts as a Meeting-place of Cultures*, Oxford: Bodleian Library, pp. 21–34. 33
4 Cornell H. Fleischer (1994), 'Between the Lines: Realities of Scribal Life in the Sixteenth Century', C. Heywood and C. Imber (eds), *Studies in Ottoman History in Honour of Professor V.L. Ménage*, Istanbul: Isis, pp. 45–61. 47
5 Theodore C. Petersen (1954), 'Early Islamic Bookbindings and their Coptic Relations', *Ars Orientalis*, **1**, pp. 41–64. 65
6 Jan Just Witkam (1995), 'The Human Element between Text and Reader: The *ijāza* in Arabic Manuscripts', Yasin Dutton (ed.), *The Codicology of Islamic Manuscripts: Proceedings of the Second Conference of Al-Furqān Islamic Heritage Foundation, 4–5 December 1993*, London: Al-Furqān Islamic Heritage Foundation, **15**, pp. 123–36. 89
7 Adam Gacek (1989), 'Technical Practices and Recommendations Recorded by Classical and post-Classical Arabic Scholars Concerning the Copying and Correction of Manuscripts', F. Déroche (ed.), *Les manuscrits du Moyen-Orient: essais de codicologie et paléographie. Actes du Colloque d'Istanbul (Istanbul 1986)*, Istanbul: Institut Français d'Etudes Anatoliennes; Paris: Bibliothèque Nationale, (Varia Turcica, 8), pp. 51–60. 103
8 François Déroche (2007), 'The Copyists' Working Pace: Some Remarks towards a Reflexion on the Economy of the Book in the Islamic World', Judith Peiffer and Manfred Kropp (eds), *Theoretical Approaches to the Transmission and Edition of Oriental Manuscripts. Proceedings of a Symposium held in Istanbul, March 28–30,*

2001, Beirut: Ergon Verlag Würzburg in Kommission (Beiruter Texte und Studien, 111), pp. 203–13. 113

PART III INTRODUCTION OF PRINTING

9 Muhsin Mahdi (1995), 'From the Manuscript Age to the Age of Printed Books', G.N. Atiyeh (ed.), *The Book in the Islamic World: The Written Word and Communication in the Middle East*, Albany: State University of New York Press [for] the Library of Congress, pp. 1–15. 127

10 Orlin Sabev (Orhan Salih) (2010), 'A Virgin Deserving Paradise or a Whore Deserving Poison: Manuscript Tradition and Printed Books in Ottoman Turkish Society', Jaroslav Miller (ed.), *Friars, Nobles and Burghers – Sermons, Images and Prints: Studies of Culture and Society in Early-modern Europe in Memoriam István György Tóth*, László Kontler, Budapest: Central European University Press, pp. 389–409. 143

11 Ian Proudfoot (1997), 'Mass Producing Houri's Moles: or Aesthetics and Choice of Technology in Early Muslim Book Printing', P.G. Riddell and T. Street (eds), *Islam: Essays on Scripture, Thought and Society: A Festschrift in Honour of Anthony H. Johns*, Leiden: Brill (Islamic Philosophy, Theology and Science: Texts and Studies, 28) pp. 161–84. 165

12 Richard W. Bulliet (1987), 'Medieval Arabic *ṭarsh*: A Forgotten Chapter in the History of Printing', *Journal of the American Oriental Society*, **107**, pp. 427–38. 189

13 Stefan Reichmuth, (2001), 'Islamic Reformist Discourse in the Tulip Period (1718–30): Ibrahim Müteferriqa and his Arguments for Printing', Ali Çaksu (ed.), *International Congress on Learning and Education in the Ottoman World, Istanbul, 12–15 April 1999*, Istanbul: Research Centre for Islamic History, Art and Culture (IRCICA) (Studies and Sources on the Ottoman History Series, 6), pp. 149–61. 201

14 Diana Rowland-Smith (1989), 'The Beginnings of Hebrew Printing in Egypt', *British Library Journal*, **15**, pp. 16–22. 215

PART IV PRINTING DEVELOPMENT AND PRINT CULTURE

15 Yaron Ben Na'eh (2001), 'Hebrew Printing Houses in the Ottoman Empire', Gad Nassi (ed.), *Jewish Journalism and Printing Houses in the Ottoman Empire and Modern Turkey*, Istanbul: Isis, pp. 73–96; 141–67. 225

16 Ami Ayalon (2010), 'Arab Booksellers and Bookshops in the Age of Printing, 1850–1914', *British Journal of Middle Eastern Studies*, **37**, pp. 73–93. 277

17 Brinkley Messick (1997), 'On the Question of Lithography', *Culture & History*, **16**, pp. 158–76. 299

18 Orlin Sabev (Orhan Salih) (2009), 'Rich Men, Poor Men: Ottoman Printers and Booksellers Making Fortune or Seeking Survival (Eighteenth–Nineteenth Centuries)', *Oriens*, **37**, pp. 177–90. 319

19 J.S. Szyliowicz (1986), 'Functional Perspectives on Technology: The Case of the Printing Press in the Ottoman Empire', *Archivum Ottomanicum*, **11**, pp. 249–59. 333

20 Reinhard Schulze (1997), 'The Birth of Tradition and Modernity in 18th and 19th Century Islamic Culture – The Case of Printing', *Culture & History*, **16**, pp. 29–72. 345

21 Geoffrey Roper (2007), 'The Printing Press and Change in the Arab World', Sabrina Alcorn Baron, Eric N. Lindquist and Eleanor F. Shevlin (eds), *Agent of Change: Print Culture Studies after Elizabeth L. Eisenstein*, Amherst and Boston: University of Massachusetts Press, in association with the Center for the Study of the Book, Library of Congress, pp. 250–67. 389

22 H.A. Avakian (1978), 'Islam and the Art of Printing', *Uit bibliotheektuin en informatieveld*, Utrecht, pp. 256–69. 407

23 Reinhard Schulze (1987), 'Mass Culture and Islamic Cultural Production in 19th Century Middle East', Georg Stauth and Sami Zubaida (eds), *Mass Culture, Popular Culture, and Social Life in the Middle East*, Frankfurt am Main: Campus Verlag, pp. 189–222. 421

24 Johann Strauss (2003), 'Who Read What in the Ottoman Empire (19th–20th Centuries)?', *Middle Eastern Literatures*, **6**, pp. 39–76. 455

25 Ami Ayalon (2005), 'The Beginnings of Publishing in pre-1948 Palestine', Philip Sadgrove (ed.), *History of Printing and Publishing in the Languages and Countries of the Middle East*, Oxford: Oxford University Press, pp. 69–80. 493

26 Meliné Pehlivanian (2002), 'Mesrop's Heirs: The Early Armenian Book Printers', Eva Hanebutt-Benz, Dagmar Glass and Geoffrey Roper (eds), *Middle Eastern Languages and the Print Revolution: A Cross-Cultural Encounter*, Westhofen: Skulima, pp. 53–92. 505

27 J.F. Coakley (1995), 'Edward Breath and the Typography of Syriac', *Harvard Library Bulletin*, n.s., **6**, pp. 41–64. 545

Name Index 569

Acknowledgements

Ashgate would like to thank our researchers and the contributing authors who provided copies, along with the following for their permission to reprint copyright material.

Michael Albin for the essay: Michael W. Albin (1985), 'Islamic Book History: Parameters of a Discipline', *International Association of Orientalist Librarians Bulletin*, **26–27**, pp. 13–16.

Malachi Beit-Arié for the essay: Malachi Beit-Arié (2009), 'The Script and Book Craft in the Hebrew Medieval Codex', in Piet van Boxel and Sabine Arndt (eds), *Crossing Borders: Hebrew Manuscripts as a Meeting-place of Cultures*, Oxford: Bodleian Library, pp. 21–34. Copyright © 2009 Malachi Beit-Arié.

Richard W. Bulliet for the essay: Richard W. Bulliet (1987), 'Medieval Arabic *ṭarsh*: A Forgotten Chapter in the History of Printing', *Journal of the American Oriental Society*, **107**, pp. 427–38. Copyright © 1987 Richard W. Bulliet.

Bodleian Library, Oxford for the images: Fragment of the Hebrew text of the book of Ecclesiastes (ch. 40) from the Cairo Genizah; Rotulus, book roll preceding the codex form. Liturgical text from the Cairo Genizah; Avicenna's *Canon of Medicine* (in Arabic); Nahmanides, *Torat ha-Adam*, a comprehensive monograph on all the laws concerning death and mourning written in cursive Sephardic script (Spain, 1330); Al-Khushani, *Book of the Judges of Cordoba*; Hebrew Pentateuch written in Italian semi-cursive script (Florence, between 1441–1468); *Dinim* (ritual decisions) according to Rabbi Meir of Rothenburg; Latin missal written in a Gothic script (Bohemia or Moravia, fourteenth century); Geo-cultural entities of Hebrew medieval manuscripts indicated on a portoan chart by Bartholomeo Olives of Majorca (1575); Maimonides' autograph draft of his legal code, *Mishneh Torah*, in cursive Sephardic script (Egypt, c. 1180).

Brill for the essays: Ian Proudfoot (1997), 'Mass Producing Houri's Moles: or Aesthetics and Choice of Technology in Early Muslim Book Printing', in P.G. Riddell and T. Street (eds), *Islam: Essays on Scripture, Thought and Society: A festschrift in honour of Anthony H. Johns*, Leiden: Brill (Islamic Philosophy, Theology and Science: Texts and Studies, 28) pp. 161–84. Copyright © 1997 by Koninklijke Brill, Leiden, The Netherlands; Orlin Sabev (Orhan Salih) (2009), 'Rich Men, Poor Men: Ottoman Printers and Booksellers Making Fortune or Seeking Survival (Eighteenth–Nineteenth Centuries)', *Oriens*, **37**, pp. 177–90. Copyright © 2009 by Koninklijke Brill, Leiden, The Netherlands.

Campus Verlag for the essay: Reinhard Schulze (1987), 'Mass Culture and Islamic Cultural Production in 19th Century Middle East', Georg Stauth and Sami Zubaida (eds), *Mass Culture, Popular Culture, and Social Life in the Middle East*, Frankfurt am Main: Campus Verlag, pp. 189–222. Copyright © 1987 in Frankfurt am Main by Campus Verlag.

Central European University Press for the essay: Orlin Sabev (Orhan Salih) (2010), 'A Virgin Deserving Paradise or a Whore Deserving Poison: Manuscript Tradition and Printed Books in Ottoman Turkish Society', Jaroslav Miller (ed.), *Friars, Nobles and Burghers – Sermons, Images and Prints: Studies of Culture and Society in Early-modern Europe in Memoriam István György Tóth*, László Kontler, Budapest: Central European University Press, pp. 389–409. Copyright © 2010 Jaroslav Miller and László Kontler.

Corpus Christi College, Oxford for the image: Records of debts in Judeo-Arabic on the blank pages of as Ashkenazic prayer book (c. 1200).

Harvard College for the essay: J.F. Coakley (1995), 'Edward Breath and the Typography of Syriac', *Harvard Library Bulletin*, n.s., **6**, pp. 41–64.

Institut Français d'Etudes Anatoliennes for the essay: Adam Gacek (1989), 'Technical Practices and Recommendations Recorded by Classical and post-Classical Arabic Scholars Concerning the Copying and Correction of Manuscripts', F. Déroche (ed.), *Les manuscrits du Moyen-Orient: essais de codicologie et paléographie. Actes du Colloque d'Istanbul (Istanbul 1986).* Istanbul: Institut Français d'Etudes Anatoliennes; Paris: Bibliothèque Nationale, (Varia Turcica, 8), pp. 51–60. Copyright © 1989 Institut Français d'Etudes Anatoliennes et Bibliothèque Nationale, Paris.

The Isis Press for the essays: Cornell H. Fleischer (1994), 'Between the Lines: Realities of Scribal Life in the Sixteenth Century', C. Heywood and C. Imber (eds), *Studies in Ottoman History in Honour of Professor V.L. Ménage*, Istanbul: Isis, pp. 45–61; Yaron Ben Na'eh (2001), 'Hebrew Printing Houses in the Ottoman Empire', Gad Nassi (ed.), *Jewish Journalism and Printing Houses in the Ottoman Empire and Modern Turkey*, Istanbul: Isis, pp. 73–96; 141–67.

Orient-Institut Beirut for the essay: François Déroche (2007), 'The Copyists' Working Pace: Some Remarks towards a Reflexion on the Economy of the Book in the Islamic World', Judith Peiffer and Manfred Kropp (eds), *Theoretical Approaches to the Transmission and Edition of Oriental Manuscripts. Proceedings of a Symposium held in Istanbul, March 28–30, 2001*, Beirut: Ergon Verlag Würzburg in Kommission (Beiruter Texte und Studien, 111), pp. 203–13. Copyright © 2007 Orient-Institut Beirut.

Oxford University Press for the essay: Ami Ayalon (2005), 'The Beginnings of Publishing in pre-1948 Palestine', Philip Sadgrove (ed.), *History of Printing and Publishing in the Languages and Countries of the Middle East*, Oxford: Oxford University Press. 2005, pp. 69–80. Copyright © 2005 The University of Manchester.

Meliné Pehlivanian for the essay: Meliné Pehlivanian (2002), 'Mesrop's Heirs: The Early Armenian Book Printers', Eva Hanebutt-Benz, Dagmar Glass and Geoffrey Roper (eds), *Middle Eastern Languages and the Print Revolution: A Cross-Cultural Encounter*, Westhofen: Skulima, pp. 53–92.

Research Centre for Islamic History, Art and Culture (IRCICA) for the essay: Stefan Reichmuth (2001), 'Islamic Reformist Discourse in the Tulip Period (1718–30): Ibrahim Müteferriqa and his Arguments for Printing', Ali Çaksu (ed.), *International Congress on Learning and Education in the Ottoman World, Istanbul, 12–15 April 1999*, Istanbul: Research Centre for Islamic History, Art and Culture (IRCICA) (Studies and Sources on the Ottoman History Series, 6), pp. 149–61.

Diana Rowland-Smith for the essay: Diana Rowland-Smith (1989), 'The Beginnings of Hebrew Printing in Egypt', *British Library Journal*, **15**, pp. 16–22. Copyright © 1989 Diana Rowland-Smith.

The Smithsonian Institution for the essay: Theodore C. Petersen (1954), 'Early Islamic Bookbindings and their Coptic Relations', *Ars Orientalis*, **1**, pp. 41–64. Copyright © 1954 Freer Gallery of Art, Smithsonian Institution. All rights reserved.

Springer Media for the essay: H.A. Avakian (1978), 'Islam and the Art of Printing', *Uit bibliotheektuin en informatieveld*, Utrecht, pp. 256–69. Copyright © 1978 Universiteitsbibliotheck, Utrecht.

State University of New York (SUNY) Press for the essays: Franz Rosenthal (1995), '"Of Making Many Books There Is No End": The Classical Muslim View', G.N. Atiyeh (ed.), *The Book in the Islamic World: The Written Word and Communication in the Middle East*, Albany: State University of New York Press [for] the Library of Congress, pp. 33–55. Copyright © 1995 State University of New York; Muhsin Mahdi (1995), 'From the Manuscript Age to the Age of Printed Books', *The Book in the Islamic World: The Written Word and Communication in the Middle East*, G.N. Atiyeh (ed.), Albany: State University of New York Press [for] the Library of Congress, pp. 1–15. Copyright © 1995 State University of New York.

J.S. Szyliowicz for the essay: J.S. Szyliowicz (1986), 'Functional Perspectives on Technology: The Case of the Printing Press in the Ottoman Empire', *Archivum Ottomanicum*, **11**, pp. 249–59. Copyright © 1986 J.S. Szyliowicz.

Taylor and Francis for the essays: Ami Ayalon (2010), 'Arab Booksellers and Bookshops in the Age of Printing, 1850–1914', *British Journal of Middle Eastern Studies*, **37**, pp. 73–93. Copyright © 2010 British Society of Middle Eastern Studies; Johann Strauss (2003), 'Who Read What in the Ottoman Empire (19th–20th centuries)?', *Middle Eastern Literatures*, **6**, pp. 39–76. Copyright © 2003 Taylor and Francis Ltd.

University of Massachusetts Press for the essay: Geoffrey Roper (2007), 'The Printing Press and Change in the Arab World', Sabrina Alcorn Baron, Eric N. Lindquist and Eleanor F. Shevlin (eds), *Agent of Change: Print Culture Studies after Elizabeth L. Eisenstein*, Amherst and Boston: University of Massachusetts Press, in association with the Center for the Study of the Book, Library of Congress, pp. 250–67. Copyright © 2007 University of Massachusetts Press.

Jan Just Witkam for the essay: Jan Just Witkam (1995), 'The Human Element between Text and Reader: The *ijāza* in Arabic Manuscripts', Yasin Dutton (ed.), *The Codicology of Islamic Manuscripts: Proceedings of the Second Conference of Al-Furqān Islamic Heritage*

Foundation, 4–5 December 1993, London: Al-Furqān Islamic Heritage Foundation, **15**, pp. 123–36. Copyright © 1995 Jan Just Witkam.

Every effort has been made to trace all the copyright holders, but if any have been inadvertently overlooked the publishers will be pleased to make the necessary arrangement at the first opportunity.

Publisher's Note

The material in this volume has been reproduced using the facsimile method. This means we can retain the original pagination to facilitate easy and correct citation of the original essays. It also explains the variety of typefaces, page layouts and numbering.

Series Preface

This series on the history of the book in the East focuses attention on three areas of the world which for a long time have been undeservedly left on the margins of the global history of the book: the Middle East, South Asia and East Asia. The importance of these three regions lies not only in the sheer antiquity of printing in East Asia, where both movable type and wood blocks were used centuries before Gutenberg's invention changed the face of book production in Europe, but also in the manuscript traditions and very different responses to printing technology in the Middle East and South Asia. This series forms an important counterbalance to the Eurocentrism of the history of the book as practised in the West.

The three volumes are edited by renowned experts in the field and each includes an introduction which provides an overview of research. The series offers a significant benefit to students, lecturers and libraries as it brings together articles from disparate journals which are often difficult to locate and of limited access. Students are thus able to study leading articles side by side for comparison whilst lecturers are provided with an invaluable 'one-stop' teaching resource.

PETER KORNICKI
Series Editor
University of Cambridge, UK

Introduction

The Origins of Writing and Texts

The area which we call the 'Middle East' – essentially West Asia and North Africa – was where the practice of representing human utterances in permanent or semi-permanent form, by making marks on prepared surfaces, first originated. Whereas oral communication was limited to the evanescent here-and-now, and to the vagaries of human memory, writing enabled texts to be transmitted through both time and space, according to the medium employed. Monumental inscriptions dating from the fourth millennium BCE onwards abound in the region: these served to make permanent records, usually of the pretensions of divine and earthly powers, helping to transmit messages of authority and legitimacy down the generations.

But the requirements of administration, everyday devotion and the supply of longer texts for reading led the ancient civilizations to adopt more portable, if less durable, vehicles for writing: clay tablets and cylinders, animal skins, palm-bark and papyrus (made from Egyptian reed stems). With these, written messages could be transmitted across space, from person to person, and used as a means of social communication.[1]

The writing systems of the ancient Middle East started with pictograms, which then gradually became transmuted into patterns of signs, the meaning of which no longer necessarily bore any relation to the original pictorial representations. The earliest of these seems to have been cuneiform, used in Iraq from the third millennium BCE, consisting of wedge-shaped strokes incised on clay tablets. In Egypt, not much later, a system of hieroglyphic writing developed, which was originally purely pictographic, but became a means of representing different meanings and concepts. The key to the use of both these systems, and others which appeared, as text media was the adoption of the rebus principle, whereby the signs became identified with the sounds of words, not just the depiction of objects. It was this which enabled the development of texts, literature and eventually books.[2]

The alphabet was the next stage in the history of the book, and it too originated in the Middle East. In Ugarit in Syria in the fourteenth century BCE, a cuneiform system was developed which used only a limited number of signs, each of which represented a unit of sound, not a word or syllable, so that words could be constructed by combining them. This was followed by the Phoenician script, originating in the same area, in which each sound/letter took the form of one of a collection of 22 specific written characters, forming an alphabet as such.

The Phoenician alphabet was subsequently widely adopted, adapted and developed to form the basis of the writing systems of many languages in the Middle East and beyond, including Aramaic, Hebrew and Arabic.

---

1 For an extended discussion of the rôle of these material bases of written communications in ancient and modern civilizations, see the two seminal works of Harold A. Innis: *Empire and Communications* (1972, rep. 2007) and *The Bias of Communication* (1951, rep. 2008).

2 For a clear and concise summary of these developments, see Jean (1992, rep. 2000).

The Manuscript Tradition in the Middle East

Hebrew

The monotheism of the ancient Israelites became at an early stage a religion of the book. Various materials, including stone, ceramics, wood, metal and animal hides were used to write the Torah in the first millennium BCE, and papyrus was also used for Hebrew letters, documents, official and religious texts. Of particular importance in Judaism is the Torah scroll (*sefer Torah*), traditionally written on parchment and rolled from both ends: very early on this became a central object of devotion and focus of Jewish ritual. Elaborate rules were developed for the writing of such scrolls, codified in the Talmud and later in twelfth-century Egypt by the great scholar Maimonides in his *Mishneh Torah.* These covered the nature of the script, the materials and implements used, and the rituals to be followed by the scribe.

The earliest Hebrew scrolls to have survived are the famous Dead Sea Scrolls, discovered in caves at Qumran in Palestine. Some are of papyrus, but most are parchment, and they contain mainly biblical and other religious texts. They have been dated between the third century BCE and the first century CE. It is thought that some of the caves were used as scriptoria and libraries, and they provide evidence of the extent and diversity of Hebrew scribal culture of that period.

Parchment scrolls have continued to be used for the Torah, but other Hebrew literature, both sacred and secular, adopted the forms and materials subsequently developed in the Middle East: the codex and paper (see further below, and especially the essay by Malachi Beit-Arié reproduced here as Chapter 3). However, hardly any manuscripts survive from before the tenth century CE: this seems to be partly because of the destruction of earlier ones, and partly because of a preference for oral transmission of texts in that period. But in the following centuries there was an efflorescence of Hebrew manuscript production. Although many of the most notable surviving examples were produced in Europe, there is no doubt that Jewish communities in the Middle East were also major producers of texts in the period before printing. Cairo especially was a major centre: a fine gilt illuminated bible, thought to have been written there in the tenth century and now in the British Library,[3] bears witness to this. The quantity as well as the quality of the output is also attested by the large treasure trove of leaves and fragments preserved in the Cairo Genizah, including autographs of the works of Maimonides and others (see Reif, 2000). Iran, Iraq, Syria, Palestine, the Maghrib and Yemen also produced significant Hebrew manuscripts. The layout, illumination and in some areas even the script of these were often influenced by their Islamic contemporaries.

Coptic

In the first century CE, the ancient Egyptian language began to be written in the Greek script, and this became the norm after the widespread adoption of Christianity in the following two centuries. The Greek alphabet was augmented with some letters derived from Demotic Egyptian, and many Greek loanwords entered the vocabulary. This new written language became known as Coptic. The earliest Coptic papyri contain pagan texts, but the great majority

[3] BL Or. MS 9879. See http://www.bl.uk/onlinegallery/sacredtexts/gasterbib.html.

of Coptic manuscripts are Christian: biblical and liturgical texts, hagiography, homiletic literature, treatises, and so on.

The Copts seem to have played a crucial part in the transition from scrolls to codices – that is, to *books* in the modern sense. This development occurred in the first three Christian centuries, when folded and bound leaves of papyrus or parchment were found to be more convenient and suitable for the lengthier Biblical and religious texts (Hussein, 1970; Roberts and Skeat, 1987). The remarkable collection of fourth-century Coptic gnostic books discovered at Nag Hammadi in upper Egypt are all papyrus codices. As Theodore Petersen has shown in his essay below (Chapter 5), Coptic binding practices for codices probably later influenced the early forms of the Islamic book.

The Coptic manuscript tradition continued until modern times, but the Coptic language itself gradually fell out of use after the Arab conquest in the seventh century. Later manuscripts contained only scriptural and liturgical texts, accompanied nearly always by the Arabic translations and commentaries necessary for their understanding by the Arabized population.

Syriac

Syriac is the Semitic language used by a number of important Christian communities in Lebanon, Syria, Iraq, Iran and Turkey. It has its own script, used to write a wide range of religious and secular literature from the second century CE onwards, notably an important Syriac translation of the Bible (the *Peshitta*), homilies, theology, poetry, history and the natural sciences. An important early centre of production was Edessa (now Şanlıurfa in Turkey), but most Syriac manuscripts were written in the numerous monasteries and convents scattered throughout the area, initially on parchment and later on paper.

After the Arab conquests in the seventh and eighth centuries, Arabic gradually displaced Syriac and, after a brief revival in the thirteenth century, the latter eventually ceased to be a literary language. It continued in use, however, as a vehicle for existing sacred and liturgical texts, at least in the Maronite, Syrian Orthodox and Church of the East ('Nestorian') communities, and manuscripts continued to be produced.

The Syriac script was also used by members of these communities to write Arabic. Such texts, known as *Karshuni*, can be found in many manuscripts of the later periods.

Armenian

Another ancient Christian community of the Middle East is the Armenians. The Armenian language acquired its own script in the fifth century CE, and thereafter a vigorous scribal tradition developed. Numerous manuscripts of the Bible, the liturgies, the Church canons, translations of the Greek and Syriac fathers, chronicles, theological and philosophical works, grammars, science, law, poetry and much else were created. Many were richly illustrated and illuminated, and bindings were often finely decorated. The main centres of production were Constantinople (Istanbul), the towns of Cilician Armenia (now south-east Turkey) and Isfahan in Iran, but many were also written in the numerous monasteries throughout the area.

The colophons of Armenian manuscripts are of particular importance as historical sources: as well as recording the circumstances of their creation, they also often provide valuable information on such subjects as natural disasters, wars and other historical events. Many manuscripts were destroyed in the numerous vicissitudes of the Armenian people over the centuries, but it is estimated that about 30,000 have survived in various collections. Nearly half of these are in the Matenadaran, the national manuscripts library and archives of Armenia in Yerevan.

Arabic and Other Muslim Languages

Arabic is a Semitic language, written in a script which reached only a very imperfect state in the pre-Islamic period. Arabic literature (mainly poetry) was then entirely oral, although there are a few references in early Arabic poetry to writing on palm-bark and parchment, and the use of reed pens. By the time the Arabs felt an imperative need to create enduring but portable written texts, in the seventh century CE, the codex had already largely superseded the scroll as the normal form of the book, and it therefore became the prime vehicle for their emerging book culture. This need, and its physical expression, resulted from the impact of the new religion of Islam, conveyed through and embodied in the Qur'ān, a great book of revelation in the Arabic language.

The word *qur'ān* in Arabic means simply 'reading' or 'recitation', but the Holy Qur'ān, in the view of Muslims, contains the spoken words of the one transcendent God (Allāh), transmitted to the Prophet Muḥammad, who lived in the Hijaz (western Arabia), *c.*570–632. These words range from passages of sublimely poetical quality to narratives, liturgies, and regulations for personal and communal conduct. Together they are regarded as the final revelation and message of God to humankind, providing the ultimate source of belief and behaviour for all people who submit to Him (Muslims). Islam (literally, 'submission') is therefore, above all, a book-centred religion, in which redemption comes through obedience to a sacred text.

It is thought that Muḥammad, towards the end of his life, started the process of committing the Qur'ān to writing, probably by dictating it to scribes who wrote it down on available materials, such as stones, animal bones, or palm-leaves. Oral transmission and memorized versions, however, continued along with the written texts, of which there were differing forms. But a standard authorized recension eventually emerged, and thereafter the making of accurate copies of the Qur'ān (*muṣḥaf*, plural *maṣāḥif*) became a sacred duty, since they embodied both the divine revelation and the indispensible guide to human life. They also became reflections of the sublime beauty of the divine word, through the development of Arabic calligraphy, which evolved into the highest art form in Muslim societies. Nevertheless, educated persons still learnt the text by heart, and oral transmission continued to be of great importance, because manuscripts could not meet the universal demand among Muslims. The Qur'ān is a book that has influenced and even determined the social, moral, and intellectual life, over many centuries, of about one-fifth of the world's population.

The Qur'ān also transformed Arab society into a pre-eminently literary culture, with textuality becoming the predominant characteristic of Arab and Muslim cognitive processes. From the earliest stage, it was necessary to supplement the Qur'anic text with further sources of authority. The most important of these were the remembered and recorded sayings of the Prophet, known as *Ḥadīth*s. These were eventually elaborated, together with the regulations in the Qur'ān itself, into bodies of law, carefully recorded in writing and continually copied and recopied to serve the needs of the community and its governing authorities. At the same time, the old Arabic poetic tradition was revived and committed to writing, which in turn stimulated a new Islamic Arabic poetic and literary output, embodied in manuscripts over the following centuries.

The massive expansion of Islam in its first few centuries encompassed large, hitherto non-Arab, populations, which thereby entered this new Arabic-Islamic book culture, but at the same time introduced their own literary and intellectual heritage into it. Not only older literary traditions, but also philosophy, science, mathematics, geography, historiography and other disciplines flourished in the Muslim environment, which enthusiastically promoted the acquisition of knowledge and learning as a virtue enjoined by the Prophet. The writing and copying of texts was an essential and integral part of this, and during the eighth–eighteenth centuries in Muslim lands it reached a level unprecedented in the history of book production anywhere.

The number of manuscripts produced is impossible to compute. Today there are more than three million manuscript texts in the Arabic script, preserved in libraries and institutions throughout the world, as well as an unknown but substantial number still in private hands. Most of these copies are no more than 500 years old; this is partly because the scribal tradition lasted until quite recently, but it is also because much of the earlier written output of Muslim civilizations has been destroyed through neglect, decay, natural disasters and the belligerent destruction of significant parts of the written heritage, both by Muslims and by their enemies. This has continued right down to the present day. What remains, however, forms a substantial part of the world's intellectual and textual heritage.

Although the earliest Arabic and Muslim writings may have been on bones and palm-leaves, the normal materials in the first two centuries were papyrus and parchment. The latter was favoured for Qur'āns, for which durability was more important than portability. Some magnificent specimens, usually in oblong shape, have survived.

In the ninth century, paper production was introduced from China, and soon became widely adopted both for fine Qur'āns and for more mundane and secular texts. Many centres of paper production were established throughout the Muslim world. Paper was convenient to use, transport and store, and it was, most importantly, considerably cheaper than papyrus and parchment. This was a major factor in the explosion of book production and the transmission of knowledge in medieval Muslim societies from the tenth century onwards. Paper put books within reach of a wider class of educated readers. Its availability and use seems also to have been a major factor in the development of more cursive and legible styles of the Arabic script in that period. It provided a more convenient medium for texts other than the Qur'ān, in which functional legibility was more important than hieratic presentation.

From the fifteenth century, European (especially Italian) paper rapidly displaced the local product in most Muslim lands. Not only was it of higher quality, but it was also cheaper, being mass-produced in Europe to meet the demands of the new printing presses. This led to a further increase in the production and readership of Arabic manuscripts in the seventeenth and eighteenth centuries.

The Arabic script, driven by the need to write down the divine text of the Qur'ān, quickly developed from its rudimentary beginnings. Through a system of pointing and diacritics, it remedied its deficiencies and emerged as a functional means of rendering and recording Arabic texts, although it never became fully phonetic. At the same time, as the vehicle of the divine message, it attracted a spiritual veneration that inspired the desire to transform it into an object of sublime beauty. Calligraphy was therefore prized, and a great variety of fine script styles emerged, used primarily, but not solely, for writing the Qur'anic text. They showed considerable regional variations, reflecting the different civilizations and patrimonies across the Muslim world.

Most Arabic manuscript books, however, are written in smaller and simpler cursive styles, notably *naskh* (which later became the basis of Arabic typography). Yet, even in mundane manuscripts, aesthetic considerations were rarely abandoned altogether, and writing still had sacred connotations. Nevertheless, the cost of paper often imposed cramped page layouts, with glosses and commentaries filling the margins. Punctuation was at best rudimentary, and often non-existent. Texts normally started on the verso of the first leaf, and ended with a colophon, usually giving the date (and occasionally also the place) of copying and the copyist's name.

The illumination and decoration of manuscripts was an important Islamic art form, second only to calligraphy. The finest Qur'āns contain gilt and/or multicoloured abstract, floral and foliate decoration; and many lesser manuscripts were also illuminated, at least at their start. Bookbindings in the Muslim world were also vehicles for artistic finesse. These, and some of the other features already mentioned, underline the important role of the book in the visual, as well as the literary culture of Muslim societies.

The profession of scribe was an established and honourable one in Muslim society, and included people of all levels of education. Scribes sometimes operated in palace workshops, or were secretaries working in court chanceries with an exalted status. At the other end of the scale, they might be market stallholders offering their services to all and sundry. In between, there were many paid copyists working in libraries, colleges, mosques and other religious institutions. Many manuscripts, however, were not written by professionals. Some were written by authors themselves: a number of holograph copies of Muslim writings survive in libraries. Impecunious writers and scholars also often resorted to copying in order to sustain themselves; and students and other readers frequently made copies, in libraries and elsewhere, simply for their own use. Inevitably in traditional society, most scribes, whether professionals or amateurs, were male. Yet, there exist a surprising number of references to women performing this role too.

Scribal activity did not entirely displace oral transmission in the diffusion of texts, however. Written books were often created in the first place by copying from dictation or from memory. The right to transmit the text was frequently granted in the form of a licence (*ijāza*), on the basis of a satisfactory reading from the copy, which had to conform to the orally transmitted and memorized version. But, whatever the immediate source, the maintenance of accuracy has always been a problem in texts reproduced in Muslim manuscript culture, as elsewhere. Copyists were always fallible, and they could all too easily lapse into unintentional repetitions, omissions and other corruptions of the text. The corruption of texts in this way, an inevitable consequence of scribal culture, was a continual source of anxiety and insecurity in a civilization for which the authenticity and integrity of texts was of paramount importance.

Many books were copied specifically for sale. The occupation of bookseller and stationer (*warrāq*) overlapped with that of scribe. As well as trading in copies made by or for themselves, booksellers dealt in copies bought in from elsewhere; they also acted as purchasing agents, seeking out particular titles or genres on behalf of scholars or collectors. Bookshops tended to cluster in particular streets or quarters of towns, a pattern that can still often be found today. In some cities, a guild structure existed, with the book trade supervised by a *shaykh* or master.

The high importance attached to books and reading in traditional Muslim societies led to the formation of many large libraries. These belonged to rulers, mosques, educational institutions, and private individuals. The libraries in a major centre, such as Baghdad, Cairo or Cordoba, contained many tens of thousands of volumes. Catalogues were compiled, and some libraries provided facilities, and even personnel, for making new copies of texts. Many libraries in the Muslim world were established as inalienable endowments (*waqf*), so that books could not be sold or otherwise dispersed. Yet, borrowing by scholars was generally allowed, and this inevitably led to some losses.

The Qur'ān gave the Arabic language and script a central importance in Islam. The areas of western Asia, North Africa and Spain that adopted Arabic became the heartlands of book culture in the heyday or 'classical' period of Muslim civilization, from the eighth to the thirteenth centuries. As such, they have been the main focus of studies of that culture. But Islam eventually spread over a huge area from the Atlantic to the Pacific, and in later periods other, non-Arab Muslim peoples and empires became predominant. They created their own literary traditions and produced manuscript books in their own languages; but the powerful influence of Arabic was such that they adopted many Arabic loanwords and, most importantly, the Arabic script, which was adapted to write a variety of other languages. In most of these areas, however, much religious and legal literature was also written in Arabic, and many copies of the Qur'ān were made, always in the original.

Iran had a proud ancient literary tradition and, from the tenth century onwards, as well as producing magnificent Qur'āns, created a flourishing Persian manuscript culture. Poetic books were especially noteworthy, and a characteristic oblique and highly artistic form of the Arabic script was developed to write them. Rulers and wealthy patrons often commissioned exquisitely decorated and illustrated manuscripts, and Persian miniatures have become much-treasured *objets d'art*.

Ottoman Turkey became the centre of a large empire that, by the mid-sixteenth century, included most of the Arab world and much of south-eastern Europe. Having inherited the Arabic manuscript tradition, the Turks both continued it and created a Turkish book culture that also borrowed some elements of the Persian. Ottoman calligraphers became especially celebrated, both for Qur'āns and for more humble manuscripts executed with great elegance. Istanbul became the greatest centre in the world for Islamic books, and remains the largest repository of them to this day.

The writing of books by hand continued as the normal method of textual transmission for far longer in the Muslim world than elsewhere. One reason for this was the extreme reverence felt by Muslims for the handwritten word. Not only was writing regarded as a spiritual activity, but the beauty of the cursive Arabic script aroused an almost physical passion, akin to human love. Given such feelings it is not surprising that Muslims were reluctant to abandon the handwritten book. Another reason was the widespread engagement of large sections of the educated population in book-copying (and associated trades). Many wholly or partly earned their living by it. Thus, there was a substantial vested interest in retaining this method of production, whatever its limitations. A third reason, arising from the other two, was that Muslims felt supremely comfortable with manuscripts, which they regarded as an integral part of their culture and society. Even when economic and other conditions created a substantial rise in demand for books among emerging classes of society – for example, in eighteenth-century Egypt – scribal production was regarded as adequate to cope with this.

At the same time, intellectual and religious authority within Muslim society was closely linked with book production and the limited transmission of texts. Islam has no ecclesiastical organization, and the status of religious leaders, who had great authority but lacked secular power, depended essentially on their role as scholars and producers of texts. This in turn depended on maintaining the sacred character of writing and a degree of exclusiveness in and control over the creation and distribution of books. So Muslims went on writing and copying books by hand until the emergence of new patterns of state authority associated with modernizing influences coming partly from outside the Muslim world.

The Printed Book in the Middle East

Hebrew

The very first book to be printed in the Middle East, and the only incunable from the region, as far as is known, was a Hebrew code of religious laws, the *Arba'ah Ṭūrīm*, printed by David Ibn Nahmias at Istanbul in 1493. He had come from Spain, apparently bringing a type fount which he had previously used there, together with another from Italy. Further Hebrew works were printed at the same press, and others both there and in other Ottoman cities, including Salonica, Edirne, Izmir, Safad, Damascus and Cairo, during the sixteenth–eighteenth centuries, and in many other centres in the nineteenth and twentieth centuries. These developments are well surveyed in Yaron Ben Na'eh's essay below (Chapter 15).

The transition from manuscript to print does not seem to have been a problem in Jewish communities, which welcomed the opportunity to distribute multiple copies of their religious texts among the faithful. Hebrew types were also used to print secular texts in other languages used by Middle Eastern Jews, notably Judaeo-Spanish (Ladino) and Judaeo-Arabic.

Armenian

Like Hebrew, Armenian typography originated in western Europe, but was adopted in the Ottoman Empire at an early stage. In 1567, encouraged by the Armenian Patriarch, the printer Abgar Toxatec'i transferred his activities and his type-founts from Venice to Istanbul. There he printed a grammar and some Christian texts, but closed the press after two years. Armenian printing was established in Istanbul on a more permanent basis at the end of the seventeenth century, but meanwhile another press, run by monks at Isfahan in Iran, produced a number of religious books between 1636 and 1647. This was the first printing of any kind in Iran.

As Meliné Pehlivanian's essay below clearly shows (Chapter 26), Istanbul became in the eighteenth and nineteenth centuries the main centre of Armenian printing, providing texts both for wealthy local patrons and for churches and schools throughout the Ottoman Empire, including especially the Armenian homeland. There was also a press in Izmir from 1759 to 1763, and in 1771 one was founded in Armenia itself, at Echmiadzin. The nineteenth century also saw the arrival of Armenian printing in Palestine, Egypt, Syria, Azerbaijan, Iraq, Lebanon and elsewhere.[4]

---

4 A useful historical survey of Armenian presses and typography can be found in Lane (2012).

Syriac

Lebanese Maronite Catholics had been involved in printing Syriac texts in Rome from the sixteenth century onwards, and in 1610 they printed a Psalter at the Quzḥayyā monastery in Lebanon, using a press and types almost certainly brought from Rome. This was in both Syriac and Arabic in Syriac script (Karshuni). No further Syriac printing seems to have taken place in the Middle East until 1785, when a Lebanese monk brought another press from Rome and started producing liturgical texts at a different monastery. This was later moved back to Quzḥayyā, where Syriac printing continued until 1897.

Other Syriac presses also operated in Lebanon in the nineteenth century, but elsewhere Protestant and Catholic missionary presses played the leading role, particularly among the 'Chaldean' and 'Nestorian' (Church of the East) communities in Iraq and Iran. An account of one missionary typographer who played a signicant part is given by James Coakley in his essay below (Chapter 27).

Another Syriac-using church was the Syrian Orthodox, which printed books at a monastic press in southern Turkey, starting in 1890. Middle Eastern printing in Syriac continued throughout the twentieth century, producing both Christian religious texts and secular ones for the use of Syriac-speaking communities.[5]

Coptic

Before the era of printing, Coptic had already become a dead language, used only for biblical and liturgical texts. Some such texts were printed in Rome in the eighteenth century and sent to Egypt, but local printing of Coptic (apart from one mediaeval block-print) did not start until the late nineteenth century, at presses established by the Coptic Orthodox and Catholic authorities.

In the 1890s the Coptic philologist Klaudios Labib (1873–1918) sought to revive the language, and acquired a press to print Coptic teaching and reading materials. He published a series of mainly bilingual editions (Coptic and Arabic), including a dictionary, grammar, primer and religious texts, as well as a periodical. But this revival attempt was a failure, and no more such material appeared after his death.

Arabic and Other Muslim languages

To find the origins of Arabic and Muslim printing, we have to go back to the tenth century CE. As in China two or more centuries earlier, it originated in a need to mass produce religious texts, not simply or even primarily to be read, but as objects with their own religious aura, giving benefit and protection to their owners. The production of these block-printed texts, and maybe others for more practical purposes, seems to have continued for about 500 years, and then apparently disappeared at the dawn of the early modern era.

These Arabic block-prints are discussed in Richard Bulliet's essay below (Chapter 12), and have been further studied, enumerated and deciphered by Karl Schaefer (2006). They raise

---

[5] For good surveys of the whole field of Syriac printing and typography, see Coakley (2002), pp. 93–115, and (2006).

a number of questions, or clusters of questions which, in the present state of our knowledge, cannot yet be answered definitively:

1 Why was the technique of block-printing texts in multiple copies not developed to produce printed books, as in China? Was it because of an aversion on the part of literate Muslims to any mechanical reproduction of texts containing the name of God (as nearly all of them did)? In that case, why were these block-printed amulets allowed, since they all contain invocations to God, and most of them also include passages from the Qur'ān itself? Or was it due to an instinctive reluctance on the part of the *ulamā* (the learned classes) and the scribal elite to sanction a method of book production that might undermine their control of knowledge and their exercise of spiritual and intellectual authority?
2 Why did Arabic printing apparently die out just at the moment when economic and social changes, and the increased availability of cheap paper (as mentioned above), were about to usher in a new, broader, book culture, both in the Muslim world and in Europe? Why, in other words, did Arabs and Muslims have printing before print culture, and then at least some of the effects of print culture without printing? This paradox, of course, tends to cast doubt on how important the technology of printing, or its absence, really was, at least in Muslim society, and whether transcendent cultural factors did not render the actual *methods* of textual production and diffusion of lesser significance. This view has been adopted, explicitly or implicitly, by several intellectual historians, and is discussed by Orlin Sabev in his 2010 article reproduced below (Chapter 10). It may not, however, do justice to the full historical effects of printing, in the Muslim world as elsewhere.

Part of the problem has perhaps been an overemphasis on the late arrival of the printing press and movable type in the Muslim world. This question has long intrigued European historians, looking at it from a Eurocentric point of view. Why and how, they wonder, did Muslim society manage for so long without Gutenberg's invention, on which European modernity relied? The answer, of course, is that they managed as they had always done, throughout all the periods of their flourishing literate civilization, by writing and copying their texts in ever-increasing numbers of manuscript copies. The post-Gutenberg Ottoman, Safavid and Mughal states functioned and flourished for at least three centuries without printing. Not until the eighteenth and nineteenth centuries did European scientific and technical superiority, and the threat which it posed, cause them to reconsider the matter and introduce presses. What really matters is what happened *after* that point, rather than what did not happen before.

In 1979, the historian Elizabeth Eisenstein published her seminal study of the effects of printing in early modern Europe, titled *The Printing Press as an Agent of Change.* As her title suggests, she assigned a crucial role to print in the development of modernity. This has caused some other historians to accuse her of fallacious technological determinism – not least because of the different experience of non-European societies such as that of the Muslim world, where printing did not bring about such change in the same period.

This may be a sterile argument about causes versus consequences, the classic conundrum of the chicken and the egg. Did Gutenberg's invention in the fifteenth century bring about the ensuing cultural and intellectual changes? Or did Europe's cultural readiness for those changes lead to the invention, and its subsequent widespread adoption? Rather than endlessly debating such enigmas, it makes more sense to regard them as reciprocal effects, or as a continuum of cause and effect. The same applies in the Muslim world: the timing and circumstances of the arrival there of the printing press were of course contingent on the interrelationship of cultural patterns and outside stimuli. But once it *had* arrived, its effects came into operation – although not necessarily in quite the same way, or at the same rate – as they had previously done in Europe.

Eisenstein's analytical framework is a valuable and useful tool, when considering these effects. She identified three principal changes, or clusters of changes, associated with the use of printing. What follows is a brief sketch of how these operated in the Arab and Muslim context.

The first is the increased **dissemination** of texts. This is a fairly obvious point, but it is surprisingly often overlooked. As early as the eighteenth century, Müteferrika's press in Istanbul produced ten or eleven thousand books in the twenty or so years of its existence, and, contrary to what is sometimes asserted, the great majority of them were sold and reached local readers (as Sabev has demonstrated in Chapters 10 and 18, and in an important (2004) monograph). After the print revolution reached the Arab world in the nineteenth century, hundreds of thousands of copies of old and new texts came into the hands of readers on a scale well beyond what had ever been achieved in the manuscript era. This both stimulated, and was stimulated by, the growth of education and literacy in that period.

The proliferation of printed books also enabled them to cross borders to an unprecedented extent. Not only was there an international trade in Arabic books, for example, both within the Ottoman sphere and beyond, but printing greatly increased the viability of translations and the demand for them. There was therefore a new spread of ideas from outside the Muslim world, and an increased possibility of what has been called 'cognitive contamination' of the ideas and belief systems of what had been previously a relatively enclosed and inward-looking intellectual arena. This in turn gave rise to the idea of knowledge as a boundless and infinitely extendable, rather than a circumscribed, domain.

The trajectory of all this, however, was not only in the direction of humanism and liberalism. Printing was also used to increase the circulation of traditional texts and old ideas, including narrow doctrinal and dogmatic ones, which were also brought to a new mass readership. This tended towards a new fundamentalism, partly in reaction against the modernizing tendencies already mentioned.

The printing of the Qur'ān itself was for a long time resisted, but this too eventually entered fully into the domain of print culture, after the publication of the standard Al-Azhar edition in Cairo in 1924. This, and its numerous subsequent reprints throughout the Muslim world, had the effect of bringing it into the everyday lives and households of many ordinary Muslims. Its use thereby changed: no longer was it mainly a source of memorized ritual – instead it became a direct source of guidance and doctrine. For some, this meant a new freedom of interpretation and action; for others, it brought a more rigid obedience to perceptions of the divine will.

The second of Eisenstein's clusters of changes is the **standardization** of texts and their presentation through typography. I emphasize the word *typography* here, rather than printing, because in the nineteenth-century Muslim world, many texts, especially traditional ones, first appeared in print not by typesetting, but by lithography, which enabled as it were the mechanical multiplication of manuscript texts. This effectively bypassed the typographical standardization identified by Eisenstein, in a manner which had no precedent in Europe.

Nevertheless, this was only a partial and temporary phenomenon. Typographic standardization did affect most texts published in Turkey and the Arab world.

This applied to the content of the texts themselves. Although many early editions were not based on thorough editing processes, eventually the practice grew of collating different manuscripts and establishing authoritative editions of classical texts in a manner quite different from the copying which took place in the scribal era.

There was also a re-standardization of the Arabic language. The development of written vernacular texts (in manuscript) which had taken place in the preceding centuries was largely halted. What was regarded as *rakāka* – feeble and insipid style – was also rejected and classical norms were reimposed in response to the challenge of creating printed texts aimed at a large educated readership. At the same time, in original writing, a new simplicity and directness was adopted, and there was a decline in what has been called the 'magic garden' mentality of obscure literary verbiage.

After an initial period when, as with Gutenberg, printed books imitated the appearance of manuscripts, texts were also eventually made clearer and more readable by more spacious book designs and page layouts, the use of title and contents pages, and the elimination of marginal glosses and commentaries. This created a new 'esprit de système', as Eisenstein calls it, which undoubtedly changed reading habits and catered for new classes of readers, as well as engendering different approaches to accessing knowledge.

Eisenstein's third 'cluster of changes' concerns printing's role in the **preservation** of texts. As mentioned earlier, large numbers of Islamic manuscripts, and the texts which they contained, have perished down the ages, through both neglect and malicious destruction. But once texts were printed in thousands of copies, the likelihood of their loss was, if not eliminated, then at least greatly reduced. Even texts which were not lost, but survived in only one or a few copies, could thereby be restored to a wide readership which had no access to them previously.

This also means that the time and energies of the literate and scholarly classes could be redirected to new avenues of thought, research and creative writing, instead of copying the old texts which could now be consulted in printed editions. Such new literature and thought could also be made widely available, and preserved for posterity.

The new availability of classical Arabic literature in printed editions in the nineteenth century, together with the diffusion of new writing, almost certainly helped to create the new self-awareness and perhaps even national consciousness which gave rise to the Arab renaissance of that period, which is called the *Nahḍa*. Similar changes occurred in Turkey, Iran and other areas of the Muslim world.

References

Coakley, J.F. (2002), 'Printing in Syriac, 1539–1985', in E. Hanebutt-Benz, D. Glass and G. Roper (eds), *Middle Eastern Languages and the Print Revolution: A Cross-Cultural Encounter*, Westhofen: WVA-Verlag Skulima, pp. 93–115.

Coakley, J.F. (2006), *The Typography of Syriac*, New Castle, DE: Oak Knoll Press..

Eisenstein, E. (1979), *The Printing Press as an Agent of Change: Communications and Cultural Transformations in Early-Modern Europe*, Cambridge: Cambridge University Press.

Hussein, M.A. (1970), *Origins of the Book: Egypt's Contribution to the Development of the Book from Papyrus to Codex*, Leipzig: Edition Leipzig.
Innis, H.A. (1951, 2008), *The Bias of Communication*, Toronto: University of Toronto Press.
Innis, H.A. (1972, 2007), *Empire and Communications*, rev. M.Q. Innis, Toronto: University of Toronto Press.
Jean, G. (1992, 2000), *Writing: The Story of Alphabets and Scripts*, trans. J. Oates, London: Thames & Hudson.
Lane, J.A. (2012), *The Diaspora of Armenian Printing 1512–2012*, Amsterdam and Yerevan: Special Collections of the University of Amsterdam.
Reif, S.C. (2000), *A Jewish Archive from Old Cairo: The History of Cambridge University's Genizah Collection*, Richmond, Surrey: Curzon Press.
Roberts, C.H. and T.C. Skeat (1987), *The Birth of the Codex*, 2nd edn, London: Oxford University Press for the British Academy.
[Sabev, O.] Орлин Събев (2004), *Първото Османско пътешествие в света на печатната книга (1726–1746)*, Sofia. Turkish translation: Orlin Sabev (Orhan Salih) (2006), *İbrahim Müteferrika ya da ilk Osmanlı matbaa serüveni (1726–1746)*, Istanbul: Yeditepe.
Schaefer, K. (2006), *Enigmatic Charms: Medieval Arabic Block Printed Amulets in American and European Libraries and Museums*, Leiden: Brill.

Part I
General and Introductory

[1]

ISLAMIC BOOK HISTORY: PARAMETERS OF A DISCIPLINE

Michael W. Albin

This paper is about something that doesn't exist. I am going to talk about a discipline whose outlines are so vague as to be as yet indiscernible in the literature of Oriental studies, even though they take form in the fertile loam of the humanities. The discipline has come to be called book history, a direct translation of the French term *histoire du livre* because it is the French who have led the way in setting out the techniques of research. Yet, even in France, as in England and the United States, the study of the book is still in its incunabular stage — which is not to say that important work has not been done in limning the boundaries of the study. In the course of this presentation I will be referring to some of these efforts. What I am proposing is that the experience of Occidental book historians be brought to bear on the book in the Islamic world.

It should be a source of wonder that the book, *al-kitāb*, a word charged with such ponderous cultural freight in the Islamic lands, should itself have gone nearly unnoticed for so long by Orientalists and, for that matter, by Muslims too. It is not that books have been neglected by scholars, but that the book as social, economic and cultural artifact has been ignored. The book, of course, has never gone unheralded as an important, even sanctified, component of Islamic society. On the contrary, the value of books, reading and writing is recognized in the Koran itself (*Nun! Wa-al-Qalam wa mā-yasṭurūna*, for example, and *Iqra' bism rabbika alladhī khalaqa*, etc.), the Hadith, and by Muslims through the ages. Much has been written about the importance of books to education, wisdom and piety. Books and syllabi are a principal feature of biographical dictionaries and are recorded in painstaking and sometimes deadpan detail, as in the *Fihrist*, whose third chapter contains "accounts of the scholars and the names of the books they composed, including accounts of court companions, associates, men of letters, singers, buffoons, slap-takers and jesters and the names of their books." But enough; I need not elaborate for this audience on the importance of the book in Islam.

A word is needed about what the history of the book is not. The history of the book is not, first and above all, bibliography. I intend no disparagement of bibliography, and far be it from me to deflect admiration from the immortal Brockelmann, from Professor Sezgin or Professor Hunwick, whose project on West African Arabic bibliography is vital to the study of universal Islam. But bibliography is not the history of the book, any more than a three-by-five inch catalog card is the book itself.

Nor, in my opinion, is the history of the book a pedantic reformulation of the dicta of Marshall McLuhan. The principal weakness of McLuhan as a model is that he is simply irrelevant to Islam. A McLuhanite thinks in simple contrasts: hot-cool, linear-enveloping, written-oral, electronic-printed, nationalism-global village. These concepts have no bearing on the way Muslims handled their social intercourse or communications, in other words, their media. Technological determinism has no place here.

Book history is, then, neither bibliography and its associated vices — antiquarianism and bibliolotry — nor the concoction of theories explaining why Muslims behave the way they do because their script is cursive and therefore inherently harder to read than ours. (You would be surprised at how many visitors to Egypt find it impossible to comprehend that an Egyptian can read Arabic as facilely as we read English.) Moreover, the study I am talking about has few links to art history, although on the surface book history and art history share an interest in book arts such as binding, calligraphy and book decoration. Book history can certainly use with profit the exhaustive research on these matters produced by art historians, but book history addresses social rather than aesthetic questions and problems. Book history is more closely associated with the concerns of the members of American Oriental Society, for it is text-based and as much concerned with the intellectual contents as with the physical properties of the book.

What do I mean by the history of the Islamic book? I am talking about a discipline (or group of disciplines) which concerns itself with the creation, manufacture and use of the book in its written or printed form. It's as simple as that. By concentrating on the written medium of transmission of Islamic civilization we may discover new perspectives for the analysis of the civilization as a whole. The manuscript is the very confluence of the contradiction between Islamic egalitarianism and the elite occupations of learning, teaching and judging. Likewise, the study of the Islamic book in the classical or post-classical age can offer new insights into illiteracy in a bibliolatrous civilization, and how society came to accomodate itself to this sort of *kufr*. The study of text production and dispersal can offer new ways to penetrate the influence of ideas and change within Islam. I think, for example, Professor Peter Gran is on the right track when he claims to discern the dawn of modernizing rationalism in the writings of the Egyptian *'alims* of the late 18th and early 19th century. It will take years of painstaking work by book historians to articulate the changes adumbrated by Gran.

While offering insights into these civilizational issues book history can also enlighten the study of a given Islamic society or epoch. Focus on the book as economic or social object allows scholars to explore such questions as: What were the economic advantages of paper over papyrus, or of the codex over the scroll? Was there a Fatimid printed book? And what is the role of the printing press in technological change and socio-economic development?

Now, to be very frank with you, I must say that my own personal interest is in the history of the printed book. What concerns me is what Bacon called in the *Novum Organum* the "force, effect, and consequences" of the printing press; and the question which has bothered me for years is why the Islamic peoples shunned the printing press for nearly four hundred years. It is the most oft-repeated of truisms about printing that the miracle of the invention lies in the principle of replication. This observation refers only to technical potentialities. Book history takes this observation one step further. If replication is the nature of printing, what makes printers start printing in the first place, and what makes them stop printing? What truly differentiates one printed product (i.e., book) from all others?

The history of printing as a subdivision of the history of the book has been blessed in the past decade with noteworthy contributions by American scholars whose work might point the way for students of the Islamic book. I refer to the works of Robert Darnton whose *The Business of Enlightenment*, the history of the publishing of the *Encyclopédie* is a perfect example of the kind of enlightment that can take place when a worthy subject, bountiful source material and a gifted writer and historian come together. There is also the work of Elizabeth Eisenstein, *The Printing Press as an Agent of Change*, which bids to become a classic and shape the discipline of book history for decades to come. I am tempted to quote at length from Eisenstein's book, but will limit myself to but one example of her method. In her chapter on the Copernican Revolution she links the introverted Polish scholar to the intellectual currents of his time by means of the books he read and the books he wrote — and eventually published — and connects astronomy, mathematics, calendar fixing, printed charts, and the transmittal of Arab science to produce a rich mixture of historiographic specualtion. With Eisenstein, in contrast to the French book historians, it is not her certainties which illuminate our studies, but her doubts.

In Islamic studies there is no Needham to lead the way in the history of technology. Useful studies of the book do, of course, exist, but in isolation. One must therefore welcome the translation of Pedersen's *The Arabic Book* (Reviewed in IAOL *Bulletin* 24-25, 1984), even though the work is seriously out of date and narrow in its focus. And it is a pleasure also to mention Minorsky's translation of Qadi Ahmad's treatise on calligraphy and painters and Levey's translations of Ibn Badis and al-Sufyani. But there is not much interest in printing history. To some it may seem of merely antiquarian interest if Iran's first printed book appeared in 1812 or 1817, or if printing was introduced permanently into Egypt in 1822, or into Iraq in 1856, and so forth. But I think that it is a matter of importance that printing in Egypt began as a fully articulated industry, vertically organized from the collection of rags and old army uniforms to make paper to the distribution of the finished books to consumers through schools and bookstores, in contrast to the experience of other countries, where early printing was less organized, more haphazard. Similarly it tells us much if the first books were lithographed rather than printed with metal types. (We must not forget that lithography is still widespread in the Muslim world today.) The Persians, Indians and North Africans seemed unable to leave their script behind when it came to replication. Fortunately, a technique appeared in Europe around 1800 which suited their needs precisely. The surmise as developed by Fr. Demeerseman of the Institut des belles lettres arabes in Tunis is that lithography combined the cultural attributes of the manuscript with the advantages of mass production. Furthermore, it makes a difference *what* was being printed and published. At Muhammad Ali Pasha's presses, for example, the thrust was toward the new utilitarian sciences. My research is coming to show that religious and to some extent literary titles were indeed done at the Bulaq Press — but at private expense. Finally, it is not inconsequential in the context of modern Arab cultural history that Morocco's first printer was an Egyptian journeyman hired in Cairo by an agent of Sidi Muhammad II (r. 1859-1873). We await the forthcoming research of Fawzi Abdulrazak to have the ramifications of this early inter-Arab technology transfer elaborated.

Before closing I must address briefly the issue of sources. For the manuscript period the book historian uses most of the same sources as the bibliographer, philologist or historian. The codices themselves constitute the primary source, and here I include the physical, chemical, inconographic and textual contents. In addition, there are many invaluable sources. Ibn Nadim has already been mentioned. There are also biographical dictionaries and the great *adab* compendia like al-ᶜ*Iqd al-Farīd* and *Ṣubḥ al-*ᶜ*A*ᶜ*shā*. Manuscript catalogs are major sources, as are Brockelmann, Sezgin, and Graf and Nasrallah for Christians in Islamic lands. We need many more studies like Levey's and Minorsky's, to repeat the beautifully produced examples cited above.

In the epoch of the early printed book, one turns to the books themselves. Their introductions and colophons are full of information about the conditions under which they were produced and distributed. In the case of Egypt, the central archives are fairly bursting with material on the advent of printing under Muhammad Ali and its progress under ᶜAbbās, Saᶜīd and Ismāᶜīl. The archives were put to excellent use by Abū Futūḥ Raḍwān in his *Tārīkh Maṭbaᶜat Bulāq*. For the time being, his transcription and quotation of documents will be our most comprehensive look at these primary materials because, unfortunately, in the transfer of Dār al-Wathā'iq from the Abdin Palace to the Citadel the numbering system was altered and one must now start from scratch, moving through the dossiers one by one, as I did in the late winter of 1985. Precious little of lasting value has been done on any other Arab country, although one can sometimes pick up a tip here and there from a Moroccan, Iraqi or Lebanese historian. And one holds out hope that Dr. Wahid Gdoura in Tunisia will maintain his interest in printing history. The brightest spot is most certainly Turkey, where book and printing history have been widely researched and discussed in popular as well as scholarly publications. I should single out the volume issued in 1980 by the Turkish Librarians Association on the 250th anniversary of the opening of Muteferrika's press as an example of the work of Turkish scholars. By contrast, in some countries of the Peninsula it is still possible to interview the pioneers of printing, men who were instrumental in breaking the manuscript barrier or helped their countries break away from absolute dependency on books imported from Beirut, Cairo or Bombay. Further east, in India, Muslim printing is covered in the forthcoming nine-volume *Printers and Printing in the East Indies to 1850* by Katharine Smith Diehl.

Finally, you will note that I have neglected to cover the history of the Islamic book in more contemporary times. In deference to what I perceive to be the predilection of our society for the earlier periods, or, to phrase it another way, the more enduring issues, I will not even try to sketch the rich treasures which await modern historians. I only hope that I have, as it were, opened the book to your observation and careful study.

—Paper read at American Oriental Society Meetings, March, 1986.

[2]

"Of Making Many Books There Is No End:" The Classical Muslim View

Franz Rosenthal

In our time, we seem to have reached the point where we may well ask ourselves whether the incessant production of books might not be too much of a good thing. The more books we throw away (actually or figuratively), the more there are to take their place. It is no longer unjustified to hope against hope that book production could be limited, even if, on the face of it, it clearly involves an uphill battle comparable to the limitation of population growth. Of course, those in the book business, whether out in front or in the rear echelons, do not welcome the prospect of reduced production and consider the idea as anything from eccentric to scurrilous to outright dangerous.

Books have been valuable and cherished possessions all through history. For the first time, their devaluation as material objects could possibly have occurred in medieval Islam, what with the introduction of a rather cheap, yet durable, writing material and the feverish and almost global activity in science and scholarship.[1] This could conceivably have happened, but it did not. Before the Muslim era, no realistic opportunity existed for the feeling to arise that just too many books might be around. The famous verse of Ecclesiastes 12:12: "Of making many books there is no end, and much study is a weariness of flesh," at the most expresses a tentative apprehension as to theoretically uncontrollable quantities of books, and so do other putative complaints about the vastness of existing knowledge.[2] The biblical verse presents many difficulties for the understanding and lends itself to various interpretations. To the best of my—admittedly very limited—knowledge, no unanimity has as yet been reached as to what it really meant in its historical context. Whatever it did mean originally, it does not contain evidence that already in ancient times, people complained about too many books as physical objects being around. There were not, and could not have been.

The fact that Eccl. 12:12 is widely considered a later addition poses a further problem,[3] but this is a minor matter. Among the principal difficulties is, for one, the great variety of meanings of the Hebrew verb "to make" and, in the second colon, the meaning of the hapax legomenon *lahag*. Recent translations include a conservative "book learning" for "to make=to use,"[4] or "a thing of no purpose" for "no end,"[5] as well as more radical suggestions such as assuming that *lahag* is in fact parallel to "no end"[6] or re-interpreting the entire passage as "Und lass dich, mein Sohn, von ihnen gut belehren, viele Bücher ohne Unterlass zu benutzen und viel zu meditieren bis zur Körpermüdigkeit."[7] The question of the applicability of "to make" to "books" appears to have been settled by the existence of an equivalent idiom in Aramaic meaning "producing. . .a document (spr znh zy 'nh ʿbdt)" and the Akkadian usage of *ennešu* as a stage in the bookmaking process.[8] The possibility that "making" here might mean "collecting" (with reference to Eccl. 2:8 "I got me singers")[9] must be put on hold for the time being, although it would go well with the Arabic idiom of *ikthār min al-kutub* for collecting many books.[10] However, the production or overproduction of books would seem to be connected in Eccl. 12:12 to the physical process of writing rather than the intellectual task of composing works.

Lahag, translated traditionally as "study" reflecting the Greek translation and a combination with Arabic *lahija* "to be deeply engaged in something" (preferably, in study)[11] remains uncertain. The derivation from the root *hāgāh* (or a Ugaritic *hg*)[12] cannot be dismissed offhand but leaves room for doubt. Rabbinical associations of *lahag* with *l-ʿ-g* and *h-g-wy* are as much guesswork as modern theories. It should, however, be noted that both *l-ʿ-g* and *h-g-wy* are based upon the uttering of sounds, such as stammering or scoffing. The Targum speaks of "(making) books of wisdom" as parallel to "(the occupation with and understanding of) the *words* of the Torah."[13] More to the point, the Syriac translation has *man(l)la* which is most readily understood as "speech." Following this lead, a Syriac commentary of Ecclesiastes used "words (*melle*)."[14] And Arabic knows a noun *lahjah* in the meaning of "tongue, speech, dialect," whose history, however, is not quite clear.[15] It is thus possible that *lahag*, whatever its derivation, refers to some sort of oral expression. This was suspected also by M. V. Fox who states that "either 'study' or 'utter' would make sense here, because study in the ancient world was essentially oral recitation."[16] Taking it all together, we may conclude that Eccl. 12:12 indeed referred originally to the combination of two modes of study, the reading and reproduction of written materials and oral discussion. Whatever mode was used committed, in the eyes of the author, the student to an endless and painful task.

It may be worth noting that Eccl. 12:12 seems to be more famous now than it was in premodern times. Generally speaking, the verse was not much discussed and, again speaking generally, it was not frequently cited. From the medieval Muslim environment, we have a comment by the tenth-century Karaite Salmon ibn Yeruham, paraphrased by G. Vajda: "Et garde-toi encore des livres innombrables qui ont été faits." Man must not attempt to become too wise.

Nobody should make the rounds of cities and markets to search for philosophical and heretical works.[17] Reflecting further the attitude of certain segments of Muslim scholarship, Abū al-Barakāt al-Baghdādī (d. ca. 547/1166) interprets Eccl. 12:12 as a warning against wasting time on books that are an outgrowth of the human imagination, whose study could take up more than a human lifetime. Abū al-Barakāt translates *lahag* as *hadhayān* "talking nonsense."[18]

It was too much knowledge, not too many books, that was complained about in ancient times and continued to be complained about through medieval Islam. Knowledge, especially in certain fields, could not be mastered in its entirety; of books there were, in a way, never enough. In the course of time, we often hear it said that works in a given discipline were "many." For example, Ibn Khallikān (d. 682/1282) said that he did not intend to include caliphs among his biographees, because "the many works on them are sufficient."[19] Works on history were so many that they obviously could not all be listed.[20] And, in particular, anything connected with ḥadīth and other religious subjects produced an enormous literature.[21] When an eighth/fourteenth-century scholar wrote a commentary of al-Bukhārī's *Ṣaḥīḥ*, he was able to draw on 300 earlier commentaries;[22] for him, this was a boast rather than a complaint. This superabundance of specialized works also led to an unwholesome restriction to standard works.[23]

Despair in the face of an overwhelming amount of existing knowledge was the almost universal complaint and the situation most generally referred to. The physical problem of the multitude of books was much less obvious. There were many reasons for this state of affairs. In the first place, it has to do with the character of our sources. They were the work of authors who naturally would not wish to play down the desirability of making more books—preferably, of course, their own. Like ourselves, they would rarely be willing to admit that anything of theirs could be superfluous, let alone harmful. In their forewords, the one thing they generally avoided was referring to an existing glut of other works on the subject.[24] A second, more objective reason was the frequent lack of books in a given environment and the constant need to replenish the stock. In an area as vast and diversified as the Muslim world, imbalances in the supply of books were unavoidable. Books that were plentiful in one place were hardly known and accessible in another.[25] Since books were expensive, scholars, with rare exceptions, had to build up their libraries by copying materials with their own hands; this was so not only at the beginning of their careers, but usually continued throughout their lives. Not many were so fortunate as to be able to buy (or inherit) books or have others do the copying for them as a favor or inexpensively, and it was probably quite unique for a scholar to have a wife whom he could train in proper copying.[26]

A third reason is peculiar to Muslim civilization and of great import for the attitude toward books. It resulted from the never abandoned fiction—very soon to be enshrined in the very center of Muslim intellectual activity, the science of ḥadīth—of the primacy of the spoken word. Books were seen as innovations that came about only after the year 120/738 when the true models of scholarship, the men around Muḥammad and most men of the second generation, were dead,[27] and so on. In fact, of course, written books were indispensable almost from the outset, as was admitted in various ways, for instance, by claiming that memory had been good enough among the ancient Arabs to suffice for preserving and safely transmitting all knowledge; among later generations, this was no longer the case.[28] It became a matter of pride to own, or, at least, have access to, as many books as possible. Yet the deep conviction lingered that there was, in addition, something else that was essential for civilization, no matter how many, or how few, books were around. As a result, their numbers were basically inconsequential. Yet even in this climate, subdued feelings not only about the very existence of books but also about their numbers can be observed on occasion. Religious scholars would complain that once knowledge was committed to writing, there developed an unending process of writing "book after book after book,"[29] the implication being that oral transmission was more restricted and thus less contaminated and more reliable than the endless array of written material. Even for secular scholars, the great increase in books *(al-kutub wa-al-taṣānīf)* made it possible for ignoramuses to infiltrate the ranks of qualified intellectuals, and actually diminish the quality of books.[30] In a way, this can be read, as another faint complaint about the proliferation of literature.

There were other ways in which feelings of this sort tried sporadically to work their way to the surface. This is the subject of the following pages.

The formation of large libraries which was eagerly pursued inevitably led to problems caused by quantity and variety. Selectivity in forming a library, be it that of a private individual or one of semi-public character, was indicated.[31] It was an occasional problem then and, needless to say, has remained one to this day. Not discarding any book was considered the better part of wisdom, even if it was a book on a subject beyond the owner's interest and competence. The brief chapter on "the amassing of books *(al-ikthār min al-kutub)*" in the Khaṭīb al-Baghdādī's (d. 464/1071) *Taqyīd al-ʿilm* "The written fixation of knowledge" contains the essence of medieval thought on the importance of each single book for the educated. As the title suggests, the *Taqyīd* ultimately comes out in favor of the written word but balances and, in a way, conceals the message by first presenting a full array of negative attitudes toward books. The chapter in question deals with three considerations that work against selling any of the books in one's library or not buying books one has the opportunity of buying. Anecdotal as it is, it is best reported in the Khaṭīb's own words.[32]

The first of the three considerations is that a book deemed disposable may later on turn out to be badly needed: "As remarked by some scholar, a person must hoard all kinds of subjects, even subjects he does not know. He must amass works on very many subjects. He must not believe that he can dispense with any subject. If he can dispense with some books on one occasion, he may need them on another. If he is unhappy with them at one time, he may enjoy them at another. If he has no time for them on a given day, he may have time for them on another day. He must not act in a hurry (to sell a book or pass up the opportunity to buy one), lest he later regret very much to have done so. It could happen that someone discards a book and then wants it badly but cannot get hold of it. This may cause him great trouble and many sleepless nights. We have a story about a certain scholar who said: 'Once I sold a book thinking that I did not need it. Then I thought of some matter that was dealt with in that book. I looked for it among all my books but could not find it. I decided to ask some scholar about it the next morning, and I stayed up on my feet all night.' When he was asked why he did not sit down rather than stand, he replied: 'I was so perturbed that I could not get a wink of sleep.' "

This scholar only lost a night's sleep and apparently was able to find a replacement in a colleague's library. But it could also be terribly frustrating and expensive to sell or discard a book, as described by the Khaṭīb in the following two stories: "Someone sold a book thinking that he did not need it. Then he needed and looked for a copy but could not find any either to loan or to buy. The man to whom he had sold his copy had left for his place of residence. He went to him and told him that he would like to cancel the sale and return the purchase price. When the man refused, he asked him to lend him the book, so that he could copy the passage he was interested in. Again, he received a negative response, so he went home frustrated and swore that he would never again sell a book. There was someone else who sold a book which he thought he did not need, but later he did need a passage from it. He went to the new owner and asked him to let him copy the passage in question but was told: 'You won't copy it unless you pav me the price of the entire book.' So he had no choice but to return the price of the book, in order to copy the passage he wanted."[33] The words of someone who was asked why he did not sell the books he did not need sums it all up: "If I do not need them today, I may need them the next day."

The second consideration is that books in fields with which their owner is unfamiliar at the moment may give him the opportunity to familiarize himself with that field. Of course, any field of scholarship has its special interest: "When someone bought a book outside his own special field and asked why he did that, he replied: 'When I buy a book outside my own field of learning, I do it in order to make that particular field part of my knowledge.' And when someone else was asked why he did not buy books to have them in his house, he replied that it was his lack of knowledge that prevented him from building up a library. He was told that one who does not know buys books in order to know. Again, someone else who used to buy every book he saw replied to the question why he bought books he did not need: 'I may need (at some time) what I don't need (now).' "[34] We may add here that the Khaṭīb's chapter ends with an anecdote about the great bibliophile al-Jāḥiẓ (d. 255/868) to the same effect, with the stress on the idea that all written materials should be investigated as to whether they contain information not found elsewhere. Nothing should ever be dismissed offhand.[35]

The third consideration concerns books as a scholar's indispensable tools. He should therefore have them handy at all times: "A judge," the story goes, "used to go into debt to buy books. Questioned about it he replied: 'Should I not buy something that has taken me so far (in the world, i.e., to a judgeship)?' "[36] Further in the same vein: "A carpenter had to sell his ax and saw. He was sad about it and regretted having sold his tools, until one day he saw a scholar, a neighbor of his, in the booksellers' market selling a book. Now he was consoled. He remarked: 'If a scholar can sell his tools, a craftsman is certainly excusable, or even more so, when he sells his.' "

We may conclude from this discourse in praise of books—which is one among many—that books were often so plentiful that one could think of discarding some, but this was generally considered wrong and something one was not supposed to do. There was, however, a dissenting voice if a rather lonely one according to our knowledge. The well-known physician and scientist in eleventh-century Egypt, Ibn Riḍwān, tells us that he either sold the books for which he had no use or stored them away in chests. Selling them, he contends, was preferable to storing them.[37] It is not quite clear whether he meant that it was better to put unneeded books back into circulation rather than keeping them out of sight. It is, however, more likely given, Ibn Riḍwān's great concern with his finances, that he was unwilling to pass up an opportunity to make some more money. He was well known as the champion of the hotly debated view that learning from books was better than by means of oral instruction. It does not seem that he was complaining about owning too many books, or more than he was able to cope with, although this could have easily been the case.

Large semi-public libraries faced a bigger problem as to what to do with their holdings when they grew too large. Books being valuable, the most common danger for libraries, not the least the libraries of which every college had one with a scholarly librarian, was frequent inroads into their holdings by neglect and theft (the always present danger of accidental destruction by fire or water damage does not concern us here). When large libraries were dissolved, it proved a bonanza for scholars who could acquire or appropriate books cheap or sell worthless or made to appear worthless, library books for their own benefit.[38] The failure to return books borrowed from libraries or individuals was often bemoaned in verse and prose. It was thus probably much more difficult to hold together large libraries than trying to weed out unwanted materials. However, we also hear about an author's hesitancy as to whether his works would be accepted for incorporation into a large library.[39] Selectivity was always practiced by collectors and was required in forming a *waqf* library.[40]

The deliberate destruction by fire or other means such as erasing (*maḥā*), washing off (*ghasala*), tearing up (*kharraqa*), or burying (*dafana*) should be mentioned here, even if it had other motives than the weeding out of books when they had become too many. Regrettably, as elsewhere in the world, book burnings were not unheard of in Islam. They affected principally books adjudged heretical or otherwise religiously objectionable.[41] This contributed to the virtual disappearance of manuscripts of such works over the centuries. Where there were both fervent partisans and violent opponents in substantial numbers, of course, the situation was different. This, for instance, is shown by Ibn ʿArabī's (d. 638/1240) voluminous corpus. Even if there were those who wrote *fatwā*s permitting the destruction of all books by him,[42] or who went to such scurrilous lengths as tying the *Kitāb al-Fuṣūṣ* to the tail of a dog,[43] his innumerable followers saw to it that copies of his works survived. An instructive story on the destruction of a work of presumably literary merit is reported in connection with a book by the blind poet al-Maʿarrī (d. 449/1057) which supposedly criticized the Qur'ān. A librarian, of all people, destroyed it. He was challenged by al-Wajīh al-Naḥwī (532–612/1137[8]–1215) with a witty argument: If the work was indeed equal to, or better than, the Qur'ān, it would be untouchable; on the other hand, if it was, as there could be no doubt, inferior to it, it ought to be preserved as a witness to the inimitability of the Holy Book.[44] Perhaps, the underlying and unexpressed moral of the al-Wajīh's remark was disapproval of the destruction of books in general.

The destruction of valuable property such as books expectedly found the attention of jurists. Strict Hanbalite opinion, for instance, was expressed by a scholar of the stature of Ibn Qayyim al-Jawzīyah (d. 751/1350). Other schools and individuals saw the matter differently.[45] Ibn Qayyim al-Jawzīyah held that no financial responsibility resulted from the destruction of books. It was as legal and free from liability as the destruction of everything connected with wine. Ibn Qayyim al-Jawzīyah's basic tradition is one of Abū Bakr al-Marrūdhī (al-Marwazī) (d. 275/888) who consulted Ibn Ḥanbal (d. 241/855) on whether he thought that he could burn or tear up a book he had borrowed that contained objectionable matters. Ibn Ḥanbal expressed the view that it was permissible, quoting a tradition to the effect that the Messenger of God once saw a book in ʿUmar's hand in which ʿUmar had written down material from the Torah that had pleased him because it agreed with the Qur'ān. The Prophet's face showed such anger that ʿUmar rushed to the furnace and threw the book into it. How then, Ibn Qayyim al-Jawzīyah continued, would the Prophet have felt had he been able to see books which contradicted the Qur'ān and his Sunnah as were published later. Only the Qur'ān and the ḥadīth were permitted to be put down in writing, and this is presented as the view of Ibn Ḥanbal himself.

All books on *ra'y*—here, approximately, dogmatic and juridical speculation—and all the more so, all books on other subjects were anathema as leading to error. To err is human, Ibn Ḥanbal is said to have opined, but the most prone to error are those who write books. While the composition of books was seen as a complicated legal problem, Ibn Ḥanbal and his followers were adamantly opposed to books that were in conflict with the Qur'ān and the Sunnah. It was, however, different with works written against those books; they could fall into any of the positive legal classifications as necessary, preferable, or permitted.[46] It does not take much to realize that we have here a good example of the eternal problem of censorship. Once set in motion, does it have proper limits, and can they be observed without detriment to intellectual life and growth? We do not know the answer.

Another common theme is that of an author himself burning his books or ordering their destructions. Among littérateurs, Abū Ḥayyān al-Tawḥīdī (d. after 400/1009) is famous or infamous for having "burned his books at the end of his life because they served no longer any purpose and he did not want those who did not appreciate their worth to have them after his death." In a letter, in which he defends his action, he speaks of burning his valuable books or washing them off. Having lost everybody near and dear to him, he says, "I found it difficult to leave them to people who would play around with them, besmirch my honor when looking into them, gloat over my oversights and mistakes when studying them more closely, and look at each other (and say how) incompetent I am."[47] This makes it clear that al-Tawḥīdī speaks about his own books and not about books by others in his library. It would seem a bit curious that he would burn his own works when they included books that had been published and had been in general circulation for a long time. Therefore, speaking about his own "books," there can be no doubt that he had in mind his unpublished manuscripts and, in particular, his notebooks and drafts.[48] This also applies to, and is confirmed by, his list of those early Muslims who served as model and excuse for his action. The earliest name in al-Tawḥīdī's list is Abū ʿAmr ibn al-ʿAlā' who buried his books. A Ṣūfī, Dāwūd al-Ṭā'ī (d. 205/821), threw his books into the river,[49] while Yūsuf ibn Asbāṭ locked his away in a mountain cave.[50] Another Ṣūfī, Abū Sulaymān al-Dārānī, burned his books in a furnace.[51] The great Sufyān al-Thawrī (d. 161/778) tore his manuscripts to pieces and scattered the pieces in the wind.[52] The last name in the list is that of a teacher of al-Tawḥīdī' Abū Saʿīd al-Sīrāfī (d. 369/979), who exhorted his son (Abū) Muḥammad[53] to burn his books if they turned out to play him and others false and distract them from acquiring religious merit; as in the numerous examples from modern times for requests to destroy the literary Nachlass of famous men, this request, of course, may or may not have been honored. The variety of ways for the disposal of books we find in al-Tawḥīdī's list is owed to his sense of style, and not necessarily to the sources from which he derived his information.

With the possible exception of Abū Sa'īd al-Sīrāfī who, however, was highly praised for his asceticism, all these men were famous exemplars of Muslim piety and religious commitment. Their alleged actions expressed their suspicion of the written word in general. But they hardly were appropriate models for al-Tawḥīdī who, in spite of pietistic episodes in his life, produced mainly works that were quite worldly in character. As other sources make abundantly clear, the destruction of one's written materials is a topos of the science of ḥadīth and of mysticism. How much reality was connected with the topos, we cannot judge. Later biographers showed a certain lack of enthusiasm for reporting these data.

We thus hear it said already about the first/seventh-century 'Abīdah al-Salmānī that he called for his "books" and erased them when he lay on his deathbed. Asked for his reason, he replied that he feared that some people might get hold of them who would not treat them properly (*yaḍa'ūnahā ghayr mawāḍī'ihā*).[54] This seems to be the earliest and, superfluous to say, fictitious example within the tradition of ḥadīth scholarship. The Khaṭīb al-Baghdādī mentions already Ibn Mas'ūd among his many examples of men who erased written ḥadīth material.[55] He tells of Abū Qilābah that he willed his "books" to another scholar if the latter survived him; if not, they were to be burned or, according to another recension, torn up.[56] A certain Yūnus ibn'Īsá meant to burn his books.[57] Shu'bah ibn al-Ḥajjāj (d. 160/777) directed his son Sa'd to wash off and bury his "books" after his death, which was done.[58] Others buried eighteen chests and baskets of books for Bishr al-Ḥāfī. It is to the credit of Ibn Ḥanbal that he could not see any sense in burning books.[60]

These and similar data continued to have a long life. The seventeenth-century Ḥājjī Khalīfah has a list that includes al-Tawḥīdī's Abū 'Amr ibn al-'Alā', Dāwūd al-Ṭā'ī, and Sufyān al-Thawrīi. He took their names not from al-Tawḥīdī but from other sources which he indicates, but which I have been unable to check. He added the Sūfī Ibn Abū al-Ḥawārī (6th/12th century) from the *Ḥilyah* of Abū Nu'aym al-Iṣfahānī (d. 430/103Q). The *Ḥilyah* presents different recensions, all of which agree that Ibn Abī al-Ḥawārī was motivated by his conviction that books may serve as guides to gnosis but become superfluous as soon as a person attains gnosis and reaches the Lord.[61]

It is to Ḥājjī Khalīfah's credit that he clearly distinguished between the two strands that defined all the statements about the destruction of "books." One of them, he realized, was the need of ḥadīth theoreticians to produce telling evidence for the alleged superiority of oral over written transmission. The other was the persistent claim of pious individuals and devoted mystics to have direct access to the divine which made any material medium such as books altogether unnecessary and undesirable.[62] Ḥājjī Khalīfh considers the view expressed by Ibn Ḥajar in connection with Dāwūd al-Ṭā'ī that the motivation for the destruction of their books by men like him was the prevention of their transmission in a way that might lead to their being branded as "weak transmitters." On his part, Ḥājjī Khalīfah realized that more was involved here: "This explanation," he says, "would not hold for the destruction of their notebooks (*dafātir*) by Ibn Abī al-Ḥawārī and his ilk. Dāwūd al-Ṭā'ī did what he did because he was concerned about the resulting weakness of his *isnād*. On the other hand, Ibn Abī al-Ḥawārī did it because of his asceticism and devotion to God. The explanation why he (and others like him) chose to destroy (their books, instead of selling them or giving them away) might perhaps be (sought in their fear) that, if they had divested themselves of the possession of their *dafātir* through gift or sale, their emotional (*qalbī*) attachment to them would not have been severed completely and they could not be sure that they might not at some time get the urge to go back to them and study them, thereby occupying themselves with something other than God."[63]

In historical cases, the evidence for such destruction is occasionally ambiguous. Thus, we hear that Aḥmad ibn Ismā'īl ibn Abī al-Su'ūd (814–870/1412–66) reached the point, probably because of religious scruples (?), where he wanted to give up all his literary activities, and he washed off all his poetical and prose writings, so that only his previously published works survived. However, another source maintains that this did not happen intentionally. When Ibn Abī al-Su'ūd was in the process of sorting out the poems he did not like in order to destroy them, a colleague appeared unexpectedly and he went out to meet him. Meanwhile, he ordered someone to destroy the papers on the right in his study. That individual became confused and destroyed the papers which Ibn Abī al-Su'ūd wanted to keep. When Ibn Abī al-Su'ūd came back and saw what had happened, he was very dismayed (*suqiṭa fī yadihi*) and destroyed the rest.[64]

Such destruction of papers and notes, or books in our sense, whether historical or not, did not reflect on the size of book production. This, I feel, probably also applies to a statement telling us that, at the time it was made, there were people who disapproved of all authorship (*al-taṣnīf wa-al-ta'līf*), even of those who were qualified and knowledgeable enough to write books. So far, I have been unable to trace this statement to any source earlier than Badr al-Dīn ibn Jamā'ah (639–733/1241–1333) who mentions it in his well-known treatise on education, entitled *Tadhkirat al-sāmi' wa-al-mutakallim*[65] Ibn Jamā'ah strongly disapproves of this attitude. If, he argues, there is no legal disapproval of the written fixation of poetry and entertaining stories, provided no indecency is involved, why, then, should the writing of books on useful religious subjects be disapproved? It is obvious that unqualified people should never be allowed to write books on any subject. As Ibn Jamā'ah sees it, the only possible explanation for the disapproval of authoring books is the constant envy and competitiveness among generations (*al-taḥāsud bayna ahl al-a'ṣār*).[66] Quoting Ibn Jamā'ah's view, Ḥājjī Khalīfah then goes on to criticize it as a reflection of the popular attitude that considers only the achievements of earlier generations as important and routinely holds contemporary scholars in low esteem, and he treats his readers to the verses:

You who think nothing of contemporaries,
considering the ancients to be out in front:
The ancients were once young/new,
And the young/new will stay on and become ancient.[67]

Neither Ibn Jamāʿah nor Ḥājjī Khalīfah seem to be correct. The disapproval of composing books may also here be rooted rather in the pietistic/mystic attitude and the long tradition of philosophers (such as Socrates) and, above all, mystics who feel revulsion at the thought of profaning their insights. It is not impossible that the expression could be explained as a complaint about the proliferation of books, but this does not really seem plausible.

The problem of overproduction is more directly addressed in the strong sentiment in favor of abridgements and brief handbooks as against long, comprehensive, and scholarly works. The latter were, of course, always produced in large numbers. They were, in fact, quite characteristic products of medieval Muslim civilization. However, the attitude, serious in part and in part a snobbish pretense, that big books are a nuisance was old and deeply engrained. al-Tawḥīdī put it succinctly: "Big books are boring *(al-kutub al-ṭiwāl mus'imah)*.[68] As A. Mez stressed long ago, writers of Muslim civilization's so-called golden age feared nothing more than boring the reader.[69] This fear persisted through the centuries and found expression in the frequently professed aversion to unnecessary length and the claim of having exercised restraint for the sake of brevity. While conciseness had special meaning for the entertaining literature, it soon invaded the scholarly and scientific community where it led to the popularity of compendia. Resistance to the trend never faltered entirely. For instance, in the introduction of his long geographical dictionary, Yāqūt (d. 627/1229) expressed himself with strong emotion against any attempt to shorten his work, quoting al-Jāḥiẓ as having been of the same mind when he stated forcefully that an author is "like a painter; his work is a painting representing its subject perfectly, and the idea of abridging it means atrocious mutilation.[70] The practice (often also indulged in by us) of exploiting large works for educational and/or commercial reasons by compiling shortened versions, which, as noted by Yāqūt, stood a better chance of achieving wide dissemination, was part and parcel of medieval Muslim life.

It was recognized that progress dictated the creation of larger and better works. Treatments of new and as yet unexplored subjects tended to start out small and then grow to ever larger size in the course of time.[71] Originality was stressed as the fundamental purpose of and justification for writing and was one of the guiding principles of research.[72] The remark, already used by Abū

Tammām (d. 231/846) the poet as a cento,[73] was constantly repeated: "How much did the ancients leave for later generations (*kam taraka al-awwalu lil-ākhiri*)." al-Jāḥiẓ is quoted again by Yāqūt as having stated that nothing is more harmful to science and scholarship than the opposite contention that the ancients did not leave anything for later generations, as this had a discouraging and debilitating effect.[74] The consequence, however, was the constant creation of new disciplines and subdisciplines, small at first and then often expanding to barely manageable proportions. With the technical means then available, they were probably unmanageable and required forgetting and discarding. More, and better, techniques are available now and offer a certain, possibly deceptive, measure of hope that we shall be able to keep up with the accumulation of knowledge and of books.

The theoretical approach of philosophers to the overwhelming mass and variety of knowledge put into writing was to suggest, as did al-Tawḥīdī and al-Miskawayh (d. 422/1030), that "since the particulars (*juz'īvāt*) are infinite, and whatever is infinite cannot achieve existence, it is the generalities of each discipline, which comprise all its particulars *in potentia*, that should be aimed at."[75] Deprived of its technical philosophical trimmings, the idea also lived on and found expression, for instance, in al-Zarkashī's (d. 794/1391) detailed elaboration of the different Qur'ānic sciences. Since, he claims, "the *'ulūm al-Qur'ān* are innumerable and the Qur'ān's meanings are inexhaustible, one must deal with them (not exhaustively but) to the degree possible." And "since earlier scholars composed no work comprising the different topics (*anwā'*) of Qur'ānic science in the way it was done in relation to the science of ḥadīth," he wrote his comprehensive work covering forty-six topics, but, he says,

> I am aware that every one of these topics cannot be dealt with exhaustively by any human being. If anyone tried, the whole of his life would be spent, and yet, he would not accomplish his task. Therefore, we have restricted ourselves to the principles (*uṣūl*) of each topic, with (only) occasional hints at the details (*fuṣūl*), for—quoting Hippocrates without naming him—"the craft is long and life is short."[76] We have dealt with as much as can possibly be achieved by imperfect speech, in accordance with the verse:
>
> > They said: Take the essence/eye (*'ayn*) of everything! I replied: There is excellence in the essence/eye, but the beholder of the essence/the glance of the eye (is imperfect).[77]

In the popular and entertaining literature, a simpler analogy was proposed in a saying which, like the philosophical approach, also had its roots in classical antiquity: Like a bee, an author should select the best flower. A more direct version of the same idea was attributed to ancient Muslims such as 'Abd Allah ibn 'Abbās (d. 68/686) and Ibn Sīrīn (d. 110/728): "Knowledge is too much for being comprehended in its entirety. Thus, take the best of every knowledge!"[78]

The statement of Ibn ʿAbbās was combined later with another one attributed to al-Shaʿbī who, like Ibn Sīrīn, lived a generation after Ibn ʿAbbās. al-Shaʿbī (d. 105/723) supposedly also alluded to Hippocrates without naming him. As he phrased it: "Knowledge is much, and life is little. Thus, take of knowledge the variety of its inner spirit (*arwāḥ*)—that is, its essences (*ʿuyūn*)—and leave alone its outward expression (*ḥurūf*)!"[79]

This advice was meant for the creative scholar and intellectual. For the mass of the educated, the compendium, the short exposition of the essentials or high points of a subject or the selective presentation of details, promised a better approach toward the elusive mastery of knowledge in its infinite variety. Another approach was for an author to justify writing a book by suggesting that his work, being an original product, would serve to replace all other works in the field[80]—this, we might say, being one way of dealing with the avalanche of books. In writing his great chronological work, al-Bīrūnī (d. 440/1048), for instance, claimed that the highly educated person who asked him to compose such a work did so in order to have a book that would make it superfluous for him to consult a large number of sources.[81] More commonly, authors expressed on their own the hope or conviction that they were about to replace any need to consult all the earlier works that had dealt with their subject. The large number of titles such as *al-Mughnī*, it may be noted, also attests to this motivation. On the other hand, it could also happen that a would-be author originally thought that the existing literature was exhaustive and made another work on the same subject unnecessary. After much research, however, he discovered that this was not the case, and he was justified in going ahead with his project and compose a more complete work likely to supplant all his predecessors' efforts. He reflected, at the end, "how much the ancients had left for later generations to do."[82]

The production of compendia in order to cope with the great amount of material to be read and digested and to make the acquisition of knowledge easier for the student eventually found full discussion in both its positive and its negative aspects in Ibn Khaldūn's *Muqaddimah*.[83] As Ibn Khaldūn (d. 808/1406) saw it, the great number of scholarly works, coupled with the refinement and sophistication reached in many fields, is an obstacle to scholarship, while the great number of brief handbooks is detrimental to the formation of a sound scholarly habit and thus of outstanding scholars. In many disciplines such as grammar[84] the literature is too vast for everything to be perused. More recently, says Ibn Khaldūn, this has also come to apply to the many writings on literary criticism which were produced in addition to the four standard works on the subject.[85] An even more crowded field, the science of ḥadīth, had developed an enormous amount of books and this had the consequence that a limited number of basic works was exclusively used for reference.[86] Ibn Khaldūn, it seems, considered this a rather dubious development. He did not go as far as to suggest that there were too many books on the market, but he clearly intimated that something was wrong with the prevailing situation and called for remedies if such could be found. Focusing his attention on the handbooks, abridgements, and compendia, he acknowledged that one of the legitimate purposes of authorship was generally recognized the production of brief and succinct abridgements.[87] The custom, he said, had become popular in his time (although it was, of course, widely practiced in preceding centuries). He considered such abridgements as often awkward but did not object to them as such. He pointed out that on the one hand, they tended to be too succinct and complicated for beginners, while, on the other, they were likely to stultify genuine scholarly minds, for true scholarship, he argued, required the painstaking study of long and detailed works over a considerable extent of time. It is clsar that for Ibn Khaldūn and those who followed him, the issue was not seen simply as the superabundance of books, although he realized that it caused a problem. It was rather a question of the proper methods and goals of scholarly and literary activity which were appropriate for a highly developed civilization such as his. These methods and goals, however, happened unavoidably to be dependent on the relentless production and wide availability of books. By his time and very probably much earlier, their numbers had come to seem threatening.

Ibn Khaldūn's discussion greatly impressed Ḥājjī Khalīfah who utilized it in the introduction of his large catalogue of Arabic books in Istanbul or otherwise known in his time.[88] In his capacity as a bibliographer, Ḥājjī Khalīfah might well have had special feelings about the cultural significance of the riches of book production in Islam. About seven centuries earlier, the situation was different. In his famous *Fihrist*, Ibn al-Nadīm (d. 380/990) had already vast numbers of titles to report on, but there was no real reason for him to sense, let alone comment on, too many books. So he concerned himself in his opening pages with the technical aspects of bookmaking which to him meant handwriting and scripts in their various forms and historical development. In the century before Ḥājjī Khalīfah, Ṭāshköprüzādeh produced a mammoth catalogue of the sciences, entitled *Miftāḥ al-sa'ādah*. His interest lay in the enormous amount of what he classified as special disciplines that together constituted the sum total of written knowledge no longer to be mastered in its entirety; he had occasion to mention only a limited number of standard works. It is due to Ṭāshköprüzādeh's influence that Ḥājjī Khalīfah in his introduction discourses lengthily on knowledge and its multiple disciplines, instead of book production as would have been logical. Thus, he misses out on the opportunity to speculate on the subiect that interests us here most. He remarks, however, in the beginning that an exhaustive bibliography such as his had become finally necessary, "because the scholarly disciplines *and books are many*, and the lives of individuals are preciously short."[89]

In conclusion, let me state that the feeling that there are simply too many books in the world remains a present-day phenomenon and is left to us not only to ponder but also to try to do something about it, if this is in our power. Possibly the fate of our civilization depends on it. In medieval Islam, books as physical objects were valuable since, for the ordinary individual, they were difficult to obtain and to amass; although plentiful in some locations, they could be scarce in others. The censorial destruction of books for one reason or another did occur at times, to the detriment of modern scholarship, but contributed little to limiting the constant increase in the number of books. The relationship between knowledge and books remained determined by a fictitious and, from our point of view, unfortunate distinction between oral and written information. Again, this did not contribute much to diminishing book production. It did, however, give some slight encouragement to the age-old tradition that some type of special secret or sacred knowledge was better left unwritten. Still, in the face of the pretended belief in the superiority of oral transmission, it was generally recognized that all knowledge was important and would disappear without books. This recognition often extended to the realization that all written materials were valuable and required preservation. The only practical attempts, however, to regulate, if modestly, the flood of books consisted of the production of works that were supposed to take the place of all the previous publications in a given field, and of the composition of handbooks and compendia, but the value and efficacy of these procedures did not remain unquestioned. Before the age of printing and modern technology, this was probably the most that could be done. The Muslim scholars cited here deserve credit for having been aware, if ever so dimly, of the problems resulting from the overproduction of books as an unintended by-product of the intellectual flourishing of their civilization. As it turned out, of making many books there was no end in medieval Islam, and we have every reason to be glad that this was so.

Notes

1. A good brief survey of contemporary scholarship on all aspects of bookmaking is by G. Endress, in *Grundriss der arabischen Philologie*, ed. by Wolfdietrich Fischer (Wiesbaden, 1983), 1:271ff.

2. While I was working on this paper, the Book Review section of the *New York Times* of 20 March 1989 published an essay by Arthur Krystal, "On Writing: Let There Be Less," dealing interestingly with our subject as reflected through the ages. Krystal mentions the Ancient Egyptian statement of Khakheperre-sonbe, which reads in the translation of W.K. Simpson: "He said: Would that I had unknown speeches, erudite phrases in new language which has not yet been used, free from the usual repetitions, not the phrases of past speech which (our) forefathers spoke." See W.K. Simpson (ed.), *The Literature of Ancient Egypt* (New Haven and London, 1972, 1973), pp. 230–33. This should

not be understood as a complaint about the existence of too much literature. Rather, it is an expression of the author's desire to be original. Expectedly, the modern plea for fewer books elicited heated responses among the essay's readers, as shown by letters to the *Book Review* of 30 April 1989, p. 5.

3. An exception is Michael V. Fox, *Qohelet and his Contradictions* (Sheffield, 1989. Bible and Literature Series 18), p. 311. I am grateful to Robert R. Wilson for bibliographical guidance through the vast ocean of biblical studies.

4. Cf. R.B.Y. Scott's commentary on Ecclesiastes in the Anchor Bible (Garden City, NY, 1963).

5. Fox, op. cit., 237.

6. According to M. Dahood, cf. H.L. Ginsberg, *Koheleth* (Tel Aviv 1961), p. 139.

7. Osweld Loretz, *Qohelet und der Alte Orient* (Freiburg-Basel-Wien, 1964), p. 139.

8. Cf. Ginsberg, loc. cit.; Michael Fishbane, *Biblical Interpretation in Ancient Israel* (Oxford, 1985), pp. 30 32; Fox, op. cit., p. 328f.

9. The presence of a possessive pronoun, which strengthens the meaning of collecting, would hardly be needed or fit into the syntax of Eccles. 12:12.

10. It seems as yet undecided whether *harbeh* (=Aram. Saggi) is used here as an adjective or as an adverb (cf. J. Goldin, "The end of Ecclesiastes," in A. Altmann, ed., *Biblical Motifs* [Cambridge, 1966], pp. 135–58.) The adverbial combination, lit., "the much making of books," appears preferable. In Semitic languages there is no easy distinction between "much" and "too much." Thus, *harbeh* in Eccles. 7:16 is translated by Ginsberg "don't overdo," cf. his *The Five Megilloth* (Philadelphia,1969), p. 68.

11. Cf. for instance Muḥammad ibn al-Raḥmān al-Sakhāwī, *al-Ḍaw' al-lāmi' li-ahl al-Qarn al-Tāsi'*, 12 vols. (Cairo, 1353–55/1934–36), 9:259, "*lahija bi-ṭalab al-ḥadīth wa-al-qirā'ah.*"

12. See above, n. 6, and M. Dahood, "Canaanite-Phoenician influence in Qoheleth," in *Biblica* 33 (1952), p. 219.

13. According to the publication of A. Sperber, *The Bible in Aramaic*, 4 vols. in 5, (Leiden. 1968), 5:167.

14. Cf. W. Strothmann (ed.), *Kohelet-Kommentar des Johannes von Apamea* (Wiesbaden, 1988. Gottinger Orientforschungen, I Reihe: Syriaca, Band 30), p. 182. It is, however, not surprising to find *huggaya* "meditation" as a translation of *lahag*, cf. W. Strothmann, *Kohelet-Kommentar des Dionvsius bār Ṣalībī* (Wiesbaden, 1988, Band 31).

15. I am greatly obligated to M. Ullmann for communicating to me his Wörterbuch entries for *lahjah*. They seem to leave doubts in his mind as to the relationship between the root *l-h-j* and *lahjah*.

16. Fox, op. cit., p. 328.

17. Cf. G. Vajda, *Deux Commentaires Karaïtes sur l'Ecclesiaste* (Leiden, 1971), pp. 61, 75.

18. Abū al-Barakāt Hibat Allah al-Baghdādī, *al-Muʿtabar*, 3 vols. (Hyderabad, 1357–58/1938–39), 2:347, line 12ff. I owe this reference to Moshe Perlmann.

In the following generation, Moses Maimonides interpreted the Mishnaic expression "heretical books (*sefarim hitsonim*) as including books on history and *adab* which constitute a waste of time, cf. his commentary on the Mishna Sanhedrin, X, 1, ed. J. Qafih (Jerusalem, 1934), p. 210.

19. Ibn Khallikān, *Wafayāt al-a ʿyān*, 8 vols., ed. Iḥsān ʿAbbās (Beirut, 1968–72), 1:20.

20. Cf. al-Ījī and al-Sakhāwī as quoted in F. Rosenthal, *A History of Muslim Historiography*² (Leiden. 1968), pp. 242ff., 388.

21. Cf. Murtaḍā al-Zabīdī, *Itḥāf al-Sādah*, 10 vols. (Cairo, 1311/1893). Reprinted in Beirut, 1:273, line 14ff.

22. Cf. al-Sakhāwī, *Ḍaw'*, 10:21. The number 300 appears again in connection with al-Khirāqī's *Mukhtaṣar*. See *The Encyclopedia of Islam*, 2nd ed. (EI²), s.v Hanabila, 3:159, col. 1, line 30 and again s.v. al-Khiraki (H. Laoust), 5:10, col. 1, line 23, but, of course, other figures appear as well. In all cases, it can be assumed to have been a boast about the large number of sources consudted.

23. Cf. Ibn Khaldūn, *Muqaddimah*, tr. by F. Rosenthal, 3 vols. (New York, 1958; Princeton, 1967), 2:455. See below, p. 43.

24. See the most useful dissertation by Peter Freimark on *Das Vorwort als literarische Form in der arabischen Literatur* (Münster, 1967). Writing on *Latin Prose Prefaces* (Stockholm, 1964, *Acta Universitatis Stockholmianiae, Studia Latina Stockholmiana* 13), Toe Janson apparently found nothing in his material on the overwhelming amount of available books on a given subject, nor did Freimark in Arabic.

25. Murtaḍā al-Zabīdī, *Itḥāf*, 1:274, line 12f.

26. Al-Sakhāwī, *Ḍaw'*, 2:180, line 4 from bottom.

27. Al-Ghazzālī, *Iḥyā' 'ulūm al-dīn*, 4 vols. in 2 (Cairo, 1372/1953), 1:70, line 4ff., from Abū Ṭālib al-Makkī, *Qūt al-qulūb*, 2 vols. (Cairo, 1310/1892), 1:159; 4 vols. in 2 (Cairo, 1351/1932), 2:37.

28. See, for instance, Ibn 'Abd al-Barr, *Jāmi' bayān al-'ilm*, 2 vols., (Cairo, n.d.), 1:69f.

29. Ibn Qayyim al-Jawzīyah, *al-Ṭurūq al-ḥukmīyah* (Cairo, 1372/1953), p. 277.

30. Abū al-Barakāt Hibat Allah al-Baghdādī, *al-Mu'tabar fī al-ḥikmah*, 3 vols., (Hyderabad, 1938–39), 1:3.

31. See below p. 000.

32. al-Khaṭīb al-Baghdādī, *Taqyīd al-'ilm*, ed. Youssef Eche (Yūsuf al-'Ishsh) (Damascus, 1949, reprint 1975), pp. 136–38.

33. Some trickery might be used by a rare book dealer, in order to raise the fee for lending a book to what the price of the entire book should have been, cf. al-Sakhāwī, *Ḍaw'*, 9:148. The owners of lending libraries as a rule would seem to have been honest and often generous.

34. Here follow verses attributed to al-Sārī ibn Aḥmad al-Kindī, i.e., al-Sārī al-Raffā'. They are not included in the 1355/1936 and 1981 editions of his *dīwān* They deal with the widespread topos of the lasting value of all knowledge and have little to do directly with the subject of books.

35. Cf. also, for instance, Ibn Ḥazm, *Marātib al-'ul*ūm, in Anwar Chejne, *Ibn Hazm* (Chicago, 1982), text, 234, trans., p. 202f. Ibn Ḥazm also called it an error to decry the amassing of books.

36. Al-Jāḥiẓ already discussed at length the "pleasure" of spending money on books, if it was done for the sake of scholarship and not for purposes of religious ostentation as, he claims, was done by the Manichaeans. Cf. *Kitāb al-Ḥayawān*, 7 vols., ed. ʿAbd al-Salām M. Hārūn (Cairo, 1938–45), 1:56. See also Ibn Ḥazm, loc. cit.

37. Cf. J. Schacht and M. Meyerhof, *The Medico-Philosophical Controversy between Ibn Butlan and Ibn Ridwan of Cairo*, Arabic text 5 (Cairo, 1937), p. 38, from Ibn Abī Uṣaybiʿah; F. Rosenthal, "Die arabische Autobiographie," *Studia Arabica* I (Rome, 1937, Analecta Orientalia 14), p. 22, from the manuscript of Ibn Riḍwān's autobiography. The eighteenth-century Murtaḍá al-Zabīdī, *Itḥāf*, 1:66, lines 15–67, line 11, still found the passage interesting enough to quote it.

38. Cf. Youssef Eche, *Les Bibliothèques arabes* (Damascus, 1967), p. 250. Selling books "by the lot (*bi-al-ʿadad*)" from a bookseller's estate might have been necessitated by their large numbers but, above all, indicated general ignorance and a lack of discrimination by potential buyers, cf. al-Sakhāwī, *Ḍaw'*, 3:150, line 6. An ignorant (*mutakhallif*?) son of Ibn Yūnus would sell the books and works of his father left to him "by the pound (*bi-al-arṭāl*)," cf. Al-Ṣafadī, *Wāfī* (Stuttgart, 1988. Bibliotheca Islamica 6u) 21:226, line 8.

39. Cf. Eche, op. cit., 104 from Yāqūt, *Irshād al-arīb*, ed. D.S. Margoliouth, 7 vols. (Leiden-London, 1907–27), 1:242; ed. A.F. Rifāʿī, 20 vols. (Cairo, 1355–57/1936–1938), 4:6.

40. Eche, op. cit., 198, from al-Qifṭī, *Ikhbār al-ʿulamā' bi-akhbār al-ḥukamā'*, ed. J. Lippert (Leipzig, 1903), p. 269.

41. The justification for book burnings was probably always sought in lèse-religion. The sad case of a grandson of ʿAbd al-Qādir al-Jīlānī, ʿAbd al-Salām ibn ʿAbd al-Wahhāb (548–611/1154–1214), whose books on magic and star worship were publicly burned, illustrates the blend of personal, academic, and religious politics with suspicions of heresy that could lead to legal proceedings and autodafés, cf. Ibn al-ʿImad, *Shadharāt al-Dhahab*, 8 vols. (Cairo, 1350–51/1931–32), 5:45f.

42. Cf. al-Sakhāwī, *Ḍaw'*, 3:32, line 17.

43. Cf. Ibn Ḥajar, *Inbā'*, 9 vols, (Hyderabad, 1387–96/1967–76), 7:394, anno 823, quoted by al-Sakhāwī, *Ḍaw'*, 3:31.

44. Cf. Eche, op. cit., 188, following Yāqūt, *Irshād*, ed. Margoliouth, 6:235; ed. Rifā'ī, 27:59f.

45. See ibn al-Jamā'ah, below, p. 42. (regarding the attitude towards the disapproval of writing books.)

46. Cf. Ibn Qayyim al-Jawzīyah, *al-Ṭurūq al-ḥukmīyah*, pp. 275–77.

47. Cf. Yāqūt, *Irshād*, ed. Margouliouth, 5:386ff.; ed. Rifā'ī, 15:16, 9:21ff.

48. Ḥājjī Khalīfah, *Kashf al-Ẓunūn*, ed. Serefettin Yaltkaya, 2 vols. (Istanbul, 1945–47), vol. 1, intro., col. 52b, quotes the section of *Kunā* from Ibn 'Asākir's *History of Damascus* as using *dafātir* in connection with Sufyān al-Thawrī (below no. 52). Although historically, *daftar* had different meanings (see EI², s.v. "Daftar" [B. Lewis]), in our context "notebooks" is intended. It need hardly be stated expressly that the range of meanings of Arabic *Kitāb* is not coextensive with our "book."

49. According to al-Khaṭīb al-Baghdādī, *Tārīkh Baghdād*, 14 vols., (Cairo, 1349/1931), 8:348, line 2f., Dāwūd al-Ṭā'ī did so after he felt sure that he no longer needed the books and was ready to devote himself conclusively to solitary divine worship.

50. Mention of the mountain cave is not found in the biographical notices. They say that he buried his books, with unhappy results for the reliability of his traditions. See al-Bukhārī, *Tārīkh*, 8 vols. (Hyderabad,1360–78/1941–58), 4 pt. 2:385; Ibn Abī Ḥātim al-Rāzī, *Jarh* (Hyderabad, 1941–53), 4 pt. 2:218 on the authority of his father Abū Ḥātim al-Rāzī; al-Dhahabī, *Mīzān al-I'tidāl*, 4 vols. (Cairo, 1382/1963), 4:162; Ibn Ḥajar, *Tahdhīb al-tahdhīb*, 12 vols. (Hyderabad, 1325–27/1907–9), 11:408. This does not necessarily indicate that al-Tawḥīdī invented the mountain cave for artistic effect—he could have found it in some other source—but it is quite likely.

51. Abū Sulaymān al-Dārānī was an authority of Ibn Abī al-Ḥawārī (below, no. 61), who was a contemporary of Sufyān al-Thawrī.

52. I have not gone through the large literature on Sufyān to find out whether this information is repeated elsewhere.

53. The text has Muḥammad, but he is presumably Abū Sa'īd's son Abū Muḥammad ibn al-Ḥasan (whose name is occasionally distorted), see Ibn al-Nadīm, *al-Fihrist*, p. 62f., also 31, line 23, as well as Bayard Dodge's English

translation, 2 vols. (New York, 1970), 1:136, and the Persian translation by M. Riḍā Tajaddud (Teheran, 1343/1965), p. 106; ʿAlī ibn Yūsuf al-Qifṭī *Inbāh al-rūwāh*, ed. M. Abū al-Fadl Ibrāhīm, 4 vols. (Cairo, 1369–93/1950–73), 1:314; Ibn Khallikān, *Wafayāt*, ed. Iḥsān ʿAbbās, 2:79; Sezgin, *GAS*, 9:98; al-Sīrāfī's long biography in Yāqūt, *Irshād*, ed. Margoliouth, 3:48–125; ed Rifāʿī, 8:142–232, draws on al-Tawḥīdī's works, but the request to have his books burned is not mentioned there. On Abū Saʿīd al-Sīrāfī, see also, more recently, G. Endress, "Grammatik und Logik" in Burkhard Moisisch (ed.), *Sprachphilosophie in Antike und Mittelalter* (Amsterdam, 1987, Bochumer Studien zurr Philosophie 3).

54. Ibn Saʿd, *Ṭabaqāt*, ed. E. Sachau and others, 9 vols. (Leiden, 1904–40), 4:63, lines 17ff.; al-Khaṭīb al-Baghdādī, *Taqyīd*, p. 61; Ibn ʿAbd al-Barr, *Jāmiʿ bayān al-ʿilm*, 1:67, etc.

55. *Taqyīd*, p. 39, line 11f. Ibn Masʿūd was put on the spot for transmitting a ḥadīth differently from what his son had written down.

56. *Taqyīd*, p.62.

57. Ibid. Yūnus ibn ʿĪsā was an authority on Bishr al-Ḥāfī.

58. Ibid.

59. *Taqyīd*, p. 63. According to Ibn Ḥajar, *Tahdhīb*, 1:445, Bishr disliked the transmission of ḥadīth and therefore buried his books. Abū Nuʿaym has nothing on the subject.

60. Ibid.

61. Abū Nuʿaym, *Ḥilyat al-awliyā'*, 10 vols. (Reprint Beirut, 1387/1967), 10:6f.

62. On the other hand, scholars were considered foolish to brag about composing works without recourse to relevant literature. Such disregard of their predecessors meant that they would not know what distinguished their works from those of others, cf. al-Zarkashī, *al-Burhān fī ʿulūm al-Qur'an*, 4 vols. (Cairo, 1376/1957), 1:16.

63. Cf. Ḥājjī Khalīfah, *Kashf*, 1:intro., col. 32f. The wish to approach God (*qaṣd wajh Allah*) was generally accepted goal and precondition for any successful study. Without it, collecting books would be useless, see, for instance, Yūsuf al-Balāwī, *Kitāb alif bā'*, 2 vols. (Būlāq, 1287/1870), 1:17, line 2f.

64. See al-Sakhāwī, *Ḍaw'*, 1:232f.

65. See Ibn Jamā'ah, *Tadhkirah* (Hyderabad, 1953), p. 30. In the context, Ibn Jamā'ah mentions al-Khaṭīb al-Baghdādī, but the quoted statement is apparently not included in the reference. In a somewhat shortened form, with the omission of the qualified and knowledgeable persons, the statement is quoted by Ḥājjī Khalīifah, 1:intro., col. 39. On his own, it seems Ḥājjī Khalīfah adds *muṭlaqan* "absolutely (disapproved)." *Taṣnīf* usually referred to the original composition of books. Cf., for instance, al-Sakhāwī, *Ḍaw'*, 1:46, line 19ff., on the very learned Ibrāhīm ibn Khiḍr: "In spite of his learning, he did not occupy himself with *taṣnīf*, although he made valuable notes on many books." Cf. also Ibn Ḥajar, *al-Durar al-kāminah*, 1st ed., 4 vols. (Hyderabad, 1348–50/1929–31), 3:490; idem, *Inbā'*, 1:184, or al-Sakhāwī, *Ḍaw'*, 2:79.

66. One may compare, from a different time and situation, al-Jāḥiẓ's remark about an ignoramus who progressed from finding fault with al-Jāḥiẓ's works to condemning the writing of books in general (*Kitāb al-Ḥayawān*, ed. Hārūn, 1:19, 37–38).

67. See also below, p. 44.

68. Cf. al-Tawḥīdī, *al Imtā' wa al mu'ānasah*, ed. Aḥmad Amīn and Aḥmad al-Zayn, 3 vols. (Cairo, 1939–44), 2:194, line 6.

69. Cf. Mez's introduction to his edition of *Abulḳāsim, ein bagdäder Sittenbild* (Heidleberg, 1902), viii f.

70. Cf. Yāqūt, *Mu'jam al-buldān*, ed. F. Wüstenfeld (Göttingen, 1866–73), 1:11f., trans. Wadie Jwaideh, *The Introductory Chapters of Yāqūt's Mu'jam al-Buldan* (Leiden, 1959), p. 16.

71. Cf. F. Rosenthal, *The Technique and Approach of Muslim Scholarship* (Rome, 1947. Analecta Orientalia 24), p. 43a, and idem, *A History of Muslim Historiography*², p. 71, n.3.

72. As indicated in the enumeration of items that justify the writing of books, see below, n. 87.

73. See Yāqūt, trans. Jwaideh, p. 9, n. 4.

74. See Yāqūt, *Mu'jam*, 1:6, trans. Jwaideh, p. 9. Jwaideh notes that the statement recurs in the biography of al-Jāḥiẓ in Yāqūt, *Irshād*, ed. Margoliouth, 6:58, ed. Rifā'ī, 16:78.

75. Al-Tawḥīdī and Miskawayh, *al-Ḥawāmil wa-al-shawāmil*, ed. Aḥmad Amīn and al-Sayyid Aḥmad Ṣaqr (Cairo, 1370/1951), p. 268f.

76. Below, in the reference by al-Sha'bi to the common idea that human life is all too short to know everything, it is not as certain as it is here and elsewhere that the first aphorism is indeed the inspiration, but it seems highly probable.

77. This appears to be the correct interpretation of the verse to be read: . . .*wa-lakin nāziru al-'ayni*. See al-Zarkashī, *Burhān*, 1:9, 12, quoted in part by al-Suyūṭī, *Itqān*, 2 vols. in 1 (Cairo, 1317/1899), 1:5.

78. Cf. Freimark, p. 64, referring to al-Washshā', *Muwashshá*, for Ibn 'Abbās, and to Ibn 'Abd Rabbih, *'Iqd*, for Ibn Sīrīn. This latter ascription appears also in al-Balāwī, *Kitāb alif bā'*, 1:14, line 19.

79. See 'Alī al-Ghuzūlī, *Maṭāli' al-budūr*, 2 vols. in 1 (Cairo, 1299–1300/1881) 1:7.

80. Cf. Freimark, pp. 40ff., 164.

81. Cf. al-Bīrūnī, *al-Athār al-bāqiyah*, ed. Sachau (Leipzig, 1878), p. 4, line 5 quoted by Freimark, p. 142.

82. Cf. Ibn al-Athīr, *al-Nihāyah fī gharīb al-ḥadīth*, 5 vols. (Cairo, 1322/1904), 1:15, line 15f.; 6, line 18; 8, line 15ff.; 9, line 17.

83. Ibn Khaldūn, *Muqaddimah*, trans., F. Rosenthal, 3:288–91.

84. Op. cit., 3:324.

85. Op. cit., 3:340f.

86. Op. cit., 2:455.

87. Op. cit., 3:287. See 284, n. 1123, for parallels. Ibn Khaldūn mentions the writing of abridgements as the last of the seven justifications for authorship. Al-Maqarrī, *Azhār al-riyāḍ*, 3 vols. (Cairo, 1358/1939), 3:34, puts abridgements in the sixth place. They were promoted to fourth place in Ḥājjī Khalīfah, 1:intro., col. 35.

88. Ḥājjī Khalīfah, *Kashf*, 1:intro., col. 43f.

89. Op. cit., 1:intro., col. 1. For the allusion to Hippocrates, see above, n. 76.

Part II
Manuscripts

[3]

The Script and Book Craft in the Hebrew Medieval Codex

Malachi Beit-Arié

The extraordinary historical circumstances that scattered the Jewish communities around the Mediterranean basin and further to the east, north and west brought them into contact with diversified civilizations, religions and societies. The mobility of individual Jews – either by choice or by economic necessity – and of entire communities – by force – made them agents of cross-cultural contacts and influences. Their manuscripts are, therefore, significant artefacts for studying the history of the handwritten book in all the other civilizations around the Mediterranean, predominantly those of Islam and Christianity. Due to the far-flung territorial dispersion of the Jews, and their adherence to their national script, medieval manuscripts written in Hebrew characters were produced in a territorial range larger than that of their Greek, Latin or even Arabic counterparts. Hebrew handwritten books were manufactured and disseminated within and across all these main and other, more minor, booklore zones. The intricate and complex reality of the Jewish existence in the Middle Ages is reflected in MS. Oxford, Corpus Christi College 133, a daily prayer book in an Ashkenazic (northern European) hand. At the end of the manuscript a creditor recorded in Arabic, written in Hebrew characters, in a cursive Sephardic (Spanish) type of script, payments made to him by English debtors, apparently while a moneylender in England (figure 8).

Hebrew manuscripts shared along with other manuscripts of the codex civilizations – in particularly with the Islamic and Christian booklores – the basic structure of the codex form of the book: the same anatomy, the same materials and therefore similar proportions and formats, a molecular structure of quiring achieved by folding a certain number of bifolia, and the employment of means for ensuring the right sequence of the quires or the bifolia and folios within the

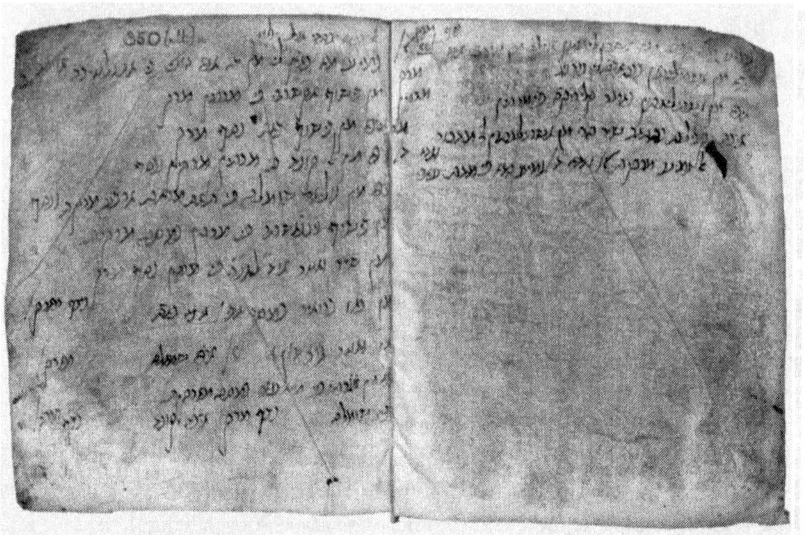

Figure 8
Record of debts in Judeo-Arabic on the blank pages of an Ashkenazic prayer book (*c.* 1200). Oxford, Corpus Christi College, MS. 133, fols 349v–350r.

quires, located on the margins. As with Latin, Greek or Arabic, the designs were planned and the parchment was ruled in preparation for copying. Scribal practices aimed at an aesthetic and legible presentation of the text, and parts of the manuscripts were decorated and illuminated in the margins or within the written space.

Moreover, due to the wide dispersion of Hebrew book production, the similarity between the appearance, writing styles, writing material, technical making and text configuration of the Hebrew codices and those of the non-Hebrew codices produced in their surrounding culture is greater than their similarity to Hebrew manuscripts produced in another geocultural region despite their shared script and texts. Yet the social circumstances of their production, dissemination and consumption were different, particularly from those of the Christian world.

Until the central Middle Ages Latin handwritten books were mainly produced in monastic centres, where books were copied in scriptoria according to ecclesiastical needs and functions or by order of other monasteries. The books were usually stored, used and studied in the location where they were made. Later, they were also conceived and produced in cathedral schools and universities. It was only in the thirteenth century that Latin manuscript production extended beyond the monastic and ecclesiastical framework and gradually handed over to commercial enterprise, mostly centred in ateliers.

The fundamental difference between Hebrew and Latin, Greek and to some extent Arabic book production stemmed from two cardinal factors of medieval Jewish life in the East and West: general literacy and the lack of political power and organization. It is often claimed that – unlike the Christian societies of the West and Byzantium, where literacy was confined to the clergy in monasteries and cathedral schools, then in universities, and in the late Middle Ages reaching also the lay aristocracy, the upper classes and the bourgeois merchants – the majority of Jewish males were literate. The egalitarian system of elementary education, financed and administered by the autonomous Jewish communities, made nearly all male children competent in reading (probably less in writing) Hebrew, acquainted them at least with the basic religious, liturgical and legal texts, and encouraged further advanced education. Lack of political structure and the vast dispersion over different political entities prevented the emergence of centralized Jewish establishments and religious or secular leadership, despite communal self-government, internal social and juridical autonomy, and the powerful authority of individual sages.

These two factors affected and moulded book production and text reproduction. General literacy and the lack of centralized political or intellectual establishments shaped the individual and personal nature of Hebrew book production and precluded the standardization of the reproduced texts.

Medieval Hebrew books were not produced, preserved or disseminated by any specific establishment or upon its initiative. They did not emerge from any religious, academic or lay institutional copying centres, nor were they produced by large-scale commercial enterprises; they were not collected, preserved or made accessible in any public or sectarian institutions, but were privately and individually produced and used. Books were either produced by professional or semi-professional scribes commissioned by private individuals, or were made by the users themselves. The recording and systematic study of almost all extant Hebrew manuscripts with dated colophons indicate that at least half of them were personal user-produced books, copied by educated persons for their own needs, and only half, or probably less than half, were written by hired copyists, who in many cases were not professional scribes. Whereas the institutional and centralized character of Latin book making and text dissemination – whether carried out in, or initiated by, monasteries, cathedral schools, universities or commercial outlets – enabled supervision and control over the propagation of texts and the standardization of versions, no authoritative guidelines or monitoring procedure could have been involved in the private transmission of texts written in Hebrew characters.

The number of surviving medieval books of the Jewish minority is naturally much smaller than that of extant Latin or Arabic ones.

Figure 9
Fragment of the Hebrew text of the book of Ecclesiastes (ch. 40) from the Cairo Genizah. Oxford, Bodleian Library, MS. Heb. e. 62, fol. a.

Figure 10 *right*
Rotulus, book roll preceding the codex form. Liturgical text from the Cairo Genizah. Oxford, Bodleian Library, MS. Heb. a. 3, fol. 33v.

However, the extant manuscripts probably represent only a small proportion of the total Jewish book production, very likely much smaller than the proportion of Latin manuscripts relative to total Latin book production. The loss of the majority of the codices was not the consequence of historical conditions alone. Not only were Hebrew books destroyed or abandoned through wanderings, emigrations, persecutions and expulsions, or confiscated and burned in Christian countries; they were above all worn out by use. The discovery of the so-called Cairo Genizah in the Palestinian Synagogue in Fustat (old Cairo) provides us with a tangible sample of the extent of book consumption and literacy among medieval Jews. The bulk of the approximately 200,000, mostly literary, fragments was stored mainly over a period of about 250 years, apparently between 1025 and 1266 and constitutes the remains of some 30,000 books which were used until they were eventually worn out and finally disposed of by one sector of the three Jewish communities in one city alone (figures 9 and 10).

Moreover, the roughly 100,000 extant medieval Hebrew codices and their consolidated scattered fragments represent the output of only the last six centuries of medieval book production. The revolutionary codex form of the book, which was adopted and diffused by Christians already in the first centuries of our era and replaced the old roll form in the areas around the Mediterranean from about 300, was employed by the Jews much later, as is attested both by findings and by textual evidence. Between the abundant finds of

Hebrew books from Late Antiquity – the Dead Sea Scrolls from the Qumran caves and the Judean desert of the Hellenistic and early Roman period – and the earliest dated and datable surviving Hebrew codices, there is a gap of some 800 years almost entirely without evidence of the Hebrew book, in either roll or codex form. The late employment of the codex may very well reflect the basically oral nature of the transmission of Hebrew post-Biblical literature.

The earliest extant categorically dated Hebrew codices were written at the beginning of the tenth century, all of them in the Middle East. However, in the structural shaping and artistic design of the copied texts, in their harmonious scripts and shared styles, these earliest manuscripts demonstrate elaborate craftsmanship and regularity, attesting to a long-established tradition of codex design and production, probably from the ninth century onwards. Dated eleventh-century manuscripts have survived from Italy and the Maghreb – present Morocco, Algeria and Tunisia – whilst those produced in the Iberian peninsula, France, Germany, England and Byzantium date from the twelfth century onwards. Until the thirteenth century their number is rather small, particularly outside the Middle East, but thereafter it grows, reaching a peak in the fifteenth century.

Though we do have significant information on the earlier stages of book production and script in the Orient, we lack such knowledge concerning the formation period in the Christian world. This applies to western and central Europe and the Byzantine zone, as well as in North Africa and Muslim Spain. Yet, some 80 per cent of the extant dated manuscripts were produced within the orbit of the Christian world, and only about 20 per cent in the Muslim lands. The development of early handwritten books in Christian territories in the central Middle Ages must have been inspired by the Oriental codex, with book production becoming more developed and elaborate in the late Middle Ages. Diversified techniques, script types, shapes and layouts evolved; transparency of the text, which enabled the users to find their way around it, was enhanced; and decoration and illumination were integrated in the production of books in this period.

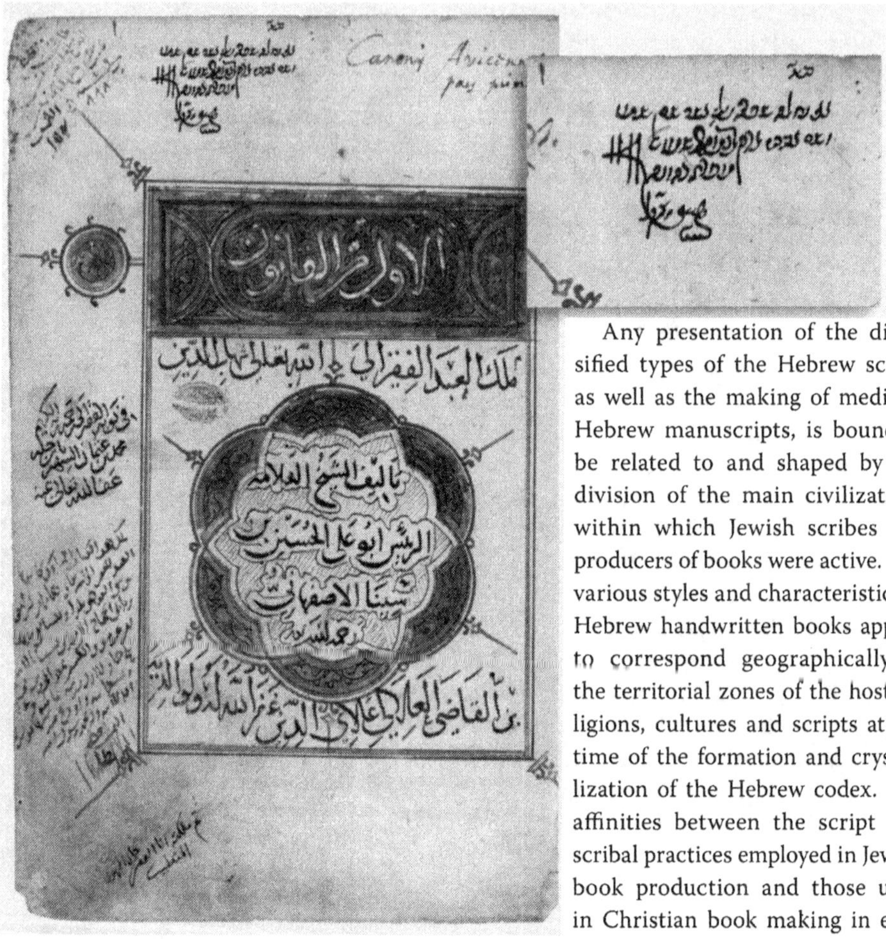

Figure 11
Avicenna's *Canon of Medicine* (in Arabic). The title page has five owners' notes in Arabic and one in Hebrew (Egypt, fifteenth century). Oxford, Bodleian Library, MS. Poc. 131, fol. 1r.

Any presentation of the diversified types of the Hebrew script, as well as the making of medieval Hebrew manuscripts, is bound to be related to and shaped by the division of the main civilizations within which Jewish scribes and producers of books were active. The various styles and characteristics of Hebrew handwritten books appear to correspond geographically to the territorial zones of the host religions, cultures and scripts at the time of the formation and crystallization of the Hebrew codex. The affinities between the script and scribal practices employed in Jewish book production and those used in Christian book making in each geocultural area which encompassed Jewish populations may contribute tangible evidence in measuring the degree of acculturation or segregation of the (usually oppressed) Jewish communities contained within Christian societies. They may also help in clarifying the direct symbiotic or indirect osmotic nature of the contacts between Hebrew and Latin scribes.

The distinctive calligraphic and codicological Hebrew traditions cluster in accordance with the three main literate medieval civilizations which flourished around the Mediterranean basin – Islam and its Arabic script, Western Christendom and its Latin script, and Byzantine Christianity and its Greek script. The geographical distribution of those distinctive characteristics corresponds to the geopolitical orbits of Islam, the Latin West and the Greek East in the formative periods of the Hebrew codex. The division of the Jewish

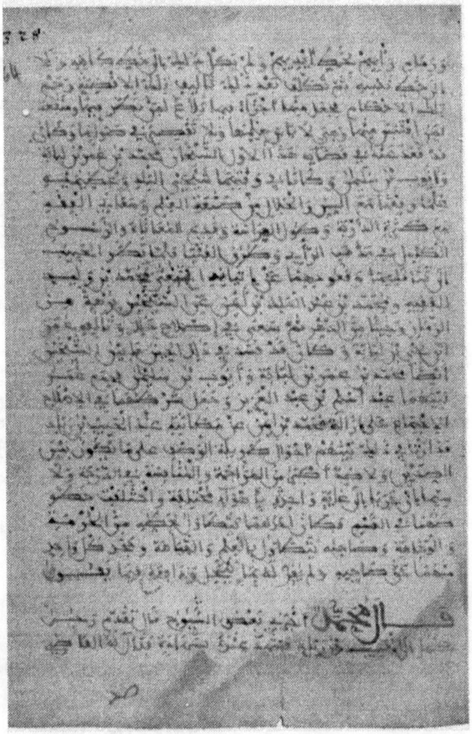

Figure 12 *above left* Nahmanides, *Torat ha-Adam*, a comprehensive monograph on all the laws concerning death and mourning written in cursive Sephardic script (Spain, 1330). Oxford, Bodleian Library, MS. Mich. 496, fol. 55r.

Figure 13 *above right* Al-Khushani, *Book of the Judges of Cordoba.* Written in Maghribi script, the Arabic script characteristic of Spain and North Africa (Spain, 1296). MS. Marsh 288, fol. 164r.

traditions generally persisted until the end of the Middle Ages, notwithstanding major changes in the encompassing geopolitical structure and cultural domination.

Thus Jewish scribal fashions and practices can be grouped into three basic branches. The first is the branch of writing and book making practised in the territories under Muslim rule in the East as well as in the West. Basically this branch shared the same archetypes of script, ductus and the reed as a writing instrument, and were strongly influenced by Arabic calligraphy and book production (figure 11). The second branch includes writing and book production in the territories of Western Europe, which shared the same archetypes of script, ductus and the quill as a writing instrument, and shows a resemblance to the styles and ductus of Latin scripts and Western booklore. The third is the branch of writing and book craft in the areas of the Byzantine Empire before its decline, which seem to have been influenced by Greek script and Byzantine booklore.

Hebrew book script and production of the Islamic domination is clearly divisible into two, namely Eastern and Western, palaeographical and codicological entities. The Eastern Islamic entity – which we

Figure 14 *right*
Hebrew Pentateuch written in Italian semi-cursive script (Florence, between 1441–1468). Oxford, Bodleian Library, MS. Canon. Or. 22, fol. 111r.

Figure 15 *far right*
Justin's *Epitome of the 'Philippic History' of Pompeius Trogus*, a work on ancient history. Written in humanistic script, which developed in Italy in the early fifteenth century (Milan (?), 1468). MS. Canon. Class. Lat. 148, fol. 120v.

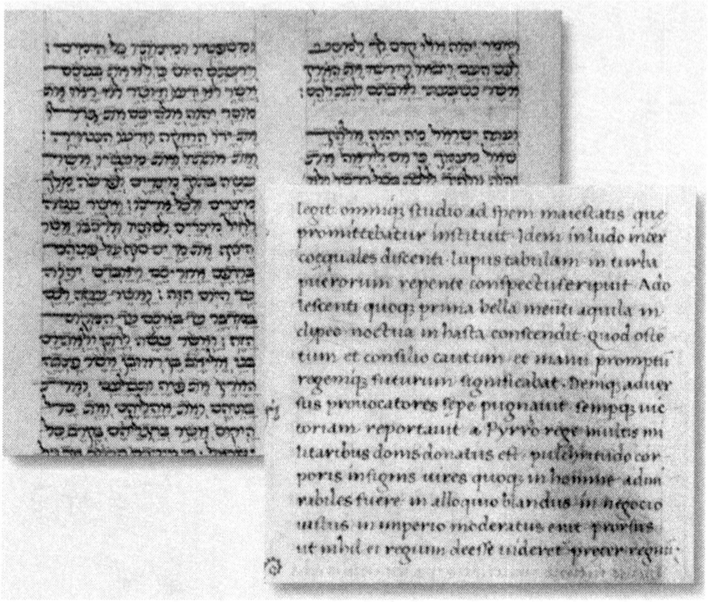

term Oriental – clusters the Hebrew manuscripts produced in the Near East and Central Asia, within the present boundaries of Iran, Uzbekistan, Iraq, East Turkey, Syria, Lebanon, Israel and the West Bank, Egypt, Yemen and Libya, which at the time when the Hebrew codex was being formed were all contained in one political unit under the Abbasid Caliphate. In general, so far as script is concerned, one can detect differences between the eastern part of the Orient and the western one encompassing Syria, Palestine and Egypt, which may have developed since the late tenth century, when these countries were ruled by the Fatimid dynasty.

The Western Islamic entity of Jewish booklore contains the Iberian peninsula and the Maghreb, which, with the exception of the northern part of Spain, were under Muslim rule, that of the Umayyad Kingdom in Spain, and of the Aghlabids in North Africa, in its formative years. We designate this jewish scribal entity by the term Sephardic (figures 12 and 13). Though the Oriental and Sephardic entities of the Islamic branch have much in common in graphic style and book design, particularly where parchment codices are concerned, each has distinctive types of script and entirely different codicological practices.

The Eastern zone of the Islamic branch is less influenced by Arabic calligraphy, but shows a stronger affinity to Arabic Oriental technical practices, such as the method of processing the writing material, quiring and ruling techniques, and book design and decoration.

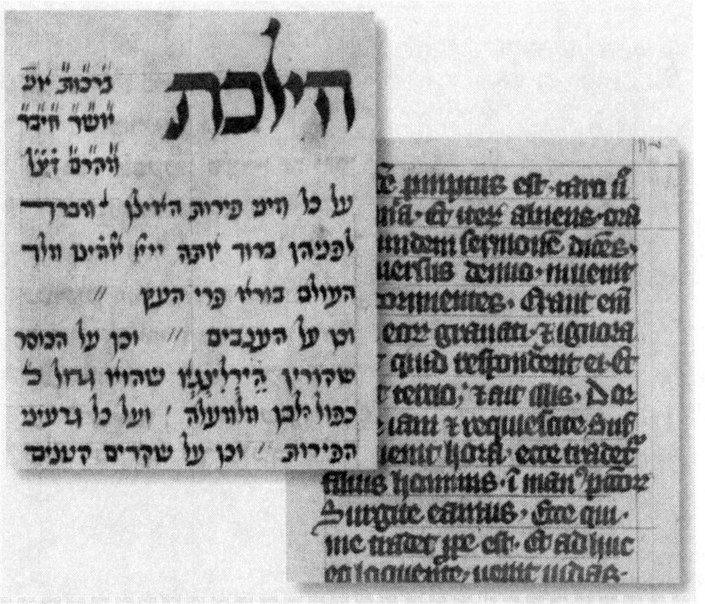

Figure 16 *far left*
Dinim (ritual decisions) according to Rabbi Meir of Rothenburg. Written in Ashkenazic Hebrew script, which is clearly influenced by Latin Gothic script (Germany, 1342).Oxford, Bodleian Library, MS. Bodl. Or. 146, fol. 39v.

Figure 17 *left*
Latin missal written in a Gothic script (Bohemia or Moravia, fourteenth century). Oxford, Bodleian Library, MS. Lat. liturg. d. 11, fol. 89v.

The Hebrew booklore encompassed by the territories dominated by Christianity in Western Europe and by the Latin script prevailed in northern France, medieval Germany, England and Italy. This Jewish scribal branch is clearly split into two entities – that of the areas extending north and east from the Alps, and that of Italy. Though certain variations in the style of script and in some codicological features can be discerned between manuscripts produced in France and Germany, and apparently also England, they all cluster into one scribal entity which we term Ashkenazic (Franco-German). The consolidated Ashkenazic scribal entity is probably rooted in the Carolingian period, as its wide sphere corresponds, *grosso modo*, to the territories embraced by the Empire of Charlemagne, which unified Western Christianity at the beginning of the ninth century. England was naturally a later insular extension of this continental tradition. Gradual migration of Jews from Germany eastward extended the Ashkenazic scribal entity to central and Slavic Eastern Europe in the late Middle Ages. Italian manuscripts exhibit distinctive scripts as well as scribal and technical characteristics within the Occidental branch of Hebrew booklore (figures 14 and 15).

The Occidental branch, especially the Ashkenazic entity, displays a clear affinity to styles of Latin script, in particular the Gothic fashions (figures 16 and 17). So far as technical features are concerned the affinities between Hebrew and Latin practices are more complex. Although Ashkenazic manuscripts share with their Latin counterparts

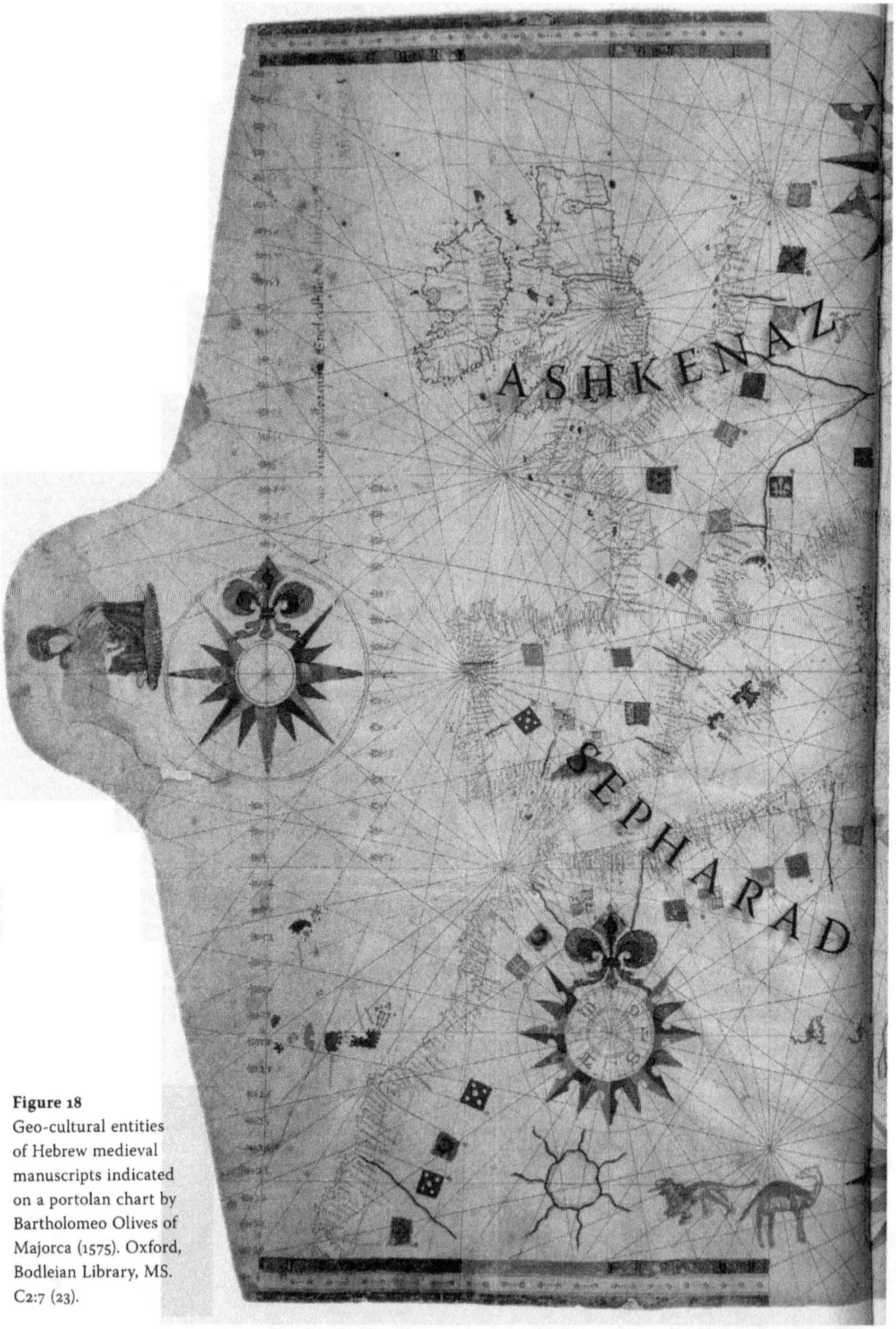

Figure 18
Geo-cultural entities of Hebrew medieval manuscripts indicated on a portolan chart by Bartholomeo Olives of Majorca (1575). Oxford, Bodleian Library, MS. C2:7 (23).

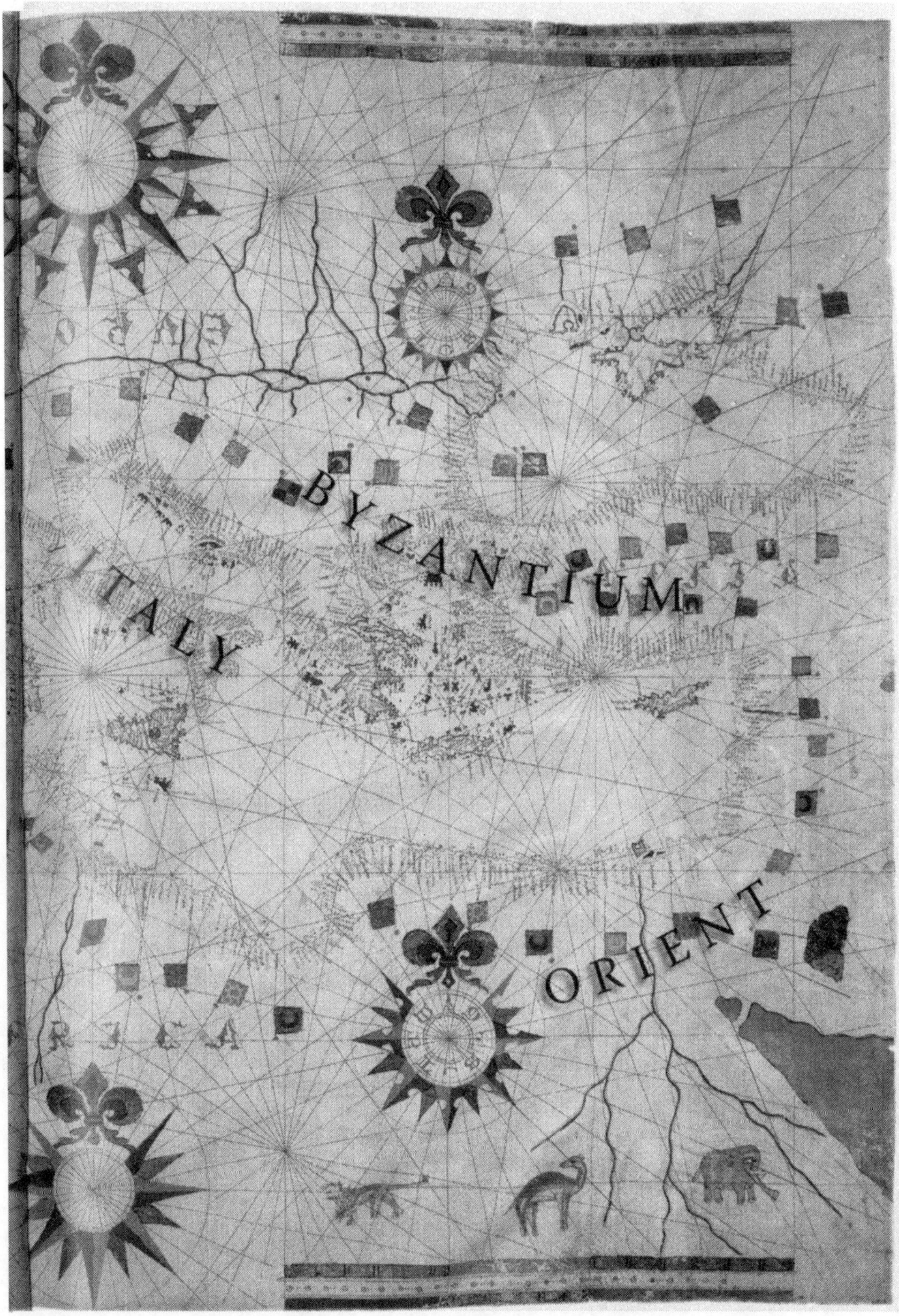
BYZANTIUM
ITALY
ORIENT

the same kind of parchment writing material, their ruling techniques do not correspond to those of Latin manuscripts. Where there is correspondence, it is evident that the appearance of such shared practices did not coincide chronologically. The employment of plummet for ruling is illuminating, since it clearly demonstrates that Jewish scribes indeed borrowed this new technology, which was introduced into Latin manuscripts as early as the eleventh century, but only after a significant lapse of time. That Jewish scribes followed the Latin ones is evident not only from the very lateness of the use of the plummet, but from literary sources which show that the new technique had been well known among Jews as early as the twelfth century, but was rejected because of halakhic considerations. The subsequent emergence of the literary genre of biblical texts surrounded by their commentaries and glossed halakhic compilations and scholarly needs promoted the adoption of the new ruling instrument by Franco-German Hebrew scribes.

Hence Hebrew medieval booklore may be classified into five main geocultural entities: Ashkenazic, Italian, Byzantine, Sephardic and Oriental (figure 18). However, conspicuous local peculiarities of script, and in some cases scribal practices, fully justify the singling out of two Oriental sub-entities, that of Iran and its neighbours, such as Uzbekistan, which we term Persian type, and that of South Arabia, designated as Yemenite type.

The various types of the medieval Hebrew book script have three fundamental operational modes – square, semi-cursive and cursive. The three modes were simultaneously employed in most of the geocultural entities and types of script, but only in the Sephardic territories had a fully current cursive developed by the twelfth century. In other types of script, the Ashkenazic and the Italian, for instance, current cursive writing emerged only in the sixteenth century, while the Oriental script never really acquired such a mode, and its later development was the result of the diffusion of the Sephardic scripts around the Mediterranean basin following the expulsion of the Jews from Spain and Portugal at the end of the fifteenth century. Following the settle-ment of expelled Spanish Jews in Italy, and particularly in Greece, the Balkans, Turkey, Syria, Palestine and Egypt, and their intellectual domination, the medieval typology of the Hebrew script was shaken and reshaped under the strong impact of the Sephardic scripts on the local ones. Later migrations of many *conversos* from Spain and particularly Portugal, to the Netherlands, Hamburg, and southern France introduced the Sephardic writings even into Ashkenaz. It seems that gradually a new type of script evolved all over the Ottoman Empire, a mixture of the Sephardic, the Oriental and Byzantine types that may be called an Ottoman type of Hebrew script.

The differences between the modes of each type basically involve the number of strokes required in producing the shape of a letter. The letters of the square scripts are formed by many more strokes than those of the semi-cursive ones; those of the cursive scripts are executed by an even smaller number of strokes, while the number of strokes is reduced to one for most letters in the current cursive shapes. However, cursiveness was not always achieved by reducing the number of strokes, but accomplished by quicker writing which combined several strokes without lifting the reed or quill pen. In the cursive grade of writing, noticeably in the Sephardic type, part of one letter or the entire letter would be combined with the following letter, or even several letters, all executed without lifting the pen (figure 19).

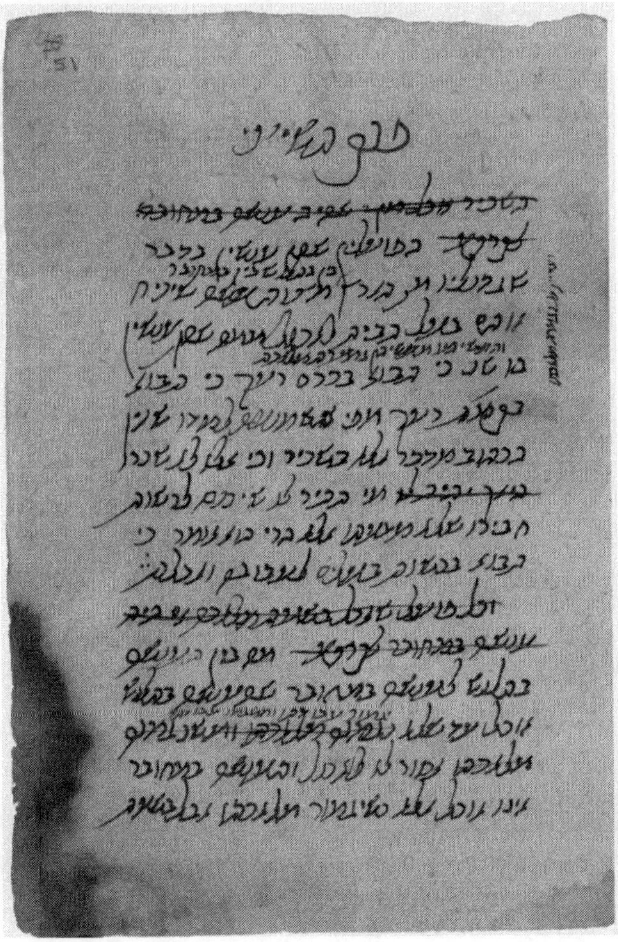

Figure 19
Maimonides' autograph draft of his legal code, *Mishneh Torah*, in cursive Sephardic script (Egypt, *c.* 1180). Oxford, Bodleian Library, MS. Heb. d. 32, fol. 51r.

In general, the square mode, which must have crystallized in the Orient as a calligraphic script for formal copies of the masoretic version of the Bible before the tenth century, and whose inception can be noticed already in the late formal script of the Dead Sea Scrolls and the Byzantine Hebrew papyri, was employed in all regions in the production of elegant or deluxe copies, particularly of biblical, liturgical and Talmudic texts, or for singling out glossed texts incorporated into commentaries. The cursive mode, which first evolved as an informal script used for private records, drafts and letters, was partly adopted as a book script, mainly in owner-produced copies and compilations.

The threefold execution of Hebrew medieval book script in fact multiplies the number of its types and subtypes, as the shapes of most of the letters in each mode of a type are entirely different from each other. Consequently, the number of distinctive shapes of writing increases to fifteen species, disregarding considerable transformations over the six centuries of extant Hebrew codices.

References

M. Beit-Arié, *Hebrew Codicology: Tentative Typology of Technical Practices Employed in Hebrew Dated Medieval Manuscripts* (Jerusalem, 1981).

— *Hebrew Manuscripts of East and West: Towards a Comparative Codicology* (The Panizzi Lectures) (London, 1993).

— *The Makings of the Medieval Hebrew Book: Studies in Palaeography and Codicology* (Jerusalem, 1993).

[4]

BETWEEN THE LINES: REALITIES OF SCRIBAL LIFE IN THE SIXTEENTH CENTURY

Cornell H. FLEISCHER

"Al-kâtib kâdhib;" "Who writes, lies." The Arabic aphorism invoked by such critical participants in the bureaucratic expansion of the sixteenth-century Ottoman Empire as Mustafa Âli points at once to Ottoman awareness of the singular social and political importance of the scribal arts, and to the humanity of the wielder of the pen. Behind the impersonal, apparently seamless fabric of the imperial orders, financial registers, and formal memoranda produced by more or less literate, and more or less privileged, members of the Ottoman ruling apparatus, lie less orderly and more variegated histories. The scribal career as such, and the expansion and regularization of bureaucratic functions that were among the most notable developments in Ottoman administrative history of the sixteenth century, are subjects that have attracted a certain amount of scholarly interest in the last decade.[1] These studies, by and large, have focussed either on the larger institutional frameworks within which the *"Ottoman kâtib"* is presumed to have functioned, or on the careers of extraordinary individuals associated with the scribal class, careers which, implicitly or explicitly, are treated within the context of pervasive assumptions that there must have existed something like the ideal *kâtib* and the typical scribal professional path. "The typical Ottoman bureaucrat" has become a sufficiently powerful topos in modern historiography as to obscure the differences between the financial clerk of the

---

[1]Linda T. Darling, "Ottoman Salary Registers as a Source for Economic and Social History, " *Turkish Studies Association Bulletin*, 14/1 (1990), 13-33; C. H. Fleischer, *Bureaucrat and Intellectual in the Ottoman Empire: The Historian Mustafa Âli (1541-1600)*, Princeton, 1986; idem, "Preliminaries to the Study of the Ottoman Bureaucracy," in Ş. Tekin et. al., eds., *Ra'iyyet Rüsumu: Essays Presented to Halil İnalcık on his Seventieth Birthday by his Colleagues and Students*, 2. vols. Cambridge, 1986, vol. 1, 135-41; D. A. Howard, "The Historical Development of the Ottoman Imperial Registry (Defter-i hakanî): Mid-Fifteenth to Mid-Seventeenth Centuries," *Archivum Ottomanicum* 11 (1986 [1988]), 213-30; Christine Woodhead, "From scribe to litterateur: the career of a sixteenth-century Ottoman kâtib," *Bulletin of the British Society for Middle Eastern Studies*, 9/1 (1982), pp. 55-74.

fifteenth century and his counterpart of the eighteenth, let alone the social, economic, and political chasm separating the bureau chief of the sixteenth century from his subordinate.

Such distinctions must be relevant to the historian, and to no one more than the student of Ottoman "classicism" concerned with discovering the realities as well as the myths of the Süleymanic *saeculum aureum.* For it was during the forty-six year reign of the "Second Solomon" that the central and provincial bureaucracies of the Empire were suddenly expanded, with a dizzying speed that meant, among other things, that it was only toward the end of the reign, around 1555, that any significant measure of professionalism in the scribal class as a whole and regularity of procedure could take hold.[2] This was an era in which literacy gained singular importance in the process of elite recruitment, both within the bureaucratic sphere proper and more widely in the ruling class; but the manpower needs of an expansive bureaucracy and the novelty of that professional class were such that the "typical" Ottoman bureaucrat could not yet have come into existence. In the interest of demythifying the received image of the Ottoman *kâtip* and contextualizing scribal service in the Ottoman Empire in the first half of the sixteenth century, I should like to adduce information taken from three petitions found in the Topkapı Palace Archives.[3] These were written, at intervals that span roughly the first thirty years of Süleyman's reign, by functionaries whose livelihood depended on literacy and who, though otherwise unknown, were among those who carried out the most basic work of empire in the sixteenth century.

The first request comes from the resident specialist in protective occult practices in the Palace, whose particular skill is the science of letters (*ilm-i huruf*) and divine names (*ilm-i esma'*) and the production of written amulets.[4] The otherwise unidentified petitioner wrote between late 1524 and 1537; he mentions

[2]Fleischer, "Preliminaries." Cf. Howard, "Imperial Registry," p. 219, whose observation that "It is only beginning with the 960s/1550s that the *ruznamçes* take on a consistent format, evidencing standardized procedures that were introduced with the expansion of the Registry" supports (in the sphere of administrative practice) conclusions reached independently by Gülru Necipoğlu, based on art historical criteria, and C. Fleischer, based on historiographical and ideological development, that various aspects of what is commonly treated as the distinctive imperial style identified with the Süleymanic regime did not coalesce as a style until after 1550. See C. Fleischer, "The Lawgiver as Messiah," and G. Necipoğlu, "A Canon for the Arts," in Gilles Veinstein, ed., *Soliman le Magnifique et son temps*, Paris, 1992.

[3]I wish to thank the Republic of Turkey for granting me permission to carry out the research (1985, 1987) in the course of which I found these documents, and I further express my particular gratitude to the directorate of the Topkapı Palace Museum and to Ms. Ülkü Altındağ, director of the Archive. The insights and instincts of my colleague Engin Akarlı, based on his research in a later and more voluminously documented period of Ottoman bureaucratic history, have been of invaluable assistance in the interpretation of these documents. I further thank Barbara Flemming, for her interest in scribes.

[4]Topkapı Sarayı Müzesi Arşivi [TKS] E[vrak] 9998; T. Fahd, *La Divination arabe*, Leiden, 1968, pp. 219-41.

by name the princes Mehmed (b. 1521) and Selim (b. 1524),[5] and he speaks of a Muhyiddin Çelebi as the *kadıasker* of Rumeli, who in this context this must be Fenarizade.[6] He further makes reference to an impending campaign against Christendom, which would indicate a date close to 1526, 1529, 1532 or, at the latest, 1537. Our author vaunts the virtues of his craft, which in fact encompasses all forms of sacred learning, having been practiced by all the prophets and saints from the time of Adam and Idris: "There is much power in this noble science, which, when properly applied, people think to be a saintly prodigy [*velâyet*]; [one can] cause rain to fall, contrary winds to blow, a village to do things against its will, cripple a hand or a foot, blind an eye." Despite this power, our specialist, most particularly because of the demands on his services made by the Palace, which requires amulets for the sultan and princes to be produced on deadlines generated by the start of campaign seasons, faces certain practical difficulties.[7] He has grown old in the family trade and family service to the Ottoman house—his father would seem to have been at the court of Murad II— and his failing eyesight prevents him from fulfilling in time his growing list of orders. Furthermore, it seems, his education is also somewhat lacking, a fact that threatens to compromise propriety and security. Because he must consult others on the meaning or spelling of Arabic words, his interlocutors may gossip about the particular sorts of amulets required, the special needs of the sultan, and their timing.

The second of these difficulties can be solved with books; he requests that he be given two dictionaries, the *Qâmûs* (i. e., of Fîrûzâbâdî] and the *Sihâh* (i. e., of Jawharî], which will free him from reliance on others in deciphering the obscure texts that are his sources and stock in trade. The solution to the first problem is also at hand. The petitioner has an orphaned ward, named Ahmed, who is an exceptional calligrapher of *ghubâr* script and practiced in other styles as well, so skilled that he can write the *Fâtiha* or *Ikhlâs* on a grain of rice. Indeed, he has already produced talismanic armbands for the sultan and the princes Selim and Mehmed; this took place because the objects were ordered in Edirne, and at that time and place there was no one but Ahmed to inscribe them.

> At the Gate of Felicity there are scribes who receive salaries. When something is to be written, they perform the task, and spend the rest of their time praying for the benefit of the just sovereign and warrior for the faith. My request is that he [Ahmed] be made one of these, and so when

---

[5] See A. D. Alderson, *The Structure of the Ottoman Dynasty*, Oxford, 1956, Table 30.

[6] Richard Repp, *The Müfti of Istanbul*, Oxford, 1986, p. 271, provides the dates: 1523-37.

[7] I shall not dwell here on the importance of this and other aspects of the petition for an understanding of the role of magical practice and the invocation of saintly intervention in the Süleymanic regime. These subjects are dealt with in *Master of the Age: Süleyman the Lawgiver and the Remaking of Ottoman Sovereignty* (forthcoming, Princeton University Press).

something is ordered to be made by your servant for your exalted person he should be assigned the writing part of the task.

This proceeding would, like the first, help to keep confidential imperial talismanic needs.

Although the result of this request is unknown, the document suggests a number of considerations of consequence for the study of the scribal career path in the sixteenth century. First, it indicates that the paths of recruitment to the ranks of the *küttab* were at this point, relatively early in the reign of Süleyman, still open, varied, and irregular[8]; the qualifications of the orphan Ahmed would seem to lie in his calligraphic skill and foster relationship to an occult specialist who had professional and family service ties to the Palace, rather than in particular clerical skills acquired through apprenticeship or other specialized education. The onomancer's characterization of the nature of the duties of Palace salaried scribes, while perhaps exaggerated, still evokes an impression of the novelty of the accumulation of a sizeable body of stipended scribal talent (the growth and structuring of the paths of scribal service in Suleyman's reign is documented[9]), of the perception of this development as opening a new avenue of social mobility in a fiscally and numerically expansive government apparatus, and of the still relatively unstructured character of the duties of the *küttab*.

Once an aspiring candidate gained a toehold in the developing bureaucratic hierarchy, his financial and social progress was by no means assured. As the next document demonstrates with dramatic clarity, even the most persistent and devoted *kâtib* was faced with extraordinary financial obligations imposed by his superiors.[10] The first step on the ladder, for those unfortunate enough to be obliged to work their way up from the bottom rather than being appointed directly to a full scribal stipend within one of the unfolding branches of the central bureaucratic service, was to serve as apprentice, salaried or unsalaried, to a ranking scribal official. The apprentice owed his first loyalty to his master, as both the form of appointment (salaried apprentices are identified as being attached to particular individuals[11]) and this petition make clear, until such time as the aspirant attained an appointment and salary line in his own right.

The petitioner, who does not identify himself by name but may well be the Mahmud registered as one of the two apprentices of the official in question, describes himself as the "longtime apprentice of the Accountant (*muhasebeci*) Ali Çelebi; [I was] the one who actually took care of the tasks that fell to his

[8]A thesis I have advanced in *Bureaucrat*, chapters 6-8, and in "Preliminaries."

[9]See "Preliminaries."

[10]TKS E 7297.

[11]See the *ruznamçes* and *müşahere-horan* registers summarized in "Preliminaries."

office."[12] The events Mahmud relates must have taken place in 1533-35, immediately before and during the Mesopotamian campaign. When Ali Çelebi fell ill—mortally so, in the event[13] —Mahmud had asked him to confer on him the Registry of the garrison troops (*hisar erenlerinin defterleri*)[14]. (Although there seems as yet to have been no title or stipend earmarked for the functionary who fulfilled this role, acquisition of these responsibilities would presumably provide some stature as well as opportunities for gain, whether in the form of fees or graft, that would be unavailable to a *şakird*). When Ali Çelebi asked for "a little something" *[bir mikdar nesnecik taleb]* in return, Mahmud

> used whatever I owned in cash and possessions, and took out a loan using some of my mother's and sisters' possessions as collateral. One way and another, I gathered one thousand florins and gave them to [Ali Çelebi's agent] Hüseyin Çelebi[15]; he returned two hundred florins, saying that they

[12]Ali Çelebi is identified as *Rumeli muhasebecisi* (the third or fourth ranking member of the ranks of the scribes of the imperial treasury) in Basbakanlık Arşivi [BBA], Kâmil Kepeci Tasnifi [KPT] 1764, p. 145 (and elsewhere), 16 Ramazan 938/22 April 1532; according to TKS D[efter] 7843 (*müşahere-horan defteri* dating from approximately the same year—see "Preliminaries"), 7b, his salary was 40 *akçe* per day, the second-highest salary (the highest being the fifty *akçe* drawn by the two *ruznamçe*-keepers) drawn by any of the treasury secretariat. KPT 1764 further lists his yearly bonus of 3,000 *akçe*, the same as that accorded his seniors. Of all those listed as *şakirds* of the scribes of the Treasury (*şakirdan-i kâtiban-i hizane-i 'âmire*), only two are noted specifically as being apprenticed to Ali Çelebi: Abdi and Mahmud, who first occur in the lists in 938/1532 (KPT 1764, p. 145). Abdi, by 1 Şa'ban 942/25 January 1536, had become one of the *mukata'acıs* of the Treasury at 20 *akçe*, while Mahmud remained an apprentice at 4 *akçe* (BBA, Maliyeden Müdevver 552, pp. 10-11). Abdi, who is certainly Çivizade Abdullah, brother of the şeyhülislam Çivizade, later became *defterdar* of Rumeli (1548-1553— see I. H. Danişmend, *İzahlı Osmanlı Tarihi Kronolojisi*, 6 vols., Istanbul, 1971 [vol. 5., 251], and Mehmed Süreyya, *Sicill-i Osmani*, 4 vols., Istanbul, 1890-97 [III, 407]). He is an unlikely candidate for authorship of this petition, which leaves either Mahmud or one of the apprentices not identified with the name of a master who occur in the lists. For the sake of narrative I shall refer to him as Mahmud.

[13]Ali Çelebi must have died shortly before 13 Rebi' II, 940/1 November 1533; KPT 1863, p. 51, records his replacement [as *muhasebe'i-yi Rumeli*] by Hayreddin Bey, the Anatolian Accountant (*muhasebe'i-yi Anadolu*), whose 29-*akçe* salary was increased to the necessary 40.

[14]This probably refers to the functions devolving on the *kâtib* slightly later referred to as *tezkere'i-yi kıla'*. The office first occurs as a distinctive category and salary line in the archival record in Maliyeden Müdevver 7118, p. 10 (Muharrem 955/February-March 1548, where the incumbent Mustafa Çelebi is assigned a daily stipend of 12 *akçe*), and in KPT 6592, 241b-268b, which begins in 969/1561 and ends in 978/1570, and where the office is referred to as *tezkere'i-yi kıla'-ı şıkk-ı evvel;* the duties attached to the office are described in the sections of ms. Atıf Efendi 1734, reflecting the structure of the central treasury at the end of Süleyman's reign, published by Ö. L. Barkan, "H. 974-975 (M. 1567-1568) Mali Yılına ait bir Osmanlı Bütçesi," *İstanbul Üniversitesi İktisat Fakültesi Mecmuası*, 19/1-4 (1957-58), 277-332 (see p. 319). The evidence of the petition studied here suggests that in 1533-34 these functions—charge of the appointment and payment of fortress garrison troops in "Arabistan, Erzurum, and Rumeli"—were performed by the office of the Rumeli Accountant, who could presumably assign or subcontract these duties to one of his staff.

[15]Hüseyin Çelebi may be the apprentice scribe who after the death of Ali Çelebi is specifically attached to the second-ranking member of the Treasury scribal corps, the *ruznamçe'i-yi sani* (Second Day-book Keeper) Hayreddin Bey (not to be confused with his junior homonym, referred to in fn. 13 (KPT 1764, p. 174, 8 Şevval 939/3 May 1533, and p. 184, Ramazan 939/March-April 1533)). This Hüseyin Çelebi rose quickly even as an apprentice; on p. 174 he is listed as

> were under measure, and he took full measure coins to make up for these. After a few days had passed Hüseyin Çelebi told me, "I gave the thousand florins you gave me to the Efendi, so now give me thirty thousand *akçe* in addition. God willing, the matter will be put to the imperial council *[divan]* at once, and they will give it to you." Again, I begged my mother and sisters to help me however they could; they gave me what they could afford, and I was able to secure a loan for thirty thousand *akçe,* which I then handed over [to Hüseyin Çelebi].

Within a few days of this exchange, Ali Çelebi had either died or had become so incapacitated that his position was given to Hayreddin Bey, who as Anatolian Accountant was his proper successor.[16] Mahmud (assuming the correctness of this identification of our petitioner) retained his apprenticeship to the Rumeli Accountant,[17] and the garrison registers that were the object of his desires passed either to his new master's province or, which is perhaps more likely, to that of the latter's senior colleague, another Hayreddin Bey who as Second Day-book keeper was the second-ranked official within the Treasury scribal corps.[18] Mahmud applied to Hayreddin Bey for the registers, and received an equivocal answer. In the summer of 1534 he asked for them again; Hayreddin Bey responded that nothing could be done at that time since the sultan was about to depart for the east on campaign. "Right now let's give you a *haraç* register.[19]

having received a yearly bonus of 2,000 *akçe*, four times the amount granted most apprentices, and two years later (24 Şa'ban, 941/28 February 1535), having accompanied his master to the Mesopotamian front, he was awarded 1,000 *akçe* (KPT 1764, p. 214). By 1 Şa'ban 943/25 January 1536 he was the highest paid apprentice in the Treasury, with a daily stipend of 7 *akçe* (Maliyeden Müdevver 559, p. 10); 4 or 5 was normal. If this identification is correct, then it is probable that, since Hüseyin Çelebi continues to play a pivotal role in Mahmud's narrative even after the death of Ali Çelebi, my tentative identification of the Hayreddin Bey to whom our scribe applies as the successor of Ali Çelebi is incorrect, and that the garrison registers were made the province of the *ruznamçe'i-yi sani.*

[16]Within the Treasury scribal hierarchy, for most of the reign of Süleyman the division of functions into Rumelian, Anatolian, and Arab zones implied by the appointment of a *defterdar* for each area was a consistent principle of organization as the financial bureaucracy expanded. The hierarchy inherent to this order was also applied throughout the scribal corps, as a survey of appointment records makes clear. Just as it was a normal, or organizationally most "natural" mode of progress for the *defterdar* of Anatolia, on promotion, to become *defterdar* of Rumeli (who was in fact the chief of the entire financial establishment), so would the *muhasebe'i-yi 'Arab* be promoted to the accountancy of Anatolia, and then to that of Rumeli. It must be remembered, of course, that this represents one of several possible patterns, rather than a rule. For a summary of the development of the financial apparatus of the Ottoman central government in the sixteenth century see Fleischer, *Bureaucrat,* Appendix A.

[17]Maliyeden Müdevver 559, p. 10, where he is listed as a 4-*akçe* apprentice to the *muhasebe'i* (1 Şa'ban, 942/25 January 1536).

[18]See note 13.

[19]Assignment of such precise revenue-collecting duties, based on the register of a particular region, on an annual basis to members of the imperial cavalry units was a common mechanism through which taxes (particularly those levied on non-Muslims) were collected and salaries provided in the sixteenth century; the *ruznamçe* registers of the period are filled with references to the practice. Such assignments were also commonly awarded to appointees attached to the Palace who were not members of the *kapıkulu* (imperial cavalry) corps (a particularly striking, though

Go collect [the taxes due from the non-Muslims of the region in question], and you'll also escape the rigors of the campaign. When you come back, you'll get those registers or we'll give you something better." Mahmud set of to the east, collected the assigned *haraç* dues, and also "did all I could further to gather a little gift [for Hayreddin Bey]." While on his way back to the court, which was then in the vicinity of Tabriz (late 1534-early 1535), he encountered between Khoy and Marand a group of Kızılbaş who took all of his possessions, including his two slaves and three pack animals; whether they also deprived him of the taxes he had collected or he had otherwise disposed of these is unclear. Mahmud went to pay his respects to Hayreddin Bey, kissing his hand; but the latter brushed him off, saying "What's this? You haven't brought us a present?"

Once again, Hüseyin Çelebi took a hand. He had a financial agent (*vekil-i harc*), another Hüseyin who was also a member of the elite Palace cavalry corps of the Sons of the Sipahis (*sipahi oğlanları*). This Hüseyin approached Mahmud with advice and a proposition.

> "Whatever you do, give the Bey a gift," he said to me. "God willing, then he will look out for and forward your interests, whatever they might be." I said, "What resources do I have now, that I should give a gift?" "Come," he said, "I have a slave boy. Let me give him to you, and you give him to the Bey." He sold him to me for ten thousand *akçe*, the sale witnessed by muslims, and I undertook to pay the money back in Istanbul. The slave boy remained with me for a week; since I had no slave [of my own], I did not really want to give him up. I sent him out for provisions; when he was to return, they [i.e., Hayreddin Bey] took him and the goods he had with him, saying '[I am doing this] because you haven't given him to me [as you were supposed to].' Later, they will get the money from me before witnesses. It is my sultan's to dispose."

Mahmud's personal and professional entanglements did not end with the woes recounted above. He had further, in a complicated fashion, acquired responsibility for a 200,000 *akçe*-per-annum tax assignment for the flour revenues of Ilıca (probably the Ilıca near Bergama is meant), for which he had formally registered a 140,000 *akçe* deposit with the deputy magistrate (*kadı na'ibi*) of the town. Mahmud explains the reasons for the 60,000-*akçe* deficit, and the mode of his acquisition of this responsibility, as follows.

---

by no means unixue, example occurs in BBA Büyük Ruznamçe Defteri 2, p. 10, which records the receipt of 23, 579 *akçe* in *cizye* arrears from Filibe delivered by the famous dragoman Yunus Bey and Mücellid Memi, one of the imperial book-binders, acting respectively as trustee (*emin*) and clerk (*kâtib*) of the mission (25 Muharrem 956/23 February 1549). It was often the case that members of the Outside Services of the Palace would collect their own salaries for a year or more in this fashion. For a published example of this practice see İ. H. Uzunçarşılı, *Osmanlı Devletinin Merkez ve Bahriye Teşkilatı*, Ankara, 1948, pp. 348-9.

A friend of his, one Nesimi who was attached to the Palace corps of the Salaried (*ulufeciler*), had been staying with him in his home (presumably in Istanbul). Nesimi had contracted for the one-year flour registry (*un defteri*) of Ilıca, at five hundred thousand *akçe*, as a tax-farm (*iltizam*); when he collected the revenues he was 60,000 *akçe* short of the promised amount. "He begged me, 'Please, if you have a friend among the retainers of Abdi Çelebi[20], make me his friend too.'" Mahmud arranged for an introduction to Mahmud Kethuda. Nesimi then suggested that they (i.e., he and our *kâtib* Mahmud) consult with the *efendi* (here clearly meaning Abdi Çelebi Efendi) and propose that if he would award the flour registers of Ilıca in *iltizam* contract for 200, 000 *akçe*, they would give the *bey* (presumably Hayreddin Bey) 60,000 *akçe*. It seems that in this way he would at once make up the deficit from his original contract, although he would be paying the amount to an individual rather than to the state, and procure the same revenue source for another year at a much more profitable rate than that originally established.

The offer was accepted, and the cash demanded. Nesimi put together the required amount from his own stores of coin (600 gold florins, 51 unminted florins, 16,000 *akçe*) and objects made of precious metals, and delivered the full 60,000. Just as Nesimi was to be given formal designation as tax-farmer of the flour revenues of Ilıca, he died of the plague, but not before declaring Mahmud his legatee in front of witnesses, The latter requested that the 60,000 *akçe* be restored to him, since the tax-farm had not been conferred on Nesimi and therefore the gift-money still belonged to Nesimi's estate. He was asked to forego the sum, to deny his claims to it. Mahmud refused to acquiesce, saying that it was his legal property, but he did suggest that he would perform the collection duties for which the money had been payment as a means to resolve the dispute. Although the authorities at first protested that this would be an "unfair" burden on Mahmud, he insisted and made an additional request that Nesimi's brother, who was also a member of the Salaried Corps, be given "a little *defter*" (i.e., revenue collection assignment) that could be considered compensation to him for loss of his brother and his inheritance. Ultimately, the award was agreed to, but at tax-collection time (*haraç vakti*) Mahmud found that it was not a tax-farm (*defter... emaneti ve kitâbeti ile*) but a legally less lucrative assignment as a salaried tax collector (*emanet*) with no licit claims on the revenues exceeding the amount stipulated in a tax-farm contract. When he turned in his taxes together with his warrant (*berat*), questions arose about the amount he surrendered, since this was 60,000 *akçe* short. Therefore Mahmud procured a receipt for the funds (140,000 *akçe*) from the deputy of the magistrate (*kadı na'ibi*) of Ilıca and

[20] Abdi Çelebi is either the Arab Accountant (*muhasebe'i-yi 'Arab*) or the former colleague of Mahmud who was promoted from apprenticeship to the post of *mukata'acı* in early 1536; see note 12 above. The latter case is the more likely, since the revenue source under discussion is clearly a *mukata'a*; this would make the date of final composition and submission of the document something after late January, 1536.

refrained from pressing his own greater claims, "with the thought that he [Hayreddin Bey] is an important person [*bir sahib-devletdür*], and [if I oblige him now] later he will remember me kindly." His petition, undoubtedly, served as further documentation of the propriety of his action.

One of the most remarkable aspects of this document, for all the horrors reported by our *kâtib*, is the conspicuous absence of that more vigorous language of complaint—complaint about venality of office, complaint about abuse of position, complaint about violation of imperial ideals enshrined in *kanun*, dynastic edict—that would fill the pages of similar petitions penned by a slightly later generation.[21] Here, the tone—in an era that is generally supposed to have represented a golden age of meritocratic expectations and relative freedom from such personal impositions—is rather one of explanation, apology, and open-ended appeal for personal assistance, assistance that is requested not because the subject has been wronged by greedy and immoral individuals, but because circumstances in an otherwise normal situation have conspired to place him in a difficult position.[22] The matter-of-fact recounting of the events, and the lack of explicit rancor against those who have wronged him—even the defunct Ali Çelebi—suggest that it would be erroneous to read Mahmud's petition as the sort of protest against corruption of an established, commonly understood system that would be characteristic of a somewhat later era. At this point, relatively early in Süleyman's reign, the relationships that structured the central administrative apparatus were still understood to be highly personalized ones within which the culture of exchange of "gifts" was taken as natural, if occasionally problematic. The gift had not yet become a bribe, and Mahmud's letter has as much the weight and tone of a report as of a complaint.

---

[21] See, for example, the angry reports of informants and petitioners for redress of grievance written by a number of functionaries who felt unfairly treated by Rüstem Paşa, the grand vezir (1544-53, 1555-61) canonized in Ottoman historiography as the institutionalizer of venality of office in Ottoman government: M.T. Gökbilgin, "Rüstem Paşa ve Hakkındaki İthamlar," *Tarih Dergisi* 8/11-12 (1955), 11-50). See also the fulminations of Mustafa Âli, cited in Fleischer, *Bureaucrat*, pp. 120-21.

[22] Ahmet Mumcu, *Osmanlı Devletinde Rüşvet*, Ankara, 1969, has noted that the age of Süleyman is largely considered to have been extraordinarily free of venal practice in government until the last years of the ruler (pp. 84-85, 111), in contrast to the usage common in earlier and subsequent reigns. Other studies generally reinforce the general perception of "corruption" as a post- or late Süleymanic development, often because they rely on both narrative and archival sources that begin to display some depth and breadth only after 1550. See, for example, K. Röhrborn, *Untersuchungen zur osmanischen Verwaltungsgeschichte*, Berlin, 1973, pp. 114-53. I would suggest that in terms of actual practice, exception of the first part of the reign from the rule of what our age would call graft is unwarranted. What merits attention is the enhancement of the language used to describe such practice as immoral and improper that occurs in the second half of the sixteenth century. For treatment from another perspective of the change in moral and social consciousness that this linguistic shift betokens, see C. Fleischer "Cultural Origins of the Ottoman *Nasihatname*," *Proceedings of the Third Congress on the Social and Economic History of Turkey*, Princeton 1983, The Isis Press, Istanbul 1990, pp. 67-78.

In the face of orderly, schematic representations of the hierarchy of rank and responsibility according to which Ottoman government has been regularly described—beginning, perhaps, with the Lawcode of the Conqueror and continuing to the present—we tend to assimilate to it our modern understanding of the nature and function of bureaucracy.[23] But certain notions central to this modern understanding, such as exclusivity of service and compensation, definition of function and responsibility within a single chain of command, and a depersonalized service ethic, are most definitely not part of the bureaucratic world of the early sixteenth century, whether in the Ottoman Empire or in Europe.[24] Our scribe's narrative lays out an intriguing picture of the complex web of personal and economic relationships through which Süleyman's government functioned, and brings into relief the degree to which such relationships were recognized as normal, even "legal," despite the apparent dictates of the logic of the bureaucratized (or, more properly at this point, bureaucratizing) structure within which they developed. Ali Çelebi's apprentice not only acted as his master's agent in private financial dealings, he also acted on his own behalf (in demanding payment from Mahmud), and himself had a financial agent who was also a salaried member of the most prestigious of the Palace cavalry units. Neither the function nor the income of Ottoman functionaries was delimited by their membership in the imperial patrimonial household; they could simultaneously serve several masters and in several capacities without their appropriateness for appointment, the way in which they fulfilled their ostensible tasks, or the propriety of their maintaining several levels or forms of employment and loyalty being questioned. It was sufficiently natural for Nesimi to use his friendship with an apprentice clerk to gain access to authority, in order to be able literally to invest in his own future, for Mahmud to detail the transaction without shame and to use it as the basis of a legal claim on property. Nesimi acknowledged the economic and quasi-familial nature of his relationship with another member of his class by making Mahmud his heir, and the latter did the same by entering a plea for Nesimi's *ulufeci* brother.

Mahmud pleads that he be accorded some of the perquisites that accrued to other members of his class (such as supplemental duty-revenue assignments) rather than denouncing capricious and venal abuse of a hierarchical structure based on function and merit. His petition also demonstrates that, for all that his account implies the destitution of his family as a result of his master's demands for payment for provision of an office, the implicit and explicit references to wealth and poverty that regularly occur in the petitions of literate Ottomans of

[23]For an eloquent recent example see H. İnalcık, *The Ottoman Empire: The Classical Age 1300-1600* (New York, 1973), p. 46.

[24]For comparison with cognate bureaucratic phenomena in Western Europe see, *inter alia*, R. Burr Litchfield, *Emergence of a Bureaucracy: The Florentine Patricians, 1530-1790* (Princeton, 1986), pp. 157-8, 175-81; K. W. Swart, *The Sale of Offices in the Seventeenth Century*, The Hague, 1949.

the sixteenth century (see also the next document) must be interpreted within the context of the high expectations and sense of entitlement that were part and parcel of the sensibility of all those associated with the apparatus of Ottoman government. Despite his debts (which he clearly hoped to be able to repay with interest once he received the supplementary assignments he desired), Mahmud had a dwelling in which he was able to lodge guests and, presumably, slaves. Furthermore, he was able to support himself on his small daily stipend (four *akçe*) and on reserve resources for quite some time before he received the *haraç* register, and he owned pack animals and slaves that he ultimately lost to Safavi marauders. His reluctance to do without a slave, despite his understanding that his professional interests lay in giving the boy as a gift, bears poignant witness to the sense of even a scribal apprentice of what constituted an acceptable standard of living for an Ottoman gentleman.[25]

The personal resources and sense of propriety of function of such stipendiary office-holders were clearly not limited, in fact or in expectation, by their office and the daily wage attached to it. Rather, their appointments and stipends (these latter being as much a badge of membership in the ruling class and a means of assigning relative rank and status as a reward for service and means of maintenance) provided access, and entitlement, to important contacts and additional means of attaining advancement and income. Mahmud and his friend Nesimi could not only negotiate for lucrative revenue-collecting assignments considered one of the normal perquisites of Palace service, they could also be absent from Istanbul and from their "posts" for considerable periods in order to carry out these supplemental duties. The relative proportions, within an individual's personal fortune, represented by stipendial and non-stipendial (but clearly licit) sources are suggested by the document. Mahmud had a daily stipend of four *akçe*, or 1,400/year. Nevertheless, he was able to secure loans for over sixty-five times that amount (calculating the *akçe* at 60/ducat) with apparent confidence that, once appointed to the Registry of Garrisons (at something like 4,380 *akçe* yearly,[26] exclusive of bonuses) he would be able quickly to repay the loan with interest. Nesimi's precise salary is not known, but in the year 1530 the average salary of members of the two Salaried Corps was eleven *akçe*.[27] Even so, Nesimi had at his immediate disposal cash and valuables worth fifteen times his probable annual salary. This amount may represent the sum that was missing

[25]Mahmud's lifestyle, as extrapolated here, would seem rather more luxurious that that deemed appropriate for an apprentice *kâtib* by a social critic of the late sixteenth century; see Andreas Tietze, "Mustafâ 'Âlî on Luxury and the Status Symbols of Ottoman Gentlemen," *Studia Turcologica Memoriae Alexii Bombaci Dicata*, Naples, 1982, pp. 577-90. However, two accounts dating from the 1530's indicate that full secretaries of the chancery expected, or were expected, to own at least two slaves: see the reports of Ramberti (abbreviated) and Yunus Bey published as appendices to A. H. Lybyer, *The Goverment of the Ottoman Empire in the Time of Suleiman the Magnificent*, Cambridge, 1913, pp. 247, 266.

[26]See note 14 above.

[27]Maliyeden Müdevver 23, 27b, Zu'l-ka'de 936.

from the 500,000 *akçe* he had contracted to collect (the figure obviously did not practically allow him to secure an appropriate profit), but even so his plan to procure the assignment again, negotiated at a lower rate of 200,000, gives a clear sense of the magnitude of potential gains at stake. Since he was apparently able to secure at least 440,000 *akçe* in Ilıca, a new contract at 200,000, after deduction of his expenses (including the 60,000 payment to the *bey*), would leave him with at least 180,000—forty times his annual stipend. It seems safe to assume that Mahmud, who ultimately did the collecting and admitted to retaining 60,000 *akçe*, profited very handsomely and felt it right that he should do so. Official salary, for such men on their way up, was the least part of what they could expect to earn as members of the ruling class.

The third and final document[28] was submitted during one of Rüstem Paşa's two terms as grand vezir (1544-53, 1555-61) by a certain Kasım, whose father was apparently known as Helvacıoğlu. Kasım's story sheds light on other dimensions of scribal life and the class consciousness of elite Ottomans:

> ...your poor, downtrodden servant, being possessed of a pen-case [i.e., literate], had for fourteen years been an unsalaried apprentice scribe for the Pillars of the State[29]. [Then] when an imperial order of the glorious sovereign left the Harem (*içrüden*] that a [particular] book be copied outside, that task was given to your prostrate servant. It was copied by my hand and submitted to you, and when you asked, "Who wrote [i.e., copied] this book?" the answer was, "Your servant Kasim, who is one of the apprentice scribes serving the great men of state [*erkân*], has written it." You responded, "How much is his salary?" and they answered, "He has no salary." You commanded, "Let him have a salary of six *akçe* [per day]; and the imperial order that resulted [from this exchange] is now extant in the offices of the Pillars of Felicity.[30]
>
> This being the case, it was then submitted to the dust of your blessed feet that "The other scribes [of this sort] are not stipended; the imperial law

---

[28] TKS E 12129.

[29] *Erkân-i devlet*; I take the reference to be to those scribes described in the pay lists as *kâtibân-ı dîvân tâbi'-i tevkî'î*, and late in the reign as *kâtibân-ı dîvân-ı 'âlî* i.e., chancery clerks working under the chancellor (*nisanci, tevkî'î*), although it is conceivable that the chancery scribes attached to the *defterdars* are meant (*kâtibân-ı dîvân tâbi'-i defterdârân*); see "Preliminaries," pp. 138-39. On balance, the first possibility seems the more likely since, were the second the case, Kasım could be expected to use the terminology current in the financial service that dealt with the the payment of salaries rather than the more general (or perhaps colloquial) *erkân-i devlet*. In any case, the *erkân* here in question are clearly the heads of the bureaucracy proper, rather than the ministers of state (*vüzera*), to whom such terminology at this date would more commonly be understood to apply. See also following note.

[30] *Erkânî* [sic] *sa'âdet;* this reference, and the following one, to the written records of his several appointments support the supposition advanced in the preceding note on the contextual meaning of *erkân* in this document.

[*kanun-ı padişahi*] is that they be compensated with *timar*-grants."[31] Thus it was ordered that I be given a *timar*, and this order too is preserved perfectly in the offices of the *erkân*. After I had served under these circumstances for some time it happened that the office of Intendant Registrar of Anatolia[32] fell vacant and was given to this your servant.

As I was serving in this capacity, one of Rüstem Pasa's retainers came and petitioned through his connections [*iltimas*] for my poor position; in justification he said, "This person's [i.e., Kasim's] father was not someone entitled to a post[33]; he's the son of a sweet-maker." On this pretext, that person took my poor living [*bunun dirlüciğin*] without there being any reason for my dismissal [*bilâ sebebden*]. Though my father never held a stipended post, he occupied himself with learning; but my grandfather was one of the Confectioners [*helvacı*] of the late Sultan Bayezid, and therefore [my father] was called by this name [i.e., Helvacıoğlu].

My hope is that you will save this, your abashed servant, from shame among the populace and will return again the wretched post won by my pen-case; otherwise, lovely lord, I will not have the face to return home. It is my sultan's to dispose.

Kasım's patronymic, his heredity, and his family's history of imperial service bear discussion. The trajectory of that history— from a father, who may have had servile status and was attached to the Palace, to a son who became a scholar, to a grandson who became a clerical bureaucrat after long years of unsalaried apprenticeship—demonstrates that at this epoch what have been called the "Ottoman career paths" of Sword, Learning, and Pen were, intergenerationally, mutually permeable and interpenetrating rather than rigid and exclusive.[34] At this juncture, it seems likely that affiliation with the class of servitors broadly considered was a more significant determinant of an individual's career prospects than membership in a particular professional category; these categories, after all, were clearly articulated only after the reign of the Lawgiver, and the evidence lies in favor of their being less formed and more porous in the

[31]This statement would seem to fly in the face of the ample documentation showing that *kâtibs* were salaried as well as (later) *timared*. Kasim can only mean that scribes of his sort—whatever subcategory of the species that may represent—were to be paid by *timar* assignment. The language here suggests that a *kanunname* is actually being quoted: *sâ'ir kâtibler 'ulûfeyle değildir kanun-ı pâdişâhî timâr ile olmakdur.*

[32]*Emin-i defter-i Anadolu;* this was a provincial rather than a central bureaucratic post, signifying headship of that office within the provincial administration that supervised matters of land registry that were the ultimate province of the *Defter-i hakani* in Istanbul; see Howard, "Imperial Registry," (218-19). Its incumbent was paid by *timar*.

[33]*Ehl-i mensûb* [sic., = *munsıb*] *değil idi.*

[34]*Bureaucrat*, ch. 8.

first half of the sixteenth century than in the second. In place of, or in addition to, the received models of the operative lines of inclusion and cleavage in Ottoman society (*askerî/re'âyâ* [ruling class/ tax-paying subjects], *seyf/ilm/kalem*, slave/non-slave, muslim/non-muslim), the document gives a name to a more elastic, but no less useful concept: the *ehl-i mansıb*, those entitled by heredity, among other criteria, to appointment within the ranks of the non-tax-paying elite (*askerî*) whatever the particulars of the individual's career path or his legal status.

It seems clear that we must fully redraw our modern image of the structure of the ruling elite of the "classical" Ottoman Empire. This image, though modified in particulars, is still pervaded by romantic notions, derived largely from Christian European sources, of the upper class as primarily non-aristocratic, normally (or ideally) monogenerational and meritocratic in nature, and implicitly servile in origin or actual status, a service elite of the most fundamental sort. Victor Ménage[35] and Metin Kunt[36] have addressed the question of how strictly we should interpret contemporary European descriptions of the Ottoman governing order of the sixteenth century. The work of these scholars focuses on members of the military-administrative career within which it has been assumed, as stated by contemporary Christian commentators, that men of *devşirme* or otherwise servile origins would predominate and so preclude the formation of an elite that could function as something like an aristocracy of blood as well as of service. Ménage and Kunt have shown that servile status was not an absolute requirement for entry to the elite administrative orders. Indeed, it may only have been a preferred qualification at very restricted and particular points in imperial history, for example, during the decade or decade and a half during which Süleyman felt it necessary to begin training a cadre of his own that would replace the upper echelons of the old guard of servitors inherited from his father and grandfather.[37] Even so, and even at that juncture, Süleyman had still to acknowledge the force and weight of these countervalent principles; his famous proclamation to the *timar*-holders of the Empire of 1531, confirming the hereditary rights to preferential status of the descendants of *sipahi*s, spoke directly to the question of transgenerational claims upon dynastic largesse.[38]

The evidence of Kasım's story indicates that the perceptions of privileged class identity and hereditary entitlement that informed the conflicts that provoked the 1531 edict were not confined to the military caste, but pervaded other sectors

[35] "Some Notes on the Devşirme," *BSOAS* 29 (1966), 64-78.

[36] *The Sultan's Servants: The Transformation of Ottoman Provincial Government*, New York, 1983, pp. 33-44.

[37] C. Fleischer, paper delivered at the Süleyman the Magnificent Symposium, Chicago, 1987.

[38] M.T. Gökbilgin, "Kanuni Sultan Süleyman'ın Timar ve Zeamet tevcihi ile İlgili Fermanları," *Tarih Dergisi* 17 (1967), 35-48.

of the ruling class as well. The numbers of those with claims to membership in the class to which appointments, stipends, prebends, and status were to be distributed grew, and so did the ideological articulation of that class consciousness; the historiographical florescence of the second half of the sixteenth century is a striking example of this latter phenomenon. The threat to social stability represented by natural increase in elite families was limited by mortality and the enhanced absorptive capacity of a geographically and demographically expansive administrative apparatus. Still, once that apparatus was in place, the challenge facing ever more vocal Ottomans threatened with increased competition for dynastic rewards would be to renogotiate, in each generation, the criteria by which inclusion and exclusion from the ruling class and its particular components would be adjudicated. The factional violence that became so marked a part of elite life at the end of the sixteenth century represented one dimension of this process, that whereby the upper echelons of the *askerî* would sort out these matters internally.

Another dimension of the process, of course, was a tension, which became acute toward the end of Süleyman's reign, between the dynasty and the increasingly bureaucratized elite that ostensibly served it. At issue here was the locus of authority to pronounce on questions pertaining to the ideals, identity, and practice of the dynastic state, particularly in matters of ideological representation, elite reproduction, and distribution of resources. With the arrival in the upper ranks of men like Rüstem Paşa, senior statesmen who were wholly the products and the carriers of the burgeoning imperial culture that was forged during the reign of the Lawgiver, the balance of power shifted in favor of the administrators.[39] These men were furthermore strengthened in their stance by those very developments initiated by the architects of the Süleymanic regime as supports for dynastic authority: codification of law, regularization of administrative practice and elite recruitment procedures, a move toward depersonalization of politics, and inculcation of expectations of regularity and reward based on common subscription to a system (as opposed to individual judgment) that determined standards of merit and entitlement.

It is therefore significant that Kasım should insist upon the fact that the orders governing his changes of status were written down, recorded, and registered in their proper place. The degree of orderliness and detail that the Süleymanic

[39]The struggle for control of representation of the dynastic image between the dynasty and the bureaucratized elite is best illustrated in the simultaneous appearance of two distinct historiographical streams in the early 1550's, one a classicizing high style purveyed by loyal but independent bureaucrats such as Ramazanzade and Celalzade, the other the courtly Persian panegyric of the official *şehname*-writers. In the writing of history, as in politics, the bureaucrats won. See Christine Woodhead, "An Experiment in Official Historiography: The Post of Şehnameci in the Ottoman Empire, "*Wiener Zeitschrift für die Kunde des Morgenlandes* 75 (1983), 157-82, and Fleischer, "Messiah."

regime brought to record-keeping was probably still somewhat novel in Kasım's day. Furthermore, the registration of these orders in the central repository of the bureaucracy represented institutional protection against the predations of Kasım's less scrupulous fellows (predations that seem to have been more common in previous reigns). These records, Kasım's exposition suggests, constituted a powerful instrument of bureaucratic authority whereby the livelihood and security of status of members of the ruling class could be protected and the corporate rights and identity of that class asserted. It is equally significant in this context that our *kâtib* relates that the chief bureaucrats objected to and corrected the sovereign's command that Kasım be given a salaried position, invoking the priority of the impersonal principle of imperial law over individual dynastic decree.

These few scribal narratives (one hopes that more such will appear), seemingly frank and unpolished as they are, afford evocative and tantalizing glimpses into the professional and family lives of men who might be described as "ordinary" Ottomans. These were low-to-middle ranking members of the privileged sector of society whose aspirations were focussed on the imperial court in Istanbul in an era when the scribal service was only just taking full form and offered opportunities for mobility to the literate. It remains only to say a few words about the nature of that literacy as it is displayed by the documents.

For the *kâtib*s or would-be scribes whose stories have been told here, calligraphic skill would seem to have been their primary claim to scribal expertise, which was not necessarily buttressed by greater learning in the literary arts or philology. This was clearly the case with Ahmed. Although Kasım's father ostensibly occupied himself with the acquisition of religious learning, he was either poorly schooled or disinclined to make a paying profession of his scholarship, since he was appointed to no stipended post. This professional decision, voluntary or otherwise, signified a break in an incipient family tradition of service to the dynasty, a break that would ultimately count against—temporarily, one hopes— Kasım's chances for advancement. In any event, Kasım's father established no great family tradition of learning, for his son's petition is filled with egregious spelling errors that show, if nothing else, that his acquaintance with Arabic and Persian must have been rudimentary at best. (This judgment, of course, assumes that he, rather than a professional writer of petitions, actually penned the document; but if he did have it written for him, sufficiently significant questions arise about why he should have done so as to render the judgment reasonably valid). While Kasım's calligraphy may have been impressive, as he suggests, he was clearly at a loss when required to compose a document without a written model before him. His fourteen years of apprenticeship seem to have done him little good in this regard; like a fair number of his colleagues who learned their writing skills on the job rather than in the *medrese*-college, Kasım remained only partly literate outside his restricted area of competence. Mahmud's orthography is somewhat better than Kasım's (though by no means perfect), but his style is as unpolished as that of his colleague.

The "Ottoman bureaucrat," at this epoch of expansion when the description of an individual with appropriate connections as "a good hand with a pen" or "useful wielder of the reed" (*yarar ehl-i kalemdür*) was often enough to secure a scribal appointment, was not necessarily a highly educated person. Nor, does it seem, were there consistent standards of professionalism yet applied to the motley corps of the *küttab*. The observations of some Ottoman observers on the tremendous difference in the educational levels and literacy of college- and non-college-trained bureaucrats should be taken with some measure of seriousness and not dismissed as the self-aggrandizing grumbling of disaffected intellectuals.[40] The "Ottoman bureaucrat" was not one type, but several, and there was a world of difference between the Ottoman gentleman and the educated Ottoman gentleman, although they shared professional space and class affiliation.

University of Chicago

[40]See, for example, the comments of Âli summarized in *Bureaucrat*, pp. 214-31.

[5]

EARLY ISLAMIC BOOKBINDINGS AND THEIR COPTIC RELATIONS

BY THEODORE C. PETERSEN

WHILE THE BELIEF WIDELY PREVAILS THAT Islamic bookbinding owed much of its early artistic inspiration and technical skill to Coptic, Sasanian, and Hellenistic sources, a full demonstration of such indebtedness could not be undertaken so long as few or no bookbindings of the early days of Islamic history were known to have survived. Now, thanks to a fortunate recent discovery and the patient and painstaking study of the findings by Georges Marçais and Louis Poinssot, the long-delayed demonstration has been attempted and is presented in the first fascicle of an imposing work, *Objets Kairouanais, IXe au XIIIe Siècle,* published by the "Direction des Antiquités et Arts," Tunis, 1948.

This first fascicle (364 pages of text with 67 drawings by L. Gaillard and P. Carrère, and 54 plates) deals exclusively with "Reliures de Kairouan." Under 156 numbers, some 179 ancient bookbindings and remnants of bookbindings are minutely described. While none of these bindings dates from the earliest period of Islamic history, 58 of them are assigned to the ninth century, 19 to the tenth, 71 to the eleventh, and 31 to the twelfth and thirteenth centuries. All the 77 bindings dating from the ninth and tenth centuries and 58 or 59 of those dating from the eleventh are of the "format à l'italienne" (wider than high). The smallest of them (No. 10) measures 105 x 52 mm. The two largest (Nos. 22 and 23) measure 368 x 274 mm. and 370 x 270 mm., respectively. Twelve or 13 of the bindings assigned to the eleventh century and all the bindings assigned to the twelfth and thirteenth centuries are of the "format à la française" (higher than wide). The smallest of the latter group (No. 113) measures about 100 x 122 mm., the largest (No. 116) measures 344 x 405 mm.

The greater portion of these bindings, including all those of the ninth and tenth centuries, was discovered a few years ago by L. Poinssot in one of the storerooms flanking the north side of the court of the Grand Mosque of Kairouan. The room had been used for many years as a pigeon house and its floor was covered high with bird manure, but some forty or more years earlier someone had deposited here the discarded debris of the library of the Grand Mosque. This debris, regarded, most likely, as too venerable to be destroyed, consisted of some badly damaged leaves from early manuscripts of the Koran and a large number of torn-off old book covers, most of them broken and worm-eaten. When found, these book covers lay scattered pell-mell over the floor and were partly covered with manure. As their age and character were immediately recognized, they were taken to the Museum of Bardo, where they were carefully cleaned and prepared for permanent preservation.

Since these bindings were no longer attached to the books for which they were made, they could reveal little about the methods by which their several quires of leaves had been sewn into gathered books (*figs. 1–4*) and about the methods by which the gathered books had been attached to the covers.[1] But

[1] The lower cover of the ninth-century binding, No. 5, still holds the remnants of a quire of parchment leaves attached to it. The sewing of this quire was done in three stitches. The sewing holes of the longer middle stitch lie flush with the two holes found in the hinging edge of the wooden board, i.e., the holes into which the sewing threads of the book were laced in commencing and terminating the sewing op-

they reveal that most of the oldest book covers were made of wooden boards which were covered with brown leather showing elaborate patterns of interlaced decoration done in blind-tooling and stamping.[2]

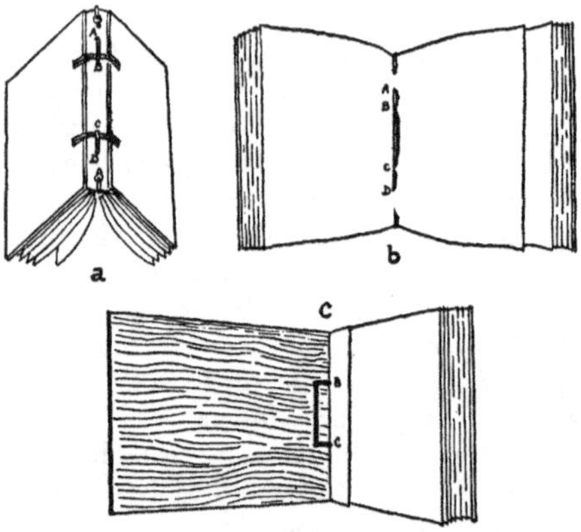

FIG. 1—SEWING OF KAIROUAN BINDING NO. 5 (97 x 142 MM.), A CODEX SEWN IN SINGLE QUIRE

(After Gaillard.)

The inner sides of the boards had in most instances been lined with parchment sheets. Some of the latter were recognizable as being the unwritten first leaves of the first quires, or last leaves of the last quires, of the manuscripts bound within those boards. The gluing of these end leaves onto the inner faces of the boards was possibly intended to give added strength to the hinging of the covers. Another fact observable in these bindings was that most of them (perhaps all those having wooden boards) had been provided with clasps consisting of looped thongs and staples, i.e., of loops of thong fastened in the edge of the lower (left) cover and being just long enough to be clasped tightly to the head of a peg or staple driven into the rim of the upper (right) cover.[3]

A good number of the bindings dating from the twelfth and thirteenth centuries, of the "format à la française," show that they were provided with pentagonal flaps extending from the fore edge of the lower left covers and being wide enough, after having been folded over the fore edge of the book, to be tucked under the upper covers down to half their widths, similar to the flaps still used in modern Islamic bindings.

Most of the older Kairouan bindings, however (chiefly those of the "format à l'italienne"), were provided with what in their present broken condition appear to be narrow leather flaps attached to the head, tail, and fore edges of the lower covers. While most of these flaps are partly or wholly broken off and lost, those which remain are of a width no greater than needed to cover the fore edges of the respective books for which they were made. Only in three instances is the leather of these flaps seen to be of single thickness,[4] while in all other instances it is of double thick-

---

eration. The hinging edges of a smaller number of the Kairouan boards lack those lacing holes, thus indicating that they were fastened to their gathered books not by lacing but only by means of glued strips of cloth, i.e., by a technique at variance with the general Coptic practice. That the latter practice of gluing books into "cased covers" was not unknown in Coptic Egypt, is shown, however, by such early evidence as the two detached wooden covers (Beatty early book covers I and II) with bone or ivory inlay, from Egypt, probably of the fourth century A.D. which had been hinged to their manuscript contents only with glued strips of linen and which came to the Chester Beatty Library together with the famous group of fourth-century Biblical Papyri, discovered in 1931.

[2] Four of these boards have been identified as being of Aleppo pine, four others of fig, three of white poplar, one each of black poplar, laurel, and tamarisk.

[3] Metal staples were used in 25 of the Kairouan bindings, the numbers of staples used in any single binding varying from two to six. In two bindings the staples are of silver, in nine, of bronze, in the others, of iron.

[4] In bindings 104 A and 106 A and D (not Nos. 116 A and D, as misprinted on p. 17, note 1).

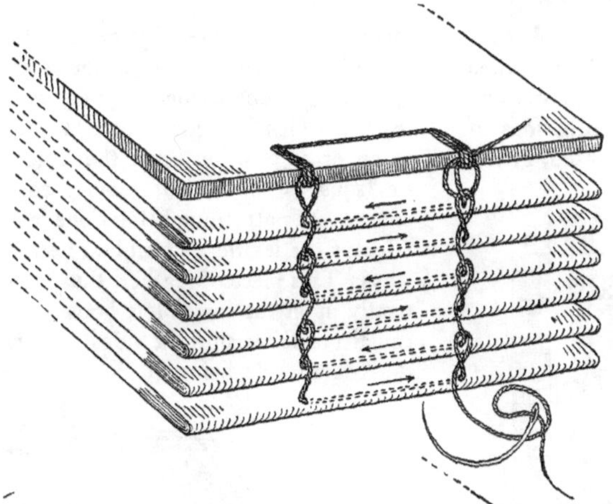

FIG. 2—RECONSTRUCTED SEWING OF KAIROUAN BINDING NO. 5 AFTER MARÇAIS' DESCRIPTION AS A MULTIPLE-QUIRE CODEX SEWN WITH THREE STITCHES

As the thread at the outermost sewing holes was not hinged to the covers, the drawing omits the usual interquire, chain-stitch linking at these two sewing holes. One should expect the codex to be sewn with four chain-stitch linkings, even though the covers were attached only to the second and third of the chain-stitch bands.

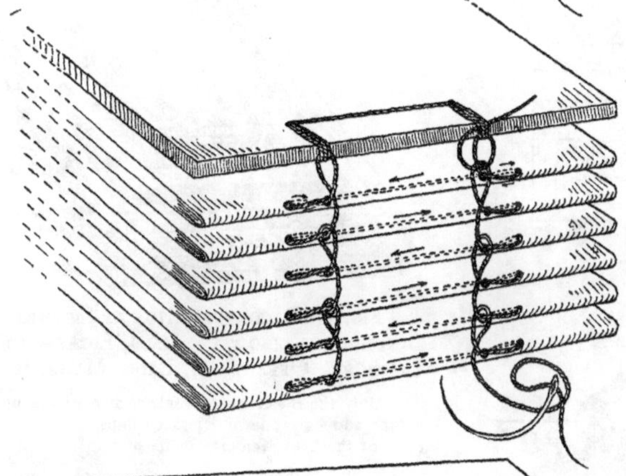

FIG. 3—SEWING OF THE MAGHREB PARCHMENT *Koran* MANUSCRIPT W 556 (146 x 160 MM.), TWELFTH TO THIRTEENTH CENTURY. BALTIMORE, WALTERS ART GALLERY

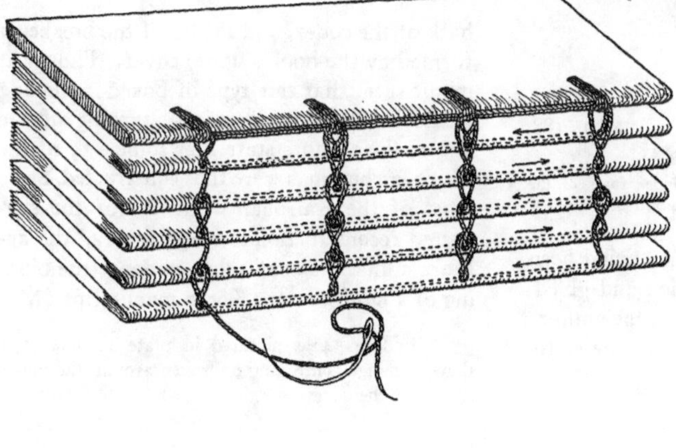

FIG. 4—SEWING OF COPTIC *Lectionary*, MS. MORGAN NO. 634 (320 x 270 MM.), NINTH CENTURY

ness, the leather having been folded over against itself, flesh side to flesh side, and then tightly glued together so as to make a stiff and solid flange. In many instances both sides of this flange are seen to be ornamented, generally with fillets, the ornamenting having been done before the flange was folded and glued. Three of the bindings [5] are cited by the authors as offering sufficient proof to support the statement that these fore-edge extensions were attached to the lower covers, not as three separate flanges but as one continuous length of leather which was glued at right angles, i.e., in an erect position upon the inside margins or "squares" of the three outer edges of the covers—the attaching being done by the lower edge of the leather, which had been bent sideways. This piece of leather, thus fastened vertically upon the lower left book cover, would constitute three upright sides of a rigid box, the fourth side being formed by the flexible back of the codex, and the lid of the box being formed by the book's upper cover. Though it might seem that this type of boxed-in binding would not lend itself to easy turning of the pages, the authors state that some 125 of the Kairouan bindings were thus constructed. Since most of the Kairouan evidence for the suggested reconstruction is fragmentary,[6] the authors adduce as confirming evidence the binding of a ninth-century Koran manuscript (Ma-

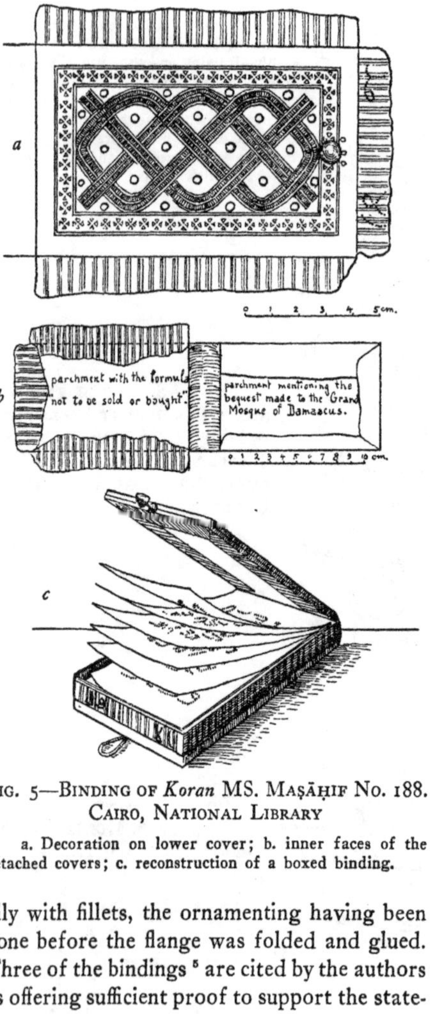

FIG. 5—BINDING OF *Koran* MS. MAṢĀḤIF NO. 188. CAIRO, NATIONAL LIBRARY

a. Decoration on lower cover; b. inner faces of the detached covers; c. reconstruction of a boxed binding.

FIG. 6—RECONSTRUCTION OF IBSCHER'S COPTIC BINDING (CA. 440 x 330 MM.), EIGHTH TO TENTH CENTURY. OFFENBACH, LEDER-MUSEUM

Only the lower cover (here shown facing upward) is extant and only one of its three flaps, the one of the tail edge of the book, remains in its place.

[5] Bindings Nos. 41, 54, and 94 *bis*.

[6] Binding 54 as pictured in plate 14 (*fig. 14*) shows a flange continuing unbroken around the lower corner of the cover.

ṣāḥif No. 188) of the Cairo Library, described in T. W. Arnold and A. Grohmann, *The Islamic Book*, p. 45 (*fig. 5*) and a Coptic bookbinding (also cited by T. W. Arnold), the property of Hugo Ibscher (*fig. 6*). It is only fair, however, to state that the published descriptions of these two bindings speak of the added leather strips not as the upright sides of a box but as "fore-edge flaps," which conceivably would fold outward when the book was opened and fold up against the fore edge when the book was closed.[7] Where book clasps were provided, the flaps would be held securely in place as soon as the clasps were fastened. The Kairouan bindings 64 and 77, being of this construction, were provided with three clasps, binding No. 94 *bis* with four clasps, binding 94-A with six clasps, and the

FIG. 7—METAL COVERS OF AN *Evangelion* MS. MOUNT SINAI 207 (305 x 240 MM.), TWELFTH CENTURY

The covers with the three metal fore-edge flaps are not as old as the manuscript (traced from Library of Congress photographs).

Byzantine bindings with metal-encrusted covers. For a fine specimen, compare with the silver binding of the Evangelion MS. Mt. Sinai 207 (*fig. 7*). A sixteenth-century Spanish *Book of hours*, MS. 31 of the Pierpont Morgan Library, has a red leather binding of this type. Its three flaps are attached to the lower cover and when folded up are held in place by two silver clasps at the fore edge and by one clasp each at the ends.

[7] Flaps of this latter type were often used in

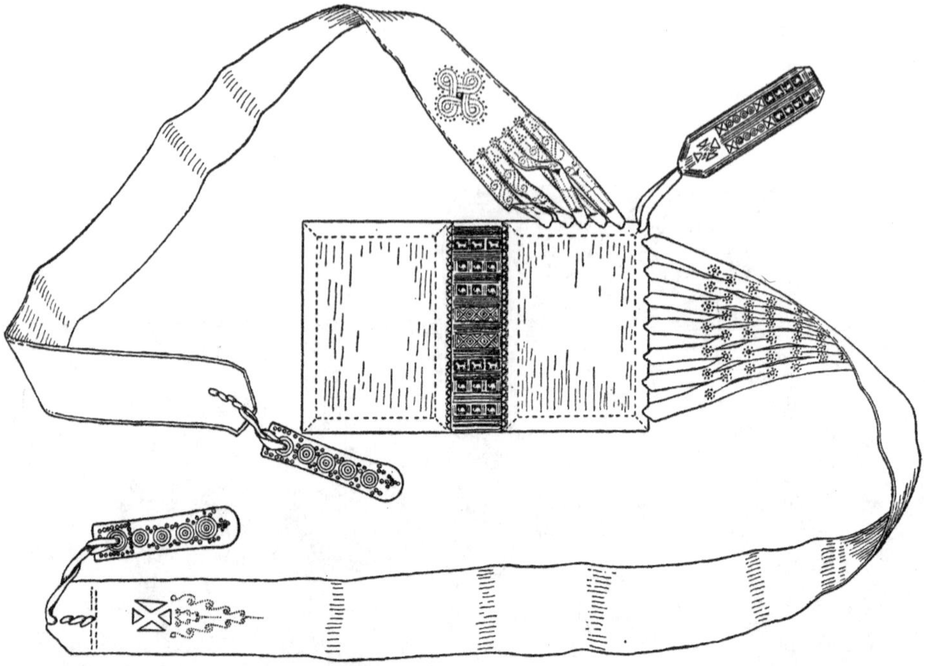

FIG. 8—C. T. LAMACRAFT'S RECONSTRUCTION OF THE BINDING OF MS. CHESTER BEATTY COPTIC B, *Acts and St. John* (120 x 102 MM.), CA. A.D. 600 OR EARLIER

(Drawn from photograph of a facsimile in the Library of the University of Michigan.)

Ibscher Coptic binding, cited above, with seven or nine clasps.[8]

[8] A more detailed description of the Ibscher binding (since 1931 in the possession of the Leder-Museum in Offenbach) is found in the eighth installment of Paul Adam's article ***Die Griechische Einbandkunst und das früh-christliche Buch,*** Archiv für Buchbinderei, vol. 24, Heft 9 (Sept. 1924), p. 81. There is evidence of the use of three flaps, but only the flap attached to the tail is preserved. The clasps in this binding had been seven in number: three along the fore edge, two each at head and tail, and besides these there is evidence at the outer corners of the lower cover of additional triple-platted thongs which, as Ibscher thought, may have been used as corner clasps, but which could also have served for the attaching of book markers such as are seen in the Chester Beatty sixth-century bindings Coptic A and B (*fig. 8*).

It is clear, however, that the ancient Cairo binding, Maṣāḥif No. 188, and most of the Kairouan bindings resembling it were fastened with only a single clasp across the short fore edge and may, therefore, have deserved the special style of "boxed-in" fore-edge protection seen in so many of the Kairouan bindings.

What will, no doubt, most interest the student of early Islamic bookbinding in the old Kairouan bindings is the richness and variety of the very specialized style of tooled and stamped ornamentation found in their leather coverings. The many different decorative elements produced here in blind-tooling—the various types of braid, twisted rope, "chenille" garland, basketweave, ringlet, and flagstone patterns, interlacings, combinations of several of these elements, and a host of intricate panel traceries—all these have been carefully classified, minutely analyzed, described, and pictured in line drawings. Then the large number of varied dies or stamps, some 240 of them, used for enlivening the tooled designs—roundels (concave and convex), annules, squares, lozenges, stars, fleurons, rosettes, heart-shaped dies and others with figures or inscriptions, cut in intaglio—have likewise been classified, analyzed, described, and pictured. And what may at times seem like a labor of supererogation, the origin, diffusion, and uses of some of these decorative elements have been traced through many lands and many centuries down to the Middle Ages. The "torsade" or twisted rope is documented (pp. 290–95) as having been used from the fourth and third millenniums B.C., in Susa, in Lower Mesopotamia, by the Sumerians, the Elamites, and later by the Syrians, Phoenicians, Greeks, Romans, and Gauls. The "tresse à quatre brins" or four-banded braid and various types of interlacing are likewise shown to be not Islamic inventions but heirlooms passed down from very ancient times and cultivated in more recent times by Syrian and Coptic artists. Here a number of patterns found in wall decorations in the Coptic monastery of Bawit are cited and presented in illustrations to show that they are not only similar to, but nearly identical with, those used by the book decorators of Kairouan (*fig. 9*).[9]

The general plan of the Kairouan tooled decorations always consisted of a panel framed by borders. In most of the bindings the panels as well as the borders were filled with "twisted rope" ornament. Within the panel areas the "twisted rope" was often arranged in elaborate, interlaced patterns, including circular, triangular, quadrangular, hexagonal, and octagonal motifs (*figs. 10–19*). Among the exceptions to this more common plan of ornamentation were some of the earliest covers,

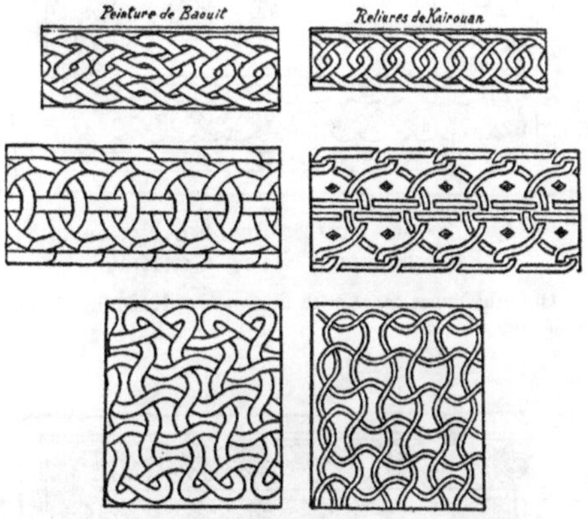

FIG. 9—DECORATIVE PATTERNS IN THE SIXTH (?)-CENTURY MURAL PAINTINGS OF THE COPTIC MONASTERY OF BAWIT AND SIMILAR PATTERNS IN THE NINTH-CENTURY BOOKBINDINGS OF KAIROUAN.

including two with panels that are bare of all ornament, one with a panel containing only two insignificant garlands, five with panels showing no other tooled ornamentation than short eulogies in large Kufic characters. These read: ما شاء on the upper cover (*fig. 10*) and الله on the lower cover—meaning together "what God wills," or بسم on the upper and الله on the lower cover, that is, "in the name of God." There are also fifteen eleventh-century bindings showing within their panels only

[9] Other such parallels could be found in Coptic manuscript illuminations and also in Coptic bookbindings. The border pattern of the Kairouan binding (*fig. 15*) can be matched with the open-work frieze pattern on the upper cover of the Coptic binding, Vienna Inv. No. 34 (*fig. 28*), and the platted-band design of Kairouan binding 98 (*fig. 17*) with the inked ornamentation of the binding of the Beatty MS. Coptic C (*fig. 23*).

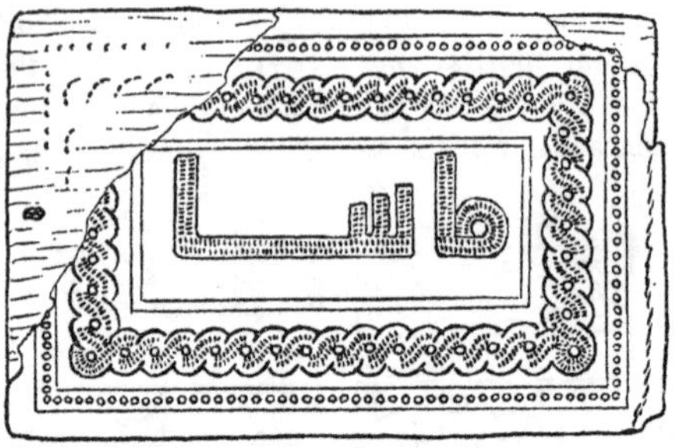

FIG. 10—KAIROUAN BINDING NO. 1a
(83 x 130 MM.), NINTH CENTURY

Only the upper cover with first part of Kufic inscription is shown.

FIG. 12—KAIROUAN BINDING NO. 16
(156 x 219 MM.), NINTH CENTURY

Lower cover only is extant.

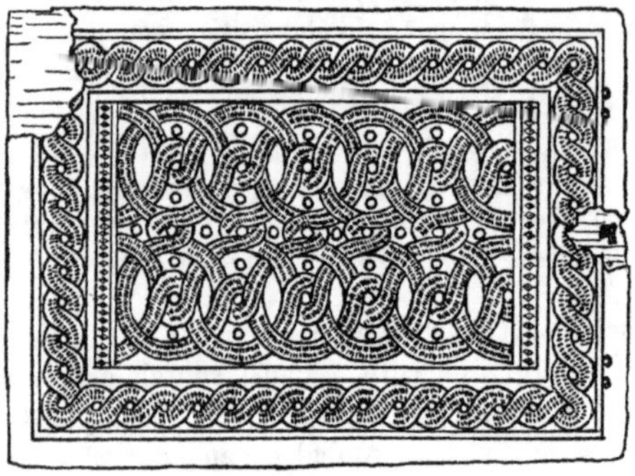

FIG. 11—KAIROUAN BINDING NO. 14
(152 x 217 MM.), NINTH CENTURY

Lower cover only is extant.

FIG. 13—KAIROUAN BINDING NO. 41
(116 x 174 MM.), NINTH CENTURY

Lower cover only is extant.

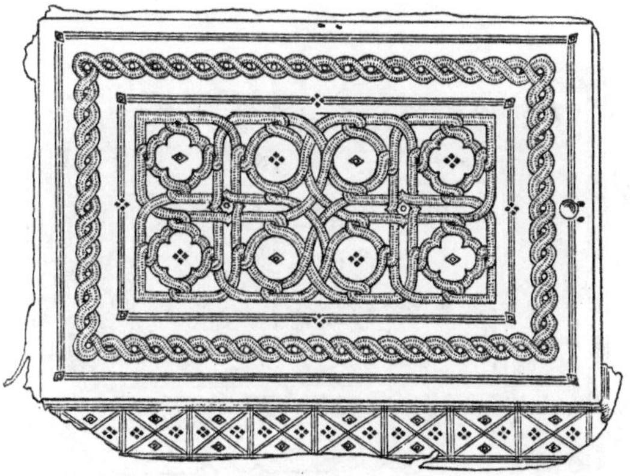

FIG. 14—KAIROUAN BINDING NO. 54 (157 X 236 MM.), NINTH CENTURY

Lower cover only is extant.

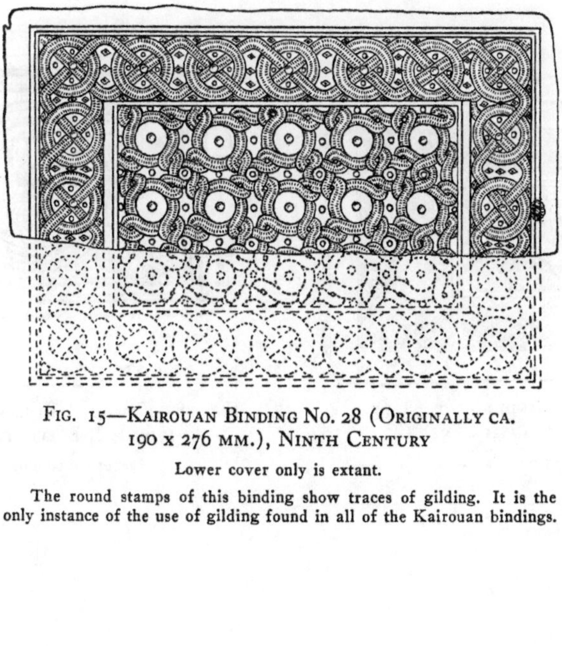

FIG. 15—KAIROUAN BINDING NO. 28 (ORIGINALLY CA. 190 X 276 MM.), NINTH CENTURY

Lower cover only is extant.

The round stamps of this binding show traces of gilding. It is the only instance of the use of gilding found in all of the Kairouan bindings.

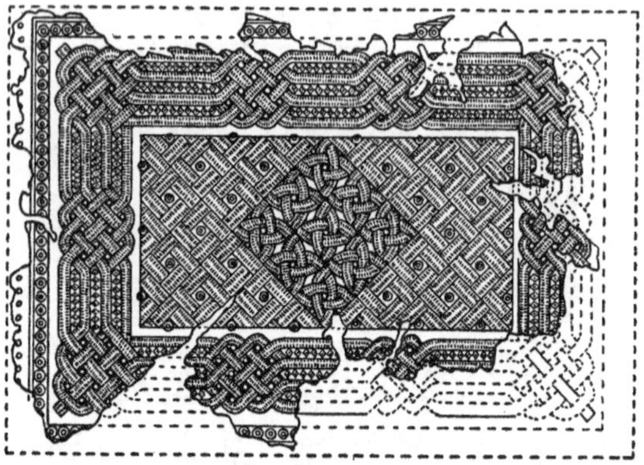

FIG. 16—KAIROUAN BINDING NO. 72 (ORIGINALLY CA. 215 x 300 MM.), TENTH CENTURY

Upper cover only is extant.

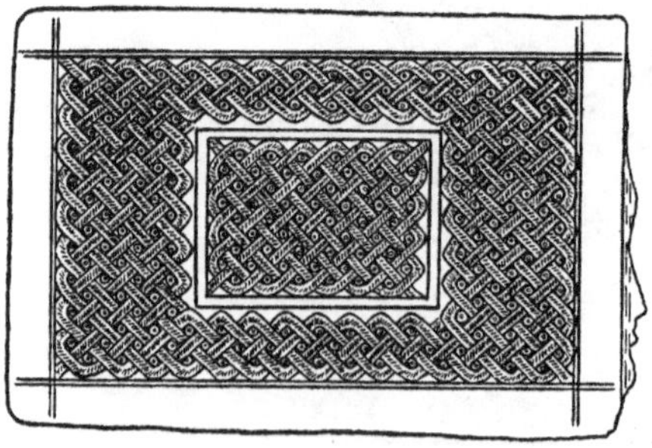

FIG. 17—KAIROUAN BINDING NO. 98 (113 x 176 MM.), ELEVENTH CENTURY

Upper cover only is extant.

FIG. 18—KAIROUAN BINDING NO. 119a (115 x 176 MM.), ELEVENTH CENTURY

Lower cover only is extant.

small central ornamentations of circular, diamond, or star-shaped contours.

Another deviation from the general plan of decoration is found in a group of nine eleventh-century bindings (Nos. 118 to 126) which show embossed ornamentation. The decorative designs of these bindings, after having been outlined on the wooden boards, were

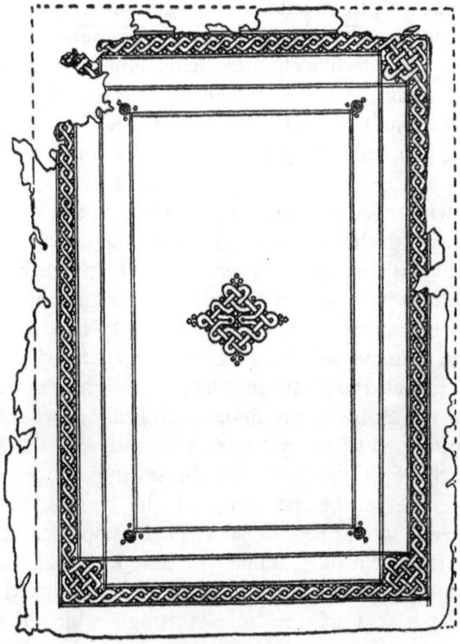

FIG. 19—KAIROUAN BINDING NO. 144 (255 x 180 MM.), THIRTEENTH CENTURY

Both covers are extant. The lower cover shows a different tooling of plain fillets without the "twisted rope" pattern.

made to appear in relief by the device of retracing and overlaying them, line by line, with pieces of cord (3 mm. thick) heavily soaked with glue. After the glued-down cords were sufficiently dried and hardened, the leather covering was glued and firmly pressed over them. Then as the pattern of the underlying cords appeared on the face of the leather as a design of gentle ridges, it was further accentuated by running a tooled line close to either side of the ridges, thereby bringing these into stronger relief.[10]

While in four of these latter bindings (Nos. 123–126) the decoration of the borders was confined to straight lines and that of the centers of the panels to circular lines, binding No. 118 was given a "twisted rope" pattern in its border and a circular shield in its panel. Bindings Nos. 119 to 122 were given palmette designs in the panels (*fig. 18*) and, in addition, Nos. 121 and 122 were given floral ornaments in the corners of the borders.

A further enlivening of the line-tooling was accomplished in the greater portion of the bindings by the free use of stamp impressions placed either singly within the meshes of the "platted band" decorations or used in continuous rows to supply frieze decoration to the borders. (Samples of some of these stamps are shown in fig. 20, A, *a–k,* and most of the stamps were used in identical forms in early Coptic leather bindings.)

In any comparison of the Kairouan bindings with earlier leather bindings of Christian Egypt it should be remembered that prac-

[10] A good-sized specimen of Egyptian leather of the late thirteenth or fourteenth century (perhaps part of a saddle) decorated in this technique, in the collection of R. Ettinghausen, clearly reveals ends of the modeling cords protruding from the embossed design, where the leather has suffered from abrasion. While this type of embossed ornament is not found on any of the early Coptic book covers extant, it was part of the Coptic leatherworker's stock-in-trade. It would be of great interest to know if the famous binding of the seventh-century St. Cuthbert codex at Stonyhurst College, England, which, according to Berthe van Regemorter's description in her article *La reliure des manuscrits de S. Cuthbert et de S. Boniface,* Scriptorium, vol. 3 (1949), p. 46, shows other resemblances to early Coptic bookbinding, also had its embossed ornament executed in a technique familiar to early Coptic leatherworkers and, somewhat later, to the bookbinders of Kairouan.

tically all the 120 or more ancient Coptic bindings available for a comparison were found, not in the ruins of large populous cities such as Kairouan in Tunis, or Alexandria, Memphis, and Cairo in Egypt, where professional scribes and bookbinders would be conversant with the latest trends of artistic book production and eager to excel in inventiveness and quality of workmanship, but in the ruins of

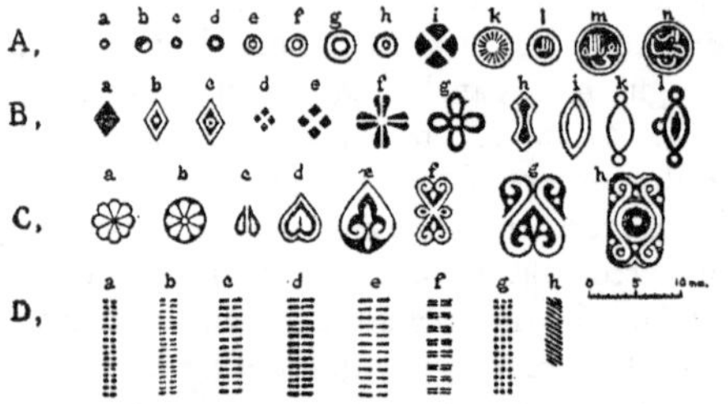

FIG. 20—DECORATIVE STAMPS USED BY THE KAIROUAN BOOKBINDERS

The inscription بقي بالله: "Duration is to God—God is Eternal," of stamp A *m*, is used on bindings Nos. 75, 113, and 127a. The binder's name ابن حسان, Son of Ḥassān, of stamp A *n*, is used on binding 144 (*fig. 19*). Of the 50 or more "chenille" stampings cited and pictured by Marçais, 8 are given here; and of these D *a* was used in binding No. 41 (*fig. 13*); D *b* in binding No. 54 (*fig. 14*); D *c* in binding No. 1a (*fig. 10*); D *d* in binding No. 72 (*fig. 16*), D *f* in binding No. 28 (*fig. 15*); D *h* in binding No. 98 (*fig. 17*). Marçais holds that the "chenille" stamps had their origin in the Coptic use of narrow strips of parchment which were threaded through rows of closely repeated slits made in the band ornaments of the leather covering, to enliven and emphasize these bands within the scheme of decoration (*figs. 27, 28, 33*).

monasteries along the edge of the deserts of Upper Egypt and the Fayum, where the copying and binding of books was done for the most part within convent walls and where the ornamenting of book covers would consist not so much in the inventing and perfecting of new designs as in the copying of tested older patterns of an established Hellenistic tradition.

The format of early Coptic codices, as well as of early Greek, Latin, and Syriac books, was uniformly vertical—oblong, with only a few exceptions which approach the square form, the Berlin manuscript Or. oct. 987 of the *Proverbs of Solomon,* Achmimic (13 x 14.5 cm.) being one of these.

The basic operations executed by Coptic monastic bookbinders at the time of the Islamic invasion were the same as those that had been used in Egypt certainly since the fourth century. Where multiple-quire codices were to be bound, the written sheets, arranged in gatherings usually of four sheets, were sewn with from two to five stitches, their number depending upon the size of the book. If the book was very small one stitch might suffice. The sewing proceeded lengthwise along the fold of the gathering, and at every thread hole, where the sewing cord was drawn out toward the back of the gathering, it would be linked or chain-stitched tightly to the sewing of the preceding gathering before it was drawn back again to form another stitch inside the fold of either the same or the next gathering (*figs. 3* and *4*), When all the gatherings had been tightly sewn into book form, the chain-stitch linkings would appear as so many braids fastened across the back of the book. When the sewing also was to include the attaching of the covers, the thread would first be laced to the upper cover in the form of a number of hinging loops, to which the book sewing would then be linked. The places of the holes through which the hinging loops were laced were near the back edge of the cover opposite each of the several thread holes made by the sewing of the first gathering. When the sewing of all the gatherings of a book was completed, the thread would then be laced through the series of holes along the hinging edge of the lower cover, but on having been looped through each one of these holes the thread would be tightly linked by a separate stitch to the respective chain-stitch sewing of the adjoining last gathering, thereby hinging the cover to the book.

The use of wooden boards for book covers

by Coptic bookbinders can be documented from the fourth century down to the Middle Ages,[11] although the greater number of the extant early Coptic bindings are seen to be constructed with boards that were built up of waste papyrus material.

After the book was sewn to its covers, a piece of heavy linen was glued over the back of the book, and this linen was made wide enough for the flanges on either side to be glued a width of an inch or more over the hinging edges of the two covers. After this was done, the sewing of the headbands was undertaken. The sewing thread, once it was firmly laced onto the corner of the hinging edge of the upper cover, was made to pass, by short single stitches, from the head of the sewn book into the inner fold of each successive gathering; and when, after each of these stitches, it was returned through the linen-covered back to the head of the book, it was linked or chain-stitched around the chain-stitch mesh protruding from the head of the preceding gathering in such a way that the whole series of chain-stitches, beginning at the hinging edge of the upper cover and terminating at the hinging edge of the lower cover, would form a braid similar to the chain-stitch band formed by the sewing of the gatherings into book form (*fig. 22*). This form of headband lacing, with some inevitable slight modifications in the loopings of the braid and with the occasional use of colored threads, served in early times as the normal headband sewing, though as time went on more elaborate techniques of braiding, with several guide threads serving as warp and two or three sewing threads of different colors serving as weft, were used for more pretentious bindings.[12]

The use of leather for covering the boards of codices can be documented by Coptic bookbindings as far back as the fourth century.[13]

The cutting of the leather coverings to proper size, allowing for the turn-ins on inner margins, and for the caps at head and tail of the back of the books has remained to the present day what it was in Egypt during the early centuries of the Christian era. The

[11] The following early wooden book covers from Egypt can be cited: Those of a fourth-century Manichaean papyrus codex of the *Kephalaia* in Coptic, now in Berlin; those of the fifth-century parchment codex of the *Gospels,* in Greek, with covers bearing the painted figures of the Four Evangelists, now in the Freer Gallery in Washington; the sixth-century parchment codex of the books of *Ecclesiasticus* and *Wisdom of Solomon,* in Coptic, now in Turin; the two sixth-century parchment codices containing (1) the *Epistles of St. Paul,* (2) the *Acts of the Apostles* and *Gospel of St. John,* in Coptic, now in the Chester Beatty Library in Dublin (*fig. 8*); a sixth- or seventh-century codex of *Theological questions and answers,* in Coptic, now in the Phillipps Library in Cheltenham; also four detached covers, perhaps third- or fourth-century, which came to the Chester Beatty Library together with the twelve early *Biblical* papyrus codices, in Greek, discovered in 1930; the large covers with beautifully tooled and stamped leather, which contain a seventh-century Syriac *Biblical* manuscript now in Milan (Ambros. C 313 inf., *fig. 21*), but which at an earlier time, according to the tooled inscription on the two covers, contained the first tome of a manuscript of the *Old and New Testaments,* in Greek. This binding came from the Syrian Monastery in the Wādī al-Naṭrūn, Egypt. The Keep of the chapel of al-'Adhrā, in the St. Macarius monastery in the Wādī al-Naṭrūn also preserves a large detached old book cover of acacia wood, lined with untooled black leather, of undetermined age.

[12] P. Adam, *Über türkisch-arabisch-persische Manuskripte und deren Einbände,* Archiv für Buchbinderei, vol. 4 (Jan. 1905), p. 149.

[13] Some of the oldest extant Coptic leather-covered bindings are: The one covering the fourth-century papyrus codex containing *Deuteronomy, Jonah,* and the *Acts of the Apostles* (Brit. Mus. Or. 7594) in plain kidskin, varnished; that which covered the fourth-century papyrus book containing *The first letter of Clement* (Berlin Or. fol. 3065), with tooled decorations; and that which covered the fourth- or fifth-century papyrus book containing *The Martyrdoms of St. Peter and St. Paul* (now in the Moscow Museum of Fine Arts).

FIG. 21—LOWER COVER OF THE BINDING OF MS. SYR. C 313 FOL. (CA. 340 x 270 MM.), SIXTH-SEVENTH (?) CENTURY. MILAN, AMBROSIAN LIBRARY

gluing-down of the leather covering over the back of the book and over the outer faces and inner margins of the boards has likewise remained the same. The turn-ins on the inner margins were not mitered but cut off at right angles at the corners of the board and then glued one over the other, the turn-in along the fore edge being placed uppermost.

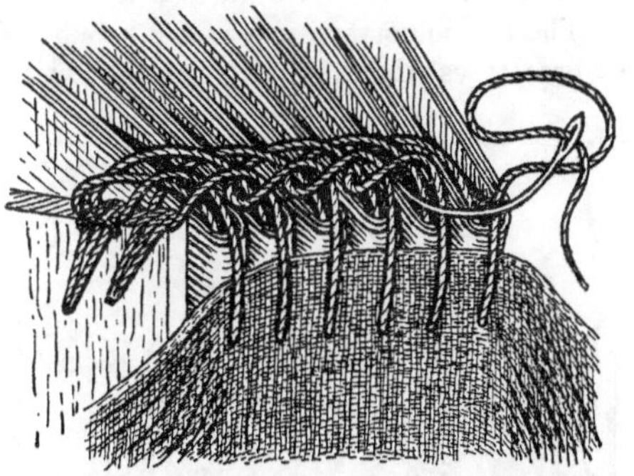

FIG. 22—DRAWING OF THE USUAL PLAIN COPTIC HEADBAND SEWING

When the threads were pulled tight they would appear as shown in the headband of the Ibscher binding (*fig. 6*).

In many old Coptic codices extra flyleaves are seen to have been "guarded" around the front of the first and the rear of the last gathering. These were generally unwritten leaves or leaves from which old writing had been washed off, and they were intended to be pasted down on the inner faces of the book covers after the book clasps had finally been rooted in the edges of the covers and the binding had thus been completed.

The earliest method of decorating the leather coverings of books was probably that of blind-tooling and blind-stamping, although the decorating with inked and painted ornament [14] and with cut-out openwork backed with pieces of painted or gilded parchment may also have been tried very early, since these techniques of ornamenting were known in Egypt long before books were bound in codex form.[15]

FIG. 23—BINDING OF MS. BEATTY COPTIC C CONTAINING *Psalms 1–50* (105 x 85 MM.) CA. A.D. 600 OR EARLIER

The design is inked on red leather.

Whenever the decorating was to consist of openwork with parchment backing it had to be done before the leather covering, already

[14] Inked ornamenting is found on the red leather bindings of the sixth-century *Psalter* codex, Chester Beatty Coptic C (*fig. 23*) and the eighth-century Greek *Poll-tax Book,* Brit. Mus. Papyrus Inv. 1442 (*fig. 24*). Painted ornamenting is found on the tenth-century binding of MS. Morgan 601 (*fig. 25*), and painted and inked ornamenting on the eighth(?)-century detached binding Berlin P. 1416 (*fig. 26*). The painting of the covers of the Freer *Gospels* was done not on leather coverings but on the wooden boards.

[15] Cf. H. Frauberger, *Antike und frühmittelalterliche Fussbekleidungen aus Achmim-Panopolis,* Düsseldorf, n.d., pls. 7–9, 18, 20–21. The three finest extant specimens of this "openwork" type of Coptic book ornamentation are seen in the binding of the *Gospels,* Morgan MS. (*fig. 27*), and the two detached bindings: Vienna Erzherzog Rainer Inv. No. 34 (*fig. 28*) and Berlin Mus. Papyrus 14018. Two leather coverings, each with a large cut-out in the form of a potented cross backed with parchment, on which a twisted rope pattern in red and yellow colors is painted, are extant in Morgan Coptic binding 670 *bis* (*fig. 29*).

cut to size, was glued to the boards. When the decorating was to be done by tooling and stamping, it likewise had to be done before the leather was glued to the boards, whenever these latter were not wooden boards but

FIG. 24—BINDING, BRIT. MUS. INV. NO. 1442, OF A PAPYRUS *Poll-Tax Book*, GREEK, FROM APHRODITO, EGYPT (340 x 295 MM.), FIRST HALF OF EIGHTH CENTURY

The design is inked on reddish leather. There is also a fore-edge flap 7 cm. wide.

boards built up of fragile papyrus material that could not withstand the pressure of tooling and hammering. The tooling was done with unheated irons and on moistened leather, according to the expert judgment of P. Adam and H. Ibscher, who closely examined and described the Coptic bindings in the Berlin Museum. Since the Kairouan bookbinders were using wooden boards, they did their tooling and stamping only after the coverings had been glued in place. The imprint of their stamping can still be seen in places where the leather has been torn from the boards.

The last important step in the bookbinding process was that of providing clasps which

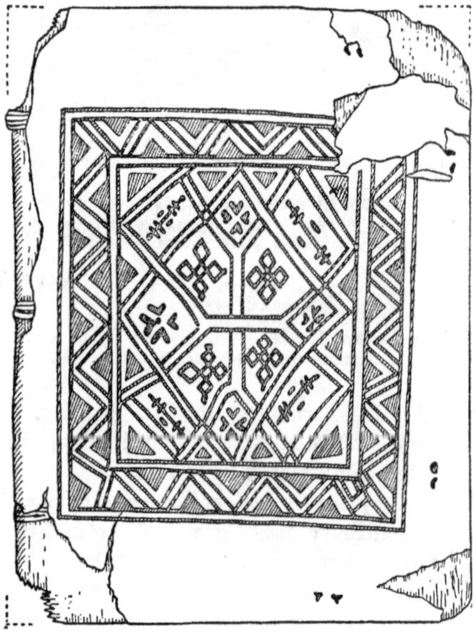

FIG. 25—BINDING OF MS. MORGAN 601, *Catholic Epistles*, COPTIC (330 x 260 MM.), NINTH TO TENTH CENTURY

The design is crudely painted with yellow on brown leather.

would hold the book firmly together when it was closed. Some of the earlier Coptic books were provided with leather thongs long enough to be tied around the books.[16]

[16] Eleven Gnostic third- and fourth-century papyrus books, found in 1946 at the site of ancient Chenoboskion in Upper Egypt (now in the Coptic Museum in Cairo), are bound in flexible leather covers and

FIG. 26—RECONSTRUCTION BY HUGO IBSCHER OF A FRAGMENTARY COPTIC BINDING, BERLIN MUS. P. 14016 (CA. 310 x 225 MM.), EIGHTH TO TENTH CENTURY

The design is painted or inked in black on reddish-brown leather.

FIG. 27—BINDING OF MS. MORGAN 569, ***The Four Gospels,*** COPTIC (385 x 295 MM.), EIGHTH CENTURY

The decoration is of openwork in red leather, over a gilt parchment base. The framework of the design is made by threading narrow ribbons of parchment through rows of closely cut slits, thus producing lanes of alternating patches of red leather and white parchment.

FIG. 28—DETACHED BINDING, VIENNA INV. NO. 34 (370 x 270 MM.), FROM ARSINOE IN THE FAYUM, SEVENTH (?) CENTURY. THE DECORATION IS THE SAME IN ITS TECHNIQUE AS MS. MORGAN 569

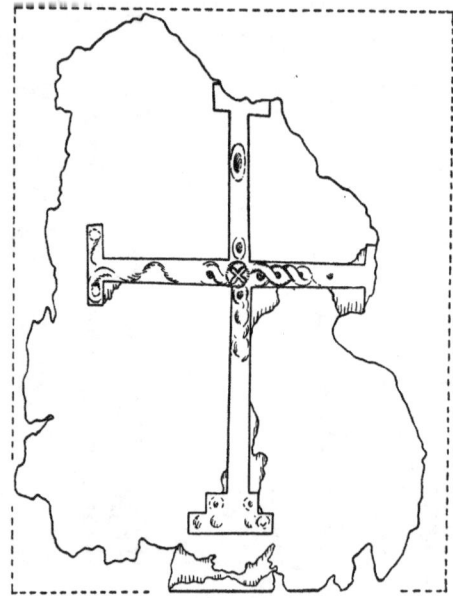

FIG. 29—DETACHED BINDING WITH A POTENTED CROSS CUT OUT OF REDDISH-BROWN LEATHER AND UNDERLAID WITH PAINTED PARCHMENT. MORGAN 670 BIS [4] (320 x 225 MM.), NINTH CENTURY

FIG. 30—BINDING OF MS. BRIT. MUS. OR. 5000, *Psalter* COPTIC (298 x 215 MM.), SIXTH-SEVENTH CENTURY

But most extant Coptic bindings are seen to have been furnished with clasps which, reaching only across the fore edge of the book, hook the front cover to the rear cover. The standard form of this type of clasp consisted of a loop of braided thong which was rooted near the edge of the upper cover and was long enough to reach the lower cover and to be slipped over the head of a metal or bone peg

have long, narrow leather straps fastened to the pentagonal flaps which extend from the fore edge of their lower covers. Some of these books had similar long straps fastened also near the top edge of the lower covers. The straps were provided for the purpose of having them tied vertically and horizontally around the books when the latter were not in use. Similar thongs are to be seen on the elaborately decorated binding of a large sixth- or seventh-century papyrus book of the *Psalter* in Coptic (Brit. Mus. Or. 5000) (*fig. 30*). This binding also has a flap extending from the lower cover. The straps fastened along the fore edge of the lower cover are three in number, while two straps are placed along both the head and tail edges of the same cover. Metal rings, into which these straps could be tied, are provided in the respective places near the edges of the upper cover.

A wider type of wrapping bands was provided for the sixth-century Chester Beatty Coptic Codices A and B (*fig. 8*) and also for the painted covers of the fifth- or sixth-century Freer *Gospels*. These bands had their attached ends slit for a short distance into a series of parallel thongs which then had been spread apart to be rooted and glued into a series of holes made in the fore edge and top edge of the upper cover. The extant portions of the bands which belong to the Beatty Coptic codices show that each of the bands was long enough to be wrapped twice around the binding and that the bone slips attached to the free ends of the bands served to pull the bands tight and to fasten them.

that was rooted and riveted in the edge of the lower cover.[17]

Another form of Coptic clasp consisted of plain, single leather thongs fastened in the upper cover and terminating at their free ends in knotted knobs which, reaching over the edge of the lower cover, could be buttoned into short clasp loops or "eyes" made of leather and fastened in the lower cover about an inch away from its edge.[18]

It is more than likely that at the time when Islam came to power the above-mentioned basic operations of the bookbinding technique of Coptic Egypt were being used throughout the Greco-Roman world and the provinces of the Near East. It would seem almost

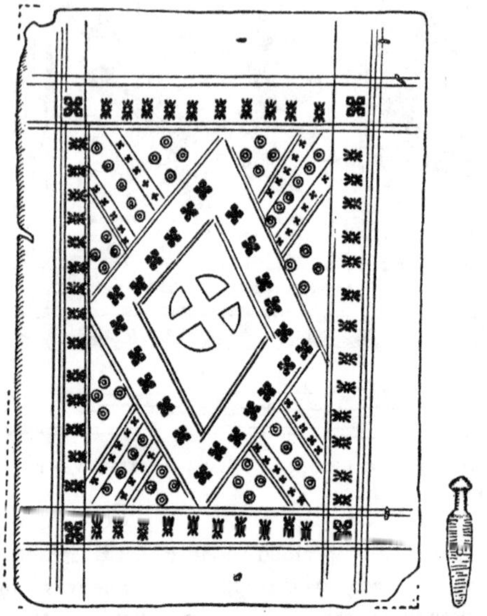

FIG. 31—BINDING OF MS. BRIT. MUS. OR. 6801, *Lectionary* FOR THE FEAST OF ST. MERCURIUS, COPTIC (279 x 215 MM.), ABOUT A.D. 1000

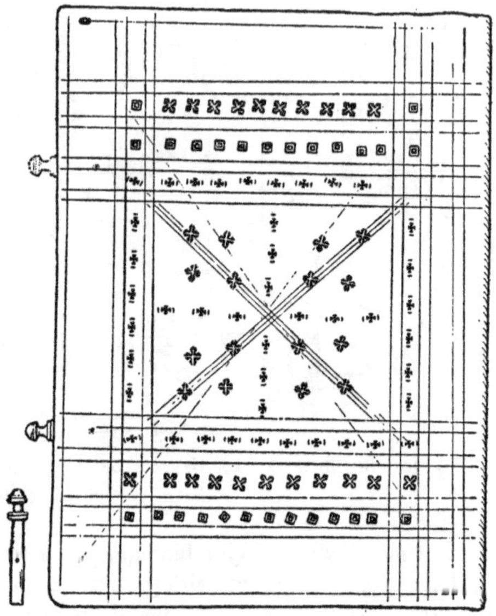

FIG. 32—BINDING OF MS. BRIT. MUS. OR. 7597, *Lectionary*, COPTIC (292 x 222 MM.), SECOND HALF OF TENTH CENTURY

[17] In the binding of the large *Gospel* codex, MS. Morgan 569 (*fig. 27*), seven clasps with seven bronze pegs were provided. The binding of the book of *The martyrdom of St. Mercurius,* Brit. Mus. Or. 6801, was fitted with four clasps and four iron pegs (*fig. 31*). The binding of a book of *Discourses,* Brit. Mus. Or. 7597 (*fig. 32*) was fitted with two clasps and two bone pegs, and at least nine of the ninth-century Coptic codices of the Pierpont Morgan Library were fitted with four or five clasps and four or five bone pegs.

[18] Four clasps of this form were used in the fifth(?)-century Leyden codex, Anastasy 9 (*fig. 33*). From four to seven of these clasps were used in fifteen or more of the ninth-century Coptic bindings in the Pierpont Morgan Library, also in several of the ninth- and tenth-century Coptic bindings preserved in the British Museum, London, and the Coptic Museum, Cairo. The small thirteenth-century Bohairic *Prayer book,* Morgan 671(1) had only one such clasp (*fig. 34*). This form of clasp has been used in Coptic bindings down to the past century (*fig. 35*).

inevitable, therefore, that the Islamic conquerors, insofar as they were not already acquainted with classical and Hellenistic methods of bookbinding, should speedily have learned of them and adopted them for their own use. There would likewise be little doubt that the Islamic invaders, on having become

FIG. 33—BINDING OF MS. LEYDEN, ANASTASY 9, *Prayers and Exorcism,* COPTIC (217 x 140 MM.), FIFTH CENTURY

experienced masters in their own right, would remember their native patrimony of artistic resources and begin to modify and change to their own taste and fancy much of what they took and used out of the abundance of their newly gained Hellenistic, Coptic, and Sasanian heritage.

They retained their fine, flowing Arabic script and their way of writing from right to left throughout the book and across each page. But when they had begun to use their writing as a feature of architectural decoration and had fashioned it into the monumental forms of the Kufic script, they began to use this latter script also in the copying of their Korans and thereupon to change the traditional format of their books to a more suitable horizontal oblong. For this change they had no Western

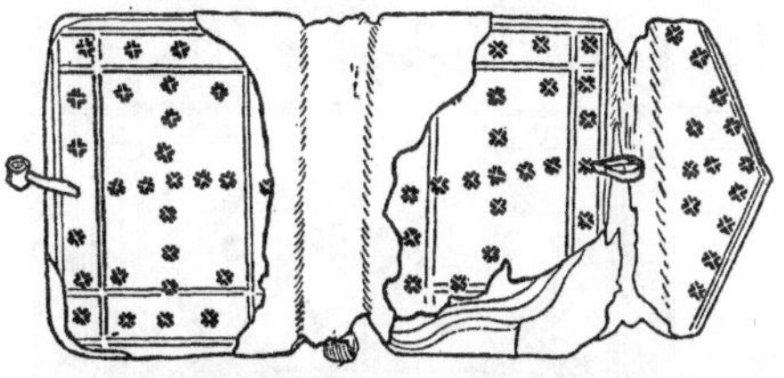

FIG. 34—BINDING OF MS. MORGAN 671 (1), COPTIC *Prayer Book* (105 x 80 MM.), THIRTEENTH (?) CENTURY

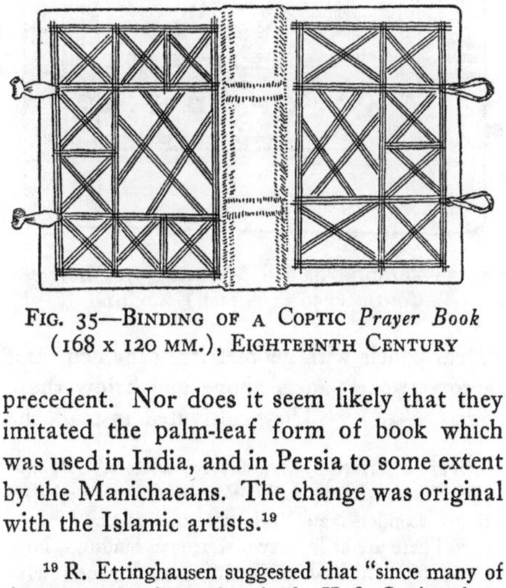

FIG. 35—BINDING OF A COPTIC *Prayer Book* (168 x 120 MM.), EIGHTEENTH CENTURY

precedent. Nor does it seem likely that they imitated the palm-leaf form of book which was used in India, and in Persia to some extent by the Manichaeans. The change was original with the Islamic artists.[19]

[19] R. Ettinghausen suggested that "since many of the manuscript decorations in the Kufic Qur'ans have a definite architectural character, such as arcades and patterns which seem to copy mosaic pavements, it is perhaps justifiable to assume that these Qur'ans [of the horizontal oblong format] may have imitated the horizontal Qur'anic inscription panels in the mosques

In designing their tooled ornamentations the Islamic bookbinders proved themselves likewise to be masters and not mere copyists. They turned away from the Coptic and Greco-Roman tradition of preferably drawing square central panels with geometrical ornament and narrow frieze panels above and below these (*figs. 36–38*).[20] They cultivated instead the plan of single oblong panels filled with twisted, platted, and intertwined, all-over band ornament, and they freely used twisted-rope patterns also on the borders (*figs. 10–14*). In this also they were most likely innovators, for there are no early Coptic book covers in existence that show similarly tooled ornament

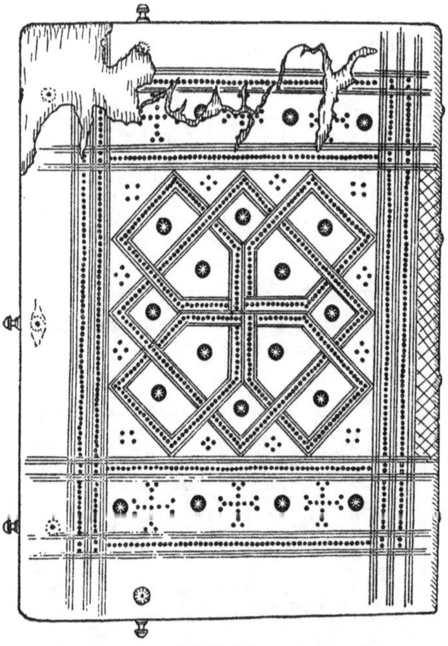

FIG. 36—BINDING OF MS. MORGAN 597, *Discourses*, COPTIC (350 x 268 MM.), A.D. 914

FIG. 37—BINDING HAMOULI IA IN COPTIC MUSEUM, CAIRO (BELONGING TO MS. MORGAN 568, *Isaias*, COPTIC) 355 x 276 MM., NOT LATER THAN A.D. 850

which are described by several Arab writers." (*Manuscript illumination* in A. U. Pope's, *A survey of Persian art*, London-New York, vol. 3, p. 1942.)

[20] There are at least two Kairouan bindings, Nos. 64 and 65, which show square central panels with the rosette or star decorations found so commonly in Coptic bindings; and there are at least three other bindings, Nos. 14, 15, and 28, in each of which an oblong central panel is flanked at either short end, inside the decorative border, not by the customary Coptic frieze panels but by narrow bands ornamented with stampings. M. Marçais, *op. cit.*, p. 82, n. 2, states it as his belief that these bands are due to a faulty composition of the panel decoration. A look, however, at binding No. 14 (*fig. 11*) should make it clear that by omitting the two narrow flanking bands the bookbinder would have been able to complete his intertwined panel design so as to make it symmetrical. May it not be that the binder in introducing the narrow flanking bands sought to retain something of the esthetic effect which he felt to have its source in the traditional Coptic panel arrangement?

from which the Kairouan patterns could have been copied. If it should be true that the bookbinders of Lower Egypt used such patterns at the time of the Islamic conquest, it is regret-

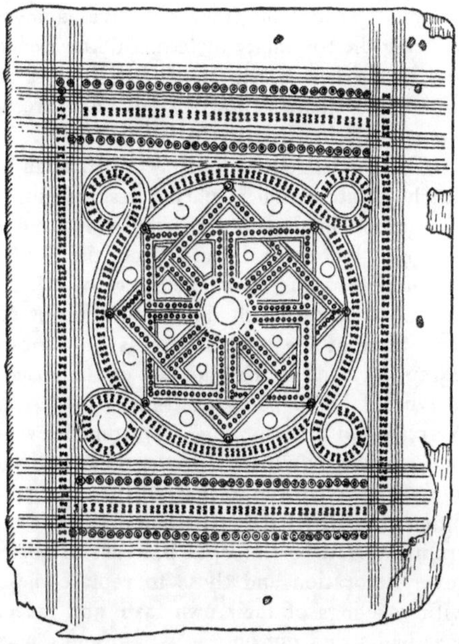

FIG. 38—BINDING OF MS. MORGAN 590, *Lectionary* FOR THE FEAST OF ST. MENAS, COPTIC (352 x 269 MM.), A.D. 893

table that none of their bindings (and for that matter none of the manuscripts written in the Bohairic dialect of Lower Egypt, older than the ninth century) have been preserved for us.[21]

It is true that some of the ornamental title frames and decorative headpieces and tail-

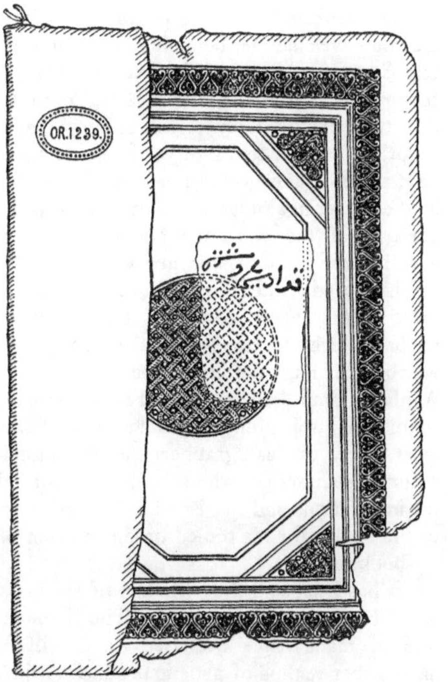

FIG. 39—BINDING OF MS. BRIT. MUS. OR. 1239, *Anaphoras,* COPTIC (BOHAIRIC), (222 x 140 MM.), THIRTEENTH CENTURY

The central circular ornament, very indistinct in the photograph, is given here as a simple platting, while the original has a more complicated interlacing.

pieces found in Coptic manuscripts resemble the platted-band ornament fancied by the

[21] Here it should be noted that possible future discoveries, like those made at Kairouan, may throw further light upon the early bookbinders' art in Lower (Northern) Egypt. The vaulted hall of the tower of the Syrian Monastery in the Wādī al-Naṭrūn was reported to contain many early elaborately tooled torn-off book covers; but while all the loose manuscript leaves found with them were salvaged and their texts published, the bookbindings were left to their fate and no description of them was given other than to suggest that they resembled the bindings figured in Budge's *Miscellaneous Coptic texts,* London, 1915, and that they could once have belonged to the early Syriac manuscripts which during the eighteenth and nineteenth centuries were taken to the Vatican and the British Museum. Cf. Hugh G. Evelyn White, *The monasteries of the Wadi n'Natrun,* Part I, New York, 1926, p. XLVII, note 4.

bookbinders of Kairouan. It is true also that extant Bohairic book covers of the later Middle Ages (*fig. 39*) resemble those made by Islamic bookbinders of their time, and it is true that even in older bookbindings from Central Egypt (as in that of the sixth- to seventh-century manuscript, Chester Beatty Coptic C, and that of the early eighth-century manuscript, Brit. Mus. Inv. No. 1442 (*figs. 23* and *24*), platted-band decorations inked upon the leather coverings suggest a relationship to the patterns of the Kairouan bookbinders. An equally close relationship, however, can easily be discovered also in the interlaced-band ornament of the carved panels of the teakwood minbar which was made for the Mosque of Kairouan at Baghdad in 863, on orders of the Aghlabid Emir Abū Ibrāhīm. From whatever source the inspirations may have come, it was most likely the calligrapher and the illuminator of manuscripts who seized and recorded the inspirations and furnished a draft of them to the binder for his tooled ornamentation of the book covers.

It has been said that "the art of the book is the basis of all oriental art. The illuminators of manuscripts exercised their skill in many other realms of artistic production, just as in Italy during the Renaissance and it was they, the illuminators, who furnished the plans for most of the creations of oriental art." [22]

[22] F. R. Martin, *Miniaturen und Buchkunst,* Die Ausstellung von Meisterwerken Muhammedanischer Kunst in München 1910, ed. by F. Sarre and F. R. Martin, München, 1912, vol. 1, p. III.

Not all the Kairouan bindings demanded the intervention of artists. None of them compare in excellence of workmanship and general sumptuousness with the magnificent books produced in the Islamic East during the Mamluk period, but they are invaluable in showing the continuity of technical knowledge and proficiency in the bookbinders' craft as they were handed down from the Greco-Roman-Coptic world to the Islamic world.

Early Islamic bookbinding in Kairouan in nearly all its technical particulars resembled Coptic bookbinding of the eighth and ninth centuries. Where it deviated from the Coptic technical tradition, as in the choice of a horizontal format (which deviation was not so much that of the bookbinders as of the calligraphers) and in the adoption of the boxed-in type of bookbinding described by Messrs. Marçais and Poinssot (*fig. 5, c*), it made eventual amends by abandoning these innovations again in favor of the formats of the older tradition. But where the Islamic binders deviated from the traditional Coptic patterns of book-cover decoration and chose to replace these with weavings of their own taste and fancy, they had struck out on a new path and a new adventure which, though at first it led them only a few steps away from the Coptic heritage, was eventually to lead them to heights of inventiveness, elegance, and sumptuousness which has never been excelled before or after by anything in "bookbinding art" the world has ever seen.

[6]

THE HUMAN ELEMENT BETWEEN TEXT AND READER

THE *IJĀZA* IN ARABIC MANUSCRIPTS

JAN JUST WITKAM

The *ijāza* is the certificate of reading or hearing which is sometimes written on manuscripts, usually near the colophon or on the title page. It confers upon the recipient the right to transmit a text, or to teach, or to issue legal opinions. It also bears witness to attendance at a reading session. The *ijāzat al-tadrīs*, the licence to teach, and the *ijāzat al-samā'*, the certificate of attendance at a reading session and hence the licence to transmit the text read, should not be confused. Our attention here will be focused on the *ijāzat al-samā'*, the protocols of reading sessions which were often added to a text, as these in particular provide us with ample information on the human element in the transmission of texts.

The *ijāza* is a conspicuous feature of Arabic manuscripts and it illustrates how a text functions in an educational, scientific or cultural environment. Studying *ijāza*s increases our knowledge of the human element in the use of texts and manuscripts. For a better understanding of the *ijāza* it is also important also to be aware of the individual and personal element in the transmission of Muslim scholarship: we, therefore, deal with this subject briefly in the following section. Finally, we suggest a proposal for collecting and analysing *ijāzāt al-samā'* in Arabic manuscripts.[1]

---

[1] There is no monograph devoted to the *ijāza*, nor is there a published corpus of texts. Some useful sources which provide a wealth of material on the subject are: 'Abd Allāh Fayyāḍ, *al-Ijāzāt al-'ilmiyya 'inda al-muslimīn* (Baghdad, 1967) (with emphasis on the Shi'a); P.A. MacKay, *Certificates of Transmission on a Manuscript of the* Maqāmāt *of Ḥarīrī, MS.* Cairo, Adab 105, Transactions of the American Philosophical Society, New Series, LXI/4

Personal approach and continuity in Islamic scholarship

It has often been stated that in Islam there is no hierarchic structure comparable with the church-like organisation of the Christians. Strictly speaking, this is true. Islam does not have an infallible pope nor does it have a clergy with an intricately differentiated hierarchic structure who claim to occupy a position between God and the believer and dispense sacraments and pretend to possess the monopoly of doctrine. This does not, of course, mean that clerical organisation is totally lacking in Islam. It is only that the dynamics of continuity — since organisation produces continuity — in Islam have developed in a different way. In Islam no intermediary between God and man is necessary. And just as a Muslim's relationship with God is direct and personal, so too is a man's way of procuring religious knowledge. In Islam it is the personal relationship between teacher and pupil that, through the generations of scholars, has produced a powerful driving force that ensures a continuity of its own.

Several genres of Islamic literature have developed in the course of time, which reflect this individual and personal attitude. It started very early indeed, with the emergence of Islamic tradition, *ḥadīth*. As important as the content of the Tradition is the chain of authorities, the *isnād*, which precedes each tradition. The early collections are even organised not according to subject matter but to their authorities, and hence referred to by the name *Musnad*. Half of Islamic Tradition is *ʿilm al-rijāl*, the "knowledge of the transmitters". Only an authentic chain of trustworthy authorities validates the text of a *ḥadīth*. Without it a *ḥadīth* is suspended in space and is incomplete — at least that is the

(Philadelphia, 1971); Ṣalāḥ al-Dīn al-Munajjid, "Ijāzāt al-samāʿ fī al-makhṭūṭāṭ al-qadīma", *Majallat Maʿhad al-Makhṭūṭāt al-ʿArabiyya (MMMA)*, I (1375/1955), 232-51; J. Pedersen, *The Arabic Book* (Princeton, 1984), esp. 31-4; Qāsim Aḥmad al-Sāmarrāʾī, "Al-ijāza wa-taṭawwuruhā al-tārīkhī", *ʿĀlam al-Kutub*, II (1981), 278-85. Many illustrations of *ijāzāt* are found in A. J. Arberry, *A Handlist of the Arabic Manuscripts of the Chester Beatty Library* (8 vols., Dublin, 1955-66). The use of the *ijāza* in the Islamic educational system has been treated by George Makdisi, *The Rise of Colleges. Institutions of Learning in Islam and the West* (Edinburgh, 1981), while Georges Vajda, *Les certificats de lecture et de transmission dans les manuscrits arabes de la Bibliothèque Nationale de Paris* (Paris, 1956), gives an analysis of the contents of a great number of *ijāzāt* in 72 manuscripts. I also wish to thank Léon Buskens for putting at my disposal a number of published *ijāzāt* or *ijāza*-related texts from his private library.

opinion of the early Muslim scholars. For practical reasons these Tradition texts and chains of authorities were written down, but, according to the old ideals, religious knowledge was best disseminated orally. The *isnad*s can thus be read as protocols of successive instances and sessions in which learning was transmitted. The written form of *ḥadīth* is thus but one dimension of the Tradition: the human factor in the transmission and continuity of knowledge is as important as the recorded message itself . The saying that "knowledge is in the breasts [of men], not in the lines [of books]" (*al-ʿilm fī al-ṣudūr lā fī al-suṭūr*) aptly summarises this idea.[2]

The rapid expansion of Islam and the enormous diversification of the different disciplines of learning made it impossible to maintain oral transmission as the only vehicle for passing on knowledge. The Word of God, the divine revelation, had to be written down, since the early carriers of the Holy Word died on the battlefields of the expansion wars. At a later stage, historical and Tradition texts were written down as well, initially in all sorts of personal notebooks[3] of transmitters, later in more organised collections that were intended for a wider audience. Though, in the end, books became accepted as the ordinary medium, the individual and personal approach nevertheless remained intact. Just reading a book in order to grasp its contents, as we do nowadays, was not enough. In the classical period, it was thought, a book should be read with a teacher, preferably the author himself, or else it should be studied with an authoritative and respected professor. Reading, or rather studying, was not a solitary affair. It was also a social event, as we shall see.

Biographical literature emerged in Islam as one of the consequences of this individual and personal approach. The genre was not new around the Mediterranean. In classical antiquity biographical literature such as the "Parallel Lives" of Plutarch served historical, didactic, moralistic and sometimes ideological purposes. Some of the Islamic biographical literature had a similar purpose but there was an extra dimension. The "science of men", or *ʿilm al-rijāl*, developed into a critical method

---

[2] See Ibn al-Akfānī, *Irshād al-qāṣid ilā asnā al-maqāṣid*, ed. J. J. Witkam (Leiden, 1989), 446, no. 191.

[3] For their use, and the distrust they evoked, see al-Balkhī (d. *ca.* 319/913), *Kitāb Qabūl al-akhbār wa-maʿrifat al-rijāl,* MS Cairo, Dār al-Kutub al-Miṣriyya, *Muṣṭalaḥ* 14M, *passim.* An edition of this text by myself is in an advanced stage of preparation.

for the assessment of scholarly authority. Many biographical works were concerned with describing networks of scholarship and chains of transmission. A clear example of this is the *Tahdhīb al-tahdhīb* by Ibn Ḥajar al-ʿAsqalānī (d. 852/1449), which is a biographical dictionary of trustworthy transmitters of Islamic Tradition.[4] The usual structure of a biography in this work breaks down into three parts: firstly the full name and some other pertinent life data of the subject are given, then follow enumerations of earlier authorities from whom he transmits Tradition, and then of those later authorities who in turn transmit from him. The biographee is thereby presented in the centre of an activity of transmission of knowledge. This particular work by Ibn Ḥajar is exclusively concerned with traditionists and this particular approach can, therefore, be observed here very clearly. Other biographical works, even those that are not so exclusively concerned with traditionists, often contain similar bits of network information.

Literary genres of an individual and personal nature

Other individual and personal genres evolved. The *fahrasa*,[5] which developed in al-Andalus and the Maghreb, is one of these. This genre, in which a scholar enumerates his shaykhs and the works he read with them, can be read as a scholarly curriculum vitae. The *thabat,* which is not confined to the Maghreb, is a list compiled by a relater of traditions in which he mentions his shaykhs and the scope of his transmissions on their authority. Likewise, in the *riḥla,* or travel account, attention shifted from geography and ethnography in the classical period to the personal relationships of scholars. Especially in later times it became much more than just a travel account. In it, the itinerant author has ample opportunity to enumerate the scholars he has met, the lessons he has taken and the authorisations he has received during his travels. And the purpose of his travels was, of course, not touristic but of a much more edifying nature, namely the pilgrimage to Makka.[6] Yet another type of personalised text is

---

4 Published in 12 volumes in Hyderabad, 1325-7 [1907-9].

5 See Ch. Pellat, s.v. "Fahrasa", *Encyclopaedia of Islam*, 2nd ed (*EI²*), (Leiden and London, 1960-), II, 743-4.

6 This genre of travel accounts became specially developed in the Western part of the Islamic world. The great distance from the Arabian Peninsula must have contributed to this development.

the *silsila*, the spiritual or scholarly genealogy.[7] The *barnāmaj*[8] and the *mashyakha* have a function very similar to that of the *fahrasa*, and sometimes contain accounts of travels in search of knowledge, the *ṭalab al-ʿilm*, just as in the *riḥla*. One of the most conspicuous types of compilation of biographical data are the works describing the *ṭabaqāt* ("the layers") of scholars, which list the successive generations of persons active in a certain field. This treatment "by generation" kept intact both the synchronic and diachronic connections in the history of a field of scholarship.

Especially in later times, such enumerations were compiled as a sort of scholarly autobiography. Sometimes the main attention is directed to the texts which were read with teachers, as in the *barnāmaj*, and sometimes the shaykhs themselves are the main object of attention, as in the *mashyakha*. Often these texts were compiled by the subjects themselves and were written in the first person, although the third person is used in the autobiography as well. When others took care of the compilation of such a list of subjects taught or authorities met by their shaykh, such a survey could simply be called *al-Taʿrīf bi-*..., followed by the name of the shaykh in question. The same applies to works which are entitled *Tarjamat* ..., followed by the name of the biographee. Titles such as *al-Sanad al-muttaṣil ilā* ..., followed by the name of an early authority, occur as well. Compilations with the word *asānīd* in the title serve a similar purpose in describing the chains of authorities by which a certain scholar is connected to the great imams of an earlier period. At a much later stage, probably only as late as the 12th/18th century, separate booklets with titles including the word *ijāza* began to appear. At first sight these seem to belong to the category of educational *ijāzāt* rather than that of readers' certificates but there are also connections between the two types of texts since the later diplomas frequently contain a *silsila* of learned predecessors, often putting the Prophet Muḥammad at the beginning of the *silsila* and the student to whom the booklet was issued at its end. Elaborately adorned, impressively calligraphed and elegantly worded, these diplomas can be considered to constitute the final stage of the *ijāza* and its

---

7 Many *silsila*s are known. The Sufis have their own sets of *silsila*s. I have published and analysed the *silsila* of the Bosnian Ḥanafī scholar Ḥasan Kāfī al-Aqḥiṣārī (d. 1025/1616) in *Manuscripts of the Middle East (MME)*, IV (1989), 85-114.

8 For this type of book, see ʿAbd al-ʿAzīz al-Ahwānī, "Kutub barāmij al-ʿulamāʾ fī al-Andalus", *MMMA*, I (1955), 91-120, 252-71.

finest artistic expression. Because of them, the *ijāza* has become an independent literary genre.[9]

Yet another special literary genre that developed from this practice is the *juz'*, a short text usually consisting of not much more than one quire, and often small enough for it to be easily carried. It could happen that only a very small part of a scholar's work was read and taught in a session in which an *ijāza* was going to be granted. In that case the issuer of the *ijāza* had the choice between two options. He could confer upon his pupil, or a visiting scholar, the right to transmit the whole of a book by him, or his transmissions (*marwiyyāt*), or his own orally received knowledge (*masmū'āt*), or the works for which he himself had already acquired certificates (*mustajāzāt*), or of any other of his works even if they had only been partially read or not read at all. Such *ijāzāt 'āmma* abound.

The other option was that the short text or the specific collection of transmissions which had been read could be written out separately. Such shorter collections of part of the repertoire of a shaykh often bear the title *juz'*.[10] Sometimes these *ajzā'* are provided with a more detailed specification and a more meaningful title.[11]

---

9 Such booklets are available in numerous libraries. The MS Montreal, McGill University Library, No. AC 156 is such a separate diploma. Its content was analysed and published by Adam Gacek, "The Diploma of the Egyptian Calligrapher Ḥasan al-Rushdī", *MME*, IV (1989), 44–55. Another one is MS Leiden, University Library, Or. 11.121. This thin volume, which probably originates from Istanbul, contains an *ijāza* in the readings of the Qur'ān conferred upon Abū Bakr Luṭfī Afandī b. al-Sayyid 'Umar al-Sanūbī by his teacher Ismā'īl Ḥaqqī b. 'Alī in *Muḥarram* 1260/1844.

10 It is not impossible that the *juz'* as an independent genre developed from the old practice of writing *ijāzāt, samā'āt* and the like on each *juz'*, here more or less meaning quire, or gathering, of a manuscript. Such manuscripts are referred to as *mujazza'*, divided into *ajzā'*. This feature is by no means rare. It can be attested by the Leiden manuscripts Or. 122 (*Makārim al-Akhlāq)* and Or. 12.644 (*Tārīkh Madīnat Dimashq*). These manuscripts contain on each gathering a number of almost identical certificates. The gatherings have title pages of their own and break up the text into parts of more or less equal length which have no connection with any division into chapters and sections that the text may also have. This latter characteristic is shared, of course, with the Qur'ān, which has a formal division into *ajzā'* and, at the same time, a division into chapters, or *sūras*.

11 *Ajzā'* with *samā'āt* are mentioned by Ṣalāḥ al-Dīn al-Munajjid, "Ijāzāt al-samā'", nos. 10 and 11.

When a scholar's trust in his colleague or student was great, it could happen that he conferred upon him the right to transmit all his works, even if they had not been the subject of a teaching session. In such a case the *ijāza* may contain the titles of most or all of the teacher's works and be, in effect, an autobibliography. Such lists of titles of books in the *ijāza*, or elsewhere in a manuscript for that matter, are have hardly been explored as yet.[12] There are many more works, often with more flowery titles, which serve the same purpose, namely to record and assess a scholar's authority. When one starts searching for this type of book the supply is seemingly endless. The common features that may be observed in all of them are the enumerations of scholars visited, of books read, and of authorisations (*ijāzāt*) received. In this context the *ijāza* is the conclusion of a meeting between two scholars which simultaneously contains an account of their scholarly antecedents. By virtue of it, the recipient is invested with the authority to transmit or teach part or whole of the work of the scholar who has issued the *ijāza.* The whole process is not unlike the diplomas which students of present day universities consider as the culmination of their study, the difference being that these *ijāzāt* reflect the relationship between two natural persons, rather than between a student and his institution of education.

Finally, we may note that the alphabetical arrangement of biographical material, such as in Ibn Ḥajar's *Taḥdhīb al-taḥdhīb*, encompassed all previous developments. This type of arrangement was, of course, the only organisational answer to an ever increasing corpus of material, although we do also find limitations of a chronological or geographical nature within alphabetically arranged biographical dictionaries.

[12] See my "Lists of Books in Arabic Manuscripts", *MME*, V (1990-1), 121–36, especially the section on '*Ijāzāt and autobibliography*' on pp. 126–30 where I discuss an 8/14th century document of such a nature. Another autobibliography which takes the shape of an *ijāza*, dated Damascus, 1169/1756, is found in MS Dublin, Chester Beatty Library, no. 3488 (cf. Arberry, *Handlist*, II, plate 63).

Codicology and the ijāza in Arabic manuscripts

What, one might ask, has all this to do with manuscripts and, more particularly, with codicology? The latter science is sometimes described as the specialism that devotes attention to all aspects of a manuscript other than the contents of the text it contains. In more positive wording, it is sometimes designated as the science that focusses exclusively on the physical features of the handwritten book. These are useful definitions but as summarised here they are too simplified. Indeed, there are often more things to be learned from a manuscript volume than the philological aspects of the text which is contained in it. One cannot, however, make such a simple schematic distinction between immaterial text and physical manuscript, between soul and body, so to speak. There is always an interaction between the two aspects, as is illustrated by, for example, the occurrence of a great variety of indications of personal use that can be found in many manuscripts. Each manuscript is, of course, a personally made artefact and contains information — always implicitly and sometimes explicitly — on the maker and sometimes on the users of the manuscript as well. On the whole, features such as the colophon, copyist's verses, owner's marks and reader's certificates enable us to gain an idea of the functioning of a certain text in general and the use of a certain manuscript volume in particular. Therefore, the study of these features, which belongs to the field of codicology in as much as the study of writing materials and script are part of it, gives a text an extra dimension and places it in its cultural context. Only this overall and integrated approach to the manuscript does justice to its features in coherence with one another. It is philology in the widest sense of the word, involving all these aspects and also the interaction between the text and the environment in which it was launched.

One usually finds *ijāzāt*, or copies of them,[13] added at the end of a text or written on the title page preceding the text for which the authorisation is granted. Sometimes the *ijāza* consists of a few lines only but sometimes they can be quite elaborate. They may be combined with readers' certificates. To add *ijāzāt* to texts was a time honoured practice in Arabic manuscripts which remained in use for a number of centuries. By looking at the manuscripts in which they are written, one can gain an idea of how this system of authorisation to teach operated. In addition to this, an *ijāza* can

13 Copies (*mithāl* or *ṣūra*) are often not recognised as such.

reveal much about the way a certain text or manuscript was used. Quite surprisingly, as yet very little has been done by way of a systematic collection of the data contained in the *ijāzāt* in Arabic manuscripts.[14] A corpus of such texts with an analysis of both their formulaic peculiarities and their content would be highly desirable. The fact that such a corpus would indeed be useful is illustrated by the discovery by Ebied and Young of the etymology of the term "baccalaureate": by scrutinising the Arabic wording of the *ijāzāt* in a number of manuscripts they found evidence for their thesis that the well known European academic term is in fact derived from the Arabic term *bi-ḥaqq al-riwāya.*[15]

Examples of some important ijāzāt

The *ijāza* originated within the Islamic educational system in which the Islamic religious sciences were taught. Its use, however, has by no means remained restricted to that field. Of the 72 manuscripts listed by Vajda, 59 have a "traditional Islamic" content, that is disciplines that are part of the *madrasa* curriculum, whereas 13 do not have a directly religious content but deal with such topics as medicine, literature and the sciences. This is still a high proportion in view of the fact that there are so many more manuscripts of the first category. Vajda's geographical register reveals that Damascus and Cairo are the places from where most manuscripts with *ijāzāt* on them originate. Baghdad, Makka and Aleppo are the runners up as places where *ijāzāt* were most frequently issued. Most other places are also situated in the Mashreq. Eighty percent of Vajda's corpus dates from the 6–9th/12–15th centuries, with a more or less even distribution over this period.[16]

One of the most outstanding sets of *ijāzāt* is found not in an Islamic scholarly text, but in what is probably the most prestigious text of Arabic imaginative literature, the *Maqāmāt* of

---

14 MacKay's extensive analysis of the *ijāzāt* in MS Cairo, Dār al-Kutub al-Miṣriyya, *Adab* 105 (see n. 1 above), which contains a contemporary copy of the *Maqāmāt* of al-Ḥarīrī (d. 512/1122), makes ample reference to secondary manuscripts and is exemplary both in this respect and from the methodological point of view. Vajda's collection of certificates (see n. 1 above) also provides a wealth of information.

15 R. Y. Ebied & M. J. L. Young, "New Light on the Origin of the Term 'Baccalaureate'", *The Islamic Quarterly*, XVIII (1974), 3-7.

16 See Vajda, *Certificats de lecture*, 65–6.

al-Ḥarīrī. This becomes clear from the *ijāzāt* found on the authoritative manuscript of the text, copied from al-Ḥarīrī's own copy. In the principal and contemporaneous *ijāza* on this manuscript the names of some 38 scholars, a number of whom are identified as distinguished notables of Baghdad, are mentioned as having been present at the reading of the entire work, which took more than a month of intermittent sessions to complete.[17] MacKay's meticulous analysis of the numerous *ijāzāt* in this manuscript has, in fact, reconstructed a period of almost two centuries of cultural life in Baghdad, Aleppo and Damascus. It all started in Baghdad in the year 504/1111, when the first reading of a copy of the author's autograph took place. That reading was followed by a number of subsequent readings, all in Baghdad. In the 60 or so years since the first reading, the manuscript had become quite heavy with *samā'* notes. After a period of 40 years, which remains unaccounted for, it came into the possession of the Aleppan historian Kamāl al-Dīn Ibn al-'Adīm (d. 660/1262). The manuscript then remained for more than 30 years in Aleppo, and bears numerous names of members of the best Aleppan families as auditors at sessions at which the manuscript was read. Finally, the manuscript bears certificates of reading sessions held in Damascus in the course of the year 683/1284. The manuscript then fades from view until, almost exactly six centuries later, it was acquired in 1875 by Dār al-Kutub al-Miṣriyya, where it still is.

When one looks at the more than 200 names of those involved in reading and listening to the manuscript, one is struck by the fact that many of them are related by family ties. The history of the transmission of the text in this manuscript often goes hand in hand with the history of generations of scholars and literary men who occupied themselves with it.

One of the earliest known *ijāzāt* is that found in the unique manuscript of *al-Nāsikh wa-l-mansūkh fī al-Qur'ān* by Abū 'Ubayd al-Qāsim b. Sallām (d. 223/837).[18] Here we do indeed

---

17 See MacKay, *Certificates of Transmission*, 9.

18 MS Istanbul, Topkapı Sarayı Library, Ahmet III A 143. The *ijāza* itself appears to be a copy (*mithāl*). A facsimile edition of the manuscript was published by Fuat Sezgin, Publications of the Institute for the History of Arabic-Islamic Science, Series C, XII (Frankfurt am Main, 1985). Pp. 418-9 of the facsimile edition contain the *ijāzāt*. The text was edited by John Burton, *Abū 'Ubaid al-Qāsim b. Sallām's* K. al-nāsikh wa-l-mansūkh *(MS. Istanbul, Topkapı, Ahmet III A 143)*, E. J. W. Gibb Memorial Series, New Series, XXX (Cambridge, 1987). Burton gives the readers' certificates

have a work which belongs to the core of Islamic sciences, the knowledge of the abrogating and abrogated verses of the Qur'an. The earliest *samāʿ* in it dates from 392/1001-2, while the latest dates from 587/1191. In one of *samāʿāt* in this manuscript a place is mentioned: al-Jāmiʿ al-ʿAtīq bi-Miṣr.[19] Here, too, several members of the same family are mentioned, including a father, his sons, and several brothers. Just as in the previously mentioned example of al-Ḥarīrī's *Maqāmāt*, it becomes clear that transmitting a text was a social event and sometimes also a family affair. In either case the personal element is clearly present. Comparison of the *ijāzāt* at the end of the Istanbul manuscript of Abū ʿUbayd's *al-Nāsikh wa-l-mansūkh* with the list of *riwāyāt* on the title page of another Istanbul manuscript, the *Kitāb al-Mujālasa* by Abū Bakr al-Dīnawarī,[20] reveals the occurrence of the same person in both manuscripts, namely, the otherwise unknown scholar Abū ʿAbd Allāh M. b. Ḥamd b. Ḥāmid b. Mufarraj b. Ghiyāth al-Artājī. In the very old manuscript of Abū ʿUbayd's *al-Nāsikh wa-l-mansukh,* he is active as *musmiʿ* in 587/1191, while in the copy of al-Dīnawarī's *Kitāb al-Mujālasa,* copied in 671/1272, he is one of the transmitters of the text preceding the manufacture of the manuscript. This shows that it is rewarding to accumulate the data of *ijāzāt, samāʿāt, riwāyāt* and the like, with the present example, for instance, revealing the beginning of a scholarly network.

The *ijāzāt* given by Ibn al-Jawālīqī (d. 539/1144), one of the foremost philologists in Baghdad,[21] can be found in a number of manuscripts. A manuscript in Dublin contains on its title page a certificate of reading signed by Ibn al-Jawālīqī in 514/1120.[22] A

---

of the Topkapı manuscript on pp. 101-3 of his edition, with an analysis of their contents and an identification of most persons mentioned in them on pp. 52-3 of his introduction.

19 This must be the manuscript to which Ṣalāḥ al-Dīn al-Munajjid refers ("Ijāzāt al-samāʿ", 233, n. 1). The date which he gives there, 372 AH, is apparently a misreading for the clearly written date of 392 AH.

20 MS Istanbul, Topkapı Sarayı Library, Ahmet III, No. 618. Facsimile edition by Fuat Sezgin, Publications of the Institute of the History of Arabic-Islamic Science, Series C, XXXVIII (Frankfurt am Main, 1986).

21 See C. Brockelmann, *Geschichte der arabischen Litteratur*, I (Weimar, 1898), 280.

22 Chester Beatty Library, No. 3009 (Arberry, *Handlist*, I, plate 1). See also S. A. Bonebakker, "Notes on Some Old Manuscripts of the *Adab al-kātib* of Ibn Qutayba, the *Kitāb aṣ-ṣināʿatayn* of Abū Hilāl al-ʿAskarī and the *Mathal as-sāʾir* of Ḍiyāʾ ad-Dīn ibn al-Athīr", *Oriens*, XIII-XIV (1960–

Leiden manuscript containing Abū al-ʻAlāʼ al-Maʻarrī's *Luzūm mā lā yalzam* was copied by Ibn al-Jawālīqī before 496/1102-3.[23] His handwriting is easily identified and the date can be established from an autograph note by his teacher and predecessor at the Niẓāmiyya school in Baghdad, al-Khaṭīb al-Tabrīzī (d. 502/1108).[24] Other reading notes in the same manuscript reveal the reading by a pupil, Ibn al-Khashshāb, in the course of the year 519/1125. The manuscript then travelled from Baghdad to Cairo, as is borne out by notes about its new owner, the grammarian Ibn al-Naḥḥās (d. 698/1299).[25] Another Leiden manuscript containing the philological work *Kitāb al-Alfāẓ* by ʻAbd al-Raḥmān b. ʻĪsá al-Hamadhānī (d. 320/932), was copied in 522/1128.[26] It, too, contains an autograph *qirāʼa* note by Ibn al-Jawālīqī on the title page. The manuscript itself contains notes of *bulūgh* and *muqābala* at fairly regular intervals and from these the length of the reading sessions can be approximately measured, each probably lasting around one or two hours. A late copy (11th/17th century?) of a *qirāʼa* note by Ibn al-Jawālīqī, dated *Ṣafar* 501/1107, is available in MS Leiden Or. 403, f. 430b, which contains the *Dīwān* of Abū Tammām with a commentary by al-Khaṭīb al-Tabrīzī.[27] The impression one gets from Ibn al-Jawālīqī's notes is that his transmissions were probably not as much of a social event as were the previous cases. It would appear that he had a predilection for a smaller group to whom he taught the important texts of his time. His copy of al-Maʻarrī's *Luzūmiyyāt*, with only his teacher al-Khaṭīb al-Tabrīzī between the author and himself, is an eloquent witness of this.

1), 159-94. The note in the Dublin manuscript is edited by Bonebakker on p. 165.

23 University Library, Or. 100. See also S. M. Stern, "Some Noteworthy Manuscripts of the Poems of Abu'l-ʻAlāʼ al-Maʻarrī", *Oriens*, VII (1954), 322-47, especially 339-44.

24 The *qirāʼa* note was published by me in *Seven Specimens of Arabic Manuscripts* (Leiden, 1978), 11.

25 See Stern, "Some Noteworthy Manuscripts", 343–4.

26 MS Leiden Or. 1070 (P. Voorhoeve, *Handlist of Arabic Manuscripts in the Library of the University of Leiden and Other Collections in the Netherlands* [Leiden, 1957], 10).

27 Voorhoeve, *Handlist*, 62.

Conclusions and perspectives

Two aspects of the *ijāza* have been dealt with, one from the point of view of cultural history, the other with codicological considerations taken into account. Both are necessary and the two complement one another by interaction. The *ijāza* itself is a good example for proving that these two orientations cannot be isolated from one another. The *ijāza* is an important source for the history of scholarly and cultural networks and gives the details by which an entire cultural environment can be reconstructed.

The *ijāza* as a mechanism in the distribution of learning deserves to be studied on a much wider scale than has hitherto been the case. Librarians should collect the *ijāzāt* in their manuscripts and publish them. Such publications should not only consist of an analysis of the data of the certificates, as Vajda and MacKay have done, but should also contain as complete a transcript as possible of the Arabic texts themselves. Only then can the most important work begin, namely, the compilation of a cumulative index of all the bio-bibliographical information contained in such certificates, which would be a valuable addition to existing bio-bibliographical reference works. The publication of a large corpus of *ijāzāt* will enable us to make a survey of the technical terminology employed which, in turn, will deepen our knowledge of the function of the *ijāza* in Arabic manuscripts.

The minimal requirements for such a corpus are, firstly, the full texts, with good photographs, of a great number of *ijāzāt*. These would constitute the main body of the work. Secondly, such a corpus should also contain a number of research aids: summary descriptions of the manuscripts in question, an index of persons with their functions in the process of the issuing of the *ijāzāt*, an index of the places to where the manuscripts in which the *ijāzāt* are found peregrinated in the course of time, and a glossary of the technical terminology employed.

This is not an easy task to perform, since the scholarly certificates are often written in the least legible of scripts. The study of the *ijāza* will only be fruitful if the student of the *ijāzāt* is well acquainted with the formal requirements of these certificates[28] and the educational environment from which they stem, and if at the same time he has a wide experience in working with manuscripts. In the ongoing development towards an increased

---

[28] As sketched by Ṣalāḥ al-Dīn al-Munajjid, "Ijāzāt al-samā'", 234–41.

professionalisation of the science of manuscripts, it is only natural that such a corpus of *ijāzāt* should be compiled by a professional codicologist.

[7]

TECHNICAL PRACTICES AND RECOMMENDATIONS RECORDED BY CLASSICAL AND POST-CLASSICAL ARABIC SCHOLARS CONCERNING THE COPYING AND CORRECTION OF MANUSCRIPTS

Adam GACEK

Some of the practices and recommendations of the early scholars of *Ḥadīṯ* and *al-ʿUlūm al-Šarʿīyah* are recorded and arranged here in order to give a better understanding of the Arabic codex and of the practices of the scribes. The main topics are the text itself, orthography (in particular different practices of pointing), abbreviations, collation and *apparatus criticus*.

Quelques pratiques et recommandations de spécialistes anciens de *ḥadīt* et d'*al-ʿulūm al-šarʿīyah* sont répertoriées et arrangées de manière à faciliter la compréhension du manuscrit arabe et des pratiques des copistes. Les thèmes principaux sont le texte lui-même, l'orthographe (en particulier les différentes manières de pointer les lettres), les abréviations, la collation et l'apparat critique.

It is well known that in the early years of Islam reliance on memory (*ḥifẓ*) was widespread, and it took almost a century before the *sunnah* of the Prophet Muhammad began in earnest to be committed to writing (*tadwīn, taqyīd bi-al-kitāb*)[1]. The recording of *ḥadīth* in this period was made on sheets (*ṣuḥuf*) and in booklets (*dafātir*), mostly for personal use and as *aides-mémoire* for teachers and preachers. Even though a number of non-*ḥadīth* compilations and translations certainly existed as early as the second half of the first/seventh century, the Qur'ān must have been the only book in those days copied for wider dissemination[2]. It has to be remembered at the same time that there existed from the beginning of Islam an art of letter-writing. The administrative machinery, which necessarily accompanied the early Arab/Islamic state, was responsible for the production of many documents. It fell, therefore, to the official amanuensis (*kātib*) to initiate the first rules for their composition and copying. The existing practices were then brought together and a literary genre, *adab al-kātib*, came into being[3].

The secretary was often a copyist of religious and literary works. Indeed, the *kuttāb* were associated with the manuscript codex from its inception. According to classical authors it was Zayd ibn Thābit, Muhammad's private secretary, who was given the task of collating and "editing" the original Qur'ān-codex (*muṣḥaf*). Later the Qur'ān, the first Arabic book *par excellence*, naturally became a model for the copyist. Innovations, therefore, introduced in the way it was transcribed and embellished had undoubtedly an impact on manuscript production as a whole. But because it was a Holy Book (*al-Kitāb*), whose careful copying would attract many blessings for the believer, copies made of its *textus receptus*, i.e. the ʿUthmanic text, largely excluded the possibility of corruption. The variants (*qirā'āt*) caused in the main by the lack of diacritical marks and vocalisation ceased to exist by the middle of the fourth/tenth century, and there was no need therefore for the scholars to work out rules and safeguards for its correct transmission[4].

The problem of tranmission of knowledge (*taḥammul al-ʿilm*) became evident first and foremost in *ḥadith*-literature. When the written body of the Prophet's *sunnah* began to grow it was more than ever necessary to ensure its authenticity. As a result a new discipline, *ʿulūm al-ḥadīth*, was born. It is this branch of knowledge which was forced to grapple with all kinds of problems connected with the text, its copying and correction. The rules established by traditionists (*muḥaddithūn*) for the written transmission of *ḥadīth*, and thus the *apparatus criticus*, were later applied in other disciplines, notably in jurisprudence, philology and theology. And today, when looking at the way Arabic manuscript codices were transcribed and corrected, one cannot fail to notice that, irrespective of subject matter, many rules elaborated by the early *ḥadīth*-scholars are clearly visible in manuscripts produced even as late as the twentieth century A.D.

The corpus of literature dealing with the transmis-

1) G.H.A. Juynboll, *The authenticity of the tradition literature: discussions in modern Egypt* (Leiden, 1969), pp. 47-54; Aḥmad ibn ʿAlī al-Khaṭīb al-Baghdādī, *Taqyīd al-ʿilm* (= *La transmission écrite du hadith*), ed. by Yūsuf al-ʿIshsh (Eche) (Damascus, 1949), pp. 5-10; Qāsim Aḥmad al-Samarrā'ī, "al-Ijāzāt wa-taṭawwuruhā al-ta'rīkhī", *ʿĀlam al-kutub*, 2, no. 2 (1981), pp. 279-281.

2) ʿAbd al-Sattār al-Ḥalwajī, *al-Makhṭūṭ al-ʿarabī mundhu nash'atih ilā ākhir al-qarn al-rābiʿ al-hijrī* (Riyadh, 1978), pp. 97-123; *idem*, "al-Kitāb al-ʿarabī al-makhṭūṭ fī nash'atih wa-taṭawwurih ilā ākhir al-qarn al-rābiʿ", *Majallat Maʿhad al-Makhṭūṭāt al-ʿArabīyah*, 13 (1967), pp. 207-293. It is interesting to note here that, as far as our present knowledge goes, all extant and dated non-Qur'anic codices go back only to third century hijrah. Kūrkīs ʿAwwād in his *Aqdam al-makhṭūṭāt al-ʿarabīyah fi maktabāt al-ʿālam* (Baghdad, 1982) enumerates some fifteen of these: nos 187 and 706 (dated 249/863), 202 (243/857), 376 (298-9/910-11), 382 (265/878), 423 (270/883), 493 and 512 (232/846), 500 (252/866), 507 (279/892), 543 (200/815), 562 (293/907), 584 (280/893), 617 (266/879), 619 (249/863), 639 (266/879), and 691 (277/890). These figures exclude two Christian codices: one dated 155/775 (nos 425 and 560) and the other 264/877 (nos 663 and 673).

3) For diplomatic and epistolography see *Encyclopaedia of Islam*, 2nd ed. s.v. "Diplomatic" (v. 2, pp. 301-316), "Inshā'" (v. 3, pp. 1241-1244) and "Kātib" (v. 4, pp. 754-760). See also M.A. Muid Khan, "The literary and social role of the Arab amanuenses during the Middle Ages", *Islamic Culture*, 26, n. 1 (1952), pp. 180-203 and J. Sadan, "Nouveaux documents sur scribes et copistes'', *Revue des études islamiques*, 45 (1977), pp. 41-87.

4) *Encyclopaedia of Islam*, 2nd ed. s.v. "al-Ḳur'ān" (v. 5, pp. 404-409) and "Ḳir'ā"(v. 5, pp. 126-129).

sion of *ḥadīth* is quite substantial. The earliest and most important texts containing information on some aspects of copying and correction of *ḥadīth*-compilations come from Ibn Khallād al-Rāmahurmuzī (d. 360/970)[5], al-Khaṭīb al-Baghdādī (d. 463/1071)[6], al-Qāḍī ʿIyāḍ al-Yaḥṣubī (d. 544/1149)[7], ʿAbd al-Karīm al-Samʿānī (d. 562/1166)[8], Ibn al-Ṣalāḥ al-Shahrazūrī (d. 643/1243)[9], and Ibn Jamāʿah (d. 733/1333)[10]. Later, in the tenth/sixteenth century, based on the information supplied by the afore-mentioned authors, and in particular Ibn Jamāʿah, Abū al-Ḥasan al-Samhūdī (d. 911/1506)[11], Badr al-Dīn al-Ghazzī (d. 984/1577)[12], and al-Shahīd al-Thānī al-ʿĀmilī (d. 966/1558)[13], each composed a chapter on this subject entitled "*fī al-ādāb maʿ al-kutub allatī hiya ālat al-ʿilm*". By far the most important and most comprehensive of these is the *bāb al-sādis* of *al-Durr al-naḍīd fī ādāb al-mufīd wa-al-mustafīd* by al-Ghazzī.

The present paper is an attempt to collect, arrange and analyse some of these practices and recommendations in order to make the Arabic codex more easily understood by the student of Arabic palaeography. Although it draws heavily on the text published in the Appendix, it does not deal with every point in it. It concentrates rather on the factual information of relevance to the copying and correction of codices.

1. Preliminary and closing formulae[14]

The overwhelming majority of Arabic manuscripts begin with the invocation of the name of God (*Bism Allāh al-Raḥmān al-Raḥīm*), the formula which is known as *al-basmalah* or *al-tasmiyah*. According to various authorities[15] the use of the *basmalah* goes back to the Prophet Muhammad himself, who, after Sūrat Hūd was revealed to him, ordered that at the beginning of his letters *Bism Allāh* should be written. This was to replace the phrase *Bismika Allāhumma* used by the Quraysh in pre-Islamic times. The use of the full formula came after the revelation of Sūrat al-Naml, āyah 30: "*Innahu min Sulaymān wa-innahu bism Allāh al-Raḥmān al-Raḥīm*". Muhammad is also quoted as saying, "*Kull amr dhī bālin lā yubtada' fīhi bism Allāh al-Raḥmān al-Raḥīm aqṭaʿ*"[16] and "*Bism Allāh al-Raḥman al-Rahīm miftāḥ kull kitāb*"[17]. Nothing should be written on the line of the *basmalah*, says al-Samʿānī, who also gives detailed instructions on how to execute it[18].

According to some authorities, not every text had to begin with the *basmalah*. Ibn Jamāʿah and al-Ghazzī[19]

5) Al-Ḥasan ibn ʿAbd al-Raḥmān ibn Khallād al-Rāmahurmuzī, *al-Muḥaddith al-fāṣil bayna al-rāwī wa-al-wāʿī*, ed. by Muḥammad ʿAjjāj al-Khaṭīb (Beirut, 1391/1971).

6) Aḥmad ibn ʿAlī al-Khaṭīb al-Baghdādī, *al-Jāmiʿ li-akhlāq al-rāwī wa-ādāb al-sāmiʿ*. 2 vols (Riyadh, 1403/1983); *idem*, *al-Kifāyah fī ʿilm al-riwāyah* (Hyderabad, 1390/1970).

7) ʿIyāḍ ibn Mūsā al-Yaḥṣubī, *al-Ilmāʿ ilā maʿrifat uṣūl al-riwāyah wa-taqyīd al-samāʿ*, ed. by Aḥmad Ṣaqr (Cairo; Tunis, 1389/1970).

8) ʿAbd al-Karīm ibn Muḥammad al-Samʿānī, *Adab al-imlā' wa-al-istimlā'* (= *Die Methodik des Diktatkollegs*), herausgegeben von Max Weisweiler (Leiden, 1952). See also M. Weisweiler, "Das Amt des Mustamlī in der arabischen Wissenschaft", *Oriens*, 4 (1951), pp. 27-57.

9) ʿUthmān ibn ʿAbd al-Raḥmān ibn al-Ṣalāḥ al-Shahrazūrī, *Muqaddimat Ibn al-Ṣalāḥ fī ʿulūm al-ḥadīth* (Damascus, 1972). This work was abridged by Yaḥyā ibn Sharaf al-Nawawī (d. 676/1277) under the title *al-Taqrīb wa-al-taysīr li-maʿrifat sunan al-bashīr al-nadhīr*, ed. by Muḥammad ʿUthmān al-Kasht (Beirut, 1405/1985). French translation: W. Marçais, *Le Taqrîb de en-Nawawi* (Paris, 1902). Probably the best commentary on the above is: ʿAbd al-Raḥmān ibn Abī Bakr al-Suyūṭī (d. 911/1505), *Tadrīb al-rāwī fī sharḥ Taqrīb al-Nawawī*, ed. by ʿAbd al-Wahhāb ʿAbd al-Laṭīf (Cairo, 1385/1966).

10) Muḥammad ibn Ibrāhīm ibn Jamāʿah, *Tadhkirat al-sāmiʿ wa-al-mutakallim fī ādāb al-ʿālim wa-al-mutaʿallim* (Hyderabad, 1353 H.). See also *idem*, "al-Manhal al-rawī fī mukhtaṣar ʿulūm al-ḥadīth al-nabawī", *Majallat Maʿhad al-Makhṭūṭāt al-ʿArabīyah*, 21 (1975), pp. 29-116 and 196-255.

11) ʿAlī ibn ʿAbd Allāh al-Samhūdī, "Jawāhir al-ʿiqdayn fī faḍl al-sharafayn" (MS, Leiden Or. 790, dated 904/1499), the relevant chapter (*al-faṣl al-sābiʿ*) is to be found on fol. 68b-70b. This chapter was reproduced almost verbatim by al-Ḥusayn ibn Amīr al-Mu'minīn al-Manṣūr bi Allāh al-Qāsim (d. 1050/1640) in his *Ādāb al-ʿulamā' wa-al-mutaʿallimīn* (Beirut, 1406/1985), pp. 91-98.

12) Muḥammad ibn Muḥammad al-Ghazzī composed *al-Durr al-naḍīd* before 947/1540-1 (see Appendix). The section in question, i.e. *al-bāb al-sādis*, was partially edited (questions 16-23) on the basis of one manuscript by Muḥammad Mursī al-Khūlī in his "Naṣṣ fī ḍabṭ al-kutub wa-taṣḥīḥihā wa-dhikr al-rumūz wa-al-iṣṭilāḥāt al-wāridah fīhā lil-ʿAllāmah Badr al-Dīn al-Ghazzī", *Majallat Maʿhad al-Makhṭūṭāt al-ʿArabīyah*, 10 (1964), pp. 167-184. In view of the importance of this chapter, as well as the fact that we now have a manuscript which was collated in the presence of al-Ghazzī himself, it has been reproduced in the Appendix. *Al-Durr al-naḍīd* itself has not yet been edited. Instead, an abridgement of it made by ʿAbd al-Bāsiṭ ibn Mūsā al-ʿAlmawī (d. 981/1573) and entitled *al-Muʿīd fī adab al-mufīd wa-al-mustafīd*, ed. by Aḥmad ʿUbayd, was published in Damascus in 1349 H. For the English translation of the chapter from *al-Muʿīd* see Franz Rosenthal, *The technique and approach of Muslim scholarship* (Rome, 1947), pp. 8-18.

13) Zayn al-Dīn ibn ʿAlī al-Shahīd al-Thānī al-ʿĀmilī, *Munyat al-murīd fī ādāb al-mufīd wa-al-mustafīd*, ed. by Aḥmad al-Ḥusaynī (Beirut, 1981). This work was composed in 956/1549 and contains a chapter (*al-bāb al-rābiʿ*) similar to, albeit much shorter than, the one in *al-Durr al-naḍīd*.

14) The preliminary and closing matter in codices and documents are called *fawātiḥ* (sg. *fātiḥah*) and *khawātim* (sg. *khātimah*) or *awā'il* (sg. *awwal*) and *awākhir* (sg. *ākhir*) respectively. Other terms used are *ṣadr* (or *taṣdīr*) and *ʿajz*. The word *muqaddimah* is mainly employed in the sense of an introduction proper.

15) See e.g. Muḥammad ibn Yaḥyā al-Ṣūlī (d. 335/946), *Adab al-kuttāb*, ed. by Muḥammad Bahjah al-Atharī (Baghdad, 1341 H.), p. 31 and D. Sourdel, "Le 'livre des secrétaires' de ʿAbdallāh al-Baġdādī", *Bulletin d'études orientales*, 14 (1952-54), p. 132.

16) Al-Samʿānī, *Adab al-imlā'*, p. 51.

17) Al-Khaṭīb al-Baghdādī, *al-Jāmiʿ*, v. 1, p. 264.

18) Al-Samʿānī, op. cit., pp. 170-171; see also al-Ṣulī, op. cit., pp. 32-36 and al-Khaṭīb al-Baghdādī, ibid., v. 1, pp. 265-268.

19) Ibn Jamāʿah, *Tadhkirat al-sāmiʿ*, p. 173 and al-Ghazzī, *al-Durr al-naḍīd*, fol. 144b-145a.

make the use of it compulsory if the work consists of a *khuṭbah*[20], whose components are the *ḥamdalah* (*al-ḥamd lil-Lāh*) and *taṣliyah* (*ṣallā Allāh ʿalayhi wa-sallam* or *ṣallā Allāh ʿalayhi wa-ālihi wa-sallam*). Furthermore, al-Khaṭīb al-Baghdādī informs us that some *ḥadīth*-scholars differed as to its usage in collections of poetry: some recommended it and others disliked it, although al-Khaṭīb himself deems it desirable[21]. Al-ʿAlmawī has no hesitation about its usage: should the author omit it, he says, it ought to be provided by the copyist[22].

Al-Shahīd al-Thānī, in turn, instructs the copyist to begin the work with the *basmalah*, followed by the *ḥamdalah* and *taṣliyah*, even if these formulae were not provided by the author himself[23].

For the early traditionist the *basmalah* ought to be followed by the name of the shaykh through whom the book is being transmitted (*mumli'*, *musmiʿ* or *musammiʿ*, *rāwin*). This preliminary statement is known as the *sanad* or *riwāyah* of a book and can be expressed in the following way: *ḥaddathanā Abū Fulān ibn Fulān ibn Fulān al-Fulānī qāla ḥaddathanā Fulān*...[24] The audition-note (*samāʿ*, *tasmīʿ*, *ṭabaqat al-samāʿ*), containing the title of the book (*al-kitāb al-masmūʿ*), names of auditors (*sāmiʿūn*) and the date of audition (*ta'rīkh al-samāʿ*), should be inscribed (*thabata, kataba*) in the margin of the first page, at the beginning of the book (*ʿalā* or *fī ẓahr al-kitāb*), or at its end (*ākhir al-kitāb*). It can be written in the hand of the *musmiʿ* or attested by him (*ithbāt*)[25]. This practice of providing a book with the *sanad* slowly wanes. Al-Ghazzi, for example, instructs the copyist to write simply *qāla al-muṣannif* or *qāla al-shaykh* after the *basmalah*, if the words which follow belong to the author[26].

The body of the text proper, or any part thereof, should end with the *ḥamdalah* and *taṣliyah*. The end of each part (*juz'*) or volume (*jild*) should be indicated by saying, for example, *ākhir al-juz' al-awwal wa-yatlūhu kadhā wa-kadhā*, and when the book is finished: *tamma al-kitāb*[27].

2. Dates and dating

It is interesting to note that neither the early *ḥadīth*-works nor the later compilations of Ibn Jamāʿah, al-Samhūdī and al-Ghazzī touch upon the question of dates and dating (*ta'rīkh*). The colophon (*jard al-matn*) is completely overlooked. The reason for this may lie in the fact that chronology was sufficiently well dealt with in the *adab al-kātib* literature. There are indeed extensive sections on *ta'rīkh* in such works as *Adab al-kuttāb* of al-Ṣūlī, *Kitāb al-kuttāb* of Ibn Durustūyah and *Ṣubḥ al-aʿshā* of al-Qalqashandī[28].

20) The *khuṭbah* in books, also known as *dībājāh*, is properly speaking a preface. It usually consists of the following formulae or parts: *al-basmalah* (*al-tasmiyah*), *al-ḥamdalah* (*al-taḥmīd*) or *al-tasbīḥ*, *al-taṣliyah* (*al-ṣalwalah*, *al-ṣalāh wa-al-taslīm*), *al-tashahhud* (*al-shahādah*, *kalimat al-tawḥīd*), *al-baʿdīyah* (*faṣl al-khiṭāb*), *ism* (*tasmiyat*) *al-kitāb*, *tartīb* (*tabwīb*) and *rumūz*. It is worth observing here that the choice of words for the *incipit* is often indicative of, or alludes to, the subject of a given work. In rhetoric this is referred to as *barāʿat al-istihlāl* or *ḥusn al-iftitāḥ* (see e.g. Aḥmad ibn ʿAlī al-Qalqashandī, d. 821/1418, *Subḥ al-aʿshā fī ṣināʿat al-inshā*, Cairo, 1383/1963, v. 6, pp. 274-278 and *Encyclopaedia of Islam*, 2nd ed., s.v. "Ibtidā'", v. 3, p. 1006).

21) Al-Khaṭīb al-Baghdādī, *al-Jāmiʿ*, v. 1, pp. 267-268; see also al-Samʿānī, *Adab al-imlā'*, p. 169.

22) Al-ʿAlmawī, *al-Muʿīd*, p. 132.

23) Al-Shahīd al-Thānī, *Munyat al-murīd*, p. 177.

24) Al-Khaṭīb al-Baghdādī, op. cit., v. 1, p. 268; al-Samʿānī, op. cit., p. 53; Ibn al-Ṣalāḥ, *Muqaddimah*, p. 100; Ibn Jamāʿah, *al-Manhal al-rawī*, p. 105. For specimens of *riwāyāt* see e.g. al-Rāmahurmuzī, *al-Muḥaddith al-fāṣil*, pp. 44-49.

25) See in particular Ibn al-Ṣalāḥ, *Muqaddimah*, pp. 100-102. Audition notes are *de facto* kinds of certificates giving authorization to transmit the contents of a given book, irrespective of whether the words *ajāza* or *istajāza* are used. They usually begin with either the word *samiʿa* (*samiʿtu*) or *qara'a* (*qara'tu, quri'a*) and, therefore, are often referred to as *samāʿāt* and *qirā'āt* respectively. The *samāʿ* or *qirā'ah* with an explicit authorization to transmit a given text (*ajāza lahu*) thus becomes, properly speaking, *ijāzat al-samāʿ* or *ijazat al-qirā'ah*. The formulae of attestation are e.g. *ṣaḥḥa* (*ṣaḥīḥ*) *dhālika wa-kataba (hu)*..., *ṣaḥḥa dhālika wa-thabata*... and *hādhā ṣaḥīḥ wa-kataba*... For the different modes of transmission of *ḥadīth* as well as an analysis of certificates of transmission see Ibn al-Ṣalāh, op. cit., pp. 60-87; Muḥammad ibn Khayr al-Ishbīlī (d. 575/1179), *Fahrasat mā rawāhu ʿan shuyūkhih*... (Beirut, 1399/1979), pp. 12-16; Ibn Jamāʿah, *al-Manhal al-rawī*, pp. 89-100; G. Vajda, *La transmission du savoir en Islam (VIIᵉ-XVIIIᵉ siècles)*, ed. by N. Cottart (London, 1983), pp. 1-9; Ṣalāḥ al-Dīn al-Munajjid, "Ijāzāt al-samāʿ fī al-makhṭūṭāt al-qadīmah", *Majallat Maʿhad al-Makhṭūṭāt al-ʿArabīyah*, 1 (1955), pp. 232-251; al-Samarrā'ī, "al-Ijāzāt", pp. 279-284; ʿAbd Allāh Fayyāḍ, *al-Ijāzāt al-ʿilmīyah ʿinda al-Muslimīn* (Baghdad, 1967).

26) Al-Ghazzī, *al-Durr al-naḍīd*, fol. 144b-145a. One often encounters the expression *qāla* (*yaqūlu*) *al-shaykh* after *ammā (wa-) baʿdu fa-*. Its being placed here and not after the *basmalah* may imply that the opening section was provided later by someone other than the author. See also al-Shahīd al-Thānī, *Munyat al-murīd*, p. 177.

27) Ibn Jamāʿah, *Tadhkirat al-sāmiʿ*, pp. 173-174; al-Ghazzī, ibid., fol. 145a; al-ʿAlmawī, *al-Muʿīd*, p. 132; al-Shahīd al-Thānī, ibid., p. 177. The synonyms of the word *tamma* often encountered in manuscripts are: *khatama*, *intahā*, *kamula* (*kamala*), *najaza* and *faragha*. The verb *faragha* is usually used in its *maṣdar*-form, namely *farāgh*, in combination with any of the following: *kāna*, *ḥaṣala*, *wāfaqa* and *ittafaqa*. The *finis*, i.e. the very end of the colophon is also often expressed by the word *tamma(t)*. Other words used are *intahā*, *faqaṭ* and *amīn*, the latter not infrequently in its ligatured form, thus .

28) Al-Ṣūlī, *Adab al-kuttāb*, pp. 178-186; ʿAbd Allāh ibn Jaʿfar ibn Durustūyah (d. 347/956), *Kitāb al-kuttāb*, ed. by Ibrāhīm al-Samarrā'ī and ʿAbd al-Ḥusayn al-Fatlī (Kuwait, 1977), pp. 133-151; al-Qalqashandī, *Ṣubḥ al-aʿsha*, v. 6, pp. 234-262; see also ʿAbd al-Raḥmān ibn Abī Bakr al-Suyūṭī, *al-Shamārīkh fī ʿilm al-ta'rīkh*, ed. by Ibrāhīm al-Samarrā'ī (Baghdad, 1971); ʿAlī ibn Ismāʿīl ibn Sīdah (d. 458/1065), *Kitāb al-mukhaṣṣaṣ* (Beirut, n.d., repr. Cairo, 1321 H.), v. 2, sifr 9, pp. 42-48 and v. 5, sifr 17, pp. 127-128; Aḥmad ibn al-Ḥasan ibn ʿArḍūn (992/1584), *al-Lā'iq li-muʿallim al-wathā'iq*, lithog. ed. (Fez, n.d.), pp. [34-37].

Dates in Arabic manuscripts are usually recorded in words and/or figures, giving the day, month and year. Al-Qalqashandī divides this traditional dating into two categories: *al-ta'rīkh bi-al-māḍī* (for those dates which use the verbs *maḍā* or *khalā* to indicate how many days have elapsed in a month), and *al-ta'rīkh bi-al-bāqī* (for those dates which employ the verb *baqiya* to show the number of days remaining till the end of a month). For example: *li-ʿishrīn laylah maḍat (khalat) min shahr*... or *li-arbaʿa ʿashrata laylah (in) baqiyat min shahr*...[29]. In a less precise date the copyist would indicate in which third (i.e. unit of ten days) of the month he finished his work. Thus the following expressions were used: *al-ʿashr al-ūlā (al-ʿashr al-uwal), al-ʿashr al-wusṭā (al-ʿashr al-wusaṭ), al-ʿashr al-ukhrā (al-ʿashr al-ukhar, al-ʿashr al-ākhirah, al-ʿashr al-awākhir)*. Other words used in this connection are: *shafaq* (first hour of night), *ṣabāḥ* (last hour of night), *shurūq* (first hour of day), *ghurūb* (last hour of day), *ẓuhr* (noon), *ʿaṣr (afternoon)*, *ghurrah* (first night of a month), *salkh* or *insilākh* (last night of a month), *ghurar* (first three nights) and *da'ādī* (last three nights)[30].

The numerical values of the letters of the alphabet (*abjad*) were also made use of, from the earliest period, as an alternative to numerals (*arqām*) and for the creation of chronograms (*ḥisāb al-jummal*). Arithmomancy or gematria, as it is properly termed, consists of adding numerical values of letters to arrive at a given date[31]. The *ḥisāb al-jummal* was also used for cryptographic dating. Al-Jazā'irī distinguishes two types of this dating: *al-ta'rīkh al-mudhayyal* or *al-taʿmiyah bi-al-ziyādah* (when more than the last *miṣrāʿ* of a *bayt* is counted), and *al-ta'rīkh al-mustathnā* or *al-taʿmiyah bi-al-naqṣ* (when the value of one word or letter from the first *miṣrāʿ* is substracted from the cumulative value of the second *miṣrāʿ*)[32].

The tenth/sixteenth century ushers in another type of cryptographic dating referred to by al-Jazā'irī as *al-ta'rīkh al-kinā'ī* (dating by allusion, metonymy), or *al-ta'rīkh bi-al-kusūr* (dating by fractions)[33]. This way of dating was most probably introduced by Ibn Kamāl Pāshā, also known as Kemāl Pāshā-zāde (d. 940/1534), whence it is also called *ta'rīkh Ibn Kamāl*[34].

3. Formulae of glorification and benediction

All authorities agree that the name of Allāh, whenever mentioned, should be followed by a formula of glorification (*taʿẓīm, tajlīl, tamjīd*), such as *taʿālā, subḥānahu, ʿazza wa-jalla, tabāraka, taqaddasa*[35]. Formulae of benediction and eulogies (*ad ʿiyah*) should follow names of prophets, angels, companions of the Prophet Muhammad, Imams and other authorities and famous individuals. The name of the Prophet ought to be followed by the *taṣliyah* in its unabbreviated form. Abbreviations of the *taṣliyah* did abound, however, for Ibn Jamaʿah, al-Ghazzī, al-ʿAlmawī and al-Shahīd al-Thani mention as many as six varieties: *ṣlʿm, ṣlm, ṣlʿ, ṣm, ṣlsm, ṣlh*[36].

Other optative formulae required after proper names are: *al-taraḍḍī (raḍiya Allāh ʿanhu* or *riḍwān Allāh ʿalayhi)*, used mainly for the companions of the Prophet, *al-taraḥḥum (raḥimahu Allāh, raḥmat Allāh ʿalayhi, taghammadahu Allāh bi-raḥmatih)* and *al-salām* or *al-taslīm (ʿalayhi al-salām)*[37].

4. Lines and rubrics

In order to produce straight lines (*suṭūr*), leaves (*waraqāt, awrāq*) were ruled in blind either by means of the fingernails (*taẓfīr*) or by using a device called

29-30) See the references in n. 28 and in particular al-Qalqashandī, loc. cit. and A. Grohmann, "Arabische Chronologie", *Handbuch der Orientalistik*, Abteilung 1, Ergänzungsband 2 (Leiden, 1966), pp. 1-48.

31) *Encyclopaedia of Islam*, 2nd ed. s.v. "Abdjad" (v. 1, pp. 97-98) and "Ḥisāb al-djummal" (v. 3, p. 468); Georges Ifrah, *Histoire universelle des chiffres* (Paris, 1981), pp. 298-305.

32) Ṭāhir ibn Ṣaliḥ al-Jazā'irī (d. 1338/1920), *Tashīl al-majāz ilā fann al-muʿammā wa-al-alghāz* (Damascus, 1303 H.), pp. 47-48.

33) Al-Jazā'irī, ibid., pp. 49-55. As far as we know there are three commentaries on dating by fractions, by a) the afore-mentioned al-Jazā'irī; b) Ismāʿīl Ḥaqqī al-Brūsawī (Brusavi, d. 1127/1715), "Sharḥ ta'rīkh Ibn Kamāl", in his *Maqālāt* (published with his *Dīwān*, Istanbul, 1288 H.), pp. 10-12; c) a certain Ṣadrī Afandī, "Sharḥ ta'rīkh Ibn Kamāl Pāshā", *Catalogue of Arabic manuscripts in the library of The Institute of Ismaili Studies* by A. Gacek (London, 1985), v. 2, p. 178 (facsimile reproduction). Al-Jazā'irī's commentary was translated by H. Ritter in his "Philologica XII: Datierung durch Brüche", *Oriens*, 1 (1948), pp. 237-247. More examples of this dating can be found in A. Dietrich, "Zur Datierung durch Brüche in arabischen Handschriften", *Nachrichten der Akademie der Wissenschaften in Göttingen*, Band 1, Phil. Hist. Klasse 2 (Göttingen, 1961), pp. 27-33 and Gacek, ibid., v. 2, p. xi.

34) The date quoted as an example in the three above-mentioned texts is 19 Ṣafar 926, i.e. the date of composition of the ninth volume of Ibn Kamāl's "History of the Ottomans". It is an enigma in itself why this dating should have been invented. V. Ménage calls it "a literary conceit" (see *Encyclopaedia of Islam*, 2nd ed., s.v. "Kemāl Pāshā-zāde").

35) See e.g. Ibn Jamāʿah, *Tadhkirat al-sāmiʿ*, p. 175 and al-Ghazzī, *al-Durr al-naḍīd*, fol. 145a.

36) Ibn Jamāʿah, ibid., p. 176; al-Ghazzī, ibid., fol. 145a-146a; al-ʿAlmawī, *al-Muʿīd*, pp. 132-133; al-Shahīd al-Thānī, *Munyat al-murīd*, pp. 177-178.

37) Ibn Jamaʿah and others, as above. No abbreviations of *al-taʿẓīm, al-taraḍḍī, al-taraḥḥum* and *al-taslīm* are mentioned, even though they are commonly encountered in manuscripts (see e.g. Gacek, *Catalogue*, v. 1, p. xiii and v. 2, p. xiv). It is also somewhat surprising that al-Shahīd al-Thānī, being a Shiite author, does not mention the most commonly used Shiite *duʿā'*, namely *al-taqdīs (qaddasa Allāh sirrahu, qaddasa Allāh rūḥahu, quddisa sirruhu)*.

mistarah[38]. As far as possible, lines should be justified, that is the words should align at the left. In order to achieve this the copyist is instructed either to elongate the letters (*madd, matt, mashq*) or to contract them (*jamʿ, qaṣr*)[39]. Word-division (*faṣl*) is disapproved of, and so is the breaking of meaningful constructions such as the construct state (*iḍāfah*), particularly if the latter contains the name of God, e.g. ʿAbd al-Raḥmān, Rasūl Allāh and so forth[40].

In order to achieve greater clarity in the body of the text, the use of chapter headings (*tarājim, abwāb, fuṣūl*), rubrics (*kitābah bi-al-ḥumrah*) and bold characters (*qalam ghalīẓ*) are recommended[41]. The use of red ink is suitable for proper names, abbreviations (*rumūz*), quotations (*aqwāl*), numbers (*aʿdād*), technical terms (*lughāt*) and other key-words. In a comment-text book (*sharḥ mamzūj bi-al-matn*), the *matn* should be written in red or overlined in red ink. The overlining can either be a straight line or, says al-Ghazzī, can look like this: ـــر[42].

4. Punctuation

Classical Arabic did not use punctuation in its modern sense. Some marks (*fawāṣil*) were, however, used to indicate a different section or paragraph, or a meaningful phrase. One of the earliest marks of this kind was a circle (*dārah, dā'irah*), introduced by the *ḥadīth*-scholar to separate one *ḥadīth* from another[43]. Al-Khaṭīb al-Baghdādī informs us that it was desirable to leave the circle empty, so that when the *ḥadīth* was collated, a dot (*nuqṭah*) or some other mark (*khaṭṭ*) could be placed in it[44]. Thus, depending on the amount of times a particular *ḥadīth* was heard (*masmūʿ*) or read (*maqrū'*), a *dārah* could contain one, two or more dots[45]. Al-Khaṭīb also reports another practice of indicating the end of a group of ten *ḥadīth* by a drawing a circle with dots on its circumference[46].

5. Handwriting

For the traditionists, accuracy and clarity of handwriting were more important than its calligraphic quality (*ḥusn al-khaṭṭ*). Clear, bold handwriting (*khaṭṭ ghalīẓ*) was, therefore, recommended. *Mashq* (i.e. a hasty hand with elongated letter-forms) and *taʿlīq* (i.e. a hand characterised by joining those letter forms, which normally should be written separately, thus, in a way, the opposite of the *mashq*) ought to be avoided. A very fine handwriting (*khaṭṭ daqīq, kitābah daqīqah, qarmaṭah*) was allowed, for example, if paper was in short supply or the person could not afford its price, or because he intended to travel and large books would be difficult to carry[47].

6. Abbreviations

Abbreviations (*rumūz, mukhtaṣarāt, muṣṭalāḥāt*), whether in the form of contractions, suspensions or *sigla*, abound in Arabic manuscripts, even if some, such as those of the afore-mentioned *taṣliyah*, were disapproved

38) Ibn Jamāʿah, *Tadhkirat al-sāmiʿ*, p. 172; al-Ghazzī, *al-Durr al-naḍīd*, fol. 144b; al-Qalqashandī, *Ṣubḥ al-aʿshā*, v. 2, p. 482; Sadan, "Nouveaux documents", p. 53, n. 66.

39) Ibn Durustūyah, *Kitāb al-kuttāb*, pp. 121-127; al-Ṣūlī, *Adab al-kuttāb*, p. 119; ʿAbd al-Raḥīm ibn ʿAlī ibn Shīth al-Qurashī (fl.6/11th cent.), *Maʿālim al-kitābah wa-maghānim al-iṣābah*, ed. by al-Khūrī Qusṭanṭīn al-Bāshā al-Mukhliṣī (Beirut, 1913), pp. 55-59; al-Qalqashandī, ibid., v. 3, pp. 140-146.

40) For a more detailed account see al-Ghazzī, op. cit., fol. 146b-147a and al-Qalqashandī, ibid., v. 3, pp. 147-148.

41) Ibn Jamāʿah, *Tadhkirat al-sāmiʿ*, pp. 191-192; al-Ghazzī, *al-Durr al-naḍīd*, fol. 154b-155a; al-ʿAlmawī, *al-Muʿīd*, p. 139; al-Shahīd al-Thānī, *Munyat al-murīd*, p. 187. The use of red ink did not, however, meet with unanimous approval. Burhān al-Islām al-Zarnūjī (fl. ca. 600/1203) says, for example, "*Wa-yanbaghī an lā yakūn fī al-kitāb shay' min al-ḥumrah fa-innahu ṣanīʿ al-falāsifah lā ṣanīʿ al-salaf*" (see his *Taʿlīm al-mutaʿallim ṭarīq al-taʿallum*, ed. by Marwān Qabbānī, Beirut, 1981, p. 85).

42) Ibn Jamāʿah, al-Ghazzī etc., as above. In early manuscripts we also encounter ⁄— as a form of overlining. For different practices of distinguishing the original text from a commentary or gloss see Gacek, *Catalogue*, v. 2, p. xi.

43) Al-Rāmahurmuzī, *al-Muḥaddith al-fāṣil*, p. 206; al-Khaṭīb al-Baghdādī, *al-Jāmiʿ*, v. 1, pp. 272-274; al-Samʿānī, *Adab al-imlā'*, p. 173; Ibn al-Ṣalāḥ, *Muqaddimah*, pp. 90-91; al-Ghazzī, *al-Durr al-naḍīd*, fol. 152b-153a. "This sign [o, i.e. circle], says A. Grohmann, is well known from old Qur'an-manuscripts..., and very probably borrowed from a Persian scribal custom, for already Pahlavi papyri show the division of sentences by means of a plain circle" (*From the world of Arabic papyri*, Cairo, 1952, p. 91). See also al-Qalqashandī, *Ṣubḥ al-aʿshā*, v. 3, pp. 145-146 and Aḥmad ibn ʿAbd al-Wahhāb al-Nuwayrī (d. 733/1333), *Nihayat al-arab fī funūn al-adab* (Cairo, n.d.), v. 9, p. 214.

44-45) Al-Khaṭīb al-Baghdādī, ibid., v. 1, pp. 272-273; al-Shahīd al-Thānī, *Munyat al-murīd*, p. 186.

46) See also al-Samʿānī, op. cit., p. 173. We do not know to what extent the dot was used as a collation mark. It seems that for some the circle and the dot constituted simply a paragraph mark (see al-Ghazzī, op. cit., fol. 153a and al-ʿAlmawī, op. cit., p. 138 ("*wa-ṣūratuhu hākadhā* ")). As regards punctuation in Qur'an-codices, Jalāl al-Dīn al-Suyūṭī says, "*Awwalu mā aḥdathū al-nuqaṭ ʿinda ākhir al-āy thumma al-fawātiḥ wa-al-khawātim wa-qāla Yaḥyā ibn Abī Kathīr mā kānū yaʿrifūn shay'an mimmā uḥditha fī al-maṣāḥif illā al-nuqaṭ al-thalāth, ʿalā ru'ūs al-āyāt*" (*al-Itqān fī ʿulūm al-Qur'ān*, Osnabrück, 1980, repr. Calcutta, 1852-54, v. 2, pp. 869-870).

47) Al-Khaṭīb al-Baghdādī, op. cit., v. 1, p. 262; al-Samʿānī, op. cit., pp. 166-169; Ibn al-Ṣalāḥ, op. cit., pp. 89-90; al-Ghazzī, op. cit., fol. 146a; Ibn Shīth, *Maʿālim al-kitābah*, pp. 42-43. The verb *ʿallaqa* was originally used as a synonym of *kataba*, i.e. joining letters one to another (see Sadan, "Nouveaux documents", p. 63). It is often found used in this sense in colophons. The description of *taʿlīq* as given in the above works corresponds to one of the characteristics of a chancery hand bearing the same name. For the analysis of *mashq* as one of the earliest Arabic scripts see Nabia Abbott, *The rise of the North Arabic script and its kur'ānic development* (Chicago, 1939), pp. 24-28.

of. *Ḥadīth*-literature was a fertile ground for various and on the whole arbitrary abbreviations. The most commonly abbreviated words were *ḥaddathanā* and *akhbaranā*. There was, however, no standard practice. Al-Khaṭīb al-Baghdādī reports, for example, that Abū al-Walīd al-Ṭayālisī (d. 227/841), when taking down a dictation, was using the following abbreviations: *khā'* for *akhbaranā*, *sīn* for *samiʿtu*, and *ḥā'* for *ḥaddathanā*[48]. Other abbreviations reported in the texts under discussion are: *nā, thnā, dthnā, dnā* (= *ḥaddathanā*); *anā, arnā, abnā, rnā* (= *akhbaranā*); *thnī, dthnī* (= *ḥaddathanī*); *q* (= *qāla*) and *qthnā* (= *qāla ḥaddathanā*)[49]. In order to separate one *isnād* (*sanad*) from another, the practice was to write the letter *ḥā'* (isolated form), an abbreviation of *taḥwīl* or *ḥā'il* or *ḥadīth* or *ṣaḥḥa*[50].

Abbreviations, when used in a manuscript, ought to be spelled out in the preface, the recommendation which was often followed as regards proper names and titles of books. Al-Ghazzī gives the following list: *khā'* = al-Bukhārī, *mīm* = Muslim or al-Imām Mālik, *tā'* = al-Tirmidhī, *dāl* = Abū Dā'ūd, *nūn* = al-Nasā'ī, *jh* or *q* = Ibn Mājah al-Qazwīnī, *ḥb* = Ibn Ḥabbān, *ṭā'* = al-Dāraquṭnī, *ḥā'* = Abū Ḥanīfah, *a* (*alif*) = al-Imām Aḥmad and *shīn* = al-Shāfiʿī. He also reports that the non-Arabs (i.e. Persians) were in the habit of using such abbreviations as: *al-mṭ* = *al-maṭlūb*, *mḥ* = *muḥāl*, *bṭ* = *bāṭil*, *wa-ḥ* = *wa-ḥīna'idhin*, *fa-ḥ* = *fa-ḥīna'idhin*, *alkh* = *ilā ākhirih* and *al-muṣ* = *al-muṣannif*[51].

7. Collation

The classical Arabic scholar attached great importance to the collation of texts (*muʿāraḍah, muqābalah*)[52]. This can be seen in a sizeable amount of sayings, some attributed to the Prophet himself, which can be gleaned from *ḥadīth*-literature[53]. Indeed, the collation of a witness (*farʿ*) with a correct and authenticated exemplar (*aṣl, umm*) was obligatory. The transmission (*riwāyah, naql*) of a *ḥadīth* could not be effected without it. Ibn al-Ṣalāḥ tells us that the best collation is made during an audition (*samāʿ*), when the master and pupil both hold their copies and most certainly when the master happens to be the author of the work[54]. Other possibilities, adds al-Ghazzī, are when a copy is collated in the presence of a master holding a holograph or a copy collated with the author, and attested in his hand[55]. The purpose of the collation is to make sure that a pupil's copy is an exact image (*ṣūrah*) of the exemplar or archetype and thus faithful to the author's original (*dustūr, musawwadah, mubayyaḍah*).

Manuscripts were usually collated in one or a number of sessions (*majālis, mawāʿīd*), depending on their length. Probably the earliest way of marking the spot at which the collation broke off was by placing a dot or some other mark in the circle (see par. 4). This collation mark (*ʿalāmat al-balāgh*) was very much part and parcel of the circle and the early *samāʿ*-sessions. It is for this reason, therefore, that the *dārah* was referred to as *ijāzah*[56]. Another way of indicating that the text was collated was by writing the word *balagha* or *balaghat* or *balagha al-ʿarḍ*. And if the collation was made during an audition of *ḥadīth*, the expression *balagha fī al-miʿād al-awwal* or *al-thānī* etc. would be used. Al-Shahīd al-Thānī adds that it was better if the *balāgh*-note was written by the shaykh[57].

48) Al-Khaṭīb al-Baghdādī, *al-Jāmiʿ*, v. 1, p. 262.

49) Al-Khaṭīb al-Baghdādī, ibid., v. 1, pp. 261-262; Ibn al-Ṣalāḥ, op. cit., pp. 99-100; al-Ghazzī, op. cit., fol. 153a-154b; al-ʿAlmawī, op. cit., pp. 138-139.

50) For the different explanations of what the *ḥā'* stands for, see in particular Ibn al-Ṣalāḥ, loc. cit. and al-Ghazzī, loc. cit.

51) Al-Ghazzī, loc. cit. There is no mention of abbreviations in al-Shahīd al-Thānī's *Munyat al-murīd*. A more extensive list of abbreviations found in manuscripts of Shiite provenance is included in Gacek, *Catalogue*, v. 2, pp. xiii-xiv. See also Jamāl al-Dīn al-Qāsimī, *Qawāʿid al-taḥdīth min funūn muṣṭalaḥ al-ḥadīth* (Damascus, 1352/1935), pp. 229-230, giving the *rumūz* used by Ibn Ḥajar al-ʿAsqalānī in his *Taqrīb al-tadhhīb* and al-Suyūṭī in his *al-Jāmiʿ al-kabīr* and *al-Jāmiʿ al-ṣaghīr*.

52) The word *muʿāraḍah* (also *ʿarḍ, ʿarḍah, ʿirāḍ, ʿirāḍah*) signifies, according to *ḥadīth*-scholars, a presentation of a text by a pupil personally to the author or shaykh, either through recitation or reading (*al-qirā'ah ʿalā al-shaykh*, see e.g. Marçais, *Taqrīb*, p. 105, n. 3). *Sard*, by contrast, is a type of *qirā'ah* effected either by the *shaykh al-musmiʿ* or the *qāriʿ* (prelector) without going into the linguistic or other analysis of the text (see al-Qāsimī, ibid., p. 221). The word *muqābalah* is very often used as a synonym of *muʿāraḍah*, though strictly speaking it is a broader term relating to a collation with the exemplar not necessarily in the presence of a shaykh. Note the phrase "*Idhā suḥḥiḥa al-kitāb bi-al-muqābalah ʿalā aṣlihi aw ʿalā al-shaykh...*" (al-Ghazzī, op. cit., fol. 148a).

53) Al-Samʿānī, *Adab al-imlā'*, pp. 77-79; al-Rāmahurmuzī, *al-Muḥaddith al-fāṣil*, p. 544; al-Khaṭīb al-Baghdādī, *al-Kifāyah*, pp. 315-318; al-Ghazzī, *al-Durr al-naḍīd*, fol. 148a. On the value of manuscript collation in Islamic literature, however, see Rosenthal, *Technique*, p. 31.

54) Ibn al-Ṣalāḥ, op. cit., pp. 92-94; see also al-Yaḥṣubī, *al-Ilmāʿ*, pp. 158-161; Ibn Jamāʿah, *Tadhirat al-sāmiʿ*, p. 180; *idem*, *al-Manhal al-rawī*, p. 102; al-Suyūṭī, *Tadrīb al-rāwī*, pp. 77-79; al-Khaṭīb al-Baghdādī, *al-Jāmiʿ*, v. 1, pp. 275-276.

55) Al-Ghazzī, op. cit., fol. 147b-148a; al-Shahīd al-Thānī, op. cit., p. 186. A good example of this is the text of al-Ghazzī reproduced in the Appendix.

56) Al-Khaṭīb al-Baghdādī, op. cit., v. 1, p. 274.

57) Al-Ghazzī, op. cit., fol. 152b; al-Shahīd al-Thānī, op. cit., p. 186. Al-Khaṭīb al-Baghdādī (loc. cit.) also reports: "*Kāna Zuhayr ibn Muʿāwiyah idhā samiʿa al-ḥadīth marratayn kataba ʿalayhi qad faraghtu*". Other expressions used in this connection are *qūbila* and *ʿūriḍa*. The *balāgh*-note often indicates the mode in which collation was made, for example, *muqābalatan, qibālan, qirā'atan, baḥthan, fahman, samāʿan, darsan, taṣḥīḥan, ḍabṭan, iʿrāban* (see e.g. Gacek, *Catalogue*, v. 2, p. xii).

8. Diacritical marks and vowelisation

The most common mistakes made in Arabic manuscripts are termed *taḥrīf* and *taṣḥīf*, that is a misplacement of either vowels or diacritical marks, or an outright misspelling. In order to avoid them the copyist is instructed to point (*naqṭ, iʿjām*) and vocalise (*shakl, iʿrāb*), in the first place, those words which were unclear or ambiguous, and proper names. For many a scholar the pointing of letters was not enough. The pointed letters (*al-ḥurūf al-muʿjamah, al-muʿjamāt*) were often distinguished from the unpointed ones (*al-ḥurūf al-muhmalah, al-muhmalāt*), by providing the latter category with an additional sign called *ʿalāmat al-ihmāl*. The texts under discussion record the following practices of indicating a *muhmal*-letter:

a) placing a dot under the letter (with the exception of the letter *ḥā'*, which, when pointed in this way, becomes *jīm*). For the letter *sīn* three dots were written under its "teeth", either in a row or like this: ∵
b) writing a miniature version of the same letter, either under it or in the loop of its descender,
c) writing above the letter a small mark, resembling a crescent (*hilāl*) or a nail-clipping (*qulāmat al-ẓufr*),
d) writing above the letter a small sign (*khaṭṭ ṣaghīr*) resembling a *fatḥah*,
e) placing a small *hamzah* (*nabrah*) above the letter[58].

To this list al-Ghazzī adds the writing of a small *kāf* or *hamzah* in the medial form of the letter *kāf* and the writing of *lam* (*lam, alif* and *mīm*) in the letter *lam*, since the *kāf* was often written without the stroke on its ascender and could thus be confused with *lām*[59].

9. Corrections and emendations

One of the ways of indicating an error (*khaṭa', ghalaṭ*) and making a correction (*taṣḥīḥ, iṣlāḥ*) is by writing a small *kadhā* (i.e. sic) in the body of the text, and *ṣawābuhu kadhā* (if the correction is certain) or *laʿalluhu kadhā* (if a conjecture) in the margin[60]. The correction which is beyond doubt can also be indicated by placing the word *ṣaḥḥa* above or next to it. The *ṣaḥḥa* becomes thus a correction mark (*ʿalāmat al-taṣḥīḥ*). In other words, the *ṣaḥḥa* signifies that the word which it accompanies is correct as regards its meaning and transmission, even though there may appear to be some doubt about it. Al-Qāḍī ʿIyāḍ and Ibn al-Ṣalāḥ inform us that any doubtful or incorrect words or passages, whether found in the original composition or a copy, and irrespective of the fact that their transmission has been established, should be indicated by putting a "bolt" (*ḍabbah*) over them[61]. The *ḍabbah*, also known as *ʿalāmat al-taḍbīb* or *al-tamrīḍ*, looks like the initial *ṣād* with a prolonged horizontal stroke (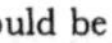). It should be written above the word (without touching it), so as not to confuse it with a cancellation mark (see par. 11). This process is called *taḍbīb* or *tamrīḍ*, the latter clearly implying that the word in question may be corrupt. Al-Qāḍī ʿIyāḍ and others quote the philologian Abū al-Qāsim Ibrāhīm ibn Muḥammad, known as Ibn al-Iflīlī (d. 441/1049), who gives the following definition of the *ḍabbah*: "Like the door-bolt, [this mark] locks the word, thus preventing its reading"[62].

Because of the resemblance of the *ḍabbah* to the initial form of the letter *ṣād*, this mark was regarded by some as an abbreviated form of *ṣaḥḥa*. It is for this reason that Ibn Jamāʿah, al-Ghazzī and others instruct the pupil to add the letter *ḥā'* to it when it is to be confirmed that this is the correct version of the word, otherwise the correct version should be written in the margin[63]. Both al-Ghazzī and al-Shahīd al-Thānī add that instead of the *ṣād* (*al-ṣād al-muhmalah*), a *ḍād* (*al-ṣād al-muʿjamah*), an abbreviation of *ḍabbabtuhu*, could be used[64].

Letters are normally pointed in the next. However, for greater clarity, or because of the lack of space bet-

58) Al-Rāmahurmuzī, *al-Muḥaddith al-fāṣil*, pp. 608-609; al-Khaṭīb al-Baghdādī, *al-Jāmiʿ*, v. 1, pp. 269-270, 276; al-Samʿānī, *Adab al-imlā'*, pp. 171-172; Ibn Jamāʿah, *Tadhkirat al-sāmiʿ*, pp. 180-182; al-Ghazzī, *al-Durr al-naḍīd*, fol. 148a-149b.

59) Al-Ghazzī, ibid., fol. 149b. See also al-Qalqashandī, *Ṣubḥ al-aʿshā*, v. 3, pp. 149-167, who gives the Maghribi orthography of the letter *fā'* (written with one dot underneath) and *qāf* (one dot above). For other practices see e.g. W. Wright, *A grammar of the Arabic language*, 3rd ed. (London, 1979), p. 4.

60) Ibn Jamāʿah, *Tadhkirat al-sāmiʿ*, p. 182; al-Ghazzī, op. cit., fol. 149b; al-Shahīd al-Thānī, op. cit., p. 182. *Laʿallahu kadhā* and *kadhā fī al-aṣl* are sometimes abbreviated in the margin *as ʿayn and kāf* respectively (see ʿAbd al-Salām Hārūn, *Taḥqīq al-nuṣūṣ wa-nashruhā*, Kuwait, 1969, p. 52).

61) Al-Yaḥṣubī, *al-Ilmaʿ*, pp. 166-169; Ibn al-Ṣalāḥ *Muqaddimah*, pp. 95-96.

62) Al-Yaḥsubī, ibid., p. 169. Ibn al-Iflīlī's explanation of *ṣaḥḥa* and *ḍabbah* is also reported by Yāqūt ibn ʿAbd Allāh al-Ḥamawī (d. 626/1228) in his *Muʿjam al-udabā'* (Cairo, n.d.), v. 2, pp. 5-6. Yāqūt also informs us of the practice of ʿAlī ibn Muḥammad al-Asadī, known as Ibn al-Kūfī (d. 343/959), who wrote *ṣaḥḥa* several times above a doubtful word ("*Wa-yaktub ʿalā al-kalimah al-shukūk fīhā ʿiddat mirār ṣaḥḥa ṣaḥḥa sahha*" - ibid., v. 14, pp. 153-154).

63) Ibn Jamāʿah, op. cit., p. 182; al-Ghazzī, op. cit., fol. 149b-150a; al-ʿAlmawī, op. cit., p. 136; al-Shahīd al-Thānī, op. cit., p. 182.

64) Clearly, the *ṣaḥḥa* and *ṣād* (or *ḍabbah*) may, in some cases, take on the function similar to the above-mentioned *kadhā*. Additionally, the letter *ṣād*, when accompanying a word in the margin, can be used instead of *ṣaḥḥa* for a certain correction such as an insertion (see par. 10), or as a conjecture. In the latter case it is synonymous with the letter *ẓā'*, which is usually explained as standing for *ẓann* (*aẓunn*) or *ẓāhir* (see G. Endress, "Handschriftenkunde", *Grundriss der arabischen Philologie*, Band I, herausgegeben von W. Fischer, Wiesbaden, 1982, p. 285; Gacek, *Catalogue*, v. 1, pp. xiv-xv, v. 2, pp. 12-13; Hārūn, *Taḥqīq*, p. 52).

ween the lines, one can repeat the relevant word in the margin in its correct form, either by writing it out using the unconnected forms of the letters, or spelling it out using correct appellations of individual letters (e.g. *al-ḥā' al-muhmalah wa-al-bā' al-muwaḥḥadah wa-al-thā' al-muthallathah*). It is also recommendable to repeat in the margin those words which were smudged or clumsily written. If the word has thus been explained in the margin, it ought to be accompanied by the word *bayān* or the letter *nūn*[65].

10. Omissions and insertions

Words omitted in the process of transcription (*saqaṭ, isqāṭ, naqṣ*) should be inserted between the lines, if space allows, or written in the margin (*takhrīj*). The omission thus restored becomes in effect an insertion (*laḥaq*)[66]. Al-Ghazzī instructs the copyist to use the right-hand margin for this purpose. The left-hand margin should be used for those omissions which occur towards the end of the line. The writing of the *laḥaq*, whether in the right- or left-hand margin, ought to proceed upwards, from the line of omission, in view of the fact that if there is another insertion to be made, there may not be enough space left for it. The words should be counted, and if they add up to more than two lines they should be written from the upper margin (*ṭurrah*) downwards[67].

There were different practices for indicating the end of an insertion. Al-Rāmahurmuzī, for example, advocates the writing of the next word in the line, thus connecting the insertion with the place of omission[68]. Ibn al-Ṣalāḥ opposes this practice, saying that it is an "erroneous extension" (*taṭwīl mūham*)[69]. Al-Qāḍi ʿIyāḍ adds to it other practices, such as the writing of *ṣaḥḥa, ṣaḥḥa rujiʿa, rujiʿa*, and *intahā al-laḥaq*[70]. But others wrote *ṣaḥḥa* and the next word in the line. This practice met with the approval of al-Ghazzī, who advocates the use of *ṣaḥḥa*, or better still, its abbreviated form (*taṣghīr*), namely *ṣād*[71].

In order to indicate the place in the line where the omission occurred (*mawḍiʿ al-naqṣ, mawḍiʿ al-sāqiṭ*) a reference mark (*khaṭṭ al-takhrīj, ʿalāmat al-takhrīj, takhrījah*) is necessary. Al-Rāmahurmuzī advocates the use of a line linking the place of omission with the insertion. This method, however, was disliked by al-Qāḍī ʿIyāḍ and Ibn al-Ṣalāḥ, who rightly point out that it was not satisfactory as it could obscure the text, particularly if many insertions were to be made[72]. The best way is to draw a small line (*ʿaṭfah*) from the place of omission upwards, curving towards the insertion and thus indicating its position in the margin (⌝ or ⌜)[73]. The drawing of a line linking the insertion with the right place in the text may be necessary, however, if the insertion is placed not on the line where the omission occured, but in some other part of the margin. In this case, says al-Ghazzī, instead of drawing a line, one can write "*yatlūhu kadhā fī al-maḥall al-fulānī*". The omission mark should be placed between the words and not on the word, as the latter could indicate a variant reading (*ikhtilāf al-riwāyah, ikhtilāf al-nuskhah*), error or gloss[74].

11. Erasures and cancellations

Superfluous words (*ziyādah, takrār*) can be removed by means of:

a) *kashṭ*, i.e. erasure with a penknife, also known as *bashr* (scraping) or *ḥakk* (rubbing). This method is preferable for e.g. removing a diacritical point (*nuqṭah*) or vowel (*shaklah*). It was discouraged, however, by many early authorities on the grounds that what was erased may turn out to be correct in another recension (*riwāyah ukhrā*)[75].

b) *maḥw*, i.e. obliteration or removing the ink by means other than a penknife, for example a cloth eraser (*khir-*

65) Ibn Jamāʿah, *Tadhkirat al-sāmiʿ*, p. 181; al-Ghazzī, *Al-Durr al-naḍīd*, fol. 148b-149a; al-ʿAlmawī, *al-Muʿīd*, p. 136; al-Shahīd al-Thānī, *Munyat al-murīd*, p. 181.

66) The word *takhrīj* (also *ikhrāj, mukhraj*) is primarily associated with omissions/insertions and thus synonymous with *laḥaq* (also *ilḥāq, mulḥaq*). E. Fagnan (*Additions aux dictionnaires arabes*, Beirut, n.d., p. 44) defines *kharraja* as "*rejeter en marge, en note*", hence *takhrījah* (ibid., p. 45), "note marginale".

67) See in particular Ibn Jamāʿah, op. cit., pp. 185-186; al-Ghazzī, op. cit., fol. 151b-152b; and Ibn ʿArḍūn, *al-Lā'iq*, pp. [40-41]. In diplomatic and epistolography the word *ṭurrah* (pl. *ṭurar*) means the matter preceding the *basmalah* (see J.S. Nielsen, "A note on the origin of the ṭurra in early Mamluk chancery practice", *Der Islam*, 57, 1980, p. 288. In the Maghribi usage *ṭurrah* also means a margin (not necessarily an upper margin) or gloss, and is thus synonymous with *ḥāshiyah* or *hāmish*. According to ʿAbd al-Karīm al-Amīn, it also means "the title-page" of a manuscript (*ṣafḥat ʿunwān al-makhṭūṭ*), see his "Mulāḥaẓāt fī qawāʿid fahrasat al-makhṭūṭāt", *al-Mawrid*, 5 (1976), p. 154.

68) Al-Rāmahurmuzī, *al-Muḥaddith al-fāṣil*, pp. 606-607; al-Khaṭīb al-Baghdādī, *al-Jāmiʿ*, v. 1, pp. 278-279.

69) Ibn al-Ṣalāḥ, *Muqaddimmah*, pp. 94-95.

70) Al-Yaḥṣubī, *al-Ilmāʿ*, pp. 162-165.

71) Al-Ghazzī, *al-Durr al-naḍīd*, fol. 152b. Other ways of indicating the end of an insertion are, for example, writing the word *aṣl*, *ṣaḥḥa aṣl*, or *ṣaḥḥa matn* (see Hārūn, *Taḥqīq*, p. 51; J.J. Witkam, *Seven specimens of Arabic manuscripts*, Leiden, 1978, p. 4).

72) Al-Rāmahurmuzī, op. cit., pp. 606-607; al-Yaḥṣubī, op. cit., pp. 162-165; Ibn al-Salāḥ, op. cit., pp. 94-95.

73) In later manuscripts we often find what looks like an inverted caret (∨ , see e.g. Gacek, *Catalogue*, v. 1, p. xv and v. 2, p. xiii). Caret is the Latin for "it needs", and was used in medieval European manuscripts (and now in proof-reading) to mark a place in the line of text where something was to be inserted. Compare also the use of a similar mark to indicate a *muhmal*-letter (see par. 8).

74) Ibn al-Ṣalāh, op. cit., p. 94; al-Ghazzī, op. cit., fol. 154b.

75) Al-Ghazzī, op. cit., fol. 150a-151b; al-Yaḥṣubī, op. cit., pp. 170-173; Ibn al-Ṣalāḥ, op. cit., pp. 96-98; Al-Rāmahurmuzī, op. cit., pp. 607-608.

qah) or by licking when the ink is still moist. Ibn al-Ṣalāḥ and al-Ghazzī quote Ibrāhīm al-Nakhaᶜī (d. 96/714) as saying, "One of the traits of manliness is the ink on a man's clothes and lips"[76]. This method is better than the *kashṭ* as it inflicts less damage on the writing surface.

c) *ḍarb*, i.e. cancellation. This method is better than the previous two and can be effected in the following ways:
- by drawing a continuous line (*khaṭṭ mumtadd, khaṭṭ muttaṣil*) over the word(s) to be cancelled, known in the Maghreb as *al-shaqq*.
- by drawing, in a similar fashion, an interrupted line (*khaṭṭ munfaṣil*). Al-Rāmahurmuzī says that the best way is to draw a line above the word, without touching it, so that it is still possible to read it[77].
- by drawing a line curved at both ends, resembling an inverted *bā'*.
- by writing the words *lā* (or *min*, or both: *lā min*) above the beginning of the cancellation, and the word *ilā* at the end of it.
- by placing at the beginning and the end of the cancellation a semi-circle (*nisf al-dā'irah*) and thus putting the word(s) to be cancelled in "parentheses" (*taḥwīq*). If there is not enough space between the words, the *taḥwīq* should be placed above the line.
- by placing a zero (*ṣifr*) at the beginning and the end of the cancellation. The *ṣifr* should be put above the line if there is not enough space.
- by writting a dotted line (*nuqaṭ mutatāliyah*) above the cancellation[78].

The use of some of these methods of cancellation was disapproved of. For example, it was thought that the semi-circle could be confused with the letter *dāl* or an omission mark, or the zero could be taken for the letter *hā'* or the circle (i.e. the punctuation-mark). If the word or passage was cancelled by mistake, the word *ṣaḥḥa* should be written at the beginning and the end of the cancellation, or next to the struck out cancellation-marks[79].

12. Variant readings

After having copied the *matn* of the work based on a particular recension (*riwāyah khāṣṣah*), says Ibn al-Ṣalāḥ, any additions or interpolations (*ziyādah*), omissions (*naqṣ*) and variants (*khilāf al-kutub*) found in other recensions should be indicated in the margin or elsewhere, specifying the full name of the transmitter (*rāwin*)[80]. If abbreviated forms of transmitters' names are used, they ought to be spelled out either at the beginning or the end of the book. The use of abbreviations (*rumūz*) is necessary if there are many recensions of the same work.

One way of distinguishing a different *riwāyah* was to write the variant in red ink (*ḥumrah*). Ibn al-Ṣalāḥ informs us that this was, for example, the practice of Abū Dharr al-Harawī (d. 434/1043) and Abū al-Ḥasan al-Qābisī (d. 403/1012). He adds that if the other recension contained an addition it should be written in red, and if the addition or omission was to be found in the *riwāyah* chosen for copying it ought to be placed in "round brackets" (*ḥawwaqa*) written in red[81].

13. Glosses and scholia

Glosses and annotations (*ḥawāshin, fawā'id, tanbīhāt*) concerning mistakes, variants and the like, say Ibn Jamāᶜah and al-Ghazzī, may be written in the margin[82]. Margins should not be obscured by strange and irrelevant notes, they add. The end of a gloss should not be indicated by writing *ṣaḥḥa*. Instead, a circle (*dārah*) can be used for this purpose[83]. The reference mark ought to be written above the word concerned and not between the words, and can, for example, be a numeral. This is in order to distinguish a gloss from an insertion (see par. 10). Glosses are often indicated by writing above them or at their ends *ḥāshiyah, fā'idah*, the letter *ḥā'* (initial form) or *ḥā'* and *shīn* (joined together)[84].

76) Ibn al-Ṣalāḥ, op. cit., p. 98; al-Ghazzī, op. cit., fol. 150a-150b.

77) Al-Rāmahurmuzī, op. cit., p. 606; same in al-Khaṭīb al-Baghdādī, op. cit., v. 1, p. 278.

78) A combination of both a dotted line and a continuous line was also used (see Ibn Jamāᶜah, *Tadhkirat al-sāmiᶜ*, p. 185, n. 1). For the above practices see also al-ᶜAlmawī, op. cit., pp. 136-137; al-Shahīd al-Thānī, op. cit., pp. 182-184; Ibn al-Manṣūr bi-Allāh al-Qāsim, *Adāb al-ᶜulamā'*, p. 96.

79) For this and other rules governing cancellations see al-Ghazzī, op. cit., fol. 151a-151b and al-Shadīd al-Thānī, op. cit., p. 184. One other category of common mistake made in transcribing manuscripts is transposition (*al-taqdīm wa-al-ta'khīr*). Although mentioned by al-Rāmahurmuzī, al-Qāḍī ᶜIyāḍ and others, it is not discussed in any detail. Transpositions are usually indicated by the letters *khā'* (*mu'akhkhar*), *qāf* (*muqaddam* or *qablā*), *mīm* (*muqaddam*), *mīm mīm* (for both *muqaddam* and *mu'akhkhar*) or *bā'* (*baᶜdu*). See e.g. Wright, *Grammar*, pp. 25-26; Hārūn, *Taḥqīq*, p. 52; Gacek, *Catalogue*, v. 1, p. xv; M. Ben Cheneb, "Liste des abréviations employées par les auteurs arabes", *Revue africaine*, 302-303 (1920), pp. 134-138.

80) Ibn al-Ṣalāḥ, *Muqaddimah*, pp. 98-99. No other text used for this paper discusses variant readings, neither is there any mention of abbreviations used to indicate a variant. We know, however, that the use of e.g. *khā'*, *lām*, and *khā' lām* (for *nuskhah ukhrā*, *badal* and *nuskhah badal* respectively) is very common in this connection (see Gacek, *Catalogue*, v. 1, p. xv and v. 2, p. xiii).

81) Ibn al-Ṣalāḥ, ibid., pp. 99. For a discussion on variants see also Rosenthal, *Technique*, pp. 30-31.

82) Ibn Jamāᶜh, *Tadhkirat al-sāmiᶜ*, pp. 186-191; al-Ghazzī, *al-Durr al-naḍīd*, fol. 154b.

83) Ibn al-Manṣūr bi-Allāh al-Qāsim, *Adāb al-ᶜulamā'*, p. 97. The *dārah* in this case is most certainly the letter *hā'*, an abbreviation of *intahā*. For other practices see Gacek, *Catalogue*, v. 2, p. xiii).

84) Al-Ghazzī, op. cit., fol. 154b; al-Shahīd al-Thānī, op. cit., p. 187. In Maghribi manuscripts, it is the letter *ṭā'* (for *ṭurrah*, i.e. gloss) which is used for this purpose.

Appendix

Al-Bāb al-sādis min al-Durr al-naḍīd
lil-ʿAllāmah Badr al-Dīn al-Ghazzī
(MS, Princeton 1375)*

Pl. XX B - XXXII B

Al-Durr al-naḍīd forms part of a composite volume, which contains two other works of al-Ghazzī copied in the same hand, namely *Sharḥ al-raḥbīyah fī al-farāʾiḍ* (fol. 1a-30b) and *al-Marāḥ fī al-muzāḥ* (fol. 31a-53b). The *Durr al-naḍīd* begins on fol. 54a and ends abruptly on fol. 162b. Although Chapter Six is complete, the work itself is imperfect, containing a number of lacunae. The manuscript was copied around 947/1540-1 (not 927 as in Mach's *Catalogue*), which is the date of copying of *Sharḥ al-raḥbīyah* (see fol. 30a). The name of the copyist is contained in several collation statements (e.g. fols. 10b, 40b, 53b, 72b) written in the author's hand. It is given as Shams al-Dīn ibn al-Rajīḥī. The author's signature can be seen at the end of a collation statement given on fol. 53b, on the right-hand side of the colophon. The statement runs as follows:
Al-ḥamd lil-Lāh// balagha kātibuhu al-Shaykh al-ʿÂlim Shams al-Dīn ibn al-Rajīḥī// nafaʿa Allāh bihim qirāʾatan ʿalayya wa-muqābalatan// bi-al-aṣl kh [katabahu] muʾallifuhu Muḥammad ibn Muḥammad ibn Muḥammad// al-Ghazzī al-ʿÂmirī al-Shāfiʿī ʿafā Allāh ʿanhum// wa-ʿan sāʾir al-muslimīn wa-al-ḥamd lil-Lāh wa-ṣallā Allāh ʿalā Muḥammad wa-sallam.

* See R. March, *Catalogue of Arabic manuscripts (Yahuda Section) in the Garret collection, Princeton University Library* (Princeton, 1977), no. 29. Published with permission of Princeton University Library.

[8]

The copyists' working pace: Some remarks towards a reflexion on the economy of the book in the Islamic world

François Déroche

> Les copistes sont en grand nombre en Perse, surtout dans les grandes villes; mais le métier leur donne à peine du pain; ils n'y gagnent d'ordinaire que 15 sols par jour, à écrire du matin jusqu'au soir. Le plus qu'on puisse écrire, quand on est très expert et qu'on travaille sans interruption, est de cinq à six cents distiques par jour ... [Le plus grand inconvénient] consiste en la multiplication des fautes, qui souvent sont telles, qu'on ne trouve point de sens à ce qu'on lit. Ces fautes arrivent par l'ignorance des copistes, et par leur inattention, à force d'aller vite, en ne prenant pas garde à leur original, et en ne relisant pas.[1]

From these remarks by Chardin who travelled to Persia during the 18th century, it appears that the speed with which the scribes were working was not without consequences on the transmission of the texts. Within the scope of this conference, I felt that this topic could be addressed, since the actual conditions of the copyists' work and more generally the whole economy of the handwritten book should not be neglected by the philologist. In some instances, they might even provide him with a clue for what he is actually seeing on the manuscript.

At the beginning of the Islamic period, scholars started discussing whether it was lawful or not to receive wages for the copying of the text of the Qur'ān:[2] professional copyists, that is persons making a living out of the copying of texts, were already at work and their work was perceived as part of the economic sphere. The speed with which they were copying became obviously part of the issue. That this question was addressed at an early date makes one hopeful that data relating to the cost of the copy, to the price of the books and so on would have been collected over a long period of time and duly commented upon by scholars. Unfortunately, things evolved differently and, as we shall see, information about the wages of the professionals who were transcribing texts are lacking, and that about the organisation of their work is very limited and scattered. Understanding how professional copyists were working will certainly take much more time and effort; I shall limit myself here to a low-key approach of the pace with which the texts were written, that is only a part of the larger question of the economy of the book. I only intend to offer a few comments on the conditions under which the copyists were working and on the sources available to estimate their working pace.

---

1 Chardin 1811, 281-282.

2 Ibn Abī Da'ūd, *Kitāb al-maṣāḥif,* 131-133.

In order to answer the latter question, one has first to note that all copyists were not working under the same conditions. Among those who contributed to the enormous handwritten heritage of the Islamic world, some were earning a living by copying texts for paying customers whereas others were amateurs transcribing texts for their own use, or for a relative or a friend.[3] This does not mean that the quality of the copies made by copyists belonging to the latter group was always inferior, as far as writing is concerned for instance. Since one of the goals of classical education was precisely to achieve a certain level of proficiency in calligraphy, it is no wonder that copies made by 'amateurs' for their own use reached sometimes very high standards. But time was not a factor as important for them as it was for those who were expecting some money for their work – and Chardin's text indicates that they were in a real predicament in the 18th century. It is to this group that we shall devote our attention, as far as we can identify them: a scholar or a student who was earning a living in this way could also make copies for private use, becoming 'amateur' for a while. In later times, we know instances of this kind, but when we rely only on the colophons to decide if the manuscript was the work of a professional or not, things tend to become difficult.

Working conditions are influencing heavily the copying pace: we shall briefly recall some of the most obvious factors, beginning with a definition of the sources used. Quite often, the manuscripts we are dealing with are the result of the transcription from an original which the copyist had in front of him; this 'normal' situation becomes sometimes more 'real' when the colophon describes his model.[4] Anyhow, copying is not reproducing exactly the original: it is indeed unusual to find copies of the same work with identical features (page setting, for instance) on each single page. In the introduction to this translation of the *Fihrist*, Bayard Dodge wrote: "Arabic scholars have explained that when a medieval scribe copied a manuscript he reproduced not only the words, but also the handwriting of the author and the arrangement of the page."[5] This remark was probably an explanation of the note found on the oldest extant copy of Ibn al-Nadīm's work, ms Dublin, CBL 3315, where a note (*ḥikāya khaṭṭ al-muṣannif*) found on the title page of various chapters suggests that the copy was a facsimile. However, this situation is quite exceptional and in fact we can wonder whether the note was not meant to enhance the value of the manuscript. For the copyist, trying to reproduce the script or the layout would obviously have been an hindering factor. An opposite situation has been analysed by Michele Bernardini who suggested that copies of Hātifī's work were customized, the work being adapted to the particular wishes of the patron – in this case affluent people but

3 Cf. for instance *FiMMOD* n° 40, 55, 56, 57...
4 Şeşen 1997, 202-203, n° 24, 26, 27; see also Rosenthal 1947, 23.
5 Dodge 1970, XXVII.

in no way high-ranking individuals.[6] Under such circumstances, the work would have been obviously slower.

Copyists are not only relying on written models. Dictation also played a role as shown by an anecdote about al-Farrā' (died 207/822): during public talks, he was transmitting the text of a *tafsīr* while two *warrāq* were writing down his words.[7] Colophons actually note that the text was dictated by a transmitter, as is the case in a manuscript dated 649/1251 now in Tashkent.[8] In our first example, it is evident that professional copyists, here *warrāq*, were working in this way. We also have to take into account that in a society which was giving a very important role to the memory in the educational process, some copyists knew by heart the text they were transcribing, the more so when they were copying it frequently. The case of the Qur'ān is particularly interesting in this respect. And to make things more simple, the possibility of a double source (dictation and copy from a model) should not be left aside.

Economic factors also influenced the pace of the work: time is money and affluent patrons could spend money in order to have a copyist devote the time needed for the best result. There are many anecdotes about famous calligraphers spending much time in order to copy a text – even if things may have been quite different in real life. According to D. James, between twelve and eighteen months were needed in order to complete the first seven *juz'* of the Qur'ān which Öljeytü had ordered for his mausoleum.[9] But this example is very far from the daily experience of the common copyist in the Islamic world.

One also has to take into account the possible team work, which completely altered the pace of the copying process – either working in turns, or dividing the copy between people working simultaneously. In the great majority of the cases, copying was a solitary experience: the same man or woman usually transcribed the text by him or herself from beginning to end. But instances of collective work do exist, even if it is sometimes difficult to reach a certainty when there is no colophon. When dealing with copies of the highest calligraphic level, there may be a doubt. One of the goals of the student calligrapher was to reproduce the script of his master:[10] the great Egyptian calligrapher Ibn al-Waḥīd, in the 7th/13th century, had his students copy the text, then added his name at the end; they received almost nothing from him, but he was paid huge fees by the patron.

---

6 Paper on "Late Timurid literary patronage" read during the conference on *Le patronage dans la culture indo-persane*, Paris, 21-23 March 2001.

7 Pedersen 1984, 45.

8 *FiMMOD* n° 250 (IOB 3105).

9 James 1988, 95.

10 See for instance Déroche 1995, 83.

As recalled by Rosemarie Quiring-Zoche[11] or Ayman Fu'ād Sayyid,[12] instances of team work are rather numerous, even in the earliest period. Two fragments in the *ḥijāzī* style, one in Sanaa,[13] the other one in Paris,[14] were respectively transcribed by three and by two persons; in both cases, the various copyists did not even bother to find a common style. Later manuscripts of an ordinary level of craftsmanship may also be the result of team work: a copy of the *Wiqāya* by Maḥbūb b. Ṣadr al-Sharī'a is particularly interesting in this respect. In 996/1587, 25 copyists started working jointly in Focha:[15] they seem to have been all 'amateurs,' but the same situation on a more limited scale may have occurred in workshops.

There is a last element which should also be investigated, since it may have been interfering with the pace of the copying process. In the BNF collection, an 'Abd al-Wāḥid b. Mawlānā 'Arab Marvdashī transcribed twice the same historical text, while Mirzā 'Alī b. Muẓaffar Ja'far Kātib Khātūnābādī copied an impressive list of historical texts between 1588 and 1627.[16] Were both men copyists specialised in historical works? Were there in the Islamic world copyists who were specialists of certain texts? This of course has been the case with the Qur'ānic manuscripts, but it might have happened with other texts.

Where did our copyists work? Here again, a wide range of situations can be identified. The workshop/studio close to the royal patron is well attested in the sources and the manuscripts. Integrated commercial workshops like those of Shīrāz in the 10th/16th century are for the moment an isolated instance: "in every house of this city the wife is a copyist, the husband a miniaturist, the daughter an illuminator and the son a binder; thus any kind of book can be produced within one family."[17] But the trades involved in the process suggest that the Shīrāzī workshops were producing only higher quality manuscripts; were the texts accurately transcribed or were the conditions so poor that the books were full of errors, like those in Chardin's time?

Copyists were usually working alone, in a variety of places.[18] For many professional copyists, home or possibly a small shop was the working place. Quite a few colophons witness this situation: for instance, a section of the *Jāmi' al-ṣaḥīḥ* was completed by Aḥmad b. Muḥammad ... al-Wadī-Ashī in his house, close to

---

11 Quiring-Zoche 2003.

12 See his paper in this volume.

13 DAM Inv. 01-25-1 (*Maṣāḥif Ṣan'ā'* 1985, 60).

14 BNF Arabe 328a (Déroche 1983, 59-60, n° 2; see the facsimile Déroche & Noja Noseda 1998).

15 Ms Sarajevo, HBB 142, 155-159 (Dobraca 1972).

16 I owe this example to F. Richard – to whom I express my thanks. It is illustrated, *inter alia*, by the mss Paris BNF Suppl. persan 225 and 164.

17 Akimushkin & Ivanov 1979, 50.

18 See a short survey in Déroche *et al.* 2000, 204-209.

the Great Mosque in Almeria, in 723/1323.[19] Texts also document situations of this kind: Yāqūt tells of Ibrāhīm al-Ḥarbī who was spending his time meditating and transcribing texts in his poor dwelling.[20]

A first answer to our question about the copyists' pace can be gleaned in the texts. According to biographical sources, Ibn al-Jawzī is said to have covered daily four quires with his writing, some sources even stating that it was actually nine quires;[21] but the man being also an author, it is difficult to distinguish between his work as a copyist and that of original literary composition. Not unfrequently, the treatises on calligraphy record the number of Qur'āns and/or of other texts which were transcribed by such and such calligrapher during his life. al-Zabīdī's *Ḥikmat al-ishrāq* which was written towards the middle of the 12th/18th century took over a fair amount of information from an Ottoman model as yet unidentified.[22] Some of the entries include the number of Qur'āns written by a calligrapher, but always remain vague about other texts (either Qur'ānic extracts or devotional works); the only exception in the latter case being Şeyh Hamdullah who is said to have copied thousand books of this kind.[23] Are the figures reliable? A closer look shows that the same Şeyh Hamdullah transcribed 44 Qur'āns, but Derviş Ali, nicknamed 'the second Şeyh' wrote significantly enough twice as much, that is 88![24] A few lines later we even hear that this 88th Qur'ān was in fact completed by a student of Derviş Ali, Ismail Efendi Halife, who was himself responsible for 44 copies of the text.[25] A Ramazan b. Ismail is even said to have produced 360 Qur'āns![26] From the generation after Şeyh Hamdullah, Muhyi al-Din Celal-zade transcribed 97 times the Qur'ān, Hüsam al-Din Halife 89 and Recep Halife 93.[27]

When we turn to the period closer to the author's time, we find that Ahmad Ef. Kazancizade only wrote 19 Qur'āns and Ahmad Ef. Şeyhzade 17.[28] al-Zabīdī's almost contemporary Ḥusayn Ef. al-Jazā'irī wrote a Qur'ān in 30 *juz'* and 2 one-volume Qur'āns;[29] he even started writing the third when he died, so that it was left to his pupil, Ḥasan al-Ḍiyā'ī to complete it.[30] From this short sample, we can conclude first that figures were obviously important to people interested in calligraphy; they conveyed information which helped estimating a calligrapher's

19 *The Qur'an* 1999, 40, n° 20.
20 *Kitāb al-irshād*, 39.
21 Hartmann 1989, 25; Ibn Khallikān, 141.
22 al-Zabīdī, 62-98.
23 al-Zabīdī, 89.
24 al-Zabīdī, 92.
25 al-Zabīdī, 93.
26 al-Zabīdī, 92.
27 al-Zabīdī, 89 and 90.
28 al-Zabīdī, 93 and 94.
29 al-Zabīdī, 94.
30 al-Zabīdī, 94.

status. They were then to some extent symbolic as indicated by some of the figures. They were however not completely alien to the actual production of a copyist – except in the case of Ramazan b. Ismail; the information from the colophons of Ottoman Qur'āns give almost the same results – the symbolic left aside.

But all these texts record preferably the exceptional, they pay more attention to the records – speed as well as slowness. Anecdotes relying on this kind of feats are more likely to be found than what is close to the usual. At the beginning of the 13th/19th century, a professional, Fāzil *dīvāna* ('the mad'), is said to have transcribed in 40 days a manuscript of a text by Bidîl which had been ordered by the emir of Bukharā; in the same time, but during the night, he made an abridged copy of the same work for his own use.[31] According to a catalogue describing a copy of the latter, it contained the *Nikāt, dīwān* and *qaṣā'id*, which even abridged were certainly still a fair amount of verse. Another man, who was *muftī* and *mudarris*, was able to copy in one night the *Mukhtaṣar* of the *Wiqāya.*[32]

Chardin's text is another source of information about the copyists' pace: travellers in the East saw these men at work, and when they were themselves trying to buy manuscripts they were sometimes interested in the way in which the copyists were actually working. From Chardin's report, we hear that a daily output of 500 to 600 *bayt* was the most which could be achieved; O. Akimushkin, A. Khalidov and E. Rezvan consider that 160 to 210 was the normal amount of verse copied in a day, adding that it was even less if the copy was carefully written.[33] The *vaqfiyya* of Ragıb Paşa reminds us that other sources of income (in this case teaching) were available and took time off from the transcription of texts.[34]

Archive documents provide important information about the work in the palace workshops; they concern a limited part of the production, usually outstanding manuscripts which are of little help when it comes to evaluating the average copyist's pace. The arrangements set out in Rashīd al-Dīn's *vaqfiyya* are nevertheless interesting as they give an idea of what a powerful and wealthy patron could ask for:[35] every year, it was expected that two carefully executed copies – one in Arabic, one in Persian – of each of the six treatises which the Ilkhanid vizier had written should be produced; some of the works extending over a few volumes. The *vaqfiyya* includes very carefully defined specifications on the copying process, but the task of recruiting the copyists was apparently left to the supervisor of the foundation. Their number was not stated in the document; Sheila Blair notes that they were not enjoying a high status.[36] The whole process

31 Vahidov & Erkinov 1999, 147.
32 *Ibid.*
33 *De Bagdad à Ispahan* 1994, 49.
34 See N. Kaya's paper in this volume.
35 Afshar & Minovi 1356/1978 (eds); trans. in Blair 1995, 114-115.
36 Blair (in press).

seems however to have taken more time than foreseen and Rashīd al-Dīn had to put pressure on his staff. One wonders if the copyist of the *Majmū'a* now in the BNF, who styled himself "the speedy writer from Baghdad" (*zūd-navīs al-Baghdādī*) was hired on account of his ability to write fast.[37]

Other documents contain relevant information about our subject. It is the case of the catalogue written by the end of the 13th/19th century and beginning of the 14th/20th in Central Asia by the bibliophile Ṣadr-i Dhiyā.'[38] He often included in this register information about the number of works which the copyists he knew and hired now and then had transcribed. A Dāmullā Mīrzā 'Abd al-Raḥmān A'lām Mullā copied 1000 works on various topics, Ṣiddīq-Jān 500, Dāmullā Raḥīm-Jān 200, 'Ināyatallāh more than 150 and his brother Mīrzā Ḥikmatallāh Maḥmūd over 370.[39] Unfortunately, these figures cover works of various sizes, so that they cannot help us in evaluating the production rate of these men.

Let's now turn to the manuscripts themselves. The colophons are an important if yet underused source of information. These short texts provide us with data ranging from the more general indications to an accurate evaluation of the pace with which a precise manuscript has been written. As 'general information,' I would mention here the Ottoman Qur'āns since the calligraphers often state that the copy they just completed was number X in their production. Here are a few instances. The manuscript Leiden, University Library Or. 12454 was copied in Iran or Anatolia by Ibn Muḥammad Ḥusayn Muḥammad Ṣādiq in 1083/1672-3: it was the copyist's 69th Qur'ān.[40] Hafiz Salih Çemsir finished his 125th Qur'ān in 1213/1798-9.[41] As for Kayiszade Hafiz Osman Efendi, he completed his 60th Qur'ān in 1290/1873;[42] according to Uğur Derman, he copied another 46 Qur'āns during the 21 years he was to live after this date, which means that he needed 5 or 6 months to transcribe a Qur'ān. If we take what I called the standard Ottoman Qur'ān (=*ayet ber-kenar* system) as the basis for an estimate, it means that the last mentioned calligrapher wrote daily from 3 to 4 pages of 15 lines. In order to make comparisons easier, this can be converted into letters per day: according to one of our sources, the Qur'ān contains 321.250 letters, which means that a page of our standard Ottoman Qur'ān contains roughly 535 letters. Three pages are then the equivalent of 1605 letters, four to 2140. This kind of information is valuable, but relies too heavily on estimates. Was the calligrapher devoting part of his time to other works? In the afore mentioned instances, the copyists seem to have been working at least continuously, even if they did not spend all the day on the transcription of texts. We also have to consider the

37 Paris, BNF Arabe 2324.
38 Vahidov & Erkinov 1999.
39 Vahidov & Erkinov 1999, 147.
40 Witkam 1993, 62.
41 *L'empire des sultans* 1995, 70.
42 *Calligraphies ottomanes* 2000, 130.

possibility of interruptions for various reasons: five years were necessary to copy the Il-khanid Mosul Qur'ān, but the *juz'* of the first half of the text were completed in 706/1306-07, those of the second half bearing dates from various months of 710/1310-11.[43]

We can even get a little closer to the actual conditions of the copyists' work with other colophons which indicate not only the day on which the copy was completed, but also the day when it was begun – or the number of days devoted to the transcription. It is then no longer a question of estimates, we can compute the pace at which the work has been progressing. The copyist of BNF Persian 266 thus says that he spent 15 days transcribing the 273 folios of Jalāl al-Dīn Rūmī's *Mathnavī*;[44] with almost 450 lines per day, he is closer to what Chardin reported than what Akimushkin, Khalidov and Rezvan's estimate. In the colophon of a Qur'ān completed in Dhū al-Qa'da 912/March 1507, 'Abd al-Raḥmān al-Ṣāliḥī al-Dimashqī states that three months and twenty days were necessary for the copying and illumination of the manuscript, which means that he wrote the equivalent of almost 82 lines of standard Ottoman Qur'ān per day at least (the time devoted to the illumination has to be taken into account), or 2915 letters.[45] This figure is slightly higher than Kayiszade Hafız Osman Efendi's output, and closer to the estimates by Akimushkin and his colleagues. There still remains a doubt about both copyists' status: the colophon contains nothing which could allow us to conclude that they were indeed professional; and we had to rely on a highly subjective estimate of their work in terms of legibility and regularity to decide about it.

Still more interesting for our purpose are the manuscripts with intermediary colophons: in the case of works divided into broad textual units (books, sections and so on), the copyists sometimes indicated the date of completion of each unit. This is for instance the case of the manuscript BNF Arabe 3280 with six colophons dated between the last Wednesday of Rajab 616/9 October 1219 and the last Friday of Shawwāl in the same year/3 January 1220.[46] We can therefore follow the progress of the work for the last five sections – the copyist does not indicate when he started working. His pace is somewhat irregular, varying from 1,32 pages to 2,9 pages (that is almost 3 pages) per day, the average running at 1,95 pages (almost 2 pages), that is 41 lines of text (which are roughly equivalent to 2870 letters, the lines in bigger letter size being excluded of this calculation). This figure is lower than the lower speed indicated by Akimushkin, Khalidov and Rezvan, but the two best results by our man (namely for section 3 already mentioned and section 5 with 2,7 pages per day) are well within their estimates. On the other hand, this average speed is very close to 'Abd al-Raḥmān al-Dimashqī's

---

43 James 1988, 101.
44 Richard 1989, 277.
45 *Rares manuscrits* 1999, lot I.
46 See *FiMMOD* n° 142.

pace. Why these variations? Obviously, many parameters are lacking: illness, feasts... Moreover, the copyist of Arabe 3280 was working for himself.

The Qur'ānic manuscripts are obviously a field for further research, even if one could object that they are too specific and would distort the picture of book production in the Islamic world. There is a number of Qur'āns in multi-volume sets, of which the *juz'* are certainly giving the most detailed view of a copyist's work. In the BNF collection, one can find the *juz'* 23 to 29 of an Egyptian Qur'ān from the 12th/18th century.[47] The size of the text in each volume is almost equivalent, which greatly helps estimating the copyist's speed. Our man was working rather regularly: he needed nine days to complete *juz'* 24, eight days for *juz'* 25 to 27, seven days for *juz'* 28 but twelve days for *juz'* 29. On the other hand, his pace is rather slow: if we consider that he has been working every day, his output does not exceed two folios of nine lines, which seems quite low. The completion of the whole Qur'ānic text can be tentatively estimated on the basis of a *juz'* in eight days; 240 days were therefore necessary and the rubricated frames for the text were certainly not delaying the progress of the copy. Anyhow, he was slower than this 'Abdallāh mentioned earlier who transcribed the same text in less than 4 months, than Kayiszade Hafiz Osman Ef. who needed 5 to 6 months; if we convert this amount into letters per day, he wrote only 1340 letters against the former's 2915 and between 1605 and 2140 for the latter. And our copyist cannot even claim that the high quality of his script explains his slowness. Others are certainly working even at a slower pace, like the calligrapher in charge of the huge Qur'ān which Öljeytü ordered for his mausoleum: as indicated previously, the first 7 *juz'* were completed in at least 12 months - but the script is really of outstanding level.[48]

It is of course impossible to reduce the copying of manuscripts to figures. Many factors should obviously be taken into account when trying to evaluate this process; some of them are closely connected with the individual's history and will therefore definitively remain outside of our reach. Others are known, but difficult to assess: this is for instance the case of calligraphy which might have been slowing down the copyists' pace in a variable proportion. The actual conditions under which the manuscripts were transcribed need to be better investigated in order to get a better understanding first of the transmission of the texts, then more broadly of the economy of the book in the Islamic world which was aptly described by Muhammad Arkoun as a "société du livre." But this goal can only be reached if more attention is paid to these "minute details" of the manuscripts which are so relevant for the historian of the book.

The Arabic script allowed copyists to write faster than their colleagues from other Middle Eastern manuscript traditions: such was the opinion of al-Kindī,

47 Ms Arabe 534-536, 538-540 (see Déroche 1985, 80-81).
48 James 1988, 95.

quoted by Ibn al-Nadīm in the IVth/Xth century: "[The Arabic writing] makes possible greater speed than can be attained in other forms of writing."[49] Did it make our copyists' lot happier? Chardin's remarks suggest that they only tried to write faster.

References

Afshār, Īraj & Mīnovī, M. (eds), 1356/1978. *Vaqfnāma-yi Rab'-i Rashīdī.* Tehran.

Akimushkin, Oleg & Ivanov, Anatoly 1979. "The art of illumination." In: B. Gray (ed.). *The arts of the book in Central Asia, 14th-16th centuries.* Paris/London, 35-57.

De Bagdad à Ispahan 1994: *De Bagdad à Ispahan, Manuscrits islamiques de la Filiale de Saint-Pétersbourg de l'Institut d'Etudes orientales, Académie des sciences de Russie.* Paris.

Blair, Sheila S. 1995: *A Compendium of Chronicles, Rashid al-Din's Illustrated History of the World* (The N.D. Khalili collection of Islamic art, 27). London.

Blair, Sheila S. (in press): "Scribes and artists in the Ilkhanid scriptorium." Not yet published in: Komaroff, Linda (ed.). *Beyond the Legacy of Genghis Khan.* Leiden. (In press).

Calligraphies ottomanes 2000: *Calligraphies ottomanes, Collection du musée Sakıp Sabancı, Université Sabancı, Istanbul.* Paris.

Chardin, Jean 1811: *Voyage du Chevalier Chardin en Perse et autres lieux de l'Orient...* vol. IV. Nouvelle édition par L. Langlès. Paris.

Déroche, François 1983: *Catalogue des manuscrits arabes, 2e partie ... I,1, Les manuscrits du Coran : Aux origines de la calligraphie coranique.* Paris.

Déroche, François 1985: *Catalogue des manuscrits arabes, 2e partie ... I,2, Les manuscrits du Coran : Du Maghreb à l'Insulinde.* Paris.

Déroche, François 1995: "Maîtres et disciples: la transmission de la culture calligraphique dans le monde ottoman." *Revue du monde musulman et de la Méditerranée* 75-76 (1995), 81-90.

Déroche, François et al. 2000: *Manuel de codicologie des manuscrits en écriture arabe.* Paris.

Déroche, François & Noja Noseda, Sergio 1998: *Le manuscrit arabe 328 (a) de la Bibliothèque nationale de France.* Lesa.

Dobraca, K. 1972: "Scriptorij u Foci u XVI stoljecu." *Anali Gazi Husrev-Begove Biblioteke* I (1972), 67-74.

Dodge, Bayard 1970: *The Fibrist of al-Nadîm, A tenth century survey of Muslim culture I.* New York/London.

L'empire des sultans 1995: *L'empire des sultans, L'art ottoman dans la collection de Nasser D. Khalili.* Genève.

49 Ibn al-Nadīm, *Kitāb al-fihrist*, ed. Flügel, 10; ed. Tajaddud, 13; (trans.) Dodge 1970, 19.

FiMMOD: *Fichier des manuscrits moyen-orientaux datés.*

Hartmann, Angelika 1989: "Codicologie comme source biographique. A propos d'un autographe inédit d'Ibn al-Jauzī." In: Déroche, François 1989 (ed). *Les manuscrits du Moyen-Orient, Essais de codicologie et de paléographie. Actes du Colloque d'Istanbul (Istanbul, 26-29 mai 1986).* Istanbul/Paris, 23-30.

Ibn Abī Da'ūd. *Kitāb al-maṣāḥif.* Ed. Arthur Jeffery (Materials for the history of the text of the Qur'ân). Leiden, 1937.

Ibn Khallikān. *Wafayāt al-a'yān wa-anbā' abnā' al-zamān.* Vol. III. Ed. Iḥsān 'Abbās. Beirut, n.d.

Ibn al-Nadīm. *Kitāb al-fihrist.* Ed. Gustav Flügel. Vol. I, Leipzig, 1871; ed. Riḍā Tajaddud, Tehran, 1350/1971.

James, David 1988: *Qur'âns of the Mamlûks.* London.

Maṣāḥif Ṣan'ā' 1985: *Maṣāḥif Ṣan'ā'.* Kuwait.

Pedersen, Johannes 1984: *The Arabic Book.* Ed. with an introduction by R. Hillenbrand. Princeton (NJ).

Quiring-Zoche, Rosemarie: "A manuscript copied in teamwork?" *Manuscripta Orientalia* 9,4 (2003), 65-72.

The Qur'an 1999: *The Qur'an, scholarship and the Islamic arts of the book.* London.

Rares manuscrits 1999: *Rares manuscrits orientaux chrétiens et islamiques.* Vente aux enchères, Paris, 7 juin 1999.

Richard, Francis 1989: *Catalogue des manuscrits persans I, Ancien fonds.* Paris.

Rosenthal, Franz 1947: *The technique and approach of Muslim scholarship.* Rome.

Şeşen, Ramazan 1997: "Esquisse d'une histoire du développement des colophons dans les manuscrits musulmans." In: Déroche, François & Richard, Francis 1997 (eds.). *Scribes et manuscrits du Moyen-Orient.* Paris, 190-221.

Vahidov, Shadman & Erkinov, Aftandil 1999: "Le fihrist (catalogue) de la bibliothèque de Ṣadr-i Dhiyâ': une image de la vie intellectuelle dans le Mavarannahr (fin XIX - début XX siècle)." *Cahiers d'Asie Centrale* 7 (1999) (Patrimoine manuscrit et vie intellectuelle de l'Asie centrale islamique), 141-73.

Witkam, Jan Just 1993: "De handschriften van de Koran." In: Buitelaar, Mario & Motzki, Harald 1993 (eds). *De Koran: ontstann, interpretatie en praktijk.* Muiderberg, 56-64.

Yāqūt. *Kitāb irshād al-arīb ilā ma'rifat al-adīb* I. Ed. D.S. Margoliouth [E.J.W. Gibb memorial series, 6], 2nd ed. London, 1923.

al-Zabīdī. "Ḥikmat al-ishrāq ilā kuttāb al-āfāq." Ed. A.S. Hārūn. In: *Nawādir al-makhṭūṭāt* 5 (1973/1954), 62-98.

Part III
Introduction of Printing

[9]

From the Manuscript Age to the Age of Printed Books

Muhsin Mahdi

The period of transition from the manuscript age to the age of printed books is the second and less important transitional epoch in the history of the book in the Islamic world. The first and more important epoch was the initial emergence of the book during the first two centuries of the Islamic era, the seventh and eighth centuries of the common era. The seriousness and persistence with which scribes and scholars in the Islamic world were able during that period to preserve and transmit the text of the most important of all books in that world, the Koran, and, next, the traditional collections of the sayings and deeds of the Prophet of Islam, meant that, once codified, their preservation and transmission could remain free of the many problems besetting the preservation and transmission of most other books, both religious and secular, during the transition from the manuscript age to the age of printed books.

In contrast, the disturbing manner in which European printers took liberties with the text of the Koran (when compared to the care taken in printing the Gutenberg Bible, for instance) could not but raise doubts among Muslims regarding the virtues of printing when they first came into contact with the new technology. One look at the title page of the Koran printed in Hamburg in 1694 (figure 1.1) must have made Muslim readers of the Koran think that only the Devil himself could have produced such an ugly and faulty version of their Holy Book; and the same must have been the impression made on them by Alessandro de Paganino's Venice Koran printed in the 1530s, where the printer, perhaps following some contemporary Arabic vernacular, did not distinguish between certain letters of the alphabet, such as the *dāl* and the *dhāl* (figure 1.2). One would expect a handbook on medicine and medicaments, such as the Arabic text of Avicenna's *Canon*, to be free of printing errors, since errors in a book of this nature can easily lead to unfortunate results. Yet the Medici edition (Rome, 1593) of this work commits a serious grammatical fault, to say nothing of the syntactical infelicities, on the title page itself (figure 1.3). Unlike

Fig. 1.1. The Koran printed in Hamburg, Germany in 1694 by Officina Schultzio-Schilleriana. Copy in Library of Congress.

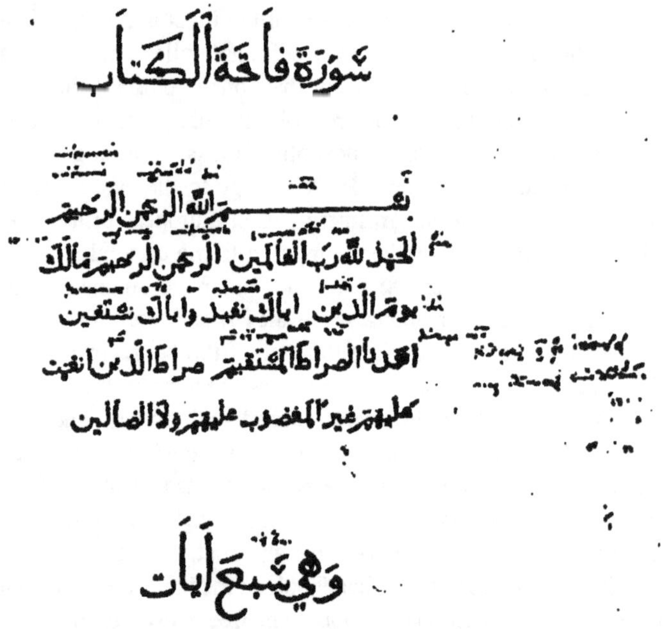

Fig. 1.2. The "Opening" of the first printed Koran in Europe (Venice, ca. 1537) by Alessandro de Paganino.

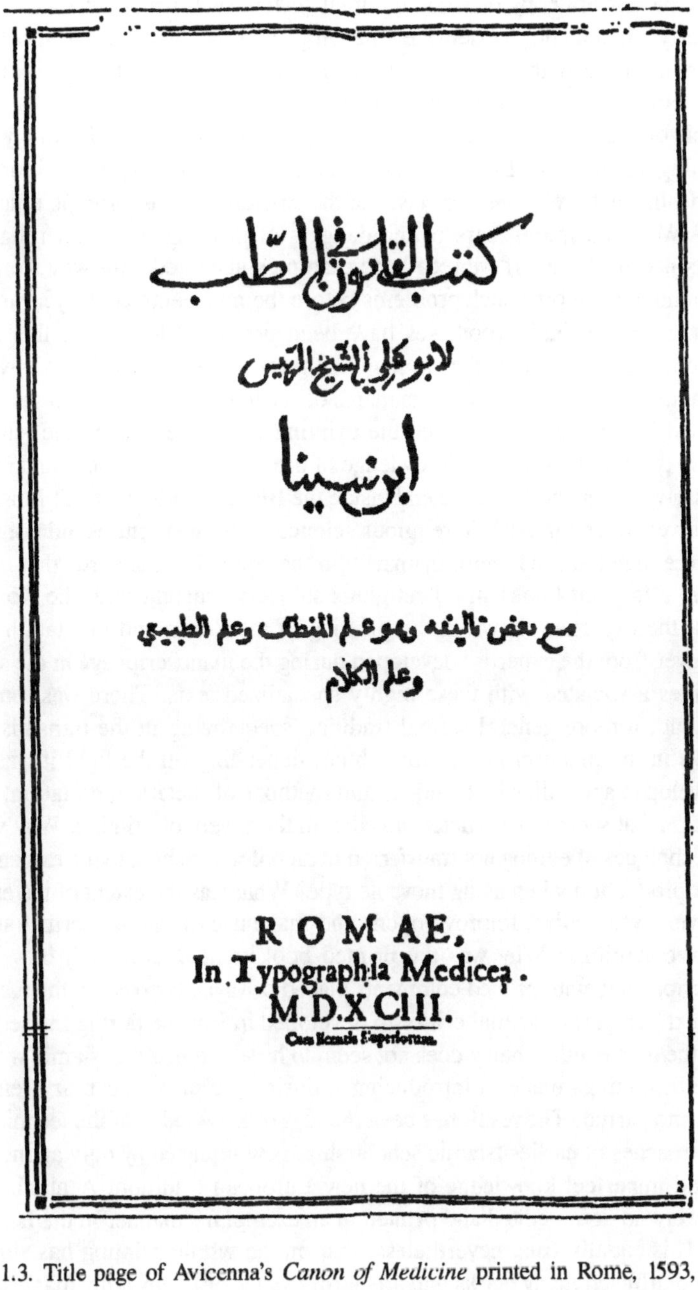

كتب القانون في الطب

لابو علي الشيخ الرئيس

ابن سينا

مع بعض تاليفه وهو علم المنطق وعلم الطبيعي
وعلم الكلام

ROMAE,
In Typographia Medicea.
M.D.XCIII.
Cum licentia Superiorum.

Fig. 1.3. Title page of Avicenna's *Canon of Medicine* printed in Rome, 1593, by the Medici Press.

a faulty manuscript copy by some ignorant scribe, such printed books involve an orderly organization, extensive financing, and the distribution of a large number of copies with the same errors, making it less easy to dismiss them as unimportant or inconsequential incidents.[1]

This brings us to the frequently cited objections made in the Islamic world to printing when it was first introduced, delays in introducing the printing of books dealing with religious subjects, and the strictures against printing religious works.[2] Were the initial fears of the dangers of printing books on religious subjects justified? Yes, if we recall the examples just cited. But why were no ways found to overcome such problems before the nineteenth century? Various economic or doctrinal hypotheses have been presented to explain this phenomenon. What is clear is that in many cultural centers in the Islamic world a scribal tradition flourished with standards of accuracy that could not be assured in printed books, especially when the printing was done outside the Islamic world by printers with limited knowledge of the languages involved; and many of the early printers both outside and inside the Islamic world were not Muslims and not well versed in Islamic religious sciences. These strictures did not last; ways were found around them, primarily in the control of standards that made it possible to print books in all religious subjects, starting with the Koran.

But the expertise shown in the printing of the Koran and the ḥadīth was a carryover from the expertise developed during the manuscript age in the strict disciplines associated with these highly specialized texts. There was, on the other hand, a more general scribal tradition specializing in the transmission of books in the manuscript age and which, depending on the field it was in, had developed specialized techniques and methods of dictation, collation, and illustration that seem to have deteriorated with the advent of printing. Why were those techniques of editing not transferred in an orderly fashion to the exigencies of book production when using movable type? What was the extent of the effort to recover, systematize, improve upon, and make use of the old scribal art in the new conditions? Why was the printed book treated as though it were a manuscript copy, with printed comments placed or variants noted on the margin of the text? The art of textual criticism developed in Europe during the second half of the nineteenth century does not seem to have reached the Islamic world, and the beginnings made in introducing it during the present century remain limited and partial. The result has been the loss of knowledge of the techniques and approaches of earlier Islamic scholarship, now replaced by only an incomplete and imperfect knowledge of the new European tradition. A number of works were no doubt edited and printed in an exemplary manner in the Islamic world. It is equally true, nevertheless, that on the whole printing has simply fixed and diffused many books that are hardly superior to any stray manuscript copy untouched by a careful scholarly hand, and others whose scholarly form is mere pretension.

From the Manuscript to the Age of Printed Books 5

The period of transition from the manuscript age to the age of printed books in the Islamic world was long and tortuous, extending over centuries and presenting the student of the history of the book with different sorts of problems from one century to another and from one region of the Islamic world to another. Then, after it largely came to an end sometime during the last half of the nineteenth century and the beginning of the twentieth, a new problem arose: the Islamic world slowly forgot what it meant to depend on scribes and manuscript copies for the creation, diffusion, and transmission of knowledge. In the mind of the vast public at least, printed books came to represent a degree of solidity and authority that went far beyond the solidity and authority of the manuscript copy or copies of the same book. Not only has the manuscript age by now come to an end in the mind of the public—hardly anyone copies an entire manuscript by hand anymore (unless it is in preparation for printing it, and photographic reproduction and printing have in some cases made even this effort unnecessary)—the manuscript tradition has for all intents and purposes ceased to be alive and to develop as it had done for more than a millennium.

It is impossible, of course, to cover, or even touch upon, all the problems arising from every aspect of the period of transition from the manuscript age to the age of printed books. Indeed, it is foolish even to try to do so, given how much remains unknown about the cultural, social, and economic history of the period and how risky it is to establish any causal relation between the introduction and spread of printed books in the Islamic world and particular social, economic, and cultural factors that may have interacted with the introduction of printing and the spread of printed books. Nevertheless, it may be useful to raise some of the questions that need to be answered if one is to gain a fuller picture of what happened during the period of transition and learn about the issues involved in the transformation of books already there in manuscript form into printed books in particular.

There are, to begin with, the numerous cultural and social implications of the transition from the manuscript age to the age of printed books: the spread of printing in the second half of the nineteenth century went hand in hand with the rise of national sentiment among the various Muslim peoples and, as happened in Europe earlier, Muslims became less and less likely to speak or be able to read more than their own national language and had to have translations from other Islamic languages in order to preserve some of the cultural homogeneity of the Islamic world. There is the role of the state in encouraging translations and the spread of secular culture through control of some of the early presses. There are the new cultural vistas and literary forms opened up through printing. And there is the role of non-Muslim communities in spreading the printing of books, first in Europe and then inside the Islamic world.

Then there are the authors (leaders of mystical fraternities, leading thinkers, reformers, and pamphleteers) who wrote original works during the nineteenth century and made a massive contribution to cultural change through printed books. There are a number of interesting questions to be asked about the diffusion of the works of those contemporary authors. How many of the original works printed during the period of transition survive today? How did the transition help create a new profession, that of the author engaged not merely in writing or dictating an original copy of his work and presenting it to a prince in the hope of financial reward and otherwise hoping for the best as to its survival and diffusion in manuscript form, but the author who could see his work printed, corrected, published, diffused in many copies, and sold, establishing himself slowly as a professional writer whose works are read immediately upon their publication by wider circles of readers?

To what extent and how fast did such contemporary works, be they literary, scientific, or religious, replace older ones? Who were the authors who commanded large audiences? When did the reading public become so large that only printing could satisfy it? Did printed books create the mass culture and the standardization of reading habits, or was it the emergence of a mass of educated readers that led to the spread of printing? Who was buying or reading the newly printed books? Did the transition merely expand readership or did it change its character as well? How was the expansion of readership connected with the change in the educational system and the emergence of new classes of professionals and educated people, the change from the time students of religion and bureaucrats were the main readers to the time after the emergence of new free professions—teachers and students of the new secular schools, new types of lawyers, doctors, engineers—who began increasingly to collect and read printed books?

Then there is the impact of translations and the role of printing in encouraging the paraphrase and translation of foreign books, especially those from European languages, which were instrumental in introducing modern science and technology to the Islamic world. Finally, one needs to consider such questions as the importance of the press in the diffusion of scientific literature, whether ancient or contemporary and Western, and of technical manuals of medicine, military science and strategy engineering, and so forth.

Then there are the political and economic aspects of the production of printed books. It was precisely that so many identical copies could be made of printed books which made printing into a mass medium, drew the attention of public authorities, religious and secular, and made it possible to exploit printed books as instruments of state policy, to censor them, or to forbid their diffusion when they were thought not to agree with, or to run counter to, the policy of the state, something not easy to accomplish in the manuscript age. But the state also came to own presses; it was able to distribute copies of printed books free of charge; and it acquired the authority to decide which books should be printed for use in its educational system. The state and the mystical fraternities seem to have been the initial sponsors of the printed book in secular and religious fields, respectively. In the case of the state, a ready clientele, consisting of functionaries and students of technical and generally of secular schools, and government subsidies, made the printing of books on non-religious subjects economically feasible. But the role of the mystical orders in spreading the printing of religious books is a subject that is well worth investigating also. Like the state, they had a ready market in their membership, which made it less risky to undertake the printing of books. Some mystical fraternities had vast memberships spreading out in many countries of the Islamic world, a readership that made the printing of literature of interest to these mystical fraternities economically feasible. When and to what extent did printed religious books begin to compete with printed secular literature, both ancient and contemporary? How did the proportion of the latter grow relative to the total?

To answer such questions, it is important to collect, preserve, and study the archives of publishers wherever they can still be found in the Islamic world, but especially in major centers of printing such as Istanbul, Cairo, and Teheran. One needs to study not only the fact of a book's publication, but how many editions and printings there were, the size of each, and the pricing of copies. We may even learn from these archives how slow or rapid the transition was from the manuscript age to the age of printed books in each major center. In general, one expects the new technologies to have exceeded by far the old in making books both widely accessible and accessible at greatly reduced prices, and to have penetrated new markets and social and economic strata of society. But did any of this happen? To what extent and at what point? What was the weight of the role of the state as against such private institutions as religious fraternities or private commercial enterprises? Which books were promoted by which sector? Which books were in demand by which sector of the reading public? What proportion of printed books were read by members of each of the two educational systems, the religious and the scientific or secular, after they parted company, and what portion by the wider public?

Then there is the impact of printing on the development of language. At the beginning of the transition from the manuscript age to the age of printed books in the Islamic world, the Arabic language was still the international Islamic language in the religious and secular sciences, even though works on modern European science and technology were translated into national languages other than Arabic, such as Turkish and Persian as well. What happened after the introduction of printing? To what extend did Arabic maintain its position? Was Arabic gradually replaced by the other national languages? When did this take place in the case of each nation with a native tongue other than Arabic, and in what fields? That is to say, when and how did languages like Persian, Turkish, and Urdu, in the main vehicles of literary culture and of the administration, become vehicles of modern scientific disciplines as well? How is it that even today, in matters of common concern to the Islamic world, works are written in Arabic by writers from countries such as Iran, India, and Pakistan?[3]

Then there is the impact of printing on the orthography, structure, and vocabulary of each of the languages of the Islamic world. To what extent did printing contribute to simplification and uniformity in any of these aspects of each of these languages? Would the problem of orthography have come to the fore in Turkey without the spread of printing? Would the problem of orthography in Arabic, that is, the unsuccessful campaign for the use of Latin characters, have been even thinkable without the spread of printing? How did printing contribute to the spread and use of punctuation, and why is it that the only strict punctuation system remains the one employed in printing the Koran, while one faces utter confusion, in Arabic at least, in the punctuation of books printed with movable type? Similar questions need to be asked regarding other aspects of scholarly form and techniques, such as the use of abbreviations. What explains the rise and decline of strict standards of typography, of orthography, punctuation, and design?

Then there is the role of linguistic and literary renaissance in the case of each of the national languages during the nineteenth century in the recovery and diffusion of older works of prose, poetry, narrative—in some cases recovered from rare manuscript collections or libraries not accessible beyond small circles of owners and scholars who happened to be in, or to have traveled to, the place where the collection or library was located. To what extent did printing contribute to the resurrection of works forgotten for a long time and made for another age, with its own taste and preoccupations? How was the development of printing related to the development of language education and literacy? And how important was government intervention in the spread of printing (e.g., the availability of printed readers, grammars, dictionaries)? Above all, to what extent was the diffusion of older works through printing a sign that these works were being read, not merely acquired as collectibles?

It is characteristic of the transformation for the manuscript age to the age of printed books in the Islamic world that it was a continuous process rather than a violent turning point. Originally, the book in the Islamic world had co-existed with an oral tradition in which memory played an important role and writing was intended as an aid to memory. Yet writing is supposed to decrease reliance on memory. The question is the extent to which printing may have accelerated this trend. Apart from the question of memory, however, the writing of books itself underwent many changes as to organization, the materials on and with which books were written, and the techniques used by scribes and readers to assure the book's integrity and correctness. This scribal and scholarly tradition underwent certain changes over time in the material it used, in the scripts it developed, and in the organization of book production; and local sub-traditions developed in various parts of the Islamic world, in different languages, and in different disciplines. By the time printing had become more than a curiosity in the Islamic world, a strong scribal and scholarly tradition was in place which was devoted to the book in manuscript form; and one of the most urgent tasks of the students of the transition from the manuscript age to the age of printed books in the Islamic world is to find out precisely what this scribal and scholarly tradition consisted of in the main centers of Islamic civilization during the eighteenth century its transformation during, the nineteenth, and its role in the introduction of printing. For it is that tradition which was instrumental initially in making the transition to the age of printed books.

One needs to ask, therefore, what were the technical and organizational features of the book reproduction industry, not during the manuscript age in general, but at the end of the manuscript age in particular: who engaged in it, patronized it, subsidized it, helped sell the scribes' works, and supplied the materials necessary for the exercise of the profession? Were they merchants, technicians, learned men, calligraphers? Were there *scriptoria* for the mass production of manuscript copies? What was the market for manuscript copies like in places such as Istanbul, Cairo, or Isfahan? How far did manuscript copies travel, and in which direction? Was the trade confined to the Islamic world? Did the manuscript copies of certain books tend to remain in certain localities and not cross certain borders? For instance, to what extent was the experience of the Ottoman statesman and man of letters Rāgib Mehmed Paşa (1699–1763), in looking for Mullā Sadrā's *Asfār*, unique? Rāgib Paşa was a voracious book collector who travelled through the Ottoman Empire and occupied important political positions in Syria, Egypt, and Iraq. Yet he tells us that this comprehensive work of illuminationist philosophy and mysticism was not well known in Anatolia and that he had to bring a copy from Iraq, from which then one or two copies were made.[4] Since it is known that a vast number of manuscript copies produced in the Safavid Empire reached Constantinople, and that this particular work was well known throughout the Safavid Empire and the Indian subcontinent, was the absence of this particular book from the book market in Istanbul and the libraries of Anatolia due to its subject matter and doctrinal content? And why even now can one hardly find a lithographic copy of it in Egypt, for instance, when it had served as the basic textbook of philosophy in many schools in Iran and India?[5]

Let us turn to the printing and diffusion of books surviving from the manuscript age. Of the millions of manuscript copies existing at the time when printing began to spread in the Islamic world, not all could be printed; a selection had to be made. By whom and on what basis was this selection made? By the political authority aiming to spread knowledge of the practical arts necessary for building a modern state? By booksellers with a view to large printings and profit? What works and what literary forms disappeared from view without being remembered except by a new generation of specialists? Were the books most widely diffused in the Islamic world in manuscript form at the time printing was introduced the ones printed? That is, did printing simply continue to feed people's interest in books that were the most widely read before? Who were the ancient Muslim authors selected and printed? How did the ancient Muslim authors not usually read at the end of the manuscript age fare with their new audiences? One could learn a great deal about such questions from studying the holdings of libraries in Istanbul, Cairo, and Teheran that ceased to grow as printing became widespread, provided one realizes that most of the mosque and school libraries did not contain many types of books—popular literature, practical disciplines, astrology, forbidden things—that were diffused and tended to be widely read outside the schools and scholarly circles, and that such books were also the ones more likely to perish. In general, then, one needs to find out what the impact of printing was on the literary culture of the time. To what extent did printing change the type of books available to readers, as compared to before the introduction of printing? How and why did this change take place? What kinds of books were involved? How much of the earlier literature became more widely available? Was this partly due to the ease with which the text of rare manuscript copies of a book could now be multiplied, to access to libraries and collections in places that had been inaccessible before, or to the printing and diffusion of information about manuscript copies through printing in general and manuscript catalogues in particular?

It is a mistake to think that the scribal and scholarly tradition still alive when the transition to printed books was taking place in the Islamic world was as competent or achieved the same high standard when transcribing *every* kind of book. In addition to the text of the Koran and the Traditions of the Prophet, there were certain disciplines in which accurate and correct transmission was essential. This was largely true of manuscript copies of books in scientific fields, such as astronomy, medicine, and mathematics, where mistakes and corruption could be easily detected by experts and render the manuscript copy almost worthless as far as they were concerned. Many scribes copying manuscripts in these disciplines were themselves experts to some extent or had developed a method of copying that reproduced the exemplar with an unusual degree of precision. In other fields (a vast majority of manuscript copies are in literary fields, such as narratives, history, and geography) the language and sometimes even the content of the work was consciously or unconsciously modernized as manuscripts were copied from one generation to another. Much of the so-called Middle Arabic features found in manuscript copies of books by early authors can be attributed to this tendency.

In the age of printed books, the *muṣaḥḥiḥ*—literally the person in charge of producing a "correct" printed version—performed a task similar to that of the scribe in the manuscript age, that is, he corrected and sometimes revised the language of the manuscript copy before it was sent to the printer, and the same person contributed to assuring that the proofs were properly corrected and a list of errata was appended to the printed book. Especially during the period of the renaissance of linguistic learning (of the *fuṣḥá* in Arabic, for instance), it was the function of the *muṣaḥḥiḥ* to make sure that the language of the manuscript copy prepared for the printer was free of grammatical mistakes and stylistic blunders. But by "good" Arabic during the eighteenth and nineteenth centuries one did not mean the stage the language had reached in the eighth or ninth under the Umayyad or Abbasid dynasties; it was already a neoclassical Arabic with its own features.[6] Thus, while the attempt was made to stem the tide of so-called Middle Arabic, and in most cases much of this kind of Arabic was eliminated, there was no assurance that it was replaced by the Arabic current during the second or third century of the Islamic era. And sometimes the attempt to reverse the evolution of the language led to making the printed book more archaic than its author had meant it to be. The revision of the language of all the first four printed versions of *The Thousand and One Nights* is quite instructive in this respect.

It is therefore also important to trace the fortunes of this scribal and scholarly tradition as printing came to be widespread in the Islamic world; study the role of its representatives as publishers, editors, and proofreaders in printing establishments; and learn about their educational background, first in the religious institutions and then as part of the new Europeanized educational system, where as scholars, teachers, and students they continued to play a significant role in transforming the culture of the manuscript age into the culture of printed books. This will require careful study of the techniques used in preparing the manuscript for the printer; what manuscript material was reproduced and what manuscript material was not reproduced (the fate of marginal corrections, conjectures, variant readings, and comments) when a manuscript was copied and corrected in preparation for being printed; the extent to which these were reproduced or suppressed or placed in a different position on the page; and whether dispensing with variant readings and the comments in printed books was due to technical or economic reasons.

A systematic study of early printings can instruct us on whether and to what extent the printed text was a better or worse scientific instrument that a manuscript copy of the same book current before the introduction of printing.[7] Yet the printed copy, which may not have been better than an imperfect manuscript copy, was now published in hundreds if not thousands of copies, sought by everyone interested in that book, and taken by the public to represent *the* book itself, the book to which reference is made and from which quotations are reproduced. It came to have the authority and finality only the author's copy could have claimed in the manuscript age. It is therefore important to find out when and to what extent printed books relegated manuscripts to a secondary position so that readers came to be psychologically oriented to look for, and expect to read, a printed book rather than a manuscript copy; and when and to what extent the habit of reading a manuscript copy—the ability to handle a manuscript copy with ease, interact with it, and learn from it—disappeared from the reading public and became a specialty confined to a few scholars and to those planning to transform the book from manuscript to print. Here again, a study of libraries, public and private, and their use over time, especially those that froze at a particular point in time, could help clarify such questions.[8]

Nevertheless, the transition from the manuscript age to the age of printed books in the Islamic world is not something that took place in the past only. Even though a lot has happened during the past two centuries or so, in certain respects the transition is still with us. Books in manuscript form continue to be transformed into printed books, and this process will continue for the foreseeable future, since a vast number of books produced during the manuscript age in the Islamic world remain in manuscript form and their transformation, by way of printing, editing, and re-editing, is not likely to come to an end very soon. Indeed, it is hard to conceive of a future date when the Islamic world will cease to be concerned with the question of the transition from the manuscript age to the age of printed books and with the many problems connected with the transformation of its heritage at the hand of printers and editors. One can only hope that, slowly, the transition will be controlled by scholars with increasingly better knowledge of the scribal and scholarly tradition that produced the books in the manuscript age, rather than by predators in search of gain or fame.

Nor has the transformation always been directly from the book in manuscript form to the printed book. We recall, for instance, the continuous role played in the transformation of manuscript copies into printed books by photography, microfilming, xeroxing, and, more recently, word processing. Think, for instance, of the accuracy and ease with which photographic reproductions of manuscript copies are now being printed. Is the product of this process a manuscript copy or a printed book? Then there are other techniques, some of which once played a significant intermediary role between the book in manuscript form and books printed with movable type: lithography, xylography, metal plates—processes that were once current in India, Iran, Egypt, and Morocco. Their use in printing books of common prayers, the Koran, religious tracts of all sorts, and secular books as well, is known.

Just at a time when the Islamic world seems to be reaping the benefits of the technological and cultural revolution brought about by printing, that revolution is being increasingly superseded by another revolution, one that is replacing both the manuscript book and the printed book with the electronic, machine-readable book. This is perhaps the most significant question we must keep in mind as we look at the transition from the manuscript age to that of printed books. But we need to remember also that, even without this recent technological revolution, at least since the beginning of this century the printed book began to lose some of its hold on the human race. One could say that until about 1914 there was no other "mass" communication medium (apart from the human voice of narrators, teachers, and preachers) besides the book, the pamphlet, or the flier. There was no radio or television, no record or tape, no film, to compete to any significant extent with printed matter. Pictures played only a limited role, and illustrations were rather rare and expensive. The printed/written word held a preeminent position; there were as yet no serious competitors to reckon with. Whenever a serious question was disputed in the Islamic community—Wahhābism, coffee drinking, smoking—the dispute was enshrined in printed books, pamphlets, and fliers.

In some respects, the book in electronic, machine-readable form will mean a return to one of the main features of the manuscript age: copies can be made and subjected to continuous change and improvement, free of the fixed form introduced by printing and movable type. With the use of various means of communication, it will be possible to make what is initially a single copy available immediately across the globe and as far as humans can reach beyond this globe, with the possibility that, from one copy, an infinite number of copies can be made, used, and disposed of.

The potential of this revolution is, or should be, of particular interest to those engaged in the effort to collect and organize information about the enormous surviving manuscript heritage of the Islamic world in all Islamic languages. This potential extends far beyond the use currently made of it in cataloging books and manuscripts. Sooner or later, the electronic, machine-readable book—consisting of digitized text, digitized graphics, or a mixture of digitized text and graphics—is likely to replace both the book as it was known in the manuscript age and the book in print; for it will be the most convenient way to access the content of books, including books that exist already in manuscript form or in print. And the electronic, machine-readable form will in turn determine the most convenient ways of packaging the book, just as it was the manuscript and printing that determined its characteristic material components.

Given the speed with which the technology is changing, however, it remains to be seen how many forms the new electronic, machine-readable book will take. It seems certain that the main advantages of the printed book, wide diffusion and an affordable price, will continue to favor certain types of printed books, perhaps those that are popular. Otherwise, many scholarly works, and generally all works of specialized interest, including illustrations, will be available in electronic form, more easily accessible across the globe, not requiring the publication of a large number of hard copies. The other function of the printed book, that of reproducing the content of books existing in manuscript form, and certainly much of the body of books produced in the manuscript age on which scholars are likely to be working in the future, will be transferred directly from the original manuscript form to electronic, machine-readable form, rather than going through the printing stage, which can now clearly be seen to have been yet another intermediate stage. But whether this transition is carried out successfully or we end up with another mess on our hands depends on how willing we are to learn more about the book in the manuscript age, how willing we are to learn the lessons of the delays and problems encountered during the transition from the manuscript age to the age of printed books, and how determined we are to face and overcome the difficulties encountered during the transition to the age of the electronic, machine-readable book.

NOTES

1. To see that such problems can arise in books edited in more recent times by authors who could not be accused of ignorance or malice, one can consult the edition of the work on the proof of prophecies by the tenth-century Isma'īlī thinker Abū Ya'qūb al-Sijistānī, *Ithbāt al-nubūwāt*, ed. 'Ārif Tāmir (Beirut, 1966), p.76, where the editor took the liberty of rewriting a paragraph of the original text in twentieth-century Arabic.

2. The relevant decrees, legal opinions, and related documents have been discussed recently by Wahid Gdoura, *Le Début de l'imprimerie arabe à Istanbul et en Syrie* (Tunis, 1985), pt. 1, ch. 2, pt. 2, ch. 2; and Fawzi Abdulrazak, "The Kingdom of the Book," PhD Dissertation, Boston University, 1990, ch. 4.

3. Consider, for instance, the Arabic writings of thinkers like Khomeini, Mawdūdī and S.S. Nadvi.

4. Rāgib Paşa, *Safīnat al-Rāghib* (Bulaq, 1282/1865 or 66), p. 322.

5. The single lithographic copy of the work I came across in Egypt had been brought there by an Indian scholar and reached the marketplace when his library was sold after his death.

6. Once, in the manuscript reading room of the old Dār al-Kutub Library building in the Bāb al-Khalq, in Cairo, I saw across the table a blind Azharite scholar with a youngster next to him reading from an old manuscript copy and holding a ballpoint pen in his hand to transcribe the text of the manuscript in

a notebook. The youngster read aloud as he transcribed the manuscript while the scholar listened, sometimes nodding in approval but frequently instructing the youngster not to transcribe what was in the manuscript copy but what was to the scholar's mind a more correct version of the text. Worse than this, he seems to have arranged with the youngster that the latter should also correct the text of the manuscript itself with his ballpoint pen. Whether because the scholar was eminent or influential, I do not know, but the keeper of manuscripts at Dār al-Kutub, the late Fuʿād Sayyid, did not dare protest the practice.

7. Modern editors treat printed books of which they cannot find the manuscript source as just another manuscript copy, with all the potential virtues and defects of a manuscript copy.

8. I recall, for instance, having to consult some Arabic manuscript copies in the Küprülü Library in Istanbul, where the only other users of the tables and chairs in the reading room. were high school students reading (modern Turkish) school books they had brought with them rather than any of the manuscript copies for which that library is known to users like myself.

[10]

A Virgin Deserving Paradise or a Whore Deserving Poison: Manuscript Tradition and Printed Books in Ottoman Turkish Society

ORLIN SABEV (ORHAN SALIH)[1]

Over a century after the introduction of typography into Ottoman Turkish society in the 1720s by Ibrahim Müteferrika, a Hungarian-born convert to Islam, it seems that printing was still considered an instrument of the devil. During his visit to Istanbul in 1844 Charles White observed that the Istanbul booksellers considered that manuscript copyists deserved to go to paradise after their demise, while the printing press was made of the poisonous plant oleander.[2] In fact, this attitude strikingly resembles early western suspicions toward printing. A late fifteenth-century Dominican friar, Filippo De Strata, for example, voiced the opinion that "the pen is a virgin; the printing press is a whore."[3] Apparently not everybody welcomed the coming of the printing press, and it is unquestionable that printing did not replace the manuscript tradition immediately and without any resistance. The shift from script to print was not simply a physical shift from pen to type, but equally a mental shift from an old to a new view of the nature of the book.

Elizabeth Eisenstein, a prominent researcher in the field of book history, put forth the idea that the printing press was an "agent of change"

[1] Orhan Salih is Orlin Sabev's original Turkish name.

[2] Charles White, *Three Years in Constantinople or Domestic Manners of the Turks in 1844* (London: Henry Colburn, 1845). Quoted after Yahya Erdem, "Sahhaflar ve Seyyahlar: Osmanlı'da Kitapçılık,"[Booksellers and travellers: the Ottoman book trade] in Gülen Eren (ed.), *Osmanlı* (Ankara: Yeni Türkiye, 1999), 11, pp. 720–738.

[3] Filippo De Strata, *Polemic against Printing*, trans. Shelagh Grier, ed. Martin Lowry (Birmingham: Hayloft, 1986). Quoted after S. A. Baron, "The Guises of Dissemination of Early Seventeenth-century England: News in Manuscript and Print," in B. Dooley–S. S. Baron (eds.), *The Politics of Information in Early Modern Europe* (London–New York: Routledge, 2001), p. 41.

that sparked a "communications revolution."[4] She went on to explain that her particular notion of "revolution" is inspired by Raymond Williams's oxymoronic expression "long revolution,"[5] in the sense that it is not about a fast change as a result of a single act but rather a continuous but irreversible process, whose effects become visible in the course of its development.[6] Later scholarship in the field of book history, however, has not fully endorsed Eisenstein's "revolution" theory, criticizing her non-contextualized approach according to which the advent of printing with movable type in itself created a print culture, and insisting that when the issue of printing is studied within a given socio-cultural context it becomes apparent that manuscript copying and printing continued to exist side by side or as competing technologies until well into the eighteenth century.[7]

However, when discussing the introduction of printing into the world of Islam and into Ottoman Turkish society in particular,[8] most scholars have remained bound to the "print revolution" paradigm, with a few ex-

[4] Elizabeth L. Eisenstein, *The Printing Press as an Agent of Change: Communications and Cultural Transformations in Early-Modern Europe* (Cambridge: Cambridge University Press, 1979), p. 44. See also Idem, *The Printing Revolution in Early Modern Europe* (Cambridge: Cambridge University Press, 1983).

[5] Raymond Williams, *The Long Revolution* (London: Hogarth, 1992).

[6] Elizabeth L. Eisenstein, "The Fifteenth Century Book Revolution, Some Causes and Consequences of the Advent of Printing in Western Europe," in *Le Livre dans les sociétés pré-industrielles* (Athens: Kentron Neoelleon Ereunon, 1982), pp. 57–76; Idem, "From Scriptoria to Printing Shops: Evolution and Revolution in the Early Printing Book Trade," in K. E. Carpenter (ed.), *Books and Society in History, Papers of the Association of College and Research Libraries Rare Books and Manuscripts Preconference, 24–28 June, 1980, Boston, Massachusetts* (New York–London: Bowker, 1983), pp. 29–42.

[7] Jacques le Goff, *Les intellectuels au Moyen Âge* (Paris: Éditions du Seuil, 1985), p. 187; Robert A. Houston, *Literacy in Early Modern Europe: Culture and Education 1500–1800* (London–New York: Longman, 1988), pp. 160–163; Brian Richardson, *Printing, Writers and Readers in Renaissance Italy* (Cambridge: Cambridge University Press, 1999), p. 9; Adrian Johns, *The Nature of the Book: Print and Knowledge in the Making* (Chicago–London: The University of Chicago Press, 1998); Diederick Raven, "Elizabeth Eisenstein and the Impact of Printing," *European Review of History/Revue européene d'Histoire* 6/2 (1999), pp. 223–234; Nicholas Hudson, "Challenging Eisenstein: Recent Studies in Print Culture," *Eighteenth-Century Life* 26/2 (2002), pp. 83–95; Asa Briggs and Peter Burke, *A Social History of the Media: From Gutenberg to the Internet* (Cambridge: Polity Press, 2003), pp. 15–73; David McKitterick, *Print, Manuscript and the Search for Order, 1450–1830* (Cambridge: Cambridge University Press, 2003).

[8] See Eva Hagebutt-Benz–Dagmar Glass–Geoffrey Roper (eds.), *Sprachen des Nahen Ostens und die Druckrevolution: eine interculturelle Begegnung/Middle Eastern Languages and the Print Revolution: a Cross-cultural Encounter. A Catalogue and Companion to the Exhibition* (Mainz: Johann Gutenberg Museum, 2002).

ceptions in which that introduction is interpreted within the framework of a cultural "evolution."[9] In the context of this controversy the question whether or not Ibrahim Müteferrika's printing enterprise was an "agent of change" in the world of Islam has received conflicting replies. Previous scholarship has tended to give a negative answer to this question since Ibrahim did not sell the total number of copies he printed, and since his enterprise was suspended after his death. However, the present article seeks to show that Ibrahim Müteferrika's printing press was indeed an agent of change—though not an agent of *immediate* change.

To be sure, the transition from scribal to print culture was a slow, gradual and arduous process. In this regard, as Brian Richardson notes, old habits die hard.[10] What is important here is to find a plausible answer to the question when exactly one could claim that a certain print culture already exists. For this we first need a definition of the term "print culture" which would then allow us to fix unambiguously the time of its real domination over scribal culture. Traditionally the so-called "print-culture scholarship" has satisfied itself in pointing out that once printing technology with movable type was introduced the spread of printed books caused profound transformations in all social spheres. But is the establishment of a printing press enough in itself to enable us to speak about a print culture? A more significant sign of a developed and dominant print culture is probably the existence of a social conviction of the necessity of printed modes of transmission of knowledge and information. Thus the establishment of a printing house is certainly a starting point in the formation of print culture, but within different social contexts the process of overcoming the strongly entrenched manuscript tradition took place in the shorter or longer term.

However, in this discussion of the agents and the opponents of printing--that is, the printers on the one hand, and the copyists or other traditionalists on the other—what has rather tended to be ignored is the role of a "third party": the reading public. The coexistence and interaction between manuscript culture and print culture depended not only on the spread and development of printing presses across Europe, or in this case

[9] See André Demeerseman, "Un mémoire célèbre qui préfigure l'évolution moderne en Islam," *Revue de l'Institut des belles lettres arabes* (IBLA) XVIII (1955), pp. 5–32; Wahid Gdoura, *Le début de l'imprimerie arabe à Istanbul et en Syrie. Évolution de l'environnement culturel (1706–1787)* (Tunis: Institut Superieur de Documentation, 1985).

[10] Richardson, *Printing, Writers and Readers*, p. 77.

the Ottoman Empire, but on the reception of printed books by the traditional or newly emerging reading public. Little has been discovered so far about how the various segments of that public considered printed books, or about how far and how fast printed materials penetrated public and private spheres respectively. The answers of these questions, however, could reveal a trend in the reception of printing by readers which proves to be at variance more or less to the speed of the spread of printing as a technology per se.

As a matter of fact, the starting point in the formation of the Ottoman Turkish attitude towards printing does not coincide with the introduction of Ottoman Turkish printing, but with the dawn of European printing with movable type in the second half of the fifteenth century. In fact, this attitude was sometimes ambivalent, revealing a variation between the official and non-official attitudes, as both non-Ottoman and Ottoman sources reveal.

At least two western travelers, André Thevet, who journeyed to the Orient in 1549, and Paul Ricaut, who was in Istanbul in the 1660s, claimed that printing was forbidden by the Ottoman rulers. Thevet claims that Sultan Bayezid II (1481-1512) issued a decree in 1483 stipulating the death penalty for those who dared to print books, and that the succeeding sultan, Selim I (1512-1520), confirmed the previous decree in 1515.[11] As a matter of fact, scholars have been reluctant to consider these claims historically correct because no documentary confirmation has so far been found.[12] Such claims have probably something to do with the known restrictions set on non-Muslim printing houses that were operating on Ottoman soil regarding the printing of books in Arabic script.[13] Ricaut, however, claims that the Ottoman sultans banned printing because it would bring in-depth knowledge that could threaten their tyrannical rule. Moreover, he gave still another reason, namely concern for the livelihood of

[11] André Thevet, *Histoire des plus illustres et scavans hommes de leurs siècles* (Paris: Manger, 1671), 2, p. 111. Quoted after Gdoura, *Le début de l'imprimerie arabe*, p. 86.

[12] See Efdaleddin, "Memalik-i Osmaniye'de Tıbaatın Kadimi" [History of printing in the Ottoman state], *Tarih-i Osmanî Encümeni Mecmuası* 40 (1332 [1916]), pp. 242–249; A. D. Jeltyakov, *Türkiye'nin Sosyo-Politik ve Kültürel Hayatında Basın (1729–1908 Yılları)* [Printing in the socio-political and and cultural life of Turkey (1729–1908)] (Ankara: Basın Yayın Genel Müdürülüğü, 1979), p. 20; Gdoura, *Le début de l'imprimerie arabe*, p. 88.

[13] John-Paul Ghobrial, "Diglossia and the 'Methodology' of Arabic Print," paper presented at the 2nd International Symposium History of Printing and Publishing in the Languages and Countries of the Middle East, 2–4 November 2005, Bibliothèque nationale de France, Paris.

manuscript copyists and the eventual decline of calligraphy, an art in which the Turks are, according to him, superior over other nations.[14]

Ricaut's claims are supported by Giovanni Donado, whose account of the literature of the Turks was published in 1688, where he states that the Ottoman sultans have banned printing in Oriental languages in order to secure the copyists' livelihood. Donado adds, however, that the Turks regard the printing press as a Christian invention and printed books as "blasphemy," although the latter attitude was not loudly voiced.[15] But the claims of Ricaut and Donado are only partly supported by the Conte di Marsigli, an Italian nobleman who visited Istanbul in the late 1670s and early 1690s. In his book on the military state of the Ottoman Empire published in 1732, Marsigli claims that if the Turks do not print their books this is not because of any specific prohibition but because of their concern for the livelihood of the numerous copyists.[16] In other words, where Ricaut and Donado speak of the official prohibition of printing, Marsigli implies rather a non-official abstention from printing.

In the 1780s Mouradgea D'Ohsson, an Istanbul Armenian, also holds the copyists responsible for the delay in the introduction of Ottoman printing.[17] Manuscript copyists were certainly unhappy at the prospect of competition from printing, and according to the accounts of a contemporary of Ibrahim Müteferrika, the Swiss nobleman César de Saussure, Ibrahim's intention to launch a printing venture met with a severe reaction from the religious and as well from the copyists, who appealed to the Grand Vizier to put a stop to such an undertaking which threatened their livelihood.[18]

[14] Paul Ricaut, *The Present State of the Ottoman Empire* (London: 1668), p. 32.

[15] Franz Babinger, "18. Yüzyılda İstanbul'da Kitabiyat" [Printing in eighteenth-century Istanbul], in N. Kuran-Burçoğlu (trans. and ed.), *Müteferrika ve Osmanlı Matbaası* [Müteferrika and the Ottoman printing press] (İstanbul: Tarih Vakfı Yurt Yayınları, 2004), p. 9.

[16] Signore conte di Marsigli/Mr. Le Compte de Marsigli, *Stato militare dell'Impero Ottomanno incremento e decremento del medesimo/L'Etat militaire de l'Empire ottoman, ses progrès et sa décadence* (The Hague–Amsterdam: 1732), p. 40; Gyula Káldy-Nagy, "Beginnings of the Arabic-Letter Printing in the Muslim World," in Gyula Káldy-Nagy (ed.), *The Muslim East, Studies in Honour of Julius Germann, Loránd Eötvös* (Budapest: Loránd Eötvös University, 1974), pp. 204–205; İsmet Binark, "Türkiye'ye Matbaanın Geç Girişinin Sebepleri Üzerine" [On the reasons for the late introduction of printing to Turkey], *Türk Kültürü* 65 (1968), pp. 295–304.

[17] Ignace Mouradgea D'Ohsson, *Tableau général de l'Empire Othoman* (Paris: 1787), 1, p. 298.

[18] Coloman de Thály (trans. and ed.), *Lettres de Turquie (1730–1739) et Notices (1740) de César de Saussure* (Budapest: Academie hongroise des sciences, 1909), p. 94.

Donado is not the only western traveler to put emphasis on the religious aspect of the printing issue. The Austrian envoy to Istanbul, Ogier Ghiselin de Busbecq (1522–1592), who shared in a number of letters the impressions from his stay there in the period of 1555–1562, wrote that the Ottomans had not adopted the technology of printing from the Europeans for fear of committing disrespect to their holy books.[19] In his history of printing Thomas Francis Carter is inclined to put the Muslim bias against printing down to conservativeness, suggesting that since the Koran was preserved in manuscript form not only its text but also its form was considered unchangeable.[20] Such an explanation might seem plausible, but late nineteenth-century findings in the Fayyum oasis in Egypt of fragments of block-printed texts with Arabic script, among them verses from the Koran dating from the tenth to the thirteenth century,[21] may indicate that such conservatism was not always a force. Certainly, one should distinguish between the printing of sacred texts and the printing of secular matters. If in regard to the former there were religious obstacles, the latter seems much more acceptable, as seems to have been the case during the reign of the Umayyad Caliph Abd ar-Rahman an-Nasir (912-961), who reportedly sent his orders to the provincial governors of Andalusia in printed form.[22]

It is interesting, further, to take a look at what Ottoman Turkish sources reveal about official and non-official attitudes towards printing. An edition of the Arabic commentary on Euclid's *Elements of Geometry* by Nasireddin al-Tusi (d. 1274), printed in 1594 at the *Tipographia Medicea* in Rome, includes the text of a decree issued by Sultan Murad III (1574–1595) in 1588. The decree reveals that two European traders had imported into the Ottoman state among other goods books printed in Arabic and Persian,[23] on the basis of a decree allowing them to do so. However, the two traders complained that their stock had been plundered at the dock by the locals who had been seriously offended by the fact that the two foreign traders had such books. The decree of 1588 ordained that all

[19] See Gdoura, *Le début de l'imprimerie arabe*, p. 103.

[20] Thomas Francis Carter, *The Invention of Printing in China and Its Spread Westward* (New York: Columbia University Press, 1931), p. 112.

[21] See Robert W. Bulliet, "Medieval Arabic *Tarsh*: A Forgotten Chapter in the History of Printing," *Journal of the American Oriental Society* 107/3 (1987), pp. 427–438.

[22] *Ibid.*; Káldy-Nagy, "Beginnings of the Arabic-Letter Printing in the Muslim World," p. 201.

[23] For western prints in Arabic script see Josée Balagna, *L'imprimerie arabe en Occident: XVIe, XVIIe et XVIIIe siècle* (Paris: Editions Maisonneuve & Larose, 1984).

responsible Ottoman authorities should in future take steps to prevent such plundering, which was contradictory to Muslim sacred law and to the capitulations that were in force.[24] The decree is a good illustration of the two sides of the coin. Officially, the Ottoman authorities allowed the trade in Arabic books printed abroad; but the wider public was, to a certain extent at least, hostile towards such prints. This hostility must have been especially true for European prints of the Koran. During the seventeenth century it is reported that a large shipment of Koran prints imported to Ottoman shores by an Englishman were thrown into the Sea of Marmara by the locals.[25]

But if for the common people such prints might have been offensive to a greater or lesser extent, those who were in need of such texts were much more open-minded and secured copies. As evidence for this I am able to refer to another print, a copy of Avicenna's *Canon in Medicine* printed in 1593 at the *Tipographia Medicea* and preserved at the Oriental Department of the Bulgarian National Library in Sofia. Its title page contains three ownership inscriptions: one of them is dated 1639-1640 and pertains to a certain Zeynulabidin son of Halil, who was Muslim judge in Galata (today, part of Istanbul), while the other two are of a certain El-Hajj Mehmed al-Garbi saying that he purchased the copy in 1695-1696 from the estate of the late El- Hajj Mahmud, mufti of Trabzon.[26] In this case one can identify at least two representatives of the Ottoman religious class of relatively high rank who were not prejudiced towards printed books in Arabic, even though these were the products of a western printing house.

However, such western prints in Arabic script had not proved generally successful as items of trade in the Orient, as Antoine Galland admitted in his preface to Herbelo de Mollenville's *Oriental Library*, printed in Paris in 1697. Galland, who was for a while in Istanbul in 1672–1673, refers to western prints of Avicenna, Euclid and "a geographical work" (in fact, the famous geographical work of al-Idrisi) which he says were targeted not at

[24] See the English translation of the text in George N. Atiyeh (ed.), *The Book in the Islamic World: The Written Word and Communication in the Middle East* (Albany: State University of New York Press, 1995), p. 283.

[25] Franz Babinger, *Stambuler Buchwesen im 18. Jahrhundert* (Leipzig: Breitkopf und Haertel, 1919), p. 8.

[26] Sofia, National Library, Oriental Department: Rare Books Collection, O II 160, *Kitâbü'l-Kânûn fi't-tıbb li-Abu 'Ali eş-Şeyh er-Reis İbn-i Sînâ* (Romae: Tipographia Medicea, 1593). See the facsimile of the page in question in Stoyanka Kenderova–Zorka Ivanova, *From the Collections of Ottoman Libraries in Bulgaria during the 18th–19th Centuries* (Sofia: National Library Printing Press, 1999), p. 95.

westerners familiar with Arabic but the reading public in the Orient. However, trade in them proved unsuccessful because Muslims still preferred manuscripts, even at a higher price, to printed books.[27] One may trust both of Galland's claims. As shown above, such prints were indeed traded in the Ottoman book market. On the other hand, they had seemingly drawn less attention than initially expected. This lack of interest in what printing had to offer is clearly detectable when we read between the lines of a pair of texts written by two prominent seventeenth-century Ottoman intellectuals, Ibrahim Peçevi (1574-1650) and Katib Çelebi (1609-1657).

In his *History*, Peçevi deals in brief with the development of European printing and describes it as a strange but efficient art.[28] Katib Çelebi, on the other hand, refers to ancient Chinese printing in his famous geographical work, *Mirror of the World*.[29] Yet Çelebi complains of being restricted from including in his book all the maps he wished, since the art of printing was not in use in his country and therefore it was a problem to reproduce even a single page of illustration.[30] For all that, Katib Çelebi does not (as Orhan Koloğlu has pointed out) recommend his compatriots adopt the technology of printing.[31] Nor did Ibrahim Peçevi. These two narratives leave the impression that well into the early eighteenth century even Ottoman intellectuals did not so much as address the question of whether to print or not to print. And the lack of such concern is indicative enough of a corresponding lack of a need. Or to be precise, with regard to Katib Çelebi's complaints one may assume that some mid-seventeenth century Ottoman Turkish intellectuals felt that there was a use for printing not in general but in particular and specific cases, for example, for map-making in this instance.

[27] Quoted after Selim Nüzhet Gerçek, *Türk Matbaacılığı* [Turkish printing], vol. I, *Müteferrika Matbaası* [Müteferrika's press] (Istanbul: MfV, 1939), pp. 18–19.

[28] Peçevi İbrahim Efendi, *Peçevi Tarihi* [Peçevi's history], ed. B. S. Baykal (Ankara: Kültür Bakanlığı, 1981), 1, pp. 82–83.

[29] Orhan Şaik Gökyay, *Katip Çelebi'den Seçmeler* [Selections from Katip Çelebi] (İstanbul: MEB, 1968), p. 124.

[30] Hamit S. Selen, "Cihannümā," in *Kâtip Çelebi Hayatı ve Eserleri Hakkında İncelemeler* [Studies on Katip Çelebi's life and writings] (Ankara: TTK, 1991), p. 131; Osman Ersoy, *Türkiye'ye Matbaanın Girişi ve İlk Basılan Eserler* [The introduction of printing to Turkey and the first printed books] (Ankara: A. Ü. Dil ve Tarih-Coğrafya Fakültesi, 1959), p. 30 (the author quotes Selen's publication but misrepresents Katib Çelebi's words in claiming that printing has been forbidden).

[31] Orhan Koloğlu, *Basımevi ve Basının Gecikme Sebepleri ve Sonuçları* [The reasons for the late introduction of printing and the printing press and their consequences] (İstanbul: İstanbul Gazeteciler Cemiyeti, 1987), p. 30.

To summarize, the tradition of hand copying seems to have been quite adequate to satisfy the need for written materials in the Ottoman Empire and in the wider world of Islam. If there were psychological, cultural, religious, and social concerns that made the Ottomans refrain from adopting printing, equally it seems that they felt no great or vital need of printing, at least to such a degree that might make them overcome the alleged concerns. Scholars dealing with Ottoman history point out that there was never an "iron curtain" between the Ottoman elite and their European counterparts to prevent the exchange of new ideas, but make it clear that the Ottomans adopted foreign cultural patterns only if they were really needed.[32]

The eventual adoption of printing technology by the Ottomans was closely connected with the socio-cultural developments during the so-called Tulip Period (1718-1730), when some trend of Westernization was sparked by the first long-term Ottoman embassy to any country, namely France. The almost one-year long embassy (1720-1721) provoked among the Ottoman elite a remarkable interest in western culture, luxurious life-style, architectural styles (such as rococo and baroque) and discoveries in the fields of geography, astronomy, biology and medicine.[33] The western influence, however, did not replace immediately and completely the traditional Ottoman culture. It was adapted rather than merely adopted, thus creating, in Fatma Müge Göçek's words, a "cultural dichotomy"[34] or, in Rifaat Ali Abou-el-Haj's expression, a "cultural symbiosis."[35] In such a cultural atmosphere, the Ottoman elite (or at least a part of it), now much more open to western culture as compared with previous times and inclined to make use of selected western achievements, supported the introduction of typography to print books for the Turkish-speaking Muslim reading public.

[32] Rifaat Ali Abou-el-Haj, *Formation of the Modern State: The Ottoman Empire Sixteenth to Eighteenth Centuries* (Albany: State University of New York Press, 1991), p. 68; Ekmeleddin İhsanoğlu, "Ottoman Science in the Classical Period and Early Contacts with European Science and Technology," in Ekmeleddin İhsanoğlu (ed.), *Transfer of Modern Science & Technology to the Muslim World: Proceedings of the International Symposium on "Modern Sciences and the Muslim World. Science and Technology Transfer from the West to the Muslim World from the Renaissance to the Beginning of the XIXth Century" (Istanbul 2–4 September 1987)* (İstanbul: IRCICA, 1992), pp. 25, 29.

[33] For the Tulip Period see Fatma Müge Göçek, *East Encounters West: France and the Ottoman Empire in the Eighteenth Century* (New York–Oxford: Oxford University Press, 1987).

[34] *Ibid.*, p. 81.

[35] Abou-el-Haj, *Formation of the Modern State*, p. 67.

Indeed, the Ottoman authorities did not initiate, but supported, the establishment of a printing press, which was completely the private and personal undertaking of Ibrahim Müteferrika, who enjoyed in the beginning the moral and financial support of Said Efendi, one of the officials who took part in the embassy to France.

Ibrahim Müteferrika was a Transylvanian-born Hungarian Unitarian who graduated from a college in Kolozsvár. During the revolt of Imre Thököly against the Austrian occupation of Transylvania in the early 1690s he become an Ottoman subject and later converted to Islam, taking the name Ibrahim.[36] He acquired his byname after he was elevated in 1716 to the position of permanent *müteferrika*, a term deriving from the name of a corps at the Ottoman court whose members were especially closely attached to the person of the sultan and who were used for more or less important public or political missions. Ibrahim Müteferrika, in particular, was employed on diplomatic missions and had certain bureaucratic responsibilities. His last office seems to be the direction of the presumably first Ottoman papermill at Yalova, near Istanbul, in the years 1744–1747.[37] Ibrahim passed away at the end of January 1747,[38] and an inventory of all his possessions, including the unsold copies of the books printed by him, were listed in a probate record dated April 1, 1747. That record, however, became known only recently.[39]

[36] Thály, *Lettres de Turquie (1730–1739)*, pp. 93–94; Gérald Duverdier, "Savary de Brèves et Ibrahim Müteferrika: deux drogmans culturels à l'origine de l'imprimerie turque," *Bulletin du Bibliophile* 3 (1987), pp. 322–359.

[37] Details on the biography of Ibrahim Müteferrika are provided in T. Halasi Kun, "İbrâhim Müteferrika," *İslâm Ansiklopedisi* (İstanbul: MEB, 1950), 5/2, pp. 896–900; Niyazi Berkes, "Ibrahim Müteferrika," in B. Lewis et al. (eds.), *The Encyclopaedia of Islam*, New Edition (Leiden: E. J. Brill, 1971), 3, pp. 996–998; Erhan Afyoncu, "İlk Türk Matbaasının Kurucusu Hakkında Yeni Bilgiler," [New data about the founder of the first Turkish printing press] *Belleten* 243 (2001), pp. 607–622.

[38] According to different views Müteferrika died in 1745, 1746 or 1747. See the latest articles on this issue: Kemal Beydilli, "Müteferrika ve Osmanlı Matbaası. 18. Yüzyılda İstanbul'da Kitabiyat" [Müteferrika and Ottoman printing: Printing in eighteenth-century Istanbul], *Toplumsal Tarih* 128 (2004), pp. 44–52; Erhan Afyoncu, "İbrahim Müteferrika'nın Yeni Yayınlanan Terekesi ve Ölüm Tarihi Üzerine" [The newly published probate inventory of Ibrahim Müteferrika], *Türklük Araştırmaları Dergisi* 15 (2004), pp. 349–362.

[39] This record is preserved in the archive of the Mufti of Istanbul: *İstanbul Müftülüğü Şeriye Sicilleri, Kısmet-i Askeriye Mahkemesi*, Defter 98, fol. 39a–40b. A transcription in modern Turkish is given in my monograph on the first Ottoman Turkish printing press. See Orlin Sabev, *First Ottoman Journey in the World of Printed Books (1726–1746): A Reassessment* (Sofia: Avangard Prima, 2004), pp. 340–348.

It was not as a *müteferrika* that Ibrahim Müteferrika became famous both among his contemporaries and in history but as the first Ottoman printer. His boundless enthusiasm for printing helped him to overcome the obstacles set in his path by those who had reason to oppose it, like scribes, manuscript copyists and religious men. In order to convince the authorities to support his undertaking, Ibrahim wrote a treatise in 1726 entitled *The Utility of Printing*. In it Ibrahim pleaded his case, setting forth the likely benefits of printing for Muslims and for the future of the Ottoman state. He undertook, however, that he would not print religious texts, but rather dictionaries and books on history, medicine, physics, astronomy and geography.[40]

Besides this treatise, Ibrahim submitted to the Grand Vizier an application for an official permit to run his printing house. The Grand Vizier approved the application, then the Grand Mufti issued an official religious opinion (*fetvā*) allowing printing as a useful way of enabling the duplication of books, and finally, in the beginning of July 1727, Sultan Ahmed III (1703–1730) signed a special decree, giving to Ibrahim and Said Efendi an official permit to run the printing house.[41] Said Efendi, however, effectively withdrew in the early 1730s, leaving Müteferrika to run the enterprise on his own.

Between the years 1727 and 1742 Müteferrika printed all in all sixteen editions in twenty two volumes. One of them, a manual of the Turkish language, was intended not for the Ottoman–Muslim but the Francophone reading public. Two of the remaining editions are dictionaries, ten deal with history, another two combine historical and geographical themes, one title is completely geographical, one deals with physics, and one is on political and military issues. Some of the works were written in and others translated from Latin by the printer himself.[42]

Since the total print of most of Müteferrika's books was clearly indicated in one of his last books, one can presume that the total number of all

[40] See the English translation of the text in Atiyeh, *The Book in the Islamic World*, pp. 286–292.

[41] *Ibid.*, pp. 284–285.

[42] Ibrahim Müteferrika's good command of Latin was because of his Hungarian origin and college level educational background. Latin was either an official or unofficial spoken language in Europe, and Hungary in particular, well into the first half of the nineteenth century. See István Gy. Tóth, "Latin as a Spoken Language in Hungary during the Seventeenth and Eighteenth Centuries," *CEU History Department Yearbook 1997–1998* (Budapest, 1999), pp. 93–111; Idem, *Literacy and Written Culture in Early Modern Central Europe* (Budapest–New York: Central European University Press, 2000), p. 131; Houston, *Literacy in Early Modern Europe*, p. 24.

the printed copies was in the range of 10,000–11,000. If we compare this figure to the number of unsold copies that Müteferrika left upon his death, which the probate record gives as 2981, we could infer that 69.3 percent of the output of his press was sold. On the basis of these figures one could argue that Ibrahim Müteferrika's printing enterprise was either a qualified success or a qualified failure. But however we interpret them, it can be inferred that what Müteferrika was offering to the public (actually, a rather limited segment of that public) was books the demand for which was created because of their rareness and unavailability or because of the scarcity of relatively current information, but which were aside from the traditional reading taste.

Some insight into what the Ottoman Muslim reading public's taste was can be gained by examining probate records that mention titles of books. Such an approach is by no means without its problems. The surviving documentation is incomplete, and yet even what has survived is so bulky that it is impossible for a single researcher to undertake the huge project of consulting all the available materials.[43] In any case, the probate records reflect the situation at the time of death, so it is difficult to ascertain whether the deceased had not owned more books than he/she left at the time of his/her death: some book owners may have previously sold, given away, or donated some or all of their books. In any case, the number of book owners found in such records does not fully account for the number of actual readers, since many who might have been readers may not themselves have owned books.

Given the many problems related to the sources, the best that a researcher can do is to limit the scope of such a study in terms of chronology, geographical focus, and items studied. There are already several case-studies exploring reading tastes in particular places and times: in the capital Istanbul (seventeenth[44] and first half of the eighteenth century[45]), the neighborhood of Eyüp (eighteenth century),[46] as well as in

[43] The *Kısmet-i Askeriye Mahkemesi* collection, for example, includes 2144 registers of the period 1000/1591–92–1342/1924. See Ahmet Akgündüz, ed., *Şer'iye Sicilleri: Mahiyeti, Toplu Kataloğu ve Seçme Hükümler* [The Sharia Records: Specifics, overall catalogue and selections] (İstanbul: Türk Dünyası Araştırmaları Vakfı, 1988), pp. 100–116.

[44] Said Öztürk, *Askeri Kassama Ait Onyedinci Asır İstanbul Tereke Defterleri (Sosyo-Ekonomik Tahlil)* [Seventeenth-century probate inventories from the office of the military distributor of inheritance shares in Istanbul] (Istanbul: OSAV, 1995), pp. 174–184.

[45] Sabev, *First Ottoman Journey*, pp. 243–251.

[46] Tülay Artan, "Terekeler Işığında 18. Yüzyıl Ortasında Eyüp'te Yaşam Tarzı ve Standartlarına Bir Bakış: Orta Halliliğin Aynası" [A glance at the lifestyle and standard

some important Balkan, Anatolian and Arab provincial centers such as Sofia (1671–1833),[47] Rusçuk (1695–1786),[48] and Salonika (nineteenth century)[49]; Bursa (fifteenth–sixteenth century)[50]; Sinop, Samsun, Trabzon, Giresun, and Çorum (eighteenth–nineteenth centuries)[51]; Damascus (1686–1717)[52]; and Cairo (sixteenth to the eighteenth century).[53] These all reveal that the majority of identified book owners possessed predominantly religious literature, mainly in Arabic, and selections of poetry in Persian, Arabic and Turkish. Among religious books the most popular were, naturally, the Koran; then, a small collection of the most popular Koran chapters (*sura*) entitled *En^cām-i Şerīf* after the sura *En^cām* (*The Camel*); the *Muhammediye*, a verse biography of the prophet Muhammad written by Yazıcıoğlu Mehmed in 1444; and the *Vasiyetnāme* (*Book of Wills*) of Mehmed Birgivi (sixteenth century), a book on religious dogma and practice. The latter two writings were by Ottoman Turkish authors whose popularity was to a great extent due to the accessibility of the language in which they wrote. As for books on history and geography, the most popular were again those related to Islamic history, such as the *History of al-Tabari* which relates the life of Muhammad and

of living in mid-eighteenth-century Eyüp in the light of probate inventories: A mirror of the middle class], in Tülay Artan (ed.), *18. Yüzyıl Kadı Sicilleri Işığında Eyüp'te Sosyal Yaşam* [Social life in Eyüp in the light of eighteenth-century Sharia records] (Istanbul: Tarih Vakfı, 1998), pp. 49–64.

47 Orlin Sabev, "Private Book Collections in Ottoman Sofia, 1671–1833 (Preliminary notes)," *Études balkaniques* 1 (2003), pp. 34–82.

48 Orlin Sabev, "Knigata v ejednevieto na müsülmanite v Ruse (1695–1786) [The book in the daily life of the Rusçuk Muslims (1695–1786)]," *Almanah za istoriyata na Ruse* 4 (2002), pp. 380–394.

49 Meropi Anastassiadou, "Livres et 'bibliothèques' dans les inventaires après décès de Salonique au XIXe siècle," *Revue des mondes musulmans et de la Méditerranée* 87–88 (1999), pp. 111–141; Meropi Anastassiadou, "Des défunts hors du commun: les possesseurs de livres dans les inventaires après décès musulmans de Salonique," *Turcica* 32 (2000), pp. 197–252.

50 Ali İhsan Karataş, "Osmanlı Toplumunda Kitap (XIV–XVI. Yüzyıllar)" [The book in Ottoman society (14th–16th centuries)], in C. Güzel–K. Çiçek–S. Koca (eds.), *Türkler* (Ankara: Yeni Türkiye, 2002), 11: pp. 896–909.

51 Fahri Sakal, "Osmanlı Ailesinde Kitap" [The book in the Ottoman family], in Gülen Eren (ed.), *Osmanlı* (Ankara: Yeni Türkiye, 1999), 11, pp. 732–738.

52 Colette Establet and Jean-Paul Pascual, "Les livres des gens à Damas vers 1700," *Revue des mondes musulmans et de la Méditerranée* 87–88 (1999), pp. 143–175.

53 Nelly Hanna, *In Praise of Books: A Cultural History of Cairo's Middle Class, Sixteenth to the Eighteenth Century* (Cairo: The American University in Cairo Press, 2004).

the emergence and development of the early Islamic state,[54] and travelogues written by pilgrims to Mecca.[55] Old Persian epics such as *Şāhnāme* and *Hamzanāme* were also among the favorites. Dictionaries, on the other hand, are very seldom listed in these records. As for the reading public itself, it was composed mainly of men of religion (*ᶜulema*), both scholars and students, as well as administrative and military officials, and sometimes traders and craftsmen. In terms of gender, men considerably prevailed over women as readers.

Given such a reading public and taste in books, Ibrahim Müteferrika definitely filled a gap when he began by printing dictionaries. His first print, Vankulu's Arabic–Turkish redaction of Cevheri's Dictionary known as *Sihāh*, clearly became a bestseller since only one copy out of 500 copies printed is mentioned in his probate record. However, in his overall editing policy Müteferrika was much more inclined to print historical and geographical books (as outlined above). Yet in chosing texts on such subjects he ignored the traditional religious or the epic literature popular at the time. By printing works on Ottoman maritime history or the political history of Persia, the Caliphate and the Ottoman Empire, as well as books on geography, Müteferrika seems to have attempted to provide historical and geographical works of didactic value that would be useful to those involved in government. Indeed, as William Watson notes, Ibrahim's printing philosophy seems to be completely utilitarian.[56]

Hence special attention should be paid to the social and professional profile of the persons who bought Müteferrika's printed books. One can immediately observe that the first printed Ottoman books appeared in probate records very soon after they were printed. It is noteworthy that those who possessed such printed, and in the beginning relatively expensive books were not only Ottoman military and bureaucratic officials, as might be expected, but also religious functionaries.[57] The latter fact is

[54] *The History of al-Tabari: Biographies of the Prophet's Companions and Their Successors*, trans. E. Landau-Tasseron (New York: The State University of New York Press, 1998).

[55] See Menderes Coşkun, "Osmanlı Hac Seyahatnamelerinde Hac Yolculuğu" [Pilgrimage in Ottoman pilgrims' accounts], in G. Eren (ed.), *Osmanlı* (Ankara: Yeni Yürkiye, 1999), 4, pp. 506–511; Menderes Coşkun, "The Most Literary Ottoman Pilgrimage Narrative: Nabi's Tuhfetü'l-Haremeyn," *Turcica* 32 (2000), pp. 363–388.

[56] William J. Watson, "İbrāhīm Müteferrika and Turkish Incunabula," *Journal of the American Oriental Society* 88 (1968), pp. 436.

[57] More details are provided in Sabev, *First Ottoman Journey*, pp. 255–260.

significant, since it has been alleged that it was precisely religious functionaries who were the traditional opponents to the printing press.

The Ottoman Turkish experiment in printing ceased immediately after Müteferrika's death in 1747, though it enjoyed a brief afterlife with the reprint of Vankulu's dictionary in the mid-1750s (the initiative, in fact, of two Ottoman Muslim judges). Except for several books that sold well, Müteferrika's efforts in printing could seem the expression of a personal enthusiasm rather than a response to a real demand in Ottoman Turkish society for increased numbers of identical copies of books on particular topics; yet when his prints became artifacts in a world dominated by the manuscript tradition they showed people that there was an alternative way of multiplication of texts, shortening the time of the diffusion of information and widening the horizon of knowledge. Thus they set a precedent that convinced more people than ever before of the advantages of printing. In the second half of the eighteenth century the idea of printing found new promoters. For instance, Süleyman Penah Efendi in a memorandum entitled *Mecmua* addressed to Sultan Abdulhamid I (1774–1789) recommended the revival of Ottoman Turkish printing for administrative and educational purposes. By this he intended only the printing of secular texts, excluding religious texts such as the Koran and the Hadiths.[58] Süleyman Penah Efendi's proposal is remarkable evidence of the increasing need for the faster multiplication and wider dissemination of certain sorts of texts by means of printing toward the last quarter of the Ottoman eighteenth century. It is not just a co-incidence that a treatise of Müteferrika's printed in 1732 and proposing European-style military reforms was—presumably widely—copied by hand on the eve of Sultan Selim III's (1789–1807) reforms of the Ottoman army. Two surviving copies, dating from the second half of the eighteenth century and preserved in Firestone Library in Princeton[59] and in the Oriental Department in Sofia,[60] are good evidence that certain current issues such as, for example, the

[58] Cahit Telci, "Bir Osmanlı Aydının XVIII. Devlet Düzeni Hakkındaki Görüşleri: Penah Süleyman Efendi" [The views of an Ottoman intellectual about the eighteenth-century state order: Penah Süleyman Efendi] in Gülen Eren (ed.), *Osmanlı* (Ankara: Yeni Türkiye, 1999), 7, pp. 178–188.

[59] Princeton University Library: Rare Books and Special Collections, Manuscripts Division, Garrett Collection, Yahuda 5011, fol. 19b–75b. I would like to express my gratitude to the Friends of the Princeton University Library Grants Committee for providing me with a grant to carry out research on the first Ottoman Turkish printed books preserved in Firestone Library during the period June 5–23, 2006.

[60] Sofia, National Library, Oriental Department: Manuscripts Collection, OR 2296.

clear and vital need for military reforms created a demand for more available copies of texts dealing with such issues. Although in this particular case the need for further copies was met through copying by hand, some Ottoman intellectuals like Süleyman Penah Efendi were convinced that printing was a better alternative. Süleyman Penah Efendi's proposal was thus in keeping with something that was in the air at the time. For instance, in 1779 James Mario Matra (1746–1808), then secretary to the British Embassy in Istanbul, made an unsuccessful effort to reestablish an Ottoman press to print in particular the *Kamus* Dictionary, and then translations of western treatises on astronomy and mathematics.[61] It is uncertain whether Süleyman Penah Efendi's proposal had any direct effect on Sultan Abdulhamid, but the latter himself initiated the revival of Ottoman Turkish printing in 1784 using Müteferrika's old presses. The newly opened printing house was commissioned to two state officials, Raşid Mehmed Efendi and Vasıf Efendi, and operated until 1794, during which time it published eleven books, six of which served Selim III's military reforms, and the rest also being on secular subjects.[62]

At the turn of the nineteenth century (1217/1802–3) another Ottoman intellectual, Mehmed Emin Behic Efendi, wrote his *Sevānihü'l-levāyih* (*Inspired Memorandums*), in which—in contrast to Süleyman Penah Efendi—he urged the immediate printing of instructive books on Muslim religion as well as Arabic textbooks in 3,000–4,000 copy editions in order to improve mass education in religion matters by providing the pupils with cheaper textbooks. Behic Efendi also recommended the printing of regulations (*nizāmnāme*) for Muslim religious functionaries in the provinces, as well as textbooks for a school which he proposed should be opened for the special purpose of training scribes for the imperial bureaucracy. In addition, he urged the printing and disseminating of a penal code in accordance with the Sharia.[63] What is significant in Behic Efendi's proposal is the fact that he appreciates the vital role printing could play as a tool for making education accessible to a wider social layer and for improving the working of the bureaucracy and the implementation of the law.

[61] Richard Clogg, "An Attempt to Revive Turkish Printing in Istanbul in 1779," *International Journal of Middle East Studies* 10 (1979), pp. 67–70.

[62] Jale Baysal, *Müteferrika'dan Birinci Meşrutiyete Kadar Osmanlı Türklerinin Bastıkları Kitaplar* [Books printed by the Ottoman Turks from Müteferrika's time to the first constitutional period] (Istanbul: Edebiyat Fakültesi, 1968), pp. 59–60.

[63] Kemal Beydilli, "Küçük Kaynarca'dan Tanzimat'a Islahat Düşünceleri" [Reformation ideas from Küçük Kaynarca to the Tanzimat], *İlmi Araştırmalar* 8 (1999), pp. 25–64.

It seems clear that towards the turn of the nineteenth century it had become much easier than ever before to persuade Ottoman society of the public utility of printing, and the reason for this was not only the more visible need of printing but equally the precedent set earlier by Müteferrika. In other words, due to Müteferrika's printing enterprise a major shift in the public attitude toward printing occurred between the mid-seventeenth century, when it did not even enter the thoughts of intellectuals like Ibrahim Peçevi and Katib Çelebi that this technology could be introduced to the Ottomans—although their accounts outline the advantages of European or Chinese printing—and the turn of the nineteenth century when intellectuals like Süleyman Penah Efendi and Mehmed Emin Behic Efendi were deeply convinced of the necessity of printing.

After the 1784 revival Ottoman printing enjoyed a boom in the nineteenth century, serving faithfully to promote reforms in Ottoman civil, religious and military education; the improvement of Ottoman central and provincial administration; the launching of propaganda for the promotion of state reformative initiatives; and the Ottoman booksellers who had permission to print books at the state printing press. As a matter of fact, prints on religious matters began gradually prevailing over those on secular matters. This was partly due to the printing of textbooks for the reformed school system that required greater numbers of books than ever before for the sake of mass education.

The remarkable expansion of Ottoman printing in the nineteenth century did not, however, put an end to the strong manuscript tradition. It simply confirmed printing as an alternative technology, which in the course of time expanded more and more at the expense of manuscript copying. Probably nostalgia was responsible for the negative attitude of some Istanbul booksellers toward printing which Charles White observed in 1844. It is noteworthy that the probate records dating from the second half of the nineteenth century, and even the official printed catalogues of Ottoman libraries prepared during the reign of Abdulhamid II (1876–1909) still make a distinction between manuscripts and printed books by explicitly designating the latter with the term *matbu*ᶜ. Official administrative correspondence either on central or local level dating from the 1850s likewise refers to printed regulative or legislative materials as a "printed general instruction sheet" (*matbu*ᶜ *ta*ᶜ*rife-i umumiye*)[64] or "printed regula-

[64] National Library, Oriental Department (Sofia): Fund 96, a. u. 92 (*mazbata* from 1852).

tion" (*matbu*^{c} *nizāmnāme*),[65] thus explicitly underlining their being printed. In other words, in the nineteenth century the printed word was still considered in a way an extraordinary rather than ordinary phenomenon among the Ottomans.

In the course of time, however, even as the Ottomans became quite accustomed to the printed word, intellectuals like Münif Pasha (1830–1910) and Celal Nuri became concerned that printing with movable type was not really compatible with the peculiar nature of the Arabic script.[66] The problem is that printing with Arabic letters creates special difficulties which are not to be found in printing with the Latin, Greek, Armenian, Hebrew, and Cyrillic alphabets or even with Chinese hieroglyphs. The Arabic script, along with its Persian and Ottoman Turkish versions, is cursive, that is, most letters are required to be linked to the preceding and following ones, in consequence of which they have four different forms, one main one and three others, depending on the position of the letter in the word. Thus, printing in Arabic is much more difficult than other scripts, and in a sense impractical, first because it requires many more forms, and second because these forms have to be perfectly linked to each other.[67] Because of this, the typesetting process takes a much longer time, and the result is not always satisfactory, thus leaving less room for the claim that printing is a better way of duplicating texts than copying by hand. Yet printing technology had to compete with calligraphy as a supreme Islamic art.[68] By contrast, when lithography was invented in the late eighteenth century and later introduced to the world of Islam it proved to be much more satisfying to the Muslim reading public on esthetic grounds.[69] But all this did not mean that the Ottomans were to desist from printing with movable type. Quite the contrary, from the reign of Mahmud II (1808–1839) and until the end the nineteenth century at least 77 printing houses, publishing in Ottoman Turkish, were in operation in Istanbul. Of them 50

65 National Library, Oriental Department (Sofia): Fund 96A, a. u. 172 (*mazbata* from 1857–58).

66 Hüseyin Gazi Topdemir, *İbrahim Müteferrika ve Türk Matbaacılığı* [Ibrahim Müteferrika and Turkish printing] (Ankara: T.C. Kültür Bakanlığı, 2002), pp. 30–32.

67 Huda S. Abifares, *Arabic Typography: A Comprehensive Sourcebook* (London: Saqi Books, 2001), pp. 94–95; Warren Chappell, *A Short History of the Printed Word* (London: André Deutsch Ltd, 1972), p. 38.

68 See Uğur Derman–N. Çetin, *The Art of Calligraphy in the Islamic Heritage*, ed. Ekmeleddin İhsanoğlu (Istanbul: IRCICA, 1998).

69 Francis Robinson, "Technology and Religious Change: Islam and the Impact of Print," *Modern Asian Studies* 27/I (1993), pp. 229–251.

combined type-setting and lithographical printing technologies, 21 were purely type-setting, and 6 lithographical.[70] In contrast to the eastern parts of Muslim world, where lithography became the preferred mode of printing, the Ottomans persevered with movable type, lithography remaining of secondary significance. Indeed, so keen were they on printing with movable type that (oddly enough) they even went so far as making efforts to reform the very nature of the Arabic script. In 1879 the Council of Public Education (*Meclis-i Maᶜārif-i Umūmiye*) appointed a special committee to remodel the standard Arabic script to make it non-cursive in order to facilitate the process of printing. The committee's efforts, however, proved unsuccessful.[71] Later, in 1914, the so-called "Enver Pasha spelling" (*Enver Pāşā imlāsı*), which separated the Arabic characters from each other, was tested in printing for a while.[72] Finally, the introduction of a Turkish version of the Latin script in 1928 solved the whole problem.

Another major step in Ottoman Turkish print culture was taken in the 1870s, when the Koran was at last printed.[73] Ahmed Cevdet Pasha (1822–1895), a prominent nineteenth-century Ottoman intellectual, explains in his *History* how the Ottoman attitude toward printing of religious matters changed. He relates that after Müteferrika and Said Efendi were permitted to print secular books the Ottomans were reluctant to print religious texts because they were concerned that this would harm the sacredness of the "Sharia books" (which is a striking reminder of Busbecq's observation from the sixteenth century!). But the Ottomans applied the principle of

[70] See the list of these presses in Ahmed Negih Galitekin (ed.), *Osmanlı Kaynaklarına Göre İstanbul. Cami, Tekke, Medrese, Mekteb, Türbe, Hamam, Kütüphane, Matbaa, Mahalle ve Selâtin İmaretleri* [Mosques, dervish lodges, theological and elementary schools, tombs, public baths, printing houses, neighborhoods, and sultanic kitchens in Istanbul in the light of Ottoman sources] (İstanbul: İşaret Yayınları, 2003), pp. 974–983.

[71] Server İskit, *Türkiye'de Neşriyat Hareketleri Tarihine Bir Bakış* [A glance at the history of publishing activities in Turkey] (Istanbul: MfV, 1939), p. 90.

[72] *Ibid.*, pp. 145–146.

[73] See Osman Keskioğlu, "Türkiye'de Matbaa Te'sisi ve Mushaf Basımı," [The establishment of the printing press in Turkey and the printing of the Koran], *Ankara Üniversitesi İlâhiyat Fakültesi Dergisi* 15 (1967), pp. 121–139; Mahmud Gündüz, "Matbaanın Tarihçesi ve İlk Kur'anı Kerim Basmaları," [A short history of printing and the first prints of Koran], *Vakıflar Dergisi* 12 (1978), pp. 335–350; Nedret Kuran-Burcuoğlu, "Matbaacı Osman Bey: Saray'dan İlk Defa Kur'an-ı Kerim Basma İznini Alan Osmanlı Hattatı," [Osman bey the printer: The first Ottoman calligrapher who received state permission to print the Koran], *Türklük Bilgisi Araştırmaları/Journal of Turkish Studies* 26/II (2002), pp. 97–112.

analogy, observed by the Hanafi school of law, and accepted that the printing of the Koran is not a blasphemy since the binding of the Koran, which also requires pressing, is considered allowable. Therefore, for the sake of the diffusion of knowledge among students religious texts were printed in great numbers.[74]

Duplication of the Koran especially is expected to be faithful in terms of wording and orthography not only because it is considered divine revelation, but also because since the very dawn of Islam the Holy Book has been required to be read and learned by heart by every Muslim man and woman.[75] This meant that copying the Koran correctly was of vital importance for its spread among the whole Muslim community. By contrast, in Christendom the Church was in principle against the direct, unlimited or widespread access to the Bible by the common people, the message of the Scripture being disseminated to them only by the learned ecclesiastical hierarchy. That was why the Church was much concerned about the spread of vernacular Bibles even before the invention of printing in Europe, not to speak about printed versions of the Bible whose text was corrupted by errors of the printing technology itself.[76] Because of this aspect of printing duplication of the Koran requires strict faithfulness to the norm, since it would be read and learned not only by educated Muslim religious functionaries, but also by the whole community. Moreover, according to the traditional Islamic concept the very starting-point of a child's education is the reading and learning by heart of the Koran.[77] Accordingly, the main point of emphasis here was the correctness of the text itself, and the mode of duplication was expected to implement this indispensable requirement. It seems that in the beginning Muslim societies considered printing as a technology that discredited itself through the cor-

[74] *Târîh-i Cevdet* [Cevdet's history] (Der sa'âdet: Matba'a-i 'Osmâniyye, 1309 [1891]), 1, p. 76.

[75] A. L. Tibawi, *Islamic Education: Its Tradition and Modernization into the Arab National Systems* (London: Luzac, 1972), p. 24.

[76] See Raven, "Elizabeth Eisenstein and the Impact of Printing."

[77] Tibawi, *Islamic Education*, p. 26; Cevat İzgi, *Osmanlı Medreselerinde İlim* [Science in Ottoman theological schools] (Istanbul: İz Yayıncılık, 1997), 1, pp. 61–108; Ömer Özyılmaz, *Manzume-i Tertib-i Ulûm, Tertibu'l-Ulûm, Kaside Fi'l-Kütübi'l Meşhure Fi'l Ulûm, Kevakib-i Seb'a ve Erzurumlu İbrahim Hakkı'nın Tertib-i Ulûm İsimli Eserine Göre, XVII. ve XVIII. Yüzyıllarda Osmanlı Medreselerinin Eğitim Programları* [The curriculum of seventeenth- and eighteenth-century Ottoman theological schools according to *Manzume-i Tertib-i Ulûm, Tertibu'l-Ulûm, Kaside Fi'l-Kütübi'l Meşhure Fi'l Ulûm, Kevakib-i Seb'a* and Erzurumlu İbrahim Hakkı's work *Tertib-i Ulûm*] (Ankara: T.C. Kültür Bakanlığı, 2002).

rupt western prints of the Koran, and manuscript copying as still reliable and much more deserving of trust. What Muslim societies were actually waiting for was probably not printing itself but the improvement of printing so as to satisfy the specific requirements of the duplicating of the holy texts. That was probably why, in contrast to western societies, they preferred to print first secular books, then popular but non-standard religious books (e.g. Birgivi's *Vasiyetnāme*), then standard treatises related to Muslim law and dogmatics which were used in theological education, and only at the last the Koran. In other words, printing penetrated the Muslim circle of knowledge from its periphery and finally approached its very core. This was just cautious behavior in the gradual adoption of printing, allowing it to penetrate further into the world of Islamic knowledge just step by step. It was a mutual process: printing overcame its shortcomings and proved that it could be more effective and correct; Muslims overcame their initial reluctance and suspicions. In other words, the "lewd" body of the printing press was covered with the veil of "virginity."

[11]

MASS PRODUCING HOURI'S MOLES

or Aesthetics and Choice of Technology in Early Muslim Book Printing

IAN PROUDFOOT

Transmissions of Islam have been radically affected by the use of print. Print has been as significant for Islam over the last two centuries as it has for Christianity over the past five centuries. In both cases the fires of reform and fundamentalism have been stoked by the new technology of communication. Muslims adopted his powerful technology from the West by processes that are still little understood. If the initiation of this change were better understood, we might also gain a better appreciation of why Muslims spurned print for three centuries while it flourished in Christian Europe.

My argument is that Muslims took up printing by two paths.

1. *The First Book Printing in the Middle East*

The Ottoman Government was consistently wary of printing. Early decrees in 1485 and 1515 forbade the printing of Arabic, though importation of books was allowed. Turkey's Christian and Jewish communities printed in Hebrew, Latin and Armenian from the sixteenth century, and Syrian Christians began sporadic printing in Arabic in the eighteenth century.[1] In 1728, the Ottoman court initiated Muslim printing under government sponsorship, but no independent Muslim presses were permitted until well into the nineteenth century. The press law of 1888 kept book printers and importers under tight administrative control.

The initiative of 1728 was part of the Ottoman court's project to emulate aspects of the France of Louis XV. A press was operated from 1728 to 1745 under the management of Ibrāhīm Müteferriḳa. It used imported French printing equipment with type cut and cast in Istanbul to produce rather costly books for well-placed Ottoman

[1] Oman 1989.

literati. Specifically excluded from the press were works on religion, namely the Qur'ān, *tafsīr*, *ḥadīth*, *fiqh* and *kalām*. Later, as part of a renewed military and fiscal modernisation program, semi-official printing was revived at Istanbul in 1780. With a similar purpose, a government press at Cairo was established at Būlāq in 1821–22 by Muḥammad ʿAlī, who had watched Napoleon use imported printing equipment disseminate administrative orders and proclamations in Arabic and believed that the Būlāq press would serve as an efficient means of improving the army and agriculture.[2]

The repertoire of these government-controlled presses in Cairo and Istanbul was rather restricted. The Ottoman ban on printing works of religion had been waived in 1803 for the publication of the Turkish catechism *Risāla-i Birgewī*, but the early diet of printed books overwhelmingly comprised technical manuals, dictionaries and grammars, with a few collections of *fatāwā* and works on dogma. Books on religious topics, which enjoyed longer print runs, began to be advertised for sale in the Ottoman Government gazette after 1831.[3] By 1850, about 650 editions of all kinds had appeared at Istanbul, while Būlāq under Muḥammad ʿAlī issued about 350 titles, of which about half were technical and scientific manuals, many translated from French.[4]

Marketing was primitive in this early period. There was but one book depository for Egypt, at Būlāq, with "pyramids of unsold stock". In 1831, an uncharitable French observer commented:

> . . . Books on tactics and medicine may have their uses, but address themselves to only a tiny number of readers. None of the others, with few exceptions, have any market or any circulation. They are multiplied by the press only to be stacked up in warehouses where it seems they are condemned to an eternal oblivion. No-one buys them, no-one reads them, because they do not accord with the needs of the present, nor with the spirit of the populace who require instruction and

[2] Berkes 1969, Duverdier 1987, Albin 1988.

[3] Baysal (1981:122) says a *firman* (not a *fatwa*) authorised this; Berkes (1964:127) says "the change seems to have come about gradually without fuss or a new authorisation."

[4] See Hammer 1831:7.583–595, Baysal 1981, Bianchi 1843, 1859–63, Verdery 1971, Heyworth-Dunne 1940, Albin 1988. The later fame of the Būlāq press may lead to an overestimate of its early scope and impact. Only after its disbandment and relaunching in 1861 did it take up large scale printing of books on history, language, literature and religion, in addition to technical works. Most of the Būlāq editions of Arabic classics date from the last thirty years of the nineteenth century (Crabbs 1984:201).

> enlightenment. Even at first glance it is easy to see how it stands with this printery, set up at such great cost, like so many other industries imported from Europe with insufficient care taken to adapt them to the country.[5]

The most saleable works were apparently put through the Būlāq press by private editors on their own account.

2. *Muslim Printing in India*

The picture in India is quite different.

The presence of the European press in India is very old, reaching back to the Jesuit press in Goa in 1556. However, not much printing of significance took place, beyond some Christian mission printing in Madras, until about 1780, when a fair number of presses began operating in the Presidency capitals of Calcutta, Bombay and Madras. In contrast to the Ottoman government, the English Company had an ideological preference for independent presses, whether run by Europeans or Indians. Yet Muslim involvement in this typographic printing remained marginal. The printing of literary and historical works in Persian in Calcutta (after 1781) and Bombay (after 1818) was undertaken on presses run by Europeans or Parsees respectively, with only editorial participation by Muslims. The first Muslim-sponsored printing came with the inauguration 1819 of a Royal Press by the Nawwāb Ghāzī al-Dīn Ḥaydar of Oudh. From this press over the next decade there issued several Persian works in praise of the Nawwāb, and two publications in Arabic: a *Panjsūrah* (five *sūra*s of the Qur'ān) and the first three volumes of an Arabic dictionary, *Tāj al-lughāt.*[6]

Then, suddenly, everything changed. In 1824 the Indian Company equipped each of its Presidencies with several of the recently invented lithographic presses, which it judged would provide a versatile and cheap means of printing administrative documents. Four of these presses were handed over to the Bombay School Book and School Society, and immediately applied to the printing of textbooks in Maratha, Gujarati and Hindustani (Urdu). In the first year, Indian operators were trained and 17,000 books were produced.

[5] Geiss 1907/08:212.

[6] Storey 1933, from Sprenger 1844.

Simultaneously, a history of Bengal, in Persian, was lithographed at Benares.[7] Over the next decade and a half, lithographic presses mushroomed all across northern India. The great majority of the new presses were Muslim owned and operated. They were private presses, independent of government subsidy or control—which was formally held at bay by the 1835 Press Act.[8] Major centres of Muslim publishing emerged at Lucknow-Cawnpore, Agra, Delhi, Lahore and Hyderabad (Deccan). Lucknow alone had more than a dozen lithographic presses in 1848, all in Muslim hands. By that time the presses of Lucknow-Cawnpore alone had published about 700 titles, some in up to ten editions, mainly comprising student's books, polemics, and religious tracts.[9] And the pace continued to quicken. By mid-century, Urdu was printed all over India, and practically all the important towns in northern India had their own lithographic printing presses. A contemporary observer estimated that there were about 112 such presses in different parts of the country. Lithography had become a very lucrative trade.[10] Indeed, so attractive was lithography that the Royal Press of Oudh switched to the new technique mid-way through the publication of its multi-volume Arabic dictionary.

While the marketing of books was disorganised, the conjunction of commercial drive and popular repertoire ensured strong demand. A sales agent for Ḥājj Ḥar[a]main Sharīfain, the first Muslim printer of Lucknow,

> would venture off with thousands of books in a bullock cart, going as far afield as Rawalpindi. In those days books were very rare, and a great novelty. He would be received with pomp, and could sell at any price he chose: usually Karima ma Muqiman for a few annas, Gulistan or Bostan for 3 or 4 rupee per volume. Even so, supply could not meet demand. After books had run out, it would be months before another consignment could be arranged.[11]

This sketch of Indian private enterprise in the market place is a far cry from the contemporary account of the Egyptian official press at Būlāq that was quoted earlier.

---

[7] Caresajee 1958.
[8] Govi 1977, Davis 1983.
[9] Diehl 1973.
[10] Haider 1981, Mohl 1853.
[11] Sharar 1975:107.

3. *The Influence of the Indian Model*

By mid-century, printing in Cairo and Istanbul was still a trickle beside this Indian torrent. The Indian model, with its commitment to lithography, proved influential. In Persia, after a brief flirtation with government-sponsored typography in Tabriz in 1819 and in Tehran in 1824, lithographic printing began in Tabriz 1835 and in Tehran 1844, and soon after in Isfahan and other cities. As in India, lithography spread quickly. By about 1860, any Persian town of consequence had at least one, and often several, lithographic presses.[12] As Browne remarked,

> One of the strangest things connected with the history of the art of printing in Persia from the time of its introduction until the present day is that notwithstanding the chronological priority of the introduction of typography into Persia, it entirely went out of fashion in a short while, and that for a long time (more than fifty years) the presses of Persia confined themselves exclusively to lithography . . .[13]

In Southeast Asia, where Muslim printing began in 1848, the following half-century of Muslim printing was similarly almost wholly lithographic. In both cases, Indian-style lithographic printing was focused from the outset on religious texts.

The government presses of Turkey and Egypt also employed lithography, but in the European manner. It was used for maps, illustrations, diagrams, formulae etc., a substitute for etching as an adjunct to typography; it was also used to reproduce administrative circulars, like the *Jurnāl al-Khidīw*. When we do find books printed by lithography, the presses belong to technical agencies. So when the *Dalā'il al-Khairat* was lithographed in the hand of the celebrated calligrapher Raḳīm Efendī in 1857, it was printed on the lithographic press of an Ottoman Engineers Regiment. By the 1850s lithographic book printing had begun to gain ground in Istanbul particularly, but it remained the poor cousin of typographic printing.[14]

This began to change in the 1860s. The turmoil surrounding the disbandment of the Būlāq press in 1861 made space for vigorous commercial printing for a popular religious and literary audience. A

[12] Polak 1865:279, Walther 1990:230, Avery 1991:817–819, Farmayan 1968:145. For Iraq, see Albin 1981, 1985:15.

[13] Browne 1914:9.

[14] Peron 1843, Geiss 1907/08, Hsu 1985, Walther 1990, Schlechta-Wssehrd 1853–55, Baysal 1981.

handful of private presses had been operating in Egypt in the previous decade, but private printing became significant as skilled personnel who had previously worked at the Būlāq press found their way into private printing. Private printeries using both typography and lithography proliferated, and publishers-cum-bookshops began printing works in popular demand, or commissioning them from jobbing printers. These were "private enterprise establishments, whose sole motive was profit and which published fast turn-over, dubious quality books, mostly on religion, popular reading and fiction."[15] These speculatively printed books were supplied to the book merchants who operated in the shadow of al-Azhar Mosque. They had previously specialised in providing cheaply copied manuscripts, and now saw a profitable alternative.

Muslim printing in the various centres of the Maghrib followed in the wake of these Egyptian developments, and similarly employed a combination of typography and lithography, usually under government supervision.[16]

In short, the history of early Muslim book printing reveals two separate initiations of printing, one in the Middle East, the other in India. The government-sponsored typographic printing in the Middle East is earlier, but had no influence on the rapid adoption of lithographic printing by Muslims in India. The two initiatives are further distinguished by different initial repertoires, one in which religious works are absent or marginal, and the other in which religious works are central. The power of lithography in this first era of book printing is evident. Lithography held sway from the beginning in India, Iraq, and Southeast Asia, displaced typography in Persia, and stimulated a great upsurge in the bulk and variety of printing in Turkey, Egypt, and the Maghrib.

4. *Preconditions for Printing*

This unexpectedly complex history of printing initiatives has implications for our understanding of the circumstances in which printing was adopted by Muslims. The notion that Islam was resistant to print is generally extrapolated from the Ottoman experience. The con-

[15] Rizk 1978:555.

[16] Safadi 1981, Albin 1988, Roper 1982, Demeerseman 1953:363, 1954:2.

trasting experience of Indian Muslims, however, provokes the question of how generalisable this Ottoman experience was.

Explanations that rely upon the exercise of state power need to be reconsidered. It is wholly credible that an authoritarian government whose writ ran sufficiently wide for a prohibition to have effect might well wish to avoid the immensely disruptive consequences of print that could be observed on its doorstep in Europe. No Christian government in Europe's print era ever enjoyed this option, so fragmented was political authority in Christendom.[17] Nor, significantly, did any government achieve more than fleeting control across the Indian sub-continent before 1857. It is also wholly credible that the Ottoman application of state power was shaped by its alliance with a clerical magistracy. Watt[18] reflects a general opinion when he characterises the higher grades of the Ottoman religious hierarchy as a privileged aristocracy "more interested in maintaining their own power than in promoting the welfare of the empire as a whole." He adds: "This is exemplified by their opposition to the introduction of printing." In fact the Ottoman evidence here is a little ambiguous: the high religious authorities approved, supported and administered Müteferriḳa's printing experiment.[19] The Ottoman integration of state and clerical interests, though normative in its day, was far from universally achieved in other societies in which Muslims pursued their fates, as British India and the Dutch East Indies remind us.

Or was conservatism intrinsic to the organisation of Islamic tradition itself, independent of state power?[20] Robinson takes up this question in his "Technology and Religious Change".[21] He adapts Graham's ideas of concurrent oral and written transmission,[22] in which Qur'anic recitation set the pattern for other dogmatic transmission, and "writing and literacy have always danced attention on a superior oral tradition." For Robinson the important dimension of this

[17] Realpolitik is in play here: the Christian Dutch East India Company enforced Ottoman-like restrictions on printing in Muslim Southeast Asia, where its writ ran wide, while in Europe the Dutch enjoyed perhaps Europe's freest and most diverse press. Europe's disunity undermines Duverdier's (1987:354) position on European reluctance to provide printing technology to Muslims.

[18] 1988:34.

[19] See Káldy-Nagy 1974, Mardin 1962:217, Duverdier 1987:336. Alleged protests by the scribes' guilds of Istanbul against the first experiments with printing are not well attested. Káldy-Nagy 1974:204–205.

[20] Bulliet 1987, Safadi 1981 etc.

[21] 1993.

[22] Graham 1987.

dualism is that "person to person transmission was at the heart of the transmission of Islamic knowledge. Muslim scholars travelled the world to receive in person the reliable transmission of knowledge." The written word, unexpounded, is a veil that separates the student from discovery of meaning. The principally valid transmission is from teacher to pupil, recorded in the *ijāza* awarded on completion of the study. (The same path to knowledge prevailed in the mystical orders, and among calligraphers.) Printing, by striking at person-to-person transmission, "struck right at the heart of Islamic authority". Therein, for Robinson, lies the explanation for Islam's conservatism toward print. "No Muslim was likely to adopt it until he saw a good in printing greater than the evil it might cause." This extreme situation arose, Robinson argues, under Christian colonial rule, when "Islam itself was at stake and print was a necessary weapon in defence of the faith."[23] In Robinson's view, this is why the first active involvement in religious printing is evident among Muslims in India (and in Russia).

However it is not clear that Islamic transmission was always so conservative as Robinson's sketch suggests, nor that Muslim printing is best understood as a response to any external threat. In the early nineteenth century there were Hindu revival movements, like that of Rammohan Roy, which responded to the Western challenge. They were led by English-educated Hindus, a class that had no Muslim counterpart until the later rise of Sayyid Aḥmad Khān and the Aligarh College group. Muslim printing was therefore not innovated by a déraciné élite, but—as Robinson concedes—exploited by active mainstream leaders concerned to reform and intensify Muslim belief. The notion that it was the European challenge which broke a conservative Islamic mould in India may underrate the dynamics of the Indian Muslim cultural environment.

Indeed, Levtzion and Voll identify vernacularisation as a major theme in their survey of Islamic renewal and reform in the eighteenth century in those societies with significant non-Muslim populations or residues, including India.[24] The push for vernacularisation involved experimenting with new paths of transmission. Reformist *ʿulamāʾ* and sufis who had long been challenging the old Perso-Islamic ways had begun to transmit knowledge in regional languages.

---

[23] Robinson 1993:237.

[24] Levtzion and Voll 1987.

In the eighteenth century, sufi ideas were spread through rural areas by means of mystical poems in the vernacular. "Urdu . . . became the recipient not just of many translations of the Quran and the Ḥadiths but also of dozens of classics of Islamic scholarship from al-Ghazali to Ibn Khaldun. Sufis followed suit, translating more and more of their *malfuẓāt* and *maktubāt* from Persian into Urdu so that the example of the saints could reach fresh generations. . . . This shift away from the old imperial language coincided with the introduction of the lithographic printing press."[25] The nineteenth-century rise of the press in India parallels the transformation of Hindustani into the new written vernaculars Urdu and Hindi.[26] The adoption of printing thus coincides with a great upsurge in vernacularisation, internal reform, and revival. Indeed, it is exceedingly difficult to disaggregate these concurrent developments. An example used by Robinson illustrates the point. Sayyid Aḥmad Barelvī's followers were active users of the press to promote their reformist ideas, notably through lithographic editions of *Sirāṭ al-Mustaqīm*, complied by Sayyid Aḥmad first in Persian, but soon translated and published in both Persian and Urdu, and *Taqwiyyat al-Imān* composed and printed directly in Urdu. Undoubtedly the press was critical in the momentum of this group, but the fact remains that Sayyid Aḥmad had compiled *Sirāṭ al-Mustaqīm* in 1819[27]—at a time when the only Muslim printing in India was undertaken on the Royal Press at Oudh—and so could hardly have written it for the press.

So, at the time when print was adopted there were already long-standing forces for vernacularisation, and active reformist and revivalist groups who had shown an interest in cultivating new modes of transmission, and who indeed took enthusiastically to print . . . but only in the early nineteenth century. The precise timing of the adoption of printing by Indian Muslims seems not to be wholly explained by the ideological climate. A more mundane fact cannot be overlooked: that is, that a new printing technology had just become available. It can be shown, I believe, that lithography has qualities that could explain its attractiveness to Indian Muslims who had not previously taken up typographic printing.

---

[25] Robinson 1991:124.
[26] Brass 1974:186.
[27] Metcalf 1982:56.

5. *Qualities of Two Printing Technologies*

Typographic printing and lithography are quite different technical processes. Both are means of achieving multiple reproduction of text, and carry the immense cultural and social implications which flow from that. However, the two processes have significantly different implications on the aesthetic and commercial level.

Moveable type printing has been invented twice, probably independently, once in China in the eleventh century, and again in Germany in the fifteenth. The idea is a simple extension of wood block printing which profits from the fact that the script to be reproduced is made up of independent items arranged in a line of uniform height or width. These were characteristics of both Chinese and European writing systems. Moveable type did not flourish in China but did so in Europe for reasons of economy. The major capital investment in printing using moveable type is the stock of interchangeable character types. Moveable type printing proved uneconomic for the morphemic Chinese writing system which required thousands of types. The European languages, which have alphabetic writing systems operating on the phonemic level, require about the number of characters provided on a standard typewriter.

In the Middle East early wood-block printing of Qur'anic verses and other religious formulae several centuries before Gutenberg,[28] did not develop into typography. An easy transition to moveable type was barred by the nature of the Arabic script. The Arabic writing system, though operating on the phonemic level, is neither alphabetic nor based on the linear arrangement of independent items. Its letter forms vary according to position, and in the scribal hand it abounds with non-linear ligatures and kerning. A reasonable approximation of the scribal hand might be achieved in moveable type, but only with ingenuity and at considerable cost. At the time of Turkey's script reform in 1928, a single-font printer's case for printing Turkish in upper and lower case Roman script required 99 types. For printing Turkish in Arabic script, 645 types were needed, and that after ignoring many ligatures.[29] A modest press would require at least

[28] Oman 1989:795, Bulliet 1987.

[29] Duda 1935:241–242, with illustration. Hammam (1951:158) records that in about 1950 the standard Būlāq press font had 465 letters, while private presses got by with 365, though with reduced aesthetic effect. Hourani 1982:38, cf. Ellis 1955:11–12.

a couple of type sizes, if not a couple of styles—each requiring a font of similar size. Thus the same economic barrier that crippled early Chinese typography was also a hurdle, set not quite so high, to Arabic typography.

In fact the initial demands confronting Arabic typography were more stringent than this suggests. They can be understood, perhaps, by recalling the transitional forms of early printing in Europe. In reality, European manuscript writing was not a purely linear arrangement of independent items. The prevalent Gothic manuscript hand was semi-cursive, and included a number of conventional abbreviations marked by diacritics, a few alternative medial and final letter forms, and many ligatures. Gutenberg and other early printers took as their brief the closest possible reproduction of manuscript forms. To achieve this, they cast many additional types, making the technology considerably more costly and expensive. Gutenberg's font comprised about twice as many types as became the standard later.[30] The cost was, in the beginning, a price that had to be paid if print was to satisfy the book reading and buying public. Over the first hundred years moveable type printing became increasingly alphabetised, and thereby more efficiently adapted to typography. In Gothic print, scribal abbreviations fell into disuse and ligatures were reduced in number. More radically, the Roman and Italic types (whose discrete letter forms better suited typography) began to displace the scribes' Gothic script. But it took about a hundred years until it was no longer necessary to disguise a book as a manuscript.[31] From this time, an increasing divergence between Europe's printed and handwritten scripts occurred.

No such initial concessions were made in Arabic typography. This is not surprising, since all the early typographic presses, in Europe, the Middle East and India, depended upon European technicians already accustomed to a strongly alphabetised type script, who no longer appreciated the need to make the same concessions to Arabic readers that Gutenberg had made to his European customers. In India and Southeast Asia the Christian missions were serious offenders. Early Muslim experiments, like that of Müteferriḳa or the early Būlāq press were more sympathetic, but still depended upon European

[30] Hirsch 1978.

[31] Chappell 1970:101.

technicians and faced constraints inherent in the technology.[32] A serious accommodation of manuscript reading would require a huge number of types. The capital costs would be prohibitive and the task of the type composers extremely complex. As practised, typography did not have the capacity to match the copyist's hand. The results appeared consistently ugly to readers used to manuscript styles. European-printed Arabic texts were poorly regarded. In the early eighteenth century, for instance, a Jesuit-printed copy of Ibn Sīnā's *al-Qānūn fī 'l-ṭibb* languished in an Istanbul bookshop, priced well below comparable manuscripts.[33] The problem was often conceived as one of poor type design. Undoubtedly there was enough of this. In the seventeenth century, Ibrāhīm Efendī identified this as the reason for Muslim rejection of books printed in Europe. Their many errors and poor choice of characters were no better than the writing of African Muslims![34] But whether the type fonts were cast in Europe, India or the Middle East they evoked negative reactions. The problem lay deeper. Typographic print was less dense than readers were accustomed to, while the lines of print themselves comprised dark, stilted, uniform imprints, not the subtly varied strokes and styles of the manuscript.[35] When eventually in 1906 the Būlāq press commissioned new fonts designed by a committee of calligraphers,[36] satisfaction with the outcome reflected not only improvements in letter forms and typesetting techniques, but also nearly a century of habituation to a new style of representing text.

Lithography altogether lacked the mechanical rigidities of type. Its complete flexibility in reproducing graphic forms made it an illustrator's medium in the West. This was critically important for its success in the Islamic world, for it meant lithography was capable of reproducing calligraphy, and achieved immense popularity for that reason. A book printed by lithography was essentially a manuscript reproduced. Lithography could accurately convey the grace and fluidity of

[32] The missionaries, always prescriptive, kept their fonts small by imposing alphabetic principles on to Arabic writing, equating one letter with one type element and allowing only for the canonical initial, medial and final forms. For reproductions of mission printing, see Gallop 1990. Müteferriḳa's type was aesthetically ahead of its contemporaries (Duda 1935). On Būlāq, Albin 1988:342.

[33] Roper 1988:51.

[34] Demeerseman 1954:41.

[35] Medhurst 1829, Roper 1988:43, 125 and 264, Oman 1989:803, Weil 1907:52, Baysal 1981:122.

[36] Hammam 1951.

a good manuscript, in all respects except the use of colour—and that too was achieved sometimes by overprinting, by hand rubrication, or by gilt stamping. Lithography could reproduce the nine scripts, as required.[37] By contrast, typeset printing offered a travesty of scribal form.

In case this argument seems too squeamish about aesthetic preferences, or is thought to imply an innate conservatism in Islamic attitudes, consider the uses of lithography in the West. When Senefelder discovered lithography, his first thought was that it could be used to reproduce musical notation.[38] Interestingly, musical notation, though linear in principle, is rather like Arabic script in requiring complex ligatures. Musical notation had never been reproduced successfully by moveable type, and at the end of the eighteenth century was most commonly etched. Lithography provided a practical alternative, and in the later form of photolithography became the technique of choice for printing music.[39] By contrast, lithography was never used in Europe for extensive reproduction of written text. After three and a half centuries of typography, the European eye had become habituated to the typographic style of public text, which had become markedly different from the handwriting used for private text. Lithography would reproduce handwriting, and was therefore deemed unsuitable for printing books. The results looked amateurish and untidy.[40] This conviction blinded European missionaries to the potential of lithography as a cheap and adaptable means of spreading their message. Lithography was considered for Arabic printing by the Malta mission in 1827, but rejected because the perfect standard of calligraphy required was unobtainable, "and less than perfect will not do".[41] The alternative of neat and tidy but clumsy type was considered more perfect. In Batavia, the missionary-printer Medhurst acknowledged the advantages of lithography—its flexibility, its ease of operation, its cheapness—and yet was concerned over the "irregular appearance of a book thus printed" and the fact [!]

[37] See Diehl 1973:123, Demeerseman 1953:354 and 378, Dewall 1857:194, Bianchi 1859–63:§103, Walther 1990:231.

[38] Senefelder 1819:13.

[39] Satisfactory results with typography became possible only during the nineteenth century with the development of "mosaic" type which abandoned the linear principle, required very large fonts, and involved very complex typesetting; see Poole & Krummel 1980; Humphries & Smith 1970:26–29 and 34–36.

[40] Cf. Twyman 1990:119–125.

[41] Roper 1988:125.

that lithography could not readily be combined with European letters. Knowing however that his native audience rejected the only Arabic type font available to him, Medhurst used lithography to reproduce an extremely regular stiff Arabic script that imitated an Arabic type font of his own design.[42] A comparable sensitivity to graphic conventions is at work on both sides, with opposite results: Muslim objections to an alphabetised Arabic typography because it did not resemble the handwritten manuscript, and Christian rejection of lithography for book printing precisely because it did resemble handwritten script.

6. *The Special Place of Calligraphy*

Typography's shortcomings become more marked when the wider literate landscape is considered. Books and other written materials demand varying degrees of aesthetic attention. At the lower end, on a utilitarian level, were the staples of the book trade, the products of professional scribes. Where there was an established market for books scholarly works and literature in Arabic and local languages might be copied by a professional scribe, the *warrāq* or *kātib*. A steady, clear hand was adequate. In such cases the demands placed upon print reproduction were not so onerous. Indeed, it was here that typographic print was allowed to make its first inroads, under Müteferriḳa, and the later government-run presses of Istanbul and Cairo. Nevertheless, even here, the graphic flexibility of lithography better suited the tastes of the early market place. The preface to a Lucknow literary lithograph of 1843 made this telling comparison with its typographic predecessor:

> The story was published in Calcutta and in other places more than once. But it was never brought out with such beauty and elegance as in this print which simply charms the readers . . . The print is lovely beyond praise: the title page is in white letters, so different from earlier editions. The popular stories are printed in bold letters looking like a garden with beds of flowers here and there.[43]

Lithography, not typography, could rival the scribal product—at, of course, a fraction of the price.

[42] Medhurst 1829, 1838:573. Similarly, the Singapore missionary, Keasberry, who experimented with lithography to produce multi-coloured books and magazines in the Arabic script, never used it for Roman script.

[43] Diehl 1973:123–124.

Also in this utilitarian domain lay scholarly texts. Such texts might be copied professionally or compiled by disciples of a teacher under whom the text was read and verified.[44] Again clarity rather than stylishness was uppermost. However the typical mode of instruction proceeded by commentary on an earlier master's text, and this is given form in the scribal conventions of the scholarly manuscript. The result could be a tangled skein of text on the scholar's page: text, commentary, supercommentary, or marginal or interlinear glosses, or charts and diagrams, in script of different sizes and emphasis. Lithography could reproduce all this as readily as plain text. For typography it was a struggle. It could manage to convey these functionally critical hierarchies and interconnections only rather clumsily through parentheses and marginalia. In time, typographic printing would offer compensating advantages by adopting new organising conventions, including paragraphing and punctuation, but its initial deficiencies were certainly a handicap.

Moving up the scale of social prestige and religious potency, we find the higher realms of writing in the hands of the calligrapher (*khaṭṭāṭ*). The calligrapher was as much an artist as a scribe. Few books were actually copied by calligraphers. In fact, the Qur'ān was the only full manuscript usually calligraphed, and even then usually only the first few pages would be fully decorated and illuminated. Indeed a good calligrapher might regard it as beneath his dignity to copy a whole manuscript, other than the Qur'ān, for high standards could not be maintained throughout.[45] Calligraphers generally displayed their skills, and earned a living, by writing prayers, selections of poetry, and religious icons: the *basmalah*, the names of Allah, invocations, and above all Qur'anic verses and extracts believed to have special potency. A fine piece of this kind could serve as an amulet or, put on display, fill the house of its owner with blessing.[46] Such items of calligraphic art were not only the main sources of the calligraphers' income, but also—and this must be stressed—the most

[44] Pedersen 1984: ch. 3.

[45] Sharar 1975:103–105. Sharar is amusing on this point. He relates (106) the following story, with rather fetching snobbery: "When Haji Harmain Sharifain inaugurated a printing press [probably the first private press in Lucknow], after much exhortation he got Mir Bandey Ali to agree to write out *Panj Sura*, five subsections of the Qur'ān. Mir Bandey Ali put in an immense amount of work and took many days to accomplish the task. When he took it the Haji and had a last look at it in his presence, something about it displeased him and instead of handing it over to him, he tore it up and said, 'I can't do it.'"

[46] Benjamin 1887:290, Schimmel 1984:35.

popular uses of the written word. This terrain lay well beyond the reach of typography, for no mechanical technique could emulate its subtle strokes and the intricate interlacing of graphic forms. Lithography, as an illustrator's medium, could do so.

Resistance to any typographic perversion of calligraphy was reinforced by a sense of calligraphy's contribution to Islamic cultural self-identity. The high standing of calligraphy, and its elaborate development, is peculiar to Islam. This is not just an argument that the calligrapher's writing has an aesthetic and spiritual dimension. As in Europe or China, so in Islam, skill in calligraphy was a fitting attribute of the scholar, calligraphy and medicine being the two vocational studies worthy of *ʿulamāʾ*. But in Islam the position of calligraphy was extraordinarily elevated, surpassing even the scholarly cult of calligraphic brushwork in China. In Hitti's words, "The art of calligraphy, which drew its prestige from its object to perpetuate the word of God, and enjoyed the approval of the Koran (68:1, 96:4) . . . became the most highly praised art."[47] The strictures placed upon representations of the human form, and a preference for avoiding naturalistic depictions of any kind, promoted calligraphy to the supreme visual art. As a seventeenth century Indian Muslim noted, "If someone, whether he can read or not, sees good writing, he likes to enjoy the sight of it."[48] As a hallmark of high culture, and an aristocratic recreation, calligraphy has played a role analogous to painting in the post-Renaissance West. For Ibn Khaldūn, calligraphy was "a noble craft, since it is one of the special qualities of man by which he distinguishes himself from the animals . . . The quality of writing in a town corresponds to the social organisation, civilisation, and competition for luxuries (among its inhabitants)."[49] The very authenticating symbol of authority, the equivalent of a European coat of arms, was the *ṭughrā*, an elaborately wrought monogram of a ruler's name. The practice and collection of fine calligraphy became an indulgence of the aristocratic aesthete. In such circles, a page of fine calligraphy might be worth an Arab horse.

As the deep rationale for calligraphy was embellishment of the Qur'ān, so the Qur'ān was calligraphy's most fit subject. For the people of the Book, the Qur'ān was honoured above all through

[47] Hitti 1960:423.
[48] Schimmel 1984:33.
[49] Rosenthal 1967^{2}: §5.29.

embellishment and ornamentation of its vocal performance according to the canons of *tajwīd*. But as Graham has pointed out, the Muslim tradition has been both the most oral and the most elaborately chirographic. "Muslim veneration of the written Qur'ān exemplar, or *muṣḥaf*, and delight in the elaborately calligraphed qur'anic word have been prominent parts of the highly oral Islamic milieu."[50]

This intimate association of calligraphy with the revealed Word and its role as the supreme visual art have inspired poetic and mystical imagery. Islamic poets could interpret everything as a book, and see writing everywhere. As Schimmel (1984) reminds us, a poetic trope was to compare the face of the beloved to a flawlessly written copy of the Qur'ān, mirroring the calligraphic conceits that made images of animals and men from prayers or verses of the Qur'ān. The dots of a famous calligrapher were transformed into moles on the cheeks of the houris in Paradise. The same intimacies excited sufi thinkers, who drew analogies from the creative processes of calligraphy; for instance, the relation of the Hand and the pen. Deep meditations in this vein, which allude to an abstraction of calligraphic theory to express the undifferentiated eternity, have been brought to our attention by Johns in his study of the *Daqā'iq al-Ḥurūf* of ʿAbd al-Ra'ūf of Singkel.[51]

Calligraphy was thus, at once, the most popular and the most prestigious mode of formal writing in Islamic culture, the embodiment of high culture, and the physical vehicle of the text of the Holy Book. This aesthetic citadel resisted typography, but opened its gates to lithography.

7. *A Muslim Technology*

Lithography not only met the aesthetic demands of calligraphy, but also seemed to preserve its cultural and ritual functions. When Müteferrika raised his ten points in favour of printing, the ninth was that "the making of books in Arabic or in non-Arabic languages is blessed when it is done by hands of Islam. When printing is done by infidels there will be no blessing in it." This was repeated by the

[50] Graham 1987:89 and 158.
[51] Johns 1955b:68–69 and 72.

great sufi Muḥammad Ḥaqqī's tract in praise of printing 1839.[52] The desire to keep religious literature within the fold is partly explained by the belief that merit accrued from the copying of the Qur'ān, ḥadīth and poems on the Prophet.[53] Conversely, the Qur'ān can only be touched or recited by those in a state of ritual purity. The text of *Sūra* 56:79, to this effect, is commonly displayed on the front page of manuscript and printed copies of the Qur'ān alike. The copying of the Qur'anic text therefore requires the calligrapher to renew his *wuḍū'* time and time again. Herein lies a source of concern with printing: the fear that the process of printing will defile the name of God or the word of God by exposing it to some source of impurity. In Egypt in the 1830s the belief prevailed that it was forbidden to print the Qur'ān or let it pass into the hands of a Christian.[54] The notions of printing and falling under Christian control are closely linked. Typography was after all a Western invention, and had been actively used by European and Syrian Christians to print in Arabic. The complexity of the processes and the specialised skills they required ensured that when government-sponsored printing began in the Middle East, the press equipment was imported from Europe, and European supervisors or operators were employed. Müteferriḳa was himself a Hungarian seminarian who converted to Islam after being enslaved as a prisoner of war. His press was acquired in Paris. To operate it, he hired the Jewish foreman of a Hebrew printing shop in Istanbul, and brought several French compositors from Paris. The Būlāq press was the successor of Napoleon's official press, re-equipped with Italian presses, advice and training, employing Italian printers, and run by a Lebanese Christian.[55]

As if to reinforce the impression that typography was intrinsically a Christian technology, it was actively promoted by Protestant missionaries not only as the supremely effective tool of Christian proselytising, but also as an emblem of Western scientific progress.[56] The

[52] Abdulrazak 1990:92.

[53] The benefits of copying the text of the Qur'ān are naturally the greatest: calligraphers are destined for paradise because of this work, and the pious among them would retain the wood of the pens they had used to copy the Qur'ān to use as kindling to heat the water used for their funeral ablutions. Ink washed off written fragments of Qur'anic text has healing powers (Schimmel 1984:86, 58 and 84).

[54] Lane 1836:283, Demeerseman 1954:59.

[55] Abdulrazak 1990.

[56] Once, amusingly, by the Singapore missionary Keasberry in a lithographed edition (1843). Again the complexity of the process is relevant, for typographic printing

association of government presses in Istanbul and Cairo with programs of military, administrative, and fiscal modernisation along Western lines hardly dispelled this perception. That is why, perhaps, after the Būlāq press had already been in operation for a decade, Lane could record that he was "acquainted with a bookseller here who has long been desirous of printing some books which he feels sure would bring him considerable profit, but cannot overcome his scruples as to the lawfulness of doing so."[57]

Lithography suffered from none of these associations. This cheap, accessible, and simple technology could be transparently under Muslim control.

Its simplicity was stunning. In 1806 its inventor, Senefelder, launched lithography by reproducing a note written by the crown prince of Bavaria in court before his very eyes.[58] Not fifty years later, when the first lithographic press was set up in Sumatra, its owner, Muḥammad Azharī, repeated the novelty for the visiting Dutch Assistant Resident, extemporising a poem of welcome and printing it on the spot.[59] This new technique required only the simplest of materials: grease, lampblack, water, paper, and fine limestone. Within a year or so of the first arrival of lithography in India, all requirements except paper were readily available locally. Lithographic ink was locally made, stones finer than those of Bavaria were found near Madras, and later in Sindh. Only European printing paper had to be relied upon until 1862.[60] Later in Cairo a distinctive locally-produced yellow paper gained popularity for printing copies of the Qur'ān and other religious works, perhaps as an indication that European paper was not involved.[61] Nor did skilled operators have to be imported for lithographic presses. The prime skill needed to produce good lithography is precisely the skill of the copyist or calligrapher. Indeed, the transfer of skills was so direct that in India local scribal mannerisms were carried across into lithographic imprints.[62]

was the first mass-production technology involving a high degree of craft specialisation, and thus an outstanding instance of the division of labour, which since Adam Smith's day had been recognised in the West as the foundation of European economic strength.

[57] Lane 1836:283.

[58] Senefelder 1819:65.

[59] Dewall 1857:194.

[60] Caresajee 1958:98, Butt 1988:156.

[61] Cf. the remark of the Turkish calligrapher-historian Mustaḳīmzāde that neither the Qur'ān nor a *ḥadīth* should be written on *firangī* paper (Schimmel 1984:81).

[62] Diehl 1973:120 and 126; Ahmad 1985:142 and 146.

Lithography thus acted as a direct extension of the manuscript tradition. This was important for those who scrupled over the need to reproduce the Qur'ān in writing by the pen, given the Qur'ān's own references to the pen as an instrument conveying divine instruction to mankind (68:1, 96:4). Indeed, the care lavished upon lithographed Qur'ān texts tended to blur further the boundary between manual copying and lithographic printing when the customary embellishments of coloured frames and gilt verse markers were added by hand.

The simplicity and flexibility of lithography made possible printing that was patently Muslim in style and process. It resolved aesthetic and ritual concerns over the reproduction of calligraphy, and specifically of the text of the Qur'ān. It provided a credible means of reproducing the written form of the Holy Book, and all the associated items of popular calligraphy—the *basmalah*, the names of Allah, invocations, verses and extracts of special potency.

And it was just such material that had a ready-made mass market. Lithography flourished supplying it. Popular calligraphy, along with illustrations of the Kaʿba and Shīʿite portraits of ʿAlī, Ḥusain, and Fāṭimah were being printed in Istanbul at least as early as 1851. (The printing of such ephemera, unfortunately, goes largely unrecorded.) They became a popular purchase for pilgrims, being sold in great numbers at Mecca.[63] Better attested are early printings of the Qur'ān. The Qur'ān or excerpts from it were regularly among the first books to be printed by private Muslim lithographers. The first Arabic language printing in Persia 1828 was a Qur'ān, lithographed in the hand of a famous calligrapher. As we have seen, the first private press in Lucknow, too, commissioned a Qur'ān selection again from an esteemed calligrapher. And in Southeast Asia, the second item of Muslim printing after a *mawlid* text recited to honour the birth of the Prophet, was again a Qur'ān.[64]

The reason, besides piety, was profit. There was a vast unmet demand for copies of the Qur'ān. Learning to recite the Qur'ān was the first stage in any Muslim child's education, and traditionally students were unlikely to have a copy of the Qur'ān to read from. They learned lines written by their teacher across the top of their slates, or worked from written fragments of the text made by the

[63] Demeerseman 1953:360.
[64] Browne 1914:8, Sharar 1975:106, Kaptein 1993, Dewall 1857.

teacher or senior pupils. Supply of printed copies of the Qur'ān for personal and educational use became a staple of the Muslim printing industry, with Bombay and Cairo eventually emerging as the major suppliers. In the early days of printing, profits could be substantial. Though lithographed copies of the Qur'ān had to be carefully prepared high-quality editions, they could command good prices because a hand-copied Qur'ān was very costly for the same reason. The Agra Qur'ān of 1850, in Arabic and Urdu, made its publisher a fortune at Rs 5 per copy.[65]

Where Muslims lived under colonial rule alongside significant non-Muslim populations, lithography took on a distinctly Muslim hue. As European printing was typographic, and most non-Muslim vernacular printing followed the European model, consistent use of lithography was a mark of Muslim culture. This pattern is strongly evident in both India and Southeast Asia.[66]

With this understanding of the printing technologies available and how they were applied, it seems less useful than ever to generalise about Islamic conservatism. The inadequacy of the technology of typography, especially in the alphabetised form in which it was accessible to Muslims, must be accepted as a significant factor in the long delay in the Muslim adoption of printing. When typographic printing was taken up by the Ottoman government in the face of growing European power, its ineptness and complexity, its Christian odour, and government direction of its uses all restricted its currency and scope. Consequently typographic printing remained marginal to the Muslim tradition and was making only slow headway when lithography burst upon the scene. However, once an appropriate technology for reproducing Arabic script became available, it was adopted rapidly. Lithography was launched in Europe only during the years 1806–1817, and reached India—as we have seen—in 1824. In that very year the first Muslim lithographic press was established. Twenty-five years later, the new technology was widely used in India and Persia, making headway in Turkey, Egypt, and the Maghrib, and about to arrive in Southeast Asia. Let us not forget either, that this new technology was not only speedily adopted, but was also raised to unprecedented levels of technical excellence in its application to book printing.[67]

65 Ahmad 1976:137.
66 Proudfoot 1986:108.
67 E.g. Sharar 1975:108.

Thus for most of the Muslim world, lithography provided the whole answer to printed book production. Only in the Middle East and the Maghrib did it flourish alongside a continuing use of typography, mainly by government presses, and here, Demeerseman argues,[68] lithography facilitated the wider acceptance of the principle of printing, and hence typographic printing as well. Thus, in different contexts across the Muslim world, lithography ushered in the print revolution.

8. *Why has Lithography been Neglected?*

If lithography was as important in early Muslim book printing as this survey suggests, then why has it continued to be overlooked? The reasons for this continuing blind spot lie both in the subsequent history of Muslim printing and in certain scholarly attitudes.

In South Asia, lithography has fully held its ground. To this day in India and Pakistan, lithography, or comparable means of reproducing handwritten script, remain the common technique for printing not only Muslim books of all kinds, but newspapers and magazines as well. Outside the sub-continent there has been a rationalisation of printing techniques; typography has largely captured the old field of the copyist and the new applications of print that have no precedent in the manuscript culture; lithography continues to serve in the field of calligrapher.

By the end of the nineteenth century periodicals and newspapers had become the leading print medium. The economics of this new genre required speedy production of large print runs, and this favoured typography. Commercial newspaper reading and government-printed school texts began to create a new literacy in typography free from manuscript antecedents. Also in the latter part of the nineteenth century, the Ottoman government's typographic presses became major printers of religious treatises in Arabic and the vernaculars. The prestige of books printed in Istanbul and above all in Mecca (after 1883) gave credibility to typography.[69] Meanwhile, in a development paralleling the early European experience of print, the graphic poverty of typography, which had at first made it a poor substitute for the manuscript style, was coming to be seen as having the virtue of

[68] Demeerseman 1954:45.
[69] Proudfoot 1993:41.

greater clarity. The advance of typography was noticed by Browne in Persia. In the passage quoted earlier he remarked upon the displacement of early typography by lithography. He then went on to point out that after fifty years of lithography, "typography again became current and popular" at the turn of the century. An analogous change took place in Southeast Asia, at about the same time, with lithography claiming a slowly dwindling audience.[70]

On the other hand, in the realm of the calligrapher, and especially in the printing of the Qur'ān, lithography gained ground and held it. When the Ottoman government allowed the printing of the Qur'ān with Turkish commentary for the first time in 1865, it was done with typography. But the same text was re-issued lithographically in 1879 and thereafter. Analogously in Cairo, early typographic editions of the Qur'ān from 1864 were succeeded in 1889 by lithographed editions. With few exceptions, the Qur'ān has ever since been printed using lithography or allied techniques.

These later developments have overshadowed the early days of printing. The familiarity of the periodical press, and the obvious importance of its impacts, make it too easy to overlook the ways and needs of earlier days, and forget that print was not at first used in this way at all.

Until very recently scholarship has done little to remove this blind spot.[71] Antiquarian bibliography, with its technical interests, and communications history, with its sociological interests, have found little to say to one another. This mismatch has not been mitigated by some prevalent perceptions of Muslim societies.

One is the tendency to base generalisations about Islam on a rather abstract and idealised version of Middle East realities. This may lead to misrepresentations. As we have seen, the history of early printing in the Middle East is not common to the societies in which a majority of Muslims lived. An antidote is to take a view closer to the ground in one place or another away from Istanbul, Mecca and Cairo. This is what makes Demeerseman's contribution to the history of Muslim printing so enriching. By using his local knowledge of Tunis, he was able to avoid some Orientalist ideal-types.

---

[70] Farmayan 1968:145, Walther 1990:236, Proudfoot 1993:57.

[71] Recent doctoral studies have begun to mend the rift. Roper (1988) and Abdulrazak (1990) should be mentioned.

Running deeper is another generalisation. It is the attitude described in the opening paragraph of this essay: namely, a rather too-ready willingness to characterise Islamic societies as intrinsically conservative, or at best reactive. One can avoid the need to explain a great deal by relying on this conviction. The history of lithography in Muslim hands suggests that there may often be more to be said.

* * * * *

Although I have been a student of Professor Johns and later his junior colleague, regretfully I have never had the opportunity to study Islam under him. Nevertheless, in the field of printing history—which must be tangential even to his wide-ranging interests—I have found my way lit by beacons which he has tended. These are his convictions that there are insights to be gained by "observing Islam" away from Mecca and Cairo; that a powerful source of understanding lies in the sensitive juxtaposition of Christian and Muslim experiences; and that at the heart of Muslim consciousness is the multi-faceted beauty of the Qur'ān. For these lights, I am grateful.

[12]

MEDIEVAL ARABIC *ṬARSH*: A FORGOTTEN CHAPTER IN THE HISTORY OF PRINTING

RICHARD W. BULLIET

COLUMBIA UNIVERSITY

Verses from poems by Abū Dulaf al-Khazrajī (10th cent.) and Ṣafī ad-Dīn al-Ḥillī (14th cent.) suggest that unethical amulet peddlers printed amulets from wooden blocks and cast tin plates to sell to naive buyers who thought they were getting handwritten charms. This is the likely origin of the printed amulets that have been identified in various collections since the 1890s. If the *ṭarsh* described by the poets were indeed printblocks, the verses would serve to date medieval Arabic printing and show its geographical extent. The hitherto unsuspected casting of printblocks from tin, if confirmed by technical examination, would enhance appreciation of medieval Islamic technology. The locus of printing technology among the Banū Sāsān "underworld" possibly explains the lack of broader influence and eventual disappearance of printing.

"Among us, without publicity or boasting, is the engraver of *ṭarsh*"

Abū Dulaf al-Khazrajī (tenth century)

"How many times has my hand written, by *ṭarsh* of tin,
Syriac followed by the language of phylacteries"

Ṣafī ad-Dīn al-Ḥillī (fourteenth century)

THE HISTORY OF TECHNOLOGY IS USUALLY ABOUT discovery and invention. Sometimes it is about failure. But there is a middle ground, as well, and it is in this middle ground that the history of medieval Arabic block printing lies.

Judging from palaeography and the eighth-century date of introduction of paper to the Islamic world, Arabic block printing must have begun in the ninth or tenth century.[1] It persisted into, but possibly not beyond, the fourteenth century. It had certainly disappeared without a trace by the beginning of the eighteenth century when the first printing press was established in Istanbul. Hence, with four centuries or more duration, printing certainly was not a technological failure. Yet it had so little impact on Islamic society that today only a handful of scholars are aware it ever existed, and no definite textual reference to it has been thought to survive.

The thesis proposed here, that the word *ṭarsh* meant "printblock" in the dialect of the medieval Muslim underworld, makes possible for the first time a history of medieval Arabic printing. However, were it not for the preservation of some of the actual prints, which were first identified by the orientalist Josef Karabacek in 1894,[2] this history would still be impossible. For the meaning of the word *ṭarsh* cannot be ascertained without knowledge of and reference to the prints themselves.

The authors of the few previously published articles and notes on medieval Arabic block printing[3] raised important questions about the rise and fall of the technique: Did it come from China, or was it independently invented? Could it have been the source

[1] Chinese prisoners in Samarqand are said to have taught the Arabs the art of paper making in 704. G. Káldy-Nagy, "Beginnings of the Arabic-Letter Printing in the Muslim World," in *The Muslim East: Studies in Honour of Julius Germanus*, ed. Káldy-Nagy, Budapest, 1974, p. 201. The palaeographical judgement is that of Adolf Grohman in A. Grohman and T. W. Arnold, *The Islamic Book*, [np], 1929, pp. 26–29.

[2] J. Karabacek, *Papyrus Erzherzog Rainer. Führer durch die Ausstellung*, Vienna, 1894, pp. 247–50.

[3] After Karabacek, Arabic block printing was discussed in T. F. Carter, *The Invention of Printing in China and its Spread Westward*, New York, 1925; Grohman and Arnold, op. cit.; G. Levi Della Vida, "An Arabic Block Print," *The Scientific Monthly*, LIX (Dec. 1944), pp. 473–74; P. Lunde, "A Missing Link," *Aramco World*, XXXII/2 (Mar.–Apr. 1981), pp. 26–27; and M. Krek, "Arabic Block Printing as the Precursor of Printing in Europe: Preliminary Report," *American Research Center in Egypt Newsletter*, No. 129 (Spring 1985), pp. 12–16.

from which the Europeans adopted woodblock printing in the late fourteenth century? This article will address these questions.

A more interesting question, however, is why so potentially revolutionary a technology had so little impact and disappeared virtually without a trace. Woodblock printing, after all, had a transformative impact on Chinese and Japanese cultures and prompted the invention of the equally important technique of movable-type printing in Korea, Central Asia, and Europe. Subsequently, printing revolutionized every society it encountered, including, after an abortive first experiment in Istanbul between 1729 and 1742, that of the Islamic Middle East.[4] It is indeed puzzling, therefore, that the same show that ran indefinitely, to standing room only audiences, in every other culture opened to a modest run and closed without reviews in the Islamic Middle East.

The indispensable sources for reconstructing the history of medieval Arabic block printing are the extant prints. But the two surviving literary descriptions of *ṭarsh* provide additional technical and social clues. Inasmuch as the secondary literature does not address technical matters, we will begin with a discussion of how the prints may have been produced. This discussion derives primarily from a close examination of the one specimen in the Columbia University Library and of reproductions of others held elsewhere, and from a consideration of the *ṭarsh* texts quoted at the outset of this article and the commentaries on them.

Most extant prints are amulets, that is, long, thin strips of paper bearing quotations from the Quran, lists of the names of God, and other religious texts designed to ward off evil. They were rolled and enclosed in metal cylinders worn on chains around the neck. One print of Quranic verses, however, resembles more a book page, with generous margins on all four sides;[5] and another, on a tiny square of parchment, is an amulet that was probably not rolled and encased.[6] The longest extant text seems to be the one at Columbia University (Plate I).[7] It contains 107 lines of writing, 37 on one block and 70 on another, on a single strip of paper 2″ by 11⅞″ in size, with Quranic verses in more ornamental calligraphy printed from a third block on a separate 2″ by 5⅜″ piece of paper glued to the top of the longer strip. All of the prints—some 50 in total—have apparently been found in Egypt. A few have been discovered archaeologically in tenth and eleventh century contexts; the rest are of uncertain provenance.[8] No printblocks have been found.

Scholars have assumed that the printblocks were of wood. Yet medieval Muslim die and seal carvers were highly skilled in cutting fine characters into metal and stone, and the coin-shaped glass weights of medieval Egypt, which also bore several lines of writing, were presumably cast in clay molds.

The case for wood rests on several particulars. The prints are fairly large, at least compared with a coin or seal. A 2″ by 6″ impression seems normal. But the value of the printed amulet was probably quite low. Hence the return would not have been likely to repay the efforts of a skilled die or seal cutter. In addition, metal or other non-wooden printblocks were unknown in China, where some scholars assume the Muslims learned the technique.

Most important technically to the question of the material or materials used is the fact that the lines of writing are normally printed black-on-white. White-on-black letters occur in larger calligraphic designs, often printed from separate blocks. Moreover, the black-on-white writing is often extremely tiny. The 107 printed lines of the Columbia specimen are squeezed 11–12 to the inch, and the thickness of the lines making up each of the thousands of letters is consistently one to two hundredths of an inch!

Tiny letters also appear in relief on coins and sealings, and larger ones appear on glass weights. The producers of these items engraved the letters in reverse into a metal, stone, or clay surface. The process of stamping or casting then caused the gold, silver, copper, glass, clay, etc. to which the design was to be transferred to enter the incised grooves.

To produce inked lines on paper from a printblock in which the letters have been similarly incised, as is done in engravings and etchings, requires a sophisticated understanding of ink and paper as well as a powerful press. The printer inks the block, wipes off excess ink that has not entered the incised lines, and exerts great pressure to force the ink to transfer from the grooves in the block to the paper.

[4] Káldy-Nagy, op. cit.

[5] The specimen is in the Cambridge University Library; Lunde, op. cit., p. 26.

[6] Levi Della Vida, op. cit.

[7] It is in the papyrus collection in Columbia's rare book collection, No. 705b.

[8] See contribution of D. S. Richards to W. Kubiak and G. Scanlon, *Fustat-C: Fustat Expedition, Final Report, 2* (forthcoming, 1987). I would like to express my gratitude to Prof. Scanlon for guidance in understanding the Fustat materials.

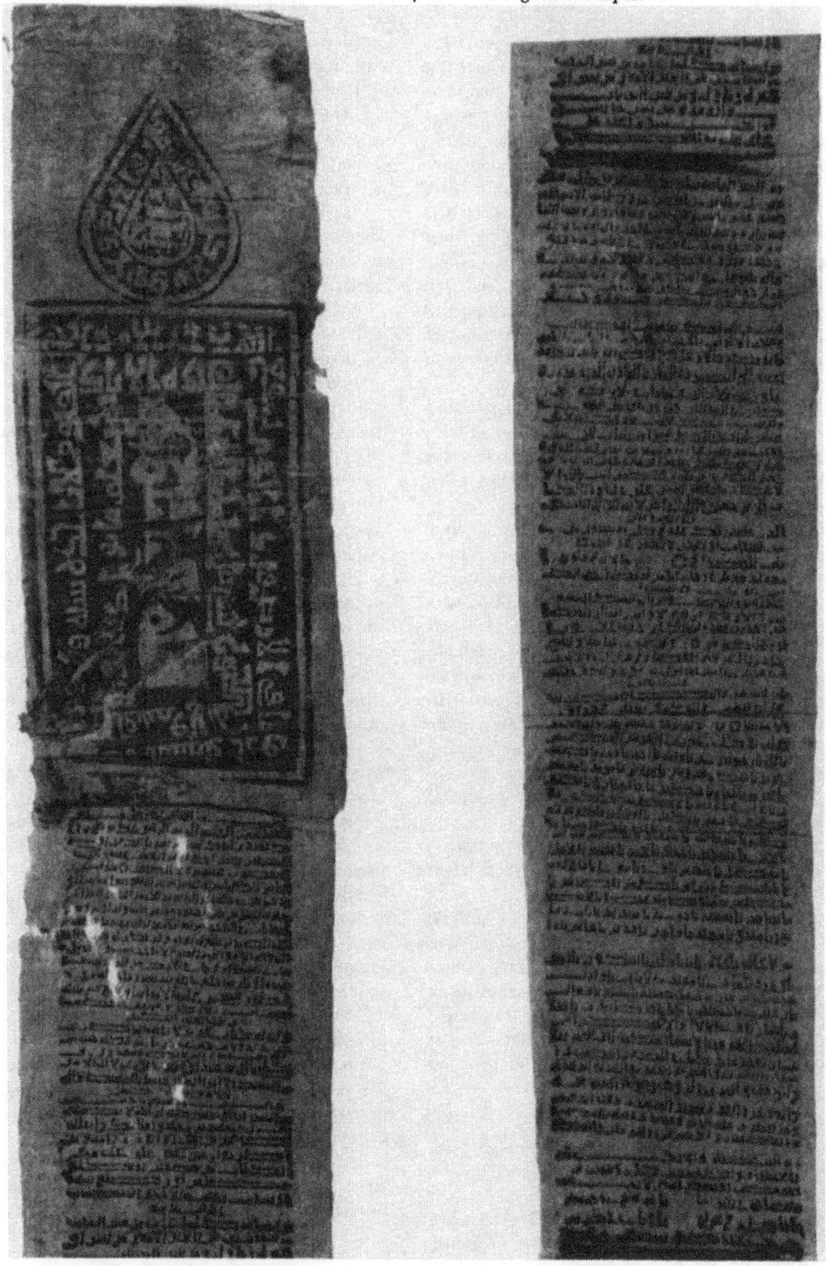

Plate I. Arabic blockprint in Columbia University Library (actual size).

Since some of the surviving amulets show a marked darkening toward the edges of the print, which the even pressure of a press would not produce, and there is no indenting of the edge of the block into the paper, which great pressure would produce, we may assume that the medieval Muslims did not print from engravings.[9] Therefore, the letters must have been raised from the surface of the printblock. In the case of a carved printblock, this requires cutting away the areas that are to remain white. Doing this in metal would have been an impossibly laborious task, and soft substances like clay or stucco would have chipped if one had tried to cut lines as fine as a hundredth of an inch. But for that matter, the fineness of detail seems too great for wood, as well!

But before investigating the problem of detail in detail, we must turn to an analysis of the *ṭarsh* texts because they strongly suggest that at least some of the printblocks were made of cast or molded metal rather than wood.

Abū Dulaf al-Khazrajī was a poet and vagabond who frequented the courts of the tenth century Iranian Buyid princes.[10] He wrote two travel accounts, one of which is totally bogus and the other replete with unlikely details. The quotation concerning *ṭarsh* is a line from his poem enumerating the types of people he counted as members of the Banū Sāsān, a medieval Islamic underworld of beggars, tricksters, and performers with whom he seems to have been quite familiar. Since his poem was filled with the argot of the Banū Sāsān, Abū Dulaf furnished his court patrons with a commentary on obscure words and practices. With the commentary his text reads:

"'Among us [the Banū Sāsān], without publicity (*jahr*) or boasting (*kharṭ*), is the engraver of *ṭarsh* [variant in two manuscripts *ṭars*].'

The engraver of *ṭarsh* is he who engraves (*yaḥfiru*) molds (*qawālib*, sing. *qālib*) for amulets (*taᶜāwīdh*, sing. *taᶜwīdh*). People who are illiterate and cannot write buy them from him. The seller keeps back (*ḥafiẓa*) the design (*naqsh*) which is on it [the *ṭarsh*] so that he exhausts his supply of amulets on the common people (*nās*) and makes them believe that he wrote them. The mold is called the *ṭarsh* [variant in two manuscripts *ṭars*]."

Prof. C. E. Bosworth has published a superb edition of Abū Dulaf's poem with a learned and exhaustive commentary and an insightful discussion of its background. However, since he did not recognize that the subject of this verse and commentary was printblocks, he assumed that a *ṭarsh* was a mold for a three-dimensional amulet, presumably figurative with writing on it in relief. His translation of the same passage reads as follows:

"'And of our number is the one who engraves a pattern for mass-producing amulets, without shaping them individually and without smoothing them down.'

Ḥāfir aṭ-ṭarsh [Engraver of *ṭarsh*]. This is the person who hollows out moulds for making amulets, and then ignorant and illiterate people buy them from him. The vendor has kept back the matrix with the pattern engraved in it, and he then sells the amulets to the common people, letting them think that he has written them out individually himself. This mould or pattern is called *aṭ-ṭarsh*."[11]

The significant differences between Bosworth's reading and that proposed here are in the verb *ḥafara* and the words *jahr* and *kharṭ*. Bosworth prefers "to hollow out" to our "to engrave," but both are normal Arabic usages. As for *jahr* and *kharṭ*, Bosworth has translated them as "shaping individually" and "smoothing down" in keeping with his assumption that a *ṭarsh* is a mold for a three-dimensional object. Abū Dulaf glossed neither word, assuming that his audience would understand them.

The verb *jahara* from which *jahr* derives has the primary meaning "to announce publicly." *Kharaṭa* means "to strip leaves from a branch and make it smooth"; by extension it commonly means "to smooth with a plane, to turn on a lathe, to brag." It is not clear what either word means in the context of Abū Dulaf's verse, but two considerations suggest the simpler interpretation proposed here.

First, since Abū Dulaf glossed the phrase "engraver of *ṭarsh*," he must have assumed that his audience was not too familiar with the technique it denoted. Hence it is unlikely that he would have used two additional descriptive words with technical meanings specific to the *ṭarsh* process without glossing them too.

Secondly, judging from his use of the pronoun "them," Bosworth seems to understand *jahr* and *kharṭ* to refer to the amulets or the molds rather than to the

[9] Arthur M. Hind, *An Introduction to a History of Woodcut With a Detailed Survey of Work Done in the Fifteenth Century*, Boston, 1935, I, pp. 3–5.

[10] R. W. Bulliet, "Abū Dolaf al-Yanbūᶜī," *Encyclopaedia Iranica*, I, pp. 271–72; C. E. Bosworth, *The Mediaeval Islamic Underworld: The Banū Sāsān in Arabic Society and Literature*, Leiden, 1976, I, pp. 48–79.

[11] Bosworth, op. cit., II, p. 201 (Arabic text p. 18).

engraver, who is the actual subject of the verse. There is no plural word in the verse for the "them" to refer to. A lack of individual smoothing and shaping would, indeed, be the mark of a shoddy charm; though the notion makes less sense in reference to a hollowed-out mold. But in either case, the Arabic words should have a pronominal suffix indicating their transitive meaning. Bosworth has supplied the "them" in his translation. While poetic requirements could have caused the deletion of the suffixes, it seems more reasonable to interpret both words as referring intransitively to the engraver.

One other difference in translation is worth noting. Bosworth's "ignorant and illiterate," instead of "who are illiterate and cannot write," plays down the commentary's specific emphasis on writing, which is repeated in the final statement that the *ṭarsh*-maker induces common people to believe he *wrote* the amulets himself. If one assumes that the amulets in question were blockprints, lack of an ability to read would have been essential in passing them off as hand-written, for it is obvious to anyone familiar with medieval Arabic handwriting that they were not written by pen. As for the word mold, *qālib* has the basic sense of "reverser." Interestingly, the earliest French and German words for woodblock carver, *tailleur de molles* and *Formschneider*, include the concept "mold" as well.[12]

Perhaps it is appropriate here to stress that this point-by-point disagreement with Prof. Bosworth is in no way intended to belittle the importance or quality of his work. *The Mediaeval Islamic Underworld* is a major scholarly achievement. Moreover, so few scholars are aware of the existence of medieval Arabic blockprints, all of which have been found in Egypt rather than Abū Dulaf's Iran, that it is not surprising that Bosworth did not realize the meaning of the passage. His linguistic note on the word *ṭarsh* indicates how close he came to the correct meaning.

"The classical lexica give for [the root] *ṭ.r.sh* essentially those meanings connected with deafness . . . but the clue to *ṭarsh* appears under [the root] *ṭ.r.s.* [the variant reading of two manuscripts], for they give *ṭarasa* as 'to write' and *ṭirs* as a written document, etc., or a paper which has been effaced and used again, i.e., a palimpsest. . . . Our jargon word . . . thus combines the ideas of something for producing writing and of rubbing into or engraving the surface of the mould. . . . [Fraenkel thought that words from *ṭ.r.s.*] must be loanwords in Arabic, since they could not be satisfactorily derived from native Arabic words, and had to fall back on the speculation that they were of Egyptian origin."[13]

The blocks for the extant amulets would obviously be a form of writing. The notion of reuse could refer to the multiple copies printed from the block, but that is not in keeping with the notion of effaced writing. Alternatively, it could mean that the worn blocks were effaced, by smoothing or melting, and used again. In any case, a hollowed-out three-dimensional mold for producing a charm in relief seems quite remote etymologically.

If the *ṭarsh* was effaced and reused, it was probably not made of wood. Wood engravers sometimes put a second carving on the back of a block, but it is much easier to prepare a fresh block of wood than to plane or sand a carved surface and reuse it. This hint that the *ṭarsh* may have been made of something other than wood is corroborated by the verse of Ṣafī ad-Dīn al-Ḥillī, which also comes from a popular poem he composed on the Banū Sāsān.

Ṣafī ad-Dīn, whose work provides the secondary focus of Bosworth's study, was an Arab from Ḥilla in Iraq who died around 1349.[14] His poetry earned him favor at the courts of the Artuqid princes of northern Iraq and the Mamluk sultans of Cairo. He was more religious and more of a scholar than Abū Dulaf, and Bosworth suggests that his poem reflects a careful study of the beggars' dialect more than personal experience. But on the matter of *ṭarsh* his information is quite independent of Abū Dulaf's. Bosworth translates the line as follows:

"And in making moulds for lead in casting amulets and charms (or: in making moulds from tin for turning out amulets and charms?), how often has my hand written on the mould in the script of Syriac and then that of phylactery-writing (sc. in Hebrew)!"[15]

The problematic first part of the verse for which Bosworth gives two versions reads in Arabic *wa bi'ṭ-ṭarsh min al-qaṣdīr*, which we translate here as "by *ṭarsh* of tin."

Bosworth observes in his linguistic commentary that *al-qaṣdīr* means tin in classical and modern Arabic.[16] But the matter is confused by the interlinear commentaries on obscure words that appear in several

[12] Hind, op. cit., I, pp. 79–80.

[13] Bosworth, op. cit., II, p. 249.

[14] Ibid., I, pp. 132–49.

[15] Ibid., II, p. 298 (Arabic text p. 49).

[16] Ibid., II, p. 327.

of the manuscripts of Ṣafī ad-Dīn's poems. The manuscripts are no more than two or three centuries old, but the original commentaries are undoubtedly older.[17] Yet they are probably not of Ṣafī ad-Dīn's own era. The chronology is important because block printing seems to have disappeared by the end of the fourteenth century. Thus the commentators may not have correctly understood the verse if they were living after the period when the prints were being made.

Three manuscripts gloss *bi'ṭ-ṭarsh* by *ḍarb al-qālib k'al-kitāba*, "the striking of the mold like [sic] writing"; and *al-qaṣdīr* is rendered by three manuscripts as "amulets (*ta*ᶜ*āwīdh* or ᶜ*uwadh*) of lead."[18]

Bosworth is understandably perplexed by these glosses since the metal indicated is clearly tin. "Lead is the obvious metal for the actual castings, but one could imagine that tin could be hammered into a matrix for producing amulets of clay and other plastic substances; I have accordingly indicated both possibilities in the translation of this verse."[19]

The interlinear commentaries on the next verse of the poem, which uses jargon words for two other types of amulets, compound the problem. One word, *jawānī*, is glossed in one manuscript as *hayākil ṣighār wa* ᶜ*uwadh raṣāṣ wa wariq*. The grammar is obscure, but this probably means "small figurines and amulets [of] lead and silver." Another gives "small figurines," and a third seems garbled giving "small lead figurines from and silver [sic]." Sellers of figurines (*hayākil*) appear in the glosses of two other verses as well, although none of the words so glossed is otherwise known to refer to figurines.[20]

The most plausible way out of this perplexity is to assume that the glosses were added to the poem at a later period by a commentator who was familiar with peddlers of lead figurines but who was unfamiliar with printed amulets. Thus the only way he could understand the explicit designation of tin *ṭarsh* was to link it to the familiar figurines which he knew to be of lead. The commentary ignores, of course, the explicit reference to writing in the second half of the verse. To the pious illiterate, Syriac and Hebrew texts undoubtedly looked like impressive prophylactics against demons.

Assuming that *ṭarsh* means something from which an amulet is printed, and that it was at least sometimes a tin plate, let us return to the prints themselves and see whether there is evidence to buttress this assumption. What can a close inspection actually determine about the process that produced them?

First, it appears that the paper was laid flat and the block pressed down upon it. When more than one block was used, they were used one at a time. This is clearly evident from Plate I. The upper block of the main text is very dark and smeared on its right edge. The lower block shows more even pressure. If the blocks had been locked together and imposed simultaneously, they would reflect the same pressure. If each block was imposed separately, the paper must have been laid on a flat surface. Otherwise, if the paper had been pressed onto first one and then the other, it would have obscured the clear view the printer would have needed to make sure the prints did not overlap.

Secondly, blocks were probably made from at least two substances. The ornamental writing on the top portion of the Columbia University specimen is verse 256 of Sura 2 of the Qur'an written around three or four uncertain words in the middle. The paper it is on is glued to the rest of the amulet. The final words of the verse are in white-on-black around the sides, and in black-on-white in the middle, of an inverted teardrop shape. The middle words are reproduced so badly that they are readable only if one knows the text. Yet the botched letters are at least twice the size of the clear black-on-white letters on the main part of the amulet.

Since the white-on-black ornaments of some other amulets also seem to have been printed from separate blocks, it seems likely that the technique that yielded tiny black-on-white letters with a good deal of precision was not the same as the one that yielded precise, and even artistic white-on-black ornamental letters. Apparently, precise black-on-white letters could not be produced by the latter technique, nor ornamental white-on-black letters by the former.

A print in the Cambridge University Library reproduced in *Aramco World* affords a partial exception to this conclusion.[21] Large, elegant, white calligraphy runs vertically across line after line of tiny horizontal black writing, all designed as a single plate with words artificially divided as needed, and fine lines added, to outline the white letters. But this is not truly white-on-black; it is essentially a fine line print yielding a white-on-white image. It strongly suggests, however,

[17] Ibid., II, pp. 291–94.

[18] Ibid., II, Arabic text p. 71.

[19] Ibid., II, p. 327.

[20] Ibid., II, Arabic text pp. 66, 70–71.

[21] Lunde, op. cit., p. 27.

that the difficulty in producing white-on-black was not the scale of the lettering but the production of large areas of black.

Thirdly, the fine lettering of the long texts must have been incised in recto on a soft medium and then reversed by transfer to a block or plate. That is, the white areas were *not* cut away leaving the black lines in relief. Under high magnification there is no sign of cutting, even on tiny rings. By comparison, early European woodcutters were frequently imprecise in cutting around closely spaced fine lines, and perfect rings were extremely difficult.[22] Yet an amulet in the library of Heidelberg University shows a dozen perfect rings, each .08″ in diameter, used to mark the end of Quranic verses. And one has a dot precisely in the center.[23]

In Chinese woodblock printing a calligrapher wrote the text in recto on thin paper. The blockcutter glued the paper upside down to the block and wet it so that the ink showed through in reverse. Then he cut away the white areas leaving the inked characters in relief. Printing converted the verso calligraphy to recto again. By this technique a good calligrapher and a precise woodcutter could produce a beautiful text. But the woodcutter's challenge was the harder. He had to follow the contours of whatever the calligrapher wrote, while the calligrapher's text was constrained only by his awareness of the technical limitations of woodcutting.

Conceivably, the Muslim amulet makers followed the same process. But if so, the calligraphers assumed that the woodcutters were incredibly skilled even though they themselves were often rather slipshod. The Kufic script of the Columbia specimen, for example, is quite mediocre and often barely legible, even under high magnification with the Quranic text at one's side for reference. Occasionally words are even left out of Quranic quotations.[24]

Plates II and III depicting a previously unpublished specimen from the Madina Collection present strong evidence that the *ṭarsh* makers did not follow the Chinese practice. The first and last letters of each line in the middle portion of the print appear to be trimmed so closely that part of each letter is missing. Since the margin of the paper is ample, the trimming must have been done on the block. But no craftsman

Plate II. Arabic blockprint in the Madina Collection, New York (No. Ca 32, 34.5 cm. × 7.5 cm.).

[22] For example, Hind, op. cit., I, figs. 40, 48.

[23] Arnold and Grohman, op. cit., pl. 15.

[24] Sura 2:256 in lines 11–15 is missing the word *dhā*, and Sura 10:81 in lines 23–25 is lacking its first three words.

Plate III. Middle portion of blockprint in the Madina Collection, New York (No. Ca 32).

would have sawn a wooden block so badly as to cut into the text. The process of putting metal in a mold is a much more plausible source of the defect.

So how was a *ṭarsh* made? We propose the following: The *ṭarsh*-engraver carefully flattened a moist clay tablet, perhaps in some way continuing the practice of the ancient Mesopotamians. With some sort of stylus, using all the writing skill he could muster, he engraved his minute text into the tablet. The depth of the engraving was probably very shallow to minimize gouging out flecks of clay that he would have to brush away. The tablet was then dried hard in the sun or baked.

He may then have taken a thin sheet of tin of the sort itinerant tinners were still purchasing in Iranian bazaars earlier in this century,[25] applied it to the tablet, and pounded the malleable metal to force it into the grooves of the letters. Or more likely he produced his plate by pouring molten tin on the tablet. Whichever technique was used, the resulting plate had to be small so it would not bend too readily, and the tiny letters in low relief on soft metal probably wore down quickly after a fairly small number of impressions. But the tin could be pounded flat, or melted, and used again.

Larger white-on-black blocks were probably cut from wood. One can only speculate as to the reason tin was not used for them too, but a likely guess is that the ink used did not adhere evenly to the large tin surface of the black areas. The question of ink, of course, cannot be addressed directly without scientific examination.[26]

The tin plate hypothesis takes into account the available evidence and also explains why the original printblocks, presumably so much more durable than the prints themselves, have not survived. A *ṭarsh* was indeed a writing made to be effaced and used again, just as its etymology indicates.

The linking of the prints and the *ṭarsh* texts through this hypothesis also locates medieval Arabic block printing in time and space and helps explain the apparent lack of impact of this remarkable technological development. Geographically, the prints are found in Egypt, where conditions for paper preservation are ideal, and the poems referring to them were written in Iran and either Iraq or Egypt.

In time, the tenth century *terminus ab quo* proposed by previous investigators on the basis of palaeography and the archaeological stratification of finds fits well with Abū Dulaf al-Khazrajī's period of activity. And the fourteenth century *terminus ad quem*, which Karabacek proposed on the weak premise that none of the manuscripts in the collection his specimens came from was dated later, fits with the career of Ṣafī ad-Dīn al-Ḥillī. A more cogent reason for regarding the fourteenth century as the end of the era of Arabic printing, however, is that European observers never noticed it in the Middle East once they had developed printing themselves, and the memory had faded entirely by the time the first Arabic books were printed in Europe in the late fifteenth century, and the first press established in the Muslim world in the early eighteenth.

The question of the lack of impact of Arabic block printing cannot be divorced from the questions of origins and consequences. Printing in Arabic appears in the Middle East within a century or so of becoming well established in China. Moreover, medieval Arabic chronicles confirm that the craft of paper making came to the Middle East from China by way of Central Asia, and one print was found in the excavation of the medieval Egyptian Red Sea port of al-Quṣair al-Qadīm where wares imported from China have also been discovered.[27]

Nevertheless, it seems more likely that Arabic block printing was an independent invention. Many prints of Buddhist texts in various Turkic languages have been discovered in Central Asia, but they date from the thirteenth century and show a familiarity with wooden movable types that would have been applicable to Arabic texts.[28] In addition, the writing is not as minute as that of the Arabic prints.

The specialized underworld use of printing, which was so unfamiliar to his dignified contemporaries that Abū Dulaf had to gloss the crucial word, also points away from China. Chinese crafts were highly admired, and Chinese products much sought after. Iranian potters, for example, sold thousands of imitations of the splash-painted sgraffiato ware of the T'ang Dynasty because genuine T'ang pieces were so rare and expensive, but enormously appealing to Iranian consumers.

[25] On the tinner's craft see H. E. Wulff, *The Traditional Crafts of Persia*, Cambridge, Mass., 1966, p. 31.

[26] Even though medieval Muslim inks were water-based, it is not impossible that oil-based ink was also used as it was for woodblock printing in China; Frank B. Wiborg, *Printing Ink: A History*, New York, 1926, p. 87.

[27] Krek, op. cit., pp. 13, 15.

[28] Pp. 20–21 of typescript of work in progress generously made available to me by Prof. Tsuen-hsuin Tsien of the University of Chicago.

It seems unlikely, therefore, that Muslim amulet hawkers could have learned about and adopted a distinctive Chinese technology without it coming to the general awareness of educated Muslims. In China, after all, printing was used for the most respectable texts, and emperors were known to sponsor special projects.

And finally, the Chinese did not print from molded or cast metal plates, though they were expert at casting bronze vessels decorated with calligraphy in relief.

The mediocre aesthetic quality of many of the Arabic prints fits better the world of itinerant tinners, rogue scribes like Abū Dulaf himself, and confidence men willing to take advantage of the piety of the gullible masses than it does the refined world of princely courts and religious scholarship. And this low social level also accounts for the insulation of this extraordinary technology from the rest of society. People of dignity did not know about *ṭarsh* and were certainly not inclined to apply the technology of their inferiors to their own lofty writings.

The only indication that printing may occasionally have caught on for purposes other than amulets comes from Muslim Spain in the tenth century. The Caliph ʿAbd ar-Raḥmān an-Nāṣir (reigned 912–961) appointed the son of a Sicilian slave to a series of high posts including the vizirate. The official's biography relates that "he used to be unique in the governorships. For official documents were written in his palace. Then he sent them for printing (*ṭabʿ*), and they were printed and sent back to him. Then they were sent [reading *tabʿathu* for *yabʿathu*] to the governors, and they acted according to his will (*ʿalā yadaihi*)."[29]

The critical root *ṭ.b.ʿ.*, taken here to connote "printing," normally means "pressing." The editor of the text remarks in a note that he believes it refers to sending documents out to receive an official seal, although there are other words that are commonly used to designate official sealing. Other scholars have interpreted it to mean "print" but have drawn no particular conclusions from the passage.[30] Whatever the word means, the vizier's practice was obviously not generally adopted.

Did the Muslims of Spain, who were in regular contact with Egypt, pick up the technology of printing and try it out in a place where it was not tainted by association with amulet peddlers? Further discoveries are needed to answer the question. If they did, however, then some of the numerous Italian traders in Egyptian ports may have done the same.

Many authors have discussed the possible origins of European printing.[31] The most popular hypotheses have been independent invention and borrowing from China, but neither has been verified. In the absence of substantial scholarship on Arabic block printing, no one has given serious consideration to the possibility of technological borrowing from the Arab world. The chronology proposed here indicates that European printing probably did begin before the practice was abandoned in the Muslim world, but there is as yet no way of verifying that the former drew in some way upon the latter.

One possible line of investigation might be the early history of tarot cards. Playing cards were popular on both sides of the Mediterranean and, on the European side, were among the earliest printed artifacts.[32] The earliest known Muslim cards, a fragment from the twelfth century and a nearly complete deck from the fifteenth century, are hand-painted.[33] Their size and shape are similar to the block dimensions of the amulets, however, and one surviving fragment of an Arabic print simply bears an arabesque decoration[34] while another has a picture of a devil that would be not inappropriate on a playing card.[35] Tarot cards, originally called *tarocchi* in Italian, are of special interest because of legends that they were introduced by gypsies, an "underworld" population that reached medieval Europe from the Middle East, and because the source of their name is unknown. Could the word tarot or *tarocco* have originally come from *ṭarsh* or *ṭars*?

Leaving this unanswerable question unanswered, we will turn to our final problem: Why did the *ṭarsh* disappear? Suggestions advanced to explain the later Muslim resistance to the printing press, such as that there were effective Muslim prohibitions on

---

[29] Ibn al-Abbār, *Al-ḥulla al-saiyarāʾ*, ed. H. Monès, Cairo, 1963, p. 253.

[30] Káldy-Nagy, op. cit., p. 201; P. Hitti, *History of the Arabs*, London, 1964 (8th ed.), p. 564. Plate IV, an unpublished specimen from the Madina Collection, may, judging from its calligraphic style, be of Spanish rather than Egyptian provenance.

[31] See works listed in note 3.

[32] Tsien, op. cit., pp. 26–27; Hind, op. cit., I, pp. 80, 84–89.

[33] L. A. Mayer, *Mamluk Playing Cards*, Leiden, 1971.

[34] Arnold and Grohman, op. cit., pl. 29.

[35] Bishr Farès, "Figures magiques," in *Aus der Welt der islamischen Kunst. Festschrift für Ernst Kühnel*, Berlin, 1959, p. 155. I am indebted to Dr. M. Krek for bringing this print to my attention.

Plate IV. Arabic blockprint in the Madina Collection, New York (No. Ca 31, 14.2 cm. × 11.2 cm.).

reproducing sacred texts or that there was resistance from a threatened scribal elite, are clearly inapplicable.[36] Printing lasted too long and was too bound up with religious texts for the former explanation to make any sense, and its encapsulation in the underworld social environment of the Banū Sāsān vitiates the latter.

Ṭarsh surely disappeared because of developments in the popular religious culture of Islam. And the popular religious development that swept the Islamic world with increasing force from the thirteenth century onward was organized Sufism. Did the Sufi *murshids* with their followings of disciples and admirers take action to curtail the shady religious practices of the Banū Sāsān? Most likely they did, because the more popular Sufis were competing for the attention and support of the same social strata, and the Sufis had a religious cachet that surely gave them the upper hand.

Sufis wrote amulets and performed similar religious services for the common people; but unlike the Banū Sāsān, if they engaged in improper practices, they risked losing their followers. Moreover, within Sufism saintliness was deemed to lie in the *baraka*, or holy aura, of the Sufi's person, and by extension of his family, tomb, personal belongings, and, of course, writing. *Ṭarsh* peddlers had little to gain from writing out each amulet personally, but for the Sufis the personal act of writing holy words was part of a wider religious claim. It is not only understandable that the Sufis would have suppressed *ṭarsh*-making, but it would be remarkable if they had not. Unfortunately, in so doing they caused one of the most ingenious medieval Muslim technologies to disappear almost without a trace.

36 Káldy-Nagy, op. cit., pp. 202–5.

[13]

ISLAMIC REFORMIST DISCOURSE IN THE TULIP PERIOD (1718-30) IBRAHIM MÜTEFERRIQA AND HIS ARGUMENTS FOR PRINTING

Stefan Reichmuth

For several years now a debate has been going on among historians and orientalists about a reassessment of the cultural and political developments of the Islamic World in the eighteenth century. The prevailing picture had been that of military weakness, economic decline and cultural ossification of the Islamic states which was only overcome, it was said, under European influence from the nineteenth century onwards. At the very best the eighteenth century was seen as foreshadowing in some respects the Muslims' opening up towards Europe which was finally and irreversibly to set in after Napoleon's invasion of Egypt. The critique of this paradigm might be traced back to the seventies and early eighties when economic and cultural developments within the Ottoman Empire, but also in India and other more peripheral regions of the Islamic world came under closer scrutiny, which revealed a good deal of internal dynamics which could not be fully explained by the push and pull of European expansion.[1] Since the late eighties the debate which was fairly heated especially in German scholarship has increasingly focused on a crucial issue of cross-cultural interpretation: Was there nothing but European rise and Islamic decline, as two sides of one coin, or are there other patterns of contact and analogous development to be identified on the two sides? Changes in worldview, a growth of rationalism, pietism and even the notion of enlightenment have been used to capture some such analogies, with results that remain quite controversial up to now.[2]

---

[1] See e.g. T. Naff, R. Owen (eds.), *Studies in Eighteenth Century Islamic History,* Carbondale, Edwardsville, London and Amsterdam 1977; P. Gran, *Islamic Roots of Capitalism: Egypt 1760-1845,* Austin, London 1979; R. Owen, *The Middle East in the World Economy,* 1800-1914, London, New York 1981; N. Levtzion, J. O. Voll (eds.), *18th century renewal and reform in Islam,* Syracuse 1987.

[2] See especially R. Schulze, "Das islamische achtzehnte Jahrhundert: Versuch einer historiographischen Kritik", *Die Welt des Islams (WI) 30, 1990, 140-59; id.,* "Was it die islamische Aufklärung?", *WI* 36, 1996, 276-325; R. Peters, "Reinhard Schulze's quest for an Islamic Enlightenment", WDI 30, 1990, 160ff.; B. Radtke, "Between Projection and Supression. Some Considerations concerning the Study of Sufism", in F. de Jong (ed.), *Shi'a Islam, Sects and Sufism,* Utrecht 1992; id., "Erleuchtung und Aufklärung. Islamische Mystik und Europäischer Rationalismus", *WI* 34, 1994, 48-66; id., "Sufism and Enlightenment. An attempt at a critical reappraisal", *WI* 36, 1996, 326-64; R. S. O'Fahey, B. Radtke, "Neo-Sufism Reconsidered", *Der Islam* 70, 1993, 52-87; T. Nagel, "Autochthone Wurzeln des islamischen Modernismus. Bemerkungen zum Werk des Damaszeners Ibn 'Abidin, *ZDMG* 146, 1996, 92-111; G. Hagen, T. Seidensticker, "Reinhard Schulzes Hypothese einer islamischen Aufklärung", *ZDMG* 148, 1998, 83-110.

The Ottoman printing press in Istanbul which was licensed by imperial decree in 1139/1727 and which began its production in 1141/1729 fully bears out this difficulty of interpretation. As printing played such a crucial role in European history and culture, the establishment of Ottoman printing has been widely seen as a major step on the road leading to the westernization of the empire. There are several points to support that view. The press was established a few years after the first major Ottoman missions to Vienna (1715) and Paris (1721). Mehmed Sa'id Efendi, the son of the ambassador to Paris who had accompanied his father, was one of the driving forces behind it. The man who was mainly responsible for the setting up and running of the press would at first glance provide an even more striking case for the European influence at work here. Ibrahim Müteferriqa (d. 1158/1745) was after all a Hungarian convert to Islam who had been a Unitarian and had even studied at a theological seminary in Hungary before he became a Muslim and exposed himself fully to the world of Ottoman learning and administration.[3] He served as liaison officer to the Hungarian allies of the Ottomans and took frequent part in diplomatic negotiations with Austria and Russia. It is even said that he obtained the equipment of his press from Vienna. As all the works which he printed were related to language, history, geography and the natural and physical sciences the impact of his Christian European background on his activities would seem to need no further confirmation.

The same could be said for the general outlook of the Ottoman court and for the cultural and political orientation of the Ottoman elite of his time. After all this was the famous Tulip Period which is connected with the Grand Vizier Dāmād Ibrāhīm Pasha (1718-30) and the rule of Sultan Ahmed III (1703-30). The lavish festivities, the garden culture of court and aristocracy, and the general passion for tulips and other flowers characterised this time which has become a symbol for the new turn of Ottoman history and for the opening up towards Europe and its culture.[4] The introduction of printing would fit fully into that trend which could be seen also in other fields, like the beginnings of Ottoman baroque

[3] See on him esp. Bursalı Mehmet Tahir, *Osmanlı Müellifleri*, İstanbul 1972-75 [İstanbul 1299/1915] III, 73-6 (in the following abbreviated as *OM);* N. Berkes, "İlk Türk Matbaası kurucusunun dinî ve fikrî kimliği", *Belleten* 26/104, 1962, 716-32; id., *The Development of Secularism in Turkey*, McGill 1964, 36-46; id., "Ibrahim Müteferriqa", *EI2* III, 996ff. (1978); W. Heinz, "Die Kultur der Tulpenzeit des Osmanischen Reiches", *WZKM* 61, 1967, 68-74; more recently G. A. Kut, "Matba'a 2. In Turkey", EI2 VI, 800f.; G. Duverdier, T. Agaroğlu, "İlk Türk Basımevinin Kuruluşunda İki Kültür Elçisi: Savary De Brèves İle İbrahim Müteferrika", *Belleten* 56, No. 215, 1992, 275-306.

[4] See esp. A. Refik, *Lale Devri*, Sadeleştiren: D. Gürlek, Istanbul 1997, N.S. Banarlı, "Bir Lâle Kervanı", appendix to A. Refik, *Lale Devri*, 127ff.; EI^2 V, 641-44 (I. Mélikoff); typical also *Türkische Kunst und Kultur aus osmanischer Zeit*, Recklinghausen 1985, I, 52 (K. Schwarz; in the following abbreviated as *TKO)*.

architecture, of manufacturing enterprise and of the translation activities which were first projected during that period. Ibrāhīm Müteferriqa is also known for his call for military reforms along European lines in his famous treatise *Usūl el-hikam* (1731).[5] He is perhaps even the author of an earlier, anonymous dialogue between an Ottoman and a Christian military officer which shows the same line of argument.[6] The play of external challenge and influence would then seem to be fairly clear in his case.

This picture of the Tulip period, conceived as the beginning of the opening up towards Europe, owes much to the late Ottoman historian and journalist Ahmed Refik Altınay (d. 1937) whose famous book on this time appeared as a serial in the Ottoman journal *Iqdām* in 1908 and was first published as a book in 1915, with several later editions in Republican Turkey.[7] Ahmed Refik adopted the notion itself from the neo-classicist poet Yahya Kemal Beyatlı (d. 1958) who had coined it during his stay in Paris.[8] Its symbolic message was strong enough: the Tulip, cherished by both Sufī poets and by the Ottoman elite in general, had been smuggled secretly out of its country. But now, in the days of Ahmed III and his vizier, it was at last finding its way back from its European exile. For all its spectacular career in Holland and its newly grown and now fully developed beauty it had never forgotten its homeland.[9]

There are several points, however, which qualify this neat picture. Further research has shown that the Tulip Period and the rule of Ahmed III were much more complex and that the development of that period shows many other cultural flows besides that from West to East.[10] Even the re-import of the tulips from the Netherlands could be seen as much as a return to older cultural patterns as an opening towards Europe. Apart from European influences there was a growing interest in the scholarly disciplines of the Islamic tradition, and the important revival of Ottoman poetry under this sultan and his Grand Vizier has been often described. Both learning and literary developments were connected with the rise of a civilian elite of scribes and Islamic scholars within the administration and within the power structures of the empire. This rise had been

---

[5] A. Şen, *İbrahim Müteferriqa ve Usûlü'l-Hikem fî Nizâmi'l-Ümem*, Ankara 1995.

[6] A.C. Schaendlinger, "Die Entdeckung des Abendlandes als Vorbild. Ein Vorschlag zur Umgestaltung des Heerwesens und der Außenpolitik des Osmanischen Reichez zu Beginn des 18. Jarhunderts", in G. Heiss/G. Klingenstein (eds.), *Das Osmanische Reich und Europa 1683 bis 1798: Konflikt, Entspannung und Austausch*, München 1983, 89-112.

[7] EI^2 V, 643 (I. Mélikoff); A Refik, *Lale devri*, introduction, 8f.

[8] N. S. Banarlı, "Bir Lâle Kervanı", 127.

[9] This is most clearly expressed by N.S. Banarlı, "Bir Lâle Kervanı".

[10] See already Heinz, "Kultur der Tulpenzeit", 116.

underway since the seventeenth century. It had a clear impact on public life and building activities, and the new pious trend in the capital, which was noticed even by European observers has to be kept in view together with the more spectacular festivities of the court if a general picture is to be drawn.[11] Also related to this pious trend might be the first issuing of coins which used the learned name *Islām-bol* instead of *Qu(n)stantīniyya* for Istanbul - this had been regarded since the 17th century by the educated classes as the "Ottoman" name of the city (vis-a-vis the Greek-derived Istanbul) but was only now introduced into coinage, to be later sanctioned by imperial decree in 1174/1760.[12]

Even the esthetics of the period which was pervaded by the admiration for the beauty of gardens and flowers might have had its religious correlates, for example in the fields of calligraphy and illumination. Ottoman, Safavid and Moghul illuminations of the Koran had developed a more naturalistic representation of flowers and leaves.[13] Ottoman painting with its realist and rational trend[14] went even further in other religious contexts. The naturalist picture of the flower was found worthy to find its place beside the sayings of the Prophet and other sacred names and texts[15]. This development still requires to be documented; it seems to have come fully into its own in the early 18th century. A striking example is the "Muhammadan Rose", a design which shows the Divine and Prophetic Names, the qualities of the Prophet and the names of his grandsons and of those companions who had been promised Paradise inscribed into carefully arranged rose flowers and buds. The earliest known example of this design is to be found in a manuscript dated 1119/1121 (1707/1709).[16] A book title falling into a similar line is "The Rose of Hundred Leaves" *(Gül-i sadberg),* a poetical commentary on a collection of 100 sayings of the Prophet, written by an Ottoman author of the time, Seyyid Ismāʿil Belīlgh (d. 1142-3/1730-31).[17] If these

---

[11] Cf. the Italian and Dalmatian sources quoted and summed up by N. Jorga, *Geschichte des Osmanischen Reiches,* Darmstadt 1990 (Gotha 1908-13) IV, 361-99.

[12] *EI²* IV, 224 (H. İnalcık); TKO I, 117f. (H. Piegeler); for examples see TKO I, 126 (H. Wilski).

[13] M. Lings, *The Quranic Art of Calligraphy and Illumination,* Westerham 1976, 189.

[14] See for this TKO II, 37f. (H.-C. Graf v. Bothmer).

[15] See *İslâm Sanatında Türkler. The Turkish Contribution to Islamic Arts,* Istanbul 1976, 77; illustrations in *Türkiye Diyanet Vakfi İslâm Ansiklopedisi,* XV, Istanbul 1997, 36f., 41, 57, 98; K. Çığ, *Hattat Hafiz Osman Efendi,* Istanbul 1948, appendix.

[16] *TKO* II, 38 (H.-C. Graf v. Bothmer); A. Schimmel, *Und Muhammad ist Sein Prophet. Die Verehrung des Propheten in der islamischen Frömmigkeit,* Düsseldorf, Köln 1981, 128; a similar design perhaps in an 18th-century ms. in the British Library, cf. M.I. Waley, "Illumination and its functions in Islamic manuscripts", in F. Déroche and F. Richard, *Scribes et manuscripts du Moyen Orient,* Paris 1997, 93.

[17] *OM* II, 56f.; E.J.W. Gibb, *A History of Ottoman Poetry,* London, repr. 1958-69 (1900-09) I, 140, IV, 117n.2. Apart from so many other connotations, the rose had become a powerful poetic symbol of the Prophet in Sufī poetry; cf. A. Schimmel, *Und Muhammad ist Sein Prophet,* Düsseldorf, Köln 1981, 32; in Ottoman poetry already in the Hilya of Khāqānī (d. 1015/1606-7), E.J.W. Gibb, *Ottoman Poetry* III, 196ff.

few hints tell us anything about the religious sentiments of the time, then the Muhammadan Rose should perhaps be added to the flowers of that era.

There are thus rather typically Islamic and "Eastern" dimensions to a cultural development which is otherwise widely seen in relation to the European world. The same can be said for Ibrāhīm Müteferriqa himself. He clearly did not belong to that group of European renegades who had joined Islam and Ottoman service for no more than practical reasons of career and fortune. Apart from his solid grounding in Ottoman learning he even wrote a passionate treatise about Islam which was directed against Catholic Christianity. It expressed his conviction that Islam was the superior religion which would remain victorious *(Risāle-i islāmiyye,* written ten years after his conversion). Even if his stand might be related as well to Hungarian opposition to Habsburg politics and to his religious convictions, Müteferriqa showed a clear interest in Islamic reform which was already noticed by Berkes.[18] This brings us to the question of how this Hungarian convert himself saw and presented his printing and publishing activities in the Ottoman context. If we look at his own testimony we find that he justified his commitment to printing in entirely Islamic terms, using arguments that later became common stock in Islamic reformist writings and movements.

This impression emerges from the introduction to his first published print, Vān Qūlī's Ottoman translation of al-Jawharī's famous Arabic dictionary *al-Sihah* which came out in two large volumes in 1141/1729[19]. The introductory part includes a foreword, then the text of the imperial decree and of the Fatwā of the Şeyhülislam which both licensed his press, and a set of 16 supporting statements (*taqārīz,* in Arabic) by prominent Qādīs and scholars. Added to this is a special treatise, called *Vesīletü t-tibā'a* in which Müteferriqa lays out all his arguments for printing and its usefulness for religion and state *(dīn-u devlet).*

The *hutbe* of the introduction[20] places the author in the world of the scribal arts and of crafts and links both of them to the order of the cosmos. God is praised as the One Who set up the Dīvān of the Universe and Who brought forth the crafts of the possible.[21] In the boundless book of the traces of His power, the whole heaven and earth provide only minor pages. Reference is then made to God's secrets which are written with the trees on leaves and flowers[22] - an

[18] *EI²*, III, 997.
[19] Vān Qūlī (al-Wānī), *Kitāb-ı lughat-ı Vān Qūlī,* Istanbul 1141/1729.
[20] Vān Qūlī 1f.
[21] *..ol münshi'i devāvīn-i ekvān ve mübdi'-i imkān...*
[22] *..eqlām-ı eshjār ile sahāyif-i evrāq ve elvāh-ı ezhār üzere...*

intriguing metaphor that evokes the spirit of the Tulip Era. After further praise of the Prophet Müteferriqa turns to the chain of the centuries since the prophetic period and to the happy days of the present 12th century. This has been graced and honoured by God with the caliphate of Ahmed III, a most virtuous Sultan. The role of the Sultan as Caliph and of the Ottoman dynasty as Caliphal family *(dūdmān-ı khilāfet)* is much stressed here, more than would have been expected, if the general opinion about the Ottomans' attitude towards that title is anything to go by. According to that opinion the title was indeed used but played only a minor role for them until the end of the 18th century when it became a welcome symbol of their continuous authority over former Muslim subjects now living outside their realm.[23] H. Gibb already described the later use of the title as implying a general claim to be a just ruler who upheld the Sharīʿa.[24] Colin Imber[25] has shown recently that the first systematic attempt to define the caliphal authority of the Sultan was made for Süleymān the Magnificent by his Şeyhülislam Abū'l-Suʿūd. The Caliphal claim became quite common also for later Sultans, based on the rights of the strongest Muslim ruler, as developed by Ibn Khaldūn.[26]

The role of the Sultan as the legitimate Caliph was stressed for Ahmed III by his Şeyhülislam as a justification for Ottoman dealings with Safavid Iran.[27] The Sultan himself used the title already around 1118/1706 in a letter to the ruler of Balkh.[28] The famous fountain which was erected by him in front of the Topkapı gate can also be seen as a symbolic expression of his religious status. The Qasīda written for it by the Ottoman poet Seyyid Vehbī[29] makes this very clear. The Sultan is praised as the source of justice, magnanimity, and sanctity, being at the same time Pādishāh and Saint, the virtues of ʿUmar, ʿAlī, and the Prophet reappearing in his person.[30] He has also become the imam of the Muslims

[23] See e.g. S.J. Shaw, *History of the Ottoman Empire and Modern Turkey*, Vol. I, Cambridge 1991 (1976), 85.

[24] H.A.R. Gibb, "Some Considerations on the Sunni Theory of the Caliphate", in dto., *Studies on the Civilisation of Islam*, Princeton 1982 (1962), 141-50.

[25] C. Imber, "Ideals and legitimation in early Ottoman history", in M. Kunt and C. Woodhead (eds.), *Süleyman the Magnificent and His Age. The Ottoman Empire in the Early Modern World*, London/New York 1995, 151ff.

[26] H. Krüger, *Fetwa und Siyar*, Wiesbaden 1978, 102ff., 154.

[27] H. Krüger, *Fetwa und Siyar*, 102 n. 394.

[28] İ.H. Uzunçarşılı, *Osmanlı Tarihi*, Ankara 1947-59, Vol. IV/2, 139.

[29] E.J.W. Gibb, *Ottoman Poetry* IV, 373ff.

[30] Gibb IV, 373:16 *ʿadl-ü kerāmet menbaʿı shems-i vilāyet matlaʿı;* 374:1f. *hem pādishāhdır hem veliyy zātında olmush münjelī * ʿadl-ı ʿOmer jūd-ı ʿAlī khulq-ı Muhammad Mustafā.*

and the helping Shadow of God, whose order is to be obeyed by Koranic injunction.[31]

The fountain was erected in 1728, that is at the same time when Ibrahim Müteferriqa was preparing his first prints. The strong religious wording seems to go beyond usual poetical flattery/hyperbole, and this suggests that Müteferriqa's use, too, reflects more than a common formality. Five of the 16 scholarly recommendations *(taqārīz)* also mention the Caliphal office of the Sultan, one even describes him as "God's Caliph in the World".[32] It would seem then that the later "pan-Islamic" use of the title, which became so common in the 19th century, had quite earlier origins in the milieu of Ottoman scholars and scribes who were since the 16th century struggling to bolster the Islamic authority and the universal sovereignty of the state.[33]

A second claim which also fits into that pattern is made here for Ahmed III, namely that he was sent by God at the beginning of the new century for the renewal of the Faith and the revival of the Sunna.[34] This is related to God's eternal providence *(ᶜināyet-i ezeliyye)* and to His habit *(ᶜādet)* to provide the necessary means for the well-being of mankind.[35] It was already Lutfī Paşa who in his *Tevārīkh-i āl-i ᶜOsmān* (after 1541) had constructed a whole series of Ottoman sultans as "Renewers of the Faith".[36] In the eighteenth century this claim of the Sultans had increasingly to compete with that of other scholars or Ṣūfīs for the status of a *mujaddid.*

The main piece of the introductory part of the book is Müteferriqa's treatise on the art of printing and the Muslims' need for a printing press, the *Vesīletü'l-tibāᶜa.*[37] It is this treatise which provides the arguments on which the imperial decree was largely based. Ibrahim stresses again God's providence, which provides groups or individuals with the necessary means to achieve their aims, once the divine will has decreed that group's or person's greatness or success. The terms used for groups here are *ümmet, cemaat, qavm,* which were to remain crucial elements in later Islamic political thought.

---

31 Gibb IV, 375:9f. oldu imām el-müslimīn zill-i khudāvend-i muᶜīn * bi-n-nass-ı qur'ān-ı mübīn emrine vājib iqtidā.
32 Vān Qūlī 5-8.
33 Cf. C. Imber, "Ideals and legitimation", 149ff.
34 *...tejdīd-i qavā'id-i dīn-i mübīn ve ihyā-yı sünen-i fakhr el-mürselīn...*
35 *...esbāb-ı khayr-u salāh āmāde edüb...*
36 C. Imber, "Ideals and legitimation", 150.
37 Vān Qūlī 9-13.

He then turns to the history of mankind and of different religions which, as he says, he studied for a long time thanks to his knowledge of different languages. In all states which he came accross in earlier and later periods until the present, there were wise and judicious men who were always concerned to find means and methods to preserve those laws and customs which were at the base of the social and political structure. Apart from engraving them in stone or metal they invented the writing and distribution of books which provided the easiest way to attain that aim.

This was true in particular for Islam, the best religion and state of all. The other religious communities, Jews as well as Christians, neglected the divine order to preserve the revealed books which had been entrusted to them. In the case of the Jews, they kept the manuscript of the Torah and of other books in the ark of the covenant in Jerusalem and did not bother much to reproduce and distribute them among the people. Therefore, when Nebukadnezar destroyed Jerusalem, most of these books were lost, and the bases of their religious laws shaken. The Christians did not collect the Injīl during ʿĪsāʿs lifetime. This is why they became divided and split over his message, when he was elevated to Heaven. Some even were misled to error and unbelief. By this scripturalist approach to religious authority, Müteferriqa's picture of the two religions of the book might perhaps reflect traces of his Unitarian protestant past.

In Islam, however, the divine book and the Sharīʿa of its Prophet were carefully preserved, collected and copied from the beginning. The spread of books made them accessible to all believers. In later periods scholars and *mujtahidūn* arose who developed the law and its principles on the basis of Koran, Sunna and Consensus of the Umma. They wrote many new and beautiful books and developed the different disciplines. Islam has thus been privileged with the authentic preservation of its message, which was made possible by the spread of knowledge through the books which were written and distributed in large numbers.

Müteferriqa complains, however about a deplorable loss of books in the Islamic world. This was related to the ongoing duty to conduct *jihād,* which involved frequent warfare. But there were other and greater disasters, especially the *fitna* of Jenghiz Khan and Hülâgü who were responsible for the destruction of books and scholarly culture in Transoxania and in the Abbasid Empire. Then al-Andalus was lost to the Franks, and this western sun of knowledge went down. The Franks secured most of the available Islamic manuscripts of the Andalusians for themselves and even extended their interest in such manuscripts to other

Islamic countries. As they acquired and secured many rare texts they contributed to the growing disappearance of important books among the Muslims. Müteferriqa complains about the diminishing interest and quality of the scribes and copyists who would nowadays hardly take it upon them to copy a multi-volume lexicon or a larger historical book.

These statements serve as background for his justification of printing which in his view would provide a welcome remedy for this deplorable situation. He describes printing as a highly useful industrial technique.[38] Bringing it closer to Ottoman readers, he says that it combines the characteristics of making coins and seals with those of writing. He then goes on to present a list of ten reasons why printing is useful. The following arguments are of particular interest for our purpose (presented in an adapted and regrouped form here):

1. Printing can serve to provide books on Arabic, especially dictionaries which are generally needed, as Arabic is the base for all arts and sciences and for a refined language. Starting from this one could then go on to increase books on other disciplines. This would be immensely useful for both elite and common people. Quite clearly, both *khavāss* and *ᶜavāmm* are his target group, and this interest in a generalised learning and education comes out in several ways in his arguments.

2. It would be important for both religion and state to edit and publish those books which were written by worthy *mujtahidūn* and other authors in order to strengthen state and religion and to bring order into the affairs of the community by their endeavour and their *ijtihād.*[39] This would encourage the writing of new books and lead to *tejdīd ve ihyā.* This call for renewal and revival would seem to imply that *ijtihād* could be resumed - a question that was already becoming a hotly disputed issue among Islamic scholars of the time!

3. Printing is much faster than copying: at the same time of copying one manuscript 1000 printed copies could be produced. That would reduce the price of the copy and would bring many books within reach of poor students. The printed text is even better and more readable as it is clearer and water-proof. There are numbers, tables of content and indices which make the use of a printed book much easier. If cheaper books are available in large numbers they could

[38] Vān Qūlī 11, *..aᶜmāl-ı sınāᶜiyyeden bir sanᶜat-ı kesīret-i menāfiᶜ olub...*

[39] Vān Qūlī 11, *...taqviyet-i dīn-u devlet ve nizām-ı mehāmm-ı ümmet-i khayr el-besher içün bunja müjtehidīn ve-müsannifīn-i kirāmin kemāl-ı saᶜy ve ijtihād ile te'līf ve tedvīn qıldıqları kütüb-i nefīseyi teksīrr ve teshīh sebebiyle...*

even be distributed in the provincial towns and in the countryside, which would increase knowledge among their inhabitants. Printing thus serves as an instruments to eradicate ignorance.[40]

4. The distribution of printed books might serve to awake the believers and to raise their pride and happiness. The author compares it to the *jihād* by which the Ottoman sultans have increased the power and the glory of the Muslims. This would pertain not only to the Muslims of the Ottoman Empire but also to all those other nations and communities in the world which have joined the religion of Islam, namely the Turks, Tatars, Turkmens, Kurds, Uzbeks, Chagatays, People of India and Sind, Persians, Yemenites, Rumis, Ethiopians and Sudanis. They are all in need of books. The introduction of such as important matter would highly increase the power and prestige of the Sultanate in the world. All Muslims would be grateful for it, and it could become a tool for their awakening.[41] This is a quite early instance of a call for a "pan-Islamic" policy of the Ottoman sultans. It is also remarkable that it comes together here with the introduction of a new means of communication.

5. Another important argument for Müteferriqa is the need for competition with the Christian powers, which also have become interested in Arabic printing and have even set their pride in it. He notes that they have already printed texts like Ibn Sīnā's *Qānūn*, al-Idrīsī's *Nuzhat al-mushtāq* and Euclides. Up to now their products are of a poor quality, as they do not rely on specialists trained in Oriental script and orthography. But they are bent on improving them and are aiming at the book market of the Islamic countries. The Muslims who have always been superior to the polytheists and unbelievers should strive to maintain that superiority also in this field. This is a call for a struggle to retain economical control over a central field of Muslim cultural production.

The treatise is concluded by references to the imperial decree and the fatwa of the Şeyhülislam which establishes the acceptability of printing within the framework of the *Sharīʿa*. Nevertheless, books on *fiqh*, *tafsīr*, hadith and *kalām* are explicitly excluded from the license. A board of four prominent scholars is established to control the printed texts before their publication. Lexicography, history, medicine, *hikma*, astronomy and geography are

---

[40] *...jehlin izālesine vesīle olur.*

[41] The term used several times in this context is the Persian word *zinde* "awake, alive".

mentioned as the main disciplines to be covered, and this was duly observed by the publishers during the eighteenth century.

Does this restriction reveal lasting apprehensions about printing? Does it establish a "secular" sector of knowledge and science which was to be more and more separated from a "religious" one? The great importance of the philological and historical works which were published later by the press would hardly justify such an interpretation. It is rather the old and accepted framework of the "auxiliary disciplines", the *ulūm-i āliyye* which came in here.

To sum up and to come back to our starting point: How are we to cope with the fact that the introduction of printing was propagated at this point of time with thoroughly Islamic arguments? Even with points that were later used in quite similar form by other Islamic thinkers and movements - presumably without any direct influence from Müteferriqa's treatise?

The 'pan-Islamic' concept and the Caliphate of the Sultan can be found here as well as the call for revival *(tajdīd, ihyā')* and - implicitly - also for the renewal of *ijtihād.* The central role of the Arabic language and the propagation of learning - religious as well as general - for everybody also come in here. The latter points might be seen as falling in line with Müteferriqa's Unitarian protestant background which perhaps partly accounts for his interest in printing as an instrument for a general awakening of the Muslims. Strangely enough, what we would otherwise put under the separate labels of "Westernisation" and "Islamic reformism" comes up here in a remarkable kind of personal union...

There are at least three possible interpretations for this strange merger of conflicting perspectives:

a) It has been most common until now to stress Ibrahim Müteferriqa's contribution to the Westernization of Turkey and to see him as the first of the Europeans who were destined to play a role in this process. Niyazi Berkes duly places him at the beginning of his "Development of Secularism in Turkey".[42] The use of an Islamic discourse would appear from this point of view to be based on expediency rather than on conviction. This would also imply the beginning of the political 'double talk' which is often assumed for the reformist writings of Ottoman politicians, bureaucrats and intellectuals in later periods.

[42] N. Berkes, *Secularism in Turkey,* 36-47.

b) The fact that Islamic reformist arguments are put forward here by a Christian convert to Islam could even be seen as confirming those who argue for a Western origin of any significant innovation which occurred in the East since the eighteenth century. This would push the argument to its very limits: even Islamic reformism was invented by former Christians from the West!

c) A third way of looking at Müteferriqa would place him at the beginning of an Islamic discourse of modernization and reform and see him also as a forerunner of pan Islamism which was to be propagated and practised by influential Ottoman reformists of the 19th century and especially by Sultan Abdülhamid II.

Which of these perspectives is to be preferred? Which vantage point is to be chosen to look at Ibrahim Müteferriqa's writings and prints? Clearly the process of cultural transfer in which he was taking part produced ambiguous results. These results can be compared with coins having faces written in different scripts and languages. Or, to use a more contemporary metaphor: they are like different overhead transparencies placed on top of each other, producing a picture which is blurred but which also shows some lines which come out stronger than before as they are reinforced by the whole set of transparencies. One of these new strong lines of both "Western" and Islamic origin is étatism, the call for a strengthening of the authority of the ruler, the bureaucratic state, and, of course, the army. A crucial "Eastern" thread running through Müteferriqa's writings is his stress on *nizām* and *intizām*, referring to the old term which links political and cosmological order in medieval political theory. All his calls for renewal and reform can actually be placed under this perspective of an Islamic étatism, which perfectly fitted the leading class of scholars and officials which he had joined. Here again, "Western" and "Eastern" transparencies or discourses reinforced each other. The story of the reformed army units of the "New Order" *(nizām-ı jedīd)* under Selīm III and Mahmūd II is too well-known to be retold here; the first reference to this term which could be identified in Ottoman writing until now appears in Müteferriqa's description of European military reforms.[43]

It may be added that Müteferriqa's political and historical reflections do not have to be regarded as isolated statements. If judged from what was reported by Dadich, discussion about the best political systems appears to have become

[43] See A. Şen, *İbrahim Müteferriqa*, 84ff., 107, 114, 147, 152, 187. For *nizām* as a central issue in Ottoman reformist thought in the 19th century, most clearly expressed in the history of Ahmed Cevdet, see C.K. Neumann, *Das indirekte Argument. Ein Plädoyer für die Tanzīmāt vermittels der Historie. Die geschichtliche Bedeutung von Ahmed Cevdet Paşas Ta'rih,* Münster 1992, 236.

quite common among Ottoman Efendis during this period.[44] He mentions their strong interest in the form of government prevailing in Venice and their idea to convert the Imperial *dīvān* into a parliamentary council of the Venetian type. Müteferriqa's outline of the three systems of government - monarchy, aristocracy, democracy - which he himself presents in his *Usūlü'l-hikem fī nizāmi'l-ümem*[45] could perhaps also be related to this kind of discussion.

The case of Ibrahim Müteferriqa reminds us that the boundaries between empires, cultures and even religions are never fully closed, and that cultural transfer might create quite unexpected fellowships. The close linkage between the mass communication media and Islamic reformism has proved to be of growing importance in Muslim societies up to the present.

[44] Jorga, *Geschichte des Osmanischen Reiches*, IV, 370f.
[45] A. Şen, *İbrahim Müteferriqa*, 130f.

[14]

THE BEGINNINGS OF HEBREW PRINTING IN EGYPT

DIANA ROWLAND-SMITH

COMPARATIVELY little scholarly interest has been taken in Hebrew printing in the Islamic World, even though some of the Jews who fled there following their expulsion from Spain in 1492 and from Portugal in 1497 brought with them their printing presses and equipment.[1] These refugees and other exiles who settled among them set up their workshops in Constantinople (1493), Salonika (1513), Fez (1516), Cairo (1557), Safed (*circa* 1577) and Damascus (1605). The reasons for the few studies on printing in the East are that these exiles were generally unable to maintain their printing activities for any length of time and usually few remains of the works that they printed have survived. In Fez, Safed, Cairo and Damascus the printing of Hebrew quickly disappeared due to the unfavourable economic conditions and probably also the influence of the adverse reaction of the Islamic World to the use of printing for religious literature. Only Constantinople, Salonika and, from 1657, Izmir succeeded in surviving as centres of Hebrew printing probably because of their relatively close ties with Western centres of influence and their greater prosperity when compared with other cities of the Ottoman Empire.

The first attempt at establishing a printing press in Egypt was made at Cairo between 1557 and 1562 by Gershom ben Eliezer Soncino, a grandson of Gershom ben Moses, the famous Italian printer who had migrated to Constantinople. The grandson Gershom moved from Constantinople to Egypt in about 1550. The only known evidence of his activity are fragments of two works, *Pitron ḥalomot* [Interpretation of Dreams], 1557, and *Refu'ot ha-Talmud*, which were discovered in the Geniza (storage place) of the old Synagogue of Cairo.[2] The latter title was probably printed by him in 1562, the year of his death.

A second attempt was made in the mid-eighteenth century when a printing press was set up in the Egyptian capital by Abraham ben Moses Yathom. Abraham Yathom had learnt the art of printing in Constantinople with Jonah ben Jacob Ashkenazi, who had been a prolific publisher of Hebrew books there during the previous decade. Abraham printed in Cairo the first edition of *Ḥoḳ le-Yiśra'el*, readings from the Bible, Mishnah, Talmud and Zohar, which the kabbalist Ḥayyim Vital had compiled as readings for each day of the week.[3] The work was edited by Isaac Baruch and published in two volumes in 1740 with the financial assistance of Abraham Zadik. The approbations dated 1740 at the beginning of the first volume are by Chief Rabbi Solomon Al-Gazi of Cairo and Rabbi

Moses Israel of Alexandria. The text of *Ḥoḳ le-Yiśra'el* is printed in two columns set within black ink rectangles—an unusual characteristic for Hebrew printed books but found in some oriental manuscripts.

In contrast to the comparatively high standard of production of the Hebrew books printed in Constantinople at this time, the typeface of *Ḥoḳ le-Yiśra'el* published in Cairo is frequently poor, some of the pages being faint and difficult to read. Probably because of the low standard of printing as well as poor economic conditions in Egypt, the press of Abraham Yathom ceased. The kabbalistic work *Ḥoḳ le-Yiśra'el* became very popular in the latter half of the eighteenth century but it was printed elsewhere, in Venice (1777), in Korets (1785), Lemberg (1788) and in other cities of Poland. It was also reprinted several times (1788, 1797-8, 1843, 1866) in Leghorn (Livorno) on the west coast of Italy. From the middle of the eighteenth century, the Hebrew press of Leghorn (founded in 1650) sought to provide for the needs of the mainly Spanish-speaking Jewish Communities around the Mediterranean basin, especially in North Africa, with whom Leghorn had close commercial ties.[4]

The attempt to establish a printing house in 1740 was thought to have been the last in Egypt until the coming of Hebrew printing to Alexandria in the second half of the nineteenth century, following an influx of Jewish refugees and immigrants from Europe and the Middle East. However, among the holdings of the British Library's Hebrew Section is an example showing that a further attempt was made at printing in Cairo in the earlier part of the nineteenth century. Among the printed books acquired after 1893 is a Haggadah or service book for the night of Passover, the Jewish Spring festival celebrating Israel's Exodus from Egypt.[5] This *Seder Haggadah shel Pesaḥ* with a Judaeo-Arabic translation was, according to the title-page (fig. 1), printed (*nidfas*) on 'the headstone with shoutings of acceptance' (Zechariah 4: 7) by the compositor (*ha-mesader*) Abraham ben Shalom ha-Levi at the new press of Moses [Ca?]stilo in Misrayim (Cairo).[6] The date given is equivalent to 1834. The reference to Zechariah 4. 7 as well as physical characteristics and the use of a cursive hand indicate that this Haggadah was lithographed.

The present volume, which measures 23 × 18 cm., consists of thirty-four folios, unpaginated but with catch words. The paper lacks watermarks and chain lines suggesting that locally made paper was used. The corners of most of the folios have been repaired and f. 30 is very severely worm-eaten. At present the volume is misbound as ff. 27–8 should be between ff. 2 and 3. Apart from this, there are two folios missing in each case between ff. 6 and 7, between ff. 12 and 13 and between ff. 22 and 23. Folios 29–34 are duplicates of earlier folios. The Hebrew text of the Haggadah is in the standard Oriental Square script. The Arabic translation and rubrics are in the Sephardi Hebrew cursive script found in North Africa. The colophon on f. 26 verso repeats the name of Abraham ben Shalom ha-Levi and adds the information that the work was printed in order to teach the young men of the Jewish Community (*na'are bene Yiśra'el*). The reference in the colophon to doing the work of the Levites may be an allusion to Abraham ben Shalom's work as a teacher in Cairo.[7]

Since at least the fourteenth century, it has been a common practice to illustrate the

סדר
הגדה של פסח
עם פתרון בל' שון
ערבי
עם כמה צורית על כל האותות והמופתים
אשר נעשו לאבותינו במצרים ועל
הים ובמדבר :
נדפס על האבן הראשה תשא"ת חן
על ידי המסדר הע"ה אברהם בכ"ר שלום הלוי
פה מצרים יע"א
שנת כנה"ה כארץ מצרים למ"ג
כו יום חדש
של משו זצשטילו ה"יו

Fig. 1. The title page of *Seder Haggadah shel Pesaḥ* (Cairo, 1834)

Haggadah with scenes from the rituals observed at Passover, the story of the Exodus and from the stories of the Rabbis mentioned in the Haggadah in order to teach and keep the younger members of the family interested. This example of the Haggadah lithographed in Cairo includes illustrations of the Passover story and employs black line historiated initials at the beginning of certain passages. A comparison of Haggadot (the plural of Haggadah) printed during this period shows that the model used was an illustrated Haggadah printed in Leghorn which, in turn, was a type based on earlier models printed in Venice in the seventeenth and eighteenth centuries. As the Haggadah was not printed with an Arabic version until ten years later in Leghorn, 1844/5, the model used must have been a Haggadah with a Ladino (Judaeo-Spanish) translation.[8] Leghorn was at this period printing many editions of the illustrated Haggadah with a Ladino translation and exporting them to Jewish Communities around the Mediterranean. Commercial ties between Egypt and Italy were particularly close at this time.[9] Indeed paper shipped via Leghorn was the most commonly used form of writing and printing material in government establishments of Egypt.[10]

The illustrated Haggadah with a Ladino translation was very popular and was produced by several Jewish printers in Leghorn, among them Ottolengi and Company, Naḥman Saʿdun and Moses Yeshua Tuviana. The Haggadot that they published vary only very slightly from each other. A comparison of the edition of Cairo 1834 with those published in the previous decade shows a particularly close similarity with those Haggadot printed by Ottolengi and Company in 1822 and by the Saʿdun brothers in 1827. However, Abraham ben Shalom of Cairo has replaced the Ladino translation and rubrics with a Judaeo-Arabic version in his own cursive script. He has omitted the evening service for Passover usually recited in the Synagogue as probably unnecessary. He has included additions to the blessing over the wine at the beginning and replaced the hymns sung at the end of the service with a hymn in Hebrew and another in Judaeo-Arabic. In this he was modifying the Haggadah to the ritual as practised among the Jews of Egypt.

The illustrations in the Haggadah of 1834 follow almost exactly those of the Leghorn imprints except that immediately after the order of the service with its mention of 'telling' (*magid*) the Passover story on f. 5, an illustration has been inserted showing the Israelites building the pyramids of Egypt (fig. 2). This additional illustration was no doubt an attempt to make the Passover story more relevant and immediate to the younger participants for whom this edition was mainly intended. It was a tradition peculiar to the Jewish Community in Egypt that their ancestors built the pyramids. Interestingly, the Israelites are dressed in European clothes although we know from the accounts of foreign travellers at this time that the Jews of Cairo—then numbering at least 3,000—wore the local dress and lived as inconspicuously as possible.[11] The style is probably an attempt to copy the remaining illustrations taken from the Leghorn Haggadot. By showing European clothes, the artist is also emphasizing that the Israelites were foreigners in Egypt.

The Passover ritual lithographed in 1834 by Abraham ben Shalom ha-Levi is not mentioned in Abraham Yaari's *Bibliography of the Passover Haggadah* and no other copy is known. The fragmentary nature of the British Library's copy suggests that the

קידוש של פסח

בָּרוּךְ אַתָּה יְיָ אֱלֹהֵינוּ מֶלֶךְ הָעוֹלָם בּוֹרֵא
מְאוֹרֵי הָאֵשׁ : בָּרוּךְ אַתָּה יְיָ אֱלֹהֵינוּ
מֶלֶךְ הָעוֹלָם הַמַּבְדִיל בֵּין קֹדֶשׁ לְחוֹל
וּבֵין אוֹר לְחשֶׁךְ · וּבֵין יִשְׂרָאֵל לָעַמִּים
וּבֵין יוֹם הַשְּׁבִיעִי לְשֵׁשֶׁת יְמֵי הַמַּעֲשֶׂה
בֵּין קְדֻשַּׁת שַׁבָּת לִקְדֻשַּׁת יוֹם טוֹב
הִבְדַּלְתָּ · וְאֶת יוֹם הַשְּׁבִיעִי מִשֵּׁשֶׁת יְמֵי הַמַּעֲשֶׂה
קִדַּשְׁתָּ · וְהִבְדַּלְתָּ וְהִקְדַּשְׁתָּ אֶת עַמְּךָ יִשְׂרָאֵל
בִּקְדֻשָּׁתֶךָ : בָּרוּךְ אַתָּה יְיָ הַמַּבְדִּיל בֵּין קֹדֶשׁ לְקֹדֶשׁ :
בָּאֵי אָמָה שֶׁ.ָ.נוּ וְקִיְּמָנוּ וְהִגִּיעָנוּ לַזְּמַן הַזֶּה :

ורחץ

כרפס

בָּאֵי ..גֶפֶן בּוֹרֵא פְּרִי הָאֲדָמָה :

יחץ

מגיד

Fig. 2. The Israelites building the Pyramids

preparation of the edition did not progress much beyond the printing of a very few samples. However, ff. 19–20 show signs of wine stains implying that at some stage these folios formed a complete copy that was used for the Passover meal.

Lithography or printing by etching on stone was a comparatively new process that had been brought to Egypt from Europe. It is likely that the educational reforms initiated by Muhammad Ali, who ruled Egypt from 1805 to 1848, and the setting up of a printing press at Bulaq in late 1821 had an influence on the Jewish Community living nearby in Cairo.[12] One of the main purposes of the government press at Bulaq was to supply Arabic and Turkish translations of European works. The Bulaq press also included a lithograph workshop used mainly for diagrams and plates. Possibly Abraham ben Shalom ha-Levi of Cairo learnt of the technique from this source.[13] A lithograph press was less demanding and cheaper than a movable type press in terms of the technical equipment required. The experiment by Abraham ben Shalom was an attempt to supply the educational need of the Jewish Community in Cairo for texts with Arabic translations. He and Moses [Ca?]stilo may have hoped that if this lithographed edition of the Haggadah were successful, it would be possible to set up a Hebrew press with movable type as happened in India, at Calcutta and Bombay, seven years later.[14] As with the two earlier presses in Cairo, the standard of reproduction of both text and illustration was poor and their product could not hope to compete with either manuscript copies or the texts printed in Leghorn. It is clear that in 1834 the financial, educational and social condition of the Jewish Community in Cairo was as yet insufficient to develop and support either a lithograph or a movable type printing press.[15]

It was only with the influx of Jews from Europe and the Near East and the rise of a large mainly immigrant community in Alexandria in the last half of the nineteenth century that Hebrew printing was able to establish itself for any length of time and to a sufficiently high standard in Egypt. Even then, Solomon Ottolengi of Leghorn only managed to print two works in Alexandria, *Naḥalah le-Yiśra'el* and *She'erit ha-naḥalah* by Israel Moses Hazan of Alexandria, in 1862, before going out of business. Three years later, Michael Hakohen and Joel Moses Solomon came from Jerusalem to Alexandria to print the last section of part two of *No'am ha-midot* by Nathan ben Ḥayyim Amram of Alexandria (the earlier part having been printed in Salonika, 1854) and *Nora' tehillot*, the Psalms with a Judaeo-Arabic version and commentaries by Ḥayyim Amram.[16] Again the press ceased before the latter work was completed. Finally Faraj Ḥayyim Mizraḥi from Persia set up his press in Alexandria in 1873 and successfully printed some fifty titles before his death in 1913. These include several editions of the Haggadah for Passover with his own Judaeo-Arabic translation, and one with that of Mevorach Baranes.[17] Especially noteworthy are the books by Raphael Aaron ben Simeon of Cairo and by Solomon Hazan of Alexandria. One example is Solomon Hazan's *ha-Ma'alot li-Shlomoh*, a biographical and bibliographical lexicon being a supplement to *Shem ha-Gedolim* by the Italian scholar Ḥayyim Joseph David Azulai, which was printed by Mizraḥi in Alexandria in 1894.[18]

In Cairo, printing in Hebrew from 1905 onwards took place in publishing houses whose main concern was printing in other languages. During the First World War, a Hebrew press in Cairo printed books, pamphlets, rules and regulations, and newspapers for the Jewish Community in Palestine. Among them was the weekly newspaper *Ḥadashot me-ha-areṣ*, *The Palestine News*, which was published in Cairo by the British Army of Occupation from 1918 to 1919.[19] After this brief period at the beginning of the twentieth century, the growth of the Jewish population in Palestine allowed Jerusalem and Tel-Aviv to become the dominant centres of Hebrew printing in the area.

1 The main reference work on the subject is by Abraham Yaari, *ha-Defus ha-'ivri be-arṣot ha-mizraḥ*, 2 pt. (Jerusalem, 1936–40).

2 A. M. Haberman, *ha-Madpisim bene Ṣoncino* (Vienna, 1933), p. 79; Yaari, ibid., pt. 1, pp. 53, 56–7. The fragments of these two works printed by Soncino are now in the Bodleian Library, Oxford, and in the Adler Collection in the Jewish Theological Seminary, New York.

3 J. Zedner (ed.), *Catalogue of the Hebrew Books in the Library of the British Museum* (London, 1869, reprinted 1967), p. 178.

4 G. Sonnino, *Storia della tipografia ebraica in Livorno* (Turin, 1912); H. D. Friedberg, *History of Hebrew Typography in Italy* [in Hebrew] (Tel-Aviv, 1956), pp. 86–7. Many of Leghorn's Jewish inhabitants were Spanish and Portuguese Jews who had moved there via North Africa.

5 BL, Oriental Collections press-mark 1971.bb.14. It will be included in the forthcoming *Second Supplementary Catalogue of Hebrew Printed Books acquired 1893–1960*, by D. Rowland-Smith.

6 The first two letters of the publisher's name are not clear.

7 Cf. Deuteronomy 33: 10.

8 The Haggadah, 1844/5, with Arabic version in the dialect of Baghdad, is not illustrated, cf. A. Yaari, *Bibliography of the Passover Haggadah* (Jerusalem, 1960), no. 637; S. Van Straalen (ed.), *Catalogue of Hebrew Books in the British Museum acquired during the years 1868–1892* (London, 1894), p. 139. The press in Leghorn was printing the illustrated Haggadah with a Judaeo-Arabic translation in 1868/9, cf. Yaari, ibid., nos. 982, 999.

9 P. J. Vatikiotis, *The Modern History of Egypt* (New York, 1969), p. 95.

10 Albert Geiss, 'Histoire de l'imprimerie en Égypte', *Bulletin de l'Institut Égyptien*, Série 5, nos. 1–2 (1907–8), p. 202.

11 J. Landau, *Jews in Nineteenth-Century Egypt* (New York and London, 1969), pp. 29–30.

12 A. Geiss, ibid., p. 196f.

13 Ibid., p. 216. In a report in the *Journal Asiatique* of 1828, two students had arrived in Paris from Egypt to study, among other printing and graphic techniques, the art of lithography. They returned to Egypt in 1831, ibid., p. 210.

14 The printing of Hebrew books began in Calcutta in 1841 with the lithographed edition of the Song of Songs, cf. A. Yaari, *ha-Defus ha-'ivri be arṣot ha-mizraḥ*, pt. 2, pp. 17, 18. In Bombay, both the Bene Yiśrael and the Iraqi Community began by producing books by the lithograph technique in 1841 and 1855 respectively. Both groups continued to use the technique for some years, cf. Yaari, ibid., p. 52f.

15 It is possible that the epidemic of 1834/5, in which nearly one fifth of the total population died, affected the work of printing, cf. A. L. al-Sayyid Marsot, *Egypt in the reign of Muhammad Ali* (Cambridge, 1984, reprinted 1988). Isaac Adolphe Crémieux, the French Jewish lawyer who visited Egypt in 1840, was shocked at the low standard of education of the Jewish Community in Cairo. With the help of the Rothschild family, he set up schools in Cairo and, later, in Alexandria. Cf. Landau, ibid., p. 73.

16 Yaari, ibid., pt. 1, pp. 55–6.

17 A. Yaari, *Bibliography of the Passover Haggadah*, nos. 1298, 1477, 1538.

18 BL, Oriental Collections press-mark 1969.g.35.

19 BL, press-mark O.P.418 (and 422). Wanting some issues of the supplements.

Part IV
Printing Development and Print Culture

[15]

HEBREW PRINTING HOUSES IN THE OTTOMAN EMPIRE

Yaron Ben Na'eh

Yaron Ben-Naeh: born in Jerusalem 1965. Researcher in the Ben-Zvi Institute for the Study of the Jewish Communities in the East (Jerusalem), and Lecturer in the Department of the History of the Jewish People, The Hebrew University, Jerusalem. Published a few articles about Ottoman Jewry. His PhD is titled "The Jewish Society in the Urban Centers of the Ottoman Empire in the 17th Century (Istanbul, Salonica & Izmir)".

ספר

מעם לועז

חלק ראשון

נדפס

בקושטאנדינה

Title page of *Me'am Loez*. Istanbul, 1748.
[From the Morit Collection]

[For other illustrations see supra, pp. *supra,* pp. 141-167].

INTRODUCTION

Printing began in Europe with Johann Gutenberg around 1445; the first printed Hebrew books appeared in Italy in the 1470's and immediately afterwards in Spain and Portugal as well. When the Jews were exiled from Spain in 1492 and later from Portugal, they arrived by the thousands in those areas which were then under Ottoman rule or soon to be conquered by Turks. Among the emigrés from the Iberian Peninsula there were experts in the art of printing; and upon settling in Constantinople they established the first Hebrew printing house there. Jews were thus the first to enter the printing trade in the whole Empire; they were followed later by other minorities such as the Armenians (1567) and the Greeks (1627).

The Turks themselves refrained from engaging in this type of work, since the printing press was viewed by Islamic leaders as the invention of heathens, and the printing of the Holy Scriptures and the Koran was considered a profanation of the sacred. Additionally, there was the adamant opposition to printing by the scribes guilds in the capital. Only in 1727, as a result of the *fatwa* of the Sheikh al-Islam which permitted the printing of books on secular subjects, was an imperial firman issued allowing for the establishment of a Turkish printing house in Istanbul. The printing presses and type moulds were purchased from the Jews and Christians, and some of their expert craftsmen were employed. This printing house was closed after fifteen years and reopened only in 1784, under Abdül-Hamit I.

The two most important centers for Jewish printing in the Ottoman Empire during the past five centuries were Istanbul and Salonica. In the 16th century printing houses operated elsewhere for very short periods, having been established by printers from Salonica or Istanbul: in Adrianople (1553-5), in Safed (1577-87), in Cairo (1557), in Damascus (1603), and later in Egypt (1740) and in Tunis (1768). Another important printing center existed in İzmir from the mid-17th century.

Until the 19th century two kinds of printing type were used. The first was the traditional square Hebrew script used for printing sacred texts such as the Bible, the *Mishnah*, the *Talmud* and prayer books. The second was the semi-cursive Sephardi type known as *Rashi* script. Until the 20th century, this script was the one most commonly used for the printing of Hebrew and Ladino works. The use of Latin letters or Arabic script was relatively rare until the late 19th century.

During the 16th century, only twenty works were printed in Ladino, known as "La'az Sefaradi", mainly for the benefit of the *Marranos* returning to Judaism in the Ottoman Empire, especially in Istanbul and Salonica. These include *Chovot Halevavot Hanhagath há-Hayyim, Shulchan Lechem ha-Panim*, and Bible translations. Until the 18th century, however, the dominant language for published works was Hebrew, although only religious scholars and sages were fluent in that language.

The publication of the famous work *Me'am Loez* in 1730 marks the beginning of a new era characterised by the increasing dominance of Ladino works intended for the general public. Among these publications were *Otioth de Rabi Akiva* (1729), *Koplas de Yosef* (1732), *Sheveth Musar* (1766) and a new translation of the Bible (1739).

Me'am Loez was a moral and exegetical commentary on the Torah written in *Ladino* which utilised all the traditional Jewish sources of rabbinical litterature. It was written in clear, easily comprehensible language and enjoyed widespread popularity. Its author, Rabbi Ya'akov Chuli, managed to complete the commentary on *Genesis* (1730) and part of *Exodus* (1733), and his work was continued by other scholars. The first edition of one thousand copies was an immediate success, and from that time onward many more editions were printed proving that Chuli had justifiable reasons for writing this work.

In his introduction, Chuli deplores the sorry state of Jewish learning. Knowledge of the Bible, the most precious heritage of the Jewish people, was decreasing, and Jews were neglecting its study in favour of other pursuits, or reading foreign literature. Being unfamiliar with Jewish sources, they could not even understand the sermons preached on the Sabbath. The works which had been printed in *Ladino* translation in the 16th century were already outdated and by now almost incomprehensible.

The 19th century opens a new chapter in the history of printing within this period of the Ottoman empire's decline. Many printing houses were established in the provinces — in the Balkans, Syria, Palestine, Egypt and North Africa, as well as on the islands in the eastern Mediterranean. In contrast with the previous periods during which Jewish refugees from Europe (mainly Italy and Poland) had dominated the printing trade, it was the local Jewish population that now ran the printing business.

More significant was the change in the character of the works printed. Until this period, printing had been confined mainly to religious literature, with a very small percentage of historical, grammatical or linguistic works, and poetic or rhetorical compositions. But from the first half of the century on, there was a increasing number of publications of a secular nature, all in *Ladino*, including translations from world literature, poetry, fiction, periodicals, pamphlets, dictionaries, manuals, official reports and forms used for private and commercial purposes.

Thus, a wide variety of printed material was produced. Religious publications, while including basic Jewish sources, consisted mainly of translations into *Ladino* of popular *halachic* compendiums as well as poems, songs, prayer books and other similar works. Alongside these, there was an increasing production of literary works in the original language and in translation, as well as a variety of journalistic publications.

It is interesting to note that towards the end of the 19th century printing houses were subject to strict censorship that in general characterized the Hamidian period, and a significant number of them operated without official licence and at great personal risk for the printers. This was the reason for the fact that in many cases the places of publication bore ficticious names.

An additional point of interest is that in İzmir and Salonica printers continued to publish religious works in significant quantities until the late 19th century, while in Istanbul, which was the greatest center of Ottoman Jewry and the seat of the Chief Rabbinate, only a few *halachic* works were printed from the 1860's onward.

There is evidence of thousands of items (books, pamphlets, journals, placards, notices, bills, letters of accredition, etc.) which were produced by the printing presses in the Ottoman Empire from the end of the 15th century onward. All traces of many printed items (sometimes even uncompleted publications) have disappeared over the years, mainly due to natural disasters which occurred from time to time. Our knowledge of some other items is fragmentary and incomplete. In this study, we shall attempt to give an overview of the work done by the important printing establishments based on preliminary research done by Ya'ari, Emmanuel and others. The period divisions below follow those of Abraham Ya'ari.

Just a few remarks before we begin:

Unlike our own times, the price of books in the 15th and 16th centuries was very high and only a few people could afford to acquire and maintain complete libraries. The printers' desire to enable the public to own the basic Jewish texts and the financial difficulties of the printing trade (the average edition of a book was one hundred and fifty to three hundred copies) led to the development of a special system of sales. In Istanbul and Salonica a considerable number of books were printed in pamphlet-segments which were distributed in the synagogues on the Sabbath in exchange for a promise of payment. Since such buyers did not always keep up their payments for all the sections of a book, or could not afford to bind them together properly, it is obvious such books could not have easily survived.

For example, in the introduction to the *Talmud* Constantinople edition of 1583, it is said :

> Every Sabbath we shall publish sections from the *Talmud* and distribute them among those who wish to buy them. They will receive these booklets each *Sabbath* and pay their price so that with God's help the *Talmud* will be in the hands of everyone in a short while and can be paid for gradually in a manner that will make the burden of payment easier to bear. The *Talmud* will then be wholly his own by payment which will amount to about twenty-five florins. Therefore, now anyone who wishes can come and get booklet after booklet and pay for them...

This method of publication, introduced at the beginning of the 16th century, continued to be used until the 19th century. At the same time, there were people who could afford to buy not only entire books but even unique and expensive editions printed on vellum (parchment). Extant today are certain books printed on vellum in Istanbul and Salonica during the first half of the 16th century.

The output of the printing houses in the Ottoman Empire until the 19th century reflects to a great extent the creative range and scope of interest shown by the intellectual elite of Ottoman Jewry. Detailed research on the printed books and their prefaces will probably reveal much about the spiritual and creative aspects of their lives, about the interconnections between the authors and their patrons and readers, and about the status of *Torah* study and *Torah* students within the Jewish society. Since the 19th century, the works printed have provided a faithful mirror of the literary tendencies and tastes of the general public.

Until the 19th century only a few Jewish printing houses existed within the boundaries of the Ottoman Empire, and these were to be found in the main cities such as Istanbul, Salonica and Izmir. Writers who wished to publish their books were forced to come to the printing centres in the Empire or outside it (mainly in Italy), and in this way strengthened the spiritual bonds among the different communities in the Empire, as well as the connections and cultural transmissions between these communities and other Sephardi communities in central and western Europe.

HEBREW PRINTING HOUSES IN CONSTANTINOPLE

a. The First Period: 1493-1530

The first Hebrew printing house in Constantinople was founded in 1493 (some date this ten years later) by David Ibn Nahmias who obtained his expertise in the Iberian Peninsula. The first undertaking was the printing of the *Arba'a Turim*. After an unexplained interruption of ten years, printing was resumed in 1505 by the Ibn Nahmias brothers who were managers of the printing house until 1511. Among the important works they published were the *Torah, Haftaroth* and *Five Megilloth* (1506), Rambam's *Mishneh Torah* (1509) and *Midrash Raba* (1512). [See illus. no. 1 p. 141].

In the following years the printing house was run by Samuel ben David Nahmias and Astruc ben Ya'akov de Toulon of Provence who had been one of the workers and later became an independent printer in Salonica from 1520 onward. Others such as Shmuel Rikomin, Yehuda ben Yosef Sasson, Yosef ben 'Ayad Kabzi, Moshe ben Shmuel Fisilino and Rabbi Shlomo ben Mazal Tov, leased the premises and kept the press going for short periods of time [See illus. no. 2 p. 141]. In those days, rich Jews who invested their funds and capital were the only ones who "supported the efforts of the workmen", though sometime the workers themselves supplied financial assistance.

During this early period more than one hundred books were published. The printers recognized the enormous importance of their enterprise against the background of the trauma of expulsion and the fury of persecution. Therefore they included among these books many of the basic texts of Judaism, some of which appeared for the first time in print: *midrashim* and various *halachic* compendiums including works by the *Geonim* and medieval sages such as Maimonides (the Rambam), Alfasi (the Rif) and Asher ben Yehiel (the Rosh). We can gain some idea of the spirit of those days and of the sentiments and intentions of the printers from the following words in the Introduction to the *Torah, Haftaroth* and *Five Megilloth* with Rashi's Commentary, Constantinople, 5265 (1506):

> Since that day when God confused the languages of the earth by the sudden and bitter expulsion from Spain ... books were also abandoned in the trauma of destruction and the confusion of sudden change, for the constant afflictions have left us as an empty shell ... and because of troubles of the times and the lack of books, people have neglected the education of their children. So that even if they have the *Chumash (Pentateuch)* they lack the Targum and if they find that, then they lack the commentaries. May their hearts inspire them to spread the knowledge of the Torah in Israel ... and to replace some of the numerous works which were destroyed ...

b. The Second Period: 1530-1553

The first half of this period is marked by the activities of the Soncino family headed by Gershom Soncino, the famous Italian printer who arrived in Constantinople after a short stay in Salonica.

Besides sacred and religious writings, they also printed general works, including scientific literature and other secular works. Among these were: *Mahbarot Emanuel* by Imanuel Ha-Romi; *Sefer Hashorashim* by David Kimhi (Radak) and *Amades de Gaula*. Altogether about forty books were printed until 1547. [See illus. no. 3 p. 142].

Over the next few years small printing houses were active in the city, but they did not survive for long. Among the well-known printers were Moshe ben El'azar of the Parnas Harofe family who took over the printing equipment of the Soncino family in 1548 and continued printing until 1553. [See illus. no. 4 p. 142].

During those same years Shmuel Helitz had settled in Constantinople. One of the founders of the printing press in Crakow, he had converted to Christianity, but returned to the Jewish faith in Constantinople in 1550 or thereabouts. He printed three books between 1551 and 1553: the Pentateuch, a commentary on Ruth, and the Book of Judith.

Research indicates that fourteen books were published in the city during this period. (According to Hacker, only ten books were printed from 1548-1560).

A noteworthy event was the printing of two books in Cairo in 1557 by Gershom ben El'azar Soncino: *Refuoth Hatalmud* and *Pitron Chalomoth* which were preserved and later discovered in the Cairo Geniza.

c. The Third Period: 1560-1598

This was the most productive period for the printers of Constantinople, and we know today of about one hundred and twenty books which were published during these years. This fertility is no doubt connected to the economic and political conditions prevailing at the time.

The period opens with the activities of three printers: Rabbi Yosef Hekim printed three books in 1560 and his son Yitzhak succeeded him in his work; Avraham ben Shmuel Hacohen of Sanguinny who brought out two books in 1560-1561; and the Ya'abetz brothers.

Most of this period is noted for the intensive activities of the Ya'abetz brothers. Shlomo and Yosef Ya'abetz printed in Salonica and in Andrianople for a short while (see below) and then their ways parted. Shlomo went to Istanbul and his brother remained in Salonica. Among the first works printed by Shlomo Ya'abetz were the *Responsa* of Rabbi Eliya Mizrahi and that of the Rabbi Yosef Ibn Lev. In 1572 Yosef also arrived in Constantinople, and it was from then onward that their printing house in Constantinople became most productive. The Ya'abetz brothers printed about seventy books. Their most important enterprise was the printing of the *Talmud*, which was never completed, in the years 1583-1593. [See illus. no. 5 p. 143]. After the burning of the *Talmud* in Italy, the Ya'abetz brothers saw its printing as a prime necessity.

In the 1570's another printer was active in Constantinople: Eliezer ben Yitzhak, who had already been employed in such work in Prague, Lublin, and Kansky-Voli (Poland). He brought with him his letter blocks and decorative printing molds and in 1575 began printing in partnership with David ben Eliahu Kashti. Among the works he printed was the prayer book for the *Days of Awe* (*Yamim Noraiim*) according to the Romaniot custom. By 1576 he was printing independently and a year later he went to Safed where he did printing for two years. He then returned to Constantinople and published, in partnership with Kashti, one additional book in 1586. He later returned to printing work in Safed.

With the closing down of the Ya'abetz brothers printing house, Dona Reyna, the widow of Don Yosef Nasi, Duke of Naxos, founded a Hebrew printing house in the Belvedere Palace on the outskirts of Constantinople, in the area called Ortaköy. The printer in charge was Yosef ben Yitzhak Ashkeloni, and he began printing in 1593. Letters were fashioned into new forms for this purpose. Over a period of four years seven books were printed there. [See illus. no. 6 p. 143].

Dona Reyna is mentioned on the title-pages of the books as "... the illustrious lady ... widow of the Duke, Minister and great leader in Israel, Don Yosef Nasi, of blessed memory ..."

For unknown reasons, the printing house was moved to Kuruçeşme, a near suburb, where eight books were printed within a two-year period. Upon her death the activity of the printing house came to an end.

Foremost among the fifteen works brought out by this printing house were books of commentary. An attempt was made to print an edition of the Talmud, (extant today is only the *Ketuboth* tractate with its commentaries), and a book in Ladino — *Libro intitulado yihus hatzadikim*, probably for the use of those intending to go on pilgrimage (*ziyara*).

d. The Fourth Period: 1639-1695

During the first half of the 17th century the Jewish community was in a state of crisis, and this had a direct influence upon cultural activities including book printing. Various attempts to renew the printing of Jewish books, even involving European intellectuals, were unsuccessful.

After a period of forty years in which printing activity ceased, Shlomo ben David Franko, a former forced convert (*Marrano*) founded a new printing house in the city in 1639. Shlomo was, as his son has testified, "a great artist" and "an expert engraver, a craftsman skilled to perfection in this work" who had acquired his skills in Spain. He managed to print no more than one book before his death. His son and son-in-law continued his work from 1641 onwards. [See illus. no. 7 p. 144].

Many of the workers in the industry were Jews who had fled from Poland after the massacres of 1648-49. Printed records of the events in 1665-66, the year of the *Sabbatean Movement*, are preserved in only two books of *Tikkunim* by Nathan of Gaza which were printed at that time. Many documents and printed works having to do with the messianic movement of Sabbetai Sevi were later destroyed in an attempt to eradicate all traces of this traumatic episode.

From 1660 onwards, for a period of three decades, printing work was done with occasional interruptions by Avraham ben Yedidia Gabbay, formerly one of the foremost printers in İzmir, sometimes in partnership with Franco. Abraham Gabbay, a scholar who arrived from Livorno, was known to have been in contact with Europeans who came to the Levant. His appointment as the translator of the Genoese Ambassador was apparently the reason for the cessation of his printing activity. He published commentaries, *responsa*, and sermons including the *Midrash Raba*, books of the *Mishnah*, the *kabbalistic* work *Hod Malkhut* by Abraham Hayachini, and two books of *Tikkunim* by Nathan of Gaza.

Altogether twenty-eight books were printed in this period.

e. The Fifth Period: 1710-1808

Yonah ben Ya'akov of Zalazitz, a Jewish refugee from Poland, was the person who re-initiated printing activity in the capital of the Ottoman Empire which became, in Ya'ari's words, "the metropolitan centre of Hebrew printing in the entire Middle East." His printing house produced most of the books printed in this period: 188 out of 210. [See illus. no. 8a, 8b p. 145].

Among the works printed here were important halachic compendiums, and works of scholarship : *Knesseth ha-Gedolah, Shearei Knesseth ha-Gedolah, Bnei Hayyai, Tikkunei Zohar, Sifrei Kavvanoth, Seder Mishmarah.* Additionally, there were a significant number of responsa including *Bnei Moshe, Eduth Biyehosef, Ginath Vradim, Bnei Ya'akov, Mate Yosef,* and many others.

A fire which broke out in Istanbul in 1712 forced him to move his printing press temporarily to the Ortaköy suburb, where seven years later he was to return and establish his enterprise. During this period the Turks founded the first Ottoman printing house with the assistance of Jews such as the above-mentioned Yonah ben Yaakov, also known as Yonah ha-Ashkenazi.

In 1728 Ashkenazi founded a printing house in İzmir as a branch of the one in Constantinople. He was active in İzmir for eleven years, printing more than thirty books. During the same period he printed sixty books in Constantinople. Another fire which broke out in 1740 caused him to interrupt operations temporarily. He resumed printing two years later in partnership with his sons who continued to do so for more than thirty years after his death in 1745.

His printing house published some of the most important books that were written in that period, among them *Knesset Hagedolah* and *Chemdat Yamim.* He was instrumental in the revival of Ladino literature — the printing of the Bible with Ladino translation, part of the book *Me'am Loez,* the Siddur (prayer book) and translations of other books, among which were those of a secular nature such as *Yosifon Ben Gurion.* He also published works written by Jews in Constantinople and also books written by scholars of Palestine, which were transferred by emissaries to Palestine.

During this period other smaller Hebrew printing houses operated in Constantinople with a relatively low output. Among these were the printing house of Avraham Franco which was activated with interruptions by his son-in-law Avraham Rozanes in the years 1711, 1719-1720; that of Avraham ben Moshe Yatom, who made a few printing attempts in the 1730s and 1740s and that of Binyamin ben Moshe Rossi of Venice who printed nine books in the years 1742-1751.

The period closes, after an interruption of twenty years, with the activities of Raphael Hayyim Pardo who was a bookseller and printer's agent. During the years 1799-1808 he published six books, including the Books of the *Zohar* which was printed and sold in installments to subscribers. These used the old type molds and printing decorations of Jonah ha-Ashkenazi of Zalazitz.

Mention should be made of the numerous single sheets printed during the 18th century, among which were the collection of Letters against Hayyoun and the correspondence between Rabbi Shimshon Wertheim and Yosef, the Sultan's physician. During this century many emissary letters were printed by order of the Eretz Israel officials in the city. In various collections are preserved some lettres calendars of that period. [see ill. no. 8c. p. 146, 8d. p. 146].

f. The Sixth Period: 1808-1863

A new printing house was founded in the city by Yitzhak ben Avraham Castro in 1808. After printing *Tikkunei Zohar,* work was stopped and resumed only in 1823. From then onwards the books were apparently prepared for publication in Castro's home and brought for printing to *El Saray del Inglez* which belonged to the Anglican missionaries. These books were mainly Ladino translations from Hebrew, a few rabbinical treatises, and two polemical works against Christianity and the English missionaries. Until his death in 1848, Castro printed more than ten books. [See illus. no. 9 p. 148].

After his death, his sons continued operating the printing house. The Nissim de Castro press printed three books during the years 1849-1850, and the Moshe de Castro press printed only two books until 1862. [See illus. no. 10 p. 149]

A printing press was founded in Ortaköy by the Armenian printer Arapoğlu Bogos and Sons. From 1822 to 1833 Jews commissioned this press to print more than eighteen books. [See illus. no. 11 p. 150].

Two other printing houses were in operation during this same period: The printing house of Ya'akov Halevi and Yosef Anavi printed two books in the years 1824-1827. Aharon Fermon and Co. printed one book in 1824.

Nissim Hayyim Piferno was a typesetter, and five of his books including the *Libriko de Moda'a, Marpeh le-Nefesh,* and *Makor Hayyim* (Pt. 3) were printed in different printing houses in the city (belonging to Jews, Greeks and Armenians) during the years 1857-1863.

g. The Seventh Period: 1865-1940

This period is characterized by the proliferation of printing houses throughout the Ottoman Empire, including in Istanbul itself. According to Ya'ari, more than two hundred and twenty books were printed, mostly in Ladino, in the fields of journalism, literature (original and translated), fiction, poetry, grammar, linguistics, etc.

Various Jewish printing houses were active during this period, including the Avraham Shalto press, 1880-1881. During the first quarter of the 20th century a number of printing houses were founded, among which were:

— The Arditi press founded in 1899 and active until 1921
— The Babuch press, 1910-1928
— The Nissim Aboab and Albert Cohen press, 1910-1921
— The Salomon Alkachir press, 1922-1940
— The Nationala Judia press, 1922-1924

Publishers such as Binyamin Raphael ben Yosef, a bookseller in Constantinople, and other publishers at the end of the 19th century printed scores of books in Ladino. More than forty books were also printed in serialized form on the pages of Jewish journals such as *Tyempo* (1873-1897); *El Nationale* (1875-1880); *El Telegrafo* (1881-1913); *El Judio* (1910-1924); *El Jugeton* (1921-1926 p.).

A considerable number of these books were printed by Armenian Christian presses — such as Boyajian, Menasian, Philipidis & Biberian and by the Greeks — Byzantes de Policrites, El Nomismatides, Thomayides and Aristobolos.* Books were also printed in the Alfred Churchill press [see ill. no. 12a p. 151]

From the 1920s onward, printing activity in Istanbul decreased considerably, yet it continues till the present day, generally in the form of offset lithography. Naturally what was printed were mostly religious texts and language study manuals. An example of such a printing house which has been functioning for decades is the Güler press which printed many books by Nissim Behar, the eminent educator. [See illus. no. 12b p. 152].

Bibliographical Sources

A. M. Haberman, *Ha-Sefer ha-Ivri be-Hitpathuto*. Jerusalem, 1958. see pp. 101, 124-126.

Y. Hacker, "Defusey Kushta be-Me'ah ha-Shesh Esrey" in *Areshet* 5 (1972), pp. 457-493.

Y. Hacker, "Shlicho shel Luis ha-Arba'a Eser be-Levant ve Tarbutam shel Yehudey ha'Imperia ha'Ot'manit be-Divuah mi-Shnat 1675" in *Zion*, 52, 1987, pp. 25-44.

Y. Vinograd, *Otzar ha-Sefer ha-Ivri* II, Jerusalem 1994, pp. 602-620.

Abraham Ya'ari, *Ha-Defus ha-Ivri be-Kushta*. Magnes Press, Jerusalem, 1957.

Salomon A. Rozanes, *Divrey Yemey Israel be-Togarma*, Dvir, Tel Aviv, 1930.

Salomon A. Rozanes, *Korot ha-Yehudim be-Turkiya ve-Artzot ha-Kedem*. Sofia, 1937-1938. See Pt. II, pp. 233-234, 236-238; Pt. III, pp. 332-333, 335-337; Pt. 4, pp. 355-358.

Avram Galanté, *Histoire des Juifs de Turquie*, V. II, Isis, Istanbul, 1985.

*I have in my possession a matchmaker's contract by the Bursa community dated in the 1920's which indicates that it was printed by "Imp. de Avila, Khalil Khan, Istanbul" This printer was not documented by Ya'ari. Other leaflets carry the name of Imp. Fratelli Haim and Imp. Izak Gabbay, Galata.

HEBREW PRINTING HOUSES IN SALONICA

a. The First Period: 1512-1530

Don Yehuda Gedaliah, also known as Ibn Gedalya, who had managed the printing house of Eliezer Toledano (Alantasi) in Lisbon, arrived in Salonica as did many other emigrés, and founded a printing house in 1512. As well as Rabbi Ya'akov Ibn Habib testifies in his introduction to Ein Ya'akov (1517) — a collection of legends from the Babylonian Talmud with commentaries by early sages — the printing work of Ibn Bedalya was of a highly important and valuable quality.

> "A worthy and reputable artist, elderly, of a kindly disposition and trustworthy, is this eminent and wise man, the honorable Rabbi Yehuda Gedaliah, may the Lord protect him and give him long life. I knew him in earlier days in Lisbon at the home of the eminent and humble sage ... the honourable Rabbi Eliezer Toledano, of blessed memory, who was like a son and brother to him and took charge of the holy work which was done at his home. And after reaching this city he expended much money to accomplish this work to perfection with great effort, and his sons and the members of his household devoted themselves wholeheartedly to this work..."

Hymns of praise and high-flown rhetoric in acclamation of Ibn Gedaliah's important work can be found in other sources. Like the printers of Constantinople, Ibn Gedaliah's family also printed important sources texts: *Pentateuchs* and other parts of the Bible with various commentaries, *midrashim* and *halachic* studies. The most important was the printing of the Babylonian Talmud with Rashi's commentary, which was never completed. [See illus. no. 13 p. 152].

About thirty books were printed by this press until the 1530s (according to Haberman until 1529, but Emmanuel claims that the printing house existed until 1535/38). These include *Yalkuth Shim'oni, Akedath Yitzhak, Tur Orach Hayyim*, *Tur Yoreh De'ah*, and some Talmud tractates with Rashi's commentary.

There was considerable printing activity in Salonica during the 1520s. Besides the Ibn Gedaliah family there were other printers whose output was far smaller. Aside from various anonymous printers, we know of Yosef ben Avraham Elnekave (1521), Astruc ben Ya'akov de Toulon (1521) and Yosef ben Yitzhak Sid (1529) who had previously worked in Gedaliah's printing house.

During this period the Italian printer Gershom Soncino, his son Eliezer and his nephew Moshe were residents of the city. They printed a few books in the years 1527-1529, and then moved on to Constantinople. Noteworthy among these were *Sefer ha-Shorashim* and many prayer books including some according to the Catalonian and Aragonese custom. From then onward there was a period of obscurity during which only a few odd books were printed. Many were completely lost in the great fire of 1545.

It seems that the general public made wide use of printing facilities, not always in accordance with the better judgement of the sages and leaders of the community. In 1529, the city elders laid down a general ruling which in effect imposed censorship on published works:

"As the rabbis of the Salonican communities noticed that unsuitable things have been printed, they have been agreed that no Jewish person will be allowed to print any text, without the permission of six of the city rabbis, and the one who transgresses will be under ban... we hereby decree that a ban will be imposed on any Jew who purchases them. In case of printing has begun, it will not be allowed to be completed without the permission of above-mentionned six Torah scholars. The permission will be granted by consensus in a specific place, signed and sealed. Any transgressor will be under ban. This day in Sunday, the 10th of Elul, 1529. I am your servant, Eliezer ha-Shimoni, Avraham Hazan, Shmuel Albukher known as Halatz, Yosef son of our eminent rabbi Shlomo Taitazak, Shlomo Cavaliere, Yaakov Tzarfati."*

b. The Second Period: 1559-1628

In the mid-1540s the Ya'abetz brothers, Shlomo and Yosef, founded a new printing house in the city. The great fire that occurred in 1545 apparently did not cause disruption in their operation, and they continued printing without interruption until 1554. In that year a terrible plague broke out, and the brothers moved to Adrianople where they established a printing house. Five years later they re-established their operation in Salonica. In 1560 Shlomo left his brother and moved to Constantinople.

The 1560s were a flourishing period for the city with the mass influx of former Marranos from the Iberian peninsula. Not surprisingly, this period was one in which printing activity reached its height with more than one hundred and twenty books published, among which were a few Ladino works.

*A. Danon, "La communauté juive de Salonique au XVIe siècle", *REJ* XLI (1900), p. 264.

In the printing house of Yosef Ya'abetz many books were printed for the purpose of *Torah* study and religious instruction. Among these were the books by Rabbi Moshe Almosnino, as well as the *Pentateuch* and *halachic* compendiums translated into Ladino. Besides religious works, Ya'abetz also printed various kinds of secular literature. Although his most important achievement was the printing of the *Talmud,* this undertaking was never completed. [See illus. no. 14 p. 153] In 1572 he left Salonica and joined his brother who had been printing since the mid-1550 s in Constantinople.

To replace this loss, David Avraham Azoviv began to make use of the typographical equipment of the Ya'abetz brothers. During the years 1578-1588 he printed over fourteen books including rabbinical *responsa* by contemporary sages, ethical works, and commentaries on the prayers. We know that he tried to bring out a new edition of the *Nevi'im* (Prophets) and the *Ketuvim* (Hagiographa) with a Ladino translation and continued the project of Talmud printing which Ya'abetz had begun. [See illus. no. 15 p. 153]

A few years later, in 1592, the printing family of Matitya Bat-Sheva arrived in Salonica from Italy. They had been persuaded to come by Rabbi Moshe de Medina, as he relates in the introduction to the collection of his father's responsa: "In an attempt to persuade them, I provided them with much gold so that they would bring their tools and all their possessions to this city... I have expended a great deal of my wealth to import paper, printing press and workers from Venice ..."

Within a few years their printing house produced more than thirty books of various kinds. [See illus. no. 16 p. 154] They printed responsa, halachic works, stories and secular works such as *Mazaloth Shel Adam, Refuath Geviyah, Minhat Yehuda Soneh ha-Nashim*, etc. Special mention should be made of the anti-Christian polemical work *Fuente Klara* which also seems to have been printed by this press.

Avraham Bat-Sheva was the first to print in Damascus, where he published *Kesef Nivhar* in 1603, but there was no one to continue his activities in this city. Later, the Bat-Sheva brothers left Salonica in 1605. Five years later the Shimon brothers, Shlomo and Moshe, made use of the typographical equipment left by their predecessors, and renewed printing activity. They, too, relied on the support of Rabbi Moshe de Medina and his son Judah. [See illus. no. 17 p. 154] Their printing house functioned until 1628 and produced more than fourteen books — *halachic* works, prayer books, and a few Talmudic tractates.

Another printer of Italian origin who was active in Salonica during this period was David ben Aharon Matza who had printed in Mantua and in other places. Today we know of only one book which was produced by his printing house in 1614: *Ya'arim Moshe* by Rabbi Moshe Hacohen, a collection of songs for *Perashat* Zachor. Other books were also printed in Salonica during these years without mentioning the printer's name.These include the *Responsa Bnei Sehmuel, Ein Yisrael, Sefer ha-Terumoth, Tsa'akat Sdom*, and others.

In fact, with the exception of a short period, Salonica did not have any well-established printing house until the end of the 17th century. From 1650-1655 Abraham Hager printed at least nine books including a few *Talmudic* tractates. [See illus. no. 18 the Proselyte, p. 155] but the quality of the printing was extremely poor.

A few other works were printed during the 1690's without any indication of the printer's name. Among these were *Machzor Katalan* (1694) and *Machzor Aragon* 1699).

c. The Third Period: 1705-1840

Towards the end of his life Avraham ben Yedidia Gabbay, the printer in Constantinople and İzmir, established a new printing house in Salonica where a number of *Talmudic* tractates were published during the first decade of the 18th century. [See illus. no. 19 p. 156]. According to Rozanes, the printing house was already established in 1694/5 by the Talmud Torah Society at the initiative of contemporary philanthropists.

After Gabbay's death the printing equipment was transferred in accordance with his will to the Talmud Torah Society in Salonica, which henceforth also dealt with book printing, mainly for its own needs. They printed *Talmud* tractates and various *responsa* by the sages of Salonica, and printing activity continued there without interruption until 1818. Avraham ben David Nahman and Yom Tov Canfelias, who had been nominated as its directors, leased the press and operated it independently [See illus. no. 20 p. 157]. When Nahman died, his place was taken by Samuel Falcon.

In 1740, Bezalel Halevi Ashkenazi who had arrived from Amsterdam leased the printing house from the *Talmud Torah Society* and renovated it. Until his death in 1756, he produced more than thirty five books which are noted for their high printing quality [See illus. no. 21 p. 158]. His sons continued to maintain the printing house until 1763.

Rabbi Judah Kal'ai and Mordechai Nahman founded a new printing house in 1753. During their thirty years of activity they printed fifty books, including a number of Talmud tractates. In their own words, these were printed:

> ... for the needs of the scholars in the Talmud Torah, may God protect them, because the Gemarot which had once been available in the Talmud Torah have now entirely disappeared...

Among the books this partnership printed were the *responsa Magen Giborim, Shulhan Gavohah,* and a book of sermons called *Yekarah de Shachvei.*

After Kal'ai's death, his son Hayyim Leon inherited his share of the business and in the five years that followed, printed a number of works. His share was then bought by David Israelije, who maintained the partnership until 1804. For the following two years Nahman managed the printing house by himself. It should be noted that he published new editions of certain parts of *Me'am Loez*. Among other works he printed were the *responsa Mayim Sha'al, Mishpath Tzedek* (Pts. 2 and 3), and a second edition of the *responsa* of Rabbi Samuel de Medina (Maharashdam).

In 1792 a new printing house was founded in the city by the Nehama brothers in partnership with Sa'adi Halevi Ashkenazi who brought in his grandfather's type molds. Rabbi Yosef Molcho joined the partnership, in 1800, which lasted for a period of three years. A year later he began printing independently with new type molds imported from Istanbul and his printing activity continued until 1829. He brought out mainly *responsa* and sermons: *Beer Mayim Chayyim, Yadav Shel Moshe, Chesed Avraham, Darkhei ha-Yam*, etc.

The other partner, Sa'adi Halevi Ashkenazi, engaged in private printing until 1815. His brother, Bezalel, continued his work until 1826, and after his death his widow took over the management of the printing house with the assistance of her sons. Printing activity continued there until the end of 1839, producing works which consisted mainly of *halachic* compendiums.

Yitzhak Jahon, who had been a worker in the printing house of Bezalel Halevi Ashkenazi, engaged in independent printing activity from 1828-1855. [See illus. no. 22 p. 159].

During this period many books were printed in Salonica, sometimes without indication of date or printer, and until today we have no knowledge as to the names of their printers.

d. The Fourth Period: 1840-1941

During this period a few printing houses were active for short periods of time in the city. These were privately owned presses by individuals working side by side with those established by various societies and associations of the Jewish community.

The most important printer in this period was Sa'adi Halevi Ashkenazi (the Second), a descendant of the veteran printing family, who continued working from 1840 to 1902. We know that he travelled to Vienna to buy new equipment for his printing press, and his longstanding occupation in the printing trade earned him the nickname "Ha[ch]am Sa'adi el de la Estampa". (Hacham Saadi, the printer). Within a period of sixty years he printed over two hundred items, including that of the print house, most of the works of Rabbi Hayyim Palachi of İzmir, rabbinical *responsa* written in the Ottoman Empire and books in Ladino. [See illus. no. 23, p. 159] His printing house brought out the first Jewish journal in the city, *El Lunar* and this was followed by his own journal, *La Epoka.* His printing house was named after him in 1875.

Smaller printing houses were active for brief periods only, and generally printed *Torah* related works. Among these we can list Hayyim Ze'ev Ashkenazi (1842); Rabbi Eliahu Faraji (1842-1843); Daniel Faraji (1842-1850); Rabbi Yitzhak Bechor Amaraji (1845-1847); and Moshe Ya'akov Ayash (1857-1858). [See illus. no. 24 p. 160].

Among those societies which engaged in printing there was the *Etz Chayyim Society* which founded a new printing house in 1875 in competition with that of Sa'adi Halevi. Until the great fire of 1917, more than one hundred and fifty books were printed there in addition to booklets, leaflets and posters. The *Gemiluth Hassadim Society* also founded a printing house which printed various works from in the late 1860's.

In the 20th century we find new printing houses which handled all types of printing work. According to Emmanuel, these include Estamparia Poliglota, Estamparia Progre, Tipografia Abraham Berudo, Tipografia David Estromsa, etc. As in Istanbul, the printing presses of Ladino journals occasionally brought out books, booklets, posters, pamphlets, calendars and invitations in Ladino. Among the names listed by Emmanuel we find: Equaroni & Bechar; Tipografi Eclaire; Imprimeria Equaroni; Estamparia Union; Estamparia la Libertad; etc. Sometimes Hebrew books were published by non-Jewish printing presses. Among these were Tipografia Moratore and the printing houses of Tintshof, Jordan Jartzif, and others.

The Nazi conquest brought a disastrous end to the large and flourishing community of Salonica. Printing activity ceased there altogether after having lasted for more than four hundred years. Although certain Hebrew calendars and Haggadot of Pesah were printed in the 1950's this was too transient an episode to record. According to Ya'ari, more than three thousand and fivc hundred titles had appeared in print in Salonica, a fact which justifies Salonika's image as "Jerusalem of the Balkans".

Bibliographical Sources

A. Elmaleh, *Le-Toldot ha-Yehudim be-Salonik.* Jerusalem, 1924.

B. Ben-Ya'kov, "Batey ha-Defus be-Saloniki" in *Saloniki: Ir va-Em be-Yisrael.* Jerusalem and Tel Aviv, 1967. See pp. 52-53.

A.M. Haberman, *Ha-Defus ha-Ivri be-Hitpathuto.* Jerusalem, 1968. See pp. 123-124.

I. Mehlman, "Perakim be-Toldot ha-Defus be-Saloniki" in *Sefunot,* 13 (Sefer Yavan 3). Jerusalem: Ben Zvi Institute, 1971-1978. See pp. 217-272.

Y. Nehama, "Saloniki Ir Hotza'a la-Or" in *Zichron Saloniki,* Vol. II (ed. D.A. Recanati). Tel Aviv: Committee for the Publication of the Salonica Community Book, 1986. See pp. 250-260.

I.S. Emmanuel, "Batey Defus u-Madpisim" in *Zichron Saloniki,* Vol. II (ed. D.A. Recanati). Tel Aviv: Committee for the Publication of the Salonica Community Book, 1986. See pp. 230-249.

Salaman A. Rozanes, *Divrey Yemey Yisrael be-Togarma.* Tel Aviv, 1930. Pt. I: pp. 319-321, 326.

Salaman A. Rozanes, *Korot ha-Yehudim be-Turkiya ve-Artsot ha-Kedem* Sofia, 1934-1038. Pt. II: pp. 234-235, 238-239; Pt. III: pp. 333-335, 337-338; Pt. IV: pp. 392-393, 395-396; Pt.V: pp. 350-354, 358-363.

I. Rivkind, "Sifrey Saloniko" in *Kiryat Sefer,* V. I (1925) pp. 294-30; Vol. III (1927), pp. 171-173; Vol. VI (1929) pp. 383-385.

V. Vinograd, Otsar Hasefer Ha-Ivri, II, Jerusalem, 1994, pp. 666-686.

HEBREW PRINTING HOUSES IN ANDRIANOPLE

Hebrew printing which existed in Andrianople during the 16th century for a very short while should be viewed mainly as an extension of Hebrew printing activity in Salonica. The printing house in the city was founded by the printer brothers Shlomo and Yosef Ya'abetz who had fled from Salonica in 1554 because of the plague.

With the printing tools they had brought with them from Salonica they printed three and began work on a fourth book which remained uncompleted. The completed books were: *Sheveth Yehuda* by Ibn Virga, *She'erith Yosef* and *Masechet Avoth* by Rabbi Yosef Ya'abetz. Apparently only a few booklets of the *Responsa of Rabbi Eliya Mizrahi* were printed [See illus. no. 25a p. 160]. In 1556 the brothers returned to Salonica and printing activity in Adrianople ceased until the 19th century.

The second period in the history of Jewish printing in Adrianople begins at the end of the 19th century. Avraham Danon, the famous scholar and researcher, revived printing activity in the city in 1887 with the publication of the weekly scholarly review *Yosef Da'ath* in Hebrew, Ladino and Turkish for the period of one year (1888) [See illus. no. 25b p. 161]. In this same year Danon published his *Maskil Leeytan,* a collection of poems in Hebrew. Books and periodicals continued to be printed in Andrianople until the 1930's.

Bibliographical Sources

S. Assaf, M Benayahu, "Andrinople" in *Ha-Encyclopedia ha-Ivrit*, Vol. I. pp. 564-568.

I. Mehlman, "Beit ha-Defus ha-Ivri be-Andrinople be-Me'ah ha-Shesh Esreh" in *Aley Sefer,* 6/7 (1979), pp. 102-106.

Salomon A. Rozanes, *Korot ha-Yehudim be-Turkiya ve-Artsot ha-Kedem*, Sofia, 1934-1938. Pt. II: p. 235.

HEBREW PRINTING HOUSES IN İZMİR

a. The First Period: 1657-1675

The first printing house to be founded in İzmir was that of Avraham ben Yedidia Gabbay in 1657. Avraham was a descendant of a famous printing family of Venice and Livorno from where he had brought the typographical equipment and skilled workmen. Gabbay used the same type molds and decorations his father had once used. These had been acquired from the Bragadine Press in Venice [See illus. no. 26 p. 162].

A noteworthy event which took place in 1659 was the printing of two books in Spanish with Latin lettering (a second edition of two books by Menashe ben Yisrael). This is the first known instance of publishing Latin characters in Western Asia [See illus. no. 27 p. 163]. These two are probably just remnants of a more intensive publishing activity in Latin characters printed for the benefit of the Portuguese Jews and European merchants residing in the city.

In 1660 and 1662 Gabbay printed in Constantinople and then ceased further printing until 1670. By 1675 he had printed another sixteen books. He left İzmir on the occasion of his appointment as dragoman to the Genoese representative. Gabbay returned to Constantinople and then moved to Salonica in 1683. After he left İzmir, all printing activity ceased for the next fifty years.

b. The Second Period: 1728-1767

Yonah ben Ya'akov of Zalazitz who had been printing in Istanbul since 1710, established a new printing house in İzmir in 1728 in partnership with a local resident, Rabbi David Hazan. This was actually a branch of the famous printing house in Constantinople, using the same letter blocks, and specializing in the publication of treatises by the learned sages of the city. Their joint enterprise lasted until 1739, ending when Hazan emigrated to Palestine, but within these brief years they managed to bring out more than thirty books [See illus. no. 28 p. 164].

Fifteen years later, in 1754, a new printing house was established by Yehuda Hazan, son of the noted Rabbi David Hazan, and Ya'akov Valensi. This was a kind of partnership in which both used the same workmen and equipment, but worked separately, each one imprinting his name on his own books. Twelve books were printed by Yehuda Hazan during the years 1754-1767, and ten books by Valensi by 1766 [See illus. no. 29 p. 165]. It is interesting to note that the same typographical equipment was later transferred to Tunis and used to print one single book, *Zer' Yitzhak*, in 1768.

The printing house of Osta Maragos, the Greek printer, was also active during this period and five books were printed there between 1755-1758: four compendiums of *halacha, derash* and *Kabbala*, and also *Meoraoth Olam* (1756) which was a collection of historical and narrative material.

Printing activity then ceased in İzmir for a period of nearly sixty years for reasons unknown.

c. The Third Period: 1838-1920

From the fourth decade of the 19th century on several printing houses were in operation in İzmir. Printing work, which had begun again after a long period of inactivity, would now continue without further interruptions.

In 1838, the English printing house of Griffith was established mainly to serve the Anglican Mission. Among the publications printed by Griffith were two Ladino journals which appeared in İzmir, and which were the first to appear in the East at all — *La Buena Esperansa* in 1842 and *Sha'arey Mizrah* four years later. Ya'ari himself notes that many of the books brought out by the Mission were never recorded. The publication by the same printer of the Christian Bible raised a great deal of controversy.

During the years 1841-1844, the printing house of Shmuel Hekim published four books. The two business partners, Yitzhak ben Siman Tov Hekim (who had worked in printing layout for Shmuel Hekim) and Hayyim Yitzhak Shaul, brought out seven books in the years 1850-1857 [See illus. no. 30 p. 166].

In the 1850's another printing house was in operation, that of the two brothers, the sons of Yehuda Shmuel Ashkenazi, who had been engaged in printing work in Livorno during the 1840's. They produced six books during the years 1852-1855, mainly *halachic* compendiums. One book, *Likutei Haamarim*, dealt with disputations with Christians and Christianity. After an interval of six years they printed five more books in partnership with Rabbi Nissim Hayyim Moda'i over a three year period, 1861-1863, all of them *halachic* and *midrashic* works.

When Avraham Ashkenazi, the younger brother, went to work for the Ottolenghi Press in Alexandria, the printing house closed. Benzion Binyamin, the son of Rabbi Yehoshu'a Moses Roditi, began printing in 1857, using the equipment of Ya'akov Ashkenazi after the latter had ceased his printing activities. Of this year, we have a book printed by Rabbi Raphael Haim Pontrimoli.

In 1862 with the assistance of the *Chevra Kadishah* (burial society) in İzmir, Roditi was given the use of a new printing house and worked in partnership with others from the 1870s onward. By 1884 he had published no less than seventy one books, among them many important religious works. One of his first publications was a new edition of *Me'am Loez*. He also brought forth many *halachic* compendiums.

Another printing house which began operating in the 1860s was that of the De Segura brothers. It was founded in 1862 and continued to exist until 1906. More than one hundred and six books and other publications were produced there. [See illus. no. 31 p. 167] These include many of the works by Rabbi Hayyim Palachi, as well as a new edition of the *Zohar*.

Avraham Pontrimoli, a member of a learned family in İzmir, together with Yaakov Poli, founded a new printing house in 1876. Their partnership broke up eight years later, and Avraham Pontrimoli continued to print until 1889. During his thirteen years of printing activity, he published thirty five books mainly religious works [See illus. no. 32 p. 167]. He also printed a few of Palachi's works as well as of other İzmir sages.

In the last quarter of the 19th century, the Armenian printer, Tatikian, also printed a few Hebrew books [See illus. no. 33 p.]. Other, smaller printing houses were those of the Shevet Ahim press, which lasted for one year only (1876), that of Mordechai ben Yitzhak Barki (1896-1897), and of Ben Senior (1921-1922) as well as the commercial printing house of the Franko press (1904-1922).

During the 20th century, the most prominent printer was Ephraim Melamed, whose printing house operated continuously from 1901 until 1924. According to Ya'ari, the place of publication for some of his books was falsified, and appeared as having been published in Vienna. Melamed specialised in Ladino textbooks and fictional works among which were many historical novels. These include: *Buketo de Istorias* (1904), *Libro de Pasatiempo i Instruksyon* (1913), *Una Vengansa Salvaje* (1913), *Libro de Instruksion Religiosa* (1916, 1924).

In İzmir, as in the other two large centers of printing which we have mentioned above, books in Ladino were occasionally published by journal printers. Among these were the printing presses of *El Novelista* (1889-1922), *El Messeret* (1897-1924), *La Esperansa* (1871-1910), *La Boz del Pueblo*, *El Progresso* and others. Naturally, these were secular works such as novels and other literary works composed in the Ladino language, some of them even in Latin characters. Hebrew printing in İzmir continued till the 1950's.

Bibliographical Sources

Abraham Ya'ari, "Ha-Defus ha-Ivri be-Izmir" in *Areshet*, 1 (1959), pp. 222-297.

Salomon A. Rozanes, *Korot ha-Yehudim be-Turkiya ve Artsot ha-Kedem*, Sofia, 1934-1938. Pt. IV: pp. 393, 396-397; Pt. V: pp. 354-355, 363-364.

Cecil Roth, "Ha-Defus ha-Ivri be-Izmir" in *Kiryat Sefer*, 28 (1953), pp. 390-393.

D. Hacohen, "Ha-Defus Ha-Ivri be-Izmir" in Kiryat Sefer, 64, 1992-1993, pp. 1403-1923.

Y. Vinograd, *Otzar Ha-Sefer Ha Ivri*, II, Jerusalem, 1994, pp. 15-19.

*Author's notice: The article was written in 1990. On the occasion of its publication the author updated the bibliography.

ספר חמישי והוא ספר
קדושה

הלכות איסורי ביאה

1. Ya'ari, *Ha-Defus ha-Ivri be-Kushta*, p. 65.

זה ספר תולדות
אדם וחוה שחברו
החכם הגדול הר
ירוחם בר משולם
זצל מפרובינציאה

2. M. Rosenthal, *Atikim u-Nedirim*, Pt. II. Jerusalem: Reuben Maas, 1988, p. 12.

3. Ya'ari, p. 97.

4. Ya'ari, p. 105.

5. Ya'ari, p. 135.

6. Ya'ari, p.141.

ספר בית ישראל

קושטאנדינה

7. Rosenthal, p. 17.

נדפס פה
קושטנדינא

8a. Author's collection.

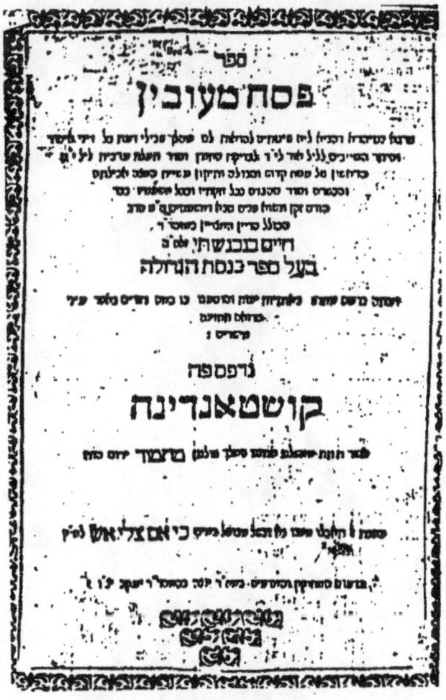
ספר
פסח מעובין
בעל ספר כנסת הגדולה
נדפס פה
קושטאנדינה

8b. Author's collection.

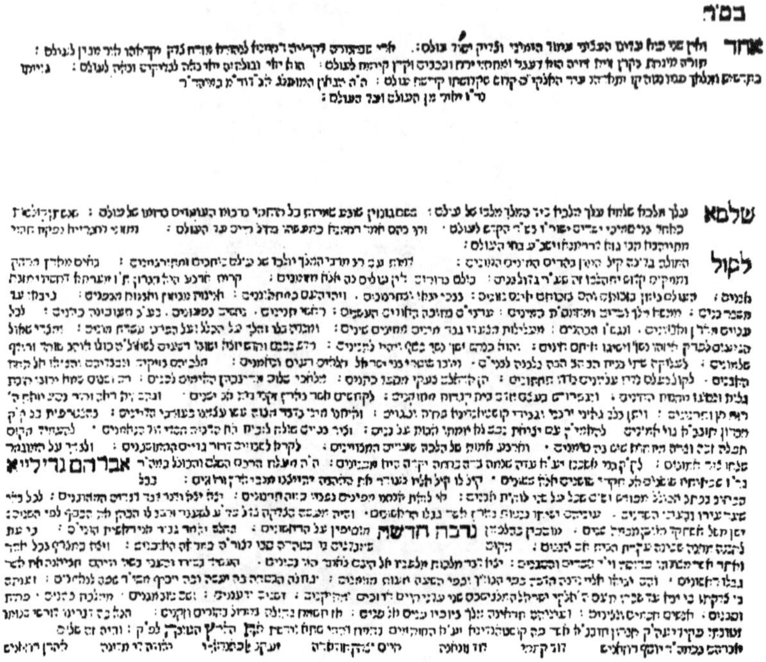

יח. פקידי חברון בקושטא, כתב שליחות, קושטא תצ״ה (1735)

8c. Mehlman's collection.

יט   לוח קיר לשנת תק"י, קושטא תק"ט (1759)

8d. Mehlman's collection.

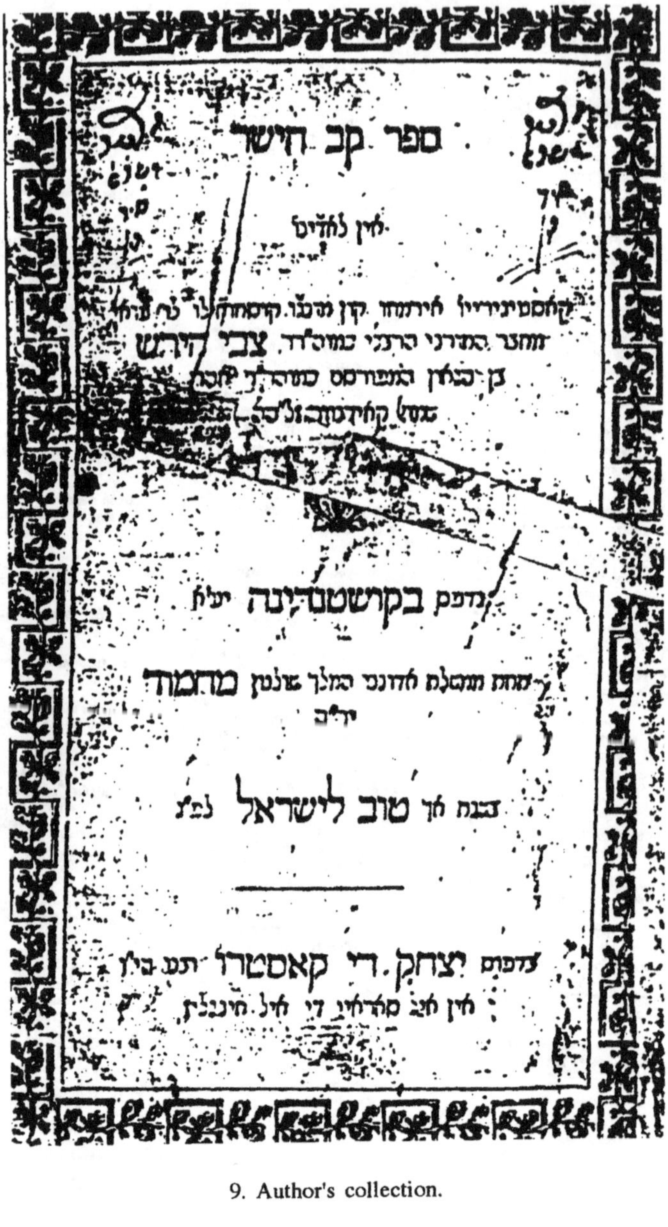
ספר קב הישר

נדפס בקושטנדינה יע"א

תחת ממשלת אדוננו המלך סולטן מחמוד יר"ה

בשנת טוב לישראל

בדפוס יצחק די קאסטרו

9. Author's collection.

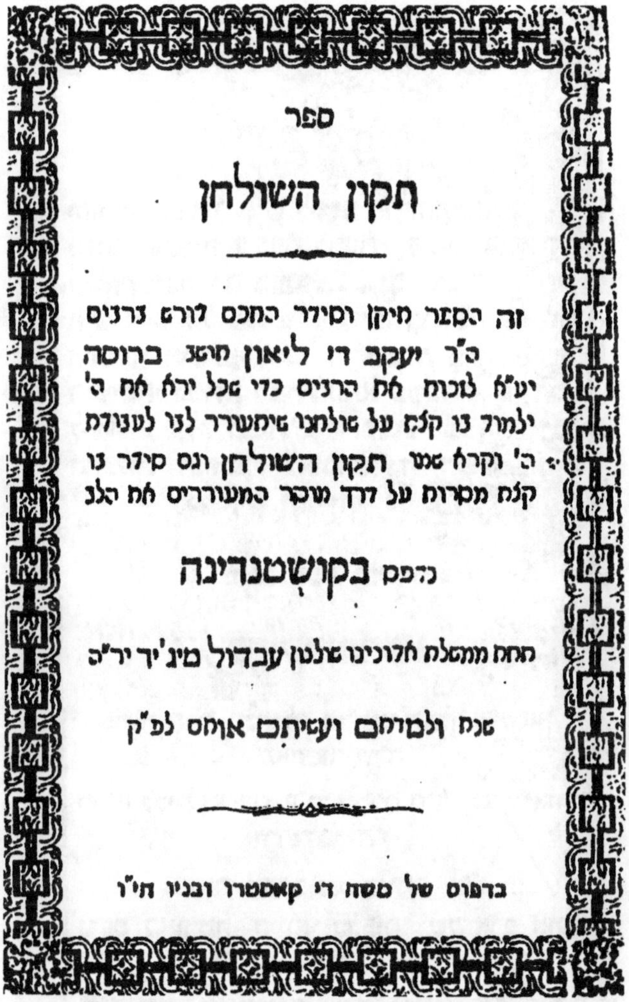
ספר

תקון השולחן

זה הספר תיקן וסידר החכם דורש ברבים
ה"ר יעקב די ליאון תושב ברוסה
יע"א לזכות את הרבים כדי שכל ירא את ה'
ילמוד בו קצת על שולחנו שיתעורר לבו לעבודת
ה' וקרא שמו תקון השולחן וגם סידר בו
קצת מסרות על דרך מוסר המעוררים את הלב

נדפס בקושטנדינה

תחת ממשלת אדונינו שולטן עבדול מג'יד יר"ה

שנת ולמדתם ועשיתם אותם לפ"ק

בדפוס של משה די קאסטרו ובניו הי"ו

10. Author's collection.

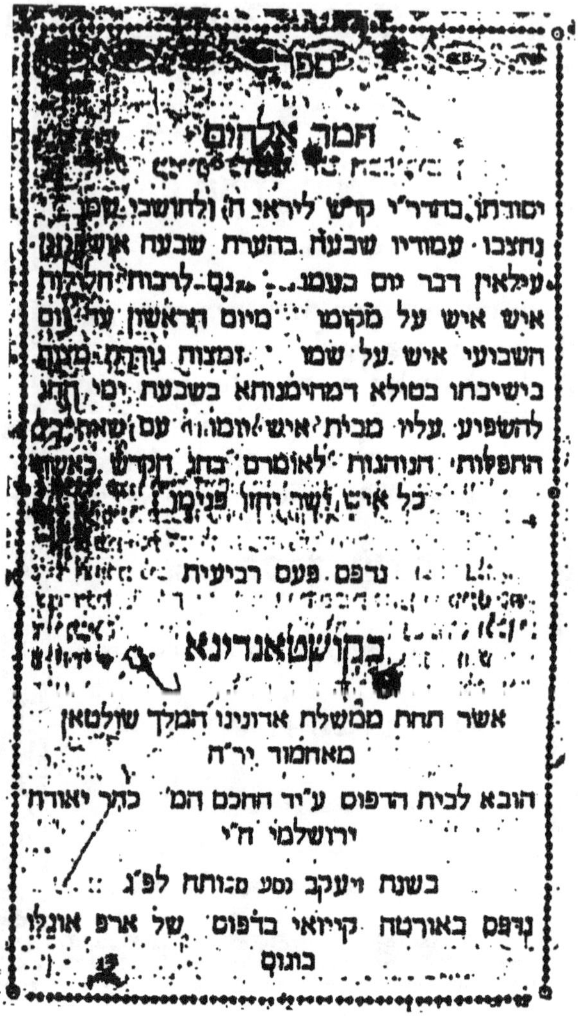
ספר
חמד אלהים
יסודתו. בהררי קדש ליראי ה' ולחושבי שמו
נחצבו עמודיו שבעה. בהערת שבעה אושפיזין
עילאין דבר יום ביומו ... גם לרבות חלוקת
איש איש על מקומו מיום הראשון עד יום
השביעי איש על שמו. זמנות
בישיבתו בטולא דמהימנותא בשבעת ימי חג
להשפיע עליו מבית איש
התפלות הנוהגות לאומרם בחג
כל איש
נדפס פעם רביעית
בקושטאנדינא
אשר תחת ממשלת אדונינו המלך שולטאן
מאחמוד יר"ה
הובא לבית הדפוס ע"י החכם המ' כה"ר יאודה
ירושלמי ה"י
בשנת ויעקב נסע סכותה לפ"ג
נדפס באורטה קיואי בדפוס של ארפ אוגלו
בתום

11. Author's collection.

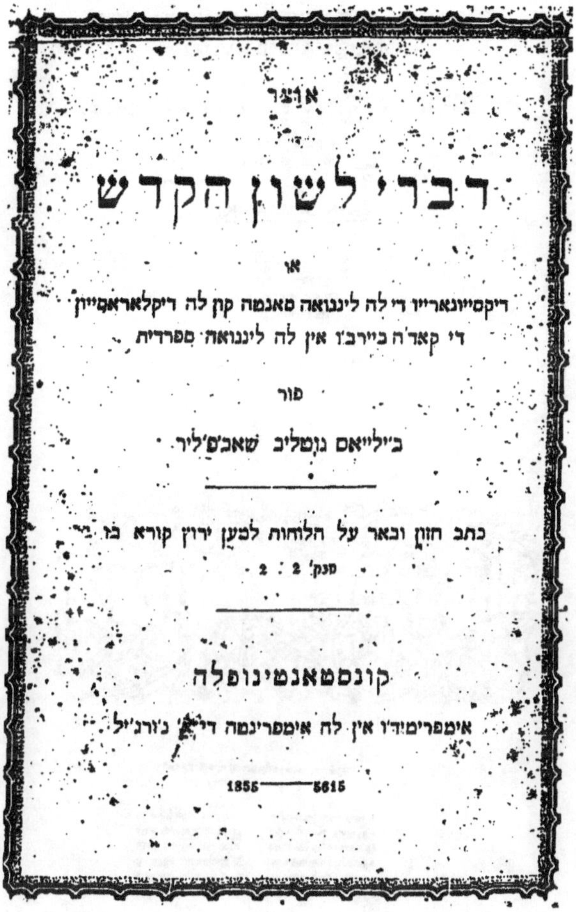

אוצר

דברי לשון הקדש

או

דיקסייונארייו די לה לינגואה סאנטה קון לה דיקלאראסייון
די קאד׳ה ביירב׳ו אין לה לינגואה ספרדית

פור

ב׳ילייאם גוטליב שאבס׳ליר

כתב חזון ובאר על הלוחות למען ירוץ קורא בו
חבק׳ 2 : 2

קונסטאנטינופלה

אימפרימיד׳ו אין לה אימפרינטה די א׳ ג׳ורג׳יל

1855———5615

12a. Author's collection.

TÜRKÇE - İSPANYOLCA - İBRANİCE
KONUŞMA KILAVUZU

MORE DEREH LANOSEİM

HAZIRLAYAN
NİSİM BEHAR
Musevi Okullarında İbranice Öğretmeni

İKİNCİ BASKI

5730 - 1969
GÜLER BASIMEVİ
İSTANBUL

12b. Author's collection.

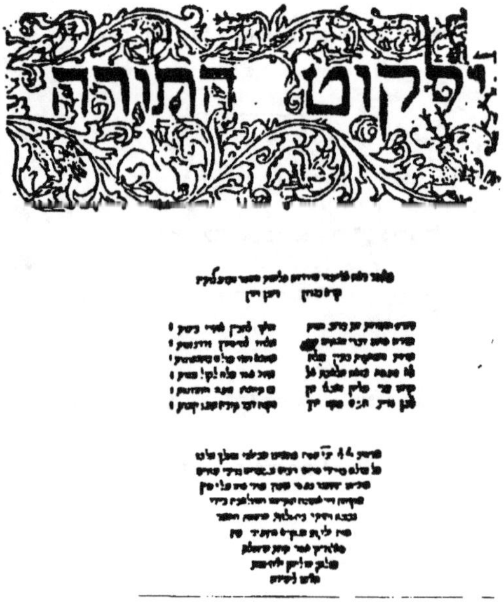
ילקוט התורה

13. Rosenthal, p. 23.

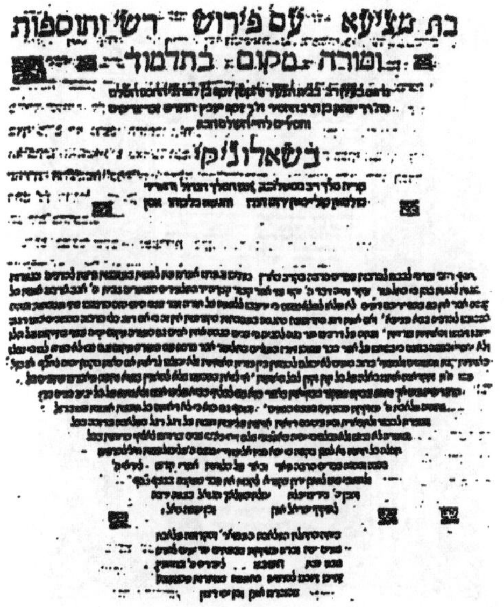

14. Mehlman, p. 226.

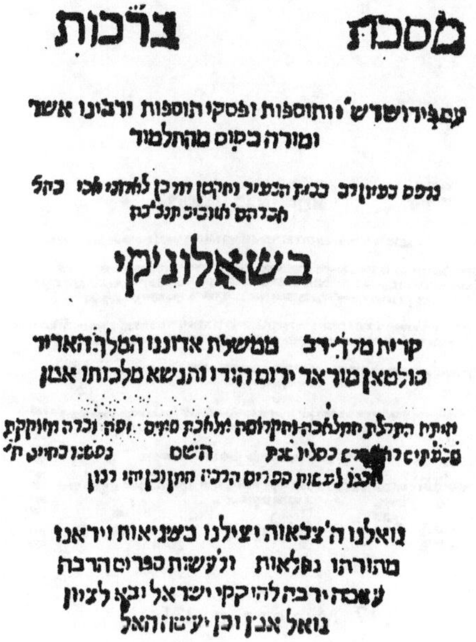

15. Rosenthal, p. 25.

שאלות ותשובות

בשאלוניקי

16. Emmanuel, p. 237.

מסכת בבא קמא

בשאלוניקי

17. Mehlman, p. 231.

ספר

שי למורא

משאלות. ותשובות

וקצת סוגיות ודברים ולשונות בעל הטורים ז״ל

מהרב המובהק כמהרר שבתי יונה זלה״ה

בשאלוניקי:

18. Rosenthal, p. 26.

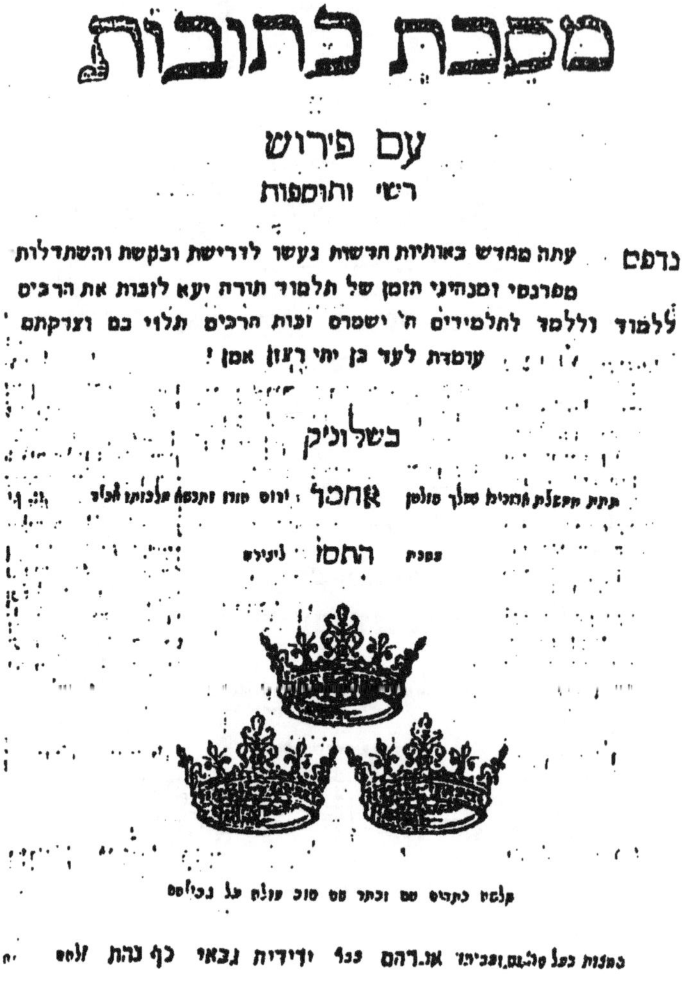

מסכת כתובות

עם פירוש

רשי ותוספות

נדפס עתה מחדש באותיות חדשות בעשר לדרישת ובקשת והשתדלות מפרנסי ומנהיגי הזמן של תלמוד תורה יעא לזכות את הרבים ללמוד וללמד לתלמידים ה' ישמרם וזכות הרבים תלוי בם וצדקתם עומדת לעד כן יהי רצון אמן!

בשלוניק

תחת ממשלת המלך סולטן אחמד ירום הודו ותנשא מלכותו

בשנת התסו

שלשה כתרים הם וכתר שם טוב עולה על גביהם

אברהם ידידיה גבאי כף נחת

19. Mehlman, p. 234.

ספר

נאמן שמואל

בשאלוניקי יע"א

20. Rosenthal, p. 27.

ספר מאיר לארץ

בשאלוניקי

21. Author's collection.

מחזור
לימים נוראים
תפארת ימים
שאלוניקי
ע״י המדפיס יצחק נאחון

22. Author's collection.

ספר
עבודת משא
יוסף איסקאפה
ראש יוסף
עבודת משא
שאלוניקי

23. Author's collection.

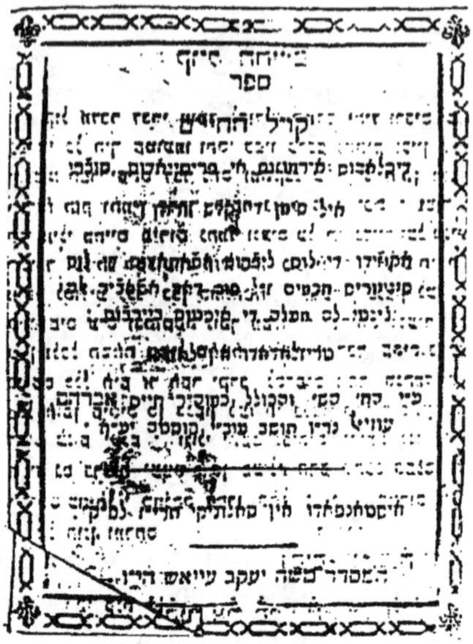
ספר
המסדר משה יעקב עיואש

24. Author's collection.

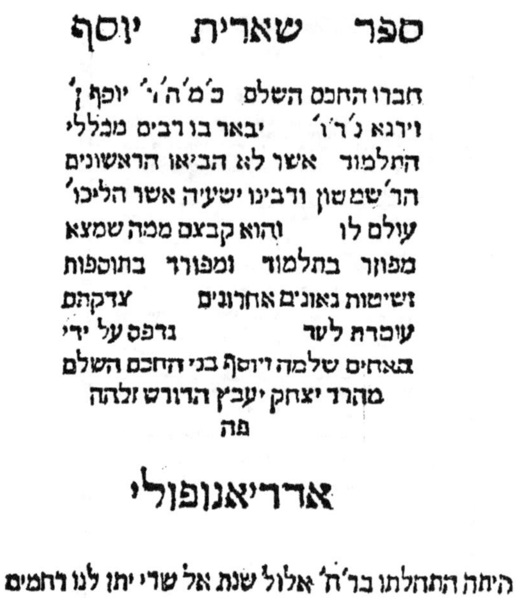
ספר שארית יוסף

חברו החכם השלם כ'מ'ה'ו' יוסף ן'
וירגא נ'ר'ו' יבאר בו רבים מכללי
התלמוד אשר לא הביאו הראשונים
הר' שמשון ורבינו ישעיה אשר הליכו'
עולם לו והוא קבצם ממה שמצא
מפוזר בתלמוד ומפורד בתוספות
ושיטות גאונים אחרונים צדקתם
עומדת לעד נדפס על ידי
באחים שלמה ויוסף בני החכם השלם
מהרר יצחק יעבץ הדורש זלהה
פה

אדריאנופולי

היתה התחלתו בר'ח' אלול שנת אל שדי יתן לנו רחמים

25a. M. Benayahu, "Makor al Megorashey Sefarad ve-Portugal ve-tzetam le-Saloniki" in *Sefunot*, 11 (Sefer Yavan 1). Jerusalem: Ben Zvi Institute, 1971-1978, p. 254.

יוסף דעת

איל פרוגריסו

מכתב-עת עברי וספרדי לתולדות ישראל על ארצות תוגרמה

יוצא לאור פעמים בחדש

על ידי

אברהם דאנון

להועלת

חברת שוחרי תושיה

באדריאנופלה

תתימה לשנה אחת

הכתבת למשלוח אגרות לנו:

Abr. Danon

Andrinople

25b. From the Ben Zvi Institute. My thanks are due to Mr. A. Attal for permission to use the photograph facing the title page of the book *Yosef Da'at.*

ספר

מקור ברוך

להרב הגדול והמופלא כמהר"ר ברוך קלעי בן להרב כמהר"ר שלמה קלעי זלה"ה
הוא תשובות לשאלות אשר נשאלו מאת הרב המחבר ז"ל והשיב לכל שאל דבר כמשפטו
בטעם טוב ודעת ה' יבא אל הדפוס בהשתדלות החכם נבון ע"י כל ברכת
תהלה כה"ר יצחק ישורון יצו לבקשת הגביר נבון ומהולל כה"ר שלמה
קלעי יצו בן להרב זלה"ה נתן לכסף כדי להוציא לאור הצלחת
הרב אבינו ז"ל ואל ברחמיו יזכו לראות בנים ובני בנים.
עוסקים בתורה ובמצות בישראל
אמן כן יהי
רצון

[illegible]

באובר

תחת ממשלת אדוננו המלך האדיר שולטן מחמד יר"ה ותנשא מלכותו ויאריך ימים
על ממלכתו.

[illegible]

[illegible]

[illegible]

26. Rosenthal, p. 31.

מקוה ישראל

Esto es,

ESPERANCA

DE ISRAEL

Obra con suma curiosidad compuesta

Por

MENASSEH BEN ISRAEL

Theologo, y Philosopho Hebreo.

Trata del admirable esparzimiento de los diez Tribus, y su infalible reduccion con los de mas a la patria: con muchos puntos, y Historias curiosas, y declaració de varias Prophecias, por el Author rectamente interpretadas.

EN AMSTERDAM.

Y de nuevo en Smirne

Impressa En La Estampa Del Caf Nahar.

5419.

APOLOGIA

Por

La noble nacion de los

IVDIOS

Y hijos de

ISRAEL

Escrita en Ingles

Por

EDVARDO NICHOLAS

Theologo Ingles.

Impressa en casa de Iuan Field en Londres.

año cIↃ cI c xI i x

Y de nuevo impressa en Smirne.

27. Ya'ari, *Ha-Defus ha-Ivri be-Izmir*, p. 102.

28. Author's collection.

29. Rosenthal, p. 33.

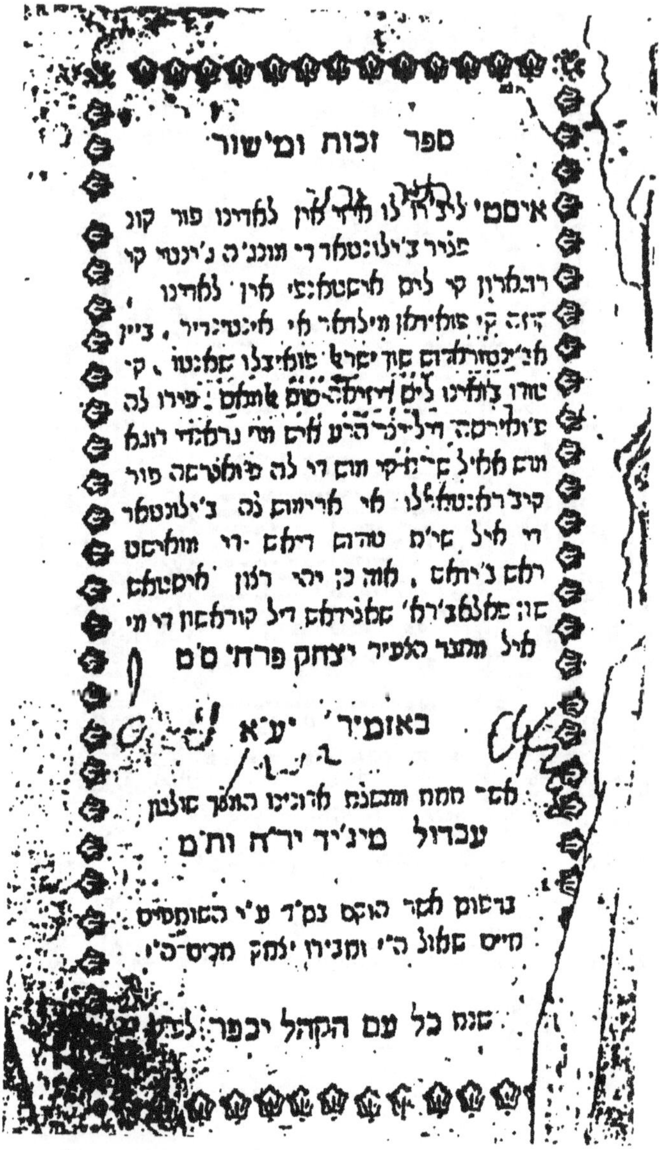
ספר זכות ומישור

באומיר יע"א

עבדול מיג'יד יר"ה ות"ם

שנת כל עם הקהל יכפר

30. Author's collection.

ספר
נכח השלחן
נדפס
פה אזמיר יע"א

31. Rosenthal, p. 35.

ספר
יעקב בעזרו
נדפס פה אזמיר

32. Author's collection.

[16]

Arab Booksellers and Bookshops in the Age of Printing, 1850–1914

AMI AYALON*

ABSTRACT *The emergence of massive printing in the Arab Middle East in the nineteenth century entailed a multiple set of changes. As well as the production of written texts in unprecedented quantities and the rise of a big reading public, that historic shift also gave birth to a range of diffusion channels-from bookshops to public libraries and from newspaper agents to reading clubs-which carried the printed works to their audiences. This article examines a small section of this scene: the growth, spreading and changing characteristics of book dealerships and bookshops in the Arab Ottoman provinces during the formative half-century prior to World War I. Exploring this mechanism casts light on the nature and pace of printing assimilation in the region, projecting it as a rather dramatic makeover.*

Introduction

Amin Hindiyya was a bookseller in Cairo's Muski quarter in the late nineteenth century. An advertisement for his shop in 1889 depicts an impressive range of items the place offered for sale. Among them were 'Arabic, Turkish, Persian, French and English books, scientific, literary, legal, historical, entertaining, and more', both handwritten and printed, from Istanbul, Syria, and Egypt. Also on sale were 'writing tools, such as paper, ink, pencils, and school needs'; as well as 'tarbushes, fitting silk buttons, light slacks (*dūblīn*), and double-sided bath robes (*ṭuqūmat ḥammām*)'.[1]

Bath robes in a bookshop—was it an oddity or a norm? And why is it important, anyway? As it happened, selling assorted goods along with books and journals under one roof was quite common at the time, if somewhat curious. But the import of this and other facets of bookselling was far greater than that of a mere curiosity. Bookselling represented a vital link in a chain of institutions and practices whose advent in the Middle East marked a major historic shift: the introduction of printing and its assimilation by the region's societies. It entailed massive production of written texts, the emergence of new diffusion channels carrying the printed products to the customers and, not least, the formation of sizeable and ever-expanding reading audience. Bearing profound socio-political and cultural implications, these changes amounted to what arguably might be considered a revolutionary cultural makeover, a development yet to be given its due scholarly consideration. The purpose of the present study is more modest: to examine

*Ami Ayalon, Department of Middle Eastern and African History, Tel Aviv University, Tel Aviv 69978, Israel. Email: aayalon@post.tau.ac.il

[1] Yusuf Asaf and Qaysar Nasr, *Dalil Misr li-'Amay 1889–1890* (Cairo, 1889), p. 228. Slightly different advertisements by Hindiyya appeared in Ibrahim 'Abd al-Masih, *Dalil Wadi al-Nil li-'Amay 1891, 1892* (Cairo, 1892), inside back cover, and in *al-Ahram*, 20 April 1889, p. 3.

a limited section of this grand scene—namely, book distribution mechanisms—with a focus on booksellers. My basic assumption is that exploring seemingly trivial ventures such as Hindiyya's shop in Cairo may yield an instructive insight into the nature, scope, and pace of that wider change.

Printing was adopted in the Middle East several centuries after it had swept Europe. A common explanation for this striking historic delay ascribes it to a distrustful attitude of sultans and 'ulama' alike toward the foreign invention, on religious as well as political grounds: they feared that machined mass-production of writings might desecrate Islam's holy texts and sacred language. If becoming widespread, it might also undermine their exclusive say in the community. Middle Eastern societies, then, did not adopt printing because their political and spiritual leaders were wary of it. The delay has also been attributed to opposition by the Empire's scribes and book copiers, presumably an influential cadre, who naturally feared for their livelihood. Of late, scholars have begun to question the plausibility of such explanations and the credibility of their underlying evidence. Recent probes into the historic Middle Eastern dislike for printing tend to look at cultural factors rather than religious and political ones. They focus mostly on the society's time-honoured preference for oral over written modes in communicating and retaining knowledge, a preference that would render the mass production of texts unnecessary. Such an explanation is perforce as tentative as the old, and seems to leave something to be desired.[2]

Be that as it may, the old aversive attitude to Gutenberg's invention began to lose ground in the eighteenth century, as a part of broader changes in the Empire's domestic and international realities. In that century, printing began hesitantly under the government's auspices in the Ottoman capital. It was followed in the nineteenth century by a more ambitious effort in Muhammad 'Ali's Egypt, where a government owned press turned out several hundred titles within a few decades, with a modest print-run and an equally modest demand.[3] The real breakthrough occurred only around mid-century, as Christian missionaries, their local pupils, and some other private individuals embarked on a vigorous publishing endeavour mostly in the Lebanon area. This outburst of non-governmental activity, and the concurrent acceleration of the Egyptian state enterprise, resulted in an unprecedented flow of written texts from these two important centres of Arabic printing. Thousands of books had appeared by 1900 in Egypt and Lebanon, in millions of copies,[4] engulfing every field of human interest. They included works from the old Arab legacy and modern pieces, original and translated, in full book size or chapbook format: religious tracts; works on history, geography, philosophy,

[2] For a survey of the scholarship on this and related issues, see Geoffrey Roper, 'The Printing Press and Change in the Arab World', in Sabrina Alcron Baron et al. (eds), *Agent of Change; Print Culture Studies After Elizabeth Eisenstein* (Boston: University of Massachusetts Press, 2007), pp. 251–267. A recent explanation is Metin Kunt, 'Reading Elite, Elite Reading,' paper presented at the Second International Symposium on the History of Printing and Publishing in the Languages and Countries of the Middle East, Paris, 2–4 November 2005.

[3] For printing under Muhammad 'Ali, see Jamal al-Din al-Shayyal, *Ta'rikh al-Tarjama wa-l-Haraka al-Thaqafiyya fi Misr fi 'Ahd Muhammad 'Ali* (Cairo: Maktabat al-Thaqafa al-Diniyya, 2000); 'Ayida Ibrahim Nusayr, *Harakat Nashr al-Kutub fi Misr fi al-Qarn al-Tasi' 'Ashar* (Cairo: al-Hay'a al-Misriyya al-'Amma li-l-Kitab, 1994), pp. 54–62, 89–93, 179–198 and 243–259.

[4] According to Nusayr, *Harakat Nashr*, pp. 53–98, over 10,000 titles were printed in Egypt by 1900 in over seven million copies. For Lebanon, Luis Shaykhu offered a partial list of 1516 titles for the period up to 1900 in his *Ta'rikh Fann al-Tiba'a fi al-Mashriq* (Beirut: Dar al-Mashriq, 1995), pp. 43–149. Shaykhu, however, chose to exclude hundreds of works that he deemed 'useless', and seems to have been unaware of numerous others. See Ami Ayalon, 'Private Publishing in the *Nahḍa*', *International Journal of Middle East Studies*, 40 (2008), pp. 561–577.

science, and language; dictionaries; general encyclopaedias; literary works and compilations of poetry; practical guides of many stripes; school texts; and so forth. Some 450 newspapers and journal had also emerged by the end of the century—and hundreds more by 1914—including many that were long-lasting and impressive in quality, featuring practical intelligence and broader knowledge. Countless other printed items, from political handbills, through commercial forms, to wedding invitations and personal *carte de visites*, came to circulate in the region with increasing frequency, changing people's lives in endless ways. All of these underlay the development known as the Arab cultural-literary 'awakening', or *nahḍa*.

The appearance of printed texts with such abundance where almost none had existed just a few decades earlier was obviously a mark of a fundamental change. A related sign was the proliferation of diffusion systems that put books and journals comfortably at the public's reach: bookshops and newspaper vendors, street peddlers and circulation agents, public libraries and reading rooms, book-lending shops, literary clubs, mail subscription, and more. With these came advertising devices of many kinds that largely enhanced distribution. They all represented indispensable support mechanisms that facilitated the change. Studying them should help in clearing the mist that shrouds the entry of Arabic-speaking societies into the era of printing.

In what follows I explore the development of Arab bookshops and book dealerships. I examine the activities of individual sellers and the emergence of the *maktaba*, a book-vending depot but actually much more than that. Selling books was anything but a clearly defined pursuit, and those engaged in it often expanded their activities in other directions, as we shall see. The probe is addressed to what may be considered the formative phase of these developments, from the mid-nineteenth century to World War I, after which the change assumed a markedly more energetic pace. As was the case with book production, distribution initiatives evolved primarily in the two major centres of cultural change: Egypt, and the area engulfing Beirut and some other towns in Mount Lebanon (to which I refer, conveniently if somewhat anachronistically, as 'Lebanon'). Similar businesses also appeared in other parts of the region but on a far smaller scale, reflecting the slower pace of their move into the era of publishing. Largely an urban phenomenon, the change also had its rural version, which is considered later on. I deal with this development as a micro case of the momentous shift to printing—an organic tissue, so to speak, that carried the genetic code of the entire process. Other aspects of this grand change must be left for other studies.

As with many institutions and practices that make up a society's life routine, bookshops are difficult to explore for their past. This is true everywhere, and in the Middle East perhaps more so. Evidence is ever a problem. Few if any bookshops from the pre-1914 Middle East have survived to our time; few have left us records of their activities. Only rarely do we find systematic book-sale data, subscriber lists, distribution figures, lending-shop reader registers, and the like. Those involved in the operation of shops as sellers or buyers hardly ever bother to record their dealings with them. In the few cases when they do, their accounts are so laconic as to tell us little: 'In Nablus was the shop of Shaykh Salih al-Khafash, with books and booklets to be lent for a fee. I used to borrow from him and read'[5]—this

[5] Muhammad 'Izzat Darwaza, *Mudhakkirat 1305–1404/1887–1984*, Vol. 1 (Beirut: Dar al-Gharb al-Islami, 1993), p. 160, referring to his childhood around 1900.

is all a keen Palestinian observer cared to say about his reading experience around 1900 in a six-volume autobiography, a brevity typical of such testimonies when they appear at all. Reports by foreign visitors are no more generous in detail. Even when the picture is somewhat better documented, it is an intricate matter to assess the relative role of each of these mechanisms in the general diffusion of printed texts. We do not know, for example, which channel contributed more to this process at a given time and place—bookshop sales or mail subscription? Or, how many readers accessed a journal copy available in a vendor's place? Much of the scene is therefore bound to remain obscure even with erudite exploration.

In the case of printed publications, however, we are a little more fortunate than in studying most other kinds of goods, thanks to the availability of two important sources. Newspapers and journals, likewise a nineteenth-century novelty that served as central conduits for marketing books (and often marketing each other), are a treasure trove of vital intelligence on the retailing of printed works. The many announcements they carry tell us a great deal about what was offered for sale, where, for what prices, and under what conditions. They also reveal much about the shops themselves, their owners, *modus operandi*, spatial spreading, and intended and actual clientele. The other kind of helpful source are the books themselves: their title-pages, colophons, and sometimes other parts, which often contain instructive details on bookseller involvement in their production and on how the books were meant to circulate. The contemporary press and printed books are, then, the two central pillars of evidence for this kind of inquiry, along with additional information occasionally appearing in local memoirs and histories by sellers, consumers, and foreign visitors. Together they relate a vibrant story.

Sellers of Printed Texts—The Beginning

For small and somewhat elitist groups in Arabic speaking and other Islamic communities, books were always a coveted commodity. For centuries, rulers, scholars, and others collected manuscript books on every conceivable topic, religious and otherwise, as precious assets.[6] They obtained items for their collections mostly in two ways, buying and copying. The trade in Arab books had a history apparently as long as that of Arab book-writing itself. That history is yet to be systematically studied, an intricate task given the paucity and piecemeal nature of the evidence for the pre-printing era. It cannot be undertaken here, nor is it really essential for a consideration of bookselling in the age of printing, as will become clear below. Fractional and unexplored as the sources are, they do tell us of bookshops and book markets operating in big cities such as Cairo, Baghdad, Basra, Aleppo, and Damascus, at least since the eleventh century CE. Book dealers travelled across the Islamic countries with their treasures; 'book criers' announced the sale of special manuscripts in city streets and markets; and booksellers were organized in guilds, along with book copiers and binders.[7] Accessing books did not necessarily entail buying them, of course, and one could read in any of the mosque or *madrasa* libraries to be found in many towns, or borrow a text form an *'ālim*. Those with the needed resources and reading skills who sought to acquire their own

[6] See, for example, Etan Kohlberg, *A Medieval Muslim Scholar at Work: Ibn Ṭāwūs and his Library* (Leiden: Brill, 1992), especially pp. 71ff.
[7] Filib di Tarrazi, *Khaza'in al-Kutub al-'Arabiyya fi al-Khafiqayn*, Vol. 3 (Beirut: Wizarat al-Tarbiyya al-Wataniyya wa-l-Funun al-Jamila, 1948), pp. 909–917.

copies could do so through a bookseller—*warrāq* or *kutubī*—who was normally also a paper dealer and a stationer. He would sell them a copy he had in stock, get them other titles through his commercial connections, or commission a copyist to reproduce a manuscript that was within reach. Hand-written, hand-illustrated, and hand-bound, books varied in value and price according to their authors' prestige, their commonness or rareness, and their physical and aesthetic quality.

The impression one gets from the sources at hand suggests that the Arab book trade before printing fluctuated between prosperity and decline in different times and places.[8] By the eve of the arrival of printing, this trade—and perhaps book collecting in general—had seemingly decreased to a point lower than in medieval times. Still, it did persist in the region's main towns, where individual book dealers operated in small numbers during the nineteenth century's first half. 'Whenever a valuable book comes into the possession of one of these persons, he goes around with it to his regular customers', Edward Lane reported from Cairo in the 1830s, conveying a sense of a humble business with a minuscule clientele.[9] Such diffusion conduits as existed were apparently sufficient for the scope of book supply and demand before printing. They were hardly prepared to accommodate the quantities of Arabic books once these became mass-produced.

Apparently the first shop in the region to sell locally printed books was the government's *kutubkhāna* in Egypt, founded in 1836 as a branch of the Education Ministry (*dīwān al-madāris*) near Cairo's al-Husayn mosque. It served as an outlet for state-published works until 1870, when its role was taken over by the Khedivial Bookshop (*al-maktaba al-khidīwiyya*).[10] Government publishing and distribution initiatives were important in blazing the trail for others, but they seem to have been of lesser cultural-historic import than were private ones. They were certainly less colourful, being official agencies that dealt primarily with school texts and state publications sold mostly, although not solely, to government-school students and to bureaucrats. Such shops did not have to struggle for economic survival or to bother much about marketing, and were in general little concerned with public tastes and wishes, with responding to them or with shaping them. Despite their pioneering role, then, they are of little interest to us here.

Private bookshops carrying printed texts first appeared in Beirut around the middle of the century, where missionary endeavour and the creativity of local, mostly Christian, individuals combined to start a dynamic publishing industry. When books were first printed there, their publishers collaborated with the few local booksellers in distributing them. Of the latter we know little beyond some names, but their businesses were apparently well known to their customers, who made up the old circle of book buyers and collectors. Adverts in the nascent local press referred these customers to shops with no identifying details; the formula '*'ind* (in [the place of]) so and so', or 'in the shop of ...' sufficed. Thus, Ibrahim Bey's history of the Ottoman Empire (1859) was sold '*'ind* al-khawājā Iliyas

[8] For some examples of such accounts, see Edward W. Lane, *Manners and Customs of the Modern Egyptians* (Cairo: Livres de France, 1978), p. 210; John Bowring, *Report on the Commercial Statistics of Syria* (New York: Arno Press, 1973 [reprint of the 1840 edition]), p. 106; Charles Warren, *Underground Jerusalem* (London: Richard Bentley, 1876), pp. 491–492; and Nelly Hanna, *In Praise of Books* (Syracuse, NY: Syracuse University Press, 2003), p. 93. For similar accounts of the Istanbul book trade prior to and in the early nineteenth century, see Ömer Faruk Yilmaz, *Tarih Boyunca Sahhāflık ve İstanbul Sahhāflar Çarşısı* (Istanbul: Sahhaflar Derneği, 2005), especially pp. 11–31 and 71–89.

[9] Lane, *Manners*, p. 210.

[10] Nusayr, *Harakat Nashr*, pp. 465–470.

Fawaz' in Beirut—a flat indication without further elaboration.[11] Khawājā Iliyas (variably also Liyas) must have been a familiar book dealer, for such concise references to his shop appeared routinely in adverts by different printers.[12] In the early 1860s he used to advertise his own business in Beirut's main newspaper, *Hadiqat al-Akhbar*, announcing books on sale at his shop for which no address was given.[13] The shop was sometimes referred to as *makhzin*, a generic name for a 'depot' carrying any kind of merchandise. This term, and its synonymous *dukkān* and *maḥall*, were regularly applied to bookshops throughout the region in those early years.[14] The name *maktaba*, which would come to distinguish bookshops from other businesses, was then still in the future.

There were others like Iliyas Fawaz whose names were advertised with no further reference, suggesting that their shop location was common knowledge. One of them was Fathallah Tajir, owner of a Beirut bookshop (*makhzin*), whose 1859 newspaper adverts indicated that he had been in the business 'for a long time'. By now he was in a position to offer products printed in Beirut itself, such as Nasif al-Yaziji's *Majma' al-Bahrayn* (1856) and a volume of the Ottoman commercial code (*Qanun al-Tijara*, 1858). He also sold Arabic and Turkish titles published in Cairo and even in Paris—in medicine, language, *ādab*, and more; no fewer than 46 items were advertised in one 1859 announcement.[15] Tajir may have been dealing in imported printed books since before the outset of printing in his own town, and it is conceivable, although not accounted for, that he had been selling handwritten works still earlier on. Such was the case with some of the other shops in the region that were already in place by the birth-hour of the Arabic press that carried their adverts, whose owners were often manuscript dealers turned into printed-text sellers, first imported and then locally made.

But the few shops operating in the city would not contain the flow of books soon to issue from the burgeoning presses. New outlets began to appear from the late 1850s onward, supplementing the old and akin to them in style and size, their newness attested to by indication of their location in press announcements. These were loose addresses, as was common then, but sufficient for navigation: '*'ind* al-khawājā As'ad al-Jamil near Burj al-Kashash'; '*'ind* 'Alwan effendi al-Ghurafi in the perfumers' (*'aṭṭārīn*) market'; or, somewhat more vaguely, 'in a shop (*dukkān*) [owner unidentified] near the commercial centre (*khān*) of al-khawājāt Bustrus'.[16]

[11] *Hadiqat al-Akhbar*, 15 December 1859, p. 4. For more examples, see: *Hadiqat al-Akhbar*, 29 December 1859, p. 4; 22 March 1860, p. 3; 20 April 1865, p. 2; and 29 February 1866, p. 4; *al-Ahram*, 11 May 1877, p. 4; *and Lisan al-Hal*, 18 May 1878, p. 4.

[12] For example, *Hadiqat al-Akhbar*, 15 March 1860, p. 3; 22 March 1860, pp. 3–4; 19 January 1865, p. 4; 20 April 1865, p. 3; and 8 February 1866, p. 3.

[13] For example, *Ibid.*, 13 November 1865, p. 4.

[14] For example, *Ibid.*, 8 September 1859, p. 4; 31 December 1859, p. 3; 15 March 1860, p. 3; 26 February 1868, p. 3; 13 November 1863, p. 4; and 20 April 1865, p. 3; *al-Najah*, 29 May 1871, p. 604; *al-Ahram*, 4 November 1876, p. 4; and *al-Watan*, 12 November 1881, p. 1; and 21 April 1883, p. 6.

[15] *Hadiqat al-Akhbar*, 8 September 1859, p. 4.

[16] For these examples, see *Hadiqat al-Akhbar*, 29 November 1859, p. 4; 15 March 1860, p. 3; and 20 April 1865, p. 3. Similarly, ibid., 15 March 1860, p. 4; 10 January 1865, p. 3; and 8 February 1866, p. 3. In Tunis a shop was called *ḥanūt* and customers were similarly referred, for example, to 'the *ḥanūt* of the bookseller (*kutubī*) Sayyid Muhammad al-Sa'idi, attached to the door of the great Zaytuna mosque on the cemetery side'; *al-Ra'id al-Tunisi*, 5 April 1865, p. 4. Similarly, *al-Ra'id al-Tunisi*, 22 June 1860, p. 1; and 12 April 1872, p. 4. For similar references in Istanbul, see *al-Jawa'ib*, 3 September 1868, p. 4. We also hear of a few merchants with alien names, apparently foreign residents who sought to profit from the rising interest in the new commodity: Fischel Rosenzweig, a bookbinder who now offered to import books on demand; Edouard du Marc 'the Frenchman', a stationer-cum-bookseller; and the somewhat more ambitious monsieur Charles Béziès—all three in Beirut. See, for example, *Hadiqat al-Akhbar*, 7 August 1858, p. 4; 28 January 1859, p. 3; 15 December 1859, p. 3; 21 May 1867, p. 3; and 19 January 1865, p. 3.

Many adverts suggest that businesses dealing primarily in other goods often added books to their sales inventory. Such, for instance, seems to have been the case with one 'Abd al-Qadir effendi al-Anja, who possessed multiple copies of a work on Arab poets and put them on sale 'in the *dukkān* of [unidentified nature, owned by] Sayyid Muhyi al-Din al-Kubba in the butter (*sammāna*) market' in Beirut.[17] The fact that quite a few of the sellers appearing in book adverts were identified by titles that could be their names or, just as well, indicate their trade, may also have hinted in that direction: books were sold by *al-sa'ātī* (watchmaker), *al-dukhānī*, *al-tunbākūjī* (both meaning tobacconist), *al-ḥakkāk* (lapidary), *al-tarābīshī* (tarbush maker), *al-ḥallāq* (barber), *al-tājir* (merchant) and the like.[18]

Other improvised ways for handling the increasing amounts of printed products characterized the transition phase. Alongside bookshops old and new, and the other businesses that became provisional outlets for printed products, books were also sold by the presses issuing them, by their advertising newspapers, and directly by the authors. Print-shops and newspapers were two vital links in the evolving chain of publishing, which during that early phase also functioned conveniently as vendors, thus playing more roles than one in book diffusion. Customers were advised to contact the office (*maktab* or *idāra*) of the printer, newspaper, or the paper's provincial agents to that end.[19] The more enterprising printers and journal-owners went a step further and opened separate bookshops beside their businesses, as we shall see later on. Somewhat less frequently, books were also sold by their authors without shop mediation: in notices on new works, potential buyers were referred directly to the author/translator for ordering them, the customary formula being *yuṭlab min mu'allifihi* ('to be ordered from its author') with reference to a location.[20] Such direct sales by printers, advertisers, and authors continued throughout the region until well into the twentieth century.

Maktaba

The term *maktaba* (pl. *maktabāt* or *makātib*) was coined apparently around the middle of the nineteenth century to denote, generally, 'a place of writings'. At first applied to libraries and book collections, the word was subsequently extended to businesses selling books, journals, and other items related to reading and writing.[21] As so often, the introduction of a new term signalled the initiation

[17] *Hadiqat al-Akhbar*, 15 March 1860, p. 4.

[18] Sometimes the title appears in addition to a three-barrel name—for example, 'Muhammad (effendi) Khalifa al-Tarabishi'—which makes this last appellation more probably the men's occupation. For these examples, see *Hadiqat al-Akhbar*, 13 November 1863, p. 4; *al-Jawa'ib*, 3 September 1868, p. 4; and 8 March 1870, p. 4; *al-Watan*, 12 November 1881, p. 1; and 21 April 1883, p. 4; *al-Janna*, 30 April 1884, p. 4; and *Misr al-Fatat*, 5 January 1909, p. 2.

[19] For some early examples, see *Hadiqat al-Akhbar*, 7 August 1858, p. 4; 30 October 1858, p. 4; 15 March 1860, p. 3; and 29 February 1866, p. 4; *al-Jinan*, 1 May 1873, inner front cover; *Thamarat al-Funun*, 20 June 1876, p. 4; and 5 September 1881, p. 1; *Lisan al-Hal*, 15 October 1879, p. 4; and 4 August 1890, p. 4; and *al-Muqtataf*, December 1882, p. 143; and March 1883, p. 223.

[20] For example, *al-Janna*, 3 September 1881, p. 4; *al-Muqtataf*, January 1886, p. 254; *Lisan al-Hal*, 14 August 1890, p. 4; *al-Hilal*, December 1892, p. 189; *al-Ahram*, 12 August 1895, p. 2; *Thamarat al-Funun*, 1 June 1896, p. 1; *al-Ra'id al-Misri*, 26 November 1897, p. 1071; and *al-Zahir*, 21 September 1904, p. 3.

[21] The term appears neither in Edward Lane's *Arabic–English Lexicon* (London: Williams & Norgate, 1863–1893) nor in A. Biberstein-Kazimirski's *Dictionnaire arabe-français* (Cairo: Impr. Egyptiènne, 1875). R. Dozy's *Supplément aux dictionnaires arabes* (Leiden: Brill, 1881), relying on mid-nineteenth century dictionaries, defines *maktaba* as 'cabinet d'étude, bibliothèque, librairie'. In Butrus al-Bustani's *Muhit al-Muhit* (1871), the term appears in the sense of 'location for placing books' (*mawḍa' waḍ' al-kutub*).

of a new practice and concept: it singled out books among other goods sold in 'shops' and lent bookselling the specificity that was called for under the new circumstances. In the 1870s *maktaba* began to be used with reference to bookshops alongside the older, more generic appellations; by the mid-1880s it had replaced all other names.[22]

A note on the semantics of '*maktaba*' is required before we proceed to consider it as an institution. As well as a name for a shop selling printed books, *maktaba* came to designate two other innovations of the new era: a stationer's shop; and a publishing house. Consequently, while contributing to specificity, the term also generated a measure of ambiguity. Library, book collection, bookshop, stationer's shop, and publishing house—all came to be expressed by one word, with the inevitable murkiness that such lax usage entails. The confusion was not merely one of name application; it was also in the practice itself, which frequently combined two or more practices in one business under the title *maktaba*. Shops selling books often carried writing tools and office needs, thus functioning as bookshops-and-stationery depots rather akin to the traditional *warrāq*'s business. Sometimes their owners engaged in modest publishing, thereby turning their *maktaba* into an enterprise that produced books rather than vending them. At other times, *maktaba*-owners dealing with book production did sell their printed products in place, thus making their business a publishing house-cum-bookshop.[23] Bearing in mind the divers applications of the term, our discussion of *maktaba* will focus primarily on the function of bookselling as a dissemination channel.

As a bookshop, *maktaba* could be a tiny newspaper-vending stand or a big business with a rich selection of printed items. The smaller ones apparently resembled humble shops of the old style, keeping to the previous modest physical setting even when shifting to a new kind of goods under a new name. The bigger places reflected the ambitious scale that would gradually come to typify certain sections of the book trade as a whole. A few of them grew into grand enterprises with regional and even international ties. Many of the new places carried, traditionally, the names of their owners: 'Maktabat Muhammad Tawfiq' in Cairo, 'al-Maktaba al-Rifa'iyya' of 'Abdallah al-Rifa'i' in Tripoli (Syria), and the like. Others adopted titles with cultural or patriotic connotations, such as 'al-Maktaba al-Adabiyya', 'Maktabat al-Taraqqi', and 'Maktabat al-Watan'.

By far the most common *maktaba*s everywhere were of the modest kind, one-man businesses whose owners sought to make a living from the sale, among other things, of the fast-proliferating printed publications for which public demand was palpably growing. 'Among other things', since at that early stage retailing newspapers, journals, books, and school texts on a local scale was usually inadequate as a source of livelihood nearly everywhere. Selling them, therefore, was often only a part of the activity of these shops. In a typical case, a *maktaba* would also carry office and school

[22] For early appearances of *maktaba* as a name for bookshop, see: in Beirut: *al-Jinan*, 29 February 1876, inner and outer back cover; *Lisan al-Hal*, 4 May 1878, p. 4; and 15 October 1879, p. 4; *al-Muqtataf*, March 1879, inner back cover; May 1880, inner front cover; August 1882, p. 87; and May 1883, p. 280; *Thamarat al-Funun*, 5 July 1882, p. 4; and 2 June 1884, p. 1. In Cairo: *al-Muqtataf*, January 1886, p. 254; and August 1886, p. 703; and Asaf and Nasr, *Dalil Misr*, pp. 189 and 228.

[23] Numerous books from the last third of the nineteenth century carried the name of a *maktaba* as publisher. For some early examples, see: Muhammad Haqi Nazli, *Khazinat al-Asrar Jalilat al-Adhkar* (Cairo: al-Maktaba al-Tijariyya al-Kubra, 1286 [1869]); Ahmad Buni, *Shams al-Ma'arif al-Kubra* (Cairo: Maktabat 'Abd al-Rahman Muhammad, 1291 [1874]); *al-Tariqa al-Wahida ila al-Bayyina al-Rajiha* (Damascus: al-Maktaba al-Salafiyya, 1299 [1882]); and Muhammad Khalil al-Muradi, *Silk al-Durar fi A'yan al-Qarn al-Thani 'Ashar* (Cairo: Maktabat al-'Arabi, 1291–1301 [1874-1883]). For the beginnings of Arab publishing, see Ayalon, 'Private Publishing'.

needs, goods usually sold by stationers whose customers would form the market for books and journals as well. Stationery, books, and journals seemed to make a natural match-up. To pick a random example, Yusuf Jirjis Shayt, who in 1880 opened a shop on Clot Bey Street in central Cairo, advertised the sale of 'paper of every kind, envelopes, European notebooks, pencils, European ink ... and so on', as well as 'numerous books printed in Egypt, Syria, and elsewhere'.[24] Such a combination could make for a solid business, especially if well located in the commercial quarter of a big city. During the early decades of bookselling we also find *maktaba* owners resorting in addition to the sale of many other goods in their shops, presumably to supplement their income. *Maktaba*s sold just about everything, from cloths and shoes to toys and holiday gifts. Amin Hindiyya's shop, we shall recall, sold books and journals along with bath robes and tarbushes. And a shop called Maktabat 'Unwan al-Najah in the tanners' market in Hamah (Syria) sold 'superb tea' alongside 'scholarly and entertaining books', and stationery.[25] Books were also sold in shops specializing in other goods; such, for example, was the case with al-Ittiḥād pharmacy (*ijzākhāna*) in Tanta, to which customers were referred for books.[26] The phenomenon was familiar from other places and times, where books, having a small market, were sold together with anything from 'quack pills and powder for the afflicted' to sports equipment and food.[27] In the Middle East it was widespread in smaller towns everywhere at least until the middle of the twentieth century.[28]

The growing quantities of locally printed texts offered more opportunities to the bold. Resourceful owners of older shops and new entrepreneurs entering the field sought to develop more ambitious book outlets. Sensing a rising public demand, they would equip their shops with a rich selection of writing paraphernalia, and bring books and periodicals in a variety of languages from elsewhere in the region and from Europe, as we have seen in a few cases.[29] They would promote their shops in the press and on book-covers—likewise a new technique—and issue sales catalogues or book lists to facilitate public access.[30] They would also undertake

[24] *Al-Muqtataf*, February 1880, back cover. For similar examples, see: *Hadiqat al-Akhbar*, 28 January 1859, p. 3; 3 December 1859, p. 3; and 21 May 1867, p. 3; *Lisan al-Hal*, 4 May 1878, p. 4; 3 May 1901, p. 1; *al-Muqtataf*, March 1885, p. 383; *Thamarat al-Funun*, 5 July 1882, p. 4; *al-Manar* (Beirut), 1 October 1898, p. 23; and *al-'Irfan*, Vol. 2 (1910–11), last page.

[25] *Lisan al-Hal*, 16 December 1913, p. 4. Similarly, a shop (*maḥall*) in Jaffa carried newpapers as well as 'English tea of the best brands'; *Filastin*, 29 January 1913, p. 4.

[26] *Al-Mu'ayyad*, 15 February 1900, p. 4. Similarly, *Thamarat al-Funun*, 23 September 1895, p. 4—references to pharmacies in Beirut.

[27] For example, Joseph Shaylor, *The Fascination of Books* (New York: G. P. Putnam's Sons, 1912), p. 136 (reference to nineteenth-century and twentieth century England); and John A. Wiseman, 'Silent Companions: the Dissemination of Books and Periodicals in Nineteenth Century Ontario', *Publishing History*, 12 (1982), pp. 18–19.

[28] See, for example, Ami Ayalon, *Reading Palestine: Printing and Literacy 1900–1948* (Austin: University of Texas Press, 2004), pp. 83ff, for twentieth-century Palestine.

[29] See the examples of Fathallah Tajir and Amin Hindiyya cited above. For similar shops, see: Ibrahim Sadir's al-Maktaba al-'Umumiyya in Beirut—Sulayman Jawish, *al-Tuhfa al-Saniyya fi Ta'rikh al-Qustantiniyya* (Beirut: Maktabat Ibrahim Sadir, 1887), shop announcement on last page; al-Maktaba al-Jami'a of Khalil and Amin al-Khuri in Beirut—*al-Hilal*, 1 July 1894, inner back cover; Jurji Zaydan's Maktabat al-Hilal in Cairo—*al-Hilal*, 1 October 1896, pp. 119–120; 'Abduh Yani's al-Maktaba al-Suriyya in Beirut—*al-Manar* (Beirut), 1 October 1898, p. 23; and 'Abdallah al-Rifa'i's al-Maktaba al-Rifa'iyya in Tripoli—Hikmat Sharif, *Sa'adat al-Ma'ad* (Tripoli: al-Maktaba al-Rifa'iyya, n.d.), p. 24, shop announcement.

[30] For example, Ibrahim Sadir's al-Maktaba al-'Umumiyya (see previous note); al-Maktaba al-Misriyya, *Qa'imat al-Kutub al-Mawjuda fi al-Maktaba al-Misriyya bi-Misr* (Cairo: al-Maktaba al-Misriyya, 1887); al-Maktaba al-Sharqiyya of Ibrahim Effendi Faris—Asaf and Nasr, *Dalil*, pp. 228–229; al-Maktaba al-Jami'a of Khalil and Amin al-Khuri in Beirut—*al-Hilal*, 15 August 1894, inner back cover; Maktabat al-Hilal—*al-Hilal*, 1 April 1897, p. 595; and Dar al-Kutub al-'Arabiyya—*al-Umma* (Damascus), 29 February 1910, p. 4.

to serve as agents for journals and newspapers, local and other, handling distribution to subscribers while increasing their commercial exposure.[31] And they would launch other creative initiatives of making books available to the public. Thus, al-Maktaba al-'Asriyya in Suez, opened in 1900, presented itself as a place for 'browsing and selling (*muṭāla'a wa-mabī'*)' of books and journals, a convenient dual service. Its owner also undertook to circulate publications sent to his shop among pilgrims passing through the town on their way to Mecca, thus underscoring its special utility as a dissemination centre.[32] Similarly, al-Maktaba al-Kuliyya in Beirut the following year invited 'whoever wishes to subscribe for reading stories, novels and the like on a monthly basis to [come and] find in [our shop] new books to gratify him'[33]—that is, a lending library as well as a bookshop. Imaginative ventures of this kind contributed to the diffusion of printed products in multiple ways beyond their mere retailing.

Book dealers engaged in yet another important kind of activity, which likewise enhanced their public prominence. They underwrote, and sometimes initiated, the production of books that they then sold in their own shops or elsewhere. Some of them went a step further, acquired printing gear and became full-fledged publishers. Such capable individuals came to play a role of great importance in the development of Arab publishing, a role that merits a separate study and can only be mentioned here very briefly. The title-pages of books thus produced usually indicated that the book was 'printed at the expense (*bi-nafaqat*) of [such and such] *maktaba*' and 'were obtainable there'. Thus, Sulayman Jawish's *al-Tuhfa al-Saniyya fi Ta'rikh al-Qustantiniyya* (1887) was 'printed at the expense of Ibrahim Sadir and his sons, owners of al-Maktaba al-'Umumiyya in Beirut' (apparently a big shop that also turned out other books);[34] and *Riwayat Yusuf al-Sadiq*, a play in five acts (Cairo, 1897), 'was printed at the expense of al-Maktaba al-Sharqiyya, owned by the *adīb* Ibrahim effendi Faris, where it is sold (*yubā' fīhā*)'.[35]

Bigger Businesses

A few especially creative individuals, of the kind we find in every trade, managed to build bigger shops that placed them in a category apart from the smaller ones considered above. Some of them designed their businesses from the start as more than just bookshops, combining wide-scale book and journal marketing with printing and publishing, bookbinding, selling stationery and other items, and providing office services. Some also published a newspaper or journal.

[31] See, for example, adverts for Nakhla Qalfaz's al-Maktaba al-Suriyya in Beirut—*al-Muqtataf*, May 1880, inner front cover; and al-Maktaba al-Sharqiyya of Ibrahim Effendi Faris—Asaf and Nasr, *Dalil*, pp. 228–229. The agent networks that newspapers spread across the region and beyond, and the many functions these agents fulfilled, seem to be important aspects of the 'awakening' yet to be systematically explored. During the last quarter of the century their number in the region reached many hundreds.

[32] *Al-Hilal*, 15 February 1900, p. 318.

[33] Notice in *Lisan al-Hal*, 3 May 1901, p. 3. Its owners were Nakhla Qalfaz (previously owner of al-Maktaba al-Suriyya; see note 34) and Salim Maydani. A shop that offered book-borrowing arrangements in turn-of-the-century Nablus is mentioned in Darwaza, *Mudhakkirat*, p. 160.

[34] In the last page of that book, Sadir announces a wholesale arrangement and advises his customers to order a catalogue of the shop's local and imported books, elegantly entitled *al-Rawda al-Bahiyya fi Asma' Kutub al-Maktaba al-'Umumiyya*.

[35] *Al-Hilal*, 1 March 1897, p. 517. For further discussion of this phenomenon and more examples, see Ayalon, 'Private Publishing'.

The publishing house of Jurji Zaydan in late-nineteenth century Cairo is a case in point. A self-made intellectual, Zaydan would become an eminent contributor to the *nahḍa*. In 1892 he started the literary-historical journal *al-Hilal* in Cairo, along with its own press, and before too long it became one of the most influential Arabic periodicals. The journal's office in the Fajjala (Faggala) quarter, Cairo's busy printing hub at the time, at first served as a sales outlet for occasional books, a common practice then as we have seen (many of the sold items were of Zaydan's own authorship). In 1896 Zaydan added a bookshop to the business, adjacent to the press, 'in response to the urging of friends and subscribers and seeking to advance the spread of knowledge'. The note enouncing the opening of Maktabat al-Hilal revealed Zaydan's farsightedness. The place would be stuffed with books, journals and newspapers from Egypt, Syria, Istanbul, Europe, and America, for customers to buy or to browse free of charge. It would also feature a lending arrangement of novels and scholarly books, to be borrowed for a monthly fee of 15 qurush (10 for *al-Hilal* subscribers), one volume at a time. Clients would be permitted to exchange books as frequently as they desired, including those residing out of Cairo when paying for postage.[36] We have little direct evidence concerning the subsequent actual performance of the shop and its various services. But routine references to the *maktaba* in later issues of *al-Hilal* (mostly as an outlet for items the journal advertised) would suggest that the shop grew into a vivid enterprise and became a success. So would the repeated printing, in later years, of the shop's catalogue, which was often said to meet with great demand and even run out of print.[37]

Jurji Zaydan began his publishing career as a salaried journalist and built his way up thanks to unusual business acumen and intellectual gift. Other sellers, just a handful of them throughout the region, entered the business while already well-off, bringing with them resources that permitted them to open large ventures. Such seems to have been the case with the Lebanese émigré in Egypt 'Aziz Zand, an intellectual of minor eminence and some wealth who opened a big bookstore in Cairo in 1887. Having bought the Alexandria daily *al-Mahrusa* with a partner the previous year, he moved the paper to the Egyptian capital and reinforced the business by adding to it a bookshop, al-Maktaba al-Misriyya.[38] The store's 28-page catalogue for 1887–88 presented an impressive range of goods and services: a rich selection of sophisticated writing tools; printed forms, contract drafts, and so forth; translation services in five languages; printing and binding; selling oil paintings by European artists—a side undertaking, as in the smaller shops; and, of course, books. The catalogue listed as many as 500 titles on sale, not including 'those yet to reach us by the end of this year and in the early part of next year from France, England, Italy, Turkey and Syria': school texts, novels, poetry, dictionaries, works in medicine, philosophy and history, language teaching guides, and more, in Arabic and in other languages. Books were offered for sale to individuals and in wholesale prices to booksellers. The shop also offered itself as a sales outlet for others wishing to sell books in any quantity and language; and

[36] *Al-Hilal*, 1 October 1896, pp. 119–120; 1 January 1897, p. 400; 1 March 1897, p. 488; and 1 April 1897, p. 595.

[37] *Ibid.*, 1 November 1897, p. 186; 15 January 1899, p. 248; 1 October 1901, p. 32; 15 February 1902, p. 324; and 1 May 1906, p. 504.

[38] Filib di Tarrazi, *Ta'rikh al-Sihafa al-'Arabiyya* (Beirut: al-Matba'a al-Adabiyya, 1913, 1914), Vol. 2, p. 8; and Vol. 3, p. 58. Zand's *maktaba* published a work by Nasif al-Yaziji to which Zand appended a *qaṣīda* he himself composed in praise of the book; *Fakihat al-Nudama' fi Murasalat al-Udaba'* (Cairo: al-Maktaba al-Misriyya, 1889). He also published at least two other books of his own authorship in the early 1890s.

pledged to find for customers any work printed abroad, thanks to its 'extensive international connections'.[39] Somewhat surprisingly, no adverts for the shop have been found in Egyptian newspapers of the time, nor is it listed among Cairo's 'most important bookstores' (*ashhar al-makātib*) in the city's business directory for 1889. It might have turned out to be short-lived for one reason or another, perhaps because its energetic owner chose to move on to another project.[40] Or, it might have been just a plan that never materialized. But even so, the impressive scope and variety of activities that the catalogue presented reflected a bold vision in book diffusion by someone who must have been affluent enough to afford it and sensed that the market was prepared for it.

We know more about the venture of another capable entrepreneur, the Lebanese Khalil Sarkis.[41] A printer, publisher, journalist and author, Sarkis played an important role in the Arab shift to print culture. He opened his first press and bookshop in 1868, in partnership with Butrus al-Bustani, then moved on to build a bigger project, al-Matbaʿa al-Adabiyya, in 1876, in Beirut. It comprised a large printing press, a book bindery, a letter casting shop, a stationery outlet, and a bookshop. The business was big enough from the start to permit the separation of the stationery wing from the other sections and moving it to a different location. For several decades thereafter Sarkis published hundreds of books, both Arab classics and contemporary works, in over a million copies, and issued the newspaper *Lisan al-Hal*, one of the region's most respected papers. Maktabat al-Matbaʿa al-Adabiyya sold the numerous titles produced in Sarkis's press (including some he himself had penned) and much else. Notices referring customers to the shop, in his and other newspapers, indicate that it was a prosperous business. Shops like those of Zaydan and Sarkis, and the one conceived by Zand, loomed large as diffusion conduits of the region's expanding publishing enterprise, overcasting the smaller shops that were popping up under their shade though evidently not preventing their rapid proliferation.

Trends of Development

Table 1 comprises all Arab booksellers and bookshops up to 1914 encountered in this study. Before glancing at its findings, a word of caution about its limitations is in order. The list is based on a close survey of most of the leading Arabic newspapers of the time, many marginal ones, and more. It is, however, a partial stock that may not reveal the full quantitative scope of the phenomenon. Book dealerships in unknown numbers operated in the region without leaving a trace, either because they were too humble to ever publicize themselves or, if they did advertise, because the media announcing their trade had not survived. We also ought to bear in mind that gaps in activity level between places may actually represent gaps in the sources: we know more about places with a periodical press that reported book dealings—Lebanon from the late 1850s, Egypt from the mid-1870s, other places after 1908—than we do about those that had none. Such gaps might have a distorting effect on the data available to us in this regard (although

[39] al-Maktaba al-Misriyya, *Qa'imat al-Kutub*.

[40] Asaf and Nasr, *Dalil Misr*, p. 189. I found no reference to the shop in *al-Ahram* of that time and in several other Egyptian newspapers. Another possibility is that Zand advertised his business mostly or solely in his own journal, *al-Mahrusa*, which was not available to me.

[41] See Ayalon, 'Private Publishing'.

Table 1. Booksellers of Printed Arabic Books, to 1914[a]

BUSINESS NAME	OWNER(S)	FIRST MENTION	LOCATION
Cairo			
Kutubkhāna	Government	1836	By al-Husayn mosque
al-Maktaba al-Khidiwiyya	Government	1870	Darb al-Jamamiz
	Hanna Saba	1877	
kutubī	Ahmad al-'Ishshi	1878	Muski
"	Hasan Kamil	1878	Khan al-Khalili
"	Khawaja Ibnir (Ebener)	1878	Azbakiyya
maḥall	Yusuf Jirjis Shayt	1880	Clot Bey St.
dukkān	Muhammad Khalifa al-Tarabishi	1881	Muski
Maktabat al-Taraqqi	Muhammad 'Ali Kamil	1883	'Abd al-'Aziz St.
maktaba	'Umar Qabil	1886	Imam Husayn St.
al-Maktaba al-Adabiyya		1886	
Maktabat al-Muqtataf	*al-Muqtataf* (journal)	1886	
Maktabat Hindiyya	Amin Hindiyya	1886	Muski
al-Maktaba al-Misriyya	'Aziz Zand	1887	Clot Bey St.
dukkān	'Ali Husni, Mahmud Sharaf	1888	By al-Azhar
Maktabat al-Watan		1888	Clot Bey St.
Maktabat al-Ahram	Murqus 'Atiyya	1889	Clot Bey St.
al-Maktaba al-Sharqiyya	Ibrahim Faris	1890	Clot Bey St.
al-Maktaba al-Inkliziyya	Father Kleine	1890	'Abd al-'Aziz St.
maktaba	Vincent Banasun	1890	al-Bawaki st.
maktaba	'Awad Hanna	1890	Kamil St.
maktaba	'Abd al-Wahid al-Tubi	1890	By al-Azhar
maktaba	Muhammad Salih	1890	"
maktaba	'Umar al-Khashshab	1890	"
maktaba	'Abd al-Khaliq al-Mahdi	1890	"
maktaba	Muhammad Sukkar	1890	"
maktaba	Mahmud al-Halabi	1890	"
maktaba	'Ali Husni Abu Zayid	1891	"
maktaba	Ahmad al-Babi al-Halabi	1890	Khan al-Khalili
l'Universe		1891	al-Bawaki st.
Maktabat Nizarat al-Ma'arif		1893	Darb al-Jamamiz
al-Maktaba al-Adabiyya		1893	Darb al-Jamamiz
Maktabat al-Hilal	*al-Hilal* (journal)	1896	Faggala
al-Maktaba al-Jadida		1899	Clot Bey St.
kutubī	Mustafa Fahmi	1901	by al-Azhar
Dar al-Kutub al-'Arabiyya	Mustafa al-Babi al-Halabi	1903	al-Sikka al-Jadida
al-Maktaba al-Azhariyya	Muhammad Sa'id al-Rifa'i	1903	al-Sikka al-Jadida
kutubī	Muhammad Maliji	1904	by al-Azhar
Maktabat al-Zahir	*al-Zahir* (newspaper)	1904	
Maktabat al-Islah	Ibrahim Fawzi	1904	
Maktabat al-Ma'arif	Najib Mitri	1908	Faggala
maktaba	'Abd al-Ghani Shihab	1909	
maḥall	Muhammad al-Sasi	1909	by governorate HQ
maḥall	Ahmad Abu al-Su'ud	1909	Khan al-Khalili
Maktabat al-Mu'ayyad	*al-Mu'ayyad* (newspaper)	1910	Muammad 'Ali St.
kutubī	Muhammad Imbabi al-Minyawi	1910	by al-Azhar
Maktabat al-Ta'lif		1910	'Abd al-'Aziz St.
maktaba	Muhammad 'Ali Sabih	1910	by al-Azhar

Continued

Table 1. *(continued)*

BUSINESS NAME	OWNER(S)	FIRST MENTION	LOCATION
Other Egyptian Towns			
Al-Maktaba al-Khadiwiyya	Jurji Gharzuzi	1868	Alexandria
Maktabat al-Amirikan		1879	Alexandria
Maktabat al-Mahrusa	Milad Asaf	1892	Alexandria
Maktabat al-Bursa		1892	Alexandria
maktaba	Mr. Dulier	1892	Alexandria
Al-Maktaba al-'Umumiyya	Mr. Scholer	1892	Alexandria
Al-Maktaba al-Swisariyya	Mr. Alberhohl	1892	Alexandria
Maktabat al-Kitab al-Muqaddas		1892	Alexandria
	'Abdallah 'Amira	1892	Mansura
maktaba	Antun Ghush	1893	Tanta
kutubī	Muhammad al-Darini	1897	Alexandria
kutubī	Sayyid 'Abd al-Latif	1899	Tanta
maktaba	Muhammad Sabri	1900	Suez
kutubī	Abu al-'Aynayn Muhammad	1904	al-Mahalla al-Kubra
Maktabat al-Mu'ayyad		1908	Alexandria
Beirut			
makhzin	Iliyas Fawaz	1859	Suq al-Sayyid
makhzin	Fathallah Tajir	1859	
dukkān	Edouard du Marc	1859	
maḥall	Fischel Rosenzweig	1859	by Khan Bayhum
	'Alwan effendi	1859	Suq al-'Attarin
	'Arab and Milha	1859	by Bab al-Saraya
	As'ad al-Jamil	1860	Burj al-Kashash
kutubī	Jirjis al-Jahil	1860	
dukkān	Habib al-Jalakh	1863	
	Jirjis Shahin	1865	Burj al-Kashshaf
al-Maktaba al-Faransawiyya	Charles Béziès	1865	
	Khalil Rubir	1866	Burj al-Kashash
kutubī	Salim Nasr	1868	
makhzin	Yusuf 'Abd al-Nur	1868	
maktab of Matba'at al-Ma'arif	Khalil Sarkis, Butrus Bustani	1868	
al-Maktaba al-Jami'a	Khalil & Amin al-Khuri	1877	Suq al-Hamidiyya
Maktabat al-Matba'a al-Adabiyya	Khalil Sarkis/Salim Nasr	1878	Suq al-Hamidiyya
	Fathallah As'ad Jawish	1878	
al-Maktaba al-'Umumiyya	Ibrahim Sadir	1879	
Maktabat al-Mursalin al-Amirikaniyyin	(Protestant mission)	1879	
al-Maktaba al-Suriyya	Nakhla Qalfaz	1880	Suq Rijal al-Arba'in
al-Maktaba al-Wataniyya	Lutfallah Zahhar, Nakhla Fawaz	1881	Suq Abi al-Nasr
Al-Maktaba al-Suriyya	(Jirjis) Nawfal & Tarrad	1882	al-Manshiyya square
Maktabat al-Funun	jam'iyat al-funun	1882	Suq al-Qawafi
Maktaba	As'ad al-Khashaf	1883	
al-Maktaba al-Sharqiyya	Khalil & Nakhla Fawaz	1883	Suq Abi al-Nasr

Table 1. *(continued)*

BUSINESS NAME	OWNER(S)	FIRST MENTION	LOCATION
	Sulayman Khuri Khayyat	1890	Suq al-Bazarkan
maktaba	'Issa 'Issu	1890	by Maronite patriarch-ate
Maktabat al-Ma'arif	Musa Sufayr	1892	
Maktabat al-Madaris	Yusuf Sufayr	1893	
maktaba	Mikha'il Rahma	1894	al-Hamidiyya square
al-Maktaba al-'Uthmaniyya	Misbah al-Lababidi	1895	Bab al-Saraya
al-Maktaba al-Unsiyya		1895	
al-Maktaba al-Suriyya	'Abduh Yani	1898	
al-Maktaba al-Ahliyya	Muhammad Jamal	1900	al-Shari' al-Jadid
al-Maktaba al-Kuliyya	Nakhla Qalfaz, Salim May-dani	1901	Suq al-Hamidiyya
Al-Maktaba al-Hamidiyya		1902	
Maktabat al-Adab	Amin al-Khuri	1911	
maktaba	Salim Bek	1913	
maktaba	Rizqallah Sarkis	1914	
Other Towns in the Region			
	Dimitri Hamawi	1859	Damascus
	Shukrallah Nasrallah Khuri	1859	Aleppo
	'Issa al-Hamawi	1870	Jaffa
kutubī	Abdallah al-Nahari	1870	Mecca
	Musa bin 'Abdallah	1876	Jaffa
maḥall	Iskandar Qabawat	1889	Damascus
al-Maktaba al-'Arabiyya	Nu'man al-A'zami	1894	Baghdad
al-Maktaba al-Lubnaniyya	Jurji Mar'i	1898	Batrun
	Muhammad al-Taji	1900	Jaffa
maktaba	Salih al-Khafash	1900	Nablus
	Muhammad Banshi	1901	Ladhiqiyya
	Muhammad al-Masri	1901	Jaffa
	'Ali Abu Taha	1901	Jaffa
al-Maktaba al-Hashimiyya	Muhammad Hashim	1902	Damascus
al-Maktaba al-Rifa'iyya	'Abdallah al-Rifa'i	1902	Tripoli
al-Maktaba al-Jami'a		1909	Damascus
Maktabat Filastin al-'Ilmiyya	Bulus & Wadi' Sa'id	1910	Jerusalem
al-Maktaba al-'Asriyya	Jamil Bakhkhash	1910	Baalbek
	Rashid al-Tibi	1911	Jaffa
	Shakir al-Shakir	1911	Jaffa
Maktabat al-'Irfan	Ahmad 'Arif al-Zayn	1911	Sidon
	Yusuf Da'ud	1911	Damascus
	Muhammad 'Umar Yamut	1913	Aleppo
maḥall	Mitri Tarrazi	1913	Jerusalem
	Hanna Jubran	1913	Jaffa
Maktabat 'Unwan al-Najah	Muhammad Sa'id Na'san	1913	Hamah
al-Maktaba al-'Umumiyya		1913	Jaffa
kutubī	Sayyid 'Abd al-Hamid	1913	Karbala'
maktaba	Yusuf Faris Asaf	1914	Haifa

[a] The list is based on a search of contemporary Arabic sources. The data on individual entries is often drawn from multiple sources, and adding references to them in the table would have made it too cumbersome. A full record of references is retained by the author.

we may sensibly assume that where no press existed, book circulation too was limited).[42] Even for those shops the sources mention, we are seldom informed of their lifespan, the range of their trade, or their clientele, let alone their actual social and cultural impact. What such a compilation of extant data provides is, more loosely, a sense of general scale of the broader trends and their main centres of gravity. These are quite clearly revealed in the table despite its inevitable shortcomings.

The list includes individuals identified as booksellers (*kutubī*, *ṣaḥḥāf*), as well as a few shop owners—especially in the earlier years—who usually traded with other goods but were reported to sell books occasionally, thereby sharing in the book diffusion endeavour, however briefly. Of the latter, I have entered only those whose names appeared on at least two different occasions. The table lists businesses identified as *maktaba* and known to have engaged in book vending, but not those *maktaba*s whose only recorded activity was publishing (as indicated on the title-pages of items they issued). As we have seen, the distinction between these last two types was often blurred, and it is possible that *maktaba*s known to us only from their published products also engaged in selling. That said, we may now attempt to mark out some of the trends the table illustrates.

The most striking phenomenon is, of course, the rapid expansion of the trade over the studied period. As against an assumed handful of book dealers in the region before printing, a total of 132 different traders in printed products have been recorded for the years 1859–1914. Of these, 14 were first encountered in the 1870s, 18 in the 1880s, 37 in the 1890s and 44 in later years, denoting a momentum of continuous growth. These businesses represented a gamut of sizes and impact. Many were unpretentious and short-lived; but quite a few were long-lasting ventures, moving on with their business from one decade to the next and displaying the vigour that marked Arabic book diffusion as a whole. New shops were simultaneously coming into being and joining those already in operation. The significance of this unmistakable trend is self-evident: it reflected the commensurate increase in Arab publishing and in public demand for its products, both beginning with remarkable verve shortly after the introduction of printing.

Another development the list mirrors is the shifting focal points of activity during the period. Lebanon was early to start, playing a pioneering role not only in book-selling but also in the region's history of printing and publishing, as we have seen. No fewer than 15 sellers had been traced in Beirut during the third quarter of the nineteenth century, as against one or two in any other place including Cairo and Alexandria. This spirited beginning resulted mostly from individual initiative of a kind that was then still in the future for Egypt, let alone the other places. During the subsequent, last quarter of the century, *maktaba*s multiplied rapidly in both Lebanon and Egypt: 20 new shops were counted in Beirut, as many as 32 in Cairo (25 of them by 1890), and 12 in Alexandria and other Egyptian towns. Egypt had now become a busier book-trade centre than Lebanon, a fact consonant with its emerging as leader in printing, publishing and journalism toward the end of the century. The massive emigration of educated Lebanese to Cairo and Alexandria

[42] A notable instance appears in the table's last section ('Other Towns in the Region'), where Jaffa has more booksellers than any town prior to 1908. This reflects the availability of a source listing bequest records of men from there who had 'engaged in bookselling', but not necessarily Jaffa's primacy over other places in that respect; see Muhammad al-Tarawna, *Qada Yafa fi al-'Ahd al-'Uthmani* (Amman: Wizarat al-Thaqafa, 2000), p. 498. After 1908, when a lively periodical press emerged throughout the region, such distortions became fewer.

was largely responsible for that change, which turned Egypt into the permanent capital of Arabic book-making. The list also exhibits the scarcity, especially prior to 1900, of such shops in other towns of the region, where printing and publishing were equally limited then. Activity there began to accelerate and spread out after the turn of the century and especially after 1908, following the Young Turk Revolution. With the outburst of printing in the towns of the Fertile Crescent from Jerusalem to Baghdad, bookshops briskly popped up where previously there had been only a few of them, or none. Twenty-six book outlets that opened from 1908 to 1914 have been traced, some of them alongside older businesses, others in places where they may have been the first ever, such as those in Hamah, Ladhiqiyya, Haifa, Sidon, and Baalbek.

Finally, spatial changes in urban bookshop distribution are also revealed by this aggregate list. Traditionally, booksellers had operated in and around town market areas, the beating heart of commercial activity. In Beirut, it was in allies of the *sūq* in the walled old city to the east of the Sarāyā; in Cairo, around Azbakiyya, Muski, Khan al-Khalili and al-Azhar. Elsewhere in the region too, bookshops were similarly located in vicinities of busy trade (in Istanbul they were concentrated near the Grand Bazaar). During the period explored here, these places continued to function as prime business centres and many of the new bookshops opened in them. But shops also appeared in newer or refashioned parts of the expanding cities, a trend most conspicuously evident in Cairo. Here new bookshops opened in areas built up during the last quarter of the century: Clot Bey Boulevard, 'Abd al-'Aziz street (north and south of Azbakiyya, respectively), and Fajjala further north—the emerging locus of book printing, publishing and selling. With printed books and journals on open display and eye-catching boards announcing their trade, such *maktaba*s projected a sense of novelty and modernity in these recently built sections.

Diffusion across the Region

A phenomenon of major significance was the circulation of printed books and journals across provincial boundaries. From the onset of Arabic publishing, items printed in one town were sold in many others near and far, and Arab places with little or no printing consumed products published elsewhere. The practice continued the time-honoured tradition of manuscripts travelling from one end of the Arabic-speaking lands to the other. Already during the first half of the nineteenth century, government-printed books were sent from Egypt to Syria and Palestine under the reign of Ibrahim bin Muhammad 'Ali, in response to a demand.[43] After mid-century, books and journals appearing in the two important printing centres and in the Ottoman capital came to be sold in towns all over the region.

As we have seen, Beirut shops carried books printed in Cairo and Istanbul as early as the 1850s, and by the 1860s they also featured items printed in

[43] A[bdul] L[atif] Tibawi, *American Interests in Syria 1800–1901* (Oxford: Clarendon Press, 1966), pp. 69–71. Tibawi traced some 1600 copies of printed works ordered from Egypt by educated people in Aleppo, Damascus, Ladhiqiyya, Tripoli, Jaffa and Gaza.

Damascus.[44] Bookshops in Cairo and Alexandria sold Beirut products from the late 1860s onward.[45] And book dealers in other towns in the region—in Damascus, Aleppo, Hamah, Tripoli, Jaffa, Tunis, and elsewhere—carried the products of Egypt and Lebanon long before printing machines were brought to them. Books and journals were not only sold away from their place of origin, they were also advertised away from their place of vending: a Beirut paper would announce the sale of a book in an Istanbul shop; a book available in Beirut would be publicized in Tunis; and an Istanbul paper would promote a volume sold in Alexandria.[46] Typical book adverts in newspapers and journals (themselves reaching far beyond their places of publication) referred potential buyers to shops in various towns all over the region. Thus, an elegant notice in rhymed prose on the front page of *al-Jawai'b*, an Istanbul weekly newspaper, advertised a work printed in Beirut and offered for sale in a *maktaba* in Alexandria.[47] And a Beirut daily promoted a work by a Damascus author, printed in Beirut, available in bookshops in Istanbul, Damascus, Tripoli and Ladhiqiyya, and composed in response to a work published earlier in Cairo.[48]

Arabic-speaking societies, or rather their reading segments, thus formed one pool of written and printed exchanges. This reality had more to it than the sale and promotion of items far from their home base. An intellectual discourse across the region was underway already before the advent of printing, as reflected, for example, in the fact that the 'Syrian Society' of science and literature (Beirut, 1847) had, alongside its local affiliates, also 'adjunct members' *(a'ḍā' murāsilīn)* from Damascus, Tripoli, Sidon, and other places.[49] Once printing emerged, this discourse expanded. Egyptian journals reviewed books published all over the region—most famously *al-Muqtataf* and *al-Hilal*, which featured regular book-review sections—and routinely announced the appearance of new Arabic periodicals everywhere. Books published through the common arrangement of prior subscription (designed to raise funds from potential customers prior to production) were offered to, and underwritten by, prospective patrons in other Arab provinces.[50] Newspapers and journals had their agent networks spread throughout the area. And reader letters to journal editors, responding to ideas they had read in the journal and to each other, likewise came in a vivid stream from Marrakesh to Baghdad.[51]

Bookshops selling titles printed in other Arab provinces were thus just one facet of the trans-regional exchanges in print. Even in places where publishing was still in the future, printed items were available to anyone able to read and capable of buying them. The gulf between Beirut, Cairo and Istanbul where printing took place, on one hand, and other towns in the region where it had yet to emerge, on

44 For example, *Hadiqat al-Akhbar*, 29 February 1866, p. 4.

45 For example, *al-Jawa'ib*, 21 April 1868, p. 1; and 7 March 1877, p. 4; *al-Muqtataf*, February 1880, back cover; *al-Ahram*, 23 June 1881, p. 4; and al-Maktaba al-Misriyya, *Qa'imat al-Kutub*, passim.

46 *Hadiqat al-Akhbar*, 8 May 1859, p. 4; *al-Ra'id al-Tunisi*, 29 Ramadan 1280 [1863], p. 3; and *al-Jawa'ib*, 20 October 1868, p. 4; and 7 March 1877, p. 4.

47 *al-Jawa'ib*, 21 April 1868, p. 1.

48 *Fasl al-Khitab aw Taflis Iblis* (a response to Qasim Amin's *Tahrir al-Mar'a*); *Lisan al-Hal*, 15 April 1901, p. 1.

49 *Al-Jam'iyya al-Suriyya li-l-'Ulum wa-l-Funun 1847–1852* (Beirut: Dar al-Hamra', 1990), pp. 17–19; and Jurji Zaydan, *Ta'rikh Adab al-Lugha al-'Arabiyya*, Vol. 4 (Cairo: al-Hay'a al-Misriyya al-'Amma li-l-Kitab, 1957), pp. 428ff.

50 For example, *Lisan al-Hal*, 7 October 1901, p. 4.

51 For further discussion of these aspects, see Ami Ayalon, 'Modern Texts and Their Readers in Late Ottoman Palestine', *Middle Eastern Studies*, 38 (October 2002), pp. 17–40.

the other, was thus apparently narrower than one would tend to assume if unaware of these exchanges. An educated townsman in Syria or Palestine, where printing was not yet extant but newspaper-agents and modest bookshops were already in place in the late nineteenth century, could avail himself of Arabic books and periodicals published faraway and become a part of the regional discourse. An illuminating instance of such access to printed products is offered by the Khalidi book collection in Jerusalem, a town that would have its own debut in printing and publishing (other than missionary endeavours) only in the last decade of the nineteenth century: publicly exposed in 1900, this collection contained not only numerous precious manuscripts but also hundreds of printed books and journal volumes from Lebanon, Egypt and beyond, accumulated for many decades by the intellectually inquisitive Khalidis.[52]

Countryside Bookselling

Bookshops, like most other features of book circulation, were a predominantly urban phenomenon. Their absence from villages, in the Middle East as elsewhere, requires no more explication than the absence from there of shops selling any other goods. It was even more obvious during the opening phase of the shift from oral modes of communication to mass literacy, a shift that began in cities. All of this, of course, does not mean that people in rural areas were not exposed to written texts. Rather, both prior to and following the arrival of printing books reached the countryside, typically works of spiritual guidance and religious inspiration, and epic stories of popular heroes. They were read there, mostly collectively, as a prime mode of pastime.[53] Still, village people who could read and wished to obtain books had to get them from sellers in the town. Bookshops of the kinds discussed above would make little sense if opened in a village.

However, we do hear of booksellers who used to come periodically with their merchandise to the countryside, trade in it and even managed to make a living out of it. The evidence on that is unsurprisingly scarce, nor are the sources that serve us in exploring the urban book trade of much avail here. Yet here and there, in memoirs and autobiographies, the practice is mentioned, sometimes in a detailed way, and the extant testimonies seem to suggest that it was not limited to just a few exceptional cases. One such informant is none other than the celebrated Egyptian writer Taha Husayn (1889–1973), who tells us in his autobiography about reading habits in rural Upper Egypt of the late nineteenth century. During his childhood in the village of 'Izbat al-Kilu near Mughagha (Minya province), he recalled, 'there were booksellers (*bā'at al-kutub*) who used to travel through villages and towns with an assorted stock of books (*asfār*)', including tales of saints, stories from the Islamic legacy, religious preaching tracts, poetry, popular epics and other stories. The people, many of them youths, 'would buy these books and devour them completely. Their brains were shaped by their contents just as their bodies were shaped by what they ate and drank'. There was a demand for books, Husayn

[52] Rashid Khalidi, *Palestinian Identity* (New York: Columbia University Press, 1997), pp. 43ff.

[53] See, for example, Muhammad Rafiq Tamimi and Muhammad Bahjat, *Wilayat Bayrut*, Vol. 1 (Beirut: Matba'at al-Iqbal, 1335 [1917]), pp. 98–100; and Sami al-Sulh, *Mudhakkirat Sami Bey al-Sulh 1890–1960*, Vol. 1 (Beirut: Maktabat al-Fikr al-'Arabi, 1960), pp. 13–14.

related, and the variety presented by the roving sellers properly fit the beliefs and world view of the villagers.[54]

A more detailed description is offered by Taha Husayn's compatriot, the religious thinker Sayyid Qutb (1903–1966), who grew up in the village of Musha (Asyut province). About the same time, or perhaps a decade later, a book peddler popularly known as Uncle Salih (*al-'ām ṣāliḥ*) used to come to the village for some three-to-four days every year, shouldering a sack full of books. 'He would set himself in the village small marketplace, sit crossed-legged on the sack after having emptied it, and spread the books for sale, some twenty or thirty of them, in front of him in rows according to their value or subject'. Among them were works of prose and poetry, classics such as the 'Thousand and One Nights' and hero epics, as well as, curiously, detective books such as Sherlock Holmes and Sinclair—a mark of the new times. These books sold for the cost of one millieme-to-two-qurush each.[55] The few days of Uncle Salih's stay in the villages were the happiest time of the year for the author, who, along with some other youngsters his age, was among the peddler's best customers. 'They would purchase from him what their budget allowed. Sometimes, for a fee of one millieme per book, they would [also] read other books, on condition that such borrowing was "local," namely, on the spot beside Uncle Salih'. The wandering dealer thus fulfilled the dual role of bookseller and book-lender for several days a year. We may assume that on other days he would visit more villages, and would come to the provincial city once in a while to replenish his stock.[56]

How widespread this practice was remains to be explored. But there can be little doubt that it obtained in other places as well. During the period under discussion, demand for books in rural areas hardly ever justified more than the periodic visits of external book dealers, who would bring in the goods fitting the modest number of customers, their limited buying power and their tastes. The countryside would remain for a long time thereafter at the margins of the developments which the introduction of printing spawned. But if marginal, it certainly was within the circle that was exposed to these developments.

Conclusion

The printing machines that set rolling in the Arab provinces and accelerated production from the 1850s onward rendered the old book diffusion conduits insufficient. Within one generation, the region witnessed a surge of bookshops small and big, geared to address the new needs. The institution that grew out of the old book dealership, the *maktaba*, resembled its predecessor in purpose and often in size but only remotely in the nature of its merchandise or the pace of vending. Sellers of the new type engaged in various other ventures of book diffusion, such as offering lending and browsing services. More significantly, many of them entered book production, and some built themselves as full-fledged publishers, with enterprises that spanned everything from tracing marketable manuscripts, through

[54] Taha Husayn, *al-Ayyam*, Vol. 1 (Cairo: Dar al-Ma'arif, 1960), pp. 97–100.

[55] In turn-of-the-century Egypt, one qurush would suffice to feed an adult for one day. A millieme equalled one-tenth of a qurush.

[56] Sayyid Qutb, *Tifl min al-Qarya, Hayat Sayyid Qutb bi-Qalamihi* (Beirut: Dar al-Hikma, 196?), pp. 118–122. There are more illuminating details on the culture of books and reading habits in the village later on in the chapter. I am grateful to Liran Yadgar for alerting me to this text.

printing them, to selling them in their shops. Others subsisted, more humbly, on retailing books, journals and newspapers along with sundry other goods. On the whole it was a highly dynamic and constantly expanding field, which by the end of the nineteenth century had reached an unprecedented scope in the Middle East. From the scanty manuscript dealer in old markets to the scores of richly furnished bookstores in modern urban quarters, the shift was striking; occurring within a few decades, it was quite dramatic.

Bookselling and its rapid expansion represented one facet of the bigger change entailed by Arab society's entry into the age of printing. Bookshops were among the many interdependent constituents of that wider cultural process, along with printing presses and newspaper peddlers, reading clubs and educational institutions, literary societies and journal agents. To assess the broad historic change credibly, we would obviously need to explore other aspects of it just as closely, from the quantitative scope of publishing, through the contents and genres of the printed output, to the scope and modes of consumption. The findings presented here enlighten us only about this modest section of the bigger scene. Still, being obviously indicative of the state of production and consumption, supply and demand, the energetic development of Arab book trade seems to suggest that the wide process spawned by the introduction of Gutenberg's invention into the Middle East was equally energetic and dynamic. It began late; but once it did, it proceeded with remarkable zeal and vigour.

Acknowledgements

Research for this study was supported by the Israel Science Foundation (Grant No. 473/05), which the author acknowledges with gratitude. The author is also grateful to the two anonymous *British Journal of Middle Eastern Studies* reviewers for their most helpful comments.

[17]

On the Question of Lithography

BRINKLEY MESSICK

While it is a well-known and extremely interesting historical fact, the late acceptance of print technology in the Muslim world has resisted adequate explanation.[1] In an important recent article, Robinson (1993:233) states that "current scholarship is unsure about why Muslims rejected printing for so long—indeed, it is a problem that seems not to have been seriously studied." Earlier on, Carter (1943) centered attention on the diffuse character of "Islam" as constituting a "barrier" to the new technology.

Robinson's analysis, based primarily on South Asian perspectives (especially Lucknow), examines both the old person-to-person mode of knowledge transmission and the close link, in the subcontinent, between Islamic revival and the utilization of the print medium. While Robinson's approach to the Muslim reception of print through consideration of issues of authoritative knowledge transmission is one that I generally endorse, I also have two specific criticisms. The first is that Robinson presents the old Muslim intellectual tradition as a unitary phenomenon and the person-to-person model as "the method of transmission not just of formal religious knowledge, but of all knowledge" (1993:239). In contrast, I have argued (Messick 1993:28,90–1,252), in connection with the different historical setting of Yemen, that a crucial distinction must be made between the authority structures of the core academic disciplines, including law and hadith, in which texts are treated in the person-to-person, "oral," or recitational-memorized paradigm of the Quran, and a large surround of other disciplines, such as

---

1 The primary sources on the question remain the formal arguments against its use, which may be consulted in the Ottoman edicts of 1485 and 1515 (E.I.2, Art. "Matba`a," p. 795).

medicine, history, etc., which are not so modeled. The initial reception of print in 1727 in the Ottoman Empire was characterized by a distinction along these lines, specifically forbidding the printing of the Quran and the texts of the core disciplines.

My second criticism concerns Robinson's apparent view that today the old person-to-person mode of authoritative knowledge transmission, "is still the method" (1993:235), and also that "print and print culture have achieved only a limited penetration of Muslim societies" (1993:250). For the central Middle East and North Africa, at least, I would argue otherwise, namely, that the old mode of intellectual transmission and its several contexts are gone, despite some contemporary practices—such as the memorization techiques of the Tabligh-i Jamaat mentioned by Robinson—which are really "new" phenomena. I think Robinson may confuse the extent of literacy, which is relatively low in some places, with the extent of print penetration. I generally agree with Dale Eickelman, who recently has documented the rapid advance of mass higher education in the Middle East (1992), and who, in an article on religion, speaks of the present as the era of "print Islam" (1989:17).

In the chapter on "Print Culture" in my book *The Calligraphic State* (1993), I examined aspects of the specific historical circumstances surrounding the advent of the printing press in the Yemeni highlands, beginning in the late 19th century. There I referred to Carsten Niebuhr[2] as a source on local antecedents, in connection with his recording of the presence, in the Yemen of the 1760s, of printed Arabic books from European presses. In a footnote, I cited his comment on this finding, which I now would like to use as a point of departure. Although such printed works were known to Yemenis of that era, Niebuhr reports that they were held in low

2 This paper originally was presented at the seminar organized by M. Harbsmeier, J. Skovgaard Peterson, and J. Baek Simonsen of The Carsten Neibuhr Institute of Near Eastern Studies. I want to express my appreciation to the organizers and to the institution for inviting me to participate in such a stimulating seminar. My research in Yemen has been supported over the years by grants from the Social Science Research Council and from Fulbright.

Niebuhr's account of his travels in Arabia remains a crucial source for the eighteenth century history of places such as Yemen, where he is well-remembered. In the town of Ibb, my general good fortune was contrasted with recollections of Niebuhr's many difficulties, including the fact that one of his colleagues died from an illness in the next town up the road on the way to the capital.

esteem. This he explained as follows: "The Arabians value chiefly a species of elegance, which consists in their manner of joining the letters, the want of which makes themselves dislike the style in which Arabic books are printed in Europe" (1792 ii:261). Niebuhr's associations with matters of "elegance" and "style" point in the direction of culturally-specific forms of writing, a direction that I want to pursue further.

A perspective close to Niebuhr's view is one of several rationales advanced to explain a separate, but related phenomenon which is part of the larger question of the Muslim reception of print technology. This phenomenon is the asserted Muslim preference, much later—in the nineteenth century—after the ban on Muslim printing in Arabic characters had been revoked, for lithography, a specialized technical process for printing that was discovered about three hundred and fifty years after Gutenberg's invention of moveable type. Lithography, from the Greek *lithos,* or stone, was discovered in the last years of the eighteenth century by Alois Senefelder, who initially employed limestone for his plate. Accordingly, the mechanical printing machine of this new type, available by the second half of the following century, was known in the Middle East and North Africa as the "stone press," *(matba`a al-hajar).*

Since the appearance in 1983 of Benedict Anderson's influential book, *Imagined Communities,* print, and especially the relationship "print-capitalism," has figured centrally in discussions of social-cultural change, the rise of literate genres such as the novel and nation-conceptualizing in the non-western world. Although sensitive to historically specific settings, Anderson's argument also stresses the "modular" (1991:4) qualities of the new forms associated with the birth of nation states in the colonial and post-colonial world. Key technology though it is, print is undifferentiated for Anderson, and we learn little about any local differences in reception.

Preference for lithography

Based upon an earlier article by Demeerseman (1953; see also 1954, 1956), the recent *Encyclopedia of Islam* entry "*matba`a,*" or printing (Oman 1989:795), maintains there are three basic reasons for the Arab Muslim preference for lithography. One concerns the technical versatility of the lithographic process. Lithography perhaps is best known in the West for the reproduction of "prints," ranging from the reproductions of Currier & Ives to other types of engravings and works of art, and it is in this role that it is discussed by Walter Benjamin (1968:219) in his seminal piece, "The Work of Art in the Age of Mechanical Reproduction." The second reason adduced is in fact termed "artistic," but it recalls Niebuhr's view in stating that lithography "lends itself remarkably well to the reproduction of writing." To this a "cultural reason" is offered as a "corollary," namely, that "lithography causes no problem to the reader who is accustomed only to the manuscript style adopted for the writing-tablets of the Qur'an school." It is on this cultural area that I intend to concentrate shortly. A third reason centers on socio-economic issues, specifically the existence of tens of thousands of hand-copyists. "In the East, the profession of copyist was highly developed, giving prestige and prosperity to a large section of the urban working class." This point is not at all specific to lithography, however, since it concerns instead the purported general resistance on the part of the scribal "lobby" to competition from any form of mechanical printing (cf. Fischer and Abedi 1990: 93n).[3] It is asserted, finally, that beyond these three reasons for the preference for lithography, "further reasons are moral, doctrinal and political" and, we are told, "these may be easily imagined."

According to the detailed history of the printing press in the central Middle East by Sabat (1966), however, when this technology began to be taken up in earnest by Muslim populations, dating from around the mid-nineteenth century, both moveable type and lithography were well-represented. Sabat follows the many local changes in equipment and makes it clear that the coming of printing machines was not a single event, but a process of ongoing local responses to a series of technical innovations. In this usage of both technologies, however, the central Middle East, including the heartland of the old Ottoman Empire, had a history different from other regions. The Indian subcontinent may represent an extreme case of the preference for lithography. Robinson (1993:239–40) states that "moveable type for Islamic cursive scripts was not widely used in South Asia until the twentieth century, and to this day has not succeeded completely in displacing lithography." According to Khalid (1994), roughly the same was true of Central Asia. In his chapter on "Printed Books," Pedersen (1984: 139) describes lithography as "particularly favored in Persia." North Africa also was devoted to lithography, as Demeerseman (1953) demonstrated for the

3 Robinson (1993:233) begins a refutation of this argument.

case of Tunisia. In Morocco the "stone press" of turn-of-the-century Fes was the famous source of that country's first locally printed works (Ayache 1964; Ben Cheneb and Levi-Provencale 1922).

Printed matters

I want to turn now to examples to bring out some technical differences between typography and lithography. My first example is a well-known, rhymed Shafi`i *fiqh* text, the *Matn al-Zubad,* by Ahmad Ibn Raslan (also known as al-Ramli), who died in 1440 C.E. This text was commonly studied in Yemen, in the Shafi`i districts of "Lower Yemen," and elsewhere, up through the 1950s and occasionally thereafter. I have photographed a manuscript version in which the poetry of the main text is complemented by a margin containing some irregularly placed, sometimes upside down, always triangularly shaped, bits of gloss and commentary. This handwritten text is one of several such texts collected together in a local scholar's study book.

I also have three printed editions from Cairo (the Shafi`i school is well-represented in Egypt). The first is from Bulaq in 1868 (third printing), in which the main text is enclosed in a rectangular space and surrounded on three sides by a margin completely filled in with commentary, set in straight lines, top to bottom. This edition was printed on a moveable type press, as was the third, issued in 1953 by Dar al-`Ahd al-Jadid. The second, however, which dates from 1884, is a lithograph. Here the poetry of the main text again is enclosed in a ruled box, but in the margins pieces of commentary are placed irregularly, at differing angles and occupying different amounts of the available margin space from page to page, as in the manuscript. Also as in a manuscript, the the word (known as the catchword) that will appear as the lead word of the text continuing on the next (left) page is placed in the lower left corner of each right hand page.[4] At the end of the lithograph text, with the date, is the statement, "Completed, with praise to God and with His help, at the press of its writer...", an individual who is named. The formulation, "at the press of its writer," underscores the key fact that lithography preserves something of the written character of a manuscript while also making possible large scale reproduction.

4 Both this 1884 lithograph and the 1953 moveable type edition are vowelled.

To my knowledge, the only Yemeni (and Lebanese) edition of the text by Ibn Raslan was published in 1988, and in moveable type, embedded in a commentary known as the *Fath al-Mannan, Sharh Zubad Ibn Raslan* (al-Mufti 1988) by a nineteenth century scholar from the town of Ibb.[5] After the title page and the page containing the publishing information, the third page of the book is a facsimile of the manuscript title page, giving the author's name and the just mentioned title of the commentary work.[6]

According to the four printed editions at my disposal, then, it is clear that the basic text in question was produced under both technical formats, moveable type and lithograph, and that the latter books retain some manuscript-like features. It would take information I do not have, however, about such important matters as comparative press runs, costs, marketing, circulation, and readership to develop this comparison further.

My second example also is a legal text, an *usul al-fiqh* manual, *Matn al-Kafil,* by Muhammad bin Yahya Bahran, a work well-known in the Zaydi school circles in Yemen.[7] The most recent edition was printed in San`a' (by Dar al-Turath al-Yamani), in 1991. It is a "lithograph," involving a reproduction of handwriting, but the technology of this modern offset press is many generations distant from the namesake, the old "stone press." The text, which nearly fills the page, is enclosed in ruled lines. There is no commentary or other marginalia, but the old device of catchwords that appear in the lower left corner of each recto page is found. In the space following the end of the handwritten-printed text is the following statement:

> With praise to God, the transcription *[naql]* of *Matn al-Kafil* was completed on the date ... in the handwriting *[khatt]* of ..., may God forgive him, from an authoritative copy *[nuskha mu`tamada]* in the handwriting and checking *[dabt]* of ..., may God forgive him and his parents, and it has been compared with a number of copies and commentaries, and God is the bringer of good fortune.

5 Muhammad bin `Ali bin Muhsin, also known in Ibb as al-Mufti. Biographical details are provided in the introduction by the editor, al-Hibshi.

6 Below this is more writing which turns out to be a legal document, dated 1897, in which a man acknowledges that he has repudiated his wife and then has this *talaq* witnessed.

7 Although evidently worthy of a new print edition, the *Matn al-Kafil,* is no longer the curriculum mainstay that it once was in local madrasas. The attention of Yemeni readers interested in shari`a law now ranges far beyond the local Zaydi (or Shafi`i) school texts to classics that span of the range of schools.

According to this statement, this contemporary printed edition of the text relies on the characteristic manuscript world technique of collation *(muqabala),* of original *(asl)* to copy, a process of comparison and checking whereby the copy may take on the authority of the original (see Messick 1993:29–30,240). In this sort of printed text two steps of reproduction are involved: the original manuscript text initially is manually copied and then this version is mechanically copied through photo-imaging in the automated technology of offset lithography. Some other works recently published in Yemen omit this intermediate stage of hand copying for eventual printing, and instead directly photo-reproduce the old manuscripts themselves in facsimile editions. I do not know why a lithographic reproduction of handwriting was chosen over the widely available type medium for this paticular 1991 edition, except perhaps to reassert the "traditional" form of the textual heritage, the *turath.*

Correctors

An earlier Yemeni edition of this same text *(Matn al-Kafil)* was printed with moveable type under the auspices of the pre-1962 Revolution imamic state. The first printing machine had been introduced into Yemen by the Ottomans in 1877 (Sabat 1966:327) and by the time the Italian Orientalist Ettore Rossi (1938) visited Yemen and examined publishing activity there, this "rudimentary" typographic press was located in the imam's palace and was still active. The Ottomans had used this moveable type machine to publish a provincial newspaper; after the end of the empire, the same equipment served the imam to print a newspaper and other government publications, including a few books. In this era the country's only other printing machine, located at the Ministry of Education and characterized by Rossi as having "few characters," was used, he notes, to print diplomas, certificates and some booklets.[8] In the early period of Yemeni printing there was no lithography.

In 1928, the press at the imam's palace produced the *Matn al-Kafil* em-

8 An example of the Ministry of Education (Ma`arif) output is the seventy-eight page *Sirat al-`Arifin,* by al-Shammahi (1356 H./ 1937), a commentary on Imam Yahya's legal opinions.

bedded in a well-known commentary known as *al-Kashif*.[9] Two statements added at the end of the publication provide information about the circumstances of its printing. The first of these, a "notice" which appears as the very last lines of the edition, following a brief biography of the commentator, addresses both the character of the source manuscript and the marked deficiencies of the available technology, the latter understandable after nearly a half century of Ottoman use. The initial comment about the manuscript language underscores how the advent of print technology began to transform the ways manuscript works would be read.

> There are to be found an expression *(lafz)* or two which is ungrammatical *(malhuna)*, not following the rule of Arabic. Or there also will be found a letter without a dot or with part [of it] not appearing, and this is due to the [fact that] the ink did not reach the letter, as occurs in many publications. Or a letter without a *hamza* when it should have a hamza, and this is due to the nonavailability of this letter. Or the absence of some dots or parts of letters is to be excused in view of the age of the type. All of this will not be concealed to one of good taste.

The second statement, located two pages earlier, before the *fihrist,* or table of contents, explains how the text came to be printed:

> Since this book is an introduction to the art of *usul [al-fiqh]*, and is among the works people are interested in due to its reputation for quality, the generality of its benefit, and the asceticism of its author, the Commander of the Faithful ... ordered its publication.

The statement continues, commenting further on problems in the transition to print, that the imam also ordered

> the correction of shortcomings in some copies of the book regarding insignificant words in a number of expressions. This is rare, and the reader should not think, if he encounters a word or words at variance with some

9 By Ahmad bin Muhammad bin Luqman bin Ahmad bin Shams al-Din bin al-Imam al-Mahdi li-Din Allah Ahmad bin Yahya bin al-Murtada. I have a copy of this book, and it is mentioned in Rossi (1938:572).

> handwritten copies, that this is an instance of typographic error. Associated with publication, investigation and interpretation have taken place, together with a review of some [manuscript] copies we believe to be accurate and of some authoritative commentaries.... (1928:271–2).

Published on the order of the imam himself, at a government controlled press in the palace, this edition is a far cry from the the independant commercial entrepreneurship of the 1991 lithograph edition. As it was produced on a typographic press, this first printed version of the book does not employ the manuscript collation language that appears at the end of the 1991 lithograph, but it does alert its readers to the minor substantive changes in the text to which they might be sensitive. In this different, typographic format another mechanism was engaged in the early years of printing to guarantee authentity and textual authority in the technological transition. The notice quoted above thus concludes by identifying two well-known Yemeni scholars who were responsible for the final "correction" *(tashih)* of the proofs prior to printing.

Significantly, such "correctors" were envisioned, early on, as a key element of the 1727 fatwa that first authorized printing in the Ottoman Empire. I quote here the text of the fatwa, which was given in response to a question about whether an individual may engage in printing several specific categories of works, including dictionaries, and treatises of logic, philosophy, and astronomy. The mufti responded:

> Supposing that one had found the art of printing correctly, with type characters of metal, the works mentioned above, furnishing a means of reducing work, of multiplying copies at low expense, thereby rendering acquisition easier and less costly, I decide that this art, by reason of its great advantages, ought to be encouraged, and its execution not be deferred, provided that one choses some capable and intelligent men who, before the works leave the press, correct them and verify them using the best originals (Omont 1895:191–2, cited Demeerseman 1954:123).

Seizing on this institution as a key, Demeerseman (1954:124–6) has documented the required presence of such "correctors," always drawn from among the scholars, to, as he puts it, "offer the desired cultural guarantee" to the early generation of Muslim typographic works. Thus, in a firman, Sultan Ahmed III named distinguished judges of Istanbul and Saloniqa and a head of a Dervish organization to verify and correct the permitted publications, ordering them to see that the printed books, "do not leave the press, except that they are complete and correct, making sure that not a single mistake slips through." Also identified are equivalent appointments to the typographic presses at Bulaq in Cairo and the l'Imprimerie Officielle in Tunis. In these correctors of printed works Demeerseman saw the new technology equivalent of the old Muslim relation of transmitters and reciters to the text of the Quran.[10]

For Muhsin Mahdi (1995:10–11), "the *musahhih*—literally the person in charge of producing a "correct" printed version—performed a task similar to that of the scribe in the manuscript age, that is, he corrected and sometimes revised the language of the manuscript copy before it was sent to the printer, and the same person contributed to assuring the proofs were properly corrected and a list of errata was appended to the printed book." As agents in the transition from manuscripts to books printed by moveable type, "correctors" applied old scholarly skills to two new necessities of the print era, the standardization of language and the certification of accuracy in printed works.

In the example lithographs from Cairo in 1884 and San`a' in 1991, and in the just discussed early Yemeni typographic edition of 1928, the statements and notices I have quoted may be considered reflective comments about the nature of the published text. They represent printed remarks about the phenomenon of print itself. Contained within the printed work, but separated off from the published "text" itself, such metacomments convey a historically and culturally specific perception of the new medium. On the one hand, aspects of the "notices" appended to the published books, such as concerning the "ancient" machine used in printing the 1928 book, are related directly to the nature of the available equipment in that period in Yemen. Such comments are associated with an historical transition in technology. Other types of comments, including both the 1991 lithograph statement about verifying the accuracy of the transcription and the 1928 typograph statement about the scholarly correctors, are statements about cultural receptions, and they are specific to the two distinct print technologies. In each case, in connection here with the specific genre of legal texts, the concern is

10 For Pedersen (1984:140), in the event that a printed book was based on a single manuscript, the "typesetter [took] the copyist place and the publisher the corrector's."

with the maintenance of textual authority through the move into the print medium.

Lithography v. Typography

To better understand the different receptions of lithography and typography, some of their contrasting features may be quickly summarized. Lithography is based directly on handwriting made for the purpose of reproduction; typography transforms handscript, or now, a typed or computer produced "manuscript," into type characters. Where, in the one, the letters in words are joined "naturally," in unbroken script, in the other they are joined mechanically. Conveyed in an idiosyncratic, individual hand, the lithograph text may be more comfortable to read, at least in certain times and places, whereas typography, employing a standard, potentially universal type form, may be relatively uncomfortable to read, again in certain times and places. (In other periods and contexts, exactly the reverse may be true, i.e., the idiosyncratic hand, or regional hands, such as the Maghrebi script, may be harder to decipher and the standard print easier.) As noted, the lithograph holds to manuscript styles and techniques, including collation devices, where the typograph embodies a stylistic and technical shift to a different world of textual authority. As Adeeb Khalid (1994:192) has remarked for the case of Central Asia, "lithographed books were printed manuscripts. Lithography allowed the age of script to continue under the guise of print."

One specific corollary of this, voweling marks aside, is that the lithograph retains indexical echoes of the recitational, oral qualities that underpinned manuscript texts in genres such as law, while the printed text eradicates, or further distances such traces. Ong's (1982:125) general statement that "manuscript culture had preserved a feeling for a book as a kind of utterance," may be extended to the mediated textual culture of lithographic print. In the context of a newly conceived "ethnography of reading" (Boyarin 1992), Fabian (1992:89) argues that we need to be more sensitive to the oral qualities of written texts. He defines "oralization" as "recourse to audible speech, actual or imagined, [as] an essential part of our ability to read texts." For Fabian, it is our "ideology of literacy" that "put[s] a taboo on revealing what we actually do when we read, for fear that oralization might subvert the authority of the written text." In our turn, we can attempt to understand the local connections of orality and reading in the Middle East and the associated choices of lithographic processes in terms of diverse regional cultures of literacy, with their differently constituted notions of textual authority.

In the Middle East, a preference for lithography, or at least a strong pattern of usage of this type of printing, also may have implications for the applicability of print-based theories of the nation state (cf. Bhabha 1990). Whereas typography, entailing the impersonality and regularity of mechanical type faces, is an appropriate medium for an emergent "imagined community" of homogeneous, interchangeable citizens, lithography, by contrast, preserves the trace of the individual, invoking, in the the art of the calligrapher, the pre-egalitarian hierarchies of scholars and manuscript culture textual specialists.

Both media, of course, share the basic feature of reproducability, the production of identical mechanical copies of originals written on stone or set in hot-metal. In a more differentiated world of "print culture," lithography brings together, in hybrid fashion, two authorities—that of the person and hand, buttressed by the human collation system, with that of the alienated truth value of mechanical reproduction. In fundamentally altering the scale of reproduction, however, even lithography works to break the old nodes of teacher and student, putting books, eventually including even law treatises and the Quran, into the hands of all readers. This vastly increased pattern of readership, associated with the previously noted transformation of schooling across the Middle East, has been central to the appearance of new textual cultures (cf. Messick 1996, in press).

In my book, I argued that the lengthy errata lists commonly found in the early printed texts from Yemen, but absent from more recent publications, revealed "the fallibility of editing and the available typography," while at the same time "subtly point[ing] up the potential perfectability, finality, and closure of the printed text" (Messick 1993:126). Rather than promoting an abstract ideal perfectability, lithography constantly recalls the imperfect qualities of human script and the particular individual. Ong (1982:132) writes generally that "print is comfortable only with finality," while manuscripts retained a relation of "dialogue with the world." This dialogue was carried out, he notes, through readers comments and glosses that could be added in the margins of manuscript works, whereas the completely filled space of printed works literally left no room for such a relation. In the intermediate form of the lithograph, however, marginalia frequently are reproduced, or, as in the example 1991 lithograph of the *Kafil,* a large empty border suitable for written reader responses is provided.[11]

Copies

To further delineate the character of lithography, I want to briefly consider the sphere of text copying and compare the movements from handwriting into two sorts of copies, the handwritten and the photocopied. The first is the mechanism by which books were reproduced prior to the advent of printing. The second, involving Xerox and other such brands of photocopying machines, is in some respects equivalent to lithography. In another sense, however, lithography represents a combination of the two processes, a hybrid.

A common contemporary copying example in Yemen is the reproduction of legal instruments such as handwritten contracts. Both types of copy by hand and by machine are known in Arabic as a *sura.* The same lexeme, in its old and new uses, covers the outcomes of two quite different processes, two distinct types of artifacts. As I stated in my book, in reference to a handwritten scribal copy made of an old register, "as a 'copy' it is virtually the same thing as the original, not because it 'looks like' the original in the photo-identity sense accomplished by mechanical reproduction..., but because it has passed through an authoritative process of human reproduction and collation" (Messick 1993:240). The collation process takes its authority from its similarity to the basic process of authoritative textual transmission, namely, the face-to-face encounter between teacher and student. In a manner analogous to the instructional exchange, in the collation activity that follows the making of a handcopy one individual reads the original text as

11 A "Letter on the Utility of Establishing a Press for Arabic Books at Tunis," addressed to a Muslim shaykh by an Orientalist in the mid-1850s, is reproduced and analysed by Demeerseman (1956). The author envisions maintaining the open responsiveness made possible by the old manuscript format. For the printing press,

> The paper must be at least as solid as that from Venice, which is used for manuscripts, and the margin must be wide, at least four fingers, so that whoever so desires may there write glosses. In this manner Muslims will acquire thc taste of purchasing printed books (1956:296).

the other listens and checks the copy. It is the medium of human presences and the associated oral-recitational channel that are the culturally specific anchors of the authentic transmission of the core texts, with the paradigms being the Quran and the mechanism for hadith transmission, the *isnad.* While mechanical reproduction produces versions outwardly identical to the original, the manual process of copying results in copies without any claim to physical identity. The claim is, rather, one of an exact substantive equivalence through verified human-to-human linkages, as conveyed in personal scripts. In the first type of *sura,* human writing is replicated by another human writing, in the second by a machine.

Yemeni photocopy studios have customized the photocopying process, narrowing the gap between hand and mechanical reproduction. Local shari`a court judgments are handwritten on verticle rolls. When they are photocopied, the copy paper is cut to the narrower width of the judgment roll and sheets are glued or taped on at the bottom to faithfully reproduce a scroll's physical quality. To enhance the copy's authenticity, the studio seal is affixed over the joints on the back of the scroll, just as the words "legal joint," are written across the joined edges of the original document paper. Except if it is signed or notarized, or otherwise reauthenticated, however, the mechanical copy suffers an inevitable drop in authority in comparison with the original, whereas handcopies, appropriately collated, could "take on" the authority *(hukm)* of the original, serving as originals in their own right (cf. Messick 1993:240). While the mechanical copy contains no written meta-reference to its status as a copy, every hand copy, whether it is a book manuscript, a register, a judgment scroll or a sale deed, comprises an appended annotation of the fact that it is a copy *(nuskha* or *sura).*

In the course of lithograph printing two copies are made. Lithography thus is a hybrid process which consists, in the first stage, of a non-identical but authoritative reproduction through handwriting and collation, and, in the second, of an identical but non-authoritative reproduction through print.

Mixed media

To further develop a more differentiated and situated approach to print culture, I now touch briefly on some print era versions of the key earlier manuscript era relation between the authoritative oral (spoken, recited) and the written (see Messick 1993). In the print era, this relation of authority may be transposed from the old oral/written to that of handwritten/print. I mentioned earlier the example of the contemporary publishing practice of including facsimilies of manuscript pages and other documents in type-printed editions. This occurs both in printings of works that formerly existed only in manuscript form and also in the modern scholarly practice of providing illustrations for a discussion.[12]

Other, less familiar examples of mixing media date from the beginning of what I have termed the "transitional" period in 20th century Yemeni history publishing (see Messick 1993:123–131). In 1929, at a press in Cairo, the Yemeni historian Muhammad Zabara published his augmented and annotated version of the two volume biographical dictionary by the famous early 19th century Yemeni jurist Muhammad al-Shawkani.[13] At the foot of the title page, below the title, the author's name, Zabara's name and other lines printed in the standard straight regularity of moveable type characters, appear a *basmala* and four compact and irregular cursive lines in the reproduced personal script of Zabara. The lines consist of a dated legal document conveying to the Cairo firm the right to publish this work of al-Shawkani together with Zabara'a notes and appendices. The lines conclude with Zabara's personal signature. Utilizing a composite of moveable type and lithograph techniques, the handwritten publishing contract becomes part of the published book, and the authority of personal script, conveying a human presence, is joined to that of the printed work.

A further example of such mixing is from the early post-Revolution years (the 1960s and 1970s), that is, at the end of the "transitional" period in modern Yemeni history writing. Printed histories by Yemenis such as Zabara and others first appeared in the 1920s, but Yemeni histories published during the next half century, into the second decade of existence of the nation state, retained some transitional qualities. These signal their intermediacy between the old discursive styles and technologies of manuscript era histories, produced by madrasa formed generalists, and the international styles and standards of scholarly history produced by university trained specialist historians. In Muhammad al-Akwa`'s history, *al-Yaman al-khadra' mahd al-hadara* ("Yemen the Verdant, Cradle of Civilization"),

12 This would include my own book and *Watha'iq yamaniyya* ("Yemeni Documents"), Cairo: al-Matba`at al-Fanniyya, 1982, by the Egyptian scholar of Yemen, Sayyid Mustafa Salim.

13 *Al-Badr al-tali`*. 2 Vols. Cairo: al-Sa`ada, 1348 A.H.

published in 1965, at the same Cairo press as al-Shawkani's biographical history, the text is printed entirely in moveable type, except for the paper-bound cover of the book which contains, on the back, a full page of reproduced handwriting. Here handwriting is retained, not for it legal value, as in the case of Zabara and the title page, but for its perceived capacity to more authoritatively convey the person. The text on the back of *al-Yaman al-khadra'* is a biographical sketch of the author al-Akwa` in his own (reproduced) script and signature, with the author's photograph appearing above the handwritten text. Presumably, by this time, the technique involved was offset lithography, which can handle both handwritten and type characters.

Two further examples concern period-specific reversals of the "normal" progression from handwriting to print. The practice in question, the hand-copying of a printed book, would only occur, I maintain, in a period during which the transitions to print usages and the elaboration of a locally specific print culture were not complete. The activity in question amounts to returning a book to manuscript form from an "original" printed edition, and it requires both the necessary skills and endurance of the manual copyist and a continuing valuation of texts in their manuscript form. We know that such actions also occured in Europe in the early years of the print revolution. In 1479, for example, a cardinal who was later to become Pope Julius II ordered scribes to copy by hand an edition of Appian's *Civil Wars* that had been printed in 1472.[14]

In my previous discussion of the persistence of the copyist tradition in twentieth century Yemen (Messick 1993:117), I referred to an acquaintance who, as a young student in the 1930s, made his own manuscript copies of an inheritance treatise and a law manual. What I did not realize until much later was that he had made his copies of the books from newly available printed editions. Although the source texts were printed, he was continuing to implement the pious and scholarly tradition of making personal manuscripts of important texts.

A different return to script occured in the 1990s but it involved an old scholar of the same generation. This was Ahmad Muhammad Zabara, son of the noted historian and the current Mufti of the Republic. The text was the last of the father's historical works, a biographical history, *Nuzhat al-nazar* ("Entertainment of the Gaze"), published posthumously in 1979,

14 Cited in *Encyclopedia Britannica* (15th Ed., Chicago, 1993), 26:96.

with Ahmad, the son, providing editorial supervision. A few years later, the book fell victim to republican censors and when I purchased a copy of the book some years later I found that numerous biographical entries on individuals connected with the pre-1962 imamic regime had been physically cut out. Ahmad Zabara did not quietly accept this mutiliation of his father's text and he set about reinserting and augmenting the removed biographies, and also adding numerous other biographies based on his own historical inquiries. He did so, however, by beginning the book over again, this time in his own handwriting, copying out his father's printed book, while adding back biographies and making his own numerous elaborations. The result of this enormous effort was four large manuscript volumes, in the "script of the author's son," as it states, to replace what originally, as of 1979, was a single volume and singly-authored printed book. Only an individual of the transitional scholarly generation that had experienced the local advent of printing would so comfortably turn to handwriting to meet the challenge of print censorship.

Conclusion

An understanding of the positive adoption of lithographic printing in various Muslim contexts must be part of a larger culturally, historically and even regionally specific analysis of relations surrounding the advent of print technologies. I have concentrated here on instances from highland Yemen where the initial technology to be introduced was moveable type, and where the form of lithography currently utilized is a modern descendant of the old "stone press." In discussing the basic differences between lithography and typography, and in drawing on a brief comparison with manual as opposed to mechanical copying, I have examined the careful human mechanisms—collation and correctors—that accompanied the first receptions of these very distinct technologies. Marking both the beginnings of new attitudes towards manuscripts and of new recognitions of the discursive horizons within the medium of print, such receptions depended fundamentally on the character and the techniques of the local textual practices of the manuscript age. Although I have not offered a new answer about the general timing of the acceptance of print technologies in the Middle East, I have argued that a simple, "modular" view of the technology itself is insufficient for understanding the various acceptances of print culture that did occur.

References

Anderson, Benedict. 1991. Imagined Communities. Rev. ed. London: Verso.

Ayache, G. 1964. "L'apparition de l'imprimerie au Maroc," Hesperis-Tamuda 5:143–61.

Bahran, Muhammad bin. Yahya. 1991. Matn al-Kafil. San`a': Mu'assasat Dar al-Turath al-Yamani.

Ben Cheneb, M. and E. Levi-Provencal. 1922. Essai de repertoire chronologique des editions de Fes. Algiers.

Benjamin, Walter. 1968. "The Work of Art in the Age of Mechanical Reproduction," *In* W. Benjamin, Illuminations. Trans. Harry Zohn. New York: Schoken Books. pp. 217–251.

Bhabha, Homi K. ed. 1990. Nation and Narration. London and New York: Routledge.

Boyarin, Jonathan. ed. 1992. The Ethnography of Reading. Berkeley: University of California Press.

Carter, Thomas F. 1943. "Islam as a Barrier to Printing," The Moslem World 33:213–16.

Demeerseman, A. 1953. "Une etape important de la culture islamique. Une parent meconnue de l'imprimerie arabe et tunisienne: la lithographie," IBLA 16(64):347–89.

__________ 1954. "Une etape decisive de la culture at de la psychologie sociale islamique. Les donnes de la controverse autour du probleme de l'imprimerie," IBLA 17(65):1–48; (66):113–40.

__________ 1956. "Une page nouvelle de l'Historie de l'imprimerie en Tunisie," IBLA 19(75):275–312,

Eickelman, Dale F. 1989. "National Identity and Religious Discourse in Contemporary Oman," International Journal of Islamic and Arabic Studies 6(1):1–20..

__________ 1992. "Mass Higher Education and the Religious Imagination in Contemporary Arab Societies," American Ethnologist 19(4):643–655.

Fabian, Johannes. 1992. "Keep Listening: Ethnography and Reading," *In* Jonathan Boyarin, ed. The Ethnography of Reading. Berkeley: University of California Press. Pp. 80–97.

Fischer, Michael M.J. and Mehdi Abedi. 1990. Debating Muslims. Madison: University of Wisconsin Press.

Khalid, Adeeb. 1994. "Printing, Publishing, and Reform in Tsarist Russia," International Journal of Middle Eastern Studies 26:187–200.
Mahdi, Muhsin. 1995. "From the Manuscript Age to the Age of Printed Books," *In* George N. Atiyeh, ed., The Book in the Islamic World. Albany: Stae University of New York Press.
Messick, Brinkley. 1993. The Calligraphic State. Berkeley: University of California Press.
________ 1996. "Media Muftis: Radio Fatwas in Yemen," *In* K. Masud, B. Messick and D. Powers, eds. Islamic Legal Interpretation. Cambridge: Harvard University Press, pp.310–320.
________ in press. "Genealogies of Reading and the Scholarly Cultures of Islam," *In* S. Humphreys, ed. Cultures of Scholarship. Ann Arbor: University of Michigan Press.
Niebuhr, Carsten. 1792. Travels Through Arabia and Other Countries in the East. Edinburgh: R. Morison and Son.
Oman, G. 1989. "Matba`a: 1. In the Arab World," Encyclopedia of Islam 2nd ed., Vol. VI, pp. 794–799.
Ong, Walter J. 1982. Orality and Literacy. London: Methuen.
Pedersen, Johannes. 1984. The Arabic Book. Princeton: Princeton University Press.
al-Ramli, Ahmad b. Husayn. n.d. Matn al-zubad. ms. (Ibb)
________ 1868. Matn al-zubad. Cairo: Bulaq.
________ 1884. Matn al-zubad. Cairo: Hasan Ahmad al-Tukhi. (lithograph)
________ 1953. Matn al-zubad. Cairo.
Robinson, Francis. 1993. "Technology and Religious Change: Islam and the Impact of Print," Modern Asian Studies 27(1):229–251.
Rossi, Ettore. 1938. "La Stampa nel Yemen," Oriente Moderno 18:568–80.
Sabat, Khalil. 1966. Ta'rikh al-Tiba`a fi al-Sharq al-cArabi. 2nd ed.Cairo: Dar al-Ma`arif bi-Masr.
al-Shamahi, `Abd Allah. 1937. Sirat al-`Arifin. San`a': Matba`at al-Ma`arif.

[18]

Rich Men, Poor Men: Ottoman Printers and Booksellers Making Fortune or Seeking Survival (Eighteenth-nineteenth Centuries)

Orlin Sabev (Orhan Salih)
Bulgarian Academy of Sciences, Institute of History, Sofia

"Are not the rich and poor brothers?" asked the young King.
"Ay," answered the man, "and the name of the rich brother is Cain."
Oscar Wilde, *The Young King*

It is an elementary truth that men of different occupation or different social background have different amounts of income and enjoy different standards of living. Further, within a given social stratum, professional group or even a family there are financial differences between its members: some of them earn or dispose of more money than the others. Yet, during one's lifetime there are sunny days, and rainy days too. In the course of time history saw emerging and declining societies, states, social or professional groups, families and individuals; and much prosperity and poverty as well. Although such a difference seems to be more than natural, it has always been an important reason for jealousy, social clashes and fratricides. The Biblical parable of the two brothers Abel and Cain is perhaps the best-known example of that. Prosperity and poverty, however, have different meanings, understandings and interpretations, as Oscar Wilde's epigram cited above suggests. What is common between them is that they cannot be taken for granted.

In the middle of the 15th century the readers and book lovers in western Europe enjoyed the birth of a new brother in the family of those involved in book production: the printer. Soon the newly emerged brother threatened the livelihood of all the traditional manuscript copyists and became one of the symbolic figures of the early modern times. The elder brothers, however, were not happy at all. A late 15th-century Dominican friar, Filippo De Strata, claimed, for example, that "the pen is a virgin; the printing press is a whore".[1]

[1] Filippo De Strata, *Polemic against Printing*, Shelagh Grier and Martin Lowry (eds.), quoted

In the Middle Ages manuscripts were copied for the sake of God and hence were believed to be an emanation of moral and as well as of orthographical purity. In other words, manuscripts were esteemed as virginally pure and perfect objects. On the contrary, not only in the very beginning of European printing but also even centuries later printed books were considered a corrupted object because of the initial orthographical imperfectness of the printing technology itself. Thus some people, especially those involved in manuscript copying, blamed the printed books for being a devil's product. Apparently not everybody welcomed the coming of the printing press and it is more than certain that printing did not replaced the manuscript tradition immediately and without any resistance.[2]

The situation long after the introduction of Ottoman Turkish typography in the 1720s was the same. Even over a century later it seems that printing was still considered *advocatis diaboli*. For example Charles White, who visited Istanbul in 1844, observed that the Istanbul booksellers esteemed, on the one hand, the manuscript copyists as deserving a place in paradise, and condemned, on the other, the printing press as being made of the poisonous oleander plant.[3]

At the initial stage of the introduction of printing manuscript copyists and printers were competitors and rivals rather than brothers cherishing the best feelings for one another. In the Ottoman case the booksellers[4] were closely and

---

from Sabrina A. Baron, "The guises of dissemination of early seventeenth-century England. News in manuscript and print", in *The Politics of Information in Early Modern Europe*, ed. by B. Dooley and S. S. Baron (London and New York: Routledge, 2001), pp. 41-56.

[2] For the long-term co-existence of the scribal and print culture see Robert A. Houston, *Literacy in Early Modern Europe. Culture and Education 1500-1800* (London and New York: Longman, 1988), pp. 160-3; Adrian Johns, *The Nature of the Book: Print and Knowledge in the Making* (Chicago and London: The University of Chicago Press, 1998); Diederick Raven, "Elizabeth Eisenstein and the impact of printing", *European Review of History — Revue européene d'histoire*, 6/2 (1999), pp. 223-34; Brian Richardson, *Printing, Writers and Readers in Renaissance Italy* (Cambridge: Cambridge University Press, 1999), p. 9; Nicholas Hudson, "Challenging Eisenstein: recent studies in print culture", *Eighteenth-Century Life*, 26/2 (2002), pp. 83-95; Assa Briggs and Peter Burke, A *Social History of the Media: From Gutenberg to the Internet* (Cambridge: Polity Press, 2003), pp. 15-73; David McKitterick, *Print, Manuscript and the Search for Order, 1450-1830* (Cambridge: Cambridge University Press, 2003 and 2004).

[3] Charles White, *Three Years in Constantinople or Domestic Manners of the Turks in 1844* (London: H. Colburn, 1845), vol. 3, pp. 155-6, quoted from Yahya Erdem, "Sahhaflar ve Seyyahlar: Osmanlı'da Kitapçılık", in G. Eren, K. Çiçek and C. Oğuz, *Osmanlı*, vol. 11 (Ankara: Yeni Türkiye, 1999), pp. 720-38.

[4] Mehmet Zeki Pakalın, "Sahhaf", in *Tarih Deyimleri ve Terimleri Sözlüğü* (Istanbul: Milli Eğitim Bakanlığı, 1954), vol. 3, p. 92; İsmet Binark, "Eski Devrin Kitapçıları: Sahhâflar", *Türk Kütüphaneciler Derneği Bülteni*, 16/3 (1967), pp. 155-62; Arslan Kaynardağ, "Eski Esnaflarımızla — Bu Arada Sahhaflıkla İlgili Bir Kitap: Letaif-i Esnaf", *Kütüphanecilik Dergisi*, 3 (1992), pp. 67-72; Erdem, "Sahhaflar ve Seyyahlar"; Ömer Faruk Yılmaz, *Tarih Boyunca Sahhaflık*

vitally related to the manuscript copyists and the early Ottoman printers were presumably nothing but unwelcome new players in the playground of book business. And business is almost all about money, whether making a fortune or seeking survival. From that point of view it is interesting to see comparatively how Ottoman manuscript sellers, on the one hand, and Ottoman printers, on the other, made their living out of the book business during their co-existence in the 18th and 19th century.

The inheritance registers provide a good opportunity to see the material condition and standard of living of a particular professional group, namely here that of the booksellers and printers. Comparison between the traditional booksellers, who well into the middle of the 19th century were associated with the manuscript trade, and the printers could reveal the impact of print culture on the social status of those who were involved in the book business. Moreover, from the middle of the 19th century on the Ottoman manuscript sellers became also printers or publishers, thus destroying the boundary that existed previously between the traditional booksellers and the printers. From this point of view it is interesting to see whether there were changes, more or less significant, in the material condition of the manuscript sellers-turned-printers, and if so, how printing technology affected their business and in what way, be it positive or negative.

It is important to remember, however, that we are not in a position to understand the exact state of affairs since we have only those inheritance inventories that have by chance survived the vicissitudes of time. At the initial stage of such a study, it is appropriate to focus on the Ottoman capital for at least three major reasons. First, we have at our disposal a rich collection of inheritance inventories of people who resided in Istanbul. Moreover, a special collection comprising the inventories of the people of *askeri* status exists because their inheritance cases were brought before a special court (*Kısmet-i Askeriye Mahkemesi*). Since all Ottoman booksellers and most of the printers enjoyed the same status it is safe to look at that collection, in which one can find sufficient registers of such people. Second, the Istanbul booksellers' guild was the largest in comparison with other parts of the empire. Let me just recall here that according to Evliya Çelebi in mid-17th-century Istanbul there were 300 booksellers and their guild had 50 bookshops.[5] Although the figures themselves could be exaggerated, they are, I would argue, used not to give the exact number of the Istanbul booksellers in middle of the 17th century, but to

ve İstanbul Sahhaflar Çarşısı (İstanbul: Sahhaflar Derneği, 2005); İsmail Erünsal, "Osmanlılarda Sahhaflık ve Sahaflar: Yeni Belge ve Bilgiler", *The Journal of Ottoman Studies*, 29 (2007), pp. 99-146.

[5] Evliya Çelebi, *Seyahatname*, vol. 1 (Dersaadet: İkdam Matbaası, 1314/1896), p. 525.

emphasize their extent. Ignace Mouradgea D'Ohsson observed the same considerable numbers in the 1780s.[6] Thirdly, Ottoman printing was introduced first in Istanbul in the first half of the 18th century with the so-called Müteferrika press and afterwards the number of printing houses operating in the Ottoman capital increased first slowly and then so rapidly that after the reign of Mahmud II (1808-39) and by the end of the 19th century at least 77 printing houses publishing in Ottoman Turkish were in operation.[7] In other words, Istanbul housed more booksellers and printers than anywhere else in the then Ottoman empire, and we have available a comparatively rich documentary basis for the study of their material condition and the extent of their well-being.

In the current article I will present my findings based on the study of the inheritance inventories of 13 Istanbul booksellers (*sahhaf*) and printers (*basmacı*) that I found in the Archive of the Grand Mufti of Istanbul (İstanbul Müftülüğü), and the inheritance registers included in the collection of the so-called *Kısmet-i Askeriye Mahkemesi*.[8] All the information I have derived from these sources in relation to the topic of the present study is presented in the table in the appendix. Five of the booksellers studied were contemporaries of the first Ottoman printer, İbrahim Müteferrika. Their inheritance inventories are dated between 1730 and 1747, while the Müteferrika press operated between 1726 and 1747. We also have extant the inheritance inventory of İbrahim Müteferrika himself.[9] Three other inheritance inventories belong to booksellers who died in the years 1804, 1805 and 1806, that is, when Ottoman printing revived as the result of a decisive state policy aimed at supporting and developing the printing facilities for important military, administrative and social purposes.[10] However, the booksellers at that period still dealt mostly

[6] Ignace Mouradgea D'Ohsson, *Tableau général de l'Empire Othoman*, vol. 1 (Paris: Imprimerie De Monsieur, 1787), p. 298.

[7] See the list of these presses in Ahmed Negih Galiptekin (ed.), *Osmanlı Kaynaklarına Göre İstanbul. Cami, Tekke, Medrese, Mekteb, Türbe, Hamam, Kütüphane, Matbaa, Mahalle ve Selâtin İmaretleri* (İstanbul: İşaret Yayınları, 2003), pp. 974-83.

[8] Their inheritance inventories are to be found in the following registers (defter): Defter No: 56 (fol. 7b), 70 (fol. 9a), 93B (fol. 25a), 93A (fol. 93b), 98 (fol. 39a), 98 (fol. 74b), 802 (fol. 57b), 802 (fol. 55b), 820 (fol. 24b), 1879 (fol. 44a), 1879 (fol. 13a), 1934 (fol. 12a), and 1934 (fol. 28a). I would like to express my gratitude to Prof. Dr. İsmail Erünsal for his generosity in providing me with information about those of the inventories which date from the 19th century.

[9] A transliteration in modern Turkish orthography of its Ottoman text is provided in Orlin Sabev, *İbrahim Müteferrika ya da İlk Osmanlı Matbaa Serüveni (1726-1746). Yeniden Değerlendirme* (İstanbul: Yeditepe Yayınevi, 2006), pp. 350-64.

[10] For a detailed study of late-18th- and early-19th-century Ottoman printing see Kemal Beydilli, *Türk Bilim ve Matbaacılık Tarihinde Mühendishâne, Mühendishâne Matbaası ve Kütüphanesi (1776-1826)* (İstanbul: Eren, 1995).

with manuscripts. And finally, we have available four further inheritance inventories of Istanbul booksellers, dating from the early 1880s and 1892, by which time all the Istanbul booksellers were united in a common trade company (*Şirket-i Sahhafiye-i Osmaniye*), which already actively printed and distributed books.[11] In other words, our last four cases have to do with booksellers-turned-printers, who represent one of the major developments in 19th-century Ottoman printing.

I will conduct my comparative analysis here from four main perspectives. The first will focus on an overall view of all the 13 cases taken into consideration in order to trace the developments in material conditions and standard of living that occurred throughout the 18th and 19th centuries. The second analysis will deal with İbrahim Müteferrika and his contemporaries. Thirdly, I will compare the traditional booksellers of the 1730s, 1740s and early 19th century with late 19th-century-booksellers-turned-printers. And finally, my fourth analysis will compare the first Ottoman printer's material condition with that of his late 19th-century colleagues.

The material condition of the booksellers and printers is examined taking into consideration the following information provided in their inheritance inventories: bookshop or printing house equipment; number, total value and average value per copy of the books listed; number, total value and average value per item of the goods listed; value of real estate, i.e. a house, if any; value of slaves, if possessed; value of the loans given and refunded; outlay, including burial expenses, dowries, debts paid and court fees; and the sum remaining after deductions (*sahhü'l baki*), number of heirs and average sum for each of them.

The latter does not represent the actual division of the remainder among the heirs because in accordance with the stipulations of the Muslim law of inheritance (*feraiz*) the heirs received not equal but different shares of the remainder depending on the nature of their relation to the deceased. For instance, if the heirs were a wife and a child the remainder was shared in proportion 1:7.[12] However, I preferred to recalculate the actual shares as stated in the inventories in averages in order to facilitate the comparison between the cases and to get some rough idea about the fortune that the dead booksellers and printers left to their heirs. In addition, again for the sake of comparison, I have rounded

[11] For the so-called *Şirket-i Sahhafiye-i Osmaniye* see Fatmagül Demirel, "Osmanlı'da Bir Kitap Şirketi Şirket-i Sahafiye-i Osmaniye", *Müteferrika*, 25 (2004), pp. 89-97; Mehmet Ö. Alkan, "Osmanlı'nın Bütün Sahafları Birleşiniz! "Şirket-i Sahafiye-i Osmaniye". Osmanlı Döneminde Sahaflar ve Yayınladıkları Kitaplar", *Müteferrika*, 29 (2006), pp. 3-44.

[12] See Said Öztürk, *Askeri Kassama Ait Onyedinci Asır İstanbul Tereke Defterleri (Sosyo-Ekonomik Tahlil)* (İstanbul: OSAV, 1995), pp. 98-100.

off all the values and given them in *guruş*, the Ottoman monetary unit which became the leading unit by the middle of the 18th century.[13] It must be pointed out that in our seventh case related to the bookseller Es-Seyyid El-Hac İsmail Efendi we deal with the appendix (*zeyl*) of his inheritance inventory written down some eight months later and in which only the total value, the refunded loans, the outlay, the remainder and the shares allotted to the heirs, respectively, are given, but not the books and goods possessed. The latter were obviously stated in the original inventory which I failed to find. However, the appendix is worth considering because of the large amount of the remainder according to which Es-Seyyid El-Hac İsmail Efendi appears to be one of the rich booksellers in the present study.

When all the 13 cases are studied from the point of view of the above-mentioned criteria, the striking finding is that in terms of value in most cases the books as a commodity and the bookshop or printing house equipment are the major part of the booksellers' and printers' property. In eight out of 12 cases (in which all the five printers are included) they constitute more than 80 percent of all the property, while in the remaining four cases they represent roughly half of the whole property (between 45 and 59 percent). This proportion between the items related to the book business and the other goods and properties shows that usually the booksellers and printers invested heavily in their book business and in eight cases these investments exceeded even the remainder to be shared by the heirs (cases 1, 2, 3, 6, 8, 9, 12, and 13). In two other cases the investments are almost the same as the remainder (cases 10 and 11), while in two cases the remainder is only slightly larger then the investments (cases 4 and 5). As for the 18th- and early 19th-century cases, in which the remainder surpassed the investments, the heirs enjoyed much bigger shares. In the late 19th-century cases, however, the picture is somewhat varied since the value of the shares depended on the number of the heirs. It is normal to assume that the fewer the heirs are in number, the bigger the share they could enjoy. However, the amount they could receive depended not only on their number, but also on the value of the remainder.

Of the booksellers and printers studied here only three invested in equipment: İbrahim Müteferrika and Es-Seyid Mustafa Esad Efendi, who possessed their own printing houses, and Sahhaf El-Hac Mustafa, who had proportionally high investments in his bookshop. The other booksellers-turned-printers presumably printed at the printing house of their common company. How-

[13] See Şevket Pamuk, *A Monetary History of the Ottoman Empire* (Cambridge: Cambridge University Press, 2000), pp. 159-71.

ever, the two printing house owners left the largest remainders to be shared by their heirs, who as a matter of fact, were the fewest in number, that is, two, as compared to the other cases.

As stated above, in all the cases studied by far the overwhelming percentage of the investments was made in books. The calculation of the average value per copy shows that the booksellers dealt with books whose average value varied between three and seven *guruş* in the 18th and early 19th century and around 11 to 13 *guruş* in the late 19th century. There are two exceptions. The first one is Sahhaf İbrahim Sadullah Efendi (1806, case 9), the average value of whose books was higher, that is, 20 *guruş*, simply because he apparently traded mainly expensive Koran copies, as listed in his inventory. In fact, among the cases studied he left the smallest remainder, that is, only 39 *guruş*, the price of one of the Koran copies listed. Obviously Sahhaf İbrahim Sadullah Efendi's book business was a complete fiasco, since he invested a great deal of money in expensive Koran copies, on the one hand, and had a great many debts, whose value even surpassed the value of his books (665,636 *guruş*), on the other. The second one is Sahhaf Hafız Ahmed Efendi (1892, case 12), who had many copies of inexpensive books printed at the printing house of the Istanbul Booksellers' Company so that the average value of his books is only 0.4 *guruş*. As a whole, it seems that investment in cheaper books was less risky and more profitable since they could sell more easily and were more affordable.

All the studied cases show that in general booksellers and printers were not inclined to live in luxury. Quite on the contrary, most of them were people of modest substance. It must be pointed out, however, that in ten out of the 13 cases the deceased left minor children which could mean that they died at a relatively young age. İbrahim Müteferrika is probably an exception, since although he left a minor daughter he is known to have died at a mature age. Being born in the early 1670s he must have been over 70 years old while on his deathbed in 1746 or early 1747. With the exception of İbrahim Müteferrika we may be dealing mostly with cases in which the deceased had no chance to live longer and to make a greater fortune, if it is true that the more you live, the more you earn. In fact, the reason that we have their inheritance inventories is precisely because upon their deaths they left minor children, for this was one of the few cases in which someone's property would be inventoried by the Shari'a court.

A cursory glance at the household goods listed in their inheritance inventories shows considerable modesty in terms of number and value. İbrahim Müteferrika possessed the largest number of goods, but their average value was comparable to that of contemporary booksellers so that he too led a rather modest lifestyle. The late 19th-century booksellers-turned-printers also possessed limited numbers of goods whose value was much higher simply because of the inflation throughout the 18th and 19th centuries.

Only three of the booksellers and printers studied possessed their own house: Sahhaf İbrahim Efendi (whose house seems to have been rather inexpensive and hence modest because of its price of 133 *guruş*, case 2), İbrahim Müteferrika (whose house is valued at 2,500 *guruş*, case 5), and Sahhaf Es-Seyid Mustafa Esad Efendi (the value of his house is not explicitly stated, case 13).

Only in two of the cases studied do we find entries of the value of female slaves, who were used as domestics. Again İbrahim Müteferrika owned three expensive female slaves of Georgian origin, and his contemporary Sahhaf El-Hac Mustafa possessed a half share of the value of a female slave (case 6).

The two also possessed some cash: upon his demise İbrahim Müteferrika left 110 *guruş*, and Sahhaf El-Hac Mustafa 40 *guruş*. However, although the latter had a half share of a slave and some cash, he had many debts to pay (77 percent of the value of his property) so that he eventually left to his two heirs a property whose value was comparable to his other colleagues who were no more than men of modest substance. The cash that İbrahim Müteferrika left upon his demise was more considerable but still insufficient to buy even a small, modest house, for instance. This sum would be insufficient even if İbrahim Müteferrika wished to buy a new press because the total value of his six used presses was estimated at 700 *guruş*, that is, 117 *guruş* per press.

In this respect Sahhaf Es-Seyyid Mustafa Esad Efendi, our last case, seems to have been the richest and luckiest of all the booksellers and printers considered in the current study. He left cash to his heirs to the considerable value of 66,090 *guruş*, a sum that surpasses several times the total value of the property of his three contemporaries. This sum seems to have been enough not only to buy new presses, the price of one of which is estimated at 200 *guruş*, but also large and luxurious houses. However, Sahhaf Es-Seyyid Mustafa Esad Efendi had to pay rather large debts valued at 129,325.5 *guruş*, so that in the end the remainder to be shared between his two heirs was even less than the value of his books. His heirs must have been enormously lucky because all his books, as well as his other possessions, were sold and they were able to share the sum received after deducting the debts and court fees, that is, 633,296 *guruş*. It must be pointed out that Sahhaf Es-Seyyid Mustafa Esad Efendi's relatively good material condition has something to do with the legacy he received from his father, the prominent Ottoman printer Karahisari El-Hac Ali Rıza Efendi. Bookselling and printing seems to have been a family business, since Mustafa Esad Efendi's son by his first wife, Mehmed Şevket Efendi, was also a bookseller, as stated in the inheritance inventory. On the other hand, besides his book business Sahhaf Es-Seyyid Mehmed Kemaleddin Efendi (case 10), who also left a considerable inheritance, had another source of regular income as a librarian at the prestigious library of the sultan Mehmed the Conqueror in Istanbul as stated in his inheritance inventory. In addition, it is unclear whether the considerable amount of the remainder left by Es-Seyyid El-Hac İsmail Efendi (case 7), calculated at 19,000 *guruş* and exceeding by at least roughly ten times those of his early-19th-century contemporaries, was due to his presumably outstandingly profitable book business or for other reasons such as, for instance, family legacy or other considerable sources of income. Interestingly, all the richer booksellers and printers in my study (cases 7, 10, and 13) appear to be *seyyids*, that is, persons belonging to the group of those claiming to be descendants of the Prophet Muhammad. It could be just a mere coincidence. However, this fact could serve as an indication for a specific social background providing more opportunities for a prosperous life.

Among the richer men İbrahim Müteferrika is an exception since he was not *seyyid*, yet he was a Hungarian convert to Islam. In comparison with all the other booksellers and printers studied he had least debts to pay, mainly monthly salaries for his workers at the printing house, but the books that remained unsold at his printing house were not auctioned or sold off but left as a legacy to his minor daughter. In other words, upon her father's demise she received no money but printed books and she had the right to receive the money made on their sale. Even so, if the estimated value of these books (20,422 *guruş*) is deducted from the value of the remainder (25,077 *guruş*) the value of 4,655 *guruş* remains to be shared between İbrahim Müteferrika's two heirs: his wife and his minor daughter. So, if not able to sell off the inherited printed books they could still rely on the other property whose value in fact surpassed by at least ten times the remainders of the contemporary booksellers studied here. It must be pointed out that in contrast to these men, whose sources of income seems to have been only the book business, İbrahim Müteferrika received a regular monthly salary for his service at the imperial court as a *müteferrika*, as well as for some additional services in the Ottoman army and by the year 1738 as a liaison officer attached to his Hungarian compatriots, who took refuge in the Ottoman empire. As a *müteferrika* he received 300 or 360 *guruş* per annum and as a liaison officer even more: 600 *guruş*. These sums are more than or roughly the same as the remainder left to be shared between the heirs of İbrahim Müteferrika's contemporary booksellers. So, it seems that the first Ottoman printer enjoyed much better material conditions and standard of living than they did. However, it is still unclear whether and to what degree his relative well-being was due to his service to the Ottoman state or to his printing activities: probably it was due to the combination of the two, since before his death he managed to sell almost 70 percent of the books produced by his printing house: a percentage that disproves the previous theories about İbrahim Müteferrika's printing fiasco.[14]

It could be inferred from the comparative analysis of the 13 booksellers and printers studied here that after their initial rejection of and opposition to printing, the Ottoman manuscript sellers accepted that it offered them positive benefits. The newly introduced and tested printing technology gave a new professional choice and created a new social behaviour. The 19th-century Ottoman booksellers preferred to print the books they sold rather than ordering their copying or to buy them from the estates of the deceased or from book owners. This shift seems to have been profitable. At least the cases studied for the present article show that the late 19th-century booksellers-turned-printers' material conditions and standard of living were much better than those of their colleagues who saw the introduction of Ottoman printing. Obviously, the traditional manuscript sellers could not resist the changing situation and had no other choice but to use the weapon of their former "enemy". In other words their parable differed slightly from the Biblical parable of Cain and Abel: in the case of Ottoman book business Cain did not kill Abel but adopted his know-how to become at least a little richer.

[14] For a detailed analysis see Sabev, *İbrahim Müteferrika*, pp. 287-303.

No	Bookseller/ Printer Year	Bookshop/ Printing House Equipment	Number of Books	Total Value of the Books	Average Value of a Copy	Number of Goods	Total Value of the Goods	Average Value of a Good	Value of House	Value of Slave Possessed	Cash	Loans Given and Refunded	Outlay: Court Fees and Debts Paid Back	Remainder	Number of Shareholders	Average Sum for a Shareholder
1	Sahhaf El-Hac Hüseyin (1730)	–	62	370 94%	6	10	23 6%	2.3	–	–	–	–	112 29%	280 71%	5	56
2	Sahhaf İbrahim Efendi (1734)	–	151	480 52%	3	51	168 18%	3	133 14%	–	–	151 16%	722 77%	210 23%	3	70
3	Sahhaf Eş-Şeyh Mehmed Efendi (1745)	–	115	350 97%	3	11	12 3%	1	–	–	–	–	190 52%	173 48%	3	58
4	Sahhaf Abdullah Efendi (1746)	–	74	507 45%	7	114	622 55%	5.5	–	–	–	–	467 41%	663 59%	3	221
5	Basmacı İbrahim Müteferrika (1747)	1,168 4.5%	2976	20,422 77%	7	258	1,639 6%	6	2,500 9.5%	600 (3) 2.5%	110 0.5%	–	1362 5%	25077 95%	2	12538.5 [2327.5]

(*cont.*)

No	Bookseller/ Printer Year	Bookshop/ Printing House Equipment	Number of Books	Total Value of the Books	Average Value of a Copy	Number of Goods	Total Value of the Goods	Average Value of a Good	Value of House	Value of Slave Possessed	Cash	Loans Given and Refunded	Outlay: Court Fees and Debts Paid Back	Remainder	Number of Shareholders	Average Sum for a Shareholder
6	Sahhaf El-Hac Mustafa (1747)	150 29%	51	160 30%	3	26	81 16%	3	–	65 (1/2) 12%	40 8%	25 5%	400 77%	121 23%	2	60.5
7	Es-Seyid El-Hac İsmail Efendi (1804-1805)	?	?	?	?	?	?	?	?	?	?	1188.5 5%	6044.5 24%	19000 76%	4	4750
8	Sahhaf Mustafa Efendi (1805)	–	43	240 57%	6	31	184 43%	6	–	–	–	–	233 55%	191 45%	2	95.5
9	Sahhaf İbrahim Sadullah Efendi (1806)	–	32	636 90%	20	7	67 10%	10	–	–	–	–	665 95%	39 5%	2	19.5

(*cont.*)

No	Bookseller/ Printer Year	Bookshop/ Printing House Equipment	Number of Books	Total Value of the Books	Average Value of a Copy	Number of Goods	Total Value of the Goods	Average Value of a Good	Value of House	Value of Slave Possessed	Cash	Loans Given and Refunded	Outlay: Court Fees and Debts Paid Back	Remainder	Number of Shareholders	Average Sum for a Shareholder
10	Sahhaf Es-Seyid Mehmed Kemaleddin Efendi (1882)	–	1739	22,948 83%	13	163	4,667 17%	29	–	–	–	–	4547 16%	23068 84%	3	7689
11	Sahhaf Hafiz Hasan Efendi (1883)	–	354	4,517 94%	13	33	270 6%	8	–	–	–	–	277 6%	4510 94%	3	1503
12	Sahhaf Hafiz Ahmed Efendi (1892)	–	33,997	12,657 82%	0.4	72	2817 18%	39	–	–	–	–	5708 37%	9766 63%	5	1953
13	Sahhaf Es-Seyid Mustafa Esad Efendi (1892)	6,800 0.8%	64,143	715,236 90%	11	430	7,217 0.9%	17	–	–	66090 8,3%	–	162046 20%	633296 80%	2	316648

Bibliography

Alkan, Mehmet Ö. "Osmanlı'nın Bütün Sahafları Birleşiniz! "Şirket-i Sahafiye-i Osmaniye". Osmanlı Döneminde Sahaflar ve Yayınladıkları Kitaplar." *Müteferrika*, 29 (2006), pp. 3-44.

Baron, Sabrina A. "The guises of dissemination of early seventeenth-century England. News in manuscript and print." In *The Politics of Information in Early Modern Europe*, ed. by B. Dooley and S. S. Baron. London: Routledge, 2001, pp. 41-56.

Beydilli, Kemal. *Türk Bilim ve Matbaacılık Tarihinde Mühendishâne, Mühendishâne Matbaası ve Kütüphanesi (1776-1826)*. İstanbul: Eren, 1995.

Binark, İsmet. "Eski Devrin Kitapçıları: Sahhâflar." *Türk Kütüphaneciler Derneği Bülteni*, 16/3 (1967), pp. 155-62.

Briggs, Assa and Peter Burke. *A Social History of the Media: From Gutenberg to the Internet*. Cambridge: Polity Press, 2003.

D'Ohsson, Ignace Mouradgea. *Tableau général de l'Empire Othoman*, vol. 1. Paris: Imprimerie De Monsieur, 1787.

Demirel, Fatmagül. "Osmanlı'da Bir Kitap Şirketi Şirket-i Sahafiye-i Osmaniye." *Müteferrika*, 25 (2004), pp. 89-97.

Erdem, Yahya. "Sahhaflar ve Seyyahlar: Osmanlı'da Kitapçılık." In *Osmanlı*, vol. 11, ed. by G. Eren, K. Çiçek and C. Oğuz. Ankara: Yeni Türkiye, 1999, pp. 720-38.

Erünsal, İsmail. "Osmanlılarda Sahhaflık ve Sahaflar: Yeni Belge ve Bilgiler." *The Journal of Ottoman Studies*, 29 (2007), pp. 99-146.

Evliya Çelebi. *Seyahatname*, vol. 1. Dersaadet: İkdam Matbaası, 1314/1896.

Galiptekin, Ahmed Negih (ed.). *Osmanlı Kaynaklarına Göre İstanbul. Cami, Tekke, Medrese, Mekteb, Türbe, Hamam, Kütüphane, Matbaa, Mahalle ve Selâtin İmaretleri*. İstanbul: İşaret Yayınları, 2003.

Houston, Robert A. *Literacy in Early Modern Europe. Culture and Education 1500-1800*. London: Longman, 1988.

Hudson, Nicholas. "Challenging Eisenstein: recent studies in print culture." *Eighteenth Century Life*, 26/2 (2002), pp. 83-95.

Johns, Adrian. *The Nature of the Book: Print and Knowledge in the Making*. Chicago: The University of Chicago Press, 1998.

Kaynardağ, Arslan. "Eski Esnaflarımızla — Bu Arada Sahhaflıkla İlgili Bir Kitap: Letaif-i Esnaf". *Kütüphanecilik Dergisi*, 3 (1992), pp. 67-72

McKitterick, David. *Print, Manuscript and the Search for Order, 1450-1830*. Cambridge: Cambridge University Press, 2003 and 2004.

Öztürk, Said. *Askeri Kassama Ait Onyedinci Asır İstanbul Tereke Defterleri (Sosyo-Ekonomik Tahlil)*. İstanbul: OSAV, 1995.

Pakalın, Mehmet Zeki. "Sahhaf." In *Tarih Deyimleri ve Terimleri Sözlüğü*, vol. 3. İstanbul: Milli Eğitim Bakanlığı, 1954.

Pamuk, Şevket. *A Monetary History of the Ottoman Empire*. Cambridge: Cambridge University Press, 2000.

Raven, Diederick. "Elizabeth Eisenstein and the impact of printing." *European Review of History — Revue europèene d'histoire*, 6/2 (1999), pp. 223-34.

Richardson, Brian. *Printing, Writers and Readers in Renaissance Italy*. Cambridge: Cambridge University Press, 1999.

Sabev, Orlin. *İbrahim Müteferrika ya da İlk Osmanlı Matbaa Serüveni* (1726-1746). *Yeniden Değerlendirme*. İstanbul: Yeditepe Yayınevi, 2006.

White, Charles. *Three Years in Constantinople or Domestic Manners of the Turks in 1844*. London: H. Colburn, 1845.

Yılmaz, Ömer Faruk. *Tarih Boyunca Sahhaflık ve İstanbul Sahhaflar Çarşısı*. İstanbul: Sahhaflar Derneği, 2005.

[19]

FUNCTIONAL PERSPECTIVES ON TECHNOLOGY: THE CASE OF THE PRINTING PRESS IN THE OTTOMAN EMPIRE*

J. S. SZYLIOWICZ

Introduction

The importance of modern science and technology is today accepted throughout the world. Some view them as forces that can solve human problems and improve the quality of life, others as elements that can destroy mankind. In the Muslim World, the debate often takes the form of whether modern science and technology are essential for the achievement of national goals or whether they are destructive of traditional values and institutions, and should be replaced by a Muslim Science. Whatever one's views on this matter, it is essential to understand the nature of science and technology and to conceptualize them accurately for, if one does not do so, the debate will be intellectually sterile. History has much to teach us in this regard. It is the purpose of this communication to identify two fundamental characteristics of technology through an analysis of the manner in which the printing press functioned in the Ottoman Empire and its impact. I shall discuss two aspects of printing — book publishing and the rise of the media — and will make some comparisons with the situation in Western Europe to illustrate my points.

* Paper presented to the International Symposium on "Modern Science and the Muslim World", Istanbul, 2-4 September 1987.

Book Publishing

Although the press was introduced into the Ottoman Empire as early as 1493 by Jewish refugees from Spain, and 37 presses had been established by minorities and missionaries by the beginning of the 18th century, it was not used by the Ottomans until 1726 when Ibrahim Müteferrika obtained permission to print books. His mandate, however, extended only to works dealing with science, language, and history; everything connected with religion was to remain the province of the Ulema. Even with these restrictions, the press continued in operation for only 15 years. When Ibrahim Müteferrika died, the press died with him. Altogether a mere 17 books were printed (about one book per year), each with a run of between 500 and 1000 copies. A second printing shop was opened in 1784 to publish textbooks for the newly established Military Engineering School, a third started operation in 1796. Now printing had at last become a permanent technological fixture in the Ottoman Empire; but the number of books printed remained quite low. Altogether it has been estimated that between 180 and 200 separate titles were published between 1729 and 1830.[1]

These developments contrast quite sharply with the situation in Western Europe along two fundamental dimensions, the degree of diffusion that took place and the type of books that were printed. The number of presses proliferated rapidly and, by 1500, were to be found throughout Italy, Germany, and other Western European countries. Over 60 German towns had presses and Venice alone had 150.[2] These presses were kept extremely busy. It has been estimated that 40,000 separate titles were published in the first fifty years after Gutenberg invented printing,[3] and that over 9 million copies were printed.[4] The Church welcomed printing and viewed it as a means of expanding its power and influence. A large percentage of all works that were published in Europe were

[1] J. Baysal, *Osmanlı Türklerin Bastıkları Kıtaplar,* (Istanbul: Istanbul Edebiyat Fakültesi Basımevi; 1968) pp. 10 ff.; N. Berkes, *The Development of Secularism in Turkey* (Montreal: McGill University Press, 1964) pp. 36 ff.; R. Davison, *Reform in the Ottoman Empire 1856-1876,* (Princeton: Princeton University Press, 1963) p. 22.; and K. Karpat "The Mass Media" in R. Ward and D. Rustow's *Modernization in Turkey and Japan* (Princeton: Princeton University Press, 196-), pp. 255 ff.

[2] "Publishing", The New Encyclopedia Britannica, Volume 26, p. 462.

[3] Baysal, *op. cit.*, p. 13.

[4] *Encyclopedia Britannica,* p. 462.

religious; secular works were considered dangerous. Church censorship was instituted to ensure that heretical secular ideas not be printed and disseminated.

In the Ottoman Empire, the situation was the reverse. There, as I have noted, the rate of diffusion was quite slow and the nature of the publications secular rather than religious. Though religious works eventually came to be published (the first Quran being printed in 1874), the emphasis remained on secular works. Overall, between 1729 and 1875, 19% of all books printed dealt with religion, 25% were literary works; in 1875 only 8% of all books published were religious whereas 33% were literary.[5]

These differences serve to illustrate a fundamental aspect of technology. It is not an autonomous or deterministic power that shapes human affairs in its own image. Nor is it an external force that lies outside society and controls our lives and institutions within. On the contrary, technology is essentially a social phenomenon whose every aspect is determined by the structure of power and the nature of the cultural, social, and other societal subsystems within which it operates. As the printing press demonstrates, any technology can be understood only in its social context. The differences between Western European and Ottoman society dictated the different patterns of diffusion and use. Specifically, when the press was introduced, the Ottoman Empire was a centralized patrimonial state with a traditional orientation, one towards the past rather than the future. Its social structure was marked by a large gap between elite and mass, and the literacy rate was quite low. And, some groups were able to exert considerable pressure against the introduction of printing. The calligraphers, an estimated 90,000, fought vigorously and effectively against an innovation which directly threatened their livelihood.[6] In other words, the environment in the Ottoman Empire was not receptive to the press in the same degree as that in Europe. Major social and cultural obstacles limited its diffusion; there was no social demand, the systems that would enable the press to flourish were simply not in place.

In the course of the nineteenth century the well known Tanzimat reforms were implemented, and the Ottoman state changed dramatically. These

[5] Baysal, *op. cit.*, pp. 53, 76.

[6] Baysal, *op. cit.*, p. 13; Berkes, *op. cit.*, p. 40.

changes impacted directly upon the role of the press which was now viewed by the elite as an important technology that could help save the Empire. In addition, great social changes created new societal interests. Beginning with the establishment of military colleges, a secular educational system came into being that expanded and diversified rapidly. By 1868 over 365,000 students were enrolled in primary schools and about 8,000 were attending *rüşdiye* schools. By 1895 over 1 million children were receiving some sort of primary education, 32,000 were in *rüşdiye* schools, and 5400 were enrolled in the *idadiye* schools. Another 100,000 students were studying in minority and foreign institutions. Although precise data are not available, it is generally estimated that the literacy rate climbed sharply from 1860 onwards, rising from about 1% in 1800 to 2% in 1868, 5% by 1876, and around 10% by 1914.[7] These developments were accompanied by rapid demographic growth (the population of Istanbul rising from 400,000 in 1800 to 1.1 million in 1914.[8] Concomitantly a new middle class emerged. To administer the many reforms that were being implemented, a new bureaucracy was required and the traditional Ottoman center grew and diversified. New professions were also developing — law, engineering, medicine, journalism, all of whose members were also part of this new class. This emerging bourgeoisie, with its new values and interests, rapidly developed a taste for reading, not only for pleasure but because printed materials provided it with the kind of information that it needed for personal advancement and success, and thus came to constitute a growing market that could not be ignored.

As a result of these societal changes the press became a fixture within the state. It was now a technology whose time had come. By 1875 there were 151 printing presses scattered throughout the Empire, 116 of which were in Istanbul; of these 77 were owned by Turks, 21 were attached to schools or ministries, and the remainder were in the hands of minorities

[7] These figures are taken from Davison, *op. cit.*, pp. 177, and 245; S.C. Antel, "Tanzimat Maarifi" in *Tanzimat* (Istanbul: Maarif Matbaasi, 1940 p. 458; and Ch. Issawi, *An Economic History of the Middle East and North Africa* (New York: Columbia University Press, 1982) pp. 113-114. Although there is some controversy over the degree of literacy in the Ottoman Empire, it is difficult to believe that higher estimates are accurate since, according to the Turkish censuses, the rate just surpassed 10% in 1927 and stood at 22% in 1940. S. Shaw and E. Shaw, *History of the Ottoman Empire and Modern Turkey*, (Cambridge: Cambridge University Press, 1976) vol. 2, p. 387.

[8] Issawi, *op. cit.*, pp. 94, and 101.

and missionaries. Not surprisingly, the number of books that were published increased greatly during these decades, rising from about 10 a year between 1803 and 1839 to 40 a year between 1839 and 1869, and 160 a year between 1869 and 1875.[9]

The Media

These developments also affected printing technology in another way. Newspapers now emerged as a major force within the state. The first paper, the *Takvim-i Vekayi* had begun publication in 1831, to meet a specific need defined by the ruling elite. It was an official organ circulated to 5,000 persons (state officials, learned men, and foreign diplomats), and its purpose was defined in traditional terms. Its first issue stated: "To know the events of the past serves to keep up the laws and character of the Empire. It is for this purpose that the government has always employed historiographers."[10] The first true paper, the *Ceride-i Havadis,* was published by an Englishman in 1843, the first Turkish newspaper, the *Tercuman-i Ahval* in 1860. Though it was short lived, it was followed, in 1862, by the *Tasvir-i Efkar.* What is particularly striking about these Turkish papers is that they were not *news* papers as such. Rather they were published by members of the Young Ottoman group in order to educate the public, in order to shape public opinion so that it would favor the kinds of reforms that they sought to implement. A knowledgeable student of the press of this period has characterized the nature of these journals as follows:[11]

> "The main feature of the paper was the editorial article. News for its own sake was not published unless it concerned the public life in its most general aspect or political condition and diplomatic relations in other countries. Provincial and city news items were published only when they could be used as a warning or a moral hint."

Once again the contrast with Europe is striking. In those countries the press performed a very different function because the society, economy, and culture there had few points in common with the Ottomans. True, in England, as in the Ottoman Empire, political actors used the press

[9] Baysal, *op. cit.*, pp. 29-44, and 55.

[10] A.E. Yalman, *The Modernization of Turkey As Measured By Its Press* (New York: Columbia University, 1914), p. 30.

[11] *Ibid.*, p. 48.

for their own purposes. Every political faction needed one if it were to prevail. In its pages it would challenge the opposition and present its own policies and views. But significant differences between the press in the two states were evident in terms of ownership and content. In England the press was controlled largely by booksellers who engaged in a wide range of business activities, and it was oriented to the commercial interests of its readers. Their needs for information about trade, commerce, developments in foreign countries were met by the papers of the day.[12]

That any technology is affected by the nature of its environment is obvious if one considers what happened to the media during the reign of Abdul Hamid II. Heavily censored, the number of dailies declined from 6 in 1891 to three in 1908, all of which received financial support from the government.[13] Since they could not print anything that was even remotely connected to politics, they were totally devoid of any news at all and contented themselves with pieces that were more or less scientific. Berkes has described the situation vividly:[14]

> As writing on political, social, and cultural subjects became susceptible to unexpected interpretations and, therefore, hazardous, the serious periodicals (even daily papers) began to stuff their pages with news, articles, and pictures that had nothing to do with such matters.... Thus, a race to publish articles and pictures on semi-scientific subjects began. A few article headings are illustrative: "A Biography of Professor Helmholtz", "Origins of the Species of Vertebrates", "How to Keep Feet Warm", "Colored Photography", "The Contribution of Arabs to Science", "Travel in Air or Under Sea", ... "The Intelligence of Cats" ... "How Much Weight a Horse can Carry", and endless articles on the life of the Lapps and Eskimos, the voyages of Christopher Columbus, the strange foods of the Chinese, the explorations of Livingstone.

When the political system changed again with the Young Turk revolution of 1908, so did the nature and functioning of the media. First, the number of publications proliferated quickly; by 1913 the number of Turkish publications had reached 161.[15] Equally, and probably even

[12] M. Harris and A. Lee, *The Press in English Society From the Seventeenth to the Nineteenth Centuries* (Rutherford, New Jersey: Farleigh Dickinson University Press, 1986) pp. 19ff.

[13] Yalman, *op. cit.*, p. 78.

[14] Berkes, *op. cit.*, p. 277.

[15] Yalman, *op. cit.*, pp. 113ff.

more significant is the change in the orientation of the media that took place in these years. The price of a paper dropped dramatically from 4c to 1c as publishers came to realize that a wide audience for their product had been created by the developments that had taken place and that, by cutting prices, they could reach many more readers and enhance their profits. Circulation promptly expanded sharply. Simultaneously, the press began to engage in a fierce competition for readers and, in doing so, they inaugurated various innovations in the existing technologies. Before 1908 no paper ever used type larger than 24pt or featured more than one headline. Anything else would have been considered "vulgar sensationalism". But, cultural restraints could not work at a time when publishers were busily competing for readers and trying to attract new ones from groups who were not accustomed to purchasing a newspaper. Accordingly, the media took on, more and more, all the trappings of a business. It was no longer the province of intellectuals but of entrepreneurs who did not hesitate to give prizes to increase their circulation or to emblazon the front page with large screaming headlines. A popular press had emerged.[16]

Impacts

The relationship between the environment and technology is not one-sided. Until now, the focus had been on technology as a social phenomenon, but it must be emphasized that technology also shapes the environment of which it is a part. Technology is not a neutral tool that can be used for good or bad. True, the press can be used to publish holy works or revolutionary tracts but, like any technology, the printing press inflicts costs and benefits that are not equitably distributed. Some individuals and groups benefit more from its introduction than others. The Sultan and the ruling elite viewed printing as a means of enhancing their power, the Young Ottomans as a way of disseminating their message and promoting the cause of reform. And, new professions, printer, journalist, publisher came to replace scribes. Whether this represented a net gain for society is not at all clear, especially if one bears in mind the behavior of the poorly paid journalists. In Yalman's words:[17]

[16] Yalman, *op. cit.*, p. 127.

[17] Yalman, *op. cit.*, p. 45.

> The journalists were distinguished more by their wild night life than anything else. They considered themselves justified in drinking to excess as they had to fulfill a delicate task and were every moment exposed to the danger of exile and prison.

Technology is not neutral in a second way. It carries its own values, a point that becomes readily apparent if one considers the kinds of impacts that have been identified by Ottoman historians.[18] The first of these is the political effect. The dissemination of books and periodicals, the emergence of the mass media, had powerful consequences for the polity. In the first place, they shaped and influenced public opinion for, as I have noted, the first Turkish newspapers were launched explicitly to generate support for reforms. In the process, a range of new concepts such as nation, liberty, natural rights, were introduced. Such ideas were subversive of traditional patterns of legitimacy, as was recognized by successive rulers who introduced censorship. Still, such efforts, even those by Abdul Hamid II, were ultimately unsuccessful; the media generated new expectations about the performance of the state, about the role and rights of citizens. Second, all these publications produced a new style of language. The traditional Ottoman form was convoluted, elaborate, and formal. The new journals, on the other hand, utilized a far more simple and direct style that was straightforward and to the point. The new language spread so quickly that by 1877 new Turkish had essentially displaced the classic Ottoman form which was reserved for news of the ruler.[19]

This change contributed to a narrowing of the marked elite–mass gap that had always characterized Ottoman society. That gap was further narrowed by the emergence of the new middle class and its growing appetite for reading. Now that literacy was increasingly widespread, people began to read for pleasure and enlightenment, as well as for professional ends. All kinds of Western works, ranging from Voltaire to Fenelon to Jules Verne, were translated and widely read, an activity that led to the development of a new Turkish literary genre. And, all these activities stimulated an interest in achieving literacy, and promoted the growth of the educational system.

[18] See the sources cited above.

[19] Yalman, *op. cit.*, p. 57.

All these impacts, however, were a function of the way in which the technology functioned in its specific environment. What remains to be noted are the consequences that resulted from the character of the technology itself. Printing embodies certain values which, whatever the context, are bound to impact upon the society in ways that are difficult to assess but are nevertheless profound and significant. Some of these were noted by Ibrahim Müteferrika when he requested permission to establish his press in 1726.[20] First, printing has preservative power. Manuscripts can be lost quite easily, for they usually exist in quite limited quantities. As Müteferrika pointed out, thousands were lost during the Mongol invasions and as a result of the Muslim expulsion from Spain. Printed matter, on the other hand, being produced in large numbers, is inherently more likely to survive. Second, printing promotes accuracy. Scribes and copyists are liable to make errors, regardless of their care and skill. Such mistakes are difficult to find and correct because of the limited number of copies that are available and the difficulties of establishing which is the correct version. And, if the scribal arts are in decline, then copyists will make many errors. This, according to Müteferrika, had happened in the Ottoman Empire. With printing editions can be more accurate, for mistakes and corruptions become more noticeable. Müteferrika pioneered in this regard, correcting Çelebi's calculations on the position of Istanbul.[21] Other advantages that would be gained from the introduction of printing, he argued, included improving learning, facilitating reading, reducing the costs of books, increasing the number of libraries, and enabling the Turks to be leaders in and protectors of learning in the Islamic world.[22]

Two other consequences of printing can be identified, each of which has important consequences for the way in which people think and perceive reality. Although it is difficult to assess the impact of new modes of thought, it is obvious that the following characteristics produced a revolution in ways of thinking throughout the world.[23] These can be summarized briefly as follows. First, printing enables the reorganization of texts and reference guides. Now data can be catalogued, codified, and

[20] Berkes, *op. cit.*, p. 40.

[21] *Idem.*

[22] Berkes, *op. cit.*, p. 40.

[23] These qualities are discussed by E.L. Eisenstein in her *The Printing Press as an Agent of Change* (Cambridge: Cambridge University Press, 1979) vol. 1, pp. 43-162.

rationalized far more easily than ever before. Indexing and cross referencing become commonplace. Moreover, maps, figures, diagrams can be incorporated easily into printed works so that technical information can be transmitted directly. And, indeed, Müteferrika did just that when adding maps and figures to Çelebi's famous geography. Second, less time had to be spent copying manuscripts and memorizing them, thus freeing scholars for more productive intellectual work. And, since texts were standardized and no longer a monopoly of professionals, students could now read for themselves; they could check the accuracy and quality of the knowledge their teachers were transmitting.

All these characteristics of printing had a profound impact everywhere that the press was introduced. Marshall McLuhan is perhaps the best known analyst of the changes which resulted, and, in his famous work, *The Gutenberg Galaxy,* he argues that the replacement of script by print transformed the social order and the way in which men see reality. Whereas society had hitherto been composed of a public that was accustomed to hearing and listening, the coming of widespread literacy and the media created a reading public that was more dispersed, atomistic, and self-centered than had ever been the case. And, since people need to identify, they found solace in new units and larger groups, including the nation state.

Conclusion

In retrospect then, it is clear that the consequences of the introduction of printing into the Ottoman Empire were profound and far-reaching, and that these consequences were a function of the nature of the technology and its interaction with the specific environment. It should be clear that any technology is a complex system that is profoundly affected by the nature of the societal context in which it operates. It does not sweep aside all before it, or work in the same way, or produce the same results in different societies. But, and this brings me to the second point that I have attempted to illustrate, though it does not exist independently of the social system which it impacts, those impacts will be determined by characteristics that inhere in the technology; any technology embodies values which cannot be controlled, and which will inevitably affect the existing culture directly and indirectly.

Given the nature of the contemporary debate in the Muslim world, and the degree to which Islamic states are engaged in transferring modern technologies from abroad, the significance of these two points extends well beyond the realm of the intellectual, and possesses important implications for policy makers and others concerned with the future shape of their societies.

[20]

The Birth of Tradition and Modernity in 18th and 19th Century Islamic Culture – The Case of Printing

REINHARD SCHULZE

Summary

This paper investigates the integration of Islamic knowledge into Muslim society made possible by the introduction of printing. Special attention is given to the publication policies of the Istanbul and Cairene printing presses from 1802 to 1848. In addition, the semantics of printing, which deeply influenced the emergence of the antonymical concepts of "tradition" and "modernity", are discussed.

Printing demanded a substantial ethical and cultural change within the Islamic culture of knowledge. It also created a social discourse in which the new reading public came to distinguish between what was regarded as "tradition" (manuscripts without a use value in the market), and what was considered "modern" (printed books). This change was rendered even more dramatic by the fact that printing was not introduced gradually in Islamic society, but emerged – like virtually all imported technologies – within a very short span of time. Once a printing press had been established, its owners, who had at their disposal the technical skills and sophisticated techniques developed in Europe since the 15th century, could print any text in a relatively short time.

In the context of Islamic culture, printing clearly marked the distinction between "tradition" and "modernity". Printing was "new", and printed Islamic texts carried the character of newness; it allowed the separation of those textual traditions that had no market value from those that attracted attention because of their material worth.

Introduction

Scholars have long recognized that terms like "tradition" require a conceptual antipode in order to convey an image of perceived reality. Hence, it can be argued that "tradition" cannot be perceived in isolation; it must be understood in reference to modernity, for it is nowadays used to delimit modernity from earlier periods of time, which survive as history. Tradition symbolizes a term of reference that is only perceptible vis-a-vis its logical antipode, namely in a synchronic modernity. By the same token, "modernity" only makes sense if it refers to a surviving historical tradition. The interdependence of tradition and modernity is, thus, an essential requisite for the weltanschauung of social groups seeking to develop a new cultural identification.

Originally, tradition and modernity do not refer to a world of objective references. Both terms constitute a single conceptual entity describing a perceived reality with regard to 'what it is' (modern) and 'what it is not' (traditional). Needless to say, a predication like 'modern' can only be applied in the environs of its logical antipode. Like other analogical terms, e.g. 'great/-small' and 'bad/good', the predication 'modern /traditional' refers to the subject, as it describes his attitude towards a perceived object, although he really wants to predicate an object of his outer world.[1]

In contrast to predicates like 'great /small' or 'bad/good', the antinomy 'traditional/modern' has a historical dimension that is important for two reasons: first, this antinomy is based on a diachronic interpretation of the world in the sense that the original conceptual base of 'what it is/what it is not' is transformed to 'what it is now/what it was formerly'. The time aspect leads to a second transformation: the predication 'what it is/what it was' is changed to a concept of 'what is/what was'. Thus, the predication 'modern/traditional' has now become an integral attribute of the subject. The originally undivided subject is split into two different states, namely into the states of tradition and modernity, or into a traditional and a modern state or society.

1 Simon Dik, *Functional Grammar*, Amsterdam [2]1979; John Lyons, *Semantics*, I–II, Cambridge 1977, p. 242 ss.; Willard Van Orman Quine, *Word and Object*, Cambridge/Mass. 1960, chapter 4.

Secondly, as the antonymy, strictly speaking, refers to those who use it and not to an object the user wants to designate, the diachronic aspects leads to a concept by means of which the subject liberates himself from history and from the social entity he, the subject, initially belonged to. This allows him to believe that he is part of a modernity, of a modern history and culture which have nothing in common with former periods and states.[2]

Throughout Islamic cultural history we find different terms that reflect the relation of contemporarity towards history, be it on the basis of law (*^{c}urf, ^{c}amal* or *^{c}âda*) or on the basis of behaviour (*taqlîd*). Urban dwellers considered the code of behaviour of nomadic tribes (*^{c}urf*) as "tradition", and contrasted it with Islamic legal system (*sharî^{c}a*), to which they attached a timeless dimension. In general, notions associated with "tradition" were originally used to reflect the historicity of the perceived reality in light of a universal ideal type developed outside the context of Islamic revelation. In this, the notion corresponds to analogous European usages, e.g.

> "non sur des croyances et des traditions populaires, mais sur la révélation d'une vérité." (Charles Seignobos, 1854–1942).

A very special use of the notion "tradition" lies in the word *ḥadîth*, reflecting a recorded narrative (in German "Überlieferung") attributed to the prophet Muhammad. These narratives too have a timeless dimension. In itself, a *ḥadîth*-tradition has no antonym. In German usages of the 18th century, however, the term tradition (as "Überlieferung") was defined in opposition to the revelation:

> "Übergebung ist auch soviel als eine Erzählung, die man vom Hörensagen weiß, nirgends aber bei einem tauglichen Schriftsteller aufgezeichnet findet, oder Menschen Satzung, davon in der Heil. Schrift nichts enthalten ist, noch gemeldet wird."

Here, we can find the term "tradition" designating something like "a consti-

2 See Jürgern Habermas, *Der philosophische Diskurs der Moderne. Zwölf Vorlesungen*, Frankfurt a.M. 1988, pp.9–33; Wolfgang Welsch, *Unsere postmoderne Moderne*, Weinheim ^{2}1988, pp. 66–77, which also deals with the history of the term "Neuzeit" and "Moderne". Cf. Reinhart Koselleck, "'Neuzeit'. Zur Semantik moderner Bewegungsbegriffe", in Reinhart Koselleck (ed.), *Studien zum Beginn der modernen Welt*, Stuttgart 1977, p. 266.

tution of men" (*Menschen Satzung*), which is contrasted with the Holy Script (*Heilige Schrift*). Owing to its specific concept, the term *ḥadîth* never turned into a more general notion of tradition as in most European languages.[3] The Arabic terms used are *taqlîd*, *ᶜâda* or *ᶜurf*, which, however, may not be summarized in a single word field, even if we are used to translating each term with the European one-word tradition.

Up to the 18th century, we cannot trace an abstract lexical unit in Islamic culture that corresponds to the western concept 'tradition'. All terms which could have been used in this sense were strictly limited to forms having a special context. A famous 14th century definition for instance reads as follows:[4]

التقليد عبارة عن اتباع الإنسان غيره فيما يقول او يفعل معتقد للحقيقة فيه من غير نظر وتأمل في الدليل كان هذا المتبع علي قوله او فعله قلادة في عنقه

("tradition is the expression of one man following another in what he says or does believing in its correctness without looking at, or reflecting on, the proof; this follower makes the other's words or deeds a necklace around his neck.")

or simply[5]:

تقليد الولاة الاعمالَ وتقليد البدنة شيئا يُعلم به أنها هدْيٌ

("to entrust rulers with the government of the provinces, to adorn a body with something known to be in fashion")

Or, the term *taqlîd* could be used in the context of *akhbâr*, 'reports', meaning the established way of reporting historical information (*taqlîd al-akhbâr*[6]). As in European cultural history, the development of an abstract and secularized term signifying "tradition" was only possible if the semantic kernel of the notion could predicate another term, or could be used as an attribute. Thus, the transformation from a concrete term ('tradition') into its abstract counterpart was only possible by using the term as a predicate, or, in a second step, as an attribute. As for the notion 'tradition', the following development in Arabic might have been expected:

3 In Islamic theology, tradition of course is supplemental to revelation.
4 ᶜAlî b. Muhammad al-Jurjânî, *kitâb at-taᶜrîfât*, Kairo 1306, s.n. (first Ottoman printing Istanbul 1253)
5 Muḥammad b. Yaᶜqûb al-Fîrûzâbâdî, *qâmûs al-muḥît*, ed. Beirut 1986, p. 399.
6 Obviously, this concept is an antonym of *ijtihâd ar-ra'y*.

a) *taqlîd*, ^{c}*âda*, ^{c}*urf* 'tradition' (used – depending on the context – mostly in the sense of "what used to be is right.")
   taqlîdî (^{c}*urfî*) [^{c}*âdî*[7]] denominization
b) predicating – attributing:
   something is *taqlîdî*, a *taqlîdî* thing or fact (in contrast with something that is not *taqlîdî*)
c) *taqlîd* 'tradition' (abstract)
   taqlîdîya 'traditionalism'
   taqâlîd (and derived forms like *taqâlîdîya*) 'old traditions', 'traditionalism' etc.

The generalization of the semantic kernel of the term tradition (*taqlîd*) presupposes objects that could be identified, i.e. predicated, by the word *taqlîdî* as traditional. Either the same object had changed its predicate from 'traditional' to 'modern', or an object predicated as 'traditional' was now regarded as obsolete and supplanted by a second object considered 'modern'. Having become an attribute, the semantic kernel of *taqlîd* had to be associated with a polar counterpart.

Originally the legal term *taqlîd* 'binding oneself to authority', had a conceptual antonym in the word *ijtihâd,* reflecting a behaviour not characterized by binding to authority, but rather by using independent judgement in a legal or theological question. As an attribute, however, the term *taqlîdî* could not be opposed to a word like *ijtihâdî*, as the former referred to situations, things and persons as well; calling an inanimate object "*ijtihâdî*" was semantically impossible. Hence, the term *taqlîd* had to be associated with a new antonym that represented in its lexical deep structure a common semantic field (like 'good/bad': scalar and polar interpretation of morality). Looking at the new antonyms, we are able to trace the revaluation of the term *taqlîd.*

In Arabic, we find several terms used as antonyms of something that is

---

7 From Koranic ^{c}Âd, "se dit des choses d'une antiquité reculée, des constructions colossales et solides, des casques énormes en acier, etc." A. de Biberstein Kazimirski, *Dictionnaire arabe-français*, Paris 1860, II, p. 400. Edward William Lane, *Arabic-English Lexicon*, London 1863, p. 2191: "Old", "ancient", also in the sense of "common".

'old': the ideal typical distinction is made by the terms *ḥadith / qadîm*; a second pair is *jadîd / khalaq/qadîm*. Whereas the first opposition judges something in accordance to its newness or oldness in time (in the sense of "once created" as opposed to eternal), the second describes its quality (-hence *khalaq* "worn"). The very specific usage of *ḥadîth* ("new"), however, seems to have prevented it from becoming the actual term for something "untraditional".[8] The first terms that paralleled usage in European languages were the words *jadîd* ("new") in Arabic and *yeni* (antonym of *eski* 'old') in Ottoman turkish.

Already in the 15th century, the Transoxanian scholars called their astronomical teachings *al-hai'a al-jadîda* ("new astronomy"). Others, like as-Suyûṭî, claimed that their "original" teaching should be labeled with *al-hai'a al-islâmîya* ("Islamic astronomy").[9] Consequently, the Paracelsian medicine was soon called *ṭibb-i jadîd* (ᶜUmar Shifâᶜî, 1704). In this context, it is interesting to compare the various titles of the first Ottoman book that contained a compilation of descriptions of the two Americas:[10]

كتابِ اقليمِ جديد (١٥٨٤)

خديثِ نو (١٥٩٠)

حديثِ نو تاريخِ هندِ غربي (ما بين ١٥٩٥ و ١٦٢٢/١٦٢٣)

تاريخِ يكي دنيا المسمى بحديثِ نو (١٦٠٠)

تاريخِ هندِ غربي المسمى بحديثِ نو (١٦٤٠)

تاريخِ يكي دنيا (١٦٩٠؟)

8 In this context, the semantic relation between the attributes *qadîm* (in the sense of *azalî*) "eternal" and *ḥadîth* "created, actual, qui paraît pour la première fois, nouveau, recent", is not under discussion. This philosophic antonymy played a role in later developments, e.g. concerning the term *ḥadâtha* ("modernity", originally "nouveauté d'une chose").

9 Reinhard Schulze, "Inqueries into Islamic Modernity Prior to the 18th Century. The Reception of the Heliocentric World among Muslim Scholars", in: A. Harrak (ed.), *Contacts between Cultures. West Asia and North Africa*, Lampeter 1992, S. 423–428 (33rd International Congress of Asian and North African Studies, Toronto 1990, Selected Papers, Vol. 1.).

10 Cf. Thomas D. Goodrich, *The Ottoman Turks and the New World. A Study of Tarih-i Hind-i Garbi and Sixteenth-Century Ottoman Americana*, Wiesbaden: Harrassowitz 1990, p. 21 ss.

ابتدا ، ظهورِ عالمِ جديد (١٦٩٠؟)

خديثِ نو تاريخِ يكي دنيا (١٦٦٧/ ١٦٦٨)

حديثِ نو (١٦٦٩ > ١٦٧٣ > ١٧٠٣)

This short list shows that Turkish *yeni* and Arabic *jadîd* were used to characterize "new facts", whereas the Persian word *new* referred to the "news" (*ḥadîth*). Still, it was difficult to apply the term *jadîd* as an antonym of *taqlîd*, as it was regarded as one of the so-called *aḍdâd* ("words with two opposite meanings"). Many a lexicographer pointed out that *jadîd* used as a passive participle could also signify "cut off"[11] and that poets loved to play with its ambiguity[12]:

أبى حُبّي سُلَيمى أن يَبِيدا   وأمسى حَبْلُها خَلَقاً جديدا

("My love of Sulaimâ has refused to perish, but her tie (of affection to me) has become worn out and cut.")

Ḥadîth also carried an ambiguous meaning: on the one hand it represented the original meaning "new", on the other it denoted a *khabar* ("what was reported", "report", "news"). This latter sense led to the concept of "tradition", i.e., something that had occurred in the past. Thus we are confronted with the paradoxical situation that something new could also signify something old, established, or even out dated. Perhaps this ambiguity prevented either term from being used as an antonym of "tradition" (in the sense of *taqlîd*). In addition, they did not cover the real meaning of the term *taqlîd*, which in the 18th century already described a concept of 'imitating/-forging'. So we find both expressions like *ᶜâdât-i jadîd* ('les usages modernes', 1846), and the antonym *jadîd/ᶜatîq* ('new/ancient, old'):

كل جديد لذيذ وكل عتيق عزيز

("tout ce qui est nouveau est agréable et tout ce qui est ancien est respectable").

11 Cf. E. W. Lane, *Arabic-English Lexicon*, London 1863, vol. I, p. 386.

12 Muḥammad Murtaḍâ az Zabîdî, *tâj al-ᶜarûs fî jawâhir al-qâmûs*, Cairo 1868, vol. II, p. 313 ss.

The following title of a collection of Ottoman treaties explicitly distinguishes between "former" and "modern" (^{c}*atîq / jadîd*):[13]

دولتِ عليه ايله دولِ متحَابه بينلرينده تيمنه ن منعقد اولان مُعاهدتِ عتيقة و جديدن مأمورينِ سلطنتِ سنيه جه مرَاجعتى لازم
گلهن فكرات عهديه يي متزمن رساله در ، استنبول ١٢٥٨ ١٨٤٢

and likewise the Arabic[14]:

قنطرة عتيقة وقنطرة جديد

whereas Suhailî, the Ottoman Turkish translator of Ahmad b. ^{c}Alî Ibn Zunbul's famous history of Egypt (written in about 1540) called his version he had completed in 1611/2 *târîkh-i Mısır qadîm ve-Mısır-ı jadîd*, thus opposing *qadîm* to *jadîd*. Here it is interesting to note that Suhailî equated the Ottoman occupation in 1516 with the beginning of a New Egypt.

Jadîd thus described the change of a quality of something. It could also mean the reestablishing of something "old", that is of something that had existed, then vanished and returned again. This is why "day and night" were called *al-jadîdân*, "the two new", and a religious scholar who wanted to restore the "authentic teachings" was named *al-mujaddid*, as he did not introduce anything new, he renewed something old.

The Turkish word *yeni* could also implicitly describe a negative state of affairs:

yenisi eskisini aratır.
("Das (schlechte) Neue läßt einen wehmütig an das (gute) Alte zurückdenken.")

Although the antonyms *jadîd/*^{c}*atîq* and *yeni/eski* include the time aspect and implicitly tend to make a value judgment about the attributed object, they did not hit the exact connotations of the terms *taqlîd / taqlîdî*. In Ottoman Turkish (and early modern Persian), the concept of *taqlîd* described a world of imitation, forgery, spectacle, duplicity but not genuine artificiality. Consequently, this concept required a notion that signified a

13 M. Seyfettin Özege, *Eski Harflerde Basılmış Türkce Eserler Katalogu*, vols. I–V, Istanbul 1971–1979, n°3920.
14 az-Zabîdî, *tâj al-*^{c}*arûs*, vol. II, p. 314.

world of originality, genuineness, authenticity and innovation. This notion of *taqlîd* was already used by al-Maqqarî when writing about the attitudes of Andalusian rulers:

وذلك أنه وَشي به للمنصور أيامَ عزمه ترك التقليد والعمل بالحديث

("[The scribe Abû Bakr Muḥammad b. ᶜAlî at-Tâjirî al-Ishbîlî died in 596/1199-1200] because he was denounced by al-Manṣûr when he decided to give up following the (bad) old and to work for the (good) new.")

Here it should be noted that al-Maqqarî used *ḥadîth* as an antonym of *taqlîd.*

In the 18th century in Ottoman Turkish usage, the term *taqlîd* designated an artificial world. In his voluminous dictionary, Mesgnien Meninski (Vienna 1680) entered the following meaning of *taqlîd*:

"*imitatio, representatio; contraffare, imitare, ne'gesti ò nel favellare, rapresentare.*"

Then he added the example:

بر كمسه نين آوازيني ويازيني تقليد ايتمك

bir kimsenin avazını ve yazını taqlîd etmek.
("to imitate someone's voice and style")

In addition, we find the following entries:
ahl-i taqlîd – "imitator, comoedus, mimus; buffone, comediante burlevole"
taqlîd oynu – "comoedia"
taqlîdji/taqlitçi, taqlîd oyuncu – "imitator, actor".

The semantic kernel "imitation" can also be found in Arabic texts of the 14th century. Ibn Khaldoun wrote:

فصار إلى تقليد الدولتَين قبلهم في وضع اسمائهم

"(And) (people) came to follow the tradition of the two preceding dynasties with regard to the use of titles."[15]

15 Ibn Khaldûn, *The Muqaddimah*, transl. by F. Rosenthal, Princeton 1967, vol. II, p. 1

In this context, however, the word *taqlîd* had to be associated with a verb denoting someone's attitude regarding a usage. Only in later time did the word *taqlîd* itself come to incorporate the meaning "imitation".

At the beginning of the 19th century at the latest, "the world of appearances" was also rendered in Arabic by the word *taqlîd*. In his dictionary published in 1828, E. Bocthor used the term *li^{c}b at-taqlîd* to translate the French "comédie". According to him, *taqlîd* could signify the meaning "imitation, copie, surtout pour ridiculiser, joue." An example may be found in Rifâ^{c}a Râfi^{c} aṭ-Ṭahṭâwî's *kitâb takhlîṣ al-ibrîz fî talkhîṣ Bârîz* (published in 1834/5): concerning the theaters of Paris, he wrote:[16]

فمن مجالس الملاهي عندهم محل تسمي التياتر والسبكتاكل وهي يُلعب فيها تقليد سائر ما وقع وفي الحقيقة أن هذه الالعاب هي جد في صورة هزل

> ("Among the places of amusement they have a place called "theater" or "spectacle". There comedies on all that happened are performed. In reality, however, these plays are tragedies in comedy form.")[17]

The negative connotation "pour ridiculiser" may be found associated with the semantic root of *taqlîd* even in early Arabic texts. Az-Zamakhsharî for example wrote:

قُلد فلانا قلادة سوء

> "Such a person was satirized with that which left upon him a lasting stigma."[18]

In Bocthor's dictionary, we also find one of the first evidences of an attributive use of *taqlîd* in the form *taqlîdî* ("imitatif") in Ottoman Turkish. In early modern Persian, however, Nâṣir-i Khusrow already used this attribute in the sense of "(an) unreasonable" or "imitating", compare his two verses (*muḍâri^{c}*)[19]:

---

16 ed. Bulaq 1249/1834–5, p. 87, ed. Muhammad ^{c}Ammâra, Cairo 1958, p. 119.

17 Cf. Reinhard Schulze, "Schauspiel oder Nachahmung? Anmerkungen zur Lektüre arabischer Reiseschriftsteller des 19. Jahrhunderts", in *Die Welt des Islams* 34 (1994).

18 Lane, *Arabic-English Lexicon*, vol. IV, p. 2557.

19 Cited in ^{c}Alî Akbar Dehkhodâ, *lughatnâme*, vol. 15, Tehran 1341, p. 849.

مپذیر قول جاهل تقلیدي　　كر چه بنام شهرهٔ دنیا شد

"Do not accept the word of an unreasonable (imitating) ignoramus
even though he might be celebrated all over the world."

and

از آن حکیم چو تقلیدي این سخن بشنود　　به جهل گفت چه دانیم ما مگر دارد (داند؟)

"When an imitator heard this word from that wise man,
he said with ignorance: What do we know? But he (pretends to know?)"

In these two cases, however, *taqlîdî* connotated someone's attitude and not the characteristic of an "imitated" (hence traditional) thing.

In summary, the term *taqlîd* developed the following field of meaning:

tying around something
↓
girding
↓
adorning
↓
adorning someone with a necklace in order to stigmatize him

↓ old
↓ bad/old
↓ binding oneself to precedent
↓ copying, imitation, simulating
counterfeiting
play acting
forging

Owing to this broad field of meaning, *taqlîd* could be used in the context of different antonymies. They represent three axes or aspects:

taqlîd	QUALITY	bad / good	*jadîd*
	TIME	old / new	*ḥadîth*
	BEHAVIOUR	bound / free	*ijtihâd*

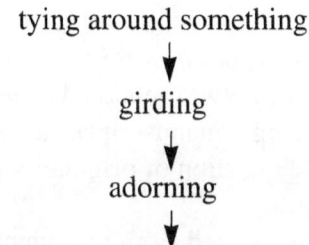

The revaluation of *taqlîd* as "bad, old and bound" at once preconditioned the existence of a concept that meant "good, new and free". Which Arabic term fulfilled these conditions?

The quality aspect has been broadened by the notion "originality /copy", which became the most important antonym of *taqlîd.* The term used to denote "originality" – being the opposite of "copy" – was *aṣl.* From its semantic kernel *aṣl* "root" Arab grammarians had derived the attribute *aṣlî* in order to signify underived Arabic words (as opposed to augmentative). The attribute *aṣlî* had a common figurative sense describing something primary or original, referring to someone's or something's natural disposition. In the stories of 1001 Nights, for instance, we find the expression:

al-bait al-aṣlî (or *al-aṣlânî*) – "the parental home".

After the term *taqlîd* had developed into a concept of imitation and copying, it was often contrasted with the word *asl* or the attribute *aṣlî*. Now, *aṣlî* was used to characterize a manuscript which had not been copied but was the original:

nuskha-yi aṣlî [*aṣlî nuskha*] or *an-nuskha al-aṣlîya.*

In Ottoman Turkish, a facsimile was rendered as *taqlîd-i khaṭṭ* ("script imitation", *khaṭṭ* usually meaning a manuscript). Accordingly, *aṣlî* was used as an antonym of *taqlîd* in the question of originality or imitation:

new	good	freed from precedent	original[20]
ḥadîth	*jadîd*	*ijtihâd(î)*	*aṣlî*

Aṣlî was embedded into the aspect system of *taqlîd.* As a result, in the 18th century *aṣlî* did not only predicate something as original, but added to this predication the connotations new/*jadîd*, good new/*ḥadîth* and freed from precedent (*ijtihâd(î)*) and falsification. The duality of originality and contemporaneousness reflected the following view of history:

20 Secularized time interpretations favoured the development of the following line:

new	good	freed from authority	modern
jadîd	*ḥadîth*	*ijtihâdî*	*ᶜaṣrî*

On the secular concept of *ᶜaṣrî*, see my article "Das islamische 18. Jahrhundert. Versuch einer historiographischen Kritik", in *Die Welt des Islams* 30 (1990), p. 140–159.

aṣl	*taqlîd*	*aṣlî*	
			→ time axis
what it was originally	what was (what is)	what is (should be)	
			→ time axis
[*târîkh*]	*taqlîd*	^{c}*aṣrî*	

Accordingly, something contemporary (^{c}*aṣrî*) could be either the original (*aslî*) or something absolutely 'new' (*ḥadîth*). The predicates that signified the state "what is / what should be" had to be derived from the perceived world and depended on the positive or negative judgement of history.

A medium that mirrored both the view of tradition and modernity was printing.[21] Printing fundamentally changed the attitudes in the Muslim world toward history, and helped to class texts with both identities.

Islamic book printing

When, in September 1803, a manuscript text dealing with theological questions was printed as a book by the newly established printing house *dâr aṭ-tibâ^{c}a al-jadîda*, the foundation was laid for a profound and momentous change within the cultural production of Islam. Since the foundation of the first official printing house in Istanbul *dâr aṭ-ṭibâ^{c}a al-ma^{c}mûra* seventy-six years earlier, the edict of Sultan Aḥmad III of 15.11.1139 /5.7.1727 had been in force. It prohibited the printing of texts that dealt with Koran, *tafsîr*,

21 See Lucien Febvre (en coop. avec J. H. Martin), *L'apparition du livre*, Paris 1958; Elisabeth L. Eisenstein, "L'avénement de l'imprimerie et la Réforme", in *Annales* 26 (1971) 6, pp. 1354–1382; Robin Myers/Michael Harris (eds.), *Spreading the Word. The Distribution Network of Print 1550–1850*, Winchester/Detroit 1990; Elisabeth L. Eisenstein, *The printing revolution in early modern Europe*, Cambridge: Cambridge UP 1990 (repr.); Michael Giesecke, *Der Buchdruck in der frühen Neuzeit*, Frankfurt a. M.: Suhrkamp 1991; Hans Bekker-Nielson (ed.), *From Script to Book: a symposium (Odense 15./16.11.1982)*, Odense: Odense UP 1986.

ḥadîth and *fiqh*. The original restricted injunction was later expanded to include the printing of any manuscripts containing Islamic texts.[22]

Until 1803, only those texts had been printed that could not be directly classed among the Islamic sciences. From 1727 to 1747, seventeen titles in twenty-one volumes had been printed, with a total circulation of 12,500. After a prolonged period of closure, the printing house was reopened in 1783/4. Still under the direct control of the Ottoman regime, the leaseholders of the printing house, Aḥmad Wâṣif and Muḥammad Rashîd, edited 29 additional titles. Whereas during the first period the Imperial history had been stressed, now dictionaries, grammars and military texts were mainly printed. For Islamic cultural production, this early printing period was of no great importance.

The production of manuscripts still occupied a monopolistic position in the field of Islamic sciences. Hence, the symbiotic concurrence of writing, copying and distribution, including permission to read a text in public (*ijâza*), was dominated by the *ᶜulamâ'* and *quḍât*, who exercised strict control over Islamic cultural production. Even though they did not directly earn their living by copying manuscripts, they controlled a large number of copyists and even the storage of manuscripts. Even after the introduction of printing, the scholars and judges were able to maintain their leading position within the system of production and distribution. The approximately forty booksellers of Istanbul, who were organized into a very highly esteemed guild, were under the scholars' and judges' control. In addition, the scholars and judges were members of the board of censors that Sultan ᶜAbdalḥamîd had created in 1784.[23]

22 Persian Islamic book printing started in India in the 1780s. The first Islamic book printed in Calcutta was perhaps Shaykh Saᶜdî Shîrâzî [died in 691/1292], *pandanâme* (on ethics), Calcutta 1788 [with an English translation by Francis Gladwin]. See C. A. Storey, "The Beginnings of Persian Printing in India", in J. D. C. Pavry, *Oriental Studies in Honour of Cursetji Erachji Pavry*, London 1933, pp. 457–461. Independent Islamic book printing started in Lucknow in 1819/20 (Aḥmad ash-Shirwânî, *al-manâqib al-ḥaidârîya*, Lucknow 1235 (1819/20)).

23 A summary of early accounts of the whole story concerning the introduction of printing in Istanbul may be found in Abbé Toderini, *Litteratur der Türken. Aus dem Italienischen mit Zusätzen und Anmerkungen von Philipp W. G. Hausleutner*, I–II, Königsberg 1790, II, p. 169 s.

Thus, the production of printed books had become a part of the existing social system without destroying its foundations. This, however, was only true for the sale and distribution of books. The most important change took place within the sphere of production. Already in the first edict issued by Sultan Aḥmad III in 1727, the fact was stressed that a printed book was much cheaper than a manuscript.

This commercial aspect was also emphasized in the decree of Sultan ᶜAbdalḥamîd. He justified the reintroduction of printing by stating that books printed during the first phase of the Istanbul press's existence (from 1727 to 1747) were no longer readily available for purchase. Moreover, if a copy were to be sold, the price was much too high, sometimes even higher than what had to be paid for a corresponding manuscript copy. As a result, the printing office was obliged to align the price of a book with the production costs and an adequate profit. Another factor in the equation was that the leaseholders of the printing office had to pay a duty for the profit on each printed sheet.

On the basis of this calculation, the production cost of one printed sheet was fixed at 1 para and it was sold for 1.5 para, giving a printed book an average cost of 5 piasters; in comparison, a manuscript copy of the same text cost 100 to 500 piasters. Thus, generally speaking, a printed book cost only a tenth of the price demanded for a manuscript or, viewed from another perspective, by using printing methods it was possible to produce ten times more copies of a text than by using manuscript techniques, although the same sum of money and less time were spent. As Ibrâhîm-i Pečuyî observed before 1640[24]:

بیک جلدک بر جلد خطّی قدر زحمت اولمز

> "Printing a thousand volumes causes less drudgery than (writing) one manuscript."

In the long run, even the scholars involved in the production of manuscripts could not ignore this commercial reality. Since they earned their living by copying manuscripts, they obviously required manuscripts to copy. As a

24 Ibrâhîm-i Pečuyî, *târîkh*, vol. I, Istanbul 1281 (1864/5), p. 363 s.

rule, their income was – at best – sufficient to purchase one major manuscript a year. By buying printed books, however, they could acquire ten texts a year at the same cost.

The edict of 1727 also gave emphasis to the fact that Islamic knowledge had become something different from non-religious knowledge. Whereas the latter could be spread through the new printing technique (which in fact was not new at all for the Ottomans) the proliferation of Islamic knowledge was restricted to production of manuscripts, a very sophisticated process.

Manuscripts and books

As long as only one printing office produced books, the manuscript tradition was not endangered fundamentally, as the printing office could not meet the general demand for texts. Thus, for years both techniques of cultural production Were complementary facets of a single process. Gradually, however, book printing gained ground. Towards the end of the eighteenth century, Indian printing offices started to print literature on Islamic subjects. It is, however, not known whether these books were sold in the Ottoman Empire.

When a printing office was opened specializing in setting texts in Arabic script was opened in Kazan in 1801, among the first works printed were the famous *at-tarîqa al-muḥammadîya*, written by Muḥammad b. Pîr ᶜAlî al-Birkawî (Birgili) (929/1523-981/1573), and translated into Tatar Turkish by the famous mystic, ᶜAbdalᶜazîz Tuqtamishoglu, and an anonymous versificated translation of al-Birkawî's *wasîyatnâma.*[25] The Russian administration had given order that the owner of this printing office, the merchant Abû

25 German summary *Ist die muhammedanische Religion an sich böse und verwerflich? Hat sie Aehnlichkeiten mit der christlichen? Verdient sie nach der christlichen den ersten Rang?*, Ratiopolis 1790. Cf. Madelaine C. Zilfi, *The Politics of Piety: The Ottoman Ulema in the Postclassical Age, 1600–1800*, Minneapolis 1988, pp. 129ss. It should be noted that the first book printed in Istanbul was a text of the Kadizadili tradition. See also Semiramis Çavuşoglu, *The Kadizadeli movement: An attempt of* şeri`at*-minded reform in the Ottoman Empire*, Ph.D., Princeton/N.J. 1990, p. 48 s. and Reinhard Schulze, "Was ist die islamische Aufklärung?", *Die Welt des Islams* 36 (1996) p. 266–325.

l-Ghâzî Bûrâshughlî, should publish "Korans, prayer books and similar books only". Bûrâshughlî published seven Islamic texts in 1801 and 1802, including extracts of the Koran, dogmatic texts for beginners (*îmân sharṭî*) and a Koran.[25a]

Al-Birkawî, who was known for his fierce attacks against those scholars who read the Koran for money, was also the first Islamic author whose books were printed in Istanbul. The owners of the new printing office in Skutari did not wait for official permission to print books dealing with Islamic subjects. Thus, they abrogated the decree of 1727 by publishing *risâla-yı Birgiwî* as the first Islamic book. This text was an Ottoman-Turkish translation of the abridged edition of al-Birkawî's *aṭ-ṭarîqa al-muḥammadîya*.

The new director of the Istanbul printing office, ᶜAbdarraḥmân Afandî, who had been appointed in 1801, seems to have been so pleased with the commercial success of the *risâla* that in June, 1804 he edited the commentary of Qâḍîzâdeh Istanbulû Aḥmad b. Muḥammad Amîn's *jauharîya-i bahîya-i aḥmadîya-i fî sharḥ al-waṣîya al-muḥammadîya*, which is a commentary on al-Birkawî's shorter treatise on morals. In the same year, he published another commentary of Qâḍîzâdeh, namely the book *farâ'id al-fawâ'id fî bayân al-ᶜaqâ'id*, a commentary on an-Nasafî written by the famous pietist preacher Qâḍîzâdeh Mehmed, 1582-1635[26]).

But whereas scholars from Kazan used the printing process to publish their own writings (they published seven volumes between 1802 and 1809)[27], the scholars in Istanbul hesitated to follow their example. Tacitly they apparently agreed, as far as their own (original) writings were concerned, to comply with the decree that had enjoined against the printing of Islamic texts.

Yet another change engendered by the introduction of printing was a new outlook toward the text itself, which was now available both as a manu-

25a For a detailed discussion of this printing office see See Michael Kemper, *Sufis und Gelehrte in Tatarien und Baschkirien 1789–1889. Der islamische Diskurs unter russischer Herrschaft*, Bochum, unpubl. Ph.D. 1997, p. 44 s., 155 s.

26 See Ibrahim Usakizadeh, *Lebensbeschreibungen berühmter Gelehter und Gottesmänner des Osmanischen Reichs im 17. Jahrhundert*, ed. Hans Joachim Kissling, Wiesbaden 1965, S. 43–45.

27 Cf. Kemper, *Sufis und Gelehrte, S.*

script and as a book. Initially the printer of a book had the same attitude towards the text as the copyist of a manuscript; he just copied the text using a new medium. Soon, however, a new factor in the equation entered the commercial publishing process, namely the distribution of the book.

The neologism used to describe the process of book distribution was *nashr* "spreading". This term had already been used to designate the spreading of the contents of a manuscript. Now, the term was restricted to the book itself. In dictionaries printed at the beginning of the 19th century, we find entries like:

édition- ------- *ṭab*^{c} *wa-nashr* (Bianchi)
éditeur ------- بر مؤلفگ كتابيني طبع ونشردن كمسنه
(s.o. who prints and spreads a book of an author, Bianchi)
édition ------- *ṭab*^{c} (Bocthor, 1828)
------- *iẓhâr al-kitâb*

Thus, the production of a book was understood at that time both as a process of printing and distribution. This view was still valid in the beginning of the 20th century.

The synchronous existence of a manuscript and a book created a problem of value and use. As soon as a text had been printed and distributed as a book, the manuscript original was stored away and lost its use value to a group that, up to that time, had established its identity on the production and management of manuscripts, namely, the scholars. It was they who now had to develop a new relation with the printed text.

In lieu of the use value, the exchange value became important and underlined the fact that a manuscript had now become a pure commodity. A book, too, was a commodity, and, as we have seen, book production had begun as a production of commodities. Just as every commodity is offered to an anonymous public, the printed book entered a new market among a much broader public.

In the European context, this process was reflected in the technical terms that describe the world of books. In the 18th century, European book production had been expanded to a lay, i.e. non-clerical, market. The term "to publish" (*publier*) was used to connotate the process of editing a book.

In German, the analogous term *veröffentlichen* came into use only in the 1830s, in accord with the specific situation of the German book market. The term *Edition*, which had been used up to then, was now restricted to the very specific sense of publishing journals and texts.

These terms can be viewed in the context of a new, organic form of social organization that had emerged in the 18th century; this was the dichotomy "public realm" / "private realm" (*Öffentlichkeit /Privatheit*). As a commodity, printed books targeted the public, who constituted the abstract body of consumerism. Manuscripts, however, were now relegated to the domain of privacy.

The relation manuscript-book, further, paralleled the concepts "old" and "new". A manuscript was old in the sense that it had been written in former times; a book was new because it was printed.

An Islamic text now had a double identity. It could be:

(Manuscript) <
- old
- rare
- belonging to the private realm
- without use value
- (later of great material value)

or it could be:

(Book) <
- new
- widely spread
- belonging to the public realm
- having a high use value
- (generally of little material value)

This double identity created the preconditions for a changing attitude towards texts. Before being printed as a book, the text had to be verified, and out of a great number of manuscript copies, the editor had to choose the one that was "true", that is the one that best represented the original text of the author. The Muslim editors spoke of *taḥqîq*, meaning verification of a text before printing. The Arabic term *aṣlî* was now applied to a text that was deemed worthy of being printed. But what was *aṣlî,* and who decided what was to be considered as *aṣlî*?

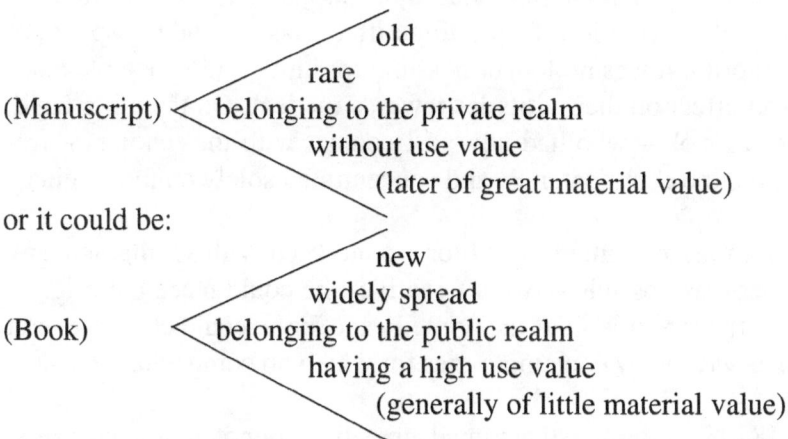

From 1803 to 1850, Islamic scholars were still the authorities who controlled the private and public libraries where thousands of manuscripts had piled up. It was their task to decide the ones to release for printing. At first, they favoured texts that could be used in the field of teaching. Consequently, they gave precedence to manuscripts that had been composed the way they were used to: the text consisted of the original, a commentary, glosses and sometimes even super-glosses (*matn, sharḥ, ḥâshiya, ta*ᶜ*lîqât*). This technique permitted timeless continuity of an original text.

However, reading a text and commenting on its contents was one matter. Anyone who had purchased a manuscript was able to read the original and the different grades of commentaries, assuring him a close link to the author. But soon the scholars had to take cognizance of the fact that printing made different demands on the text.

Unlike a manuscript penned by a learned man, the printed book was sold to an anonymous public. The scholar, who had been used to propagating the ideas in a specific text by reading it out to his pupils[28], now had to face the fact that the book, once it left the printing office, was beyond the sphere of his direct authority. It was no longer possible for him to influence the readers or have an effect on their attitudes towards the text. On the other hand, the reader of a book – who had now lost contact with the scholars – frequently ignored the commentaries, and concentrated solely on the original.

This state of affairs permitted the editor – concerned with selling as many copies of a book as possible – two alternatives: he could place the original text clearly in the foreground of the printed page, or he could choose to edit only new texts written by contemporaries for which no commentary existed.

During the 1840s, the term *aṣlî* assumed a positive connotation, contrasting originality with non-originality. Books containing original texts were more valuable than books formatted like manuscripts[29], i.e., with extensive commentaries in the margins or elsewhere.

28 In doing so he was also allowed to teach the book's contents (*ijâza khâṣṣa*).

29 In German, the word *Originalität* still reflects this attitude. It means either "original" in the sense of *aṣlî* (originär), or *originell,* with the meaning "novel", or "a novel type" of something.

This attitude contributed to the fact that, after the introduction of printing, an original text was only valid and useful if it was printed; before being printed or edited, a text no longer had any use value. As a result, thousands of manuscripts covering widely differing subjects were consigned to the background of contemporaneous cultural production because, from the viewpoint of the scholars who formed part of the new public, they represented an obsolete tradition from which the ahistorical, timeless originality of important texts needed to be distinguished.

This obsolete tradition was identified with the Islamic term *taqlîd*. But whereas this word had formerly been used to describe the behaviour of a person, it was now applied to a past period embedded in history.

History, itself, was divided into two forms of tradition: the good (*aṣlî*), and the bad (*taqlîd*). In the former, the individual's behaviour reflected the construed originality of the "new age", whereas in the latter, behaviour was characterized by eclecticism, copying, mimicry and imitation. The *taqlîd*-time separated the good tradition from the present time.

With the help of printed books, the "good" tradition could be revived or invented. The revival or invention of an original tradition, however, pertained to the world where the "up-to-date" scholars and intellectuals lived. It could be modelled according to the identification needs of those social groups seeking a new self-understanding. By choosing texts out of the thousands of manuscripts, scholars were able to create a "good" new tradition and a contemporary self-knowledge.

Themes and subjects of Early Islamic Book printing

By 1817/18, the impact of the tabu against printing books that dealt with Islamic topics had been weakened. Its effect, however, was still noticeable. From 1803 to 1817 only eight books dealing with of this type had been printed in Istanbul. An initial boom started in 1818. Within ten years, twenty-one Islamic books were printed and, according to Jale Baysal's counting[30] the figure may have been as high as thirty two. This amounted to 11.2% of the total book production of Istanbul.

After a short recession, in 1835 a second boom set in. Subsequently, manuscript production decreased significantly in Istanbul. The invention of lithographic printing by Aloys Senefelder, which enabled the first books to be published in Paris around 1816, also fundamentally influenced the spread of the printing of Islamic books.[31] This new technology was first used in Madras and Lucknow in 1820, spread to Tabriz in 1825[32] and reached Istanbul in 1830.[33]

With the help of lithography, the last tabu could be broken, namely the printing of the Koran. In Teheran, a lithographed Koran was published in 1828, one year later in Houghy/India and finally, in 1830, in Istanbul.[34] A concomitant benefit was that, due to lithographic printing, at least some famous copyists could be integrated into the printing production process. The editor of the Istanbul Koran (Sharafzâdeh) hinted at this very important fact in his postscript. Finally, since the Ottoman Sultan Maḥmūd II himself ordered the printing of the Koran, it may be assumed that the regime no longer had interest in maintaining the printing tabu.

From 1821, after the official Egyptian printing office in Bulaq had been inaugurated, no one spoke of a specific injunction against printing religious

30 Jale Baysal (Bugra), *Müteferrika'den birinci meşrutiyete kadar Osmanlı Türklerinin bastıkları kitaplar*, Stambul 1968.

31 Aloys Senefelder, *Vollständiges Handbuch der Steindruckery*, München/Wien 1818.

32 Printing at Tabriz already started in 1812 under the patronage of Crown Prince ᶜAbbâs Mîrzâ; the first book printed was the *fathnâme* (1817). The printing press known as *basmakhâne* was directed either by Mîrzâ Sâliḥ Shîrâzî, who had visited England, or Mîrzâ Zayn al-ᶜÂbidîn. Because of technical problems and esthetic considerations, Shîrâzî introduced lithographic printing in 1824/5 from Russia, cf. Y. Porter, "Arts du livre et illustration", in Y. Richard (ed.), Entre l'Iran et l'occident, Paris 1989.

33 In 1830/1, the wâlî of Iraq, Dâ'ûd Pasha, also used a lithographic press to print a history called *dauḥat al-wuzarâ'*, written by Rasûl Ḥâwî. See Michael W. Albin, "Iraq's First Printed Book", in *Libri* 31(1981), pp. 167–174.

34 In Kazan, the Koran was printed as a fourth edition of the famous St. Petersburg Koran (1st ed. probably 1787) in 1809. A new edition was published in 1817. See *Bibliothèque de M. le Baron Silvestre de Sacy*, vol. I, Paris 1842, p. 320s. (n° 1464–1467).

texts.[35] Only four years later, a new edition of Qaḍîzâdeh's commentary to al-Birkawî's *al-waṣîya al-muḥammadîya* appeared, the twelfth book to be printed at Bulaq. So the preconditions for the integration of the Islamic tradition into the new cultural production had been fulfilled both in Istanbul and in Bulaq.

A review of the Islamic books printed between 1802 and 1842 in Istanbul and between 1821 and 1842 in Bulaq indicates that the selection of the manuscripts to be printed was not random, but determined by two factors:

1. the choice of tradition as a mirror of present needs,
2. the demands of European libraries.

(in the following, only books specifically identified in the current research are dealt with[36]):

Generally speaking, the following facts can be stated:

a. Output

During the period under review, a total of eighty-one Islamic books (with the exception of historiography, natural sciences, linguistics and *adab*) were printed, forty eight in Istanbul and thirty three in Bulaq. Islamic book production reached 24% of the total in Istanbul and 13% in Bulaq (514 and 248 titles respectively). The edited number of copies ranged from 500 to 4000; the formats varied from small quarto editions to three-volume folios.

b. Subjects

The subjectsof the Islamic books printed may be classified as follows:

- dogmatics (*ᶜaqâ'id*)
- jurisprudence (*fiqh*)
- mysticism (*taṣawwuf*)
- rhetoric and logic (*bayân, manṭiq*)
- *tafsîr*
- *ḥadîth*
- other subjects.

---

35 See e.g. Anouar Abdel-Malek, *Idéologie et renaissance nationale. L'Égypte moderne*, Paris 1969, ²1975, pp. 164–185.

36 It may be assumed that the total Islamic book production in Istanbul till 1842 amounted to some 127 titles, in Kazan 201.

Islamic book printing 1802–1848

SYNOPSIS

	Istanbul[37]	Bulaq[38]	Egypt[39]	Azhar[40]
Period	1802–1842	1821–1842	1687–1797	1800–1920
Total	514	252	222	392 153
Islamic titles	48 9,4% 127 24.9%	33 13.3%	?	275 95
Subjects				
Law	8	7	65	55 29
Dogmatics	10	8	23	18 15
Logic, Rhetorics	15	3	20	8 3
Mysticism	7	10	18	26 8
Exegetics	1	1	2	2 2
Hadîth	1	1	50	5 1
Fatwa	5	0	?	3 ?
Others	1	3	?	? ?
Total	48	33	178	117 58
Language	106	38	?	8 14
Sciences etc.	134	113	37	2 5
History	21	20	?	4 0
Literature etc.	125	48	?	11 2
Grand Total	514	252	222	392 153

37 For the sources, please see the bibliography.

38 My own counting, based on the works cited in the bibliography. Nuṣair, *kutub*, p. mim, gives the following totals for Egyptian book production: in the 1820s there were 105 titles, in the 1830s, 358, and in the 1840s, 404. For the period under review she counts more than 463 books.

39 The number of manuscripts written in Egypt is derived from: ᶜAbdarraḥmân al-Jabartî, *kitâb ᶜajâ'ib al-âthâr fî t-tarâjim wa-l-akhbâr*, vol. I a. II, Bulaq 1302, as cited by J. Heyworth-Dunne, *An Introduction to the History of Education in Modern Egypt*, London (1938), p. 83. A new evalution should be made on the basis of Thomas Philipp & Guido Schwald, *A Guide to ᶜAbd al-Raḥmân al-Jabartî's History of Egypt*, Stuttgart 1994, p. 221–265.

40 Gilbert Delanoue, "Écrits et milieux d'évots dans l'Egypte du XIXe siècle", in Jacques Berque, Dominique Chevallier (eds.), *Les Arabes par leurs archives (XVIe–XXe siècles)*, Paris 1976, pp. 163–176. The first number refers to printed books, the second to manuscripts.

Nuṣair states that up to 1900, 10,405 books had been printed in Egypt alone.[41] In her counting, she includes 1346 translations (7.7% of the total book production) and entered each reedition seperately. According to her listing, the following Islamic subjects were put on the book market:

Subjects	Titles	Subject Groups	Titles	Percentage
Logic	115	Logic	115	4.2%
Ethics	42	Ethics and Philosophy	371	13.6%
Philosophy	329			
Islam (in general)	32	Islam	32	
Koran: science	19	Koran	294	11.1%
texts	40			
tajwîd	26			
Recitation	29			
asbâb an-nuzûl	1			
Lexicography	6			
i^cjâz	7			
tafsîr	166			
ḥadîth	259	*ḥadîth*	259	9.5%
Dogmatics	48	Dogmatics	61	
Sects	13			
Law	221	Law	995	35%
mâlikiya	189			
shâfi^cîya	338			
ḥanafîya	172			
ḥanbalîya	5			
Mysticism	405	Mysticism	405	14.8%
Muḥammad	198	Early History	231	8.5%
Companions	33			
Islamic Titles	2723		2723	100%
Grand Total	10,405		10405	(26.2%)

41 ^cÂyida Ibrâhîm Nuṣair, *al-kutub al-^carabîya allatî nushirat fî Misr fî l-qarn at-tâsi^c ^ca-shar*, Cairo 1990, p. mim.; as for Ottoman Turkish books, Özege counts 25554 titles printed up to the early 30s of the 20th century. He includes Ottoman Turkish books printed in Bulaq, Cairo, Paris and other places, so that this number has to be reduced considerably. This shows that in Egypt, book production at caught up with, if not surpassed, that of Istanbul by the turn of the century.

The first synopsis shows that the traditionalization of Islamic culture differed in accordance with the geographical region.[42] Whereas in Istanbul, Islamic texts dealing with rhetoric and logic were placed in the foreground, the Bulaq printing office stressed titles of Islamic mysticism. Most striking is the fact that the tradition of *ḥadîth*-writings, which had dominated the Islamic cultural production in 18th century Egypt, was clearly cut off the moment printing came into use. Until 1848, texts on *fiqh*/jurisprudence were also relatively small in number, unlike the situation in the 18th century.

Therefore, it can be said that the inception of printing marks a break within Islamic cultural history. The pillars of Islamic culture in 18th century Eypt, *ḥadîth* and *fiqh,* Were replaced by *taṣawwuf* and *ᶜaqîda*. In Istanbul, on the other hand, texts on Islamic law still retained a prominent position, but the kernel of the Islamic cultural production was logic and rhetoric literature (a situation very much like that in India).

Regarding Islamic book production, the following general observations can be made:

a. Very few books written by contemporary authors were printed either in Istanbul or in Bulaq. The scholars seem to have used the printing offices only to reproduce traditional texts. They themselves clung to the manuscript mode of production until 1850/60. Egyptian scholars seem to have used printing for their own writings prior to their Istanbul colleagues.
b. It has to be assumed that, for a limited transitional period, manuscripts and printed books were of equal worth, as some printed books predetermined the knowledge of texts still in manuscript form.
c. The number of printed commentaries or glosses of original texts was relatively small (compared to the number of written commentaries). For the period under review, 39 books containing original texts can be identified (24 in Istanbul and 23 in Bulaq; this means that the works of eight

42 In what follows, only the main tendencies of Islamic book printing prior to 1848 are discussed. Nuṣair's data indicate further and important changes in the second half of the 19th century. The high proportion of traditional Islamic subjects printed after 1850 demonstrates that by then, the manuscript tradition had been totally supplanted by printing. Even the field of law, which had preciously been transmitted mainly by manuscripts – reflecting the scholars' attitude in favour of maintaining a separate readership – was also embedded in the new market.

primary authors were printed in Istanbul as well as in Bulaq). The proportion of primary works to commentaries was 70% in Bulaq and 50% in Istanbul. Hence, originality became an important feature of Islamic book printing.

d. The fact that in Bulaq a very high portion of printed books dealt with mysticism suggests an independent tradition that should not be considered as simply a poor imitation of Istanbul. The primary works printed at Bulaq were, furthermoe, texts of Egyptian authors. Most interestingly, it apparently made no difference whether a book was printed in Ottoman Turkish or in Arabic.

e. In contrast to texts on language and linguistics, only some of the books of Istanbul were reedited in Bulaq. This may also confirm the assumption that in the field of Islamic culture, the Bulaq printing office reflected an independent Egyptian tradition.

Apart from these general trends, within each Islamic subject some common features can also be traced:

a. *^{c}aqâ'id*

Both in Istanbul and Bulaq, the field of Islamic dogmatics was one of the major printing themes. Three commentaries on al-Birkawî's writings on this subject were produced. Besides al-Birkawî, the Istanbul publishers used texts of ^{c}Umar b. Muḥammad an-Nasafî (460/1068–577/1142) and of his commentaries, as well as of the famous scholar ^{c}Adud ad-Dîn al-Îjî (died 756/1355) and his work on *kalâm* (theology), *al-mawâqif fî ^{c}ilm al-kalâm*.

Some evidence is found of a "revival" of the Mâturîdî *kalâm* tradition, which apparently also took place in Bulaq. There, among others, the famous work *as-sawâd al-a^{c}zam* of Abû l-Qâsim as-Samarqandî (died in 342/953) was edited.

Also in Bulaq, besides this Ḥanafî Mâturîdî tradition, a new tendency developed: that of printing books containing Mâlikî dogmatic texts. For instance, the *jauharat at-tauḥîd* of Ibrâhîm b. Ibrâhîm al-Laqânî (died in 1041/1631) was printed. It was also commented on by his son 'Abdassalâm and many Egyptian scholars of the 18th and 19th century had also written glosses on it.

Ibrâhîm b. Muḥammad al-Ba(i)jûrî (1198/1783–1276/1860) was one of the first scholars to avail himself of this tendency. His work on Islamic dogmatics, including a commentary on Muhammad b. Yûsuf as-Sanûsî's (died in 892/1486), was printed in Bulaq under the title *as-sanûsîya au ᶜaqîdat ahl at-tauḥîd as-sughrâ*.

b. Logic and rhetoric

In Istanbul, as in India, printing of books dealing with rhetoric and logic was very common. In Egypt, however, this subject was relegated to the background. The Istanbul printing offices[43] fell back on only four primary texts, including commentaries on them:

– al–Îjî: *risâla fî adab al-baḥth*
– al-Abharî (died in 663/1265): *kitâb al-isâghûghî* (εἰσαγωγη)
– as-Sakkâkî (555/1160–626/1226): *miftâḥ al-ᶜulûm*
– al-Kâtibî (died in 675/1276): *risâla shamsîya fî l-qawâᶜid al-manṭiqîya*

In Bulaq, once again the Maliki background of the Maghribi Ahzar scholars affected the printing in this field. The first book concerning logic to be printed was ᶜAbdarraḥman b. Muḥammad al-Akhḍarî's (920/1514-?) *as-sullam al-muraunaq yuraqqâ bihî ᶜilm al-manṭiq* (commented on by al-Bajûrî).

c. Law

Ibrâhîm b. Muḥammad al-Ḥalabî's (died in 956/1549) Ḥanafî work on the *furûᶜ* (applied *fiqh*) *multaqâ al-abḥur* and glosses and commentaries on the *kitâb munyat al-muṣallî* (written by al-Kashgharî /7th/13th century) constituted the basis for printing Ḥanafî jurisprudence literature in both Istanbul and Bulaq. In addition, the Bulaq publishers specialized in editing works of Egyptian authors, e.g. ad-Dumyâṭî (died 814/1411) and at-Timirtâshî (died 1005/1595). In Istanbul, an Ottoman-Turkish translation of as-Sarakhsî's commentary on ash-Shaibânî's famous book *kitâb as-siyar al-kabîr* was printed. In the field of jurisprudence there was naturally a close connection between both printing and the regime. It must be assumed that here the *quḍât* decided what was to be printed and not the scholars. This may ex-

43 Up till 1875, 115 printing offices had been founded in Istanbul, 6 in other parts of the Ottoman Empire (including Egypt).

plain why in the field of *fiqh*, the Bulaq printing office had very limited freedom of choice. More than half of the works on *fiqh* printed there were reeditions of Istanbul books. The publication of ad-Dumyaṭi's book on the merits of the *jihâd* (Just War) *masârî l-ashwâq* – as a complete edition or in parts – during the Morea campaign of Ibrâhîm Pasha in 1826 underlines in particular the dependency of printing law books on the concurrence of the regime.

d. Mysticism

As if the Bulaq printers were trying to demonstrate their independence, they concentrated their activities on editing different books dealing with Islamic mysticism. One book in this field that had been printed often, and which had a very wide circulation, was the *fuṣûṣ al-ḥikam* of Muḥyî d-Dîn b. ᶜArabî (died in 1240). It was printed in an Ottoman-Turkish translation. Another author favoured by publishers in Istanbul, Egypt and India was ᶜAlî b. Ḥusain al-Kâshifî (died in 909/1504), whose description of miracles of early Naqshbandî shaykhs (*rashaḥât ᶜain al-ḥayât*) had been the first book in the field of mysticism to be printed at all. In addition to these two primary works, various texts of the following *turuq* (orders) were printed: *shâdhilîya, kubrawîya, jilwatîya* and *mawlawîya.*

It may be of interest that most Arabic texts were printed in Istanbul and most Ottoman-Turkish texts (and some Persian texts) at Bulaq. This is especially true for the famous mystical encyclopaedia *maᶜrifatnâme* by Ibrâhîm Ḥaqqî-i Endurunu (1703–1780), which was printed in three editions at Bulaq (1835, 1839, 1841).[44] This shows that the market for Arabic or Ottoman-Turkish texts was not limited to the corresponding metropolises only. The exact explanation of this phenomenon, however, requires further detailed studies regarding the relationship of Arabic to Ottoman scholarship and book marketing.

e. *Other subjects*

The printing of works dealing with *tafsîr*, *ḥadîth*, and other Koranic sciences, was less frequent than in the four above-mentioned fields. Bulaq and Istanbul each produced only one book on *tafsîr* and one on *ḥadîth*. The two works on *tafsîr* were:

44 The first Istanbul edition dates to 1867.

- al-Kâshifî (Ḥusain, the father of the above-mentioned author): *tafsîr-i mawâhib* in an Ottoman translation in Istanbul.
- Ismâ^{c}îl Ḥaqqî (1063/1652–1137/1725): *rûḥ al-bayân fî tafsîr al-qur'ân* in Bulaq.

Both works belonged to the mystic *tafsîr* tradition. Regarding *ḥadîth* literature, the two works printed were:

- an-Najashî's commentary *sharḥ ash-shamâ'il* on Abû ^{c}Îsâ Muḥammad at-Tirmidhî's *kitâb ash-shamâ'il*.
- ^{c}Alî Ḥâfiz al-Qastamûnî's commentary on an-Nawawî's (631/1233 – 676/1278) famous *kitâb al-arba^{c}în ḥadîthan* (*ḥadîth-i arba^{c}în sharḥi*).

The small degree of interest in printing texts on *tafsîr* and *hadîth* may be explained by the fact that the tabu against printing religious works still exercised a certain influence. After the Koran had been printed, however, this tabu seems to have disappeared. It can be therefore assumed that books on these two subjects had no market. Only in the 1860s were books on *ḥadîth* (al-Bukhârî etc.) printed in Bulaq.

Conclusions

This very short review on the subject of early Islamic book printing in Bulaq and Istanbul leads to the following conclusions:

- Works on *ḥadîth* and *tafsîr* had no market.
- In the field of dogmatics, great importance was attached to Mâturîdî *kalâm*.
- In Istanbul, logic and rhetoric had priority over all other subjects.
- In Egypt/Bulaq, already at an early stage, a tendency towards the development of an Egyptian tradition determined the choice of texts to be printed.
- Within the field of mysticism, those texts that constituted the basis for what was formerlly called the neo-Sufic movement were given priority.
- With the development of a conscience of heritage (*turâth*) and the privatization of the book production, the Islamic book market in Egypt

boomed after 1850. The large group of Islamic jurists put their tradition on the market and dominated Islamic book printing.[45]
- The new public gained entry to Islamic tradition mainly by using mystic or philosophic texts.

Concerning printing itself, it may be concluded that the adoption of technology assisted in the development of the "commodity character" of Islamic culture in the 19th century. An average edition of a book in Bulaq – about one thousand 1000 copies, at an average price of 5 piasters – had a greater economic impact than almost any manuscript. (It may be of interest that the real prices ranged from 1 pt to 700 piasters, the latter being the price of a copy of Ismâᶜîl Ḥaqqî's Koran commentary).

Those scholars and intellectuals who were now used to reading printed books were much influenced by the proliferation of available titles. The supply itself was determined by the selection of the particular manuscripts to be printed, which involved a consciousness of tradition and heritage (*turâth*). Hence the wide distribution of printed books created a new knowledge of the past, reflecting the needs of the time. This knowledge focused on, and referred to, the subjects dealt with in printed books. It soon created an image of a new past as an invented tradition (the *aṣlî*-tradition).

The rational and market-oriented distillation of an "original" tradition engendered the reciprocal development of the consciousness of a *taqlîd*-tradi-

45 The book market for Islamic law coincided with the social structure of law culture. Cf. the following percentages (number of teachers: 1901; number of students: 1902; number of law books: 1821–1900):

School of Law (*madhhab*)	Teachers	Students	Books
Shâfiᶜîya	39.8	44.7	46
Mâlikîya	30.6	26	25.7
Ḥanafîya	28.6	28.9	23.4
Ḥanbalîya	0.8	0.3	0.7

Sources: Teachers and students: Reinhard Schulze, *Islamischer Internationalismus im 20. Jahrhundert*, Leiden 1990, p. 41, n.90; the number of law books has been derived from Nuṣair, *kutub*, passim.

tion. This "bad" tradition was not to be published, i.e. made avalable to the public, as it did not reflect the world view of the scholars and intellectuals concerned. The only material expression of the "traditional" culture, as it now called, were the manuscripts. According to the new outlook the *aṣlî*-tradition had to be published and the *taqlîd*-tradition was to be neglected.

Furthermore, the reevaluation of manuscripts affected their market value. Whereas, the use value of manuscripts diminished and they became a private affair, their exchange value rose. Having become antiquities, manuscripts now acquired a very high material worth. A somewhat ironic corollary of this reevaluation, was that the production of manuscripts became an exchange-value-oriented industrial art. As an artifact, the manuscript was part of the new tradition. Regarding its content, the public only took notice of it from the time when it was printed.

The orientation of book production to use and exchange value, however, embodied the knowledge of tradition and modernity. Printed Islamic books had to compete with the large range of secular subjects for which printing had always been the only medium. This competition had a most important and effective impact on the development of a new Islamic mass culture, which shaped the general outlook of the Islamic cultural elites during the 19th and 20th centuries. Hence, it may be concluded that in Islamic culture traditions of originality and authenticity on the one hand, and modernity on the other, were born simultaneously.

Literature

(This bibliography concerns the history of printing in the Middle East, with the exception of those books and articles dealing with the beginning of printing in the Ottoman Empire. These have been discussed by Babinger, Einführung, Weil, Drucke, Niyazi Berkez, "Ilk Türk Matbaasının Kurucunun Dinî ve Fikrî Kimlige", in Beleten cilt 26, sayi 104 (1962), pp. 715–737 and Ismet Binark, "Türkiye'ye Matbaanın Geç Girisin Içtimai-ruhî Sebepleri", in VIII. Türk tarihi kongresi, Ankara 1981, pp. 1299–1319.)

ALBIN, Michael W., "Iraq's First Printed Book", in Libri 31 (1981) 2, pp. 167–174

BABINGER, F., "Die Einführung des Buchdrucks in Persien", in Zeitschrift des Vereins des Buchwesens und Schrifttums 4 (1921), pp. 141–142

BABINGER, Franz, Stambuler Buchwesen im 18. Jahrhundert, Leipzig: Deutscher Verein für Buchwesen und Schriften 1919

BAYSAL (Bugra), Jale: Müteferrika'den birinci meşrutiyete kadar Osmanlı Türklerinin bastıkları kitaplar, Stambul 1968

BAHGAT, Mohamed Amine, "Aperçu historique sur l'imprimerie nationale égyptienne", in Gutenberg-Jahrbuch 1931, pp. 275–277

BAKHSHÂYISH, ᶜAlî, kitâb wa-kitâbkhâne-hâ zîrtabâ-yi tamaddun wa-ᶜulûm-i islâmî, Qum: čapkhânî-yi mahr 1353 (hsh) (1974)

BALAGNA, José, L'imprimerie arabe en occident (xvi, xvii et xviii siècles), Paris: Maisonneuve & Larose 1984

BEN CHENEB / LÉVI-PROVENCAL, Essai de répertoire chronologique des éditions de Fès, Alger: Carbonel 1922

BIANCHI, T.X.,"Catalogue général des livres arabes, persans et turc imprimés à Boulac en Egypte depuis l'introduction de l'imprimerie dans ce pays", in Journal Asiatique 4/2 (Juillet-Aout 1843), pp. 24-61 (continued in following vols. of the JA)

BIANCHI, T.X., Notices sur le premier ouvrage d'anatomie et de médicine imprimé en Turc à Constantinople en 1820, Paris: Cellot 1821

BIRGE, J. K., "The Printing of Books in Turkey in the Eighteenth Century", in MW 33 (1943), pp. 292–294

BOUSTANY, Salaheddine, The Press During the French Expedition in Egypt 1798–1801, Cairo 1954

CARTER, T. F., "Islam as a Barrier to Printing", in MW (1943), pp. 213–216

CHAUVIN, V., "Notes pour l'histoire de l'imprimerie à Constantinople", in Zentralblatt für das Bibliothekswesen 24 (1907), pp. 255–316

CHENOUFI, Moncef, Le problème des origines de l'imprimerie et de la presse arabes en Tunisie dans sa relation avec la renaissance Nahda (1847–1887), Paris 1974

CLOGG, R., "An Attempt to Revive Turkish Printing in Istanbul in 1779", in IJMES 10 (1979) 1, pp. 67–70

DEMEERSEMAN, A.,"Les données de la controverse autour du problème de l'imprimerie", in IBLA 17 (1954), pp. 1–48.

DEMEERSEMAN, A., "Une parente méconnue de l'imprimerie arabe et tunisienne: la lithographie", in IBLA 16 (1953), pp. 47– 85

DORN, B. "Catalogue des Ouvrages arabes, Persans et Turcs, Publiés à Constantinople, en Égypte, et en Perse, qui se trouvent au Musée Asiatique de l'Académie", in Bulletin de l'Asiatique de l'Académie Impériale des Sciences de Saint-Petersbourg, X(1860), pp. 182–199.

DUDA, H. W., "Das Druckwesen in der Türkei", in Gutenberg -Jahrbuch 1935, pp. 226–242

ERSOY, O., Türkiye'ye matbaanın girisi ve ilk basıları eserler, Ankara 1959

FLOOR, W. M., "The First Printing Press in Iran", in ZDMG 130 (1980), pp. 368–371

GDOURA, Wahid, Le début de l'imprimerie arabe à Istanboul et en Syrie: évolution de l'environnement culturel (1706–1787), Tunis 1985

GEISS, Albert, "Histoire de l'imprimerie en Egypte", in BEI 5/I, fasc. 13 (1907), pp, 132–157, (Part) II in BEI 5/II fasc. 2 (1908), pp, 195–201

GERÇEK, Selim Nüzhet, Türk Matbaacılığı, I, Istanbul: Devlet B, 1939, (1st ed. 1928)

HAMAN, M. Y., "History of Printing in Egypt", in Gutenberg -Jahrbuch 1951, pp. 156–159

HAMMER[-Purgstall], Joseph von, Geschichte des osmanischen Reiches, Siebter Band, Pest: Hartleben 1831; achter Band ibid., 1832

HAMMER-PURGSTALL, Freiherr [Joseph von], Bericht über die in den letzten vier Jahren 1845, 46, 47 und 48 zu Constantinopel gedruckten und lithographirten Werke, (Wien) 1849 [= off-print of Sitzungsberichte der kaiserlichen Akademie der Wissenschaften, October 1849.]

HAMMER-PURGSTALL, Freiherr [Joseph von], Bericht über die seit dem Jahre 1848 zu Konstantinopel gedruckten und lithographirten Werke, (Wien) 1851 [= off-print of Sitzungsberichte der philos. histor. Classe der kais. Akademie der Wissenschaften, February 1851.]

KÁLDY-NAGY, Gy., "Beginnings of the Arabic-letter Printing in the Muslim World", in Studies in honour of J. Germanus, Budapest 1974, pp. 201–211

KHALID, Adeeb, "Printing, Publishing, and the Reform in Tsarist Central Asia", in International Journal of Middle East Studies 26 (1994), pp. 187–200

KHALID, Adeeb, "Muslim Printers in Tsarist Central Asia", in Central Asian Survey 11 (1992), 113–118

KHOURY, R.G., Bibliographie rainnée des traductions publiées au Liban à partir des Langues étrangers de 1840 à jusqu'aux environs de 1905, Paris [Fac. des Lettres et Sciuences humaines, Univ. de Paris] [1965]

KREK, Miroslav, A Bibliography of Arabic Typography, Weston, Mass, 1976
KREK, Miroslav, A Gazetteer of Arabic Printing, Weston, Mass, 1977
MUSHÂR, Ḫanbâbâ, mu'allifîn-i kutub-i čâpî-yi fârisî wa-ᶜarabî az âğâz-i čâp tâ-kanûn, vol. I-VI, Tehran: n.P. 1340–44 (1961–65)
NASR, Sayyed Hossein, "Oral Transmission and the Book in Islamic Education: The Spoken and the Written Word", Journal of Islamic Studies 3 (1992), pp. 1–14
NURI ᶜUthman (ed.), majalla-yi umûr-i baladîya, I, târîkh-i tashkîlât-i baladîya, Istanbul: ᶜuthmânîya 1338/1922
NUṢAIR, ᶜÂyida Ibrâhîm [Nosseir, Aida Ibrahim], al-kutub al-ᶜarabîya allatî nushirat fî Miṣr fî l-qarn at-tâsiᶜ ᶜashar, Cairo: The American University of Cairo Press, 1990
ÖZEGE, M. Seyfettin, Eski Harflerde Başılmıs Türkçe Eserler Katalogu, vols. I-V, Istanbul 1971–1979
ORAL, Süraya, Türk Basın tarihi, Istanbul 1968
ROBINSON, Francis, "Technology and Religious Change; Islam and the Impact of Printing", in Modern Asian Studies 27 (1993), pp. 229–251
PEDERSEN, J., The Arabic Book, trns. G. French, ed. R. Hillenbrand, Princeton, N.J.: Princeton Univ. Pr. 1984
PERSON, A., "Lettre sur les écoles et l'imprimerie du pacha d'Egypte par ... à J. Mohl, 22,10,1842", in Journal asiatique 4/2 (Julliet-Aout 1843), pp. 7–23
PORTER, Y., "Arts du livre et illustration", in: Yann Richard (ed.), Entre l'Iran et l'occident, Paris 1989.
REINAUD, J., "Notice des ouvrages arabes, Persans et Turcs Imprimés en Égypte", in Journal Asiatique 2/8 (October 1831), pp. 333–344
RIḌWÂN, ᶜAbdalfutūḥ, târîkh maṭbaᶜat Bûlâq wa-lamḥa fî târîkh aṭ-ṭibâᶜa fî buldân ash-sharq al-ausaṭ, Cairo: al-amiriya 1953
RHODES, Dennis E., India, Pakistan, Ceylon, Burma and Thailand, Amsterdam 1969 [The spread of Printing. A History of Printing Outside Europe in monographs, ed. by C. Clair, vol. I/4, Amsterdam 1969 s.]
SÂBÂT, Khalîl, târîkh aṭ-ṭibâᶜa fî sh-sharq al-ᶜarabî, Cairo: dâr al-maᶜârif 1966
SÂMÎ, târîkh-i Sâmî wa-Shâkir wa-Subḥî (1730–1743), Qusṭantinîya 1198 (1783)
SHAW, Graham (W.), Printing in Calcutta to 1800. A Description and Checklist of Printing in Late 18th Century Calcutta, London: Bibliographic Society 1981

SHAYYÂL, Jamâl ad-Dîn ash-, târîkh at-tarjama wa-l-ḥaraka ath-thaqâfîya fî ᶜahd Muḥammad ᶜAlî, Cairo: al-iᶜtimâd 1951
SHURBAJÎ, Muḥammad Jamâl ad-Dîn ash-, qâ'ima bi-awâ'il al-maṭbûᶜât al-ᶜarabîya al-maḥfûza bi-dâr al-kutub, Cairo: dâr al-kutub 1383 /1963
STOREY, C. A., "The Beginning of Persian Printing in India", in Oriental Studies in Honour of Cursetij Erachji Pavry, London 1933, pp. 457–461
ṬABÂṬABÂ'Î, Muhît, târîkḥ-i taḥlîlî-yi maṭbûᶜât-i Îrân, Teheran 1878/8
WALTHER, Karl Kraus, "Die lithographische Vervielfältigung von Texten in den Ländern des Vorderen und Mittleren Orients", in Gutenberg-Jahrbuch 65 (1990), pp. 223–236
WASSEF, Amin Sami, L'information et la presse officielle en Égypte jusqu'à la fin de l'occupation française, Cairo: IFAO 1975
WEIL, Gotthold, "Die ersten Drucke der Türken", in Zentralblatt für Bibliothekswesen 24 (1907) 2, pp, 49–61
ZENKER, J. Th., Bibliotheca orientalis. Manuel de bibliographie orientale, I–II, Leipzig 1846

Annex I

OTTOMAN ISLAMIC BOOKPRINTING 1802-1848

Unless otherwise stated the books were published by the official Imperial Press.

١٨٠٣ رسالة برگوي (ويا واصيتنامه) > محمد بن پير علي برگوي > دار الطباعة الجديدة ١٢١٨ ١٨٠٣

١٨٠٤ جوهرية بهيئة احمديه في شرح الوصية المحمدية > احمد بن محمد امين قاضيزاده > ١٢١٩ ١٨٠٤ (١٢٢٣ ١٢٢٥ ١٢٤١ ١٣٣٢ ١٢٥١ ١٢٥٥ ١٢٥٨ ١٢٦٢)

١٨٠٤ شروط الصلاة (ترجمه سى) > ابن كمال > ١٢١٩ ١٨٠٤

١٨٠٧ البرهان (في المنطق) > إسماعيل بن مصطفى بن محمود الكلانبوي > ١٢٢٢ ١٨٠٧

١٨١٢ حاشية عبد الحكيم السيالكوتي على الشرح المطوّل (للتفتازاني على تخليص المفتاح لجمال الدين محمد بن عبدالرحمن القزويني من مفتاح العلوم للسكاكي)١٢٢٧ ١٨١٢ ١٢٤١ ١٨٣٦ (ولا على العقائد للنسفي GAL II/549

١٨١٧ نهجة المنازل (امور الحج) > محمد اديب بن محمد درويش > ١٢٣٢ ١٨١٧

١٨١٨ حاشية الكلانبوي (على عقائد جلالي للدواني شرح العقائد العضدية للايجي) ١٢٣٣ ١٨١٨

١٨١٩ تعليقات الكلانبوي (على ميزان الادب لمحمد خان التبريزي شرح الرسالة الوضعيه العضدية للايجي) ١٢٣٤ ١٨١٩

١٨١٩ تعليقات الكلانبوي (على حاشية مير ابى الفتح الصائدي على سير التهذيب للدواني شرح تلخيص المفتاح للتفتازاني) ١٢٣٤ ١٨١٩

١٨٢٠ تعليقات السيالكوتي (على حاشية الخيالي على شرح العقائد النسفية للتفتازاني) ١٢٣٥ ١٨٢٠

١٨٢٠ الدر الناجى (شرح كتاب الايساغوغي للابهري) > عمر بن صالح الفيضي الطوقاتي > ١٢٣٥ ١٨٢٠ ١٢٥٩ ١٨٤٣

١٨٢١ رشحات عين الحيات > عبدالله بن الحسين الواعظ الكاشفي > ترجمه: محمد بن محمد عباسي (تُوركجه) > ١٢٣٦ ١٨٢١

١٨٢٢ نتيجة الفتاوى > محمد بن احمد بن مصطفى القدوسي > ١٢٣٧ ١٨٢٢

١٨٢٢ الرسالة الشمسية في الفوائد المنطقية > تعليقات السيالكوتي (على حاشية الكوچك للجرجاني على تحرير القوائد المنطقية لمحمد بن قطب الدين الطهطاني شرح الرسالة الشمسية لنجم الدين علي بن عمر الكاتبي > ١٢٣٨ ١٨٢٢

١٨٢٢ غنية المتملي > الحلبي (شرح منية المصلي وغنية المبتدئ لسعيد الدين الكاشغاري) ١٢٣٨ ١٨٢٢

١٨٢٢ المواقف في علم الكلام > الايجي > ١٢٣٩ ١٨٢٣

١٨٢٣ اخترئ كبير > مصطفى بن شمس الدين اختري (ت ١٥٧٨) > ١٢٣٩ ١٨٢٣ / ١٢٥٦ ١٨٤٠ / ١٢٦٣ / ١٨٤٧

١٨٢٤ مجمع الانهر في شرح ملتقى الابحر > عبدالرحمن بن محمد بن سليمان شيخزاده (شرح الحلبي) ١٢٤١ ١٨٢٤

١٨٢٤ المواقف (في علم الكلام) > الايجي (مع شرحين للتفتزاني و الجرجاني) > ١٢٤١ ١٨٢٤

١٨٢٥ علمِ حال > إبراهيم حقي (من معرفتنامة) > ١٢٤٢ ١٨٢٥

١٨٢٥ ترجمة شرحِ سير الكبير > محمد بن ابي سهل احمد السرخسي (شرح السير الكبير الشيباني) : محمد منيب العينتبي > ١٢٤١ ١٨٢٥

2

١٨٣٦ تعليقات على حاشية الفناري > عبدالله بن شيخ حسن الكانجري (على حاشية على الامور العامة للفناري على > شرح الجرجاني على المواقف للايجي) ١٢٤٢ ١٨٣٦

١٨٢٧ فتاوىٰ عبدالرحيم > عبدالرحيم منتشي زاده > ١٢٤٣ ١٨٢٧ (دار الطباعة المامورة السلطانية)

١٨٢٨ در يكتا > محمد أسعد إمام زاده (ت ١٨٥٩) (دروس في امور دينية للتعليم في الرشدية) > ١٢٤٢ ١٨٢٨ > > ١٨٤٨ (١٢ ط)

١٨٢٨ حلية الناجي (حاشية الگوزلحصري على غنية المتملي للحلبي (شرح منية المصلي وغنية المبتدئ لسعيد الدين الكاشغاري) ١٢٤٢ ١٨٢٨

١٨٢٨ أسِ ظفر > محمد أسعد صحافلر شيخيزاده (ت ١٨٤٨) > ١٢٤٣ ١٨٢٨

١٨٢٩ فتاوىٰ علي افندي > علي چتلجلي شيخ الاسلام . ترتيب: ضالح بن احمد الكفوي > ١٢٤٥ ١٨٢٩

١٨٣٠ تفسير المواهب (تفسير المواكب ترجمه سى) > حسين واعظ الكاشفي > مترجم: إسماعيل فزوخ > ١٢٤٦ ١٨٣٠

١٨٣٢ تحفة الصكوك > نعمان دباغزاده > ١٢٤٨ ١٨٣٢ (ط ٢ ١٢٥٩ ١٨٤٣)

١٨٣٣ حاشية حصام الدين (بن الحسن الكاتي) (على شرح احمد بن موسى الخيالي على العقائد لابي حفص عمر بن محمد النسفي) ١٢٤٩ ١٨٣٣

١٨٣٣ رساله بركوي > ١٢٤٩ ١٨٣٣

١٨٣٥ علمِ حال > احمد علمي > ١٢٥٠ ١٨٣٥ / طبعخانۀ اميره ١٢٥٩ ١٨٤٣ (حجر) ١٢٦٢ ١٨٤٧ ١٢٦٤ ١٨٤٨ بولاق ١٢٦٠ ١٨٤٤

١٨٣٥ توسل > (شرح قصيدة البردة لمحمد مكي) > ١٢٥١ ١٨٣٥

١٨٣٥ الفروق > إسماعيل حقي بروسوي > ١٢٥١ ١٨٣٥

١٨٣٦ هديه العرفان در شرحِ بهارستان > عبدالرحمن جامي (ت ١٤٩٢) : محمد شاكر > ١٢٥٢ ١٨٣٦

١٨٣٦ عقائد دينية متعلق مسائل اعتقادية > مكتب حربية ١٢٥٢ ١٨٣٦

١٨٣٦ زبدة العرفان في وجوه القرآن > حامد بن عبدالله (عبدالفتاح) الپالوي > ١٢٥٢ ١٨٣٦

١٨٣٦ الايتلاف في وجوه (روايات) الاختلاف (في القراءات) > ١٢٥٢ ١٨٣٦ (فى هامش كتاب زبدة العرفان للپالوي)

١٨٣٦ رسالۀ عقائدِ دينيه > مكتبِ حربيه مطبعخانه سى > ١٢٥٢ ١٨٣٦

١٨٣٦ ملتقى الابحر > إبراهيم الحلبي > ١٢٥٢ ١٨٣٦

١٨٣٧ فتاوىٰ جامع الاجارتين > ترتيب : محمد عارف مشرب افندي حفيدي > ١٢٥٢ ١٨٣٧

١٨٣٧ تحفة الرشد > احمد رشدي (النقشبندي) قره اغاجي > (شرح كتاب الايساغوغى للايجي) > ١٢٥٢ ١٨٣٧

١٨٣٧ شرحِ الاربين حديثا > إمام نووي > إسماعيل حقئ بروسوي (توركچه) > ١٢٥٣ ١٨٣٧

١٨٣٧ حديقة السعدا ء > محمد بن سليمان فضولي > بولاق ١٢٥٣ ١٨٣٧ (اتنبول ١٢٧٣ ١٨٥٦)

١٨٣٧ دفتر عشق > فَضل اندروني > ١٢٥٣ ١٨٣٧

١٨٣٧ كتاب التعريفات > الجُرجاني > ١٢٥٣ ١٨٣٧

3

١٨٣٨ حبانامه > فاضل اندروني > ١٢٥٣ ١٨٣٧

١٨٣٨ حل رموز > عصمت بخاري > احمد رشدي النقشبندي > ١٢٥٢ ١٨٣٧

١٨٣٨ شرحِ دلائل خيرات (توفيقِ موفق الخيرات لِنيل البركات فى خدمتِ مِنبا ء السعادات) > ابو عبدالله محمد بن عبدالرحمن الجزولي >
داؤود > ١٢٥٤ ١٨٣٨ // ١٢٥٥ ١٨٣٩ (دلائل الخيرات وشوارق الانوار في ذكر الصلاة على النبي المختار)

١٨٣٨ كتاب التصورات > محمد بن إبراهيم الارزنجاني مفتيزاده (تعليقات على شرح الكوچك للجُرجاني على تصرير القوائد المنطقية على
(التصورات) من الرسالة الشمسية في القوائد المنطقية للكاتبي) > ١٢٥٤ ١٨٣٨

١٨٣٨ الدر اليتيم في التجويد > البركوي (مع شرح) > ١٢٥٣ ١٨٣٨

١٨٤٠ قيرق سؤال > ملا فراقي (فتاوى) > سرعسكريه ١٢٥٦ ١٨٤٠

١٨٤٠ خليليةْ حقي (الرسالة الخليلية في التصوف) > اسماعيل حقي بروسوي > ١٢٥٦ ١٨٤٠

١٨٤٠ شرح صلوات المشيش (إعانة الراغبين في الصلاة والسلام على افضل المرسلين لابي محمد عبدالسلام بن مشيش) مع شرح (لاسماعيل حقي) >
سرعسكري > ١٢٥٦ ١٨٤٠

١٨٤٠ شرح الأُصول العشرة (النجمية) >نجم الدين احمد بن عمر الكبرى الخيقاوي مع ترجمة وشرح لإسماعيل حقي > ١٢٥٦ ١٨٤٠
١٨٤٠ امثله شرحي > كوسه افندي > مط دار السلطنت السنية ١٢٥٦ ١٨٤٠

١٨٤٠ اخلاق احمدي > حسين الواعظدن احمد طيب الكاشفي > (تخليص) فارسي اخلاق حسنى > دار الخلافة العلية ١٨٤٠ ١٢٥٦

١٨٤٠ حاشية (على الرسالة) الحسينية (في فن الآداب) / ادب البحث > شاه حسين افندي الانطاقي (الشارح ؟) > ١٢٥٦ ١٨٤٠

١٨٤٠ عجائب المعاصر وغرائب النوادر > سحيلى احمد بن حمدان ١٢٥٦ ١٨٤٠

١٨٤٠ هدية الاخوان فى شرحِ شبحة الصِبيان > محمد نَجيب > ١٢٥٦ ١٨٤٠

١٨٤٠ كتاب الخطاب(في التصوف) > إسماعيل حقي بروشوي > ١٢٥٦ ١٨٤٠

١٨٤٠ وصيتنامه > شيخ احمد قدوسي > ١٢٥٦ ١٨٤٠

١٨٤٠ رسالۀ برگوى (البريقة المحمودية / مترجم: طريقتجي) > ١٢٥٦ ١٨٤٠ (مع وصيتنامه)

١٨٤١ شرح الكبائر > إسماعيل حقي بروسوي > سرعسكري > ١٢٥٧ ١٨٤١

١٨٤١ البريقة المحمودية شرح الطريقة المحمدية > محمد بن مصطفى الخَادمي > ١٢٥٧ ١٨٤١ // ١٢٦٠ ١٨٤٤

١٨٤١ الهدية الندية شرح الطريقة المحمدية > عبدالغني النابلسي > ١٢٥٧ ١٨٤١

١٨٤٢ (هُدى ريم) مفتاح الجنة (مزراكلى علمِ حال) سونونده > ابراهيم حقي اندروني > مطبعۀ بابِ حضرتِ سرعسكري ١٢٥٨ ١٨٤٢ //
طبعخانۀ اميريه ١٢٦١ ١٨٤٥

١٨٤٢ تكملۀ ترجمۀ طريقتِ محمديه > بركوي > ودادي > سرعسكري > ١٢٥٨ ١٨٤٢ (ط ٢ ١٢٦٢ ١٨٤٦)

١٨٤٢ شرحِ غرر الاحكام المسمى بدرر الحكَام > ملا خسرو > ١٢٥٨ ١٨٤٢

١٨٤٤ الطريقة المحمدية > بركوي > مع البركات المحمدية شرح الطريقة المحمدية > ١٢٦٠ ١٨٤٤

4

١٨٤٤ علمِ حال > ابراهيم حقي اندروني > بولاق ١٢٦٠ ١٨٤٤

١٨٤٤ حلبي ترجمه سى باباداغى > ابراهيم الحلبي > ابراهيم بن عبدالله بن ابراهيم البابادا‌غي > ١٢٥٥ ١٨٣٩ > ١٢٦٠ ١٨٤٤ > ١٢٦٤ ١٨٤٨

١٨٤٤ زبدة النسايح > شيخ الاسلامِ هروي > محمد رؤوف السيد ١٢٦٠ ١٨٤٤

١٨٤٤ شرحِ علمِ حال (فيض البحرين) > حلوصي شيخ الحاج مصطفى بن محمد > ١٢٦٠ ١٨٤٤

١٨٤٤ شرحِ اورادِ قادري لمستقيمزاده (عبدالقادر الجيلاني > سليمان سعدالدين مستقيمزاده) ١٢٦٠

١٨٤٥ الوسيلة الاحمدية شرح الطريقة المحمدية > رجب بن احمد > ١٢٦١ ١٨٤٥

١٨٤٥ مواهب اللدنية ترجمه سى معالم اليكين في سيرتِ سيد المرسلين (المواهب اللدنية في المِنَح المحمدية > أبو بكر احمد بن محمد القسطلاني) > عبدالباقي (شاعر باقي) > ١٢٦١ ١٨٤٥

١٨٤٥ مفتاح الجنة > علمِ حال > مزركلي > ١٢٦١ ١٨٤٥

١٨٤٥ محمود الاثر في ترجمة المستطرف المستأثر > محمد احمد الاشبيهي > اكمكجي زاده احمد > ١٢٦١ /١٢٦٣ ١٨٤٥-٤٧ (؟)

١٨٤٦ حزب الاعظم (وترجمه سى) > ١٢٦٢ ١٨٤٦

١٨٤٦ خاتمة الواردات > مصطفى رضا ء (الدين) نجارزاده شيخ > تحفة الارشاد ديوان و ديگر رساله لريله برابر > ١٢٦٢ ١٨٤٦

١٨٤٦ زبدهٔ علمِ حال > عبدالحميد بن مصطفى رشيد >١٢٦٢ ١٨٤٦

١٨٤٦ كتابِ محمديه في كمالات الاحمديه > محمد يازيجي زاده > طبعخانهٔ اميره ١٨٤٦ ١٢٦٢ (برينجي بصمه كازان شوتس ١٨٤٥)

١٨٤٧ گنجينهٔ حكمت > حكايهٔ ابو علي سينا > يحيا ضيا ء الدين سيد > بولاق ١٢٥٤ ١٨٣٨ > استنبول ١٢٦٤ ١٨٤٧

١٨٤٧ حابنامهٔ ويسي > اويس ابن [illegible] (ويسي) > بولاق ١٢٥٢ ١٨٣٦ > استنبول ١٢٦٣ ١٨٤٧

١٨٤٧ حسب حال السالك في اقوام المسالك > (حسين) حمدي > ١٢٦٣ ١٨٤٧ > طبعخانهٔ اميره

١٨٤٧ جواهر الاسلام > (اعتقاد) > ١٢٦٤ ١٨٤٧

١٨٤٧ امثله جديده > ابراهيم حسين رشدي > مكتب حربية شاهانة مطبعه سي ١٢٦٣ ١٨٤٧

١٨٤٨ الورد المفِد فِ شرح التجويد > محمد أسعد صحافلر شيخيزاده > ١٢٦٤ ١٨٤٨

١٨٤٨ حليهٔ حاقاني > محمد حاقانى > ١٢٦٤ ١٨٤٨

١٨٤٨ حزب البهير شرحى ترجُمسه سى > علي بن عبدالله الشاذلي > ١٢٦٤ ١٨٤٨

١٨٤٨ فوائد > محمد امين > ١٢٦٤ ١٨٤٨ (الورد المفيد في شرح التجويدين سونونده)

Annex II

ISLAMIC BOOK PRINTING AT BULAQ 1825-1842

Books marked with an * are reeditions of books printed at Istanbul

١٨٢٥ * [١٨٠٤] احمد بن محمد امين قاضي زاده استنبولي خواجه > جوهريه بهيه احمديه في شرح الوصية المحمدية

١٨٢٥ اللقاني > جوهرة التوحيد

١٨٢٦ * [١٨٢٦] الكانغري > تعليقات على حاشية الامور العامة للفناري (على شرح الجرجاني على المواقف للايجي) (مطبوع في بولاق سنة ١٨٢٦ كما قال همر ٨٢؟)

١٨٢٦ الدمياطي > مشارع الاشواق إلى مصارع العشاق و مشير الغرام إلى دار السلام

١٨٢٦ الاخضري > السُلَّم المرونق يرقي به علم المنطق

١٨٢٨ * [١٨٣٣؟] الكانقري > تعليقات الكانقري على حاشية الخيالي على شرح التفتازاني على العقائد للنسفي ١٢٤٤

١٨٢٨ ؟ > كتاب في الدين الإسلام (توركجه)

١٨٣٠ * [١٨٢٨] محمد أسعد إمامزاده > دُرَ يكتا (عقيدة حنِفية)

١٨٣٠ الجاحز > كتاب الاصنام

١٨٣٣ * [١٨٣٣] علي قنالي زاده > اخلاق علائي (توركجه)

١٨٣٤ * [١٨١٧] محمد اديب بن محمد درويش > نهجة المنازل ١٢٥٠ ١٨٣٤ < ١٢٥٢ ١٨٣٦ <١ ١٢٥٦ ١٨٤٠

١٨٣٥ محمد أديب > مناسك الحج

١٨٣٥ الباجوري > السنوسِية او رسالة في علم التوحيد

١٨٣٦ * [١٨٢٨] الناجي > حلية الناجي في حاشية الحلبي (مختصر غُنية المتملي في شرح مُنية المصلي للكاشغاري) للگوزل حصاري

١٨٣٦ الدمياطي/الباقي > فضائل الجهاد (= توركجه ، تخليص كتاب مشارع الاشواق)

١٨٣٦ ابراهيم حقي > معرفتنامه (توركجه)

١٨٣٦ إسماعيل حقي > (فرح الروح) شرح (طريقه،) محمديه (لمحمد يزيداوغلو) (توركجه)

١٨٣٧ عبدالله الشناوي > تجليات عرائس النصوص في مفصلات حكم الفصوص (عبدالله عبدي البوسنوي)

١٨٣٧ الحلبي ، الكاشغاري > مد يكتا (توركجه)

١٨٣٨ * [١٨٤٧] حابنامهٔ ويسي > اويس بن محمد (ويسي) > بولاق ١٢٥٢ ١٨٣٦ > استنبول ١٢٦٣ ١٨٤٧

١٨٣٨ گنجينهٔ حكمت > حكايهٔ ابو علي سينا > يحيا ضياء الدين سيد > بولاق ١٢٥٤

١٨٣٨ ابو القاسم إسحاق بن محمد (السمرقندي) > السواد الاعظم يشتمل على اسئلة وأجوبة (دن عايني توركچه)

١٨٣٨ ابن عربي > كتاب فصوص (مع شرح لعريف الله) (توركچه)

١٨٣٨ * [١٨٣٧] فضولي > حديقة السعداء (توركچه) (١٨٣٧)

١٨٣٨ ابو البقاء الكفوي > كلية ابو (!) البقاء

١٨٣٩ علي بن ابي طالب > شرحِ ديوانِ علي المرتضى كرّم الله وجهه (سليمان سعدالدين مستقيمزاده)

١٨٣٩ * [١٨٣٨ (عربي)] إبراهيم الحلبي > (الملتقى) الموقوفاتي > محمد الموقوفاتي توركچه ط ٢ ١٢٥٦ ١٨٤١ ط ٣ ب ت ط ٢ : نشر ايدن : الحاج عثمان اغا جنبلاط والحاج محمود

١٨٣٩ حسن أفندي النجشي > شرح الشمائل (لابي عيسى محمد الترمذي)

١٨٣٩ إسماعيل حقي > (فرح الروح) شرح (طريقه) محمديه (المحمد يزيداوغلو) (توركچه)

١٨٣٩ الطهطاوي > حاشِية الطهطاوي علي الدر المختار (الحصكفي) شرح تنوير الابصار وجامع البحار (التمرتاشي)

١٨٤٠ أبو البقاء > كليات أبي البقاء في جميى الىلوم ط ٢

١٨٤٠ إسماعيل حقي > روح البيان في تفسير القرآن

١٨٤٠ ابراهيم حقي > علمِ حال (توركچه) (من كتاب معرفتنامه)

١٨٤٠ ابراهيم حقي > معرفتنامه ط ٢

١٨٤٠ ابو الفضل عياض بن موسى (اليحصبي) > رفع الخفاء عن ذات الشفاء (فى تعريف حقوق المصطفى) (القَاريْ الهروي ت ١٠١٤ ١٦٠٥)

١٨٤١ الكانجري (الانقراوي) > حاشية الكانجري (على الفناري شرح الايساغوغي للابهري) (توركچه)

١٨٤١ عبدالرحمن ابو النجيب > نهج السلوك في سيَاسة الملوك ١٢٥٧ ١٨٤١

١٨٤١ البريقة المحمودية شرح الطريقة المحمدية > محمد بن مصطفى الخَادمي > ١٢٥٧ ١٨٤١

١٨٤١ محمد مصطفى البوصيري > شرح قصيدة البردة (توركچه ، عربچه دن احمد لالي)

١٨٤١ سليم أفندي > التحفة السليمية في علم التوحيد (توركجه)

١٨٤١ * [١٨٣٨] الجزولي > دلائل الخيرات (توركجه)

١٨٤١ الكنفر(و)ي (الانقراوي) > منهاج الفقراء (إسماعيل بن احمد الانقراوي المولوي) (توركجه)

١٨٤١ ابو الفضل عياض بن موسى قاضي (اليحصبي) > شفاء شريف ترجمه سى (خلاصة الوفاء في شرح الشفاء) (توركچه) > إبراهيم حنيف أفندي (من رفع الحفاء ونسيم الرياض (لاحمد بن محمد الخفاجي / ت ١٠٦٩ ١٦٥٩)

١٨٤١ * [١٨٢١] الكاشفي > رشحات (عين الحياة) (توركچه)

١٨٤٢ السمرقندي > كتاب السواد الاعظم ط ٢

١٨٤٢ * [١٨٢٦؟] الكانغري > تعليقات على حاشية الامور العامة للفناري (على شرح الجرجاني على المواقف للايجي) (مطبوع في بولاق سنة ١٨٢٦ كما قال همر ٨٢؟)

١٨٤٢ * [١٨٠٣] بركوي > رساله بركوي (شرح الطريقة المحمدية)

١٨٤٤ * [١٨٢٥] علمِ حال > ابراهيم حقي اندروني > بولاق ١٢٦٠ ١٨٤٤ ط ٣

١٨٤٦ چيورن صالح > مناقبِ اولياء مصر ، ترجمان الشهداء في ترجمتِ مرشد الزوار في زيارات الكرافة والقبور والابرار > چيورن صالح > بولاق ١٢٦٢ ١٨٤٦

Annex III

ISLAMIC BOOKS PRINTED AT BULAQ AND ISTANBUL 1825-1848

١٨٢٥ * [١٨٠٤] احمد بن محمد امين قاضيزاده استنبولو خواجه > جوهريه بهيه احمديه في شرح الوصية المحمدية

١٨٣٦ * [١٨٣٦] الكانغري > تعليقات على حاشية الامور العامة للفناري (على شرح الجرجاني على المواقف للايجي) (مطبوع في بولاق سنة ١٨٣٦ كما قال همر ٢٨٢؟)

١٨٢٨ * [١٨٣٣؟] الكانغري > تعليقات الكانغري على حاشية الخيالي على شرح التفتازاني على العقائد للنسفي ١٢٤٤

١٨٣٠ * [١٨٢٨] محمد أسعد إمامزاده > دُرّ يكتا (عقيدة حنفِية)

١٨٣٣ * [١٨٣٣] علي قنالي زاده > اخلاق علائي (توركجه)

١٨٣٤ * [١٨١٧] محمد اديب بن محمد درويش > نهجة المنازل ١٢٥٠ ١٨٣٤ > ١٢٥٢ ١٨٣٦ > ١ ١٢٥٦ ١٨٤٠

١٨٣٦ * [١٨٢٨] الناجي > حلية الناجي في حاشية الحلبي (مختصر غُنية المتملي في شرح مُنية المصلي للكاشغاري) للگوزل حصاري

١٨٣٨ * [١٨٤٧] حابنامهٔ ويسي > اويس بن محمد (ويسي) > بؤلاق ١٢٥٢ ١٨٣٦ > استنبول ١٢٦٣ ١٨٤٧

١٨٣٨ * [١٨٣٧] فضولي > حديقة السعداء (توركجه) (١٨٣٧)

١٨٣٩ * [١٨٣٨ (عربي)] إبراهيم الحلبي > (الملتقى) الموقوفاتي > محمد الموقوفاتي توركجه ط ٢ ١٢٥٦ ١٨٤١ ط ٣ ب ت ط ٢ : نشر ايدن : الحاج عثمان اغا جنبلاط والحاج محمود

١٨٤١ * [١٨٢١] الكاشفي > رشحات (عين الحياة) (توركجه)

١٨٤١ * [١٨٣٨] الجزولي > دلائل الخيرات (توركجه)

١٨٤٢ * [١٨٠٣] بركوي > رساله بركوي (شرح الطريقة المحمدية)

١٨٤٢ * [١٨٣٦؟] الكانغري > تعليقات على حاشية الامور العامة للفناري (على شرح الجرجاني على المواقف للايجي) (مطبوع في بولاق سنة ١٨٣٦ كما قال همر ٢٨٢؟)

١٨٤٤ * [١٨٢٥] علم حال > ابراهيم حقي اندروني > بولاق ١٢٦٠ ١٨٤٤ ط ٣

[21]

The Printing Press and Change in the Arab World

GEOFFREY ROPER

IN 1937 the Arab American historian Philip Hitti published his *History of the Arabs,* which quickly established itself as a classic; through its many subsequent editions up to the present, it has introduced generations of students and general readers to the broad outlines of Arab history. Its final chapter, dealing with the past two centuries, and the changes brought about by modernization and westernization, opens with a brief account of the import of a printing press by the French into Egypt in 1798. Subsequent pages give prominence to the establishment of other presses in Cairo, Beirut, and elsewhere. Clearly, for Hitti, printing was an essential ingredient of modernization in the Arab world. Nor was he alone in this view: in the following year (1938), the celebrated Arab nationalist historian George Antonius, in his influential book *The Arab Awakening,* laid great stress on the introduction of printing as a factor in that awakening. "The installation of a printing press equipped to emit books in the Arabic language," he wrote, "opened out new horizons . . . without [it], the making of a nation is in modern times inconceivable."[1]

But neither they nor most subsequent historians of the Arab world down to the last quarter century explained why printing was so important, nor did they devote any significant space or effort to tracing its progress or

This survey covers, in addition to the Arab countries, that is, those where Arabic is the main written language, some aspects of Arabic printing history in the broader sense, involving book production in all languages using the Arabic script, a historic vehicle of Islamic culture. But the many detailed studies of Ottoman Turkish printing history are not considered: for a comprehensive list of publications in this field in the period 1981–95, see M. Bülent Varlık, *Türkiye basın-yayın tarihi bibliyografyası* (Ankara: Kebikeç Yayinlan, 1995). Nor has it been possible to survey the fewer but significant specialized contributions on Persian, Urdu, Malay, and other Muslim languages.

1. Hitti, *History of the Arabs from the Earliest Times to the Present* (1937; 7th ed., London: Macmillan, 1960); Antonius, *The Arab Awakening: The Story of the Arab National Movement* (London: Hamish Hamilton, 1938), 40.

elucidating the effects that it had. Even studies of intellectual history, such as Albert Hourani's masterly and seminal *Arabic Thought in the Liberal Age* (1962), despite dealing intensively with printed texts, paid scant regard to the means and processes by which intellectual production reached its readers and achieved its potent effects. The relatively few studies of Arabic book history tended to concentrate their attention on the manuscript production of earlier eras, with printing added, if at all, merely as a postscript. The key work in this field was Johannes Pedersen's *Den Arabiske Bog* (1946; translated by Geoffrey French as *The Arabic Book,* 1984): only the last of its ten chapters considers the printed book, and this deals only with the outline history of the establishment of presses and the nature of some of the texts printed. Among the Arabs themselves, the situation was little better. Khalīl Ṣābāt's useful survey of the history of Arabic presses[2] took for granted their historical role and did not attempt to analyze the relationship between the printed output and changes in social and intellectual patterns. In 1979, the date that also marks the appearance of Elizabeth L. Eisenstein's *The Printing Press as an Agent of Change: Communications and Cultural Transformations in Early-Modern Europe* (*PPAC*), a major history of the Arabic book by Maḥmūd 'Abbās Ḥammūda allocated a mere 11 of its 280 text pages to the printed book and used them to give no more than a bare chronological summary.[3] As late as 1982, the Tunisian scholar Abdelkader Ben Cheikh, in a report to UNESCO, commented that "discontinuité et rareté des approches caractérisent l'état actuel des recherches sur le livre et la lecture dans les pays arabes."[4]

So Elizabeth Eisenstein's observation that "almost no studies are devoted to the consequences that ensued once printers had begun to ply their new trades"[5] certainly applied in full measure to the historiography of the Arab Middle East. In 1982, fresh from the excitement of reading Eisenstein, I pointed out, at the annual conference of the Middle East Librarians' Committee (MELCom) in Paris, that the systematic study of early Arabic printed books and the impact of printing on the Arab world had yet to achieve any significant recognition as a discipline to be pursued by either historians or bibliographers, and I appealed for new initiatives in

2. Ṣābāt, *Tārīkh al-ṭibā'a fī 'l-Sharq al-'Arabī* [History of printing in the Arab East], 2nd ed. (Cairo: Dar al-Ma'ārif, 1966).

3. Ḥammūda, *Tārīkh al-kitāb al-Islāmī* [History of the Islamic book] (Cairo: Dār al-Thaqāfa, 1979).

4. ["discontinuity and scarcity of approaches characterize the current state of research on the book and reading in Arab countries."] Ben Cheikh, *Production des livres et lecture dans le monde arabe* [Production of books and reading in the Arab world] (Paris: UNESCO, 1982), 49.

5. Eisenstein, *PPAC,* 4.

this field.[6] Three years later, Michael Albin of the Library of Congress corroborated some of what I had said by setting out, in a paper to the American Oriental Society,[7] the parameters of the discipline of Islamic book history, which he claimed did not then exist. By "Islamic" he was referring not to the religion as such but to Muslim culture in all its manifestations, as mediated through the Arabic script and the texts written in it; he gave the term "book history" as a direct translation of *histoire du livre,* the discipline developed by French scholars, particularly Lucien Febvre and Henri-Jean Martin.[8] But he also pointed especially to Elizabeth Eisenstein, whose work he considered would "shape the discipline of book history for decades to come" and therefore "might point the way for students of the Islamic book." There was, however, a note of ambivalence in this recommendation: as well as firmly rejecting "technological determinism" (although he did not, like some others, openly accuse Eisenstein of this), Albin noted that it was "not her certainties which illuminate our studies, but her doubts."[9] This ambivalence is reflected in some subsequent work in the history of Arab and Muslim modernization, and the role of printing in it, as I indicate in what follows.

The Historiography of Arabic Printing since 1979

In the past two decades the state of knowledge in this field has been transformed, quantitatively and qualitatively. The historical incidence and development of Arabic printing and presses, since their introduction to the Arab world in the eighteenth century, have attracted a steady procession of researchers where previously they were few and far between. There is space here to mention only a few highlights and examples. In 1982 the major reference manual *Grundriss der arabischen Philologie* included a section titled "Die Anfänge der arabischen Typographie und die Ablösung der Handschrift durch den Buchdruck," by the noted German scholar of Islamic studies Gerhard Endress. Although somewhat sketchy and inaccurate, it presented to the traditional world of European philological scholarship a useful survey of the print revolution in Arab countries as it affected the physical presentation of texts.[10]

6. Geoffrey Roper, "Arabic Incunabula," *L'arabisant* 21 (1982): 21–4.

7. Albin, "Islamic Book History: Parameters of a Discipline," *International Association of Orientalist Librarians Bulletin* 26–27 (1985): 13–16.

8. Febvre and Martin, *L'apparition du livre* (Paris: A. Michel, 1958), edited by Geoffrey Nowell-Smith and David Wootton, translated by David Gerard as *The Coming of the Book: The Impact of Printing 1450–1800* (London: N.L.B., 1976; reissued, London: Verso, 1990).

9. Albin, "Islamic Book History," 13–15.

10. Endress, "Die Anfänge," in *Grundriss der arabischen Philologie,* vol. 1, ed. Wolfdietrich Fischer and Helmut Gätje (Wiesbaden: Reichert, 1982), 291–6, 312–4.

In 1985 the Tunisian scholar Wahid Gdoura took a major step forward with his study of the beginnings of Arabic-script printing in eighteenth-century Syria, Lebanon, and Turkey. Although most of his book was devoted to the background, initiation, and development of the early presses, and an enumeration of their output, the final section did give a brief assessment of the place of printed books in the intellectual milieu of the time, their use as an agent of reform and modernization, and their limited role until the later, more widespread adoption of printing became "le facteur moteur des grandes rénovations intellectuelles . . . du XIXème siècle."[11] Written in French, it later gained a wider Arab readership in an Arabic version.[12] In the same year (1985), the Iraqi writer and educator Bihnām Faḍīl ʿAffāṣ produced a substantial synoptic account of the history of printing and presses in his country, providing much useful new data. Although he notes in his introduction that printing was the "foundation stone" of the nineteenth-century Arab Renaissance (*Nahḍa*), in Iraq as elsewhere, he did not attempt any analysis of its specific role in intellectual or social change.[13] The same was true of later studies such as those of Aḥmad Muḥammad al-Qalāl (1994) on publishers and publishing (with particular reference to Libya) and Maḥmūd Muḥammad al-Ṭanāḥī (1996) on the Egyptian printed book in the nineteenth century. This last was also the theme of a major monograph by the distinguished Egyptian librarian and bibliographer ʿĀʾida Ibrāhīm Nuṣayr (1994). Drawing on her previous work on the enumerative bibliography of the period,[14] she set out at some length the intellectual currents discernible in the printed books and their physical characteristics. She also analyzed the nature and role of their publishers: governmental presses, private individuals, learned and literary societies, commercial companies, and the like, as well as the channels of distribution.[15] By doing so, she has made a significant contribution to our knowledge and understanding of early Egyptian printed book production;

11. ["the driving factor in the great intellectual renewals . . . of the 19th century."] Gdoura, *Le début de l'imprimerie arabe à Istanbul et en Syrie: Évolution de l'environnement culturel (1706–1787)* [The beginning of Arabic printing in Istanbul and Syria: Evolution of the cultural environment (1706–1787)] (Tunis: Institut Supérieur de Documentation, 1985), 247.

12. Waḥīd Qadūra, *Bidāyat al-ṭibāʿa al-ʿArabīya fī Istānbūl wa-Bilād al-Shām: Taṭawwur al-muḥīṭ al-thaqāfī* (Zaghouan: Muʾassasat al-Tamīmī lil-Baḥth al-ʿIlmī wa-al-Maʿlūmāt, 1992).

13. Bihnām Faḍīl ʿAffāṣ, *Tārīkh al-ṭibāʿa wa-ʾl-maṭbūʿāt al-ʿIrāqīya* [History of Iraqi printing and printed publications] (Baghdad: Maṭbaʿat al-Adīb al-Baghdādīya, 1985).

14. Nuṣayr, *Al-kutub al-ʿArabīya allatī nushirat fī Miṣr fī ʾl-qarn al-tāsiʿ ʿashar* [Arabic books published in Egypt in the nineteenth century] (Cairo: Qism al-Nashr bi-ʾl-Jāmiʿa al-Amirīkīya bi-ʾl-Qāhira, 1990).

15. Nuṣayr, *Ḥarakat nashr al-kutub fī Miṣr fī ʾl-qarn al-tāsiʿ ʿashar* [The book-publishing movement in Egypt in the nineteenth century] (Cairo: al-Hayʾa al-Miṣrīya al-ʿĀmma li-l-Kitāb, 1994).

but she did not attempt any Eisensteinian analysis of how this production may have, in itself, been an agent of change.

The physical characteristics of early Arabic books printed in Egypt were more particularly the focus of a major and groundbreaking study in analytical bibliography by Jīhān Maḥmūd al-Sayyid, published in 2000.[16] Her detailed treatment ranges from title pages to colophons and includes tables of contents, preliminaries, text-blocks, and watermarks. But there is little discussion of the cognitive and social effects of these features and their development. More recently, two significant monographs, by Yaḥyá Maḥmūd ibn Junayd and ʿAbbās ibn Ṣāliḥ Ṭāshkandī, have added greatly to our knowledge of the history of printing in the Arabian peninsula.[17] But, like the others already mentioned, they do not try to trace the emergence of print culture in the area.

Apart from such monographic treatment, the growth of interest in Middle Eastern printing history has also been reflected in several conferences and exhibitions. In 1989 Eleazar Birnbaum and a group of his colleagues organized a major exhibition in the Thomas Fisher Rare Book Library of the University of Toronto, with seventy-nine exhibits carefully chosen to illustrate the transition from the scribal to the printed production of Muslim texts.[18] In 1995 the Jumʿa al-Mājid Centre in Dubai and the Cultural Foundation in Abu Dhabi jointly convened a symposium (*nadwa*) on the history of Arabic printing up to the end of the nineteenth century. Twelve papers by distinguished Arab scholars covered different Arab countries and areas, Europe, the Americas, the Indian subcontinent, Iran, and the Russian empire, as well as the role of orientalists and trends in text editing in the late nineteenth century. But the stated aims of the symposium did not include consideration of the effects of the spread of printing, nor did this consideration feature, to any great extent, in the contributions.[19] It did, however, in another conference held the fol-

16. Sayyid, *Al-bibliyūjrāfiyā al-taḥlīlīya: dirāsa fī awāʾil al-maṭbūʿāt al-ʿArabīya* [Analytical bibliography: A study in early Arabic printed books] (Alexandria: Dār al-Thaqāfa al-ʿIlmīya, 2000).

17. Ibn Junayd, *Al-ṭibāʿa fī shibh al-jazīra al-ʿArabīya fī ʾl-qarn al-tāsiʿ ʿashar al-Mīlādī (1297–1317 H)* [Printing in the Arabian Peninsula in the nineteenth century] (Riyadh: Maktabat al-Malik Fahd al-Waṭanī, 1998); Ṭāshkandī, *Al-ṭibāʿa fī ʾl-Mamlaka al-ʿArabīya al-Saʿūdīya 1300 H–1419 H* [Printing in Saudi Arabia, 1882–1999] (Riyadh: Maktabat al-Malik Fahd al-Waṭanī, 1999).

18. Birnbaum, Virginia Aksan, Michael McCaffrey, and Noha Sadek, *From Manuscript to Printed Book in the Islamic World: Catalogue of an Exhibition, Thomas Fisher Rare Book Library, University of Toronto* (Toronto: Univ. of Toronto, 1989).

19. *Nadwat Tārīkh al-ṭbāʿa al-ʿArabīya ḥattá intihāʾ al-qarn al-tāsiʿ ʿashar . . . 1416 H . . . 1995 M.: al-waqāʾiʿ wa-ʾl-buḥūth allatī ulqiyat fīhā* [Symposium on the history of printing up to the end of the nineteenth century, 1995: Documents and studies delivered] (Abu Dhabi: Cultural Foundation, 1996).

lowing year (1996) in Copenhagen on the topic "The Introduction of the Printing Press in the Middle East." There a small group of mainly Western scholars presented papers that analyzed in some detail the role of printing in eighteenth- and nineteenth-century Islamic culture, and the use that was made of it by rulers and ruled in a number of different countries of the Middle East.[20] Some of them are considered in the discussion that follows.

The opening years of the twenty-first century have seen further activity in this arena. In 2001 the twenty-first Deutscher Orientalistentag of the Deutsche Morgenländische Gesellschaft, held in Bamberg, included a special panel, "Zur frühen Druckgeschichte in den Ländern des Vorderen Orients." As in Copenhagen, a select group of specialist scholars, in this instance German, considered analytically the impact of the earlier presses and the role of their protagonists.[21] This was accompanied by a notable exhibition of early imprints, organized by Klaus Kreiser, which included a few carefully chosen rarities in Arabic from Italy and Lebanon, described in detail in the catalogue.[22]

Then in 2002 Middle Eastern printing history came to the very birthplace of the printing press, when a major exhibition was installed at the Gutenberg Museum in Mainz, titled "Middle Eastern Languages and the Print Revolution: A Cross-Cultural Encounter." Organized jointly by the director of the museum, Eva Hanebutt-Benz, and two Arabic specialists, Dagmar Glass and Geoffrey Roper, the exhibition aimed to present not just the earliest imprints (although these were present) but also representative specimens of the range and development of printed material, in Arabic and other Middle Eastern languages, as it spanned the revolutionary transition from scribal to print culture.[23] At the same time, a symposium was held in the museum, as part of the First World Congress of Middle Eastern Studies, on the topic "History of Printing and Publishing in the Languages and Countries of the Middle East." This symposium was on a larger scale than the other gatherings so far mentioned, bringing together thirty-two specialists, whose papers covered a wide range of historical and technical aspects, including some post-Eisensteinian

20. The papers were published in a special issue of *Culture & History* 16 (1997).

21. Ulrich Marzolph, ed., *Das gedruckte Buch im Vorderen Orient* (Dortmund: Verlag für Orientkunde, 2002).

22. Klaus Kreiser, ed., *The Beginnings of Printing in the Near and Middle East: Jews, Christians and Muslims* (Wiesbaden: Harrassowitz in Kommission, 2001).

23. Eva Hanebutt-Benz, Dagmar Glass, and Geoffrey Roper in collaboration with Theo Smets, eds., *Middle Eastern Languages and the Print Revolution: A Cross-Cultural Encounter / Sprachen des Nahen Ostens und die Druckrevolution: Eine interkulturelle Begegnung,* Gutenberg Museum Mainz, Internationale Gutenberg-Gesellschaft (Westhofen: WVA-Verlag Skulima, 2002).

studies of print culture.[24] In 2005 a second international symposium on the same topic was convened at the Bibliothèque nationale de France in Paris, at which twenty-eight papers were presented. So, Arabic and Middle Eastern printing history can fairly be said to have lost its Cinderella status of twenty-five years or so ago, at least in part because of the change in the general intellectual climate stimulated by Eisenstein in 1979.

The Study of Arab Print Culture

As well as histories of the introduction of printing and of the early presses and their output, such as those mentioned previously, some scholars in this period have also attempted the more demanding task of tracing the emergence of print culture in the Arab world and its effects on patterns of awareness and social interaction. In 1986 the Tunisian information scientist Abdelkader Ben Cheikh approached the subject from the perspective of literacy and education. In his book on the role of reading in social development, he devoted a substantial section to the historical impact of printing, especially in Tunisia, in which he traced the emergence of two kinds of reading in Islamic culture: sacred and ritual recitation (*qarā'a*) and desacralized, internalized reading (*muṭāla'a*). Printing spread the latter to a much wider public, opening the way to the extension and modernization of education and, ultimately, of the wider literate society.[25]

This topic was also the theme of Carter Vaughn Findley's 1989 essay on the transition to modern patterns of knowledge and education in the Middle East. He traced the passing of the "magic garden" mentality in Muslim culture, its replacement by a more rationalist discourse, and the subsequent movement toward "mass mobilization." He attributed this change to, among other factors, the nineteenth-century arrival of the "Gutenberg age" in the area and the consequent "media revolution."[26]

The 1990s saw a quickening pace in the pursuit of such lines of enquiry, although major monographic treatment was still lacking. In 1992 Brinkley Messick devoted a chapter to print culture in his book on the role of textual transmission and "textual domination" in Yemen. Some of his insights have

24. Philip Sadgrove, ed., *History of Printing and Publishing in the Languages and Countries of the Middle East, Journal of Semitic Studies*, suppl. no. 15 (2005).

25. Ben Cheikh, *Communication et société: Pouvoir lire et développement culturel* (Tunis: Publications du Centre de recherches en bibliothéconomie et sciences de l'information, 1986), 115–59.

26. Findley, "Knowledge and Education in the Modern Middle East: A Comparative View," in *The Modern Economic and Social History of the Middle East in its World Context*, ed. Georges Sabagh (Cambridge: Cambridge Univ. Press, 1989).

a much wider relevance and validity, such as his observation that, unlike traditional oral and scribal educational materials, "printed textbooks [pertained] to a curriculum system of public instruction, and the associated sociopolitical, citizen-based universe of nationalism"; nevertheless, the relatively isolated and untypical nature of Yemeni society perhaps limits the applicability of his findings to the study of the print revolution elsewhere in the Arab Middle East.[27]

The British Muslim intellectual and information scientist Ziauddin Sardar went perhaps to the other extreme in his 1993 article on the role of communication technologies in "the making and unmaking of Islamic culture." Writing in very broad terms about the whole of "Muslim history," he traced three transformations that have revolutionized the creation and transmission of knowledge (*'ilm*): the introduction, respectively, of paper, printing, and electronic media. The second of these, he considered, effectively led to the unmaking of the old knowledge-based Islamic culture because it brought about a split between traditional knowledge, which the conservative-minded Islamic scholars (*'ulamā'*) were reluctant to see in print, and the modern secular texts widely disseminated from the presses.[28] While unsupported by any systematic analysis of what texts were in fact produced by the nineteenth-century presses, this thesis perhaps reflected a synthesis of certain revisionist approaches to the emergence of Muslim print culture that can also be found in the work of several other scholars.[29]

The distinguished Arabic literary and philosophical scholar Muhsin Mahdi, in his 1995 essay, also treated printing as just one of the transitions undergone by Muslim literate culture: in his opinion, the earlier emergence of the written book was more important and "printing has simply fixed and diffused" many texts of no greater significance or value than their manuscript forerunners. He did, however, acknowledge that printed books eventually imparted "a degree of solidity and authority that went far beyond the solidity and authority of the manuscript copy or copies of the same book"; he went on to summarize some of "the numerous social and cultural implications of the transition," such as the rise of national sentiment and secular culture, the emergence of professional writers, the changing ratio of new works to old ones, the use of books as instruments of state policy, the buttressing of

27. Messick, *The Calligraphic State: Textual Domination and History in a Muslim Society* (Berkeley and Los Angeles: Univ. of California Press, 1992), 115–31.

28. Sardar, "Paper, Printing and Compact Disks: The Making and Unmaking of Islamic Culture," *Media, Culture and Society* 15 (1993): 51–5.

29. E.g., Abdullah Schleifer and Timothy Mitchell, considered in later discussions.

popular religion through the use of printing by the Sufi (mystical) orders, and the impact on the Arabic language. On nearly all these Eisensteinian topics, however, he raised questions without giving answers.[30]

In a more specialized study published in 1999, Ulrich Marzolph, after observing that "probably the most decisive event for cultural production in the Arab Middle East in the nineteenth century was the introduction of printing," went on to assert the essential continuity in the content of some kinds of book from manuscript to print production, in particular the issuing of compilations of stories. But he then traced how within print culture these compilations underwent significant shifts and changes and became "sanitized step by step in order to give way to a domesticated fantasy," presumably more in keeping with the requirements of the new middle-class market for printed books.[31]

The present century has already seen further notable contributions to the study of Middle Eastern print culture. Two examples must suffice, both from German scholars who are prominent in this field. At the 2001 Bamberg conference mentioned earlier, Dagmar Glass traced the essential role of Arabic printing presses in the nineteenth-century Renaissance (*Nahḍa*) and in the renewal of Arabic written culture.[32] Looking at the question from the point of view of the consumption of printed material, Johann Strauss has traced the development of print culture through a detailed analysis of different readerships among the various linguistic and religious groups of the Ottoman Empire, including Arabs, in the nineteenth and early twentieth centuries.[33]

Eisenstein in Studies of the Arab World

All of the studies mentioned in the previous section seem to have been written at least partly under the indirect influence of Elizabeth Eisenstein, insofar as they deal with questions of the kind originally raised in *PPAC*, and that consequently were "in the air" at the time they were written. None of them, however, cites her book or explicitly acknowledges her influence. Nor has

30. Mahdi, "From the Manuscript Age to the Age of Printed Books," in *The Book in the Islamic World: The Written Word and Communication in the Middle East,* ed. George N. Atiyeh (Albany: State Univ. of New York Press; Washington, DC: Library of Congress, 1995), 1–15.

31. Marzolph, "*Adab* in Transition: Creative Compilation in Nineteenth-Century Print Tradition," *Israel Oriental Studies* 19 (1999): 161–72.

32. Glass, "Die *Nahḍa* und ihre Technik im 19. Jahrhundert: Arabische Druckereien in Ägypten und Syrien," in *Das gedruckte Buch im Vorderen Orient,* ed. Marzolph (Dortmund: Verlag für Orientkunde, 2002).

33. Strauss, "Who Read What in the Ottoman Empire (19th–20th Centuries)?" *Middle Eastern Literatures* 6.1 (2003): 39–76.

there appeared any major monographic study of Arab print culture drawing wholly or partly on her insights, like the notable study of Russian printing history by Gary Marker.[34] There are, however, a few smaller-scale contributions that do mention her, and wholly or partly adopt a framework of inquiry that reflects her approach.

J. S. Szyliowicz in his 1986 article pointed to two of Eisenstein's findings on the role of printing in changing "the way in which people think and perceive reality": first, the reorganization of texts and reference guides to enable their more systematic use and the more rational presentation of data, and second, the reorganization of time and effort among scholars and students, away from copying and memorization toward "more productive intellectual work." He indicated, although without detailed analysis, that these trends were present also in early Ottoman printed-book production in the eighteenth and nineteenth centuries.[35] The German scholar Reinhard Schulze took up another Eisensteinian theme in a ground-breaking 1987 article on nineteenth-century Islamic cultural production. In this essay he pointed out that the concept and feeling of modernity were necessarily predicated on a rejection of the immediate past in favor of reclaiming a semi-mythical "golden age" of "timeless universality." Just as in Renaissance Europe, this shift was made much easier, and less reversible, by the use of the printing press to establish, propagate, and canonize the texts of that earlier age—those of classical antiquity in western Europe, early Islamic ones in the Arab Middle East.[36] Schulze did not mention Eisenstein here but was unmistakably influenced by her; in a later article (based on a paper at the 1996 Copenhagen conference) he made his debt clearer, citing her in support of his assertion that "printing fundamentally changed the attitudes in the Muslim world toward history."[37]

In a more specialized context, I made some use of Eisenstein's insights in my 1988 thesis on Arabic printing in nineteenth-century Malta. In it I tried to place the subject—and Arabic printing history in general—in the context of communication and book history overall: tracing its development from

34. Marker, *Publishing, Printing, and the Origins of the Intellectual Life in Russia, 1700–1800* (Princeton, NJ: Princeton Univ. Press, 1985).

35. Szyliowicz, "Functional Perspectives on Technology: The Case of the Printing Press in the Ottoman Empire," *Archivum Ottomanicum* 11 (1986): 257–8. Also in Ekmeleddin İhsanoğlu, ed., *Transfer of Modern Science & Technology to the Muslim World* (Istanbul: Research Centre for Islamic History, Art and Culture, 1992), 251–60.

36. Schulze, "Mass Culture and Islamic Cultural Production in 19th-Century Middle East," in *Mass Culture, Popular Culture, and Social Life in the Middle East,* ed. Georg Stauth and Sami Zubaida (Frankfurt am Main: Campus Verlag; Boulder, CO: Westview Press, 1987), 205–7.

37. Schulze, "The Birth of Tradition and Modernity in 18th- and 19th-Century Islamic Culture: The Case of Printing," *Culture & History* 16 (1997): 41.

Innis through McLuhan, Febvre and Martin, and culminating in Eisenstein, while noting the absence of such analysis by Middle East historians. I tried also to cast my description and analysis of the Malta output in such a way as to facilitate the consideration of those features highlighted by Eisenstein as important in the development of print culture, and I concluded with some, necessarily provisional and tentative, discussion of Eisenstein's "clusters of changes," involving the accelerated dissemination, standardization, and preservation of texts brought about by the early Arabic presses in Malta and elsewhere.[38] In later published articles, I applied these concepts to the work of one particular famous Arab writer of the period, Fāris al-Shidyāq, who worked at the Malta press and later became a leading proponent of the print revolution in the Ottoman Empire: I attempted to show how he not only transformed the delivery of both classical and modern Arabic texts but also embodied in himself, as a former scribe who became a professional author and journalist, the transition from scribal to print culture. He himself, more than a hundred years before Eisenstein, had emphasized elements of dissemination, standardization, and preservation to justify the adoption of what was still in some Arab and Muslim eyes a suspect novelty.[39] In addition, I pointed to his role in, and his opinions on, the use of the printing press in developing national awareness and civic rights, along with those of some of his contemporaries.[40] Interestingly, though, the example of Fāris al-Shidyāq has subsequently been adduced elsewhere to make a tentative counterargument against Eisensteinian notions of print-induced cultural change.[41]

Another doctoral thesis, presented by the Iraqi American librarian and scholar Fawzi Abdulrazak in 1990, also drew inspiration from Eisenstein. This was a study of early Arabic printing in Morocco, and its very title refers to printing as "an agency of change." The author stated clearly in his introduction that he had "benefited from [Eisenstein's] framework as a guide to the observation, documentation and discussion of the various effects of print-

---

38. Roper, "Arabic Printing in Malta 1825–1845: Its History and Its Place in the Development of Print Culture in the Arab Middle East" (Ph.D. thesis., Univ. of Durham, 1988), esp. 1–5, 260–9, 325–9.

39. Roper, "Fāris al-Shidyāq and the Transition from Scribal to Print Culture in the Middle East," in Atiyeh, *Book in the Islamic World*, 209–31.

40. Roper, "National Awareness, Civic Rights, and the Rôle of the Printing Press in the 19th Century: The Careers and Opinions of Fāris al-Shidyāq, His Colleagues and Patrons," in *Democracy in the Middle East: Proceedings of the Annual Conference of the British Society for Middle Eastern Studies, 8–10 July 1992, Univ. of St Andrews, Scotland* ([Durham]: BRISMES, 1992).

41. Nadia al-Bagdadi, "Print, Script, and the Limits of Free-thinking in Arabic Letters of the Nineteenth Century: The Case of Al-Shidyāq," *Al-Abhath* 48–49 (2000–1): 99–122. See further discussion in the next section.

ing technology in Morocco." His Eisensteinian approach informs the whole structure of his study, and he also explicitly compared and contrasted the role of printing in the European Renaissance, drawing on Eisenstein, with the equivalent transformation of Morocco in the nineteenth century. After tracing the different strands of intellectual, social, and political change as affected by the printed word, he concluded by asserting that "printing was not only an agent to preserve knowledge, but also an agent of change which contributed to the shaping of Moroccan history."[42] This work, while remaining unpublished in English, was translated into Arabic and published in Morocco in 1996.[43]

Eisenstein's direct influence can also be found in some smaller-scale studies from the 1990s. Francis Robinson's inaugural lecture as Professor of the History of South Asia at the University of London in 1992 deals with the impact of print on religious change in Islam, and he starts off by drawing parallels with the European Christian Reformation and Counter-Reformation, citing Eisenstein's analysis of the conflicting trends of "Erasmian" humanism and modernism on one hand and orthodox Biblical fundamentalism on the other. "Clearly," Robinson says rather ambivalently, "print has a lot to answer for."[44] He goes on to trace how printing "struck right at the heart of" traditional textual communication in Muslim society and thereby had a revolutionary impact, leading to the emergence of a kind of "Protestant or scriptural Islam," promoting pan Islamic sentiments, undermining the traditional clerics (*'ulamā'*), and eventually giving rise to the conflicting currents of modernism and fundamentalism. His main focus is on South Asian Islam, but his Eisensteinian insights have considerable relevance to other Muslim societies, including the Arab world.

A more specialized study of the use of *fatwás* (promulgated legal opinions) in nineteenth-century Egypt, by the Danish scholar Jakob Skovgaard-Petersen, appeared in 1997. In this connection he examined the use of the new print medium by Egyptian clerics (*'ulamā'*) and jurists (*fuqahā'*). Like Robinson, he was struck by the parallels with the European Reformation period and remarked that "although often accused of techno-determinism, Elizabeth Eisenstein's book *PPAC* contains a number of suggestions worthwhile reflect-

42. Abdulrazak, "The Kingdom of the Book: The History of Printing as an Agency of Change in Morocco between 1865 and 1912" (Ph.D. diss., Boston Univ., 1990), 5, 117–8, 257.

43. Fawzī 'Abd al-Razzāq, *Mamlakat al-kitāb: tārīkh al-ṭibā'a fī 'l-Maghrib 1865–1912* [*The Kingdom of the Book: The History of Printing in Morocco, 1865–1912*], trans. Khālid al-Ṣaghīr (Rabat, Morocco: Jāmi'at Muḥammad al-Khāmis, Kullīyat al-Ādāb wa-'l-'Ulūm al-Insānīya, 1996).

44. Robinson, "Technology and Religious Change: Islam and the Impact of Print," *Modern Asian Studies* 27.1 (1993): 232.

ing upon in this much later Egyptian context." The spread of printing, he observes, coincided with an important reformation in Islamic thought, and printing gave it permanence, unlike earlier ones, just as Eisenstein observed of sixteenth-century Europe. Furthermore, printing also eventually strengthened both uniformity of belief and a sense of personal responsibility and individual understanding of scripture—another Eisensteinian finding. He concludes that "the period 1850–1900 is hardly understandable without due consideration of how thoroughgoing were the changes in Egypt's cultural production," an assertion hardly to be found in the pre-Eisenstein era.[45] The French scholar Yves Gonzalez-Quijano studied a later era of Egyptian book production in his book on publishing and intellectual culture in the republican period (i.e., since 1952). His delineation of the culture of printed books, and its part in creating an autonomous role for both authors and readers, also shows the influence of Eisenstein, whose work appears in his bibliography.[46]

Another writer who invoked Eisenstein was the American Muslim professor of mass communication studies Abdullah Schleifer, although he took a rather different view of the print culture she analyzed. "As Eisenstein has so clearly documented," he wrote, "the printing press was inevitably the most potent weapon of every subversive (or 'progressive') force in the West; of worldliness, licentiousness and secularism, . . . of a plethora of sects splintering religious unity, . . . of the Enlightenment philosophers who banished God from social and scientific discourse," leading to the evils of the French Revolution. A similar fate awaited Muslim society from the nineteenth century on. But it was not just a question of the presses falling into the wrong hands, important though that was: another "inescapable component" of mass communication through printing is the desacralization of the word, in particular the word of God in the Qur'ān and the Names of God. It leads even to desecration, through the unthinking disposal of unwanted printed matter.[47] Here we find an author who accepts Eisenstein's analysis, only to stand it on its head by using it to reject the values of the print culture whose role in human progress is her central theme. Schleifer brings to this rejection the ardor of the religious convert. But other writers, too, both Muslim and non-Muslim, have been ambivalent in their attitude toward Eisensteinian print

45. Skovgaard-Petersen, *Defining Islam for the Egyptian State: Muftis and Fatwas of the Dār al-Iftā* (Leiden: Brill, 1997), 51–6.

46. Gonzalez-Quijano, *Les gens du livre: Édition et champs intellectuel dans l'Egypte républicaine* (Paris: CNRS Éditions, 1998).

47. Schleifer, "Mass Communication and the Technicalization of Muslim Societies," *Muslim Education Quarterly* 4.3 (1987): 4–12.

culture and toward the postulates of her formulation of the concept. To these we now turn.

Problems with the Eisenstein Model in the Arab World

The influence of Eisenstein on studies of Arab printing history and cultural modernization is undeniable, and she can fairly be said to have transformed the concepts of a significant number of scholars of the early modern history of the Middle East, as elsewhere. Nevertheless, there has been some reluctance to embrace in toto her model of print-induced modernity, and a tendency in some quarters to seek at least partial alternatives. This is true even of some of the scholars mentioned earlier who have been influenced by her.

A few scholars have given preference to alternative or variant European approaches, such as those of Roger Chartier. This is true, for instance, of Gonzalez-Quijano, although, as we have seen, he does not ignore Eisenstein. He places some emphasis on Chartier's view of the role of the book (and of writing and printing generally) as a social instrument, and in his study of Egyptian "book people" develops this view in the direction of the notion of a print-enabled "public space," in sociopolitical terms, using a concept of Jürgen Habermas.[48] The latter is also taken up by Juan Cole, in his 2002 article, who likewise uses the concept to extend and partly qualify the application of Eisenstein's frameworks to areas south and east of the Mediterranean.[49] Chartier's emphasis on "the many uses and plural appropriations" of print[50] is also one that has appealed to some historians of Arab print culture because the printed book, at the level of the learned culture on which Eisenstein concentrated, has never been quite as significant among Arabs and Muslims as it has been in Europe. Popular devotional texts, pamphlets, "pavement literature," and, above all, newspapers and journalism, tended to loom larger in the Middle East in the print era, as Gonzalez-Quijano suggests.[51]

There has also been, among some Middle East historians, a resistance to the "technological determinism" that has been unfairly attributed to Eisenstein. Some instances of this resistance have been noted already, but the question whether culture determines technology or technology determines

48. Gonzalez-Quijano, *Les gens du livre,* 8, 16.

49. Cole, "Printing and Urban Islam in the Mediterranean World, 1890–1920," in *Modernity and Culture, from the Mediterranean to the Indian Ocean,* ed. Leila Tarazi Fawaz and C. A. Bayly (New York: Columbia Univ. Press, 2002), 345–6, 358–9.

50. Chartier and Alain Boureau, *The Culture of Print: Power and the Uses of Print in Early Modern Europe,* trans. Lydia G. Cochrane (Princeton, NJ: Princeton Univ. Press, 1989), 2.

51. Gonzalez-Quijano, *Les gens du livre,* 11, 124, 174, 190–3, 196–7.

culture has particularly exercised scholars concerned with this part of the world. The German Ottomanist Klaus Kreiser, for instance, points out that the introduction of printing by İbrahim Müteferrika to Ottoman Muslim society in the eighteenth century "did not create a fundamental break with the past as induced by the new technology in Europe,"[52] citing Eisenstein in his discussion. Others too have attributed a decisive role to Muslim culture in the way printing was introduced and received in the Middle East, which meant that printing itself did not play such an important role in modernization: its effects were mediated by local patterns of intellectual production and authority, and the modernizing influences came from without.[53]

Nadia al-Bagdadi has used a study of part of the career and output of Fāris al-Shidyāq (the celebrated nineteenth-century Arab renaissance writer who spanned the transition from scribal to print culture) to "take up the debate among the main representatives of the 'Eisenstein school' and scholars refuting the approach laid down in Eisenstein's work, most prominently Roger Chartier."[54] In particular, she questions the idea that there could be "no *nahḍa* [Arab renaissance] without the printing press" and asks whether technology really accounts for the substantive nature of literature. To support this challenge, she considers the use made by Fāris of scribal as well as print transmission, particularly of texts that might upset religious sensibilities, such as his critique of the Christian Gospels, *Mumāḥakāt al-ta'wīl fī munāqaḍāt al-Injīl* [Disputations of interpretation in criticisms of the Gospel].[55] In her view, this indicates "sharply diverse strategies in the production and dissemination of knowledge" and typifies the co-existence of print and manuscript in nineteenth-century Arab culture. This co-existence in turn creates a "need to reconsider some of the assumptions concerning print" in relation to the Arab renaissance.[56] Beyond this one case, however, she does not produce any general or quantitative data to support her challenge. But her treatment of Fāris al-Shidyāq, while not invalidating earlier studies, including my own,[57] provides an interesting variation of emphasis, away from the Eisenstein model.

The partial shift away from Eisenstein or the limits placed on the applica-

52. Kreiser, *Beginnings of Printing*, 16.

53. Cf. Schulze, "Mass Culture"; and Timothy Mitchell, *Colonising Egypt* (Cambridge: Cambridge Univ. Press, 1988), among others.

54. Bagdadi, "Print, Script, and the Limits," 99 n. 2.

55. This work survived only in a manuscript copy kept in the Awqāf Library in Baghdad. Since the destruction of that library following the U.S. invasion in April 2003, it may now be completely lost.

56. Bagdadi, "Print, Script, and the Limits," 103, 118; the argument is further developed throughout the essay.

57. Roper, "National Awareness, Civic Rights," and "Fāris al-Shidyāq."

tion of her model to the Arab and Muslim domains are mainly attributable to three major problems in the history of Arabic textual transmission and book culture.

The Late Arrival of the Printing Press

The Arabs used printing as early as the tenth century CE, five hundred years before Gutenberg.[58] But this was to produce block-printed amulets, and it was certainly not an "agent of change." Book production remained firmly in the hands of scribes until the eighteenth century. It did not become a normal method of text transmission among Arab Muslims until the second half of the nineteenth century, despite the much earlier triumph of the print revolution elsewhere. This is a major problem for cultural historians, and, in the words of the German Arabist Hartmut Bobzin, "until today [the] Islamic world's delay in employing one of the greatest achievements of Western technology . . . has not been explained convincingly."[59] Much attention has, however, been given to the problem. In 1954 André Demeerseman, a French scholar based in Tunisia, explored the issue in an extended article. He drew a distinction between superficial (and false) reasons, such as resistance to progress, aversion to culture, inwardness, inertia, and formalism, on one hand, and essential reasons—cultural, artistic, social, moral, doctrinal, economic, political—on the other.[60] While this distinction is certainly helpful, each of these "essential reasons" requires extended treatment in itself. Others have followed these lines of inquiry, most recently Lutz Berger at the Bamberg conference in 2001. He likewise pursues sociocultural, economic, and aesthetic lines of inquiry but ends by lamenting that the "eloquent silence" of Islamic sources on the subject renders attempts to reconstruct the earlier Muslim viewpoints premature.[61]

This still unsolved problem seems not susceptible to an Eisensteinian analysis. If the printing press was such a powerful agent of change in early modern Europe, why did it not have a significant impact on the Arab world for another four centuries? It is not surprising that inquirers in this field have

58. Karl R. Schaefer, *Enigmatic Charms: Medieval Arabic Block Printed Amulets in American and European Libraries and Museums* (Leiden: Brill, 2006).

59. Bobzin, *Between Imitation and Imagination: The Beginnings of Arabic Typography in Europe* (Beirut: Orient-Institut der Deutschen Morgenländischen Gesellschaft, 1997), 3.

60. Demeerseman, *L'imprimerie en Orient et au Maghreb: Une étape décisive de la culture et de la psychologie islamiques* (Tunis: Nicolas Bascone & Sauveur Muscat, 1954), previously published in *IBLA* 17 (1954).

61. Berger, "Zur Problematik der späten Einführung des Buchdrucks in der islamischen Welt," in Marzolph, *Das gedruckte Buch im Vorderen Orient.*

tended to pursue cultural and social reasons for technological change (or lack of it) rather than seeing the technology of the printing press as itself an agent of change.

Lithography

Another feature of Arabic-script printing history that has no counterpart in earlier European experience is the prevalence for much of the nineteenth and early twentieth centuries, in areas as far apart as Morocco and Indonesia, of a hybrid method of book production: lithography. Whereas in Europe this technique was used almost entirely for pictorial and cartographical illustration, Muslims used it to reproduce entire texts written by hand. In this way they could retain most of the familiar features of Islamic manuscripts, and the calligraphic integrity of the Arabic script, and avoid expensive investments in movable types.[62] But this means that Eisenstein's insights into the conscious and subliminal effects of the standardization of text presentation, and the emergence of a new print-induced *esprit de système,* do not really apply to those societies where this method was prevalent. Yet, the effects of the much wider dissemination of these texts—mainly traditional and classical ones—was very considerable, and, as Proudfoot says, "ushered in the print revolution."[63] Hence the ambivalence—part acceptance, part rejection—of Eisensteinian analyses among those who have studied this important phase in the development of Arab and Muslim print culture.

The Relationship between Modernization and Westernization

An even more serious historiographical problem is that the widespread adoption of printing in the Arab Middle East came in the wake of major European incursions in the military, economic, and cultural domains. Modernization has often been equated with westernization, and printing treated as an aspect of the latter. An adequate assessment of this problem cannot be attempted here. Suffice it to say that this equation has led some scholars to take a negative view of the effects of the print revolution on Arab and Muslim society

62. Cf. Demeerseman, "Une étape importante de la culture islamique: Une parente de l'imprimerie arabe et tunisienne, la lithographie," *IBLA* 16 (1953): 347–89, also published separately in Tunis, 1954; Karl Klaus Walther, "Die lithographische Vervielfältigung von Texten in den Ländern des Vorderen und Mittleren Orients," *Gutenberg-Jahrbuch* 65 (1990): 223–6; Brinkley Messick, "On the Question of Lithography," *Culture & History* 16 (1997): 158–76; and Ian Proudfoot, "Mass Producing Houri's Moles, or Aesthetics and Choice of Technology in Early Muslim Book Printing," in *Islam: Essays on Scripture, Thought, and Society,* ed. Peter G. Riddell and Tony Street (Leiden: Brill, 1997), 161–84, among others.

63. Proudfoot, "Mass Producing Houri's Moles," 182.

and culture. Timothy Mitchell, for instance, considered that, because of the partly oral nature of Islamic scholarly and literary communication, and of the Arabic language and script through which it was mediated, "writing could never unambiguously represent an author's unambiguous meaning [and therefore] no proper Arab scholar would have been interested in the power of the printing press. The problem of the author's presence in writing, furthermore, corresponded to a problem in the presence of political authority in society." But in mid-nineteenth-century Egypt, Europeans effectively colonized Muslim thought by promoting a medium—print—in which "words were to lose their power" and traditional authority was to be replaced by "an apparent certainty—the effect of an unambiguous meaning—made possible by modern methods of representation."[64] The printing press was thus certainly an "agent of change" but in the direction of dependency and peripheralization, rather than autonomous modernity. Some of the writers mentioned previously in this essay have also associated the print revolution with westernization, although not always quite so negatively.[65]

I and a few others, however, have taken a different, more Eisenstein-oriented view. Regardless of its origins, I wrote in 1988, "printing has its own direct effects, as Innis, McLuhan, Febvre and Eisenstein have shown. These operate, as they have demonstrated, both on the cognitive plane, and on the socioeconomic plane. The systematic investigation of these factors might shift the historical perspective somewhat: westernization might then perhaps seem a less direct cause of some of the changes in Middle Eastern thought and society in the nineteenth century."[66] I stand by these words, and call upon my colleagues, in the spirit of Eisenstein, to devote more effort to that systematic investigation.

64. Mitchell, *Colonising Egypt*, 150–3.

65. Cf. Gdoura, *Le début de l'imprimerie;* Schulze, "Mass Culture" and "The Birth of Tradition"; Abdulrazak, *The Kingdom of the Book;* and Robinson, "Technology and Religious Change," among others.

66. Roper, "Arabic Printing in Malta" 4–5.

[22]

Islam and the Art of Printing

H.A. Avakian

The purpose of this article is not simply to explore the early history of printing in the Muslim countries of the Middle East, but particularly to examine the circumstances which led to the slow pace with which the invention of printing was harnessed to tackle the problem of spreading Muslim religious literature.

There has been relatively so little published on the subject of Muslim/Arabic printing. The little that has been published does not go beyond a dozen articles of a more or less historical nature, and having read these publications one cannot avoid the feeling that many questions have been left unanswered. We only hope that this article may be a new start in the attempt at a multidisciplinary approach to one aspect of the history of Muslim culture.

An alternative title to this article may well have been: *"Islam as a barrier to printing" revisited* (1). We intend to reconsider the conclusions of T. F. Carter in this article, and while not denying the fact that printing was used on some scale in the Muslim world only as of the eighteenth century, we hope not only to account for this fact but also to show that if we place the circumstances within the correct historical/theological context, only then shall we be able to remove the impression implicit in the writings of T. C. Carter to the effect that the whole matter is evidence of rigid conservatism of Islam as a religion and a culture. Before looking at the early history of printing in the Muslim world let us simply memorate some facts which will clarify the degree of surprise at the developments as we know them:

1. There is enough historical evidence to prove that block printing was known in the Muslim world long before it was known in Europe (as early as the tenth century A.D.). In de 1880s some block prints were found in the Fayyum province in Egypt. The finds have been carefully described by Karabacek in the catalogue of the Erzherzog Rainer Collection in

Vienna, and they were known to be housed in Vienna, Berlin and Heidelberg (2).

2. The art of making paper was known in the Arab world long before it came to Europe. There is documentary evidence that after 751 A.D. the Arabs learned the art from the Chinese and passed it on much later to Europe.
3. There has been some 'prejudice' in the Muslim world to printing. While Jews (Marranos from Spain who had taken refuge in the Ottoman Empire), and Christians of all sorts were allowed by the authorities to establish their own private printing houses within the Ottoman Empire very early in the sixteenth century A.D., (not to mention Arabic printing in European countries such as Italy and France), the first printing press run by a Muslim (convert) started production only in 1729 in Constantinople. Printing on a large scale in Arabic, Turkish and Persian by Muslims was very late, as of the nineteenth century.

A juxtaposition of these three facts causes natural bewilderment. Let us now look at the history of Arabic/Muslim printing. (We speak here of Arabic/Muslim printing in order to distinguish between printing in Arabic regardless of the country where it took place, and printing in Arabic and other languages by Muslims within the 'house of Islam' and the boundaries of the Ottoman Empire in the course of history.)

II.

The printing of the Bible has had more than one impact on the history of printing. Soon after the printing of the Gutenberg Bible it became necessary to print the Bible in various languages which reflected the text history, the well-known Polyglots. This implied the printing of the Scriptures in several Semitic and other non-European languages such as Hebrew, Syriac, Aramaic, Chaldean and Arabic. By the end of the sixteenth century various printing centres in Europe published among other religious works theological treatises, translations of the Gospels, Psalms, horologia, and all sorts of liturgical books in Arabic.

Several printing centres achieved pre-eminence in Arabic publications in Europe. The first work printed in Arabic was an horologium of the Church of Alexandria published in Fano, Italy. The Arabic press there was started at the instigation of Pope Julius II. A first edition of the Qur'ān in Arabic type was published in Fano in 1514, to be followed by another edition in 1518. (There is no extant copy of the edition of the Qur'ān in Arabic type which is said to have been printed in Venice sometime in the period 1485-1499). Another early work was the five-language Psalterium published in Genoa by P. Porrus in 1516 for François I, the king of France. The fourth decade of the sixteenth century witnessed the beginnings of Arabic printing in Vienna. Towards the end of the sixteenth century Rome was firmly established as a centre for Arabic printing under the encouragement of popes Gregorius XIII and Paulus V. Special mention should be made of the Medici press there. Ferdinand de Medici who was cardinal in Rome, was willing to spend "40,000 golden crowns" (a capital sum for the time) for luxurious publications in Oriental languages under the direction of the orientalist Raimondi de Cremone. Robert Granjon cut a special alphabet, the petit arabe, soon followed by three sets of other oriental characters. Some of the publications were illustrated by Tempesta, one of the famous illustrators of the time. Mention could also be made of the printing activities in Leiden under Erpennius in 1595 (3).

It is remarkable that these first attempts at Arabic printing took place at a time when there were no authoritative printed Arabic reference works such as grammars and dictionaries. What were the motives for these activities in Europe? If we set aside motives of studious scholarship (on which matter we do not wish to pass any judgment here), we notice that commerce and religious polemics ranged as very important motives. From the remarks of Galland (4) we learn that the printers and their patrons went through all the expense and trouble "dans la vue de faire commerce en Levant de ces livres, dessein qui échoua d'abord parce que les Mahométans ne voulurent pas recevoir les exemplaires qu'on leur porta" (5). The Society for the Propagation of the Christian Faith in Rome used the products of its presses in its attemps at missionary and polemic activities. French missionaries, on the other hand, were supposed to receive several free copies of the products of the Société Typographique de Paris as part of their equipment.

How did the Muslim world (the Ottoman Empire) react? Galland observes that the Turks rejected printing – what was offered to them – as a matter of policy.

> "Nous apprenons d'ailleurs que Selim I, empereur de Constantinople, renouvela en 1515 une ordonnance de son père Bajazeth II qui défendoit, sous peine de la vie, de se servir de livres imprimés.... Dans le Levant une infinité de personnes qui subsistent en copiant des livres, auroient été réduites à la mendicité par l'imprimerie; on a voulu depuis l'établir, on a imprimé à Constantinople plusieurs livres Turcs, mais elle a été abandonnée, et les Mahométans préfèrent toujours leurs manuscrits

à nos imprimés..." (6).

One should not forget, however, the tolerance with which the authorities in Constantinople were willing to allow their subject non-Muslim religious communities to engage in printing activities, so that next to the well-known activities of the Marrano Jews in the capital, the Armenians set up their presses in 1567 (by Apkar of Sivas), and the Greeks in 1627 (by Nicodemus Metaxas) in addition to the activities of the Arabic speaking Christians in Syria and Lebanon.
But the question may be raised, before considering the attitudes of the Muslims to the Western art of printing, whether the Muslims hat not known or engaged in printing at all. We already mentioned the cases of block printing in Egypt. But there are other intriguing instances of mention of printing in Spain during the Moorish occupation there. A first instance is that refered to by Von Hammer Purgstall in his remarks on a passage in *Kitāb al-Iḥāṭa fī Ta'rīḫ Ġarnāṭa* (a history of Granada dating from 1375 A.D.) in which a biography is given of Abū Bakr al-Qollosī. A. Geiss (7) discussed the matter to some extent. In the section on the biography of Abū Bakr al-Qollosī we read that he (Abū Bakr) wrote a work – *The hidden pearl on the beauties of Estepona* – and that he dedicated "to the vizier al-Ḥakīm a work on the properties and the fabrication of ink [?] and the instruments of printing, a work singular [?] in its contents" (8). Whether this work was kabbalistic in nature and alchemistic in character, as Geiss thinks, some consideration should also be given to the fact that an imprint of a wooden seal was found in Almería, Spain about 1850, dating from 1350 A.D., indicating that the seal was used in trade there at the time. There is also evidence from another source again from Moorish Spain. Ibn al-'Abbār mentions in his *Kitāb Ḥulla as-Siyarā'* (Torso of biographies) that Badr, the freed slave of prince 'Abdallah, who later became vizier under an-Nāṣir,

> "was in charge of the provinces; the records [or protocols] were written in his home and he would send them to be printed; they were printed and sent back to him, [who in turn] sent them to the administrators [governors]; these acted on his authority [lit. at his hands]" (9).

Geiss's general conclusion of the matter is:

> "It is impossible, in view of the actual facts, to admit that the Arabs, even as masters of Spain up to 1469, should have known the art of Gutenberg which was not introduced there in 1468, although invented

since 1440" (10).

We do not deem it impossible, since Galland mentions printing by the Moors in Morocco. While the Turks refused to avail themselves of the invention of printing in 1485 and 1515, "Les Maures furent moins scrupuleux à cet égard: on prétend qu'il y a eu des imprimeries à Maroc; mais que ces peuples se font un point de religion de ne pas laisser sortir ... leurs livres" (11). It is not impossible that these printing activities in Morocco were a continuation of what was done by the Moors in Spain once they were driven back to North Africa.
The breakthrough in the history of Muslim printing occurred in the third decade of the eighteenth century in Constantinople. William J. Watson describes the situation at the time in the following words:

> "The Ottoman Empire in the early eighteenth century was beginning to be stirred, slightly but perceptibly, by new ideas. The realization that all was not well with the world was brought on to a great extent by the alarming frequency of military setbacks in recent years. To a lesser extent the fact was dimly beginning to be perceived that Europe, until now known to be peopled by barbarians, was technologically and scientifically ahead of the Muslims. The imperial economy was in a process of continuing decline, in agriculture, in commerce, in industry. Everywhere in the empire the power of Europe was having its deleterious effect. Turks began to take an interest in Europe, and especially in France, first for a mixture of military, diplomatic and economic reasons, and then as possessors of a culture that was worth attention. The work of translation grew to include not only works from Arabic and Persian, but also from Latin, French, Italian, German. Social change was in the wind. There were some signs of what might be loosely described as a new national consciousness. It was a critical period, and one of its significant innovations was the printing press" (12).

The Turkish ambassador to Paris, Mehemet Effendi who was accompanied by his son Zaïd Aga, had undoubtedly reported upon his return to Constantinople of the benefits of printing all sorts of books and especially maps and charts. A cardinal role, however, was played by a Hungarian convert to Islam, Ibrahim Müteferriḳa (court-steward). In 1726 he wrote a pamphlet *Vesīlet üṭ-ṭibāʻa* (the means of printing) which he submitted to the Grand Vizier, the Grand Mufti and the ʻUlemā'. He also submitted a formal request to the Sultan asking for a ferman authorizing him to embark on his enterprise: to publish classical and scientific works such as dictionaries, collections on logic, philosophy, astronomy etc. by means of metallic letters. Sultan Ahmed III, according to custom, consulted his venerable pontif, the Grand Mufti of the empire, Šayḫ 'Abdullah, to find out whether Muslim jurisprudence allowed such an enterprise. (It is important to note in this context that works on religion, especially the printing of the Qur'ān, books on Quranic exegesis, traditions, theology and holy law were excluded.) It is due to this proviso that opposition from the religious camp was avoided. The Sultan issued a ferman in 1727, a Khatti humaïoun (imperial edict) in which he granted Ibrāhīm permission to go ahead. In a period of fourteen years seventeen works were published of which the total count amounted to about 13,000 volumes (13). Printing was finally granted a foothold in Muslim world. The nineteenth century witnessed further printing presses in Egypt and Persia.

III.

Having surveyed briefly the history of printing in the Muslim world of the Middle East, we have to face a number of questions which must be answered if at all we are to succeed in securing the right perspective for observation and judgment:

1. Is it bias or ignorance (or both) on the part of T. F. Carter which led him to remarks such as, "whatever the reason may be, up to today [1925] the Koran has never been printed in any Moslem country except by block printing or lithography"? (14). Memorating that Sultan Ahmed III granted permission to Ībrāhīm Müteferrika to set up a press in Constantinople in 1727, he goes on to say

   "in 1729 [a possible exception by him is granted for another earlier attempt in 1714] a history of Egypt appeared. But it awakened such opposition that until the nineteenth century no more printing was attempted in Moslem lands, and even through the nineteenth century printing has had to fight against great odds.... so far as is known, with the exception of the abortive projects of 1714 and 1729 at Constantinople, the Islamic world (the Chinese part of it excepted) never printed a book till 1825, when the first press was set up in Cairo" (15).

The facts disprove Carter's claims. Between 1729 and 1745 (with a brief interval from 1735 to 1740) no less than seventeen works came from

Müteferrika's press (the so-called Turkish incunabula). A more noteworthy disclaimant is the fact that the National Press of Egypt in Cairo was set up in 1821, and the projects which were assigned to it clearly indicate the "national" nature of the undertaking.

"L'imprimerie Nationale a été instituée en l'année 1821 sous le règne du Grand Mehemet Aly Pacha, chef de la dynastie régnante, à la même place qu'elle occupe actuellement, à Boulac. Son institution avait alors pour but d'imprimer à la lithographie, tous les imprimeries de l'Armée: lois, ordres, instructions militaires ... L'évolution de l'instruction moderne et la création de Kuttabs, d'écoles primaires, secondaires et supérieures, les réformes introduits dans l'Armée et la Marine ainsi que les nouveaux et grands projets d'irrigation, ont eu pour effet direct une augmentation énorme des imprimés faits par l'Imprimerie Nationale. Ainsi, il lui fut confié, entre autres impressions, l'impression de toutes sortes de livres scolaires, en langues française, anglaise et arabe ainsi que tous les ouvrages militaires" (16).

The 'official gazette' of Egypt dates from 1828 A.D. A detailed review of works on the history of the printing press at Constantinople (and indirectly in Egypt) up to 1907 is given by V. Chauvin (17).
The next two questions are of a somewhat intricate nature and we shall deal with them jointly.

2. Are the developments which took place within the Muslim world specific to the Muslim attitude, i.e. is it inherent to Islam as a culture and a religion that it reacted to the 'new' art of printing the way it did?
3. The interpretation which Western scholars have given to the developments and to the Muslim reaction (an interpretation which ranges from disappointment to subtle accusation of conservatism and rigidity), to what extent was it objective or sympathetic by taking into account the Muslim situation, or was it based on the presumption that the natural course of events in the Muslim world should have been somewhat similar to the course of events in Christian Western Europe?

The answers to the two questions above could be grouped in two categories:

A. Superficial, ready to hand, or "obvious" explanations -

1. The Muslims rejected the application of printing to their Scriptures (the Qur'ān), because of the unclean materials involved in the new art. T. F. Carter (18), Gy. Kaldy-Nagy (19), and H. Omont (20) relate that one possible reason for the Muslim repugnance was due to the fact that

hog's bristles were used in the brush for cleaning the block, which would involve touching the name of Allah with the brush – an act which amounts to blasphemy.

2. The Qur'ān was given in written form, and to print it would do violence to the nature or rather the tradition of revelation. Omont quotes Busbequius to the effect that "selon les Turcs, leurs livres sacrés ne seraient plus une écriture si on les imprimait" (21). (One has to ask oneself whether the Muslims in later years reconsidered this argument and decided to become modern, going ahead and printing their Scriptures.)
3. Printing would result in an increased number of harmful publications, detrimental to morals, leading to divisions and polemics, that one would not go through the trouble of copying a manuscript unless motivated by the virtuous zeal of edifying a devout and ardent seeker after knowledge.
4. The vast body of copyists formed a united front against the threat to their means of livelihood. Estimates of the number of copyists in the Ottoman Empire in the beginnings of the sixteenth century vary, but somehow scholars have assumed the plausibility of the copyists' invested interests, and therefore their resistance to join the ranks of the new profession of printers and editors, holding fast to the old values and norms.

We shall only cite R. Hirsch (22) who has written extensively on the background and circumstances which prevailed in Europe in the 100 years which ensued the discovery of the art of printing. He sees a connection between literacy and the quick spread of the art of printing in late fifteenth century Western Europe. He mentions (23) several factors

"which promoted literacy during the period which straddles the late Middle Ages and modern times ... 1. The revival of learning ... by humanists, ... the Brothers of the Common Life, the reforms of some monasteries of various orders ... and the spread of a new piety, especially among the lower classes, which increased their desire to read for themselves parts of the Bible and devotional literature.
2. Greatly improved transportation; the increased wealth of the middle classes in towns; a gradual increase in the size and number of lower and upper schools outside the control of the church.
3. The founding of new universities educating more people whose

primary or exclusive vocation was not limited to the priesthood or the professions. (Quite a few of these became printers.)
4. The lower cost of many types of manuscripts, thank to the increased production of paper, the establishment of more, at times very small, commercial scriptoria, catering not primarily to the Latin-speaking literati but to those who spoke and read only their own language."

Various explanations have also been offered to account for the invention of printing at the actual particular junction of history in Europe, ranging from reasons in the technical, or economic, or social, or the intellectual sphere. The truth of the matter lies more probably in the favourable combination of all these elements. It is with this in mind that we shall now attempt to account for the reaction of the Muslim world to the 'new' art from the 'house of war' (as the world outside the world of Islam is often refered to by Muslims).

B. Deeper, contextual reasons to be sought in the combination of the different elements we refered to above -

1. Socio-economic factors. It is evident that the body of scribes and secretaries (regardless of the fact whether they were organized as guilds) had invested interests which would have been harmed by printing books and other publications on a large scale. This body was to a great extent an alien unit in the fabric of Muslim society. Whereas the army and eventually the ruling class had grown from the original Arab elements of the Arabian peninsula (in the first centuries of Muslim history), this same class was later (especially in the Ottoman Empire) exclusively formed by a professional body recruited from Turkish and other Asiatic elements which shared only a common religion with the peoples which they ruled. The secretaries and scribes were trained in administration and especially the Arabic language (gradually Persian and Turkish too), and the elements of Musliml law and jurisprudence, particularly Muslim theology (as far as judges were concerned, from which body the grand mufti was chosen). Their job was to secure that degree of orthodoxy within the armed forces which had to be engaged in fighting the unbelievers and ruling the various peoples of the empire which had to adhere to the central authorities in the capital. Royal and princely courts had their own scribes and copyists who met the artistic needs of the elite but not those of the common people (24). In this respect there was a very limited market for books, even though this market was one with sophisticated tastes. All in all, scribes, secretaries and copyists were the most important party in the antagonism which

prevailed between those who wielded the pen over against those engaged in manual labour (whether they were peasants, merchants or soldiers).

2. Educational factors. Knowledge and wisdom have always been in high esteem in the Muslim heritage (25). Religion, especially the Qur'ān, played a major role in Muslim education, in establishing its institutions, shaping its curriculum and determining its history. Because religion, literacy and education were so important in the promotion of the printed word in Christian Europe, we have to examine the comparative components in the world of Islam.
   The Muslim institution of learning in the Middle Ages was the maktab or kuttāb (later madrasa) where primarily the Qur'ān was taught, with in addition the possibility of teaching some arts and crafts.

"As to teaching methods the oral tradition had never been suspended, and at all levels teachers continued [as of old] to rely on recitation and oral exposition, and pupils on learning by rote. Even after the whole of the Arabic-Islamic tradition was recorded, distinguished teachers in the classical age were more comfortable, and indeed more profound, without than with the aid of the written word. However, as the classical age was followed by one of less vitality and originally teachers became increasingly the slaves of texts. They conceived their task to consist of merely expounding and 'dictating' commentaries. Dictation was the more formal stage in the development of teaching methods of which we have already distinguished two others: oral transmission and exposition followed by question and answer" (26).

The pre-Islamic heritage was poetic and poetry was transmitted orally. With the advent of Islam, the miracle of the Qur'ān overshadowed all other literature. At school pupils were taught to recite short passages from the Qur'ān. Learning how to write presented two main difficulties: firstly, besides the religious motives, the Qur'ān was predominant in that it was the main written material with all that this entailed in questions of style and poetic language; and secondly, the Arabic script in the early period, "was such a chaos of symbols that a single word could be read in several different ways with only the sense as guide" (27).
If we take a look at the developments after the disruption of the historical caliphate (after the Abbassid period), we notice that Arabic, the language of the Qur'ān and the lingua franca of Islam, ceased to be official in Turkey and Persia, and it

"suffered degeneration both as a classical model and as a spoken language. Not before the beginning of the nineteenth century did its revival begin in earnest, preceding by nearly a century the restoration of Arab political independence" (28).

The school and its products would have been the natural breeding place for the impetus and the market for the production of the printing press. But unfortunately schools in Islam enter the picture in a positive sense only in the nineteenth century when modernization was necessary in the military and technological fields. Luther's assessment of universities and monastic schools of his day, however exaggerated and made with ulterior motives, to the effect that they were "Eselställe und Teufelschulen" (29) could be applied with little modification to the situation in the Muslim world.

3. Religious factors. Evidently the religious element has been decisive in the reaction of the Muslim world to the western art of printing. Most of all, the very nature of the Muslim Scriptures played a cardinal role. We have seen that the request by Ībrāhīm Müteferriḳa to print, and the permission granted by the Sultan and the Grand Mufti excluded the printing of the Qur'ān, of books on Quranic exegesis, traditions, theology, and holy law. It is interesting to note that the Qur'ān as literature has been discussed in the Muslim world on three occasions when it confronted three developments of modern times, namely printing, translating, and recording on tapes or playing records. The Qur'ān was printed in its entirety in the nineteenth century. Much discussion, often emotional, but always with a theological argumentation, had to be carried on before the Muslim world reluctantly allowed the translation, but then only of the meaning of the glorious book (so that the translation was more of a paraphrase of its contents) (30). The last confrontation took place when the Egyptian government decided to grant its support for the scientific project of recording the Qur'ān on tapes and records according to the various readings (31).

   Only when one gets a clear understanding of the Muslim's attitude to the Qur'ān as revelation primarily and not simply as literature, can one empathize with, sympathize with or explain the historical decisions made. Only then can one understand why the Bible and the Qur'ān played such radically different roles in the history of printing in Europe and the Muslim world respectively. And finally, only then could one understand why there was no 'Qur'ān pauperum', or Qur'ān in the vernacular (only as of the twentieth century). Even at the risk of precarious simplification we could say that whereas for the Christian the primary access to the Divine Presence is not through words since the "Word became flesh", for the Muslim the primary access is through the sacrament (if the Muslim will forgive this alien concept which he does not recognize) of the "written", revealed Arabic Scripture. It is within this framework that we can correctly appreciate the Muslim art of calligraphy, particularly Quranic calligraphy. Not only does the Qur'ān satisfy the artistic urge and outlet, but it also enables the appreciation of the beauty of the Arabic language and the beauty of the human voice when it is used in chanting the revelation (tanzīl and tartīl as the Qur'ān is also refered to).

> "It must not be forgotten that one of the greatest purposes of Qur'ān calligraphy is to provide a visual sacrament. It is a wide-spread practice in Islam to gaze intently at Quranic inscriptions so as to extract a blessing from them, or in other words so that through the windows of sight the soul may be penetrated by the Divine radiance of the 'signs of God', as the verses are called. Questions as to how far the object is legible and how far the subject is literature would be considered irrelevant to the validity and to the efficacy of the sacrament" (32).

We should neither judge the tastes of earlier generations by the standards of our own times, nor the theological doctrines of others by the theological doctrines to which we adhere. Certain categories of publications which were available in the Christian world were not available in the Muslim world. The latter had no equivalents of the European/Christian 'Biblia pauperum' (no condensing of the Qur'ān, nor another order of chapters or verses of the glorious book were even thinkable since they were part and parcel of the revelation), nor liturgical texts for use by the clergy, such as missals (even the concepts liturgy and clergy are alien to Muslim thinking), nor finally those publications for private devotion – the famous horaries— were known by Islam. The classical heritage in the Muslim countries had a different character compared with that of Europe; its use, moreover, was equally of a different nature.

It is with these considerations in mind that we would like to end this article by quoting R. Hirsch:

> "Today literacy is considered the sine qua non of civilized man. Those who are concerned with what man writes and what man reads, may at times still wonder whether the invention of printing was a blessing or a curse" (33).

NOTES

1. The quotation is the title of ch. 15 of a book by T. F. Carter which has also been published as an article with the same title. Thomas Francis Carter. *The invention of printing in China and its spread westward. Rev. by L. Carrington Goodrich.* (2nd ed. New York, Ronald Press Company, [1955]) 150-154. Cf. also *The Muslim World* 33 (1943) 213-216.
2. Thomas F. Carter, "The westward movement of the art of printing", *Yearbook of Oriental art and culture*, 1 (1924-1925) 25; and F. Bonola, "Note sur l'origine de l'imprimerie arabe en Europe", *Bulletin de l'Institut Egyptien*, sér. 5, 3 (1909) 75.
3. For more information one should consult, besides the sources we quote in this article, the studies by Manzoni, Mauri, Deschamps, Olski and Schnurrer. We have consulted two articles by people who lived and worked in the Middle East: F. Bonola, *Ibidem*, 74-78; and Louis Cheikho, "Tārīḫ fann aṭ-ṭibāʿa fī al-mašriq" ("History of the art of printing in the East"), *al-Mašriq*, 3 (1900) 78 ff., 174 ff., 251 ff., 355 ff., 501 ff., 706 ff., 839 ff., 998 ff.
4. Galland as quoted by Joseph de Guignes, "Essai historique sur l'origine des caractères orientaux de l'Imprimerie royale, sur les ouvrages qui ont été imprimés à Paris, en Arabe, en Syriaque, en Arménien, etc. et sur les caractères grecs de François Ier", *Notices et extraits des manuscrits de la Bibliothèque du Roi* ..., 1 (1787) xxvii-xxviii.
5. *Ibidem*, xxvii.
6. *Ibidem*, xxviii.
7. A. Geiss, "Observations de M. Geiss à la suite de la note de M. Bonola Bey", *Bulletin de l'Institut Egyptien*, sér. 5, 3 (1909) 81-84.
8. *Ibidem*, 82.
9. *Ibidem*, 83, and Cheikho, "Tārīḫ", 79. Incidentally both authors cite not only the wrong name, but also have committed errors in the quotation of the work in question. We have made direct use of the publication by R. P. A. Dozy, *Notices sur quelques manuscrits arabes*. (Leiden, Brill, 1847-1851) 137.
10. Geiss, "Observations", 84.
11. Guignes, "Essai", xxviii.
12. William J. Watson, "Ibrāhīm Müteferriḳa and Turkish incunabula", *Journal of the American Oriental Society*, 88 (1968) 435.
13. *Ibidem*, 436. For detailed information and documents cf. H. Omont, "Documents sur l'imprimerie à Constantinople au XVIIIe siècle", *Revue des bibliothèques*, 5 (1895) 185 ff., 228 ff.
14. Carter, *The invention*, 150. F. Babinger, to cite one author, mentions the printing of the Qur'ān in Teheran in 1824/1825. Cf. F. Babinger, "Die Einführung des Buchdruckes in Persien", *Zeitschrift des Deutschen Vereins für Buchwesen und Schrifttum*, 4 (1921) 141.
15. Carter, *The invention*, 151.
16. Mohamed Amine Bahgat, "Aperçu historique sur l'Imprimerie NationaleEgyptienne", *Gutenberg-Jahrbuch* (1931) 275.
17. V. Chauvin, "Notes pour l'histoire de l'imprimerie à Constantinople", *Zentralblatt für Bibliothekwesen*, 24 (1907) 255-262.
18. Carter, *The invention*, 150.
19. Gy. Kaldy-Nagy, "Beginnings of the Arabic letter printing in the Muslim world", in: *The Muslim East; studies in honour of J. Germanus*. (Buda-

pest, 1974) 203.

20. Omont as quoted by Chauvin, "Notes", 256.
21. *Ibidem.*
22. Rudolf Hirsch, *Printing, selling and reading 1450-1550.* (2nd printing. Wiesbaden, Harrassowitz, 1974.)
23. *Ibidem*, 10.
24. Cf. Claude Cahen, "Les facteurs économiques et sociaux dans l'ankylose culturelle de l'Islam", in: *Classicisme et déclin culturel dans l'histoire de l'Islam*. (Paris, Editions Besson, 1957.) 195-207.
25. There are several well-known traditions which come from the Prophet to this effect, such as "Seek knowledge even if it were in China".
26. A. L. Tibawi, *Islamic education. Its traditions and modernization into the Arab national systems*. (London, Luzac, 1972.) 33.
27. *Ibidem*, 26. It is interesting to note that the Arabic script and its suitability to teach how to write and to print have been subject to debates and discussions. Mehmed Münif Paşa was probably the first to openly raise the issue of reforming Arabic typography. In a speech in May 1862,
    "he raised the question of a reform in the alphabet, as a necessary preliminary to the advancement and dissemination of science. Ottoman orthography was hard to teach, hard to learn; worse still, it was inaccurate and ambiguous, and could easily mislead instead of informing a reader. It was unsuited to the printing press, 'the most powerful instrument for the spreading of knowledge'; compared with the Western alphabet it was expensive and inefficient, needing two or three times as many characters."
    Bernard Lewis, *The emergence of modern Turkey*. (2nd ed. London, Oxford University Press, 1968.) 427. The proposed solution was to become a radical solution, viz. of adopting the Latin alphabet in Turkey, where romanized Turkish was adopted in November 1928. Several Arab countries, however, which were also aware of the difficulties of the Arabic script, tried to find a solution to the problems by calling in the help of the Academy of Arabic Language in Cairo. After two decades of discussions and much work, there was no tangible practical result. Cf. P. Minganti, "Semplificazione dei caratteri di stampa per l'arabo nella Repubblica Araba Unita", *Oriente moderno*, 40 (1960) 656-660.
28. Tibawi, *Islamic education*, 34.
29. Hirsch, *Printing*, 10.
30. Cf. Muhammad Shakir, "On the translation of the Koran into foreign languages", transl. by F. W. Arnold, *Muslim world*, 16 (1926) 161-165. And: A. L. Tibawi, "Is the Qur'an translatable? Early Muslim opinion", *Muslim world*, 52 (1962) 4-16.
31. Labib as-Said, *The recited Koran. A history of the first recorded version. Transl. and adapted by Bernard Weiss, M. A. Rauf, and Morroe Berger.* (Princeton, N. J., Darwin Press, [1975].) This book is a wonderful existential account of how the Muslims have tried to preserve their heritage while coping with the demands (political, economic, technological and religious) of the modern times.
32. Martin Lings, *The Quranic art of calligraphy and illumination.* ([London], World of Islam Festival Trust, [1976] 16.
33. Hirsch, *Printing*, 153.

[23]

Mass Culture and Islamic Cultural Production in 19th Century Middle East

Reinhard Schulze

Up to the present day, two antinomies have determined the representation and self-representation of the cultural development of Islamic countries. It has in a linear sense been regarded as an alternating succession of eras of traditionalism and modernism, while these two notions have themselves been classified, and a value judgement attached to them, in terms of either cultural decadence or cultural renaissance. Thus, the antinomies tradition/modernity and decadence/renaissance have formed the basis of a concept of cultural history which, of course, reflected the political interpretation of historical development current in the nineteeth century.

Decadence in the Islamic Middle East was discovered by Europeans. In order to legitimate his military invasion of Egypt in 1798, Napoleon fell back on the old European image of the Orient when he said the country had been driven into barbarism and decay. But this, he maintained, was not the fault of the Arabs, but of the Turks, who had established themselves as military rulers in almost every Islamic Arab country. France, the cradle of the Enlightenment and the great humanistic revolution, would now liberate the Arabs from the yoke they had been brought under and give them back their dignity[1].

This view of Middle Eastern society had no influence on what the contemporary Islamic élites thought of themselves. For how, they asked, could "barbarians such as the French, who lacked culture", be regarded as authoritative judges of Egyptian culture? Particularly, when their daily lives consisted of nothing but thieving, sexual libertinage, the love of pleasure and idleness[2], and their general behaviour much more resembled the rabble's (ᶜamma) than that of educated men? Never could they act as a cultural model or as an acceptable cultural authority, even given that their scientific curiosity was charming, and their mania for regulating all social and political affairs on a juridical level proof they possessed "the innocence of children"[3]. In Europe, however, the reports of the numerous scientists, soldiers and daredevils, who had accompanied Napoleon on his expedition, about their experiences in Egypt seemed to confirm all that had been written in the memoirs of the travellers and Orientalists of the eighteenth century. Decadence had seized the Islamic Orient, and the subjected classes there, were only waiting for their liberation, and this had to be based upon the principles of the French revolution.[4]

Decadence, it was stated, was caused by many factors. Most responsible, however, was the religion of Islam itself, being, as Vivant Denon argued, a symbol of superstition and backwardness.[5] From the European point of view, Islam not only stood in opposition to Christianity, but, above all, to the culture of European civilization. Thus, Islam was not to be evaluated as a theology, but as a culture, in the sense employed by Herder, Kant or Schiller. As culture was used as a synonym for humanity, reason and freedom, the European spectators of the Orient had to define Islam as "un–culture", just as they described Islam as an absolutely restrictive system of rules within an Islamic environment consisting only of barbarism and slavery. Wherever the European cultural mission in the Orient (being, of course, the legitimation for the colonization of the Islamic world) gained a foothold in Islamic countries in order to open the door for modernity for the Muslim peoples, this bad oriental tradition had to be suppressed. So, the missionary aim was no longer christianization, but modernization. The tradition/modernity dichotomy was born. For the Europeans, the birth date could be said to coincide with the date of the French embarkment in Alexandria in Egypt, the 1st July, 1798.

Up to now, the division of Islamic history into the 'traditional' and the 'modern', which used Egypt as its primary example, has been retained.[6] Since it is a part of the same concept, the progressive evolution from decadence to modernity also has remained untouched. For decades European researchers and especially the Orientalists among them looked for forms of modernity in the Orient. They ferreted them out where ever the European cultural mission had been victorious: in the sphere of technology, of jurisdiction, of literature, of science, even of "everyday" culture.

Since not every aspect of Middle Eastern culture could be described by the term "modernity", the analysis of the contradictions between tradition and modernity became important. Sometimes, the diachronical division of both terms was abandoned and, instead of this, the synchronical presence of tradition and modernity was accepted (with regard to the theory of dual cultures[7], for example). When 'modernity' began, however, was not questioned at all.

Thus, owing to modernity, the Islamic world also obtained a culture. At first, it referred to modernity only, and not to tradition. But as the concept of culture was gradually generalized in Europe, thus leading to an analytic, universal concept, Islamic tradition was also associated with a culture. The essence of the partition between traditional decadence and modern renaissance, however, did not change. Thus, the European worldview served to determine Islamic identity. Recently, the study of the transition from tradition to modernity has been brought into the foreground of discussions. Just as Franz Borkenau[8] for example, had done, some researchers considered this transition as a successive historical process which paralleled the change of society from one social and economic form into another.[9] The category which served to define this transition is that of "Enlightenment". What emerged was a triad composed of three concepts: tradition, enlightenment and modernity. And it seems as if modernity had some inner coherence with tradition.[10]

After only a few decades, this categorization, as it was generally used in Europe, became an integral part of the self-understanding of Islamic intellectuals. Willingly, they accepted the thesis that the eightheenth century had been decadent and used it to legitimate their own culture production (renaissance/*nahda*). *Nahda* required a concept of cultural decadence, for how else was the claim to cultural renewal to be justified? A pre-condition was to free oneself from tradition in as far as it was regarded as being decadent. In addition, the concept of contemporary renaissance required the discovery of a 'classical' period in the distant past that might be rejuvenated in the present. Analogous to European concepts of renaissance, Islamic intellectuals in the nineteenth century fell back upon a "Golden Age" of Islam. But even here, the European Orientalists provided precious assistance by explaining to them what the classical Islamic period was, and how it was to be understood and assessed historically. Briefly, the "Dark Year" of 1258[11], which saw the conquest of Baghdad by the Mongols under Hülegü, ushered in the end of "autochtonous" Islam. Evidently, not all of Islamic history from 610, the approximate date of the first revelation, to 1258 could be described as a Golden Age, but in comparison with the "catastrophic Mongolian assault"[12] and the centuries of foreign rule which followed it, the era could be described as classical.

II.

Why did Islamic intellectuals so eagerly submit to European interpretation? How did it happen that within a few years the rich cultural tradition of Islamic societies (which European and Arab researchers have only recently started to rediscover) could fall into oblivion?

The reasons are to be traced in the social history of the Islamic societies in the nineteenth century. Till today, the history of colonialism in respect to Islamic countries has been regarded as a rectilinear process which gradually transformed the pre-colonial, traditional, social structures into modern ones. Depending on the political point of view of the observer, this process was regarded as, either beneficial or pernicious to the Islamic societies.[13] Everything and everybody, it was argued, had to change, and so had the Islamic élites, too. These élites, which formerly had stood in a specific functional relation to the traditional regimes, experienced a "crisis of orientation". The "modern" state now exacted from them something more than simply perpetuating a universal, Islamic, all-round education. They had to become specialists in order to "find answers to the challenges of the time". All of this forced them to ignore traditions within their own cultures, and after a period of self contemplation and reflection (Enlightenment) they were able to provide the "New Age" with a new cultural expression. Generally speaking, this process is called "secularization". In parallel, all social relations and economic conditions were transformed as well.[14]

Sometimes, the tables are turned. One author maintains that the "Westernization" of the Islamic élites was "inconsistent" as "it had *no* counterpart in the social structures of the respective societies"[15]. Such inconsistency provoked a "reflection" on the subject of the Islamic identity. Applied to the questions raised in this paper, this would mean that only the intellectual élites experienced a social and functional process of change which alienated them from society. Islam, therefore, offered a posibility of reintegrating them into a still traditional society.

The social history of colonialism offers a different approach. First, it has to be pointed out that the colonization of Islamic societies was both an exogenous and endogenous process. Exogenous, in as much as it was carried out and organized by European "mother–countries". The aim, in general, was to make the surplus product produced by a re–structuring of the regional economies, (to the benefit of colonial "mother–countries") available on the world market. The process also was endogenous as the regional economies had already been integrated into the world economy for decades. Within these societies, tendencies existed toward a preparation for the colonization of power and an intensification of agricultural production and of commerce with Europe. Being most important in the eighteenth century[16], this process initiated a systematic re–structuring of social conditions, not, however, in the sense of "change", but in the sense of developing social complexity[17]. Social groups were not "transformed" (tradition to modernity), but new groups came into being, in addition to the "old" ones, and occupied the state functions of the exogenous and endogenous induced colonization. One of their most important functions consisted in the formation of the colonial state itself. In contrast to the former "rent states" of the eighteenth century, whose function was the appropriation of the surplus product in favour of a regionally organised regime, the colonial state had to ensure a frictionless transfer of wealth to the "mother–countries". Because of this, the colonial state could no longer rely on common forms of cultural legitimation. This called for a new public[18] which had to give proof of the fact that Islamic societies were not just composed of barbarians unable to rule themselves, and that the "new society" had nothing in common with the *ancien régime* and the Dark Age of the eighteenth century. By keeping their distance from the past, the representatives of the new public, which was structured just like

similar publics in the colonial "mother–countries" (party politics, press etc.), saw their chance to gain safeguarded positions of power within the colonial state. The new political public resulted from of a general social disintegration which was necessary if special social spheres were to be brought into a functional relation with the colonization process. These new élites can be described in the same
terms as those used to define the "free intelligentsia" of nineteenth–century Europe. To begin with, this refers to their cultural techniques – the means the new élites used to produce culture and to promote their self–understanding ideologically.

During their three–year occupation of Egypt (1798–1801), the French had imported printing presses and published among other things two French journals (*Courrier de l'Egypte* and *La décade égyptienne*).[19] The Egyptians, of course, did not comprise the public of these journals as they were directed at the 20.000 European occupants only. True, the French published Arab leaflets, too, through which they propagandized their politics, and even edited a version of the collection of anecdotes *Luqman al–hakim*[20]. The fact, however, that such texts were no longer reproduced as manuscripts but as printed documents did not pose a special problem for the Islamic élites.[21] In 1821, the situation changed. By order of Muhammad ᶜAli, the Egyptian *wali* (Governor) of that time (1805–1849), a first printing office was established in the Qasr al–ᶜAini barracks in the western outskirts of Cairo. Shortly after, it was transferred to Bulaq, a small suburb of Cairo. It was directed by Niqula Musabiki, who the *wali* had sent to Milan to study. (Niqula Musabiki thus succeeded his father Yusuf, a Damascene Christian, who had entered the French service in 1798 and worked in the French *Imprimerie nationale* in Cairo under the direction of J.J. Marcel.) After having learnt type–setting in Italy, he returned to Cairo and was commissioned to assemble the parts of a printing and type–setting machine newly imported from France.[22] In 1831, Musabiki still directed the printing–office.

By 1842, 248 books have been printed. The respective books and booklets may be classified as follows:[23]

	Bulaq	Istanbul
sciences, military, medicine etc.	45,6%	26,1%
adab and geography	17,7%	24,3%
languages	15,3%	20,6%
Islamic studies	13,3%	24,7%
history	8,1%	4,1%

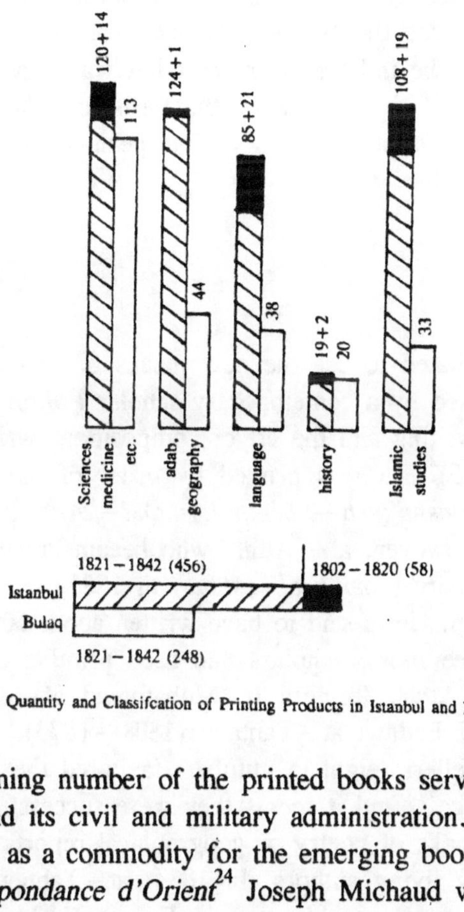

Quantity and Classifcation of Printing Products in Istanbul and Bulaq (1802/1821 – 1842)

An overwhelming number of the printed books served the direct needs of the regime and its civil and military administration. Only a small portion was produced as a commodity for the emerging book market.

In his *Correspondance d'Orient*[24] Joseph Michaud wrote that up to 1831, only three books on literature (*adab*) and four on Islamic subjects had been published.

> "The Arabic anthology (one of the *adab*—works) is a collection of the poetry of the most illustrious authors. Besides, it is a new edition. The book had already been printed in a Latin and French translation in Paris. It is a particularity of the Orient that it receives its own masterpieces by foreign procurement."[25]

The Azhar libraries and the private mosque libraries were full of manuscripts on Islamic and non—Islamic subjects. The state supervisors of the printing—office[26], however, did not utilise these manuscripts. The means of production, raw material and all, came from Europe: paper from Italy, typefaces from France *and* the Islamic *contents* from Europe. Book production did not aim at the indigenous market but was a product designed for the immediate use of the regime or the Parisian *Bibliotheque Nationale*. Hence, the the Or"att became a European commodity, with a European commodity value.

III.

The Islamic élites hesitated to use the new means of production. One of the first books composed by a contemporary scholar (*ᶜalim*) and printed at Bulaq was a text on writing and the art of composition, written by Hasan al—ᶜAttar (1766—1835)[27]. It was printed by order of the *wali* Muhammad ᶜAli in 1827/8 (*insha'(ash—Sheikh hasan)al—ᶜAttar*), and reprinted in 1835. As a rule, however, al—ᶜAttar, who became rector of the Cairene al—Azhar University (*shaikh al—Azhar*) in 1831, remained loyal to the manuscript tradition. He is said to have written about 100 works.[28]
Up to 1842, only three living scholars had used printing as a means of publishing texts: al—ᶜAttar, Ibrahim b. Muhammad al—Bajuri (1783—1860) and Rifaᶜa Rafiᶜ Badawi at—Tahtawi (1801—1873).[29] Up to 1835, the few Cairine booksellers (eight in number) favoured the private use of the Bulaq printing office[30], and it seems they were successful. From 1835 on, dozens of small books of poetry or geographical reports were printed, all of them written by living authors. In 1834, at—Tahtawi got permission to publish his memoirs of his stay in France (1826—1831) at the Bulaq printing office.[31] A book on geography compiled from French sources by at—Tahtawi was also published in the same year, and numbered 1000 copies.[32]

After the *wali*'s death in 1849, and especially owing to the economic collapse of the Ottoman Empire in 1839/40, the state monopoly on printing in Egypt was abolished. New printing offices were opened in Cairo and Bulaq at an increasing rate. In 1862, the government sold the Bulaq printing offices to a private entrepreneur, ᶜAbdarrahman Rushdi Basha. Bulaq became a stronghold of Arabic Islamic printing. Between 1872 and 1878, 300 000 copies are said to have been printed, that is as many as between 1821 and 1872.[33] Scientific and technical literature had by far the largest share of the new book production industry devoted to it. Engeneering and the agricultural sciences were particularly singled out as subjects of concern, reflecting, of course, the growing interest in colonizing Egyptian agriculture. In addition, titles, which fell specifically in the Arabic Islamic tradition, were now increasingly published. By 1890, about 750 Islamic books had been printed, among others the bulky "neoclassic" dictionary *taj al–ᶜarus min qawahir al–qamus* (1870) composed by Muhammad Murtada al–Husaini az–Zabidi (1732/3–1791) between 1761 and 1774.[34]

After the introduction of lithographic printing methods into the Muslim printing offices in the 1820s, it was possible to print the *Qur'an* (Teheran 1828, Istanbul 1830, Bulaq 1865/66 at the printing office of Ahmad at–Tukhi). The years 1864–6 marked a thorough–going change in the Bulaq printing tradition. By order of the Egyptian scholar Hasan al–ᶜIdwi (1806–1886), al–Budharis compilation of *hadiths (al–jamiᶜ as–sahih)*, one of the most important collections of Islamic literature on *hadith*, was re–edited in Bulaq after a first edition had been published in India in 1852/3.[35] From then on, a distinct increase in the printing of Islamic texts can be noted. The *shaikh al–Azhar Muhammad ᶜUlaish* changed to printing in 1864/5, publishing a book on eloquency.[36] The same year, ᶜUlaish ordered the printing of a book on malikite law at the office of Mustafa Wahbi, which was at that time the Shaikh's habitual printing office.[37] And, finally, in 1869 at–Ghazzali's great compendium *ihya' ᶜulum ad–din*[38] was printed at Bulaq, and Islamic subjects entered commodity production.[39]

All these remarks suggest that since about 1850–1860, the Islamic tradition has been integrated into the new cultural production. From then on, a manuscript was no longer ingeniously copied on demand as it would have been formerly, but it became part of market production. The market, on the one hand, comprised the learned Islamic public (for example al–Azhar), and on the other, Europe, where the great libraries bought a copy of nearly every book printed in Cairo, Bulaq or elsewhere. The manuscript tradition seemed to be on the wane. No manuscript could compete with the prestige of a printed book, unless it was produced very artisticly. Thus, a new industrial art came into being. The manuscript tradition continued but as an industrial art just as the old handicraft tradition had developed into an 'art' which was no longer orientated towards use value, after mechanical commodity production came into existence. Thus, the splitting of production into utility goods and art production, which characterized the nineteenth century economy, affected Arabic–Islamic culture, too. This development was fatal in that it was also coupled with the question of prestige. What had been produced on the basis of the manuscript tradition a few decades before now had less value than what was presented to the public in printed form. Even in regard to its contents, the value of the non–printed tradition diminished, too. The non–printed tradition was withdrawn from the public and hidden away in the magazines of mosques, universities and medreses. Instead, representatives of the new public regarded books, no matter what their contents so long as they were printed in Europe, as more valuable than the traditional cultural production.

The term 'decadence' having been coined by European Orientalists, obturned a new reality. Culture which had been produced prior to 1821, a year which can be defined as a 'break' in Egyptian cultural history, no longer had the same value as culture emanating from the post–1821 period. As the pre–1821 culture could not be "measured" by the standards of European culture, the eighteenth century had to be seen as a period of decline, as part of a universal Islamic decadence. One of the first intellectuals who articulate this problem was the Egyptian official, engineer, author and scholar ᶜAli Mubarak (1824–1893)[40]. In his novel *ᶜalam ad–din* he describes the ardent desire of the colonial élites for a new cultural self–identification. He states:[41]

> "The Nation now sheds her false ideas, frees herself from worthless concepts and gets used to the new institutions. Within a short time, all has

changed: attitudes, habits, customs, and institutions. This is what is happening in Egypt today. Anyone who saw Egypt fifty years ago and who now sees it again today will find nothing he knew from former times. He will realize that it has experienced a revolution and that it has become similar to a region of Europe."

As the possibility of producing any number of mass produced commodities grew, culture in the form, for example, of literary works, also could be reproduced on a mass scale.[42] With this development, characteristic distinctions based on the traditional culture were dropped. Formerly, these distinctions had been associated with nearly every article available in society owing to the nature of handicraft production, which helped to identify social groups. Such matter-of-factness within the cultural tradition disappeared as the new cultural producers struggled to provide their social function with a cultural identity and expression. The division between handicraft production of individual goods and the mass production of easily reproduced commodities provoked a "crisis of orientation and identity" within Egyptian society. The term crisis itself must be used with caution as it postulates a linear continuity which happened to encounter a "crisis". This, of course, was not the case. On the contrary, the necessity to identify social groups culturally within society was decisive for the new colonial élites. One of the simplest questions they asked was: Who are we? In answering this question they could refute a second argument: the Europeans' accusation that the Orient was "barbaric, despotic, irrational and unscientific".[43] Once again, this presupposed a clear line of demarcation from the hitherto accepted social tradition and thus from nearly the whole of Egyptian social culture in every respect. The point of orientation for them became the European (colonial) culture, which they initially regarded as a competing culture but one whose concepts were to change into absolute universalities, and then would be accepted as such. From 1860 on, writings by Islamic authors who attempted to answer these questions became more numerous. I shall only mention three of them: the Ottoman Namiq Kemal (1840-1888)[44], the Tunisian Khair ad-Din at-Tunisi (ca. 1829-1889)[45] and the Persian Jamal ad-Din al-Afghani (1838-1897)[46]. All three represented the new public, Kemal being the prototype of a journalist, at-Tunisi of a politician, and al-Afghani of an ideologist. They all argued in an Islamic way and they regarded Islam as the basis of their social and cultural identity. But as they were no longer able to build their own world view on their own social tradition, they had to search for an abstract, idealized, historical epoch in which there had not been any form of decadence. Kemal traced it to the time of the Saljuqs and of the conquerors of the crusaders, Salah ad–Din al–Ayyubi (Saladin, 1138–1193), and of the Ottoman Sultan Sulaiman the Magnificent (1494/5–1566). Al–Afghani had to go even further back to the time of the Prophet and the well–versed originators of Islam (*as–salaf as–salih*), i.e. the first four califs and some of Muhammad's companions. He thus perpetrated the idealization of the early period of Islam.[47] Al–Afghani's article, refuting a lecture given by Ernest Renan in Paris in 1883, might be regarded as a typical example of such a process of identification.[48]

IV.

The division between art and consumerism, the production of culture for a new market embodied by the colonial élites and, as a result, the reification (*Verdinglichung*) of Islamic tradition could no longer be halted. In accordance with this, a conceptual re–evaluation of Islam as a theology took place. Islamic self–realization, of the new élite which spanned both the period of decadence and of renaissance, had to attach itself to the "Golden Age" in the sphere of social, as well as cultural, standards. A basic condition for this to happen was the re–introduction of *ijtihad* (free reasoning in the field of jurisprudence reserved for a defined group of scholars).[49] This conceptualisation enabled intellectuals to abjure tradition while using it.

Even in 1843, in two *fatwas* (legal opinions), Muhammad ᶜUlaish still opposed every effort aimed at reintroducing *ijtihad* as a source of jurisprudence.[50] On the contrary, *taqlid*, strict binding to authority[51], was to be unconditionally retained. Hasan al–ᶜAttar also argued in this sense[52]. In an essay, at–Tahtawi published in the Egyptian journal *raudat al–madaris* in 1870[53], a moderation of the concept of *taqlid* could be observed.[54] Yet it was not before 1897, that free reasoning, competing with European rationalism, could be taught publicly once again at al–Azhar–University. This time, an Islamic scholar who was fully integrated into the new colonial public, Muhammad ᶜAbduh (1849–1905)[55] provoked a vivid discussion of the *ijtihad* concept. In his single, purely theological, work *risalat at–tauhid*, published in 1897, he demanded the full re–establishment of *ijtihad*, reserved naturally for accepted scholars. Thus, the possibility of intellectualizing Islam was born.

By abolishing *taqlid* Islamic intellectuals – i.e. scholars like Muhammad ᶜAbduh, journalists, lawyers and writers who took a stand on Islam problems – now hoped their arguments would be heard. They did not suffer any encroachments on their right to define themselves as "Islamic", and because of this, they were able to break the traditional scholars' monopoly. Outwardly, the new public represented by the "secularized" élites, still remained Islamic. They argued in an Islamic manner, propagated Islam as an ideology and regarded Islam as a suitable "response to imperialism". The fact, however, that many new Islamic intellectuals presented themselves as good Muslims, while, at the same time being members of Masonic lodges, demonstrates that they hardly understood Islam as a real theology.[56]

Fearing to loose their position of power as the new Islamic intelligentsia emerged, Islamic scholars also reacted by delimiting themselves from tradition. The object of delimitation, i.e. "tradition", however, did not fade away after the colonial public had come into existence. On the contrary, it continued vigorously. In opposition to the new public, traditional Islamic culture had at its disposal a rigid organizational structure in the form of the mystical brotherhoods (*turuq*)[57]. For centuries, mysticism, being the "second dimension of Islam", exercised one of the most important of social functions. Through mysticism (*tasawwuf* or Sufism), a direct religious experience for the greater part of the population became possible. Pure contemplation of Islam as a theology or as a form of obedience to the fundamental Islamic standards of law were not able to guarantee subjective religious experience. At the same time, mysticism offered a possibility of cultural utterance and identification for the rural and urban population. This tradition was mediated through the veneration of holy men and grave cults, by an educational system that fitted local conditions, and a system of medical care which was accessible to all. Reading and writing were not of great importance. Other cultural techniques such as chanting, magic miracles, and blessings dominated. In this field, Islam was not the object of scholarly contemplation or disputation, but was a social practice that determined the public of these localities.

Therefore it is not surprising that those social groups which were hit by colonialism (and not those which were created by colonialism) survived on the basis of mystical Islamic cultures.

Nearly every rebellion against colonialism in the early nineteenth century originated in this cultural milieu. The theological element of mystical Islam played a major role. It allowed for the appearance of saviours, of *mahdis*, who would save the Islamic community (*umma*) from European colonization. At the beginning of the eighteenth century, a thorough-going change within Islamic mystical culture appeared in outline. The sources of the movement, generally known as "neo-Sufism", are obscure, despite research done in the last decades. Neo-Sufism is characterized by a certain freedom in interpreting the Islamic system of rules as it had been handed-down generation by generation. On the basis of divine and/or prophetic emanation, some leaders of mystical orders believed that they themselves were able to decide on the character of the Islamic systems of rules.[58] Some movements of this kind, as the Arabian *wahhabiya*, rejected popular mystical culture, too. Movements which based their legitimation on neo-Sufism, however, were far more common. Among others, the following movements are worth mentioning: the Libyan *sanusiya*[59] (from about 1840 on); the Maghrebine *tijaniya*[60] (1781/2); the Sudanese *mahdiya*[61] (1881); several West African movements such as ᶜUthman dan Fodio (1754-1817) or of ᶜUmar Tal (1794-1864)[62]; the rebellion of the Daghestanian Shaikh Sham(w)il[63], and, in a shiite setting, the *babiya* (1844) and the *baha'iya* (1863) in Persia.

The mobilization of popular mystical culture against colonization was also directed against scholars and jurists, since they were one of the most important pillars of official Islamic culture.[64] In the countryside, two slogans were often heard simultaneously: 'Death to the unbelievers' and 'Death to the ᶜ*ulama*' (scholars).[65] The first slogan was directed both against the foreign colonizers and the executives of the indigenous regimes which tolerated colonization. The second slogan was aimed at the urban scholars who were suspected of collaboration. Saviours were popular heros and holy men who in the end would stop the traditional culture from vanishing. As culture was the only possibility of social utterance open to the peasants, the various mystical movements also served as a means to rescue the traditional social order. It must be pointed out however that the neo–Sufi movements did not romantize social reality. On the contrary, in fighting against the destruction of the traditional social order, they transgressed it themselves and tended to want to abolish it in favour of a new order.

Already at a very early stage, texts dealing with Islamic mysticism had been printed at Bulaq. After the state monopoly on printing had been abolished, new printing offices came into being and soon specialized on various Islamic topics. Most active with respect to mystical texts was the printing office *dar al–kutab al–^{c}arabiya al–kubra,* founded in 1855 by Mustafa al–Babi al–Halabi. Even the traditional printing office in Bulaq was sold to a private entrepreneur (1862). One of the books on mystical subjects printed at this time, was a work devoted to the miracles of the Moroccan *sufi* ^{c}Abdal^{c}Aziz ad–Dabbagh (ca. 1683–1730)[66] written by his pupil Ahmad b. Mubarak al–Lamti. It was lithographed in two volumes in 1861/2. But why, it must be asked, was this book printed at Bulaq? Which market was meant to benefit from the 200 odd copies, which cost three times the price of books printed prior to 1855? Hardly one was exported to Morocco where a text about ad–Dabbagh might have found a ready audience. But the number of copies was very limited. Up to then, a printed book dealing with the miracles of holy men like ad–Dabbagh had had hardly any use value, as those scholars, who followed ad–Dabbagh's tradition (for example, ^{c}Abdalhafiz ^{c}Ali, who died in 1896[67], or the founder of the *sanusiya*, Muhammad b. ^{c}Ali as–Sanusi, 1787–1854) disposed of their own, oral or manuscript tradition.

It is likely that the eager publishers from Bulaq drew on the inexhaustible supply of manuscripts found in the librairies of Cairine mosques and produced books for the European intellectual market. At that time, European orientalists and their agents bought nearly every book that looked like a relic of the Islamic cultural tradition. This would be a typical example of how Islamic culture became a commodity. New studies on the organization and modes of cultural production of the colonial public are required to confirm this thesis and to trace the receptive attitude of the "new society" in Islamic countries and that of European researchers and research institutions at that time. If it was possible to verify this thesis, then we would be confronted with wide–ranging consequences for Islamic historiography in Europe and thus in Islamic countries in the nineteenth century. This would mean that up to now, this historiography has been based on a random choice of sources mainly determined by market conditions. If such arbitrariness could have shaped the dissemination of Islamic culture in Europe in the nineteenth century, it would be equally plausible to argue that the same would hold good for how European historiography of Islam was received by Islamic intellectuals in the nineteenth and even twentieth centuries in the Middle East.[68]

V.

The Islamic intellectuals' selfdelimitation from the "decadent" traditional Islamic culture had widespread consequences and implications for the scholars' relation towards mysticism. With the beginning of the *ijtihad*–movement, known under the name *islah* (reform), a vehement attack against the traditional element of sufism, which contradicted Islamic idealization, was launched.

From 1820 on, a growing institutionalization and centralization of the Egyptian *sufi* orders was apparent.[69] Numerous decrees and regulations, edited on behalf of the regime by the shaikhs of the Egyptian *sufi* council, legitimated the centralization of the divided sufi order system.[70] Nearly all of the 200 orders submitted to, and accepted the al–Bakri family, as their sole authority. Since the eighteenth century the al–Bakri family had already monopolized most of the important positions in the hierarchy of the *sufi* order.[71] Devoted to the regime, members of this family resided in al–Azhar and given their double social function were able to fight off every neo–Sufic tendency. They and other scholars, condemned neo–Sufism as an apostasy, and as an attempt to loosen the ties binding the society to the regime. Best known is the condemnation of 1883 of the Sudanese *mahdiya* written by the Egyptian *mufti* Muhammad al-ᶜAbbasi al-Mahdi (1827-1897).[72] Sometimes, as the scholars as Hasan al-ᶜIdwi[73] or ᶜAbdalhafiz ᶜAli did, they accepted some elements of neo-Sufic thinking, but dissassociated themselves from any real social movement based on it.

But it was the *islah* movement at al-Azhar which openly turned against mysticism as a whole. Muhammad ᶜAbduh, himself educated by a local mystic (Shaikh Darwish), condemned mysticism as an innovation allowed in Islam (*bidᶜa*).[74] Thus, the delimitation of Islamic élites from Islamic tradition was effected. Everything that the "civilized" Europeans distrusted within Islamic culture, especially "blind belief in authority", Islamic popular culture, or the "movements of the Mad Mullahs" (i.e. neo-Sufism)[75] was abolished simply by declaring it to be unislamic. In purified form, Islam would now be able to compete with European ideologies. The Islamic scholars and intellectuals had given proof of the fact that they were not barbarians and that they had abjured their tradition. Henceforward, the Europeans could treat them as partners, or, at least, recognize them as enemies of equal standing.

VI.

In the main, Islamic cultural history was determined by the development of a cultural self-understanding on the part of the new colonial élites. In the same manner that patterns of action, behaviour and communication coined by the West were adopted by the indigenous cultural élite, the process by which it found its own cultural identity was also mediated by Europe. Its self-understanding or self-representation was bound up with "universal categories" postulated in European concepts of culture. The Islamic intellectuals, as a part of the colonial élites, were compelled to rewrite the Islamic cultural tradition to make it fit European patterns of the history of mind and culture. The adoption of the Europeans' categories such as tradition, modernity, decadence and renaissance, was most important. The last category itself represented the colonial élites' striving for a new form of cultural utterance of their own. At first, reevaluation began on the basis of Islamic categories which, however, reflected European concepts. One point of departure, beside others, was the dichotomy *taqlid–ijtihad.* Formerly these were two clearly defined forms of Islamic jurisprudence; now they became reinterpreted in following sense:

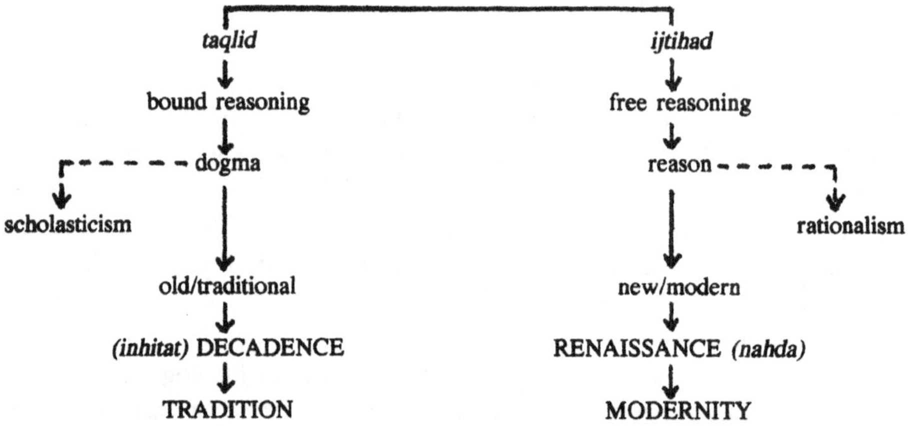

(⟶ means: identified as)

Through this concept, it was possible to integrate the European interpretation of Islamic cultural history into a self–image claimed by the colonial élites in Islamic countries. Modernity serving as a collective notion for forms of social and cultural utterance in colonial society, was joined to the negative counterpart or antinomy tradition identified as the Dark Age (661–1798 or 1258–1798). The historical process which gave birth to "modernity" was understood as a renaissance requiring, of course, an antinomy, namely decadence. In analogy with European patterns of cultural history, renaissance had to refer historically to a classical period which the Islamic intellectuals traced to the Golden Age of the revelation and (mostly) the first calife (610–661). And again in analogy to a European historiography of culture, the Golden Age was seen as a timeless universality. This caused no difficulty since in Islamic traditions, Muhammad's community was already regarded as an ideal–type or as an archetype of social organization.

But as the "Islamic classical epoch" also served to legitimate cultural modernity, reevaluation also touched the concept of the ideal – type. Thus, the social reality of modernity (expressed as the cultural self – understanding of the colonial élites) was reflected in the mirror of the ideal – type of the Muhammadan community.

Notes

1. Nicolas Turc (Niqula Turk): *Chronique d'Egypt, 1798–1804*. Ed. et trad. par G. Wiet. Le Caire 1950, p. 8 s. Conf. Harald Motzki: *Dimma et égalité. Die nichtmuslimischen Minderheiten Ägyptens (...) und die Expedition Bonapartes (1798–1801)*. Bonn 1979, p. 172 ss.

2. Rotraut Wieland: *Das Bild der Europäer in der modernen arabischen Erzähl– und Theaterliteratur*. Beirut 1980, p. 30 ss.

3. ᶜAbdarrahman b. Hasan al–Jabarti: *ta'rikh muddat al–Faransi bi–Misr*. Ed. a. transl. by S. Moreh. Leiden 1976, p. 89 s. (arab.)

4. Conf. *Description de L'Egypte*. 9 vols., in–fol. Paris 1809–1825.

5. Vivant Denon (Baron Dominique Vivant): *Voyage dans la Basse et la Haute Egypte, pendant les campagnes du général Bonaparte*. Paris an X (1802).

6. Conf. Bassam Tibi: "Der Islam, der einst eine Hochkultur war, degenerierte unter den Osmanen; weder Wissenschaft noch Literatur noch Baukultur konnten gedeihen (...)." *Die Krise des modernen Islam. Eine vorindustrielle Kultur im wissenschaftlich–technischen Zeitalter*. München 1981, p. 67.

7. For Indonesia conf.: J.H. Boeke: *Economics and Economic Policy of Dual Societies as Exemplified by Indonesia*. Haarlem 1953.

8. Franz Borkenau: *Der Übergang vom feudalen zum bürgerlichen Weltbild*. Paris 1934.

9. Peter Gran: *Islamic Roots of Capitalism. Egypt 1760–1840*. Austin/Tex. 1979.

10. Gilbert Delanoue: *Moralistes et politiques musulmans dans l'Egypte du XIXe siècle (1798–1882).* I–II. Le Caire 1982, esp. p. 561 s.

11. There are numerous examples, f.e.: Franz Taeschner: *Geschichte der arabischen Welt.* Stuttgart 1964, p. 156 s. Gerhard Endreß: *Einführung in die islamische Geschichte.* München 1982, p. 152. Hamilton Gibb/Jacob Landau: *Arabische Literaturgeschichte.* Stuttgart 1968 (1. engl. ed. 1926). Gibb's classification is: "heroic age", "golden age", "silver age", the mamluk era, followed by Landau's essay on the 20th century. This concept is still kept by Roger Allan: *The Arabic Novel. An Historical and Critical Introduction.* Manchester 1982, esp. pp. 19–25. As for Arabic interpretation, see Shukri Faisal: ^{c}asr al–inhitat, in: Salih al–^{c}Ali: *al–adab al–^{c}arabi fi athar ad–darisin.* Beirut 1981; Seyyed Hossein Nasr: Decadence, Deviation and Renaissance in the Context of Contemporary Islam, in: *Islamic Perspectives,* ed. by Khurshid Ahmad and Zafar Ishaq Ansari. London/Jeddah 1979, pp. 35–42.

12. Endreß, op.cit., p. 97.

13. F.e., Rosa Luxemburg: *Die Akkumulation des Kapitals. Ein Beitrag zur ökonomischen Erklärung des Imperialismus.* Berlin 1913. Karl Wittfogel: *Die orientalische Despotie. Eine vergleichende Untersuchung totaler Macht.* Frankfurt a.M. 1977 (1. engl. ed. 1957). Conf. Bryan Stanley Turner: *Marx and the end of orientalism.* London 1978.

14. Nadav Safran: *Egypt in Search of Political Community. An analysis of the intellectual and political evolution of Egypt, 1804–1952.* Cambridge/Mass. 1961.

15. Tibi, op.cit., p. 69.

16. I have tried to discuss this problem at some length in: Islamische Kultur und soziale Bewegung, in: *Peripherie* 18/19 (1985), pp. 60–84.

17. For the concept of "complexity" conf. Jürgen Habermas: *Zur Rekonstruktion des historischen Materialismus*. Frankfurt a.M. 1982, pp. 144–199, esp. p. 155 s.

18. The term "public" (Öffentlichkeit) is discussed in length: Oskar Negt/Alexander Kluge: *Öffentlichkeit und Erfahrung. Zur Organisationsanalyse von bürgerlicher und proletarischer Öffentlichkeit.* Frankfurt a.M. 1971, pp. 17–101.

19. Repr. as: Saladin Boustany (ed.): *The Journals of Bonaparte in Egypt, 1798–1801*, 10 vols. Cairo n.d. (1971).

20. *La décade égyptienne*, II. pp. 192–200.

21. J. Heyworth–Dunne: *An Introduction to the History of Education in Modern Egypt*. Cairo 1938, p. 99, lists 21 titles.

22. A. Greiss: Histoire de l'imprimerie en Egypt, in: *Bulletin de l'Institut d'Egypte* (le Caire) 5 (1907/8) 1, pp. 133–157 a. 2, pp. 195–320.

23. This information is taken from my article Islamische Kulturproduktion im 19. Jahrhundert, in: *Welt des Islams* (forthcoming). As for Istanbul, I only take into account the printing after 1802. At that time, the first book dealing with Islamic studies had been printed (*risala–i Birgiwi*, an abridged version of Muhammad b. Pir ^{c}Ali al–Birkawi's *at–tariqa al–muhammadiya*. Skutari September 1803). Many of the books printed at Bulaq were merely translations, among others by Yuhanna ^{c}Anhuri of Damascus and by the French physician Clot Bey (1793–1868). Cf. Yusuf Ilyas Sarkis: *mu^{c}jam al–matbu^{c}at al–^{c}arabiya wa–l–mu^{c}arraba*. al–Qahira 1346/1928, p. 1389, 1576. A language school opened in 1835. See: Luis Shaikhu al–Yasu^{c}i: *al–adab al–^{c}arabi fi l–qarn at–tasi^{c} ^{c}ashar*. 2 vol., Beirut 1924/26, i/6 ss.

24. 7 vols. Paris 1833–35.

25. Cit. in: *Mameluken, Paschas und Fellachen. Berichte aus dem Reich Mohammed Alis 1801–1849.* Hrsg. u. kommentiert von Thankmar Freiherr von Münchhausen. Tübingen 1982, p. 319.

26. Since 1837, it was administered by the *diwan al–madaris* (Ministry of Education).

27. Gran, op.cit., passim. Delanoue, op.cit., pp. 344–357.

28. Sarkis, op.cit., p. 1336. Cf. the list of his writings in Gran, op.cit., pp. 197–208. See also the (incomplete) list of early book printing at Bulaq: T.X. Bianchi: Catalogue général des livres arabes, persans et turcs, imprimés à Boulac en Egypte depuis de l'introduction de l'imprimerie dans ce pays, in: *Journal asiatique* 4 s., t.II (Paris) 1843, pp. 24–61.

29. Delanoue, op.cit., pp. 383–487, 109–118.

30. Edward William Lane: *Manners and Customs of the Modern Egyptians.* London 1895 (1. ed. 1836), p. 222, 283.

31. *takhlis al–ibriz fi talkhis Bariz* (original title: *rihlat ash–shaikh Rifa^c ya^{c}ni akhbar bilad Uruba.*)

32. *at–tarbiya as–safiya li–murid al–jughrafiya* (original title: *jughrafiya saghira.*) Cf. Delanoue, op.cit., p. 622.

33. Sarkis, op.cit., preface.

34. Concerning the tradition of Islamic–Arabic dictionaries see Stefan Wild: *Das Kitab al–^{c}Ain und die arabische Lexikographie.* Wiesbaden 1965.

35. Sarkis, op.cit.,pp. 535, 1499 ff.

36. *hashiya ^{c}ala risalat as–Sabban al–bayyaniya.*

37. *manh al–jalil ^{c}ala khtasar ash–shaikh Khalil.*

38. *ihya' ^{c}ulum ad–din*, probably written between 1096 and 1097.

39. For the history of the printing offices, cf. ^{c}Abdalfutuh ar–Ridwan: *ta'rikh matba^{c} at Bulaq*. al–Qahira 1953.
Jewish, Christian and even Ottoman printing had started much earlier:
   - printing office in Dair Qazhiya/Lebanon, founded in about 1625, Syriac letters
   - printing office in Aleppo, founded by the patriarch of Antakia in 1702 (gospel printed in 1703)
   - printing office of Dair Marhanna/Lebanon, founded in 1733 (Christian–Arabic books)
   - the Greek–Orthodox printing office in Dair al–Qadis/Lebanon, founded in 1750.
   - Printing in Istanbul started in 1727, as the Ottoman wezir Ibrahim Müteferrika (1674–1745) opened a printing office for military purposes. At first he published maps, then a dictionary and finally his own writings, among others usul al–hikam fi nizam al–umam (1731).
   - Täbris 1816.

   In Europe, printing with Arabic letters began in 1514 (Rome, Genua, Venice, here, in 1530, a first printed Quran was edited).
   Finally, mention must be made of the Jewish printing office in Istanbul, founded in 1530; from 1710 on, Arabic letters were used for Ottoman–Turkish texts published in this office.

40. Delanoue, op.cit., pp. 488–564.

41. *^{c}alam ad–din*, I/319.

42. Walter Benjamin: *Das Kunstwerk im Zeitalter seiner technischen Reproduzierbarkeit*. Frankfurt a.M. 1977, pp. 7–44.

43. Ernest Renan: *L'islamisme et la science*. Paris 1883.

44. F.A. Tansel in *Encyclopedia of Islam*, Leiden 1960 ss., IV (1978), pp. 875–879.

45. G.S. van Krieken: *Khair al–Din et la Tunisie (1850–1881)*. Leiden 1976 (gives as date of birth 1822/3); Ibrahim Abu–Lughod: The Islamic Influence of Hair ad–Din at–Tunisi, in: *Essays on Islamic Civilization*, ed. by Donald P. Little. Leiden 1976, pp. 9–24.

46. Nikki R. Keddie: *Sayyid Jamal ad–Din "al–Afghani". A political biography*. Berkely/Cal. 1972. EADEM: *An Islamic Response to Imperialism*. Berkeley/Cal. 1968. A. Albert Kudsi–Zadeh: *Sayyid Jamal al–Din al–Afghani. An annotated bibliography*. Leiden 1970.

47. See my: Die Politisierung des Islam im 19. Jahrhundert, in: *Die Welt des Islams* 22 (1982), pp. 103–116.

48. Al–Afghani: Response à Renan, in: *Journal des débats*, 18.5.1883, repr. in: Keddie, *Sayyid Jamal ad–Din*, pp. 181–187.

49. See D.B. MacDonald in *Encyclopedia of Islam*, op. cit., III/p. 1026 s.

50. Delanoue, op.cit., p. 158 s.

51. *Shorter Encyclopedia of Islam*, ed. by H.A.R. Gibb a. J.H. Kramers. Leiden 1974, pp. 562 ss.

52. Delanoue, op.cit., pp. 530 ss.

53. *al–qaul as–sadid fi l–ijtihad wa–t–tajdid*, sep. printed 1871.

54. Delanoue, op.cit., pp. 435 ss.

55. For Muhammad ᶜAbduh see: Elie Kedourie: *Afghani and 'Abduh*. London 1966. *Mudhakkirat al–imam Muhammad ᶜAbduh*. (Ed. by)

Tahir at–Tanakhi. al–Qahira n.d. Muhammad Rashid Rida: *ta'rikh al–ustadh al–imam ash–shaikh Muhammad ᶜAbduh, I–III.* al–Qahira 1925–1931.

56. f.e. al–Afghani and ᶜAbduh.

57. J. Spencer Trimingham: *Sufi Orders in Islam*. Oxford 1971.

58. B.G. Martin: *Muslim Brotherhoods in Nineteenth Century Africa*. Cambridge 1976. Baber Johansen: *Islam und Staat*. Berlin 1982, p. 25 s.

59. Martin. op.cit., pp 99 ss. Nicola Ziyadeh: *Sanusiya*. Oxford 1958.

60. Jamil M. Abun–Nasr: *The Tijaniyya. A Sufi Order in the Modern World.* London 1965.

61. Peter M. Holt: *The Mahdist State in the Sudan, 1881–1898.* Nairobi (etc.) ²1979. It is interesting to note that the *mahdi* used lithographic printing in 1883 to publish his regulations. *ar–ratib*, 1302/1883.

62. Martin. op.cit., pp. 13 ss a. 68 ss.

63. Lesley Blanch: *The Sabres of Paradise*. London 1960.

64. For the history of Islamic scholarship see: *Scholars, Saints and Sufis. Religious institutions in the Middle East since 1500.* Ed. by Nikki R. Keddie. Berkeley/Cal. 1972.

65. See my: *Die Rebellion der ägyptischen Fallahin 1919*. Berlin 1981, pp. 79–88.

66. *kitab dhahab al–ibriz min kalam Sidi ᶜAbdalᶜaziz.* Cf. Yusuf b. Ismail an–Nabhani: *jamiᶜ karamat al–auliya'*, I–II. Beirut 1974, II/273 ss.

67. Cf. his: *ghurrat as–sabah wa–zinat al–afrah*, printed at the margin of his: *luqtat al–^{c}ajlan min tunfat al–ikhwan*. al–Qahira 1323/1905.

68. Cf. the remarks of Jules Mohl in *Journal Asiatique*, 6è série/IV (July 1863), p. 50, n.2, in which he commented on the Bulaq edition of al–Bukhari's *sahih*, published in 1280/1863 in three volumes. He stressed the fact that the Bulaq publishers regarded the text as a very expensive commodity which would have lost its value if the number of copies exceeded a certain quantity. "Il y avait un incouvénient; on tirait à trop petit nombre, de sorte que les bons ouvrages s'épuisaient vite et atteignaient des prix très–élevés. En Europe on aurait remédié à cela en doublant le tirage, et l'imprimerie aurait alors payé ses frais. En Orient on procéde autrement; on a loué L'imprimerie à un fermier qui a trouvé plus simple de doubler et de tripler les prix, ce qui dispense d'un tirage plus grand."

69. F. de Jong: *Turuq and Turuq–Linked Institutions in Nineteeth Century Egypt*. Leiden 1978.

70. De Jong, op.cit., pp. 192–214.

71. Delanoue, op.cit., pp. 251 ss. For the Bakri–family see de Jong, op.cit., pp. 7 ss and passim.

72. Delanoue, op.cit., p. 181 s.

73. F.e. al–^{c}Idwi in 1880, Delanoue, op.cit., p. 604.

74. Cf. Muhammad ^{c}Abduh: *al–a^{c}mal al–kamila*, (ed. by) Muhammad ^{c}Ammara, I–VI, al–Qahira, II (^{2}1980), pp. 510–533. An early refutation of mysticism within colonial society is: Wafa Muhammad al–Quni al–Misri: *ar–radd al–mubin ^{c}ala jahalat al–mutasawwifin*. al–Qahira 1293/1876/7. Of course, this has nothing in common with the anti–Sufic propaganda of the *wahhabiya*.

75. A fine example is: Douglas Jardine: *The Mad Mullah of Somaliland*. London 1923, dealing with the Somali *mahdi* Muhammad b. ᶜAbdallah Hassan (died 1920).

References

ᶜAbduh, Muhammad, al-aᶜmal al-kamila, in: Muhammad ᶜAmmara (ed.), I-VI, al-Qahira, II ([2]1980), pp. 510-533.

Abu-Lughod, Ibrahim, The Islamic Influence of Hair ad-Din at-Tunisi, in: Donald P. Little (ed.) Essays on Islamic Civilization, Leiden 1976.

Abun-Nasr, Jamil M., The Tijaniyya. A Sufi Order in the Modern World, London 1965.

al-Birkawi, Pir ᶜAli, at-tariqa al-muhammadiya, Skutari, Sept. 1803.

al-Ghazali (ed.), ihya' ᶜulum ad-din, Bulaq 1869.

ᶜAli, ᶜAbdalhafiz, luqtat al-ᶜajlan min tuhfat al-ikhwan, al-Qahira 1323/1905.

al-Jabarti, ᶜAbdarahman b. Hasan, ta'rikh muddat al-Faransis bi-Misr, Ed. a. transl. by S. Moreh, Leiden 1976. (arab.)

al-Lamti, Ahmad b. Mubarak, kitab dhahab al-ibriz min kalam Sidi ᶜAbdalᶜaziz, 2 vol., Bulaq 1861/2.

Allan, Roger, The Arabic Novel. An Historical and Critical Introduction, Manchester 1982.

al-Quni al-Misri, Wafa Muhammad, ar-radd al-mubin ᶜala jahalat al-mutasawwifin, al-Quahira 1293/1876/7.

an-Nabhani, Yusuf b. Ismaᶜil, jamiᶜ karamat al-auliya', I-II, Beirut 1974.

ar-Ridwan, ᶜAbdalfutuh, ta'rikh matbaᶜ at Bulaq, al-Qahira 1953.

at–Tahtawi, Rifa^{c}a Rafi^{c} Badawi, takhlis al–ibriz fi talkhis Bariz, Bulaq 1834.

at–Tahtawi, Rifa^{c}a Rafi^{c} Badawi, at–tarbiya as–safiya li–murid al–jughrafiya, Bulaq 1834.

at–Tahtawi, Rifa^{c}a Rafi^{c} Badawi, al–qaul as–sadid fi l–ijtihad wa–t–tajdid, in: raudat al madaris, 1870.

at–Tanakhi, Tahir (ed.), Mudhakkirat al–imam Muhammad ^{c}Abduh, al–Qahira n.d.

Benjamin, Walter, Das Kunstwerk im Zeitalter seiner technischen Reproduzierbarkeit, Frankfurt a. M., 1977.

Bianchi, T.X., Catalogue général des livres arabes, persans et turcs, imprimés à Boulac en Egypte depuis de l'introduction de l'imprimerie dans ce pays, in: Journal asiatique 4 s., t.II (Paris) 1843, pp. 24–61.

Blanch, Lesley, The Sabres of Paradise, London 1960.

Boeke, J.H., Economics and Economic Policy of Dual Societies as Exemplified by Indonesia, Haarlem 1953.

Borkenau, Franz, Der Übergang vom feudalen zum bürgerlichen Weltbild, Paris 1934.

Boustany, Saladin (ed.), The Journals of Bonaparte in Egypt, 1798–1801, 10 vols., Cairo n.d. (1971).

Delanoue, Gilbert, Moralistes et politiques musulmans dans l'Egypte du XIXe siècle (1798–1882), I–II, Le Caire 1982.

Denon, Vivant, Voyage dans la Basse et la Haute Egypte, pendant les campagnes du général Bonaparte, Paris an X, 1802.

Description de l'Egypte. 9 vols., Paris 1809–1825.

Endreß, Gerhard, Einführung in die islamische Geschichte, München 1982.

Faisal, Shukri, ᶜasr al-inhitat, in: Salih al-ᶜAli, al-adab al-ᶜarabi fi athar ad-darisin, Beirut 1981.

Gibb, Hamilton and Jacob Landau, Arabische Literaturgeschichte, Stuttgart 1968 (1. engl. ed. 1926).

Gran, Peter, Islamic Roots of Capitalism. Egypt 1760-1840, Austin, Texas 1979.

Greiss, A., Histoire de l'imprimerie en Egypt, in: Bulletin de l'Institut d'Egypte (le Caire) 5 (1907/8) 1, pp. 133-157 a. 2, pp. 195-320.

Habermas, Jürgen, Zur Rekonstruktion des Historischen Materialismus, Frankfurt a. M. 1982.

Heyworth-Dunne, J., An Introduction to the History of Education in Modern Egypt, Cairo 1938.

Holt, P.M., The Mahdist State in the Sudan, 1881-1898, Nairobi (etc.) ^{2}1979.

Jardine, Douglas, The Mad Mullah of Somaliland, London 1923.

Johansen, Baber, Islam und Staat, Berlin 1982.

Jong, F. de, Turuq and Turuq-Linked Institutions in Nineteenth Century Egypt, Leiden 1978.

Kedouri, Elie, Afghani and 'Abduh, London 1966.

Keddie, Nikki R., An Islamic Response to Imperialism, Berkeley/Cal. 1968.

Keddie, Nikki R. (ed.), Scholars, Saints and Sufis. Religious institutions in the Middle East since 1500, Berkeley/Cal. 1972.

Keddie, Nikki R., Sayyid Jamal ad–Din "al–Afghani". A political biography, Berkeley/Cal. 1972.

Krieken, G.S. van, Khair al–din et la Tunisie (1850–1881), Leiden 1976.

Kudsi–Zadeh, A. Albert, Sayyid Jamal al–Din al–Afghani. An annotated bibliographie, Leiden 1970.

Lane, Edward Williams, Manners and Customs of the Modern Egyptians, London 1895.

Luxemburg, Rosa, Die Akkumulation des Kapitals. Ein Beitrag zur ökonomischen Erklärung des Imperialismus, Berlin 1913.

Martin, B.G., Muslim Brotherhoods in Nineteenth Century Africa, Cambridge 1976.

Michaud, Joseph, Correspondance d'Orient, 7 vol., Paris 1833–35.

Mohl, Jules, in: Journal Asiatique, 6è série/IV (July 1863), p. 50, n. 2.

Motzki, Harald, Dimma et égalité. Die nichtmuslimischen Minderheiten Ägyptens und die Expedition Bonapartes (1798–1801), Bonn 1979.

Mubarak, ᶜAli, ᶜalam ad–din, I/319.

Münchhausen, Thankmar Freiherr von (ed.), Mameluken, Paschas und Fellachen. Berichte aus dem Reich Mohammad Alis 1801–1849, Tübingen 1982.

Nasr, Seyyed Hossein, Decadence, Deviation and Renaissance in the Context of Contemporary Islam, in: Khurshid Ahmad and Zafar Ishaq Ansari (eds.), Islamic Perspectives, London/Jeddah 1979, pp. 35–42.

Negt, Oskar and Alexander Kluge, Öffentlichkeit und Erfahrung. Zur Organisationsanalyse von bürgerlicher und proletarischer Öffentlichkeit, Frankfurt a. M. 1971.

Renan, Ernest, L'islamisme et la science, Paris 1883.

Rida, Muhammad Rashid,
ta'rikh al–ustadh al–imam ash–shaikh Muhammad ᶜAbduh, I–III, al–Qahira 1925–1931.

Safran, Nadar, Egypt in Search of Political Community. An analysis of the intellectual and political evolution of Egypt, 1804–1952, Cambridge/Mass. 1961.

Sarkis, Yusuf Ilyas, muᶜjam al–matbuᶜat al–ᶜarabiya wa–l–muᶜarraba, al–Qahira 1346/1928.

Schulze, Reinhard, Die Rebellion der ägyptischen Fallahin 1919, Berlin 1981.

Schulze, Reinhard, Die Politisierung des Islam im 19. Jahrhundert, in: Die Welt des Islam 22 (1982), pp. 103–116.

Schulze, Reinhard, Islamische Kultur und soziale Bewegung, in: Peripherie 18/19 (1985), pp. 60–84.

Schulze, Reinhard, Islamische Kulturproduktion im 19. Jahrhundert, in: Welt des Islam (forthcoming) 1.

Taeschner, Franz, Geschichte der arabischen Welt, Stuttgart 1964.

Tansel, F.A., Encyclopedia of Islam, Leiden 1960 ss., IV (1978), S. 875–879.

Tibi, Bassam, Die Krise des modernen Islam. Eine vorindustrielle Kultur im wissenschaflich–technischen Zeitalter, München 1981.

Trimingham, J. Spencer, Sufi Orders in Islam, Oxford 1971.

Turc, Nicolas, Chronique d'Egypte, 1798–1804. Ed. et trad. par G. Wiet, Le Caire 1950.

Turner, Bryan Stanley, Marx and the End of Orientalism, London 1978.

ᶜUlaish, Muhammad (ed.), manh al–jalil ᶜala khtasar ash–shaikh Khalil, Bulaq 1864/5.

ᶜUlaish, Muhammad, hashiya ᶜala risalat as–Sabban al–bayyaniya, Bulaq 1864/5.

Wieland, Rotraut, Das Bild der Europäer in der modernen arabischen Erzähl– und Theaterliteratur, Beirut 1980.

Wild, Stefan, Das Kitab al–ᶜAin und die arabische Lexikographie, Wiesbaden 1965.

Wittfogel, Karl, Die Orientalische Despotie. Eine vergleichende Untersuchung totaler Macht, Frankfurt a. M. 1977.

Zidayeh, Nicola, Sanusiya, Oxford 1958.

[24]

Who Read What in the Ottoman Empire (19th–20th centuries)?

JOHANN STRAUSS

In Miss Pardoe's famous book on Istanbul and the 'domestic manners of the Turks', first published 1837,[1] we find the observation: 'Perhaps, with the single exception of Great Britain, there exists not in the world a more reading nation than Turkey ... Nearly every man throughout the Empire can read and write, and there are, at this moment, upwards of eight thousand children scattered through the different schools of the capital.' Surprising as this assessment may seem at first glance, it is less unrealistic if we consider the following: 'But the studies of the Osmanlis of both sexes have, with a few exceptions, hitherto been confined to the Koran, and to works of an inconsequent and useless description; the mere plaything of an idle hour, incapable of inspiring one novel idea, or of leaving upon the mind impressions calculated to exalt or to enlighten it.'[2]

It describes fairly well the situation prior to the revolution which took place in the Ottoman world of letters in the 19th century. The 'Osmanlis of both sexes' referred to by Miss Pardoe were, of course, the Muslim Turks. In fact, these formed just one segment of a much more larger 'reading nation' consisting also of Greeks and Bulgarians, Armenians, Jews and Arabs, 'Franks' and Levantines. Modern historians have tended to create a separate literary identity for each of them according to the Western European concept of 'national' literature. Literature is restricted to the production of one 'nation' in one single language; the established canon consists, of course, of original works, emphasizing specimens of the different genres which had developed in the West (novel, drama). The literary activity in the Ottoman Empire with its very specific features does not fit this pattern and is therefore not taken into account.[3] In particular, literatures which do not fit the nationalist paradigm, such as that of the Turkish speaking Greek-Orthodox (*Karamanlı*) or the Turcophone Armenians, fall between two stools. Generally, they are not regarded either by Turkish or by Greek and Armenian scholars as part of their literary heritage, and have been studied only by specialists.[4]

However, their significance cannot be denied. It was a *Karamanlı* author's work, 'The Spectacle of the World—The Tormentor and the Sufferer' (*Tamaşai Dünya ve Cefakiar-u Cefakeş*) published in 1870–71 that was hailed after its 'rediscovery' as the 'first Turkish novel'.[5] This assumption eventually proved to be false since it was in fact only the adaptation of a Greek work, a novel first published in 1839 in Athens but written by an Ottoman Greek from Istanbul.[6] It had been more or less ignored by historians of literature so far—despite its pioneering character.[7]

Johann Strauss, Département d'Études turques, Université Marc Bloch, 22, rue René Descartes, F-67084 Strasbourg cedex, France

A few years later there came to light another Turkish novel, 'The Story of Agapi', published almost 20 years earlier (1851) in Armenian script whose claims to originality seem to be well-founded. This Armeno–Turkish work has therefore to be considered—at least for the time being—as the first novel in Turkish.[8] Incidentally, the first Armenian novel in the vernacular—perhaps less artful than the 'Story of Agapi'[9]—*Khosrov and Makruhi* by Hovhannes Hisarian (1827–1916), was published the same year.

This is just one example of the complexity of the subject and the potential inherent in this kind of research. It also shows that there was a literary activity which deserves better than anything else the epithet 'Ottoman'. The idea of a 'literature' developing in a specifically 'Ottoman' context, and even within the borders of that multi-ethnic empire, may seem strange to those accustomed to the usual framework of 'national' literatures. But the Ottoman capital was a centre of printing and publishing very much like Paris or other European capitals. The production was by no means limited to books in Turkish.[10] To various degrees, it was a cultural centre for Greeks and Bulgarians, Armenians, Sephardic Jews and, despite the importance of a local centre such as Beirut, even for Arabs.[11] The emergence of Modern Persian literature is also closely connected with the activity of Iranians in Istanbul.[12] The different communities were much less exclusive than it may seem at first glance and various types of contacts were much more frequent than might be expected. It is true that non-Muslims usually did not study the Koran, the Holy Book of Islam, which at the time served as the first initiation into reading for a large part of the population. Until the *Tanzimat* era, they may even have met with serious obstacles to acquiring and studying Muslim books, if we are to believe certain western observers.[13] Many readers were also only familiar with one single language, but there were many channels of transmission and works which attracted a readership within all communities.

The present article attempts to describe them, starting with some of the more basic aspects of reading and literary activity in a plural society which was divided, among other things, by religion, language and script. In some important matters (circulation of books and papers, reading knowledge of western languages, etc) information is scanty and difficult to interpret. For most of the languages dealt with here we also lack comprehensive repertories of translated literature published in periodicals. These difficulties have to be taken into account when we try to give an answer to the question 'Who read what in the Ottoman Empire?' in this contribution.

The Reading Public of the Ottoman Empire

Who were the 'reading communities' of the Ottoman Empire? Which languages were understood and read? It is obvious that only linguistic communities with a written language and a proper script are susceptible of having a reading public. This basic assumption is, however, complicated by the fact the ethnic language does not always coincide with the written language used by the community, defined in the Ottoman context by religion. In other words: although many languages were spoken in the Ottoman Empire, relatively few were written (or printed) until the 19th century. Those were then basically Ottoman Turkish, Persian, Arabic, Greek, Armenian and Hebrew.[14] A significant literary production existed only in these languages.

From the 18th century onwards, Greek had become the cultural language of many educated Bulgarians and Rumanians. Nicolas Piccolos (1792–1865), of Bulgarian origin but trained in Greek colleges, was the first translator of Bernardin de St Pierre's immensely popular *Paul et Virginie* and other works of the same author—into Greek![15] Hebrew was used by many Jewish writers whose ethnic language was (Judaeo-) Spanish, Greek or something else.[16] Persian represents a special case, since it was not an ethnic language but served as a language of culture for the educated class among the Ottoman Turks. Turkish poets, including those with another mother tongue (Bosnians, Albanians, etc.) often composed part of their works in Persian. The accessibility of the literary production depended therefore to a large extent on the training of the prospective readers, and in some cases (e.g. those of Persian, Hebrew) on the readers' knowledge of what was basically a 'foreign' language.

The same applies to scripts. Muslims in Bosnia, Albania or in the Greek lands used for the—more or less important—literary production in their ethnic languages the Arabic alphabet rather than the one used by their Christian countrymen. On the other hand, Arabic-speaking Christians had kept for a long time to *karshûnî*, used originally for Syriac, before they switched to the Arabic characters. Sephardic Jews used to write their vernacular Spanish in the Hebrew based *rashi*-script. Turkish-speaking Christians used the alphabets of their religious community, mainly Greek or Armenian. At one point, books in at least three different scripts (Arabic, Greek, Armenian) were available to the Turcophone reading public.

Which Languages were Read?—19th Century Developments in Literary Languages

In the 19th century, several important developments took place which did not fail to affect reading habits.

First, classical languages were gradually replaced by more vernacular varieties (diglossia).[17] The most conspicuous case is Modern (Western) Armenian, where the classical variant (*krapar*) became more or less obsolete towards the end of the century, despite the desperate efforts of the Mekhitarists in Vienna and Venice and their followers to restore it. It also contributed to the rise of publications in Armeno-Turkish. Vartan Pasha, the author of the 'Story of Agabi', in the preface to his 'History of Napoleon Bonaparte' justifies the fact that he had written this work in Turkish with the argument that those in the Armenian *millet* who knew *krapar* were very few and that even the new literary language based on the vernacular (*ašxarhapar*) was still not sufficiently developed and too dependent on *krapar*. He concludes: 'Since in the Armenian millet those who know Turkish well but are unfamiliar with Armenian are more numerous than those who know Armenian and ignore Turkish, the Turkish language has necessarily been preferred for this work, as a sign of respect for the majority.'[18] Greeks and Arabs, on the other hand, continued to remain strongly attached to the classical models, restored more or less successfully. As far as Ottoman Turkish is concerned, the elaborate literary language developed slowly but eventually irresistably towards simplification.[19]

Secondly, ethnic languages emancipated themselves from the grip of other languages. Among the non-Muslims, Turkish becomes increasingly important as a medium of literary expression for those members of the religious (or ethnic) community who were ignorant of the dominant 'national' (or 'sacred') language. We therefore have an impressive book production and a flourishing press in both *Karamanlı* and Armeno-Turkish. A somewhat similar case is the rise of the ethnic language of the Sephardic

Jews. We not only see the development of a Jewish press in Judaeo–Spanish (and hardly any Hebrew) in Smyrna and Istanbul but also an extremely variegated literary activity, predominantly of translation. This is the more surprising, since this language was still scorned by many as a 'jargon', infinitely less prestigious than the sacred language, Hebrew, which had been the language used almost exclusively by learned men and scholars in their writings.[20]

Thirdly, new literary languages emerged. In the Ottoman context, Bulgarian is perhaps the best example. From very modest beginnings (the first book in the modern language was printed in 1806) it developed rapidly into a fully developed literary language, with a flourishing press and an intense publishing activity, in the Ottoman lands limited almost exclusively to the capital until 1878.[21]

Fourthly a new, western language, French, was introduced. French attained the status of a semi-official language in the Ottoman Empire and one of communication between the educated speakers of different linguistic communities. In the case of the Sephardic Jews, it even became the language of the upper classes.[22] Works in French were available from local booksellers and were read both by educated Muslims and non-Muslims. Although there are no comprehensive studies on this subject, it is most likely that the French press in the Ottoman Empire also had its share in the transmission of western literature and in the forming of the literary taste of the Ottoman reading public.

These issues are closely connected with a number of other developments such as the progress in public education (which will not be dealt with here) and, in particular, with the spectacular rise of printing and publishing in the Ottoman Empire in the wake of the *Tanzimat* reforms in the 19th century. These developments also provided the necessary audience for an expanded press and contributed further to the growth of the reading public.

Literary Development and Printing and Publishing

The crucial period for the development of literature(s) in the Ottoman Empire are the 1850s. This will be illustrated by the following chronological survey. As becomes clear from this list, a number of pioneering works appeared during this period, the majority of them published in the Ottoman capital:

1851 (Istanbul): Vartan Pasha, *Akabi Hikyayesi* (first novel in [Armeno-]Turkish).
1851 (Istanbul): Hovhannes Hisarian, *Khosrov ew Mak'ruhi* (first novel in Modern western Armenian, published in the literary journal *Banasêr*).
1851 (London): Stephanos Th. Xenos, *The Devil in Turkey* ('Istanbul novel').[23]
1855 (Paris): Fâris al-Shidyâq, *Al-sâq 'alâ al-sâq* (first modern novel in Arabic).[24]
1859 (Paris): Ambroise Calfa, *Telemak'* (first translation of Fénelon's *Aventures de Télémaque* into Modern Armenian).
1859 (Istanbul): Yusuf Kâmil Pasha, *Terceme-i Telemak* (first literary translation into Ottoman Turkish; published in 1862).
1859 (Istanbul): Münif Pasha, *Muhaverat-ı hikemiyye* (translation of 'Philosophical dialogues' by 18th-century French writers).
1859 (Istanbul): Şinasi, *Terceme-i manzûme* (first Turkish translation of Western poetry).
1860 (Istanbul): Vasil Drumev (1840–1901), *Neštastna familiya* ('The Unhappy Family'; first Bulgarian novel; published in the journal *Bâlgarski knižitsi*).

Significantly, several works appeared first in periodicals. In fact, the press had developed much earlier. Some of the periodicals listed below already contained reading material (translated novels, etc.) for a new type of readers. It should be noted that the publications of Protestant missionaries played a pioneering role; both the first paper in Bulgarian, and the second Armenian paper in the Ottoman Empire were published by them.

1824 (Smyrna): *Le Smyrnéen* (first French paper).[25]
1839 (Smyrna): *Štemaran Pitani Giteleac'* ('The Store of Useful Knowledge').[26]
1840 (Smyrna): *Anatolê* ('Anatolia'; *Karamanlı* paper; later transferred to Istanbul).[27]
1840 (Istanbul): *Ceride-i Havadis* (first non-offical Turkish newspaper; founded by an Englishman, William Churchill).
ca. 1842 (Smyrna): *La Buena Esperanza* (first Judaeo-Spanish paper; ephemeral).[28]
1843 (Istanbul): *Journal de Constantinople et des intérêts orientaux* (a continuation of the *Journal de Smyrne* 1828–1831).
1843 (Istanbul): *Têlegraphos tou Vosporou* ('The Telegraph of the Bosporus', Greek paper; published translations of novels: Sue, *Le Juif errand*, Dumas, *Monte-Cristo*, etc.).[29]
1844 (Smyrna): *Lyuboslovie* ('Philolology'; for the most part articles adapted from the Greek *Apothêkê ophelimôn gnôseôn*, which was also published by missionaries).[30]
1848 (Istanbul): *Tsarigradski Vestnik* (Bulgarian paper; first novels appeared from the fifties onwards: *Robinson Crusoe*, *Paul et Virginie*, etc.).[31]
1850 (Istanbul): *Anatolê.*
1852 (Istanbul): *Masis* ('Ararat'; perhaps the most influential Armenian paper).
1852 (Istanbul): *Mecmuayı havadis* ('Journal of Events'; Armeno-Turkish paper published by Vartan Pasha; ephemeral).
1853 (Istanbul): *Or Yisrael—La luz de Yisrael* (first periodical in Judaeo-Spanish published in Istanbul; ephemeral).
1858 (Beirut): *Ḥadîqat al-akhbâr* (first Arabic paper to devote a regular section to fiction; appeared also in a French version: *Hadikat-el-Akhbar. Journal de Syrie et Liban*).[32]
1860 (Istanbul): *Jurnal Yisraelit* (Judaeo-Spanish paper, founded by Yehezkel Gabbay (1825–1898).[33]
1860 (Istanbul): *Tercüman-ı Ahval* (second non-official Turkish paper, published by Şinasi and Agâh Efendi).
1860 (Istanbul): *Ruzname-i Ceride-i Havadis* (initially a supplement to the *Ceride-i havadis*; instrumental in the transmission of Western literature[34]).

One must assume that it was during that time, which coincides with the period of the Crimean War and the famous 'Firman of Reforms' (*Islâhât Fermanı*; 1856), that a literary public came into being which eventually became large enough to sustain a literature.[35] This reading public was large by comparison with previous periods, although given the limited distribution of literacy, it was of course still very far from the mass reading public of today; but the signs of modernity are visible even in contemporary fiction. In the 'Story of Agapi', for instance, Rupenig Agha's western-style salon has a big mahogany bookcase. Its contents are, however, hardly impressive: some Turkish letter writers' guides (*inşa ve tomar*), a French abecedary (*elifbe*), Armenian primers and books of instruction (*bardez ve talimat*) (p. 48); but Agapi already reads *Atala* in French (p. 58).

44 *Johann Strauss*

Who Provided the Ottoman Reading Public with (Modern) Reading Material?—Printing Presses and Editors

Until the *Tanzimat* reforms, inaugurated by the *Hatt-ı şerif* of Gülhane (1839), reading material in the different ethnic languages of the peoples of the Ottoman Empire (Turkish, Arabic, Greek, Bulgarian, Armenian, Judaeo–Spanish, etc.) was not only provided by printers and publishers of the Ottoman capital and the Danubian Principalities but also by printing presses established abroad. This applies especially to non-Muslim communities. Books intended for them were printed in a number of cities in Western Europe such as Vienna, Venice, Leipzig, Amsterdam, etc., but it should be noted that during the first half of the 19th century even for a Muslim Turkish readership, printing presses in the periphery of the Empire played a significant role; the first translations of western languages (although hardly any fiction) were printed in Egypt, and Ottoman poetry was initially available only through books printed in Cairo.[36]

Each community displays specific features. The most remarkable case is that of the Jewish community. Relatively few books of Ottoman Jewish writers were printed in Western Europe. Although books destined for a Jewish reading public were also printed in Amsterdam, Venice, Florence, Leghorn, Padua or Frankfort, the Ottoman Jews were, in particular thanks to the extremely active printers of Salonika, almost autonomous in this respect. Moreover, these printers even assumed the task of printing books commissioned by Jewish authors living in Eastern Europe.[37] In this city, Bessalel Halevy (d. 1752) founded a dynasty of printers who for 175 years made Salonika the city of books, a sort of Leipzig for Hebrew books for the whole of the East.[38]

The other extreme is the Greek case. For Greeks, prior to the Greek Revolution, books from printing presses in Europe (Venice, Vienna, Trieste, etc.), including books for the Turkish-speaking Orthodox, were absolutely dominant in the book production in terms of figures.[39] The first Modern Greek novel, strangely reminiscent of Montesquieu's *Letters Persanes*, Nicolas Mavrocordato's (1680–1730), *Philotheou Parerga* ('The Leisures of Philotheos') was written in Istanbul in 1718, but it appeared in print only in 1800 in Vienna.[40] Greek printing in the Ottoman capital was scarcely significant prior to the *Tanzimat* Reforms. It had even received a severe blow after the outbreak of the Revolution.[41] The Greeks were then the first among the Ottoman subjects to have their independent state. Their traditional providers beyond the frontiers of the Ottoman Empire, the presses in Western Europe, were thus increasingly replaced by those in the Greek Kingdom.[42] A great deal of what was read by the Greek Orthodox in the Ottoman Empire (including works in *Karamanlı* and 'Istanbul Novels'[43]) was then published in independent Greece. The Bulgarians, whose progress was to become most spectacular after the *Tanzimat* reforms, at the beginning of the 19th century had a few printing presses in Buda and Belgrade, later also in Wallachia (Bucharest and Brăila).[44]

Unlike the Greeks, the Armenians had no homeland to rely upon. For the preservation of the Armenian language and literature, the activities of the members of the Mekhitarist order, founded in 1701 in Istanbul by Mekhitar (1676–1749) from Sivas, played an outstanding rôle.[45] Thanks to their teaching and their publication of translations of European works introduced in Istanbul, the Mekhitarist Fathers of Venice and Vienna, of whom 80% were still natives of Istanbul in the 19th century, trained generations of young intellectuals, including Vartan Pasha and Hovhannes Hisarian, who were to stimulate the literary movement, press, associations and political activity of the Ottoman Armenians, particularly those of the capital.[46] At the same time, the Mekhitarists were staunch defenders of the classical language (*krapar*) which they sought to revive at all costs, even by translating contemporary novels such as *Uncle Tom's Cabin* into that language. For the dynamic Armenian community in the Ottoman Empire, this type of writings therefore became increasingly obsolete.[47] Moreover, the Armenians had many outstanding printers in the Ottoman capital.[48] These printers served diverse communities, Greeks, Bulgarians and in particular the Ottoman Turks.

Religious books for Arab Christians were printed in the pre-*Tanzimat* era mainly in Europe, in Rome or Paris. But there were also other types of literature produced in Paris. For propagandistic reasons, the French had printed a variety of Arabic and Turkish tracts and pamphlets during the Egyptian campaign, Despite their stylistic shortcomings, we can assume that not only the historian Al-Jabartî read them. The same applies to a small brochure, 'The speech of the Ottoman muezzin directed to his own coreligionists', translated by the French dragomans Belletête, Kieffer and Sylvestre de Sacy. Its Turkish version (*Müezzin-i osmanîden kendü dindaşlarına kitab olunan nutkudur*) was reproduced in the chronicle of the Ottoman historian 'Mütercim' Asım.[49] It was distributed in 6000 copies. Napoleon's *Bulletins de la Grande Armée* (1805–1806) were also translated into Turkish by several prominent Oriental scholars.[50] The Turkish Bible, which goes back to the 17th century translation of Ali Bey (i.e. Albertus Bobovius, d. 1675), was first printed in Paris (1819: New Testament and 1827: the whole Bible), revised by Daniel Kieffer (1767–1833). The same applies to the translation of the Bible from *krapar* into Modern Armenian by the Mekhitarist father Hovhannes Zohrabian, which was published in Paris in 1825. Fâris al-Shidyâq's famous novel *Al-sâq 'alâ al-sâq* appeared in Paris in 1855. In the 1860s and 1870s, Turkish residents and political émigrés (Şinasi, Ali Suavi, etc.) were very active in the French capital. They also published a few remarkable works there, such as a Turkish translation of Benjamin Franklin's immensely popular *The Way to Wealth*.[51]

Apart from Paris, Vienna too was to play a significant role in this respect. Many books in Armenian, Greek, Bulgarian and Judaeo-Spanish were printed in the Austrian capital. The famous historian Joseph von Hammer (1774–1856) published works of Turkish poets, among others. His proposition presented to Sultan Mahmud II in 1833 concerning a translation of Marcus Aurelius into Turkish has been preserved in the Ottoman archives. The dragoman and distinguished Oriental scholar Ottocar von Schlechta-Wssehrd (1825–1894) composed a treatise on the 'Law of Nations' (*Hukuk-i milel*), based on sources in German, which was printed in 1263/1847 by the Imperial Press in Vienna. It was later republished—slightly revised—in Istanbul by the press of *Al-Jawâ'ib* and later even translated into Arabic (*vide infra*). Another work by the same author, his *Manuel terminologique français-ottoman* of diplomatic and political terms (1870) enjoyed considerable esteem in the Ottoman Empire.

In London, the British scholar Charles Wells (d. 1917), a contributor to Ali Suavi's *Mukhbir*, published one of the first Turkish books on political economy.[52] London also played an important role in the context of Islamo–Christian controversy in the 19th century. Translations of K. G. Pfander's *Balance of Truth* and his 'Key of the Mysteries' (*Miftâḥ al-asrâr*) into Turkish were printed in London (1861) as well as anti-Christian polemical works in a variety of languages. A new edition of the *Tuḥfat al-Arîb fî al-radd 'alâ ahl al-ṣalîb* (1420) by the Spanish convert known as 'Abdullâh al-Tarjumân al-Mayûrqî was made by the English convert 'Murad Istanli' (presumably Baron Henry Edward John Stanley of Alderley; 1827–1903). Published in London 1290/1873, the book was also available from several *sahhafs* in Istanbul. One of the most interesting 'Istanbul novels' in Greek, 'The Devil in

Turkey; or Scenes in Constantinople' by Stephanos Th. Xenos from Smyrna (1821–1894) also appeared in the British capital.[53]

Finally there are the Missionary publications. In the 17th–18th centuries, the presses of the Propaganda in Rome were instrumental especially in providing Arab Christians with appropriate reading material.[54] In the 19th century Protestant Missions, in the first place those from the United States, took the lead. In the 1820s, Malta had become a centre of book production for the whole Middle East before its presses were transferred to Beirut and other places.[55] The French Jesuits established their *Imprimerie catholique* in 1848. The first Turkish version of *Robinson Crusoe* (1864),[56] which is said to have been translated from Arabic, may well go back to the one published in Malta in 1835.

Missionaries sometimes tended to overestimate the impact of their publications,[57] of which they kept such a meticulous record, but there can be no doubt that many written languages used in the Ottoman Empire, Bulgarian, Albanian and especially Modern Armenian,[58] owe their formation to a considerable extent to the efforts of Protestant missionaries, a fact which is little acknowledged today. The *nahḍa* in the Arab Middle East is unthinkable without the work of the Protestant missionaries, or without the efforts of Catholic institutions in Syria, Lebanon and even Iraq. A key figure of Arab modernism, Fâris al-Shidyâq (1804–1887) appears on the cover page of his *Practical Grammar of the Arabic Language* (2nd edition by the Rev. Henry G. Williams, London 1866) as 'formerly professor of Arabic at the University of Malta' and 'translator of the whole Bible into Arabic'.

Missionary publications addressed a readership among all communities of the Ottoman Empire in principle. Their impact should not be underestimated, even if mainly Christians but hardly any Jews or Muslim Turks were affected. Publications in Judaeo-Spanish, including the journal *El Manadero* ('The Source'), published by the British Mission in 1855–58, seem to have had little success. The American Board in Istanbul published very few Turkish books in Arabic script,[59] whereas the number of Turkish publications in Greek and Armenian script was considerable. To some extent, however, they also influenced Turkish print culture. The missionaries' illustrated papers attracted Turkish publishers and printers who even borrowed clichés from them.

Bookshops

The first bookstores are mentioned by western travellers in the early 19th century. Others may have existed before, but foreign travellers hardly ever managed to discover them. Armenian bookshops are said to have existed in Istanbul already in the 18th century.[60] In the early 19th century the '*Kitabcı* Markar' (1789–1845) in the Mercan Çarşısı enjoyed a particular reputation. A first Greek bookseller located at the Zindankapı, John Khapsoulas, is mentioned in 1816.[61] A few years later two French travellers, Joseph Michaud (1767–1839) and J. J. François Poujoulat (1808–1880), discovered one single, extremely small bookshop in Galata selling books 'belonging to our Western literatures'.[62] Charles White, who has left perhaps the best account of the book trade of that period,[63] is particularly interested in the dealings of the traditional *sahhafs*. He also observed that Armenian booksellers sold exclusively theological works printed in Venice. In 1847 the booktrade in Péra/Beyoğlu was limited, according to a German observer, to two bookstores, one run by a westerner, another by an Armenian. The first one, that of Wick, which had been established only recently, sold exclusively what the writer calls '*nouveautés de Paris*': novels by Eugène Sue (*Les Mystères de Paris*,

Le Juif errant), etc. but—much to the chagrin of this observer—no 'scientific things', (*wissenschaftliche Dinge*) such as a Turkish dictionary or a grammar. The second one, an Armenian named 'Iskender', had scholarly works,[64] but sold them only reluctantly. In particular, he refrained from selling books on religion since he risked more serious sanctions than simple confiscation in that case.[65]

These bookshops hardly give strong evidence of a flourishing booktrade. Their number increased, however, in the last third of the 19th century. The number of bookshops listed in the *Indicateur Ottoman*[66] was 34 in 1882, 49 in 1889 and 63 in 1912.

Catalogues

More significant by far are the first catalogues of Istanbul booksellers. These began to be published only half a century later. In 1869, the brothers Anthony and Nicholas Depasta, graduates of the University of Athens, who had founded their bookshop in Galata in 1858, published their first catalogue which was to appear regularly from then onwards. The first to venture publishing catalogues of Turkish books was the Armenian Arrakel Tozlian (d. 1912), who is known as 'Arakel the Bookseller' (*Kitabci Arakel*) among the Turks.[67] His first catalogue (1301/1884) was immensely successful and particularly appreciated by Oriental scholars in the West.[68] Later on, almost every printer or bookseller in Istanbul published his own catalogue. For Armenian books, the catalogues of the bookseller Bedros Balentz are particularly important.

The catalogues available from the *Al-Jawâ'ib* printing office were destined mainly for a Oriental readership. The *Akhtar* press of the Persian paper with the same name, founded in 1876, was also very active. Its bookstore, initially established in the *Sahhaflar Çarşısı* before it moved to the Ebuussuud Caddesi near the 'Avenue of the Sublime Porte' (*Bâb-ı âli Caddesi*), was a type of mail-order bookshop. Thanks to contacts with booksellers in Syria, Egypt, India and Persia, it was able to sell works published in these countries in the Ottoman capital. For Judaeo-Spanish books the catalogues of Salomon Israel Cherezli, who founded a bookshop in Jerusalem in 1899, are particularly valuable.[69]

Printing offices often functioned the same way as bookshops. Some of them became the meeting place for *hommes de lettres*. For the Ottoman reading public, 'Reading Rooms' (Turkish *kıraathane*) also played an crucial role. Thanks to the books and newspapers on display in the *Kıraathane-i osmanî*, opened in 1273/1857[70] on the Divan Yolu in Istanbul by the Armenian Dikran (?) Serafim Efendi, generations of Turkish writers were initiated to modern literature and were able to form their literary taste.[71]

Reading Material Published Prior to the *Tanzimat* Reforms

At the beginning of the 19th century, literature destined for the non-Muslim readership in the Ottoman Empire was still, to a great extent, a continuation of medieval traditions. Religious topics dominated and also figure prominently among the books owned by the majority of readers.[72] This is confirmed by almost all writers dealing with this subject.[73] This even applies to the 'new', translated literature. There is a type of 'Christian' canon including classical works of edification such as Thomas à Kempis' *Imitation of Christ*, said to have been one of the first books printed by Mekhitar in Pera, or Cardinal Bellarmino's *Doctrina Christiana* (1603), whose Arabic and Armenian versions had already been printed in the 17th century.[74] A penitential book, *Il Penitente istruito a ben confessarsi* by the Jesuit Paolo Segneri was translated into Arabic in the 18th century and was among the best-known books in Syria.[75] Most of these works were later also available in Turkish versions, printed in Greek or Armenian characters. Segneri's *Penitente*, for instance, was published in Armeno–Turkish by the Mekhitarists in Venice (1827).[76] Another extremely popular work, Edward Young (1683–1765)'s *Night Thoughts* were translated from Le Tourneur's French version into Armeno–Turkish by the Armenian dragoman of the Danish Legation in Istanbul, Hovhannes Yeremian.[77]

The translation movement and its fundamental role in the rise of modern literature in the Muslim Middle East, especially for Turkish and Arabic, is well known.[78] What has been observed much less often is the fact that this movement started much earlier among the non-Muslim communities. It is true that the Turkish versions of the *Doctrina Christiana* or the *Imitation of Christ*, had they been printed in Arabic script, would hardly have been very attractive for a Turkish Muslim or Jewish readership, but the intimate contact with the West also led to translations of secular works from western languages, whose number increased continuously. These were in general published in the diaspora. Greeks, in particular, were forerunners in translating European fiction and scholarly literature; they were closely followed by the Armenians. What seems important is the fact that this translation movement also affected the Turkish-speaking subjects of the Empire. If the *communis opinio* sees this movement as having started, in the Turkish case, in the late 1850s, the fact remains that the first literary translations from western languages into Turkish go back far beyond the date of 1859, regarded conventionally, as the starting point of literary translation.[79]

The concept of 'Classical' authors remained alien to the Ottoman Turks for a long time. It was first discussed in Ottoman journals at the end of the 19th century. Despite an undeniable interest in ancient Greek culture, which can be observed in the wake of the *Tanzimat* era, translations of the ancient classics, including philosophers, were never particularly popular among Muslim Turks, Arabs or Jews. An Armenian version of Aristotle's *De Causis* appeared in Istanbul already in 1750. The Mekhitarists translated Classical authors of ancient Greece in a systematic way (educated Greeks read them in their original versions), but the Ottoman Turks and Arabs made only half-hearted attempts. Homer's Iliad, for example, was available in an Armenian version from 1843, whereas no complete Ottoman Turkish version exists, despite several attempts made only a few decades later.[80] Sulaymân al-Bustânî's famous but hardly popular Arabic version, written in Istanbul at the end of the 19th century, has also remained an isolated case.[81]

As a whole, the record of ancient Greek authors translated into Ottoman Turkish in the 19th century is relatively meagre. Moreover, most of the early translations were the work of non-Muslims. The Greek Georges Rhasis translated Arrian's *Anabasis Alexandrou* (Bûlâq 1838)[82] another Greek, Vasilaki Voukas, Lucian's *Peri Parasitou* (printed in 1870).[83] The first biographical sketch of 26 ancient Greek philosophers in Turkish was due to an Armenian, Krikor Kumarian.[84] The Turkish writer Ali Suavi (1839–1878) translated the *Tabula of Cebes*, but seems to have particularly attracted by the fact that it had already been translated into Arabic by Ibn Miskawaih.[85] Turkophone non-Muslims, on the other hand, had the possibility of reading Classical authors, Greek philosophers, etc. in Turkish versions several decades earlier.[86] Just to give a few examples: the so-called *Physiognomica*, attributed to Aristotle, appeared in a *Karamanlı* translation in Istanbul as early as 1819,[87] while Epictetus's *Enchiridion* was available in an Armeno–Turkish version made by the Mekhitarists in 1837.[88]

The first works on Greek philosophers were printed in Arabic in Bûlâq and Rifâʿa al-

Ṭahṭâwî himself was involved in these translations. They were read (and sometimes even repirnted) in Istanbul. Interest in philosophy among the Ottoman Turks—both scholars and others—increased considerably in the 1860s and 1870s of the 19th century. Ahmed Midhat Efendi (1844–1912), who owes his fame especially to his novels, wrote many articles on Greek philosophers, including Diogenes, whose name had become popular thanks to Teodor Kasap's satirical paper *Diyojen* (published also in French and Greek),[89] but the treatment of western philosophy was at that time still a somewhat delicate issue, since even the term *felsefe* was proscribed in conservative religious circles.

A Greek 'philosopher' who became really popular among a Muslim readership was Aesop. He was already familiar to a Greek, Bulgarian and Armenian readership. Many Turkish versions of his fables were published under various, sometimes very flowery titles: *Kissadan hisse* ('From Tale to Moral') by Ahmed Midhat (Istanbul 1287/1870) which also contains fables of French authors; *Edebiyat ve hikâyât-ı garîbe* ('Literature and curious stories') by Hafiz Refi (Istanbul 1291/1874); and *Menakıb-ı hayevân berayı teşhîz-i ezhân* ('The Exploits of Animals for the Sharpening of the Mind') translated by Osman Râsih (1294/1877).[90] The *Terceme-i Yezopos* by one Agop Lutfî from Diyarbekir (1290/1873) was probably translated from Armenian. There are also earlier versions in *Karamanlı* and Armeno-Turkish. Curiously enough, the earliest Turkish version of Aesop's fables appeared in Cyrillc script in 1852.[91]

Among the historians, Herodotus was relatively well known and attracted readers among all communities interested in the ancient history of the Middle East. He was later considered as a major source for the early history of the Turks.[92] The history of ancient Greece was dealt with in a number of Turkish and Arabic works, some of them published relatively early.[93] Oliver Goldsmith's writings on ancient history also seem to have been popular in the Levant.[94] His *Roman History from the Foundation of the City of Rome to the Destruction of the Western Empire* (1769) even exists in an Armeno-Turkish version.[95] There seems to be no Turkish translation in Arabic script. The first comprehensive Roman history in Ottoman Turkish dates from 1887.[96]

Other works which had been known for a long time through translations by non-Muslims eventually also found their way to a Muslim readership. An interesting example is the *History of America* (1777) by the Scottish historian William Robertson.[97] It may be regarded as one of the most successful western historical works in the Levant. As early as the end of the 18th century it was translated into Armenian (from the Italian version) by the Mekhitarist father Minas Kaspariants from Artvin (Trieste 1784–86), and into Greek by George Vendotis (4 vols, Vienna 1792–1794). The first Turkish translation of the same work only appeared in 1858—in Egypt. Independently, another Turkish translation had been produced in Istanbul by a member of the 'Ottoman Academy' (*Encümen-i Daniş*, founded in 1851), which was published posthumously in 1880.[98]

Télémaque and its Readers in the Ottoman Empire

It should also be noted that Fénelon's *Aventures de Télémaque*, whose Turkish version by Yusuf Kâmil Pasha in 1859 marks the starting point of literary translation in Turkey,[99] is less striking as a choice if we consider the fact that it had been immensely popular among all communities in the Levant before.

From A. Ubicini (1818–1884) we learn that *Télémaque* was well known among the Greeks of Péra during his stay in the late 40s of the 19th century, and that it was 'the first French book that they had had in hand'. *Télémaque* was considered there as '*le livre classique par excellence*'. It had therefore been translated into all languages in the Levant. The Russian attaché in Istanbul even showed Ubicini an album with the famous beginning of the novel in 17 or 18 languages, from Turkish to 'Chaldaean'.[100] The first (printed) Greek translation dates from the the 18th century,[101] but the Mekhitarists, too, seem to have been particularly attracted by this work.[102] A version in *krapar* by Emmanuel *vardapet* Ciakciak was published in Venice in 1826; a second, more elegant translation by Edward Hürmüzian (1799–1876) appeared in 1850. The Modern Armenian version by Ambroise Calfa[103] (Paris 1859), was also published by the Mekhitarists.

Incidentally, it appeared in the same year as Yusuf Kâmil Pasha's famous Turkish version. The interest of Greeks (who regarded *Télémaque* as a sort of sequel to the Odyssey) and even Armenians in the work does not surprise us, but its impact among Muslims is striking. At one point, one has the impression that there was almost a competition among Turks, Iranians and Arabs to provide their readers with their own versions of *Télémaque*. Not only were several Turkish versions of that work published in Istanbul. Even a Persian version appeared in the paper *Akhtar*,[104] whereas the printing office of the Arabic paper *Al-Jawâ'ib* offered its readers an Arabic version.[105]

The example of *Télémaque* also shows us that many of the first translated works belong to what was considered as children's or juvenile literature at that time, or literature '*récupérée par la jeunesse*'.[106] Ambroise Calfa's Armenian version of *Télémaque*, for example, was also published in a bilingual edition to be used as a textbook in schools. An interesting case is Henri Merquam's *Promenade en Amérique, ou, Scènes instructives et pittoresques, propres à faire connaître aux enfants les mœurs, les coutumes, les monuments et les beautés naturelles de cette partie du monde* (Paris 1838). It was translated into Arabic[107] and later even into Turkish—from the Arabic.[108] Şemseddin Sami's seminal Turkish version of *Robinson Crusoe* (1886), which inaugurated a new style of translation, was translated from Ambroise Rendu's *Robinson dans son île, ou Abrégé des aventures de Robinson* (first published 1832), a book that was also used in Ottoman schools;[109] the first Turkish *Robinson (Terceme-i hikâye-i Robenson*, 1866, 1869, 1874) is said to have been translated from an Arabic version which may have been that of the missionaries. The classical works of 18th and 19th century juvenile literature by writers such as Arnaud Berquin, Joachim Heinrich Campe[110] and, in particular, Christoph von Schmid (*vide infra*), were eventually widely known and read in the Ottoman Empire.

What They Read (I): A Late 19th Century Ottoman Writer's Initiation into Reading

Many Ottoman writers have left us recollections of their first reading experiences. The case of Fatma Aliye (1864–1936), regarded as the first female Ottoman writer, is an instructive example. Thanks to her admirer Ahmed Midhat Efendi, who wrote a book on her literary career,[111] we are particularly well informed about the development of her reading skills and habits.

One has to say that there is little, if anything, specifically feminine in the canon of works she read. Fatma Aliye, the daughter of the great Ottoman historian Ahmed Cevdet Pasha (1822–1895), is said to have learnt the Koran by heart at the age of five. She was also able to read the popular catechism known as the *Mızraklı İlm-i hâl* (first printed 1842) and the poem on the birth of the prophet Muhammed (*Mevlid*) of Süleyman Çelebi (15th century). At the age of seven she read the popular epic poems of *Battal Gazi* and *Kankardeşi* (an episode from the epic of *Köroğlu*), the 'Fantasies' (*Muhayyelât*) of Aziz Efendi (18th century; a work reminiscent of Pétis de la Croix's *Mille et un Jour*) and the stories of the 'Thousand and One Nights' (*Binbir gece masalları*).

Her Turkish *hoca*, Mustafa Efendi, taught her to read the *Dürr-i Yektâ*, another popular catechism. Having reached the age of 11, she began to study French. This was apparently still rather unusual among Muslim families in the 1870s of the 19th century (the same as painting or playing the piano).[112] Her French teacher was a Christian Arab, Doctor Elias Maṭar.[113] She studied this language with the grammar of Chapsal (which was translated several times into Turkish), the pocket dictionary (*Ceb lûgati fransızcadan türkceye*, Istanbul, 1882) of Ambroise Calfa, the above-mentioned Armenian translator of the *Télémaque*, and the *Miroir des Enfants*. At the same time, Elias Maṭar had her translate passages from the Arabic press.[114] With another, less competent female teacher, she learnt the *Emsile* ('Examples'), an Arabic grammar book, and the *Tuhfe-i Vehbî*, a rhymed Persian dictionary, by heart. At that stage she was already able to read (and understand) Yusuf Kâmil Pasha's version of the *Télémaque* which is written in an extremely elaborate style.

Her first contact with 'modern' Ottoman literature dates from the same period. Ahmed Midhat's 'Amusing Stories' (*Letayif-i Rivayât*), written in a simple style, were most welcome after the cumbersome reading of the *Terceme-i Telemak*. She followed that with his novel 'Hasan the Seafarer' (*Hasan Mellâh*, 1874), which is an imitation of Dumas's *Comte de Monte Cristo*, a novel she had read before but which she had found too terrifiying. Eventually she read all of Ahmed Midhat's writings.

A similar 'canon' appears in the writings of many other Turkish writers. In the memoirs of another female writer Halide Edib [Adıvar; 1884–1964], *Battal Gazi* also figures among the first book she read.[115] The father of Turkish nationalism, Ziya Gökalp (1875–1924), also writes that at the age of seven he had been very fond of the *hikâyes* of Shah Ismail and Âşik Kerem, but that kind of reading was shunned by most of the more westernized Ottoman intellectuals in the 19th century, who were completely uninterested in popular literature and folklore. A friend advised him to read more serious books instead of these love-stories. He therefore began to read poetry, novels and literary works, and eventually scientific and philosophical books as well.[116]

The Literary Taste of the Ottoman Reading Public

As appears from these examples, popular literature lost its attractiveness for more sophisticated readers at one stage. It was then replaced by western-style fiction, but most readers were interested in the first place in translations, which were far more numerous than 'original' works. For some communities, like the Sephardic Jews, 'original' works were almost non-existent.

The dominant position of translations within the literary polysystem of Middle Eastern literature is well known. In the Ottoman Empire, translated novels (mainly from the French) were indeed immensely popular among all communities. Moreover, it can be shown that the canon of translated literature and the favourite authors were essentially the same for Turks, Greeks, Armenians and even Bulgarians and Jews. In this respect, mutual influences were not infrequent (*vide infra*).

French, of course, occupied the first place as a source language of translated novels. English played a rather insignificant role—much to the chagrin of the American missionaries. Even the works of English, Italian or German authors were usually translated from their French versions but, in fact, the situation was more complex. *Karamanlı*, Armeno–Turkish and Judaeo–Spanish writers also translated books (including some by western authors) from their 'national' languages, Greek, Armenian and Hebrew, while Bulgarians (and perhaps also others) occasionally translated from Greek. The choice made by the translators (who had in view their prospective readers) often seems rather surprising to those accustomed to a well-established canon of classical authors. Most of what was translated into Turkish, Armenian, Greek, Judaeo–Spanish and other languages were the works of French novel writers who are forgotten today, but who were extremely popular in their time.[117]

American missionaries led a desperate struggle against the influence of these '... romances whose gilded vice is the sole human interest appreciated by their authors' as one of them remarks on the reading habits of the Armenian community.[118] Turkish books fare little better in the eyes of the same observer: 'Half of the stock in trade is composed of romances of real life, of the class which has made the French novel typical of vulgarity'.[119] Catholic observers had the same objections. An Assumptionist Father in Tokat was appalled to find an Armenian translation of Sue's *Le Juif Errand* in the possession of one of his students in 1905.[120] Another observer mocked the popularity of the French novel-writer Ponson du Terrail and his *Rocambole* among a Greek readership in the Ottoman Empire.[121] French missionaries even started wondering about the usefulness of teaching the French language to their students since '*dès leur sortie de l'école on les voit en grand nombre se jeter sur toutes les malpropretés littéraires et se servir du français que nous leur avons donné pour jouir à leur aise de toutes les productions passionnées de nos romanciers les plus tristement célèbres.*'[122] Another Jesuit Father resumes the taste of the 'Oriental' reading public as follows: '*Ceux qui lisent en Orient veulent des livres divertissants, des livres sinon tout à fait immoraux du moins assez égrillards*' which the Jesuit Fathers were, of course, unable to offer in their colleges.[123]

Unsurprisingly, western Oriental scholars also shunned this production. The editors of the *Journal Asiatique* refused to list translations of French novels in the 'Notices sur les livres imprimés à Constantinople'.[124] Even members of the minorities at times showed deep concern, in particular about the absence of 'serious' authors. 'Prince' Mgrdich Dadian (1844–1911), speaking proudly about the literary progress of his compatriots,[125] in particular the translations from French into Armenian, and the 'quite considerable number of works of the great novelists, Balzac, Dumas, Victor Hugo, George Sand, Eugène Sue, etc.' but also detects 'most regrettably' a vogue for 'a licentious and utterly outdated author, the old Pigault-Lebrun'.[126]

Publishers also occasionally reassured their readers about the innocuousness of their books. In the preface to the Armeno–Turkish version of Jules Verne's *20 000 lieues sous les mers*, translated by Mihran B. Arabajian,[127] we read that 'this charming novel is free from unsuitable love stories, from insolent, terrifying and disgusting pictures of deception, horrible crimes which disturb man's mind and imagination' and that a 'wise father can let his sons and daughters read it without reserve'.[128]

Missionary Literature

The Protestant missionaries had their own canon of translated literature. Among the literary highlights were John Bunyan's (1628–1688) *The Pilgrim's Progress from this world to that which is to come* (1678). This work was perhaps the most translated book after the Bible, as one Turkish translator observes.[129] It seems to have been one of the few works to have appealed to Middle Eastern readers.[130] It was translated into Modern Syriac (Urmiyah 1848; tr. Justin Perkins) and Arabic (begun in 1834) and was also among the first works to appear in Armenian (Izmir, 1843; published first in instalments in the 'Store of useful knowledge'). There are also Turkish versions (*Kristiyan Yolculuğu*) in Armenian (1864) and Greek script (1879). The Bulgarian version by the missionary Albert Long (*Pâteshestvennikât ot toyzi svyet do onzi*) was published in Istanbul in 1866 (the first part also appeared in the journal *Zornitsa* published by the American missionaries).[131]

Another successful book, at least according to the number of translations, was Leigh Richmond's (1772–1827) *The Dairyman's Daughter* (or *The Daughter of Walbridge*).[132] It was translated into nineteen languages, among them Modern Greek (1821), Arabic (Malta, 1834), Modern Armenian (1839) and Modern Syriac (1845), but it does not seem to have enjoyed the same popularity among an Oriental readership as *Pilgrim's Progress*. Muslim Turkish readers remained for a long time unaware of Bunyan's work. A first translation in Arabic script was published only in 1905 in Bulgaria.[133]

Exchanges Between the Different Literatures

Contacts and exchanges between the different literatures took place in different ways and on different levels. As has been said, they were connected closely with the reception of western literature. The press of the Ottoman capital played an important role in the transmission and dissemination, especially of contemporary fiction. Ahmed Midhat's translation of Émile Richebourg's *La Fille Maudite* (*Merdud Kız*; 1300/1883), for instance, was inspired by the success of this novel which had been serialized in Greek and Armenian papers before.[134] Several of his *Letayif-i rivayât* were based on stories that had appeared in the French press.

Differences of script were not an insuperable obstacle. Muslim Turks occasionally learnt the Armenian alphabet and read Turkish books or papers printed in Armenian characters.[135] Advertisements can be found in newspapers where people offer to teach the alphabet to those interested in reading modern literature in Turkish. Due to its simplicity and advantages in practice, the use of the Armenian alphabet was even propagated by some high-ranking Turkish government officials.[136]

The Turkish-speaking Greek Orthodox ('*Karamanlı*') and Armenians read Turkish folk-literature[137] and even novels of contemporary writers like Ahmed Midhat Efendi (1844–1912) in Greek or Armenian characters. Ahmed Midhat seems to have enjoyed particular popularity in the Armenian community; in 1879 his novel 'Filatun Bey and Rakim Efendi' appeared in Armeno-Turkish. Two other novels by him, *Yeniçeriler* ('The Janissaries') and *Şeytan Kayası* ('The Devil's Rock') were published in Karamanlı versions in 1891. The *Karamanlı* version of his *Yeniçeriler* appeared first serialized in Misailidis's *Anatoli*, where numerous novels, mostly translated by the editor himself from Greek or French, were published. Unfortunately, no studies yet exist which elucidate the dependencies or the mode of adaptation of works available in different scripts. Interestingly enough, titles of translated works are mostly identical.

On the other hand, relatively few Armeno-Turkish writers and almost no *Karamanlı* authors published Turkish works in Arabic characters.[138] Whereas certain types of Armeno-Turkish books attracted Muslim Turkish readers, this does not seem to have been the case of writings in *Karamanlı*. Misailidis's picaresque *Tamaşai Dünya* (*vide supra*) seems to have remained largely unnoticed by the Muslim Turkish public. The same applies to Vartan Pasha's *Akabi hikâyesi* whose topic, the tragic love story between an Armenian Orthodox girl and an Armenian Catholic young man, may have had little attraction for a Muslim readership. Vartan Pasha has also left a 'History of Napoleon Bonaparte' (1861–1868) in Arabic script, first published in instalments in the *Ruzname-i Ceride-i Havadis*, which had been preceded by a considerably longer Armeno–Turkish version.[139]

A few Greeks participated in the translations of French popular novels at a relatively early period. Teodor Kasap (1835–1897), who published his famous satirical paper *Diyojen* in French, Turkish and Greek (other papers even in Armeno–Turkish and Bulgarian) is the most famous example. His Turkish version of Dumas's *Monte Cristo* (1871; first serialized in *Diyojen*) has been rightfully regarded as the first 'real' translation of a novel from a western language.[140] Other, less prestigious translators are known only by their Christian names. One 'Michalaki' figures as the translator of Eugène Sue's novel *Mathilde ou Mémoires d'une jeune femme* (1874) and of the volume 'Gourmandise' from his *Sept Péchés capitaux (Şikemperverî—Oburluk*; 1882). A certain 'Vasilaki' translated Pierre Zaccone's *Misérables de Londres* (*Londra Biçaregânı*; 2 vols, 1879) and Jules Lermina's *Fils de Monte-Cristo* (*Lord Hop*; 6 vols, 1878). In the literary journal *Envâr-ı Zekâ* ('The Lights of Intelligence'; published 1883–84) we find a remarkably high number of Greek collaborators, including the prominent *Karamanlı* writer Nikolaki Soullides.

Extensive exchanges and influences can be detected in the domain of drama, where the dominant role of the Ottoman Armenians is well known. There is, for instance, the curious case of *İkinci Arsas* (1282/1865), one of the earliest specimens of Turkish dramatic literature.[141] Its protagonist is a historical figure, the Armenian King Arshag II (French *Arsace*; 351–367) whose destiny inspired a number of prominent Armenian writers in the Ottoman Empire, such as Mgrdich Beshiktashlian (1828–1868), Emmanuel Yesaian (1839–1907), Khoren Galfayan (c.1831–1892) and Thomas Terzian (1840–1909). All of them chose this intriguing ruler as a hero for their dramas. Apart from Armenian plays, certain specimens of Modern Greek drama also seem to have tempted Muslim translators. A Muslim Cretan translated, e.g. the play 'Heracles and the Olympic games, or, Friendship and Love' by G. P. Contes.[142] Two dramas by the Greek physician Alexander Stamatiades (1838–1891), 'Osman the Victorious' (*Osman ho nikêtês*) and 'Chios enslaved' (*Chios doulê*), the latter becoming one of the most successful plays staged in Istanbul, were translated into Turkish under the titles *Osman Gazi*[143] and *Hatâ-i nisvân yahud Sakız Esirleri*,[144] respectively.

On the whole, however, one can say that the modern literature of the minorities remained to a large extent *terra incognita* for Ottoman men of letters. The Ottoman version of one of the masterpieces of early Modern Greek literature, Vincenzo Cornaro's *Erotokritos* (17th century), published in 1873, seems to have remained largely unknown, perhaps because the translators had not even furnished the author's name.[145] The same is true as far as Modern Armenian literature is concerned. We can conclude this from the reactions of several prominent writers (Abdullah Cevdet, Şahabeddin Süleyman, Süleyman Nazif) who wrote eulogies (*takriz*) for an anthology of Armenian short stories in Turkish—the first collection of its kind—which was published as late as 1913. To them this publication appeared almost as a revelation.[146]

Non-Muslim communities sometimes showed the same lack of interest as far as Ottoman Turkish literature was concerned. There seems to have been hardly any interest in Turkish language and literature among Greeks, if we are to believe the complaints of the Ottoman scholars in the community such as Alexander Constantinides, who published a highly praised Turkish anthology.[147] Ahmed Midhat Efendi even accused them once, somewhat exaggeratedly, of regarding the study of any other language than Greek as 'shameful'.[148] An exceptional case was the learned physician Michael Tsakyroglou from Izmir (1854–1920), who is known for his study on the Yürüks.[149] He was interested in Persian and Ottoman poetry and published articles on the subject in the Greek press of Smyrna. He also published a selection of the poems of Bâki (1526–1600) in Greek translation.[150]

The situation is different as far as the Armenians are concerned. They were considered by many Turks as being closest to them.[151] In fact, almost all of them were either bilingual or, in some cases, monolingual speakers of Turkish. Many of the educated may not even have needed Armenian translations to read the works of Turkish writers. A great number of teachers, lawyers, doctors and others composed works in Turkish themselves. Literary translations became more widespread after the Young Turk Revolution (1908). Diran Kélékian (1862–1915), professor at the prestigious School of Administration (*Mekteb-i Mülkiyye*), who had an excellent knowledge of the Ottoman Turkish language,[152] and himself wrote several works in Turkish, observed in his translation of Krikor Zohrab's collection of stories 'Life as it is', published in 1913,[153] that Turkish authors were now being translated increasingly into Armenian. This is also confirmed by Armenian schoolbooks from that period, which contain extracts of the works of numerous Turkish authors. A similar interest seems to have started among the Ottoman Jews, who counted some fervent partisans of Turkification already at the end of the 19th century, in particular the Turkish poets Isaac Ferera (1877–1933) and Avram Naon ('İbrahim Nom', 1878–1947).

Educated Sephardic Jews were interested mainly in French literature. Very little is known about translations from Turkish.[154] Judaeo-Spanish was read by the lower classes. This is confirmed by Elia Carmona (1870–1931), a very prolific translator, who writes: 'Having realized that those who read Spanish (i.e. Judaeo-Spanish) are those who know neither Turkish nor French, I started writing in a popular language understood even by children and old people.'[155]

Exchanges: From Turkish to Arabic

This very conspicuous lack of interest in the literature of the ruling element was not particular to Greeks and other non-Muslim communities. Literary translations from Turkish into Arabic are also extremely scarce. There are translations of historical and scholarly works, grammars, etc. from Turkish into Arabic in the 19th century but almost nothing was translated from the works of contemporary Ottoman writers.

The Arabic translation of the 'Symbols of Wisdom' (*Rümuzü l-hikem*, 1870), a much admired but somewhat old fashioned work by Abdurrahman Sami Pasha (1772–1878),[156] is one such exceptional case. Significantly enough, it was published in a bilingual edition in Tripoli in 1894. However, it cannot be said that Arab writers were unaware of the literary activities of the Turks. The fame of Yusuf Kâmil Pasha's Turkish version of Fénelon's *Télémaque*, for example, also reached Rifâʿa al-Ṭahṭâwî who had translated the same work in his Sudanese exile.[157] In Jurjî Zaydân's collection of 'Biographies of celebrities of the East in the 19th century' we find an entry on Namık Kemal (1840–1888), the great 'National Poet' (*Vatan şairi*), but it is only a summary translation of an article by a close friend of this writer and poet, the printer and publisher Ebuzzıya Tevfik (1848–1913).[158] Although some of Ahmed Midhat Efendi's works were even translated into Tatar, and his polemical writings, notably his controversy with the American missionary Henry Otis Dwight (1883), were much appreciated by the Turks of the Russian Empire, he seems to have had no impact on the Arabic-speaking world.

This needs an explanation. Was it due to a feeling of independence or even superiority? The influence of missionaries? Cultural or linguistic differences? Was Ottoman Turkish untranslatable into Arabic, as Ziya Pasha affirmed in his seminal treatise on "Poetry and Prose" (*Şiir ve İnşâ*)?[159] Or were there enough Arab readers familiar with Ottoman Turkish? An answer to this question cannot be given here. Strangely enough, Fâris al-Shidyâq, who for some 20 years published the paper *Al-Jawâ'ib* in the Ottoman capital, does not seem to have been interested in Turkish literature.[160] However, it was the *Al-Jawâ'ib* press which undertook the printing of the first Turkish novel, Şemseddin Sami's 'Love of Talât and Fitnat' (*Taaşşuk-i Tal'at ve Fitnat*, 1872). It also printed a Turkish version of Robertson's *History of America* and the Turkish translation of Khayr al-Dîn Pasha's *Muqaddima* to his *Aqwam al-masâlik fî ma'rifat al-mamâlik*.[161] The printing office also had Turkish books on offer, including a somewhat enigmatic Turkish drama, *Esther*, a book with naive woodcuts, which does not, however, seem to have been translated from Racine's famous tragedy.[162]

Curiously enough, the majority of the rather small number of Arab Turkish scholars were Christians. Khalîl Sarkîs (1842–1915), the editor of the *Ḥadîqat al-Akhbâr*, translated Abdullatif Subhî's *Tekmiletü l-İber*, a sort of continuation of Ibn Khaldûn's *Kitâb al-ʿibar*.[163] Louis Sabundji ('Yakub Sabuncuzâde Luvis Beri Efendi', 1838–1931) was a well-known figure thanks to his 'Illustrated Tour around the World' which appeared in a bilingual (Turkish–Arabic) edition.[164] Nawfal Efendi Niʿmatullâh Nawfal (1812–1887),[165] first secretary of the Arabian customs (*bâshkâtib gamârik ʿArabistân*) translated Ottocar von Schlechta-Wssehrd's *Hukuk-i Milel* into Arabic (under the title *Ḥuqûq al-umam*, Beyrut 1873), and another work on the beliefs of the Circassians, whose original is unknown (*Aṣl muʿtaqadât al-umma al-jirkisiyya*, Beirut n.d.). He also used Turkish sources for his (unpublished) chronicle—a rare case at that time.

Among the Muslim Arabs who wrote works in Turkish, the divisional general (*ferîk*) Ṣâdiq al-Mu'ayyad from the famous al-ʿAẓm family of Damascus (therefore known as 'Azımzâde' among the Turks)[166] deserves particular mention. He was a relatively active writer and has left a number of works in Turkish: the stories of 'Little Henry' (*Küçük Hanri*, Istanbul, 1880; 1890) and *Fernando* (1883) were both translated from the French. His abridged translation of al-Wâqidî's 'History of the Conquest of Syria' (*Târih-i Fütuhü ş-Şâm*, Istanbul 1302/1884–5), appreciated in particular for its military interest, was first published in Ahmed Midhat's *Tercüman-ı Hakikat*. His 'Voyage to Abyssinia' (*Habeş Seyahatnâmesi*) was published in Turkish (1904) and later translated into Arabic.[167]

Exchanges II: From Arabic to Turkish

The interest of the Ottoman Turks in the literary activity of modern Arab writers seems to have been more widespread. Classical authors (Al-Ṭabarî, Ibn Khaldûn, etc.) continued to be translated into Turkish in the 19th century. Educated Ottoman Turks were able to read Arabic. Scholars trained in the *medrese*, such as the historian Cevdet Pasha, even wrote works in Arabic themselves. We also know that Ottoman readers familiar with the 'three languages' (*elsine-i selâse*: Arabic – Persian – Turkish) but ignorant of western languages read books in Arabic which were translated from western languages, especially those printed in Egypt by the Bûlâq press.[168]

Examples of contemporary Arab writers translated into Turkish are less frequent. It should be noted, however, that Rifâ'a al-Ṭahṭâwî, who was known by the Ottoman Turks as 'el-Bedevî', was a well-known figure among them. He figures among the corresponding members of the Ottoman Academy (*Encümen-i Dâniş*), founded in 1851.[169] His travelogue *Takhlîṣ al-ibrîz ilâ talkhîṣ Bârîz* (1834) was translated into Turkish in Egypt as early as 1839 and seems to have been popular with the Ottoman reading public. In Şemseddin Sami's famous encyclopaedia *Kamusü l-Aʿlâm* (6 vols, 1889–1898), we also find an entry on Fâris al-Shidyâq who played such a significant part in the intellectual life of the Ottoman capital for several decades thanks to his paper *Al-Jawâ'ib*. His Arabic grammar textbooks were translated into Turkish but—perhaps understandably—not *Al-Sâq ʿalâ al-sâq* (the Paris edition was, however, on offer in *Al-Jawâ'ib*'s catalogue).

In the early 20th century the writings of Jurjî Zaydân (1861–1914) were influential among the Ottoman Turks, in particular his concept of an 'Islamic civilization'. The popularity of this Arab Christian writer continued even into the early Republican era. Various writings of his appeared in the journal *Mâlumat* during Abdülhamid II's reign. The Turkish translation of his 'History of Islamic Civilization' (*Ta'rîkh al-tamaddun al-islâmî*) by Zeki Meghamiz, another prominent Ottoman writer of the period,[170] was published in Istanbul after the Second Constitution (1912–1914). His historical novel on Hârûn al-Rashîd and the fall of the Barmecids, *Al-ʿAbbâsa ukht al-Rashîd* (Cairo 1906) was translated by Hasan Bedreddin (Istanbul, 1339–1342/1923).[171]

What They Read II: The Background of an Ottoman Scholar—Süleyman Pasha's *Târih-i âlem*

The following discussion is meant to show what kind of books a cultivated Ottoman writer of the period may be supposed to have read. The unfinished 'World History' (*Târih-i âlem*, first published 1876) by Süleyman Pasha (d. 1892), the unsuccessful general during the Turco-Russian war of 1877, is a typical example, as it shows the complexity of the situation.

This 'History' is preceded by a quite extensive bibliography of works used for its compilation. The author lists among its sources the works of Arab historians (Ibn al-Athîr, Ibn Khaldûn, Abû al-Fidâ', Masʿûdî's *Murûj al-dhahab*), 17th-century Ottoman historians (Müneccimbaşı, Kâtib Çelebi), Abulghazi's *Şecere-i türkî*, originally written in Eastern Turkish (Chaghatai), 19th-century Ottoman historians (Patinakizade Mehmed Atif's *Hulâsatü tevarih*), European authors such as Bouillet and his *Dictionnaire universel d'histoire et de géographie*, the universal histories of Victor Duruy and D. Lévi Alvarès, various volumes from the *Univers pittoresque*,[172] de Guignes' *Histoire des Huns*, Maspéro's *Histoire ancienne des peuples de l'Orient* and, interestingly enough, even the *Armenian History* of Michael Chamchian ('Mikail Vartabet'; 1738–1823).[173]

There are also works in Turkish translated from or based on works in western languages such as Ahmed Hilmî's *Târih-i umumî*,[174] Alexander Constantinidi's 'History of Ancient Greece', Abdullah Bey's 'Geology' or Bûlâq editions such as the 'History of Alexander the Great' (*İskender Târihi*) and the *Bidâyat al-qudamâ' wa hidâyat al-ḥukamâ'* (Bûlâq 1254/1838; reprinted 1282/1865), an Arabic work on ancient history, compiled from an unknown western source.

From this impressive list of sources we can conclude that the author was able to read French, Arabic and possibly even Armenian, but that he had a visible preference for works in Ottoman Turkish. This forms a certain contrast to writers such as Ahmed

Midhat Efendi, whose orientation was directed almost exclusively to literature in western languages (i.e. French).

What They Read III: 'Popular' Literature

The works quoted above were, of course, accessible only to educated readers familiar with several languages, including western ones. The following list of Armeno-Turkish books on sale (prices varying between 11/2 and 20 *gurush*) may provide an idea of what was really 'popular' reading material. It was stocked by the Armenian printer Hovsep Kavafian in the Çakmakçılar Yokuşu in 1889.[175]

1. *Alexianos fakırın hikyayesi.*
2. *Aşık Kerem* [ile Asli hanım hikâyesi], 1875.
3. *Aşık Garib* [türküler ile beraber], 1860.
4. *Aşık Tahir ile Zöhre* [hikâyesi], 1875.
5. *Aşık Kurbanı.*
6. [Bidari.] *İngilterra düşessalarından Kenovape nam afife kadının hekyayei garibesi*, 1886.
7. *Yemek tertibi.*
8. [Christoph von Schmid] *Yenoveva hikyayesi*, 1855, 1868, 1891.
9. [Ponsiyanos padişah ve] *Yedi alimler*, 1864.
10. *Zeycan* [ile] *Esman* [hikyayesi türküler ile beraber], 1870.
11. *Taiyar zade* [hikâyesi], 1872, 1874.
12. [Vartan Pasha] *Telegraf resalesi*, 1857.
13. [Kurban Osep] *İki kapu yoldaşlar yahud hakkı adaletin zahiri* (3 vols), 1885; 1890.
14. *Leyla ile Mecnun* [1872].
15. [Mustafa Behcet] *Hezar esrar.*
16. *Melikşah* [ile Gülli Hanım] *hikyayesi*, 1876.
17. *Nasretdin* Hoca[nın tuhaf latifeleri], 1853; 1872; 1875.
18. *Nisa tayifesi* [nin mahrem-i esrar], 1876.
19. *Şah İsmail* [ile Gülizar Hanım], 1875.
20. *Şirin ile Ferhad* [hikyayesi türküler ile], 1881.
21. [Tilkian] *Çoban kızları.*
22. [Armenag Hayguni] *Delikanlılar girdabı* [yani emraz-ı şehviyye], 1863.
23. [Vichen Tilkian] *Dürbünü aşk* [ve mahbubei milel], 4 vols, 1872.
24. *Rakkam cedveli.*
25. *Köroğlu* [hikâyesi türküler ile beraber], 1872, 1875.

This list includes different categories. The most important is that of the *hikâyes* from the Muslim tradition: the love-stories of Kerem and Aslı, Aşık Garib, Tahir and Zühre, Leyla and Mecnun; Melikşah and Gülli Hanım, Tayyarzade, Shah İsmail and Gülizar Hanım, Asüman and Zeycan,[176] Shirin and Ferhad, the epic of Köroğlu and the anecdotes of Nasreddin Hoca. Relatively few of them were also familiar to an Arab readership, such as the story of *Layla and Majnun*, or the *Thousand and One Nights*, which do not figure on this list but were also well known to Turkophones of all creeds. Nasreddin Hoca was the Juḥâ of the Arabs and the Sephardic Jews.[177]

The second category are popular works of early Christian tradition: 'The Story of Saint Alexis', or the 'History of the Emperor Pontianus and the Seven Sages' which had already been published in Armenian in Istanbul several times in the 18th century.[178]

The third category is modern western popular literature: the 'Story of Geneviève' (*vide infra*).

The fourth category is represented by translations of the writings of contemporary Armenian authors. Their titles leave little doubt about their content: 'The Keeper of Women's Secrets' (no. 18) by an unknown author; 'The Young Men's Whirlpool i.e. Venereal Diseases' (no. 22),[179] by Armenag Hayguni (1835–1866), a controversial author.[180] 'The Telescope of Love or Every Nation's Darlings' by Vichen Tilkian is a kind of Ottoman *Decamerone*. It is divided into 31 days, replete with entertaining stories on Armenian, Greek, Circassian, 'Frankish' (*alafranga*), Ottoman and other belles. This work was also published (anonymously) in Arabic script (*Âşık ile mâşuk dürbini ve her milletin güzeli*, 5 vols, 1289/1872), like Tilkian's 'The Shepherdesses' (*Çoban kızları*; 1294/1877). Kurban Osep (Hovsep Kurbanian, 1847–1903), Sultan Abdülaziz's famous ventriloquist, was the author of 'Two Fellow-servants or the Manifestation of Justice' (no. 13), a hitherto little-known novel on the life of the Istanbul Armenians.

The last category are non-fictional books of practical use: 'The Thousand Secrets' (no. 15), a sort of compendium of popular medicine written originally by the *hekimbaşı* Mustafa Behcet (1774–1833), a cookbook (no. 7), a logarithm table (no. 24) and Vartan Pasha's treatise on the telegraph.

Many of these books also exist in *Karamanlı* versions. After the Young Turk Revolution, Gerasimos Alexandratos, a Greek bookseller at the *Yüksek Kaldırım* in Istanbul, had the following books on sale.[181]

1. *Alexios.*
2. *Avraam.*
3. *Şah İsmail.*
4. *Aşık Kirem.*
5. *Kioroğlu.*
6. *Yenovefa.*
7. *Nasdradin Xotzas.*
8. *Aşık Garib.*
9. *Aşık Ömer.*
10. *Ünlü Kioroğlu.*[182]

The 'Sacrifice of Abraham' (no. 2), which goes back to a Greek work from the end of the 17th century,[183] also exists in Armeno-Turkish versions. A special case is no. 9, the divan of Âşık Ömer, who lived during the second half of the 17th century. It shows that occasionally even Turkish poets' works enjoyed popularity among Turkophone non-Muslims.[184] The story of the popular hero Köroğlu in *Karamanlı (Hikiaye-i Kioroğlu*, first published Istanbul 1872) was presumably transcribed from the Armenian (Armeno-Turkish?) version.[185]

As far as the anecdotes of Nasreddin Hoca are concerned, their popularity among non-Muslims is well known. First references by non-Muslims go back to the 18th century. Demetrius Cantemir (1673–1723) already refers to him as the 'Greek Aesop' in his 'History of the Ottoman Empire', and eight versified anecdotes by the Phanariot writer Dapontes (1713–1784) are known (contained in his *Geographikê Historia*).[186] Their attractiveness for a Muslim-Turkish readership is demonstrated by the fact that they were printed several times at the press in Bûlâq (1838, 1841), which had mainly commercial aims as far as Turkish books were concerned.

The paths of transmission and the dissemination of the first printed editions are complex but typical in the Ottoman context. Curiously enough, it was a French version, the *Trente-trois plaisanteries de Khoja Nasr-ed Din, traduites du turc en français*, published in Smyrna in 1847, which seem to have been the source of several works in Greek and other languages published in the Ottoman Empire. Moreover, it was a sort of sanitized version since the author, Nassif Mallouf, had suppressed the obscene anecdotes—which earned him the praise of western Oriental scholars: '*Ce savant orientaliste a fait … preuve de bon goût en écartant de sa traduction tout ce qui, dans le texte original, était de nature à blesser la juste susceptibilité des lecteurs*'.[187]

A Successful Writer in Smyrna: Nassif Mallouf

The Melchite Nassif Mallouf (Nâṣîf Maʿlûf; 1823–1865),[188] a native of Zabbûgha (Lebanon), was what may be called in the Ottoman context a 'successful author'. He enjoyed a high reputation during his lifetime and Jurjî Zaydân counts him among the eminent writers of the 19th century.[189] He was a teacher of Oriental languages at the College of the Lazarists in Smyrna, where he died at a relatively early age.

His mostly didactic writings do not have great literary merit, but for specific reasons they attracted a readership from the most diverse communities. Since a knowledge of the written language of the ruling class, Ottoman Turkish, was not, as has been seen, widespread among non-Muslims, works written in French were attractive to them.

Not only were Mallouf's multilingual dictionaries and conversation guides, sold at relatively low prices, very popular (some of them were later reprinted in Paris), he provided an Ottoman readership with one of the first specimens of western juvenile literature, a Turkish version of Arnaud Berquin's *Conversations, historiettes et contes*.[190] He also left an *Abrégé de géographie* (Smyrna 1851) and a *Précis de l'Histoire ottomane depuis la fondation de l'Empire* (Smyrna 1852), which was translated into Bulgarian by a prominent writer and journalist, P. R. Slaveikov (1827–1895) for use in Bulgarian schools.[191] There is also an Armeno–Turkish version of this work (*Otuzbir sultanın muxtasar tevarixi*, tr. by P. Teghtabanian), published in Istanbul in 1859.[192]

The example of Nassif Mallouf shows that not only Beirut but also Smyrna were cultural centres of the first rank. As has been seen, the French press in the Ottoman Empire had started in Smyrna. The missionaries had early on established very active printing presses there, but it was also the home of several outstanding, extremely prolific Greek and Armenian writers. Much of what was read by Greeks and Armenians in the 19th century, in particular the translations of major works of modern European fiction, stemmed from writers who lived in Smyrna.

From the 1840s onwards John Isidorides-Skylisses (1819–1890), a Greek journalist and writer, translated dozens of French novels by the most distinguished authors: Lamartine, Chateaubriand (*Atala*), Victor Hugo (*Les Misérables*), Eugène Sue (*Les Mystères de Paris*), Alexander Dumas and others. Strangely enough this writer, well known even to European scholars during his lifetime,[193] is absent from most histories of Modern Greek literature. His translations have become illegible since he composed them in archaic Greek, according to the taste of his Ottoman Greek readership.

The Armenians, too, had several outstanding writers in Smyrna.[194] Matteos Mamourian (1830–1901), perhaps the most prolific of them, left 58 volumes mainly of translations, including those of *Zadig, Micromégas, Le Barbier de Séville, Werther, Les Mystères de Paris, Les Trois Mousquetaires* and *Le Tour du monde en quatre-vingts jours*. His contemporary, Krikor Chilingirian (1839–1926), translated 27 romantic novels, including *Manon Lescaut, Raphaël, Les Confessions d'un enfant du siècle* and Sue's *Mathilde*. In Armeno-Turkish he published Chateaubriand's *Le Dernier Abencérage* (*Son Abenseracın sergüzeşti*, 1860) and Victor Hugo's *Les Misérables* (*Mağdurin*, 1863). He even sent a copy of his Armenian version of *Les Misérables* to Victor Hugo. The famous French novelist was impressed, even though he did not know the language. An equally very active Armenian printer and translator from Smyrna, Dikran H. Dedeyan (1832–1868), provided an Armenian readership with an Armenian version of Dumas's *Comte de Monte-Cristo*, among other works.

Successful Books: a Few Examples

In what follows a few examples of highly successful works shall be given, i.e. works that were translated into several different languages used by the linguistic communities of the Ottoman Empire. The modern reader may be surprised to find a number of works which are totally forgotten today; however, we have to keep in mind that in their time they were bestsellers.

The Vissicitudes of a Pseudo-autobiography: The *Manuscrit venu de Ste Hélène*

One of the earliest and most intriguing examples is a pseudo-autobiography of Napoleon Bonaparte. It was published under the title *Manuscrit venu de Ste Hélène, d'une manière inconnue* in 1817 in London. Its author was the Swiss agronomist Frédéric Lullin de Châteauvieux (1772–1842) who had written it during an inspired moment in his leisure time. He boldly sent it to London where this 'Manuscript transmitted from St. Helena in an unknown way' was immediately published. The book immediately had a tremendous success. It managed to deceive readers all over the world. Statesmen such as Wellington and Metternich believed initially in its authenticity. Napoleon protested in vain against this deception from his exile in St Helena.

Since Napoleon was a popular figure among all communities of the Ottoman Empire,[195] among Muslims due notably to the Egyptian campaign, the success of this work in the Levant need not surprise us. The first to act were the Greeks. A Greek version had been already published in 1818, under the title *Cheirographon ek tês Hagias Helenês*, translated with notes by N. Skouphos.[196] From the Greek, it was translated into Roumanian in 1828 (a printed version appeared in Bucharest in 1846).

The first Turkish translation was published in Bûlâq in 1247/1831 under the title "The summary translation of a treatise in French which has arrived from the African island of St. Helena. It contains the story of Bonaparta (sic) who has been in exile there. It was composed by Bonaparta himself and has arrived here by some means".[197]

The interest in this work is truly striking. It continued to be translated and reprinted even long after the identification of its true author (a fact which seems to have remained unnoticed by the Turkish public). A second, more 'modern' translation, also published in Egypt, dates from 1260/1844. Later, the first translation was reprinted in Istanbul (1277/1860). The *Tezkire-i Bonaparte*, as it was known to the Ottomans (a *Karamanlı* version published in 1864 bears the same title)[198] was used by the historian Ahmed Cevdet Pasha for his chronicle. It was reprinted in Istanbul for the last time in 1911.

A Modern Novel: Alexandre Dumas' *Monte-Cristo* and its Reception

The reception of Alexander Dumas' famous novel *Monte-Cristo* (first published 1845–1846) by an Ottoman readership also goes back to an early period. Ubicini, who had stayed in Turkey in the late 1840s, observed that '*Les [trois] Mousquetaires et le Comte de Monte-Cristo faisaient fureur de mon temps à Péra; deux éditions en grec moderne, publiées par livraisons, furent épuisées en moins de trois mois.*'[199] This is confirmed by other sources. A Greek version seems to have already appeared in the first Greek paper published in the Ottoman capital, 'The Telegraph of the Bosphorus'.[200] A printed version by I. Patroklos, director of a Greek school in Péra/Beyoğlu, presumably the one seen by Ubicini, dates from 1845–1846.[201] It was published by Henri Cayol (1805–1865), a pioneer of printing in Istanbul.

The same impact can be detected in other communities. *Un Çiko Montekristo* ('A little Monte Cristo'), an imitation of Dumas's *Monte-Cristo* by Joseph Israel Herrera, seems to have been one of the first novels published in Judaeo–Spanish (Salonika 1850).[202] Dedeyan's Armenian version, published in Smyrna 1866–1868, was reprinted several times, but it was the Turkish translation by Teodor Kasap (Dumas's private secretary for some time) which became without doubt the most famous version. It appeared first in the satirical paper *Diyojen* in 1871.[203] Incidentally, an Arabic version by Bishâra Shadîd appeared in the same year in Cairo. A *Karamanlı* version in 6 volumes dates from 1882.[204]

The concept of a 'novelist' still seems to have been unfamiliar to authors of the Turkish and *Karamanlı* translations; in both of them, Alexandre Dumas was introduced as 'one of the famous French poets' (*Fransa meşahir-i şuarasından*).

Capricious Choices: Silvio Pellico's *Le mie prigioni*

An interesting case is the reception of *Le mie prigioni* by the Italian writer Silvio Pellico (1788–1854) among the Ottoman readership. The author of this work had been arrested by the Austrian authorities in 1820 and imprisoned for two years at Venice. He was then condemned to death on a charge of Carbonarism but had his sentence commuted to 15 years' imprisonment in the dreadful jail on the Spielberg near Brünn/Brno in Moravia. (He was liberated in 1830). He published the account of his imprisonment under the title 'My Prisons' in 1833. Although the author was a fervent Italian patriot, the message his book conveys is one of patient suffering without rancor for the narrator's Austrian captors.

This novel enjoyed immense popularity in the 19th century. Artin Pasha Dadian (1830–1901) is said to have translated it into Armenian as early as 1851.[205] In 1862 another Armenian version by Garabed S. Ütüdjian appeared (*Bantk' im*, 2nd edition, Istanbul 1869). The Bulgarians were also attracted by this novel. The Bulgarian version (*Tâmnitsite mi*) by Dragan Tsankov (1859–1911), a journalist and Ottoman government official who had taught Ahmed Midhat Efendi French, was published in Istanbul in 1874. In the same year there also appeared a Turkish translation (from the French)[206] by the young writer Recaîzade Mahmud Ekrem (1847–1914), which had been previously published in instalments in the paper *Terakki*.

This Turkish translation (*Meprizon Tercemesi*, Istanbul 1291) was subjected to harsh criticism by Namık Kemal. It had been a strange choice indeed. Christian readers could derive some consolation from it. The Bulgarian version, for instance, was much read by the Bulgarian Revolutionaries in 1876, but the topic and the tenor of this work meant little to a Muslim readership. In fact, the choice had been fortuitous. Recaîzade Mahmud, keen to participate in the translation activity, had asked his teacher for a convenient work to translate, whereupon he had suggested Pellico's *Mes Prisons*. Unsurprisingly, the translation remained unfinished.

Western Popular Literature: Christoph von Schmid's *Genoveva*

The edifying stories of the German writer Canon Christoph von Schmid (1768–1854) were also known among all communities in the Levant; in particular the moving 'Story of Geneviève' (*Genovefa*; first published 1810), an outstanding example of feminine virtue and chastity, attracted numerous translators. Unsurprisingly, the Mekhitarist Fathers of Venice started translating Schmid's works into Armenian already in the 1840s. A rhymed Armenian version of *Geneviève* (*vide supra*) was translated into Armeno-Turkish by Mihran Arabajian (d. 1898),[207] whereas a second one (*Yenoveva hikyayesi* 1855, 1891) seems to stem from a Greek original. This Greek version, listed in the catalogue of the Brothers Depasta, was translated from the French (2nd edn, 1868). A *Karamanlı* translation by Misailidis goes back to the early 1850s. The Bulgarians were also particularly fond of von Schmid's stories.[208] The 'Story of Geneviève' appeared once more in Istanbul in that language (*Istoriyata na Genoveva*, translated by S. Bobtchev (Istanbul 1872). It was followed one year later by a Judaeo-Spanish version.[209] A translation was already available to a Turkish readership in 1868 (*Terceme-i Hikâye-i Jönevyef*, 1285).[210] A second translation by one Midhat Ibnül Ahmed from Rethymnno (*Jenovefa*) appeared in 1311/1893. Christoph von Schmid's 'Story of Genevieve' was also known to the Arab reading public. It does not surprise us that the Arabic *Riwâyat Jinifyâf*, translated from the French, was also on offer in the catalogue of *Al-Jawâ'ib*.

Christoph von Schmid's works were disseminated largely through translations among Arabs and Turks. One hundred stories were published in Arabic in Beirut (*Kitâb mi'at ḥikâya qaṣîra li-ifâdat al-ṭalaba al-aṣâghir*, translated by M. Masâbkî, 5th edn, Beirut 1888). Perhaps the most impressive edition, containing 190 stories, was published in Turkish in a sumptuous volume under the title, 'The German Realm of Examples' (*İberistân-ı almanî*, translated by Macid Pasha Keçicizade, Istanbul 1306/1889).

'Victor de Féréal': *Les Mystères de l'Inquisition*

This novel, by an otherwise almost unknown author, Madame de Suberwick (who first published it under a pseudonym in 1844) was one of the most successful books of the 19th century.[211] Some hundred editions are known. It is the love-story of Estevan de Varga and his fiancée Dolores, daughter of the governor of Sevilla during the reign of Charles V. Complications ensue because the Grand Inquisitor of Sevilla, Pedro Arbués, has also fallen in love with her. After many tribulations and persecutions she is eventually liberated. The novel displays a vast panorama of the Inquisition at the period. For obvious reasons it was of considerable interest for readers in the Ottoman Empire, Orthodox, Muslims and Jews, as an example of Catholic fanaticism and oppression, in a period where religious controversy was rife.

In Istanbul the first translation appeared in Armenian[212] by the journalist and editor of the influential paper *Masis*, Garabed Ütüjian (1823–1904), who was also one of the most active translators in the community. It had been preceded by several editions published in Tiflis, which were translations from the Russian version. It was followed by a Greek version (*Ta apokrypha tês Hieras Exetaseôs*, 1874), translated by the well-known journalist Demetrios Nicolaïdes (1843–?). A Bulgarian version, translated from the Greek by Nikola Mikhailovski (1818–1892), Censor of Bulgarian Books and Inspector of Bulgarian schools who had studied in Athens, appeared one year later (*Taynite na inkvizitsiyata*, 1875). Then came the Turkish version by Hüseyin Nazım (1854–1927), a poet and playwright, who was by then minister of police (*Enkizisyon Esrarı*, 1296/1879). As the translator explains himself in the afterword, it was done within two weeks, for the most part in the street-car.[213] Eventually the indefatigable translator David Fresco (1850–1933) even published a Judaeo–Spanish version (*Los misteryos de la enkizisyon*, 1889). The book's success story in the Ottoman Empire does not end here; a new, illustrated Turkish translation was published after the Second Constitution.[214]

The Literary Taste of the Levantine Reading Public and a Local French Novel: Jacques Loria, *Les Mystères de Péra*

The last example I would like to present in this contribution is a novel published in French in the Ottoman capital in 1897, *Les Mystères de Péra*.[215] It represents a special case in several respects since it is, first, an original work and secondly, it seems to be the only novel of this size (932 pages) ever published in French in the Ottoman Empire.

The success of this sensational novel, published in instalments of 16 pages, must have been extraordinary. According to a contemporary observer it was the major topic of discussion for months, not only in families and other groups but also in theatres, boats and even churches. Greeks and Italians both claimed that this talented but hitherto unknown author undoubtedly came from their own community.[216]

The title is, of course, reminiscent of Eugènes Sue's seminal *Mystères de Paris* (1842), one of the first serialized novels. In France it soon led to imitations such as the *Mystères de Londres* (1844) by Paul Féval (1817–1887) which like the 'Mysteries of Paris' also exist in Ottoman Turkish versions. The Ottoman Greeks produced several novels in the same vein, such as 'The Mysteries of Smyrna' (*Apokrypha ês Smyrnês kai ta taxidia tou Gerô Spanou*, Smyrna 1850) by N. Stamenes or Christopher Samartsides's 'Mysteries of Constantinople' (*Apokrypha Kônstantinoupoleôs*, 3 vols, Istanbul 1868).[217] As far as the *Mystères de Péra* are concerned, they seem to have been preceded by a similar novel in German (published in the paper *Osmanische Post*), and a Greek novel by Ep. C. Kyriakidis (*Ta Apokrypha tou Peran*, 1889) of which a *Karamanlı* version appeared in Misailidis' *Anatoli*.

The author of this novel, Jacques Loria, was in fact a teacher of the *Alliance Israélite Universelle* which had played such an important role in disseminating French language and culture among the Ottoman Jews. He wrote works in French, Judaeo–Spanish and Turkish,[218] his literary career may be regarded as typically Ottoman. It does not seem to have ended with the publication of the *Mystères de Péra*. In 1325/1909, after the Young Turk Revolution, the Imprimerie française of L. Mourkidès in Istanbul published a first instalment (*cüz*') of a new novel in Turkish, which was distributed gratis. Its title was 'The Imperial Treasure of the Topkapı Serail' (*Topkapı Hazine-i hümayunu*). Its author was once again Jacques Loria, the author of 'The Mysteries of Pera' (*Beyoğlu Esrarı müellifi*), who appears here under the pen-name Prinkipo Bey.[219] The announcement says: 'The people of Istanbul, deprived of any works of fiction, fed up with political articles, will find here nourishment for the soul. Men, women, old and young, and even young girls will hasten to read "The Treasure of the Topkapı Serail" and will spend a very pleasant time with this delightful reading-matter'.[220] We do not know whether, or in which language(s), this novel eventually appeared, but it illustrates fairly well the complex nature of literary activity in the Ottoman Empire. Moreover, the new novel *Topkapu Hazine-i hümayunu* was even termed a '*millî roman*'—a 'national novel'.

Conclusion

The context established for comparative studies in Middle Eastern literatures has conventionally been limited to Arabic, Persian and Turkish.[221] This 'Orientalist' perspective proper to the Islamic scholar may be justified for the 20th century, where the ethnic and linguistic composition of the Middle East has been radically transformed. The old multilingualism does not exist any longer.[222] Linguistic (and reading) communities such as the Spanish-speaking Sephardic Jews, or the Turcophone Armenians and Greek Orthodox, whose literary activity was, as has been seen to be, considerable and played an integral part in the transmission of knowledge, have virtually disappeared. Very few writers can still afford to use a European language as a medium of literary expression in Turkey and most of the successor states of the Ottoman Empire. After World War I and with the end of colonialism, missionary activity has also come to an end.

It is obvious that such a perspective is absolutely unable to give an appropriate and complete picture of the literary activities in the Ottoman Empire and their manifold connections and interrelations. Comprehensive studies in this domain cannot exclude the writings in Greek, Bulgarian, Armenian and other languages used in the Ottoman Empire. It is certainly more appropriate to speak of 'Literatures of the Eastern Mediterranean, as Hilary Kilpatrick does in a stimulating article,[223] But the Ottoman context also demands that Balkan literatures such as Bulgarian be taken into account. It is also absurd to discard the literary production in western languages from studies focusing on the development of literature(s) of the Middle East/Levant. As the example of Jacques Loria's *Mystères de Péra* shows, even a French novel could form an integral part of the literary life in a cosmopolitan society. In this respect, much more research has to be done. This literature may not always meet the more exacting standards of our time, but its study would allow us to obtain a new perception of the nature and characteristics of literary activity in different cultural spheres, including that of Western Europe in a not too remote past.[224]

Notes

1. Julia Pardoe (1806–1862) had accompanied her father to Istanbul in 1835. In the eyes of a certain contemporary, 'since Lady Montagu probably no woman has acquired so intimate a knowledge of Turkey'.
2. Miss Pardoe, *The City of the Sultan. Domestic Manners of the Turks*, London 1854 (first published 1837), p. 71.
3. This has led to compendious histories of literature from which, as e.g. in the case of Greek, the community's literary activity in Istanbul in the 19th century is almost absent. Cf. the standard histories by Dimaras, Polites and others.
4. For research on literature in *Karamanlı*, see now the survey by an eminent specialist, E. Balta's 'Périodisation et typologie de la production des livres *Karamanlı*', in: F. Hitzel, ed., *Livres et lecture dans le monde ottoman* (= *Revue des mondes musulmans et de la Méditerranée* 87–88 [1999]), pp. 251–75, which contains an extensive bibliography. For Armeno–Turkish works, the repertory by H. Stepanian, *Hayatař t'urk'eren girk'eri matenagitut'yun* (Erevan 1987) is useful but far from

complete. A. Hetzer's *Dačkerēn-Texte. Eine Chrestomathie aus Armenierdrucken des 19. Jahrhunderts in türkischer Sprache* (Wiesbaden 1987), deals almost exclusively with works published by the Mekhitharists and, surprisingly enough, ignores almost completely the secular literature in Armeno–Turkish.

5. See the new edition by R. Anhegger and V. Günyol, Evangelinos Misailidis, *Seyreyle Dünyayı (Temaşa-i Dünya ve Cefakâr u Cefakeş)*, 2nd edn, Istanbul 1988. In histories of Turkish literature, it is Şemseddin Sami's *Taaşşuk-i Tal'at ve Fitnat* (Istanbul 1289/1872) which has commonly been regarded as the 'first Turkish novel'.
6. This was first discovered by the Greek scholar Sula Boz. See her 'Paleoloğos/Misailidis/Favini. Üç isim, bir akrablalık', *Milliyet Sanat Dergisi* (July 1990), 36–7.
7. Henri Tonnet calls it '*le premier essai de roman complet des lettres néo-grecques*' (see his *Histoire du roman grec des origines à 1960*, Paris 1996, p. 95). Also see the new bilingual edition by the same author, Grégoire Palaiologue, *Ο πολυπαθής. L'homme aux mille mésaventures* (Paris 2000).
8. See the new edition by A. Tietze, Vartan Paşa, *Akabi Hikyayesi. İlk Türkçe Roman*, (Istanbul 1991). 'Akabi' is the (Western) Armenian form of the Greek girl's name 'Agapi'. Significantly enough, it was translated into Armenian only one century later (*Agapii patmut'yunë*, tr. by G. Kh. Stepanian, Erivan 1953).
9. Kevork B. Bardakjian calls it 'a penny dreadful novel'. See his *A Reference Guide to Modern Armenian Literature, 1500–1920*, Detroit 2000, p. 107.
10. See J. Strauss, 'Les livres et l'imprimerie à Istanbul (1800–1908)', in P. Dumont, ed., *Turquie. Livres d'hier, livres d'aujourd'hui*, Strasbourg-Istanbul 1992, pp. 5–24.
11. Cairo is not included here since in the last third of the 19th century, Egypt had *de facto* ceased to be an 'Ottoman' province. Significantly enough, it even became a centre for political refugees from the Ottoman Empire, both Muslims (Turks and Arabs) and non-Muslims, especially Armenians and Sephardic Jews, who deployed an intensive publishing activity there.
12. See J. Strauss, 'Les voies de la transmission du savoir dans un milieu cosmopolite. Lettrés et savants à Istanbul au XIXe siècle (1830–1860)', in F. Sanaugustin, ed, *Les intellectuels en Orient musulman. Statut et fonction*, Cairo 1999, pp. 109–125, 110.
13. '*Il n'y a pas encore longtemps que le même préjugé, qui interdisait aux chrétiens, et surtout aux Francs, l'achat de livres musulmans dans les bazars, leur fermait l'entrée des bibliothèques publiques, à moins d'un firman spécial*' (A. Ubicini, *Lettres sur la Turquie*, vol. 1, Paris 1853, p. 22).
14. One might add the different varieties of Church Slavonic used by Serbs, Romanians, Bulgarians, Macedonians, etc. They will not be dealt with here since hardly any works were printed in that language in the Ottoman Empire.
15. Piccolos's Greek version of *Paul et Virginie* was first published in Paris 1824 (reprinted 1841 and 1860). The first Bulgarian translation by A. Granitski (1825–1879), published in Istanbul, *Pavel i Virginiya*, dates from 1850. It was probably translated from the Greek version. See 'Bâlgarski prevodi ot grâtski', in: Manyo Stoyanov, *Stari grâtski knigi v Bâlgariya*, Sofia 1978, pp. 439–453, 443.
16. In the wake of the *Tanzimat* reforms, Turkish was to become the 'national language' (*millî lisan*) of non-Turcophone Muslims, especially in the Balkans (Bosnians, Cretans, etc.).
17. See on this subject J. Strauss, 'Diglossie dans le domaine ottoman, evolution et péripéties d'une situation linguistique', *Revue du Monde Musulman et de la Méditerranée* 75–76 (1995), pp. 221–55.
18. '... *milleti Ermeniyande, lisanı türkiye oldukca vakıf olub ibarei Ermeniyane aşna olmayanlar, lisanı Ermeniyane vakıf olarak ibareyi Türkiyeyi aşna olmayanlardan ziade olduklarından ekserietin xatırına riayeten bu te'lifimizde daxi lisanı türki bilicab tercih olunmuşdur' (Tarixi Napoleon Bonaparte imperatoru ahalii Fransa*, vol. 1 [Istanbul 1855], pp. 8–9). Moreover, Vartan Pasha had heard that what he calls respectfully 'our guides' (*bizlere rehnuma olan*), the Mekhitarists of Venice, had presented a comprehensive History of Napoleon in *krapar* to Napoleon III which was going to be printed by the Imprimerie Nationale in Paris. For this reason, the composition of another work in Armenian seemed useless (*abes*) to him. On Vartan Pasha and his 'History of Napoleon Bonaparte', also see *The Beginnings of Printing in the Near and Middle East: Jews, Christians and Muslims*, Wiesbaden 2001, pp. 64–5.
19. See on this process A. S. Levend's comprehensive survey, *Türk Dilinde Gelişme ve Sadeleşme Evreleri*, 3rd edn, Ankara 1972.
20. Cf. Joseph Nehama's remarks on the book production until the middle of the 19th century (in his *Histoire des Israélites de Salonique*, vols VI–VII, Salonika 1978, p. 711): '*Ces livres sont destinés, en*

général, au public lettré qui peut comprendre aisément l'hébreu. On ne commence à se préoccuper de la masse à demi-lettrée que lorsque les écoles ont ouvert une brèche dans les remparts dont s'entoure le fanatisme.'

21. On the importance of Istanbul as a cultural centre for Bulgarians, see N. Nachov, *Tsarigrad kato kulturen tsentâr na bâlgarite do 1877* g., Sofia 1925.
22. On the gradual Gallicization of the Sephardic culture of Istanbul see M. Şaul, 'The Mother Tongue of the Polyglot: Cosmopolitism and Nationalism among the Sepharadim of Istanbul', in: Mehmed Tütüncü (ed.), *Turkish-Jewish Encounters*, Haarlem 2001, pp. 129–66; 143ff. (A first version of this article was published in *Anthropological Linguistics* 25/3[1983] pp. 326–58).
23. *Vide infra* n. 53.
24. French title: *La vie et les aventures de Fariac, relation de ses voyages avec ses observations critiques sur les Arabes et sur les autres peuples*. Also see the French translation by René R. Khawam, *La jambe sur la jambe* (Paris 1991).
25. G. Groc and İ. Çağlar, *La presse française de Turquie de 1795 à nos jours. Histoire et catalogue*, Istanbul 1985, p. 7. Unfortunately, writings on the French press in the Ottoman Empire hardly ever deal with the literary aspects of it.
26. This was the first Armenian paper published in the Ottoman Empire after the Armenian edition of the official gazette *Takvim-i Vekayi* (founded 1831). See on the Armenian press of this period 'T'rk'ahay mamuli verelk'i handruannerë', in: Toros Azadian (ed.), *Žamanak k'arasnameay yišatakaran 1908–1948*, Istanbul 1948, p. 14.
27. See 'Synchronos hellênikê dêmosiographia', in: I. G. Sakellarides (ed.), *Ho Pharos tês Anatolês etous 1901*, Istanbul 1900, p. 390.
28. On the Jewish press in the Ottoman Empire, see now Gad Nassi (ed.), *Jewish Journalism and Printing Houses in the Ottoman Empire and Modern Turkey*, Istanbul 2001.
29. 'Historikai selides peri tou vyzantinou typou', in: I. G. Sakellarides (ed.), *Ho Pharos tês Anatolês ... etous 1902*, Istabul 1901, pp. 388–394, 390.
30. See M. Stoyanov, *Bâlgarskata vâzroždenska knižnina*, vol. I, Sofia 1957, p. 433. On the Greek paper see P. Nasioutzik, *Amerikanika oramata stê Smyrnê ton 190 aiôna, hê synantêsê tês anglo-saxonikês Skepsês metên hellênikê*, Athens 2002, p. 261–367.
31. See Nikolai Genchev, *Frantsiya v bâlgarskoto dukhovno vâzradane*, Sofia 1979, p. 336f.
32. Cf. Groc/Çağlar, *La Presse française*, pp. 62 and 107.
33. Gabbay has been characterized as '*le véritable fondateur du journalisme israélite en Turquie*' by M. Franco (*Essai sur l'histoire des Israélites de l'Empire ottoman depuis les origines jusqu'à nos jours*, Paris 1897; p. 280). He is also known for having translated works from Turkish to Judaeo-Spanish (see I. Jerushalmi, *From Ottoman Turkish to Ladino. The case of Mehmet Sadık Rifat Pasha's* Risâle-i Ahlâk and *Judge Yehezkel Gabbay's* Buen Dotrino, Cincinnati 1990).
34. It was in this article that a summary translation of Victor Hugo's *Les Misérables* was published (under the title *Mağdurîn hikâyesi*) as early as 1862, shortly after the publication of the original.
35. For similar assessments cf. e.g. R. Ostle, 'The Printing Press and the Renaissance of Modern Arabic literature' in: *The Introduction of the Printing Press in the Middle East* (= *Culture & History* 16), 1997, pp. 145–57, 147; M. Nichanian, *Âges et usages de la langue arménienne* (Paris 1989) p. 289. The Ottoman Armenians, referring to the major representatives of the 'National Awakening', used to speak of the 'Generation of 1860'; for Turkish cf. Jitka Malečková, 'Ludwig Büchner versus Nat Pinkerton: Turkish Translations from Western Languages, 1880–1914', *Mediterranean Historical Review* 9/1 (1994), pp. 73–99; 76–8. Greek literature represents a special case since it did not develop in an exclusively 'Ottoman' context after 1821.
36. Moreover, some divans have never been reprinted in Istanbul. On the role and impact of books printed in Cairo, see J. Strauss, *The Egyptian Connection in 19th Century Ottoman Intellectual History* (= *Zokak el-Blat(t)* 20), Beirut 2000, pp. 33–48.
37. '*Les commandes viennent de tous les Balkans, d'Italie, d'Allemagne, de Pologne. L'imprimerie est l'une des industries les plus prospères de la ville*' (Nehama, *Histoire*, p. 513).
38. Nehama, *Histoire*, p. 507.
39. With the exception of the Danubian principalities (Moldavia and Valachia), where the first printings presses were founded in the 17th century. These presses printed books in Greek, *Karamanlı*, Rumanian and even Arabic. On the Glykis publishing house in Venice, one of the most active ones during this period, see the excellent study by G. Veloudis, *Das griechische Druck- und Verlagshaus 'Glikis' in Venedig, 1670–1854; das griechische Buch zur Zeit der Türkenherrschaft*, Wiesbaden 1974.

40. See Tonnet, *Histoire du roman grec*, p. 60ff.
41. Significantly enough, a great 'National' dictionary remained incomplete for this reason (see *The Beginnings of Printing* [cited n. 18] 21f). We still lack a comprehensive study of Greek printing and the press in Istanbul in the 19th century.
42. Later in the century a Western observer, well informed about the issue, stated: 'On the whole the Greeks of Turkey are better equipped in this respect than any other class of Turkish subjects. They have the rapidly developing writers of Athens to rely upon' (H. O. Dwight, *Constantinople and its Problems: its Peoples, Customs, Religions and Progress*, New York, 1901, p. 252).
43. See n. 53 *infra*.
44. See Stoyanov (cited n. 30).
45. See on this order, its activities and notably its influence on the Ottoman Armenians, K. Kévorkian, 'Littérature arménienne. Constantinople et son activité littéraire au XIXe siècle', *Revue de littérature comparée*, 59/2 (1985), pp. 199–209; 205f. See also the 'defence' of the Mekhitarists' achievements against the allegations of Turkish historians by K. Pamukciyan, 'Mıhitaristler hakkında', *Tarih ve Toplum* 28 (1986), pp. 238–9.
46. Major figures of Western Armenian literature such as the poet and writer Mgrdich Beshiktashlian (1819–1876), Garabed S. Ütüdjian (1823–1904), the founder of the influential paper *Masis*, and even the modern poet Taniel Varuzhan (1876–1915), were trained by the Mekhitarists.
47. See Nichanian, *Âges et usages* ..., 298. The prices charged may have been high, too. An American missionary, naturally inclined to promote the vernacular language, speaks of '... the solemn writings of the Venetian and Viennese monks' displayed in some Istanbul bookshops, 'which some of those who are rich enough to pay the enormous prices charged can understand' (Dwight, *Constantinople*, p. 255).
48. The best source on Armenian printing in the Ottoman Empire remains the extensive repertory of Armenian printers and printing presses by 'Theotig' (i.e. Theotig Labjinjian; 1873–1928), *Tip u Taṙ* (Istanbul 1912). This brilliant example of the high standards of Armenian print culture was published in the Ottoman capital on the occasion of the anniversary of the invention of the Armenian script and the beginning of Armenian printing. On the first Armenian books printed in Istanbul, also see R. H. Kévorkian, *Catalogue des 'Incunables' arméniens (1511/1695)*, Geneva 1986, esp. pp. 112–13 and 120–39.
49. See *Tarih* I, Istanbul n.d., pp. 313–317. This text contains attacks against Russia whereas Napoleon is presented as an ally and friend of Islam.
50. They were published in Turkish under the title *Tarih-i isevînin sekiz yüz beş senesi yahud târih-i hicrînin bin iki yüz yigirmi senesinde França Devleti ile Avusturya ve Mosko(v) Devletleri beyninde Nemçe ve Avusturya memalikinde vâki olan ceng ü sefere dayir havadisnâmelerin tercümesidir.*
51. *Tarik-i refah. Amerika meşahir-i hükemasından Franklen'in bir mezadda irad olunacak yollu tertib eylediği nutukdur*, tr. by Reşad (i.e. Charles de Chateauneuf; Paris 1286/1869; reprinted Istanbul 1910). Another Turkish translation of the same work also appeared in the same year in Istanbul: *Tarik-i servet ez hikmet-i Rikardos*, tr. by the Armenian Bedros Khojasarian.
52. *İlm-i tedbir-i mülk* (London 1860).
53. *Ho Diavolos en Tourkia êtoi skênai en Konstantinoupolei* (London 1862). It was preceded by an English version published in 1851. See on this novel H. Tonnet, 'Les premiers romans grecs à sujet turc', *Revue des études néo-helléniques*, I/1 (1992), pp. 5–19.
54. See Bernard Heyberger, *Les Chrétiens du Proche-Orient au temps de la Réforme catholique*, Rome 1994, p. 440.
55. See Dagmar Glass, *Malta, Beirut, Leipzig and Beirut Again. Eli Smith, the American Syria Mission and the Spread of Arabic Typography* (= *Zokak al-Blat(t)* 16), Beirut 1997; on Turkish books printed in Malta see G. Roper, 'Turkish Printing and Publishing in Malta in the 1830s', *Turcica*, 29 (1997), pp. 413–21.
56. *Vide infra*, p. 50.
57. Cf. Dwight, *Constantinople*, 286: '... it was gratifying to perceive that to America this and almost every other great school in Turkey and Greece is indebted for its elementary books of instruction'. For a different, rather negative appreciation of the impact of books published by the Protestant missionaries, see A. Ubicini's remarks in his *Letters on Turkey*, translated by Lady Easthope, 2 vols (London 1856), II, pp. 398–400 which prompted a translator's note.
58. The first grammar of the modern language was printed in Smyrna in 1847. Its author was the American missionary Elias Riggs (1810–1901). In the preface he writes that '... the genius of the age and the best interests of humanity requir[e] that authors should no longer, as formerly, veil their ideas in a dialect accessible only to the few, but should spread them far and wide in the free

and idiomatic use of the languages vernacular to their countrymen.' (*A Brief Grammar of the Modern Armenian Language as Spoken in Constantinople and Asia Minor*, Smyrna 1847, p. 3.)

59. These books, almost all of them written by George F. Herrick (1834–1926) were: *İtikad ve ibadet yani protestanların itikad ve ibadetine göre din-i mesihî beyanındadır* (1884); *Tâlim hakkında tasavvurat-ı mütenevvia* (1301/1884), *Abraham Linkon reis-i sâdık* (1885), *İlm-i ilahî-i tabiî* (1885). See G. F. Herrick, 'Literature for Turkish Moslems', *The Moslem World* IX (1919), pp. 375–8.
60. Tuğlacı says that the first Armenian bookshops were opened in 1730. The first one was run by a certain Manuk from Erzurum. He sold the books printed by Astvadzadur Tbir (d. 1748) who had founded his press in 1699 (see P. Tuğlacı, 'Ermenilerin Türk matbaacılığına katkısı', *Tarih ve Toplum* 15 [1991], 48–56).
61. M. Gedeon, *Aposêmeiômata chronographou 1800–1913*, Athens 1932, p. 188.
62. Michaud/Poujoulat, *Correspondance d'Orient*, 7 vols, Paris 1833–35, vol. 2, 210: '*Il n'y a qu'un libraire à Constantinople qui vende des livres appartenant à nos littératures d'Occident. Je suis monté plusieurs fois dans sa boutique à Galata; cette boutique, placée presque sous les toits, a cinq ou six pied carrés.*'
63. See his *Three Years in Constantinople*, 3 vols, London 1845.
64. Among other things, he also distributed the works of the French dragoman and Oriental scholar Thomas Xavier Bianchi.
65. See 'Zustand des Buchhandels in Pera', *Zeitschrift der Deutschen Morgenländischen Gesellschaft*, 1 (1847), p. 208.
66. This commerical guide, founded by an Ottoman Jew, Raphael C. Cervati, was first published in 1868 under the title *L'Indicateur Constantinopolitain.*
67. See Lütfî Seymen, 'Erbab-ı mütalaa-ya hizmet: I. Meşrutiyet kitapçılığı ve Arakel Tozluyan Efendinin mektupları', *Müteferrika*, 1 (Autumn 1993), pp. 67–72.
68. *Arakel Kitabhanesi esami-i kütübü*, Istanbul 1301. For the success of this catalogue, Arakel's preface to the second catalogue, published in 1304/1886, is particularly interesting.
69. See R. K. Loewenthal, *Elia Carmona's Autobiography: Judeo–Spanish Popular Press and Novel Publishing Milieu in Constantinople, Ottoman Empire, circa 1860–1932*, (unpublished doctoral dissertation), University of Nebraska, Lincoln 1984, pp. 110–12.
70. See *Indicateur Ottoman Illustré*, 3rd year (Istanbul 1882), p. 353.
71. See S. Ünver, 'Yayın hayatımızda önemli yeri olan Sarafim Kıraathanesi', *Belleten*, 43 (1979), pp. 481–90. On *kıraathanes* in Istanbul, also see J. Strauss, '*Romanlar ah! O Romanlar!* Les débuts de la lecture moderne dans l'Empire ottoman', *Turcica*, 26 (1994) pp. 125–63, 140–3; and F. Georgeon, 'Les cafés à Istanbul à la fin de l'Empire ottoman', in: H. Desmet-Grégoire and F. Georgeon (eds), *Cafés d'Orient revisités*, Paris 1997, pp. 67–70.
72. In the domain of Ottoman Turkish, where the first religious work was printed, for well-known reasons, only in 1803, religious books also occupy an important place in the following period. See K. Beydilli, *Türk bilim ve matbaacılık tarihinde Mühendishâne, Mühendishâne matbaası ve kitâphanesi*, Istanbul 1995, pp. 254–59; also see R. Schulze, 'The Birth of Tradition and Modernity in 18th and 19th Century Islamic Culture—the Case of Printing', in: *Culture & History* (cited n. 35), pp. 29–72.
73. Cf., on Armenian books: '*Une part importante du marché était encore représentée, au début du siècle, par les livres religieux: Bible, Evangiles, Rituel, Bréviaire, Calendrier, poésie sacrée de Grégore de Narég et Nersès Chnorhali, hagiographie, historiens de l'Eglise, etc. tandis que la 'Nouvelle littérature', plus militante, voyait ses proportions augmenter au fil des années, et finit par supplanter définitivement la suprématie du livre d'église après 1860*' (K. Kévorkian and P. B. Paboudjian, *Les Arméniens dans l'Empire ottoman à la veille du génocide*, Paris 1992, p. 75); on Jewish books: '*Ce sont toujours les sempiternelles questions de culte et de jurisprudence civile et commerciale qui absorbent leur attention et font les frais de leurs études et de leurs recherches. Leurs œuvres constitutent, en général, une répétition des écrits de leurs predecesseurs. Ce sont des recueils de consultations juridiques et casuistiques, des variétés sur le* Talmud *et sur le* Michné Tora *de Maîmonide, des sermons*' (Nehama, *Histoire*, 542). 'Up to the 1850's Judeo–Spanish publishing consisted of works prepared by rabbis or pious writers on religious topics in Hebrew and Ladino ... In the following decades, however, works of popular fiction were translated from other languages, mostly French and Hebrew' (Loewenthal, *Elia Carmona's Autobiography*, p. 99). Similar observations have been made on *Karamanlı* works etc.
74. See Josée Balagna, *L'imprimerie arabe en Occident (XVIe, XVIIe et XVIIIe siècles)*, Paris 1984, p. 54f.; Vrej Nersessian, *Catalogue of Early Armenian Books 1512–1850*, London 1980, p. 49.

75. An Arabic translation, *Kitâb murshid al-khâṭiʾ*, was published in 1747 and 1794; also see Heyberger, *Les Chrétiens*, p. 440.
76. The Turkish title is *Tövebekyar adam eyi xosdovanank olmak için talimat.*
77. *Yung feylesofun figanleri, yaxod Yungun geceleri*, 3 vols Venice 1819; 2nd edn 1836. For specimens of this (and others translations) see Albrecht Krafft, 'Türkische Werke aus der Druckerey der Mechitaristen auf S. Lazzaro bey Venedig', *Jahrbücher der Literatur*, 95 (Vienna 1841), pp. 13–31, 14–16.
78. Cf. the contributions in Robin Ostle (ed.), *Modern Literature in the Near and Middle East 1850–1970*, London and New York 1991.
79. One should also mention certain Turkish translations published in Egypt from the 1830s onward such as that of the *Manuscrit venu de Ste Hélène* (see p. 61 f.) which provided a Turkish readership with a specimen of a new genre of personal narrative, the autobiography. On Turkish translations from Egypt see J. Strauss, 'Turkish translations from Mehmed Ali's Egypt. A pioneering effort and its results', in Translations: (re)shaping of literature and culture, edited by Saliha Paker, Istanbul, 2002, pp. 108–147.
80. These are: *İlyada eser-i Homer* (Istanbul 1301/1887), tr. by M. Naim Fraşari (1846–1900), who had been educated in a Greek college; *İlyas yahud şair-i şehîr-i Omiros* (Istanbul 1316/1898), tr. by Hilmî from Salonika. Both translations only comprise the inital parts of the *Iliad.*
81. See on this translation R. G. Khoury, 'Die arabischen literarischen Übersetzungen aus dem Griechischen, unter besonderer Berücksichtigung der Ilias von Homer', in: *Nubia et Oriens Christianus. Festschrift für Detlef G. Müller zum 60. Geburtstag*, eds P. O. Scholz and R. Stempel, Cologne 1988; pp. 163–80.
82. There is also an Arabic 'History of Alexander the Great', said to be translated from Greek (*Taʾrîkh Iskandar dhî l-qarnayn al-makdûnî*, Beirut 1886). See *Le livre et le Liban jusqu'à 1900*, Paris 1982, p. 323.
83. See on these works J. Strauss, 'The *Millets* and the Ottoman Language: The Contribution of Ottoman Greeks to Ottoman Letters (19th–20th Centuries)', *Die Welt des Islams*, 35/2 (1995), pp. 189–249.
84. *Evvel zamanda âzamü ş-şan olan filosofların imrar etmiş oldukları ömürlerinin icmalidir—Abrégé de la vie des plus illustres philosophes de l'Antiquité* (Turkish-French), Izmir, 1270/1854.
85. Ali Suavi published Ibn Miskawayh's Arabic version in Paris in 1873. His Turkish translation had appeared in 1867. It was published in the *Ruznâme-i Ceride-i Havadis*, nos 583–591 (23 Ramazan—8 Şevval 1283 [1867]). This influential paper, whose editor was an Englishman, Alfred Black Churchill, merits further study. Its columns contain numerous excerpts from classical works, particularly of a historical nature, by both Ottoman and Western (including ancient Greek and Byzantine) authors. See also n. 34.
86. See Krafft, 'Türkische Werke', pp. 13–31.
87. See on this translation R. Clogg, 'A Millet Within a Millet. The Karamanlides', in: D. Gondicas and Ch. Issawi, eds, *Ottoman Greeks in the Age of Nationalism*, Princeton, 1999, pp. 115–142, 125.
88. Turkish title: *Ebigdedos feylesofun el cüzü tercümesi*, Venice 1837.
89. See J. Strauss, 'Notes on the first satirical papers in the Ottoman Empire', in: A. Pistor-Hatam (ed.), *Amtsblatt*, vilayet gazetesi *und unabhängiges Journal: Die Anfänge der Presse im Nahen Osten*, Frankfurt etc., 2001, pp. 121–38, 131–8.
90. This author also tells us that Aesop's fables were being read as early as the 1830s in the School of Medecine in Istanbul.
91. See S. Velikov, 'Penčo Radov, éditeur de livres. Son ancienne traduction d'Ésope en turc', *Études balkaniques*, 2 (1969), pp. 99–102.
92. The Turkist writer and scholar Necib Âsım (1861–1935) translated extracts from the fourth book on the Scythians by what he calls the '*şeyhü l-müerrihîn*', Herodotus (see *Sitler*, Istanbul, 1310/1894, *Mukaddime*). First translations, however, go back to 1862/1278. They were published in the *Ruzname-i Ceride-i Havadis.*
93. e.g. Alexander Constantindi, *Târih-i Yunan-ı kadîm* (Istanbul 1286/1869).
94. Cf. the following testimony: 'I have often seen at Smyrna and on the Bosphorus an attentive group gathered round a friend reading aloud. I once examined the book whose contents so much delighted them—it was a translation in Romaic of Goldsmith's epitome of Ancient Grecian History!' (Charles MacFarlane, *Constantinople in 1828*, 2nd edn, vol. II, London 1829, p. 282).
95. *Roma tevarixi icmali. Roma şehrinin binası ve devletinin ibtidasından ğarb tarafında hükyümetinin xarabınadek*, Venice 1830; see Krafft, 'Türkische Werke', pp. 13–31; 19f. A French traveller writes: '*J'ai vu l'*Histoire romaine *et d'Angleterre de Goldsmith, et les* Nuits *d'Young traduites en turc*

et imprimés en caractères arméniens, plus aisés à lire que les caractères turcs,' (E. Poujade, *Chrétiens et Turcs. Scènes et souvenirs de la vie politique, militaire et religieuse en Orient*, Paris 1859, p. 72).

96. Cevdet, *Manzara-i iber yahud Roma Târihi*, 2 vols, Istanbul 1305. The sources of this compilation are unknown.
97. Robertson was known to Arab readers thanks to the translation of his *History of the Reign of the Emperor Charles V* into Arabic, printed in Bûlâq in 1842.
98. See Strauss, 'The Egyptian connection', p. 27.
99. See on this translation Mustafa Nihat Özön, *Türkçede roman hakkında bir deneme*, 2nd edn. by A. Kabacalı, Istanbul 1985, pp. 125–8.
100. A. Ubicini, *La Turquie actuelle*, Paris 1855, p. 456f.
101. See Tonnet, *Histoire du roman grec*, p. 81f. *Télémaque* was also read in the preparatory classes of the Medical School (*Mekteb-i tıbbiye-i şahane*, established in 1838). See Rıza Tahsin, *Mir'ât-ı Mekteb-i Tıbbiye*, vol. I, Istanbul 1328 [1912], p. 26.
102. See R. H. Kévorkian and A. Lautel, 'La diffusion de la littérature occidentale en Arménie à travers un exemple caractéristique: le *Télémaque* (de Fénelon), *Revue de littérature comparée*, 61/2 (1987), pp. 209–16. The Mekhitarists also printed a Bulgarian translation by P. Piperov, *Priklyucheniya Telemakha syna Odiseevago*, in Vienna in 1845 (Genchev, *Frantsiya* ..., p. 330).
103. Ambroise Calfa(ian) (1826–1906), a native of Istanbul, was the director of the Armenian (*Haygazian*) College in Paris. He also used the pseudonyms 'Guy de Lusignan' and 'A. de Nar Bey' which appear on the cover pages of several didactic works (dictionaries, textbooks), published in Venice, Paris, Feodosia, and Istanbul. He also translated Bernardin de St Pierre's *Paul et Virginie* into Armenian (Paris 1856).
104. Published in instalments in *Akhtar* 1879–1880; see Strauss, 'Les voies de la transmission' (cited n. 12), p. 124.
105. This was not, however, Rifâ'a al-Ṭahṭâwî's translation, which had been published in Beirut in 1867, but the one by Sa'dullâh al-Bustânî (*Riwâyat Tilîmâk*) which had been printed in Cairo (n.d.). See *Catalogue des livres arabes, turcs et persans édités à l'Imprimerie arabe 'd'El-Djavaïb' à Constantinople*, September 1884, 47. Nothing seems to be known of the identity of the translator.
106. Denise Escarpit, *La littérature d'enfance et de jeunesse*, Paris 1981, p. 51. *Pilgrim's Progress, Robinson Crusoe, Gulliver's Travels*, etc. belong to the same category.
107. *Siyâḥa fî Amrîkâ*, tr. by Sa'd Ni'âm, Bûlâq, 1262/1846.
108. *Seyahatnâme-i Amerika*, tr. by Abdullah 'Ayntabî', Istanbul 1288/1872.
109. It figures also in the catalogue of the Greek booksellers Depasta, Istanbul 1869, p. 27.
110. Campe seems to have been aware himself of the success of his works. In the preface to the 7th edition of his *Der Neue Robinson* (1779) he mentions proudly that it had been translated into all European languages from 'Cadix to Moscow', and 'even Constantinople' (see Paul Dottin, *Daniel de Foe et ses romans*, vol. 2, *Étude historique*, Paris 1924, p. 444).
111. *Fatma Aliye Hanım yahud bir muharrire-i osmaniyyenin neş'eti*, first published 1311/1893. The version in Modern Turkish by Bedia Ermat, *Fatma Aliye. Bir Osmanlı Kadın Yazarın Doğuşu*, Istanbul, 1994 has been used here.
112. *Fatma Aliye*, p. 37. Ahmed Midhat says that he knew some hundred families whose girls were taught a foreign language (p. 50).
113. Elias Maṭar (1857–1909), a native of Hasbeya/Lebanon is well known from Arabic sources (see, e.g. Sarkîs, *Mu'jam al-maṭbû'ât al-'arabiyya wa al-mu'arraba*, 2 vols, Cairo 1928–1931, p. 1458; Philippe de Ṭarrâzî, *Ta'rîkh al-ṣiḥâfa al-'arabiyya*, 4 vols, Beirut 1913–33, II, 227). During his chequered career, he also taught at the School of Medecine (*Mekteb-i Tıbbiyye*) and the Law School (*Mekteb-i Hukuk*) in Istanbul. His Arab biographers usually omit his Turkish works, mainly on medecine (*Kolera risalesi* (1883); *Usul-i hıfzu s-sıhhat-i umumiyye* (1886); *Emraz-i azâ-yi hazmiyye* [n.d.]).
114. *Fatma Aliye Hanım*, p. 43.
115. See *Memoirs of Halidé Edib* (New-York-London 1926) repr. New York 1971, p. 115.
116. See Ali Nüzhet Göksel, *Ölümünün 25inci Yildönümü Münasebetiyle Ziya Gökalp, Hayatı – Eserleri*, Istanbul 1949, p. 8.
117. See Strauss, '*Romanlar* ...' (cited n. 71), pp. 151–63.
118. Dwight, *Constantinople*, p. 255.
119. Dwight, *Constantinople*, p. 254.
120. Christiane Babot, *Missions jésuites et assomptionnistes en Anatolie à la fin de l'Empire ottoman et au début de la République turque*, Strasbourg 200 (unpublished doctoral dissertation), p. 142.

121. '*Ponson du Terrail in ispecial modo è il beniamino dei sapientoni dei borghi*' (A[urelio Palmieri], 'La crisi libraria', *Bessarione*, III/5 (1899) pp. 161–8, 162. *Rocambole* was indeed very popular with the Greek readership in the Ottoman Empire. Translations of this author's novels such as *Les Drames de Paris, Les Mystères du demi-monde, Le pacte de sang, La corde du pendu, Le dernier mot de Rocambole* were published in Smyrna and Istanbul in the 80s and 90s.
122. Babot, *Missions jésuites* ..., p. 351.
123. Ibid.
124. '*La Commission du* Journal asiatique *a cru devoir supprimer l'indication d'une vingtaine d'ouvrages qui ne sont qu'une plate traduction de romans français en vogue. Pas un de nos lecteurs ne regrettera cette élimination dans la liste recueillie avec tant de soin et de persévérance par notre savant collaborateur*' (Cl. Huart, 'Notice des livres turcs, arabes et persans impirmés à Constantinople durant la période 1299–1301 de l'hégire (1882–1884)', *Journal Asiatique* (février-mars-avril 1885), pp. 229–68; 231, n. 3).
125. See Mek.-B. Dadian, 'La société arménienne contemporaine. Les Arméniens de l'Empire ottoman', *Revue des Deux Mondes* (15 June 1867), pp. 902–28, 926.
126. Charles Antoine Guillaume Pigault-Lebrun was a writer under the Directoire who was shunned by 'serious' literary historians; cf. '... *une philosophie moqueuse et des tableaux grivois firent le succès de ses romans dont notre plume se refuse à mentionner les titres*' (F. X. de Feller, *Biographie universelle*, 8 vol. [Paris 1851], s.v.)
127. See on this writer n. 207.
128. '*Bu latif roman, münasibetsiz teaşük hekyayeleri, hiyle ve bir takım cinayatı müdhişe ile insanın fikr u xayalini taxdiş (?) iderek yüz çıkartacak, ve dehşet verecek nefretamiz menzarelerden ari olub, bir akil peder bunı bila ihtiraz kız ve erkek evladlarına okudabilir*' (*Yirmi bin farsax denizler altında seyahat*, Istanbul 1892). Almost identical remarks can be found in the edition of the same work in Arabic script. See Strauss, '*Romanlar*', p. 160.
129. '*Kitab-ı Mukaddesden maada hiç bir kitab bu kitab kadar elsine-i muhtelifeye terceme olunmamışdır.*' See *Yolcunun azîmeti bu dünyadan gelecek dünyaya. Eser-i Yuhanna Bınyan*, Shumla 1905, p. 7.
130. See P. Kawerau, *Amerika und die Orientalischen Kirchen. Ursprung und Anfang der amerikanischen Mission unter den Nationalkirchen Westasiens*, Berlin 1958, p. 392 (referring to an article published in the *Missionary Herald* in 1839).
131. Stoyanov, *Bâlgarska vâzroždenska knižnina* I, p. 426.
132. Kawerau, *Amerika und die Orientalischen Kirchen*, p. 390.
133. It was translated by the convert Johannes Awetaranian ('Abdulmesih Yuhanna Avedaranian' *alias* Mehmed Şükrü). A Modern Turkish translation by Mustafa Necati was published in 1932.
134. *Arakel Kitabhanesi esami-i kütübü* (see n. 68), p. 200.
135. See Strauss, '*Romanlar* ...', p. 133.
136. The advantages and possibilities of the Armenian script were already emphasized by the authors of a book published in the 50s, 'The Key to reading the Ottoman language in Armenian characters'. It was written 'after a proposition of respectable Ottomans desiring to learn the Armenian characters in an easy way' (*huruf-i ermeniyyenin sehil kıraat ve taallümüne arzukeş olan Osmanlılardan ekser-i zevat-ı muteberenin âcizlerine vâki olduğu teklifi üzerine*; Mesrob and Sahak [Abro], *Miftâh-ı kıraat-i huruf-i ermeniyye fî lisan-ı osmanî*, Istanbul s.d., p. 4). Also see Rekin Ertem, *Elifbe'den Alfabe'ye*, Istanbul 1991, pp. 125–7.
137. *Vide infra* p. 36ff.
138. Characteristically, Ottoman Turkish books published by Armenians often had a Muslim Turkish 'corrector' (*musahhih*).
139. See *The Beginnings of Printing*, p. 23f.
140. See İsmail Habib [Sevük], *Avrupa Edebiyatı ve Biz. Garpten tercümeler*, 2 vols, Istanbul 1940–41, II, p. 237.
141. See Metin And, *Osmanlı Tiyatrosu*, Istanbul 1999, p. 180.
142. *İraklis ve Olympiakos Agonas yahud sıdk ü hulus ve muhabbet-i hakikî*, translated by Mehmed Raşid from Candia (Istanbul, 1289/1872).
143. *Gazi Osman. Sene 709 ilâ 699. Üç fasıldan ibâret tiyatro oyunudur* (Istanbul 1294). It was translated by a Greek government official, Yanko Vazzides, who also translated a history of the Franco-Prussian war into Turkish.
144. Translated by the Cretan Rif'at Bey, 1291/1874.
145. See on this translation J. Strauss, '*Eratos ya'ni Sevdâ.* The Nineteenth Century Ottoman Translation of the *Erotokritos*', *Byzantine and Modern Greek Studies* 16 (1992), pp. 189–201.

146. S. Serents, tr., *Ermeni edebiyatı nümuneleri*, Istanbul 1328, pp. 163–82.
147. *Müntahabât-ı âsâr-ı osmaniyye*, Istanbul 1288/1871; 2nd ed. 1290/1874.
148. In his 'History of Greece' published in the series *Kâinat*, Istanbul 1298/1882, p. 126.
149. *Peri Giouroukôn, Ethnologikê meletê*, Athènes 1891; French tr. by Paul Zipcy, *Étude éthnographique sur les Yuruk*, Athens 1891.
150. *Divan-i Mpakê êtoi poêtikê syllogê tou Mpakê*, Venice 1907.
151. The Turkish writer Şahabeddin Süleyman (1885–1921) wrote in his *takriz* for S. Serents' anthology of Armenian writers (see n. 146), p. 174: 'With an Arab, I have difficulties to get on well, although we share the same religion. With one of yours, I can easily unite and establish friendship'. He also observes that 'all of you know our language'.
152. We have him to thank for a new edition of Şemseddin Sami's Turkish-French dictionary, a considerably expanded version, which continued to be reprinted until 1928. See on Kélékian, *Yaşamları ve Yapıtlarıyla Osmanlılar Ansiklopedisi*, vol. II, Istanbul 1999, p. 24.
153. *Hayat olduğu gibi* (Istanbul 1329). The original dates from 1911. Krikor Zohrab (b. 1860), deputy at the Ottoman Parliament after 1908, was killed, like Kélékian, during the deportations of 1915 (see *Osmanlılar Ansiklopedisi*, vol. II, p. 703).
154. E. Romero in her *La creación literaria en lengua sefardí* (Madrid 1992, 251) lists one single novel published in 1931 in Salonika. But cf. n. 33.
155. Loewenthal, *Elia Carmona's Autobiography*, p. 44.
156. Abdurrahman Sami Pasha was a native of the Peloponnese. After the Greek Revolution the family emigrated to Egypt where Sami Pasha pursued a remarkable career. After having presented a memorandum on the Greek Revolution to Muhammad Ali, he was appointed director of the famous Bûlâq Press.
157. See Strauss, 'The Egyptian Connection', p. 53f.
158. See his *Tarâjim mashâhîr al-sharq fî al-qarn al-tâsiʿ ʿashar*, 3rd edn, Beirut 1985 (first published 1907), II, pp. 115–21.
159. In this treatise he says that, due to the intricacies of the Ottoman chancery style, it had been impossible to find a translator in Tunisia capable of translating the Ottoman Code of laws (*Düstur*) into Arabic. For this reason 'the *vilâyet* of Tunis is unable to have the law of the state to which it belongs' [see Levend, *Türk Dilinde Gelişme* (cited n. 19), p. 119]. It should be noted that the *Düstur* was eventually translated into Arabic by a Syrian translator.
160. No translations from Turkish authors are to be found in the first volume of the *Kanz al-raghâ'ib fî muntakhabât al-Jawâ'ib (Al-fuṣûl al-laṭîfa, al-maqâmât al-ẓarîfa, al-maqâlât al-adabiyya)*, Istanbul 1288/1871.
161. See Strauss, 'Les voies de la transmission' (cited n. 12), p. 125.
162. It must have been published around 1880. On Turkish books distributed by the *Al-Jawâ'ib* Pressee also the lists in G. Roper, 'Fâris al-Shidyâq and the transition from scribal to print culture in the Middle East', in G. Atiyeh, ed., *The Book in the Islamic World*, Albany 1995, pp. 209–31, 218.
163. Y. Sarkîs, *Muʿjam*, p. 1196.
164. See *Resimli Devr-i âlem seyahatnamesi* (Istanbul 1896). Also see the photographs in *Mâlumat*, no. 71, 23 Ramazan 1314 (25 February 1897), p. 466. Cf. Sarkîs, *Muʿjam*, p. 1177f; on his Turkish writings, see Sabuncuzâde Luis Alberi, ed. M. Aydın, *Sultan II. Abdülhamid'in Hal Tercümesi*, Istanbul 1997; A. Özcan, 'Yerini bulamayan bir gazeteci: Louis Sabuncu ve İstanbul Yılları', *İstanbul Araştırmaları* 5 (Spring, 1998), pp. 117–27; esp. pp. 124–7.
165. Zaydân, *Tarâjim*, II, pp. 206–11.
166. He died 12 Şevval 1328 (18 October 1910) after having resigned from his post as *kaymakam* of Jeddah. Şâdiq al-Mu'ayyad had been for many years Sultan Abdulhamid's Aide-de-Camp. He was sent on missions to Abyssinia and the Sudan and had been commissioner for Bulgaria. See Ekrem Reşâd and Osman Ferid, 1327 *sene-i mâliyyesine mahsus musavver Nevsâl-t osmanî*, Istanbul 1327–1329 [1911], p. 216. Sarkîs (*Muʿjam*, p. 1181f) has nothing to say about his writings in Turkish.
167. See on this travelogue Ch. Herzog and R. Motika, 'Orientalism *alla turca*: Late 19th/Early 20th Century Ottoman Voyages into the Muslim "Outback"', *Die Welt des Islams* 40/2 (2000), pp. 139–195, 169ff.
168. See Strauss, 'The Egyptian connection …', p. 45f.
169. See Taceddin Kayaoğlu, *Türkiye'de tercüme müesseseleri*, Istanbul 1998, p. 68.
170. The Arab Christian Zeki Meghamiz (Aleppo 1871–Istanbul 1932) is one of the most intriguing figures in late Ottoman intellectual history. Information on him is somewhat scattered (for a first

orientation see Alâettin Gövsa, *Meşhur Adamlar. Hayatları, eserleri*, 4 vols, Istanbul 1933–36, III, p. 1028). He was one of the most active writers and journalists of the period, and is also famous for having been Pierre Loti's Turkish teacher. He published numerous articles in Turkish papers (*Saadet, İkdam, Sabah, Mâlumat, Resimli Kitab*, etc.) and played an important role in the transmission of contemporary Arabic literature. Among his translations into Turkish is Qâsim Amîn's (1865–1908) 'Woman's Liberation' (*Taḥrîr al-Marʾa*, Cairo 1899; 1905) under the title *Hürriyet-i Nisvân* (Istanbul, 1329/1913). In the Republican period his translation of Jurjî Zaydân's novel 'The Bride of Ferghana' (*ʿArûs Farghâna*; 1908) appeared under the title *Cihan Hatun. Fergane güzeli* (Istanbul 1927). Zeki Meghamiz also translated the Koran into Turkish. This translation appeared anonymously after the Second Constitution (O. N. Ergin, *Muallim M. Cevdet'in hayatı, eserleri ve kütüphanesi*, Istanbul 1928, p. 308).

171. The Turkish version was preceded by a French translation, *Al Abbassa ou la sœur du Calife*, tr. by M. Y. Bîtâr and Charles Moulié (Paris 1912).
172. This series, *Histoire et description de tous les peuples, de leurs religions, mœurs, coutumes, etc.* comprised 67 volumes, published 1834–1856 in Paris by Didot frères. It was well known to a number of Ottoman writers. It inspired Ahmed Midhat Efendi to his own collection *Kâinat* ('Universe'; 1871–1875), while Ziya Pasha's 'History of the Inquisition' (*Enkizisyon Târihi*; 1299/1881) is translated from vol. 30, Joseph Lavallée's and Adolphe Guéroult's *Espagne* (1844), pp. 453–70. Süleyman Pasha refers to the volumes *Chine* (Guillaume Pauthier), *Inde* (Dubois de Jancigny and Xavier Raymond) and *Tartarie, Béloutchistan, Boutan et Népal* (Xavier Raymond).
173. *Patmut'iwn Hayoc'*, 3 vols, Venice 1784–1786; English tr. by J. Avdall, Calcutta 1827.
174. *Târih-i umumı*, 6 vols, Istanbul (1283) 1866ff. It is based on the relevant volumes of *Chamber's Educational Course* but also includes sections from other sources (such as the chapter on Tamerlan).
175. The bibliographical data have been completed on the basis of Stepanian's repertory (cited n. 4).
176. See on this work O. Spies, 'Esman und Zejdschan. Ein türkischer Volksroman aus Kleinasien nach einem armenisch-türkischen Druck', *Anthropos*, XVIII–XIX (1923–1924), pp. 804–818; XX (1925), pp. 653–677, 1001–1031.
177. See Marie-Christine Bornes-Varol, 'Djoḥa juif dans l'Empire ottoman', in: I. Fenoglio and F. Georgeon (eds.), *L'humour en Orient* (= *Revue du Monde Musulman et de la Méditerranée* 77/78), 1996, pp. 61–74.
178. See F. Macler, *La version arménienne de l'histoire des sept sages de Rome*, Paris 1919.
179. Presumably the Turkish version of his *Gerezmank' eritasardac' kam Trp'akan hiwandut'iwnk'* (cf. Bardakjian, *Reference Guide*, p. 367).
180. Cf. Bardakjian, *Reference Guide*, p. 366f: 'His attempts to explain biological, social, and political phenomena in a scientific manner, as well as his anti-clerical views, were vigorously opposed by the Armenian Church'.
181. See E. Balta, *Karamanlidika. XXe siècle. Bibliographie analytique*, Athens 1987, p. 95; and E. Balta, *Karamanlidika. Nouvelles additions et compléments I*, Athens 1997, p. 239f.
182. See on this edition Balta (1997), p. 237.
183. See J. Eckmann, 'Die karamanische Literatur', in: *Philologiae Turcicae Fundamenta*, vol. II, Wiesbaden 1964, p. 824f.
184. *Karamanlı* poets also exist, but the Armenians had a particularly important tradition of poets and *âşıks (ashugh)*, many of them using a *mahlas* in the Turkish fashion.
185. The title page says: '*Muahhıren ermeniceden lisanı rumiye ilk yazılarak, bu defa tahsis ilan basılmışdır*'.
186. On Greek editions of Nasreddin Hoca's stories see now G. Kechagiaoglou, 'Enas Othômanos Aisôpos stên Avlê tôn Mavrokordatôn kai tou Othôna. Hoi prôtes sôzômenes hellênikes metaphraseis tou Nasrentin Chotza', *Molyvdo-Kontylo-Pelekitis*, 4 (1993), pp. 1–41, and 'Avivliographêtes ekdoseis tou Nasrentin Chotza (Smyrnê 1848, Athena 1860, 1861)', *Hellênika*, 45 (1995), pp. 362–71.
187. X. Th. Bianchi, 'Bibliographie ottomane ou Notice des ouvrages publiés dans les imprimeries turques de Constantinople, et en partie dans celles de Boulac, en Égypte, depuis les derniers mois de 1856 jusqu'a ce moment', *Journal Asiatique* (octobre–novembre 1859), pp. 287–298, 290.
188. See the entry in *Encyclopaedia of Islam*, 2nd edn, VI (1991), p. 303.
189. *Tarâjim*, pp. 276–84.
190. *Kitab der hakk-ı sıbyan ve sabâvet. Mükâlemat-ı latife ve emsal-ı sagîre ve tevarih-i muhtasare*, Istanbul 1266/1850.

191. *Skratenie na turskata istoriya ot osnovanieto na imperiyata do naše dni* (Galata 1854).
192. The pivotal role played by French appears also in other, rather elementary books on Ottoman history published in the Ottoman Empire. The *Histoire abrégée de l'Empire ottoman* (Istanbul 1869), by Caroline Furet, teacher at an Armenian college for girls in Ortaköy, was also translated into Bulgarian and seems to have inspired the author of a Greek history of the Ottoman sultans (A. Vaporides, *Viographikê historia tôn Sultanôn tês Othômanikês Avtokratorias*, 3rd edn, 2 vols, Istanbul 1894). There are also several textbooks of that type published by Ottoman Jewish writers in French (e.g. Moïse Fresco's *Histoire de l'Empire ottoman*, Istanbul 1911) or Judaeo-Spanish (on these see Romero, *La creación literaria*, p. 206f.).
193. Cf. Queux de St. Hilaire, 'Des traductions et des imitations en grec moderne, *Annuaire de l'Association pour l'encouragement des études grecques en France*, 7me année (1873), pp. 330–47, 347–55.
194. See J. Etmekjian, *The French Influence on the Western Armenian Renaissance 1843–1915*, New York 1964, p. 156.
195. The most comprehensive account about Napoleon Bonaparte written in the Ottoman Empire was, curiously enough, in Armeno-Turkish: Vartan Pasha's *Tarixi Napoleon Bonaparte (vide supra)*, but it should also be noted that Colonel Louis Calligari's biography (*Sîrat Nâpulyûn al-awwal*, Tunis 1856; Beirut 1868) figures among the first works of that kind published in Arabic.
196. See A. Camariano-Cioran, *Les Académies princières de Bucarest et de Jassy et leurs professeurs*, Salonika 1974, p. 336.
197. *Afrika cezayirinden Santa Elena nâm cezireden vâsıl olub oltarafda cezirebend olan Bonaparta'nın sergüzeştini şâmil franseviyyülibare bir kıt'a risalenin hulâsa-i tercemesidirki Bonaparta'nın kendisi tarafından tahrir olunub bir tevarüd etmişdir*, Bûlâq 1247. See on this work J. Strauss, 'The Egyption Connection', p. 25f. (with further references). In the literature on translations and the Bûlâq press, it has so far been wrongly identified as a Turkish translation of Las Cases's *Mémorial de Sainte Hélène*.
198. *Fransa İmperatorı Birinci Azim Napoleonun tezkiresi*. It was translated by Nicholas Souullides and corrected by E. Misailidis (see S. Salaville and E. Dalleggio, *Karamanlidika. Bibliographie analytique d'ouvrages en langue turque imprimés en caractères grecs II (1851–1866)*, Athens 1966, p. 68f.)
199. Ubicini, *La Turquie actuelle*, p. 457.
200. *Vide supra* n. 29.
201. *Ho komês tou Montechristo*, 5 vols, Istanbul 1845–1846.
202. Nehama, *Histoire*, p. 547.
203. *Vide supra* n. 140.
204. See S. Salaville and E. Dalleggio, *Karamanlidika. Bibliographie analytique d'ouvrages en langue turque imprimés en caractères grecs, III (1866–1900)*, Athens 1977, p. 116f.
205. Pars Tuğlacı, *The Role of the Dadian Family in Ottoman Social, Economic and Political Life*, Istanbul 1993, p. 242.
206. The French translation by P. L. Lezaud was on offer in the catalogue of the Greek booksellers Depasta (see n. 109).
207. Arabajian is an exceptional figure. He was both a poet (where he used the *mahlas* Bidari) and a translator of French popular novels. See the entry 'Bidari' (M. Sabri Koz) in *Dünden bugüne İstanbul Ansiklopedisi*, vol. II, Istanbul 1994, p. 227f.
208. Stoyanov, *Bâlgarska vâzroždenska knižnina*, I, p. 426, lists 20 translations.
209. See Romero, *La creación literaria*, p. 251 (a new translation of this '*romanso historiko moraliko amostrando el kavo de la mujer onesta*' was published in 1923).
210. It is not a translation of Lamartine's *Geneviève*, as some authors have stated; see the extract in *Yeni Türk Edebiyatı Antoloji I. 1839–1865*, Istanbul 1988, pp. 592–4.
211. On the translations into Western languages see Emil van der Vekene, *Bibliotheca bibliographica historiae Sanctae Inquisitionis*, 3 vols, Vaduz 1982–92, II, p. 415f.
212. Entitled *Gaŧnik' havatak'nnut'iwn*, 2 vols, Istanbul 1864–66; 2nd edn, 1873.
213. See Strauss, '*Romanlar*', p. 144f.
214. *Musavver enkizisyon esrarı*, translated by M. Ali Vaizzade, Istanbul 1326/1910.
215. Pera (Turkish *Beyoğlu*) is the ancient 'Frankish' quarter of the Ottoman capital, formerly inhabited by a very special, predominantly non-Muslim population (Greeks, Armenians, Levantines, Europeans, etc.).
216. See J. Strauss, 'Le livre français d'Istanbul (1730–1908)', in *Livres et lecture* (cited n. 4),

pp. 277–301, 298f.; see also *The Beginnings of Printing*, p. 31f. It was later also translated into Judaeo-Spanish (Romero, *La creación literaria*, p. 240).

217. Tonnet, 'Les premiers roman grecs à sujet turc', p. 6f. The latter novel was also translated into Bulgarian.
218. See Romero, *La creación literaria*, p. 277. I have been unable to locate some of them in the relevant repertories.
219. In fact, Loria used various pseudonyms, 'Comte de Persignac' as well as 'Prinkipo Bey'.
220. '... *her dürlü âsâr-ı hayalperverâneden mahrum kalan, makalat-ı siyasiyyeden bıkan İstanbul ahalisi bu kitabda birgıda-yı manevî bulacakdır. Erkek, kadın, ihtiyar, çocuk ve hattâ genc kızlar bile* Topkapu Hazine-i hümayunu'nu *kemal-i tehalükle okuyarak bu mutalaa-i dilfirîb ile gayet tatlı vakitler geçireceklerdir*' (*Topkapu Hazine-i hümayunu*, p. 3).
221. See, for example, the collection *Literaturen im Kontext: arabisch-persisch-türkisch* of which a first volume, *Understanding Near Eastern Literatures*, edited by Verena Klemm and Beatrice Gruendler, was published in Wiesbaden, 2000. On the other hand, even the most comprehensive general comparative literature studies and repertories of translated literature ignore the impact of Western literature in the Levant.
222. This phenomenon has been illustrated in a wonderful essay by Nora Şeni, 'Souvenirs à plusieurs voix', *Anka*, 7–8 (1989), pp. 108–9.
223. See her 'Eastern Mediterranean Literatures. Perspectives for Comparative Study' in *Understanding Near Eastern Literatures*, pp. 84–94.
224. A version of this paper was presented at the International Congress 'Travelling Texts. Exchanges between literatures: North Africa, West Asia and Europe (Zurich, 26th–28th October 2000), which was organized by the Swiss Society for Middle Eastern and Islamic Studies in cooperation with the Orientalisches Seminar of the University of Zurich.

[25]

The Beginnings of Publishing in pre-1948 Palestine

Ami Ayalon

Tel Aviv University

What happens to a printed text once it is out of the printer's shop?[1] How does it become public property and how is it consumed? After all, printing, an amazing device no doubt, is no more than a production implement and further processes are involved in turning written texts into consumer goods. Indeed, printing is a link in the chain of mechanisms by which ideas are transmitted from author to audience. Earlier links include the formulation of ideas as intelligible statements and rendering them as presentable manuscripts, and printing, in turn, is followed by publishing — advertising, distributing, and selling — which make the product accessible to the public. Where this last process ends another, equally complex process begins: consumption. Aside of reading in different modes, solitarily or collectively, quietly or vocally, the consumption of printed texts also entails their mental assimilation, sometimes debating their contents with others, and always a dialogue with the author, explicit or implied. The fate of a text once it is born thus forms a multi-phased and multicoloured tale.

Historians, sociologists, anthropologists and ethnographers have explored aspects of the production and consumption of written texts, mainly in Western societies. We already have a considerable corpus of scholarship on the history of printing and publishing in Europe and its cultural offshoots, on the evolution of libraries, bookstores, private book collecting and literary societies, as well as on who read what and how, the intercourse between writer and audience, and the formation of public opinion. In the Middle East, by contrast, work on such matters has barely begun. In cultural history, as in most other fields, the study of Arab societies still lags way behind that of Europe, not least when modern times are concerned, for reasons that are too well known to detain us here. In the pages below I propose to make a very

1 The author acknowledges the support of the Israeli Science Foundation in the preparation of this article.

modest contribution to the study of Arab publishing, focusing on one individual case, that of the Arab community in pre-1948 Palestine. The confines set for this article allow no more than a quick glimpse at two limited sections of the scene: the advent of printing and the emergence of bookshops, two central links in the chain of the publishing trade at its inception. It may be noted in passing that this is a particularly difficult terrain to plough in the Middle East, since evidence is ever wanting; and that in Palestine the problem is all the more intricate, due to the devastating impact of the 1948 *nakba* on historical evidence. Still, testimonies do exist and, when creatively exploited, they permit us to tell a meaningful story.

The development of publishing in pre-1948 Palestine had two prominent features. First, the process was short and markedly intensive. While elsewhere in the region — primarily in Egypt and the Lebanon — a vivid cultural-literary blossoming had taken place from the mid-nineteenth century onward, Palestine had remained on the sidelines of this activity until much later. A handful of precursors aside, its cultural awakening and the concomitant emergence of publishing activity were telescoped into the half-century after 1900, especially the post-World War I decades, and then cut short rather abruptly by the mid-century crisis. Second, even when such an industry began to evolve in Palestine, it was overshadowed — and actually checked — by the dynamic ventures in its neighbourhood. By the time Palestine took its first step in this arena, Egypt and, to a lesser extent, Lebanon had already become lively regional foci of creativity, potent enough to constrict the growth of local publishing industries around them. Palestine, like most of the region's other countries, thus remained a satellite of the Egyptian and Lebanese literary endeavours, whose written products were regularly consumed by the Palestinian educated class. We have few data on this influx of imported texts, but there is ample evidence to show that it was substantial, perhaps to the extent of dominating the market in Palestine, at least with regards to books.[2]

Under the circumstances, pre-1948 Arab Palestine made up a rather modest publishing arena. Of the humble yield of its products, the bulk was newspapers, a

2 For a discussion of imported texts from Palestine's neighbourhood, see Ami Ayalon, 'Modern Texts and their Readers in Late Ottoman Palestine,' *Middle Eastern Studies* 38:4 (2002), 17–40, and idem, *Reading Palestine: Texts and Audience, 1900–1948* (Austin forthcoming), Ch. 2.

novel commodity whose history in the country began only after 1900.[3] By the mid-1940s the Palestinian periodical press had reached a total circulation of perhaps 20,000, an impressive progress explainable by the growing public thirst for information, which, in turn, was generated by the rapid shifts in the country's political landscape. Books, by contrast, addressed different (and less urgent) needs and there was a small demand for them that was met, in part, by imports. Local book making was therefore very limited. A full record of it is yet to be assembled, but available data seem to suggest that it did not exceed an annual output of 20 titles on average from 1900–48 (being more energetic at the end than at the outset).[4] Notably, in some significant way book printing was a by-product of the journalistic enterprise, especially so in its early years, as we shall see.

In the discussion below we will be concerned mainly with non-periodical publishing, leaving aside the exciting story of Palestinian journalism, except when it affected the advent of the book industry. Basically, book production in Palestine represented collaborative efforts of two kinds: author-printer and author-bookseller. The former, born shortly after the introduction of printing into the country, was by far the most common type of operation until the end of the period. The latter, indeed a variation of the former, developed only in the wake of World War II.

Printing

A Jewish press had operated in Safad, northern Palestine, already in the late sixteenth century, turning out books in Hebrew for about a decade before it closed down. The country's next press was another Jewish venture, set up in 1832 in the same town by Yisrael Bak and his son Nissan, who in 1841 moved their shop to Jerusalem. It was followed by several initiatives launched by Christian evangelical societies in Jerusalem. The earliest of these, and by far the busiest depot until the end of the century, was the one founded by the Franciscans in 1846 near the Old City's New Gate. It printed scores of books and pamphlets in several languages, including Arabic,

3 That is, if we disregard a reported feeble attempt to publish an official state bulletin back in 1876, of which we know nothing other than its name. See Yusuf Khuri, *Al-Sihafa al-'Arabiyya fi Filastin 1876–1948* (Beirut 1976), 3. Another official Ottoman organ appeared briefly in 1903 (see below), but the real beginning of the Palestinian Arab press was only in 1908, following the Young Turk Revolution.

4 For a detailed discussion of this issue, see *Reading Palestine*, ibid.

dealing with a variety of subjects, from theology to geography.[5] Anglican and Protestant societies and the local Greek-Orthodox and Armenian communities in the city subsequently founded presses that printed in Arabic, all in the nineteenth century, which put out books and leaflets dealing mostly with religious-educational matters.[6] Some reports also point to the existence, alongside the missionary and communal enterprises, of several private presses in pre-1900 Jerusalem: *al-Matba'a al-Ma'muniyya* (1876), the Dumyan brothers press (1892), a printing shop owned by Martin Lasfu (1892) and *al-Matba'a al-Wataniyya,* which Alfonse Antun Alonzo ran from 1892–4. We know little about them beyond their names. Nor is there evidence to support an obscure reference in an 1898 official Ottoman publication, to similar activities taking place outside of Jerusalem.[7] Further exploration is obviously needed before this scene is clear.[8]

Yet another private printing shop that started operating around the same time was that of Jurji Habib Hananya, about which we know slightly more. Apparently a typical instance of the country's nascent publishing projects, it would be worth our while to look at it more closely. Hananya (1857–1920), a Greek-Orthodox Jerusalemite, seems to have been employed for some time in one of the presses in that

5 M.T. Petrozzi, 'The Franciscan printing press,' *Christian News from Israel,* 20:26 (1971), 64–9. A bibliography of Arabic works printed in Palestine from 1847 onward lists 65 items produced by the Franciscan press during the nineteenth century and another 51 during the first half of the twentieth; see Rasim Jabbara, *Al-Bibliyughrafiyya al-'Arabiyya fi Filastin 1847–1947* (al-Tayyiba, Israel 1996), passim. Jabara's list exists only in draft form, and I am grateful to the author for allowing me to consult it. Undoubtedly less than complete, it is nonetheless the most comprehensive record of this kind so far.

6 Details in Ya'acov Yehoshua, *Ta'rikh al-Sihafa al-'Arabiyya fi Filastin fi'l-'Ahd al-'Uthmani, 1908–1918* (Jerusalem 1974), 7–13; Muhammad Sulayman, 'al-Matabi' al-Filastiniyya wa-Atharuha al-Thaqafi fi'l-'Ahd al-Turki,' *Ru'ya* (Gaza), 13 (October 2001), 78–82; 'Abd al-Rahman Yaghi, *Hayat al-Adab al-Filastini al-Hadith, min Awwal al-Nahda hatta al-Nakba* (Beirut 1968), 77–80.

7 Sulayman, 77, quoting an Ottoman *Salnameh* from 1316/1898, which refers to private Arabic printing activity 'in the narrow alleys of old Jerusalem, Haifa and Jaffa.' This reference was first quoted by Sulayman in a study he had published in 1987 (probably adopted from Yehoshua, 7). In his 2001 article cited here, he notes that 'since the publication of that book in 1987 until today, my extensive toiling and all forms of exploring and inquiring [into the matter] have led to no [new information] worth mentioning in this regard.'

8 Yehoshua, *Ta'rikh,* ibid; Sulayman, ibid. Yehoshua also mentions two Jewish presses, that of Yitzhaq Hirschenson (1876) and that of Yitzhaq Levi (1896), both of which were equipped with Arabic characters as well as Hebrew ones. Frequent discrepancies between the secondary sources regarding dates of foundation and other details suggest that the early development of printing in Palestine is still awaiting a more systematic study. For example, Yaghi, relying on various sources, quotes impressive but somewhat dubious figures relating to the output of some pre-1900 presses in Jerusalem, for which no evidence is known to be extant. Jabbara's *Bibliyughrafiyya* mentions a modest total of 14 items printed before 1900 by Jerusalem presses other than the Franciscan (and a few others without a date of publication printed between 1847 and 1948).

city before launching his own business. In 1894 he applied for a printing license. Such a request normally entailed protracted waiting in Hamidian times, and Hananya moved ahead to begin his activities anyway, acquiring Latin characters and buying printing time from presses in the city to perform freelance jobs during the tourist season. Resourceful and ambitious, he then imported Arabic letters and a simple leg-operated machine and put them to use secretly in his home, taking private assignments from Ottoman officials and others and handling them at night while carrying on with his other commitments during the day. Repeatedly quarrelling with the authorities, Hananya persisted in this difficult routine until February 1898, when he eventually obtained the desired printing license. The following year he applied for permission to publish a newspaper, an application he would subsequently repeat numerous times and back it with sizeable bribes but to no avail. Meanwhile, he made a living from printing 'the circulars (*dafatir*) of all government departments' as well as the local Ottoman official organ, *Quds-i Sharif/al-Quds al-Sharif*, launched in 1903 and lasting for five years. More impressive, by the time the Hamidian censorship dam collapsed in summer 1908, Hananya's business had to its credit — by his own account — a total of '281 books (*kitab*^{an}), among them 83 in Arabic.'[9] Aside of Hananya's own testimony, however, no evidence has yet come to light that would confirm these remarkable but somewhat questionable figures. Most likely, a yield of this scale, if true, comprised mainly small-size pamphlets, leaflets and perhaps single-sheet products rather than real 'books'.[10]

Having gone through trial and error in rough times, Hananya was ready for the new opportunities offered under 'the rising sun of freedom.' Within six weeks of the changeover in the Ottoman capital, his semi-weekly newspaper *al-Quds* was out in the market — one of the country's very earliest periodicals. It was among 15 Arabic newspapers and journals that appeared in a frantic outburst before the end of 1908, reflecting the new liberal spirit in the empire.[11] The license to print prompted the

9 Opening article of *al-Quds* (Hananya's paper), 5–18 September 1908, quoted in Yehoshua, *Ta'rikh,* 41–4, and see also 10–11. On p. 10 Yehoshua erroneously indicates the date of the license as 1906, an error also adopted by Sulayman, 82.

10 Jabbara's bibliography lists only 5 works printed in Hananya's press (also called Matba'at *Jaridat al-Quds*), only one of them before 1908 — see below. In addition, *c.* 20 other titles are mentioned as having been printed in Jerusalem until 1908, for which no printer's name is given.

11 Details in Khuri, *al-Sihafa,* 7–15. Another 19 papers appeared in Palestine between 1909 and 1914; ibid, 16–26.

emergence of presses, set up specifically for the purpose of publishing newspaper and voicing opinion. Such were the printing shops producing *al-Insaf*, *al-Najah* and *al-Nafir* in Jerusalem, *al-Akhbar*, *Sawt al-'Uthmaniyya* and *Filastin* in Jaffa and *al-Karmil* in Haifa before 1914, all modest enterprises that used imported machinery, often second-hand, to manufacture the rudimentary organs authored by their owners. Others, eager to pronounce views but unable to buy the needed equipment, hired the services of existing presses (Hananya's own shop printed one other journal, or more, alongside his own *al-Quds*).[12] But putting out newspapers was a small operation even for these humble businesses, and they looked for additional jobs, advertising such innovative products as commercial letterheads and envelopes, personal cards, wedding invitations and the like. They would gladly print books, if and when they were available for publication.

But books were slow to appear. Pre-World War I Palestine was overwhelmingly illiterate and the size of its book-consuming audience was Lilliputian. The number of authors was still tinier. Prior to the introduction of printing into the country, members of the small educated elite had subscribed to foreign journals and bought books from neighbouring provinces and Europe; while the handful of local writers went abroad to print their composed or translated works.[13] Writing in Palestine was far too limited in scope to keep the machines of the newly launched presses rolling. Preceding the country's literary awakening, the development of printing thus had to rely mainly on publishing newspapers, a novel brand of commodity whose consumer market was yet to be formed. Hananya's business was illustrative of this activity. With a twice-weekly paper as its mainstay, the press constantly looked for more jobs but found little. 'Few as [presses in Jerusalem] are, there is no adequate work for them,' he complained.[14] In 1900 he was hired to print the catalogue of the new Khalidiyya library, an 87-page, Spartan-looking booklet.[15] Other Hananya-produced works that came down to us include a 28-page tourist guide in 1908 and three tracts on language

12 Ibid, 7; Yehoshua, *Ta'rikh,* 78, 86.

13 Husam al-Khatib, *Harakat al-Tarjamah al-Filastiniyya: min al-Nahda hatta Awakhir al-Qarn al-'Ishrin* (Beirut 1995), appendix; Nasir al-Din al-Asad, *al-Ittijahat al-Adabiyya al-Haditha fi Filastin wa'l-Urdun* (Cairo 1957), 42.

14 Quoted in Yehoshua, *Ta'rikh,* 12.

15 Al-Maktaba al-Khalidiyya, *Barnamaj al-Maktaba al-Khalidiyya al-'Umumiyya* (Jerusalem: Matba'at Jurji Habib Hananya, 1900).

from 1912, likewise skinny opuses of 60–70 pages each.[16] There might have been a few more, of which we have no trace. This was probably characteristic of the scale of private printing efforts in pre-World War I Palestine. We know little on the manner in which such works were circulated; with few bookstores around before the War (see below), the dissemination of printed items must have been slow and cumbersome, and on the whole limited in scope. Hananya himself ran into financial difficulties, typically resulting from the unfriendly market conditions, and was forced to close his business, leaving the country for Alexandria in 1913 or 1914.[17]

So much for the printer's share. To view Palestine's early publishing from the author's angle, we may look at Khalil Baydas (1875–1949), owner of the literary weekly/monthly *al-Nafa'is al-'Asriyya.*[18] A Greek-Orthodox like Hananya and a graduate of Russian missionary schools in Palestine and Syria, Baydas had translated Tolstoy and Pushkin novels and published them in Beirut and Cairo for several years prior to 1908.[19] In November of that year, three months after the Revolution, he launched his journal in Haifa, teaming up with a new local press called *al-Matba'a al-Wataniyya.* The following year he published a novel he had adapted from the Russian, hiring the same printer to bring it out.[20] In 1910 Baydas moved with his journal to Jerusalem, where he continued to publish it regularly until the War, scoring remarkable success.[21] Seeking to acquaint his readers with the treasures of Russian literature, he devoted a large portion of the journal to translations from that language, usually his own. But he also issued separate works, rendered from Russian and other tongues and often presented as *riwayat,* or short stories — apparently small-size chapbooks (as their modest price would suggest) — but also more massive works.[22] Both *al-Nafa'is al-'Asriyya* and some of these separate literary items were produced

16 Jabbara, *al-Bibliyughrafiyya,* see entries under Salim Ilyas al-Qari (1908) and Muhammad Salim Ibn Qutayna (1912).

17 Yehoshua, *Ta'rikh,* 48–50.

18 Jan Daya, 'Al-Nafa'is al-'Asriyya,' *Shu'un Filastiniyya,* 87–88 (February–March 1979), 168–80.

19 Details in al-Khatib, first page of the appendix; *al-Kitab al-'Arabi al-Filastini: Ma'rad al-Kitab al-'Arabi al-Filastini al-Awwal fi Nadi al-Ittihad al-Urthuduksi fi'l-Quds, min 11–20 Tishrin al-Awwal 1946* (Jerusalem 1946), passim.

20 *Ahwal al-Istibdad,* a translation of a book by Tolstoy (Haifa: al-Matba'a al-Wataniyya, 1909); Khatib, *al-Kitab,* ibid.

21 Daya, 'Al-Nafa'is al-'Asriyya,' 170; Yehoshua, *Ta'rikh,* 94. While in Haifa the paper was entitled *al-Nafa'is.* The name was expanded to *al-Nafa'is al-'Asriyya* once it was restarted in Jerusalem.

22 Baydas's journal used to advertise such books and booklets. See e.g. Vol. 5, issues 1 (January 1913) and 4 (April 1913), back covers, featuring 19 and 20 items respectively. Most items sold for 1.50–2.50 Franks each (equivalent to 6–10 Ottoman qurush), a rather modest price.

in Jerusalem by *Matba'at Dar al-Aytam*, the Syrian orphanage press, an ambitious endeavour which by then had acquired a reputation as the country's best.[23] The initiative in this publishing operation was most likely the author's, who selected the texts, prepared the manuscripts and then promoted the final products in his journal. Once again, with bookstores still in the future, the printed items were distributed directly by the author and potential customers were urged to order them 'from the management of *al-Nafa'is al-'Asriyya* in Jerusalem.'[24]

Palestine's political, economic and educational wheels shifted to a higher gear after World War I and private printing shops proliferated quickly. A bibliography of Arabic works published in Palestine until 1947 mentions no less than 115 presses that were involved in their production in the post-War years, including 40 in Jerusalem, 35 in Jaffa, 22 in Haifa and the rest in Acre, Nazareth, Nablus, Bethlehem, Gaza, Ramallah, Lydda, Safad and Hebron.[25] The majority of books and leaflets were produced through simple collaboration with the authors, usually initiated by the latter. Serving as his own editor and copyreader, the writer would hire the services of a press, which would also advertise the work in its own-printed or other newspaper. As for distribution, bookshops that emerged in Palestine after the War gradually became popular conduits for the purpose. Some of them also got involved in publishing, as we shall now see.

Bookstores as Publishers

Data on the front cover of *Ta'rikh Filastin,* a volume published in Palestine in 1923, reveal the story of its production. 'Its publication,' it reads, 'was handled (*'ana bi-nashrihi*) by Bulus and Wadiʿ Saʿid, owners of *Maktabat Filastin al-'Ilmiyya*, and it was 'printed in *Bayt al-Maqdis* press in Jerusalem.'[26] Production was thus a dual process, representing a joint author-bookshop-printer venture. This was a rather rare kind of undertaking at the time, but it would become quite common in the 1940s.

---

23 Yaghi, *Hayat,* 79; W.D. McCracken, *The New Palestine* (London 1922), 262. The Syrian orphanage was founded in 1860 as a German Protestant project. Among the different vocations in which the children were trained was printing, an endeavour apparently begun around the turn of the century.

24 E.g., *al-Nafa'is al-'Asriyya*, Vol. 5, issues 1 (January 1913) and 4 (April 1913), back covers.

25 Jabbara, *al-Bibliyughrafiyya*, passim.

26 'Umar Salih al-Barghuthi and Khalil Tawtah, *Ta'rikh Filastin* (Jerusalem: Matba'at Bayt al-Maqdis, 1923).

Until close to World War I, the notion of a bookstore was barely known in Palestine. A survey of Jerusalem shops in the late 1860s, conducted by a contemporary observer, found only two booksellers among the 1,932 businesses he recorded, an Armenian and a Jew.[27] Old-style individual book dealers may have operated in some places there already in the nineteenth century, circulating mainly traditional manuscripts; but given the limited demand, this could hardly have been a thriving trade. During the last third of that century, the number of visitors to the holy city was on the ascent and local traders began to cater to their needs, among others in tourist guides (primarily, of course, in foreign languages). Thus, Boulus (Bulus) Meo's famous souvenir shop near the Jaffa Gate carried, along with 'olive, wood and pearl' items, also 'tourist guidebooks,' as its front door sign indicated.[28] More such dealerships opened elsewhere in the city and possibly in the town of Jaffa, the country's main port of entry. Sometime before World War I, the brothers Bulus and Wadi' Sa'id — who would later publish *Ta'rikh Filastin* — opened their *Maktabat Filastin al-'Ilmiyya* or 'Palestine Educational Company' in Jerusalem, a firm that would become one of the country's biggest after the War.[29] A bookshop is also reported to have opened in Haifa in mid-1914, only to close down within several months due to the War.[30] Commensurate with the scanty demand, the scope of these initiatives must have been, on the whole, very small at that stage.

The number of bookshops in Palestine grew markedly after the War. But if books made in the country were few, what did they sell? Ads in the post-War press tell us that the merchandize carried by these businesses was highly variegated. In mandatory Palestine, a bookshop, or *maktaba,* represented a colourful institution. Beyond trading in local and imported books, such places often sold newspapers, school and office supplies, Christmas cards and gifts, toys, household aids, and more. Some of them offered bookbinding services. Others lent books for a periodic fee.

27 Charles Warren, *Underground Jerusalem* (London 1876), 491–2. There were also seven bookbinders, six Jews and a Muslim.

28 See Ruth Victor Hummel, 'Reality, imagination and belief: Jerusalem in 19th- and early 20th-century photographs (1839–1917),' in Sylvia Auld and Robert Hillenbrand (eds), *Ottoman Palestine* (London 2000), Vol. 1:261 (presenting a photograph from *c.* 1881 that shows the shop and its sign); Walid Khalidi, *Before Their Diaspora* (Washington DC: Institute for Palestine Studies, 1984), 62, picture no. 40 (where it appears in a section covering the period prior to 1918).

29 Their post-war ads indicated that the shop had been in operation since 1910; e.g., *Filastin,* 9 September 1921, 3; *al-Nafa'is al-'Asriyya,* 9:4 (August 1922), 111.

30 *Al-Zahra,* 2:7/8 (1922–3), 185–6.

Thus, the Saʿid brothers' company, expanding its trade to Jaffa (as well as to Cairo and Alexandria), carried 'all scholarly and cultural books in Arabic and foreign languages, writing materials, school and business supplies,' current periodicals, Arabic, English and Hebrew 'Royal' typewriters and even 'Columbia' gramophones.[31] Such businesses became quite numerous during the mandate; by 1945, when a 'union of Arab bookstore owners in Palestine' was founded, no less than 51 of them had joined in — from Acre to Jerusalem, from Tiberias to Gaza.[32] More to the point, toward the end of the period some of the more enterprising businesses began to enter into publishing, cooperating with existing presses or buying their own printing equipment.

A closer look at one such venture would illustrate this development.[33] Fawzi Yusuf, a young man from Jerusalem, moved to 'fulfil an old dream' in 1935 by opening a bookstore in the Old City, which he named *Maktabat al-Andalus.* He rented a small place, previously a shoe store, refurbished it and commenced his trade. The shop at first sold mostly writing materials, but Yusuf aspired for more. Identifying a rising demand for printed texts, he began to import Egyptian schoolbooks, literary works and journals. Within three years he already had his own bureau in Cairo, upgrading his services and acting as an agent of leading Egyptian periodicals, which he distributed through contracting shops in Jaffa, Haifa, Lydda and other towns. On the eve of World War II he introduced yet another innovative service, allowing his customers to borrow books for a monthly sum. The War cut the supplies from Egypt and forced Yusuf to close down his Cairo office. Resourceful and resilient, he moved to devise new projects that would keep him afloat on the rough waters. 'We did not remain idle with our arms crossed,' Yusuf recalled (speaking of himself in the first-person plural):

> Rather, we sought new directions for our initiative and began thinking of printing schoolbooks locally ... The idea was crowned with success. A group of teachers prepared the texts needed for our schools, each in his field of specialization, and we had the books

31 Ads in *al-Nafa'is al-'Asriyya*, ibid; *Filastin*, 9 November 1921, 4, and 30 April 1929, 7.

32 Israel State Archive, P326/630 — letter by the union's secretary to Khalil al-Sakakini dated 11 March 1945. The letter also refers to several additional bookstores that had declined to join the union.

33 This description is based on Fawzi Yusuf, *Khamsun 'Aman fi Khidam al-Haraka al-Thaqafiyya: Maktabat al-Andalus 1935–1985* (Jerusalem 1985), 16–22, 27, 30; idem, *Shay' min Hayati* (Jerusalem 1980), 47–9.

> printed locally. We thereby fulfilled a precious desire: the writing and printing of books at home became a reality ... To guarantee continued production, we began importing the required [quantities of] paper directly from the mills.
>
> Our store came to supply schools with the necessary texts ... The Department of Education encouraged this scheme, and sometimes bought quantities of them for its depositories. We also paid visits to schools and bookstores, offering them the books we printed.[34]

This was an exemplary case of a project born out of necessity. Yusuf combined forces with a well-known press, Bandali Mushahwar's *Matba'at Bayt al-Maqdis* near the Old City's Jaffa Gate (which, we shall recall, was the printer of *Ta'rikh Filastin*, mentioned above).[35] He also came up with an assortment of original paper products carrying his shop's logo, outwitting his competitors and helping his business to survive the dire circumstances. Once the war was over, *Maktabat al-Andalus* could resume its book dealings in full swing. By now it was experienced in production and in a position to become a small-size publisher, issuing school texts and children's books.

Fawzi Yusuf's story was replicated by other businesses of a similar kind that sprang up in mandatory Palestine. The bookstore-cum-stationery formula, the centrality of selling imported products, the marketing of school texts along with other works, were all features of the post-Ottoman era, which *Maktabat al-Andalus* shared with several other traders. The market of consumers developed tardily, and booksellers had to engage in diverse tactics to survive. The more creative among them became embryonic publishers, entering into book production toward the end of the period. Most active, aside of Yusuf's shop, were *al-Maktaba al-'Asriyya* and *Maktabat al-Tahir Ikhwan* in Jaffa, both founded in the 1930s, and the Jerusalem *Maktabat Filastin al-'Ilmiyya* of the veteran Sa'id brothers.[36] A growing share of the books appearing in the country during the later years of the mandate were, thus, not only distributed but also printed by these shops.

---

34 Yusuf, *Shay'*, 48; idem, *Khamsun 'Aman*, 30.

35 Jabbara's bibliography mentions 122 items published by this press between 1920 and 1948. Jabbara, *al-Bibliyughrafiyya*, passim.

36 Of the two Jaffa shops, the former produced 20 books or more during the 1940s, the latter at least 16; the Sa'ids issued at least 7 recorded titles. Figures gathered from Jabbara's bibliography, passim. See also Yaacov Shim'oni, *Aravey Eretz Yisrael* (Tel Aviv 1947), 397–8.

By 1948, Palestine had made important strides toward developing its own publishing industry. Where a mere handful of presses had existed in 1900, dozens of them were now running. Where bookstores had been rare, scores of them were now engaged in lively trade countrywide. Other changes, not discussed in this paper, were equally vital in this development: the expansion of the periodical press, a promoter of books and a public trainer in reading; the emergence of social-cultural clubs, loci of literary activities; and, perhaps most important, the dynamic spread of education. These changes provided indispensable underpinnings for the publishing edifice. On the whole, however, the achievements were modest at that early stage, as reflected in the meagre local printed harvest (this was especially conspicuous when juxtaposed with the immeasurably richer output of the country's smaller but better educated Jewish community at the time).[37] Such limited accomplishments should be hardly surprising, given the very low point of departure and the mighty impact of literary activity in neighbouring countries. The fateful events of 1948 befell Palestine while still laying the foundations for its own publishing trade, cutting short what seemed to be a promising beginning.

37 Cf. the somewhat hasty but still telling comparison by Ishaq Musa al-Husayni between Arab and Jewish publishing in mandatory Palestine. Husayni contrasted the 209 Arabic books published between 1919 and 1946, which he had managed to trace, with 349 Hebrew books published in the country in one year, 1933–4. Ishaq Musa al-Husayni, *'Awdat al-Safina* (Jerusalem 1945), 37–40. In the same vein, see E. Mills, *Census of Palestine 1931* (Alexandria, Printed for the Government of Palestine by Whitehead Morris, 1933), I:214, 219.

[26]

MESROPS ERBEN: DIE ARMENISCHEN BUCHDRUCKER DER FRÜHZEIT

MESROP'S HEIRS: THE EARLY ARMENIAN BOOK PRINTERS

Meliné Pehlivanian

1. Der kulturelle Hintergrund

Armenier haben von jeher eine besonders enge Beziehung zum geschriebenen oder gedruckten Wort. Der Mönch Mesrop Maštoc', Schöpfer des armenischen Alphabets im Jahre 405, wird als Heiliger verehrt, weil sein Werk das armenische Volk, sein Christentum und seine Kultur vor dem Untergang bewahrte. Der armenische Kirchenkalender kennt ein „Fest der Übersetzer", das der Erfindung des armenischen Alphabets und den ersten Übersetzern der Bibel ins Armenische gewidmet ist. Das handgeschriebene Buch wurde verehrt, geschmückt, vor Feinden geschätzt und begleitete die Menschen auf der Flucht.

Die Armenier, deren Geschichte mit dem Untergang des kilikischen Reiches seit 1375 bis 1918 keine Staatlichkeit mehr kennt, und deren geographische Lage am Kreuzweg vieler Kulturen und mächtiger Reiche das Volk immer wieder zum Opfer von Kriegen, Plünderungen und Zerstörungen machte, sahen von jeher in ihrem Glauben und in ihrer Sprache die Garanten des nationalen Überlebens. Doch Sprache kann nur überdauern wenn sie fixiert wird, wenn sie die nationalen Überlieferungen in handgeschriebenen, später gedruckten Büchern von Generation zu Generation weiter gibt. Adel und Klerus förderten das Entstehen von Skriptorien und Bibliotheken in den Klöstern und gaben Handschriften in Auftrag. Doch das handgeschriebene Buch war ein rares, kostbares und vor allem gefährdetes Gut. In Kriegszeiten wurden Klöster und deren Skriptorien und Bibliotheken zerstört, verloren die Menschen ihr Hab und Gut und natürlich auch ihre Bücher. Der Verlust eines Manuskriptes aber konnte den Verlust von nationalem Schriftgut, einer Chronik oder eines Gedichtes, für immer bedeuten.

1. Cultural background

Armenians have always had a particularly close affiliation to the written or printed word. The monk Mesrop Maštoc', creator of the Armenian alphabet in the year 405, is revered as a saint because his work saved the Armenian people, its Christianity and its culture from decline. The Armenian church calendar contains a "Feast of the Translator," dedicated to the invention of the Armenian alphabet and the first translators of the Bible in Armenian. Hand-written books were revered, ornamented, protected from enemies and accompanied fleeing refugees.

Armenia was stateless after the fall of the Cilician empire in 1375 till 1918 and the country's geographical location on the crossroads of many cultures and powerful empires repeatedly made its people the victims of wars, plundering and destruction. Hence, the Armenian people have always seen their belief and their language as the guarantors of national survival. But language can only survive if it is fixed; when it passes down national traditions from generation to generation in hand-written and later in printed books. The nobility and the clergy promoted the creation of scriptoria and libraries in monasteries and commissioned hand-written works. But the hand-written book was a rare, costly and above all an endangered commodity. In times of war monasteries and their scriptoria and libraries were destroyed, the people lost their belongings and of course also their books. However the loss of a manuscript could mean the permanent loss of part of the national writeen heritage, a chronicle or a poem.

2. Geschichtlicher und gesellschaftlicher Hintergrund

Als in Europa um 1450 der Buchdruck aufkam durchlebte Armenien eine der schwersten Perioden seiner Geschichte. Das 15. und 16. Jahrhundert gelten als das „dunkle Zeitalter" Armeniens. Das Land stand fast vollständig unter fremdem Joch und wurde zum Schauplatz kriegerischer Auseinandersetzungen, die die Region verwüsteten. Zu Beginn des 16. Jahrhunderts geriet der eine Teil des Landes unter persische, der andere unter osmanische Fremdherrschaft - dies sollte über dreihundert Jahre so bleiben.

In dieser Situation war die armenische Kirche mit ihrem Oberhaupt, dem Katholikos in Etschmiadzin, die letzte nationale Institution. Der Katholikos und sein Klerus allein waren in der Lage, gesamtnationale Interessen zu vertreten, um das Überleben des Volkes und seiner Kultur zu ermöglichen. Der Klerus richtete sein Augenmerk auf die Bewahrung der nationalen, christlichen Kultur in einem feindlichen Umfeld. Kulturelle Erneuerung in dem geschundenen Land konnte nur durch Bildung, Vermittlung der nationalen, religiösen und geistigen Traditionen und durch Wachhaltung der geschichtlichen Überlieferungen erreicht werden.

Dem Buch kam dabei die zentrale Bedeutung zu. Die Skriptorien jedoch verfielen, Bibliotheken waren vernichtet und am geschriebenen religiösen Buch herrschte großer Mangel. Als die Nachricht von der Gutenbergschen Erfindung nach Armenien gelangte, hoffte die Kirchenführung, durch diese neue Methode zur Vervielfältigung von Schrift und Wissen ein Mittel zum Erreichen ihres Zieles gefunden zu haben. Der Klerus, gemeinhin zu den konservativen Kräften einer Gesellschaft gehörig, wurde im armenischen Fall zum Träger eines Phänomens der gesellschaftlichen Modernisierung und kulturellen Renaissance: Bis zum Ende des 17. Jahrhunderts gingen alle Initiativen im armenischen Buchdruck vom Klerus, oft direkt vom Oberhaupt der armenisch-apostolischen Kirche, dem Katholikos in Etschmiadzin, aus.

Doch es gab noch eine andere Schicht, ohne deren Zutun die Nutzbarmachung des Buchdrucks für die armenische Gesellschaft zum Scheitern verurteilt gewesen wäre: Die armenische Kaufmannschaft in den europäischen und asiatischen Handelsmetropolen. Seit den Invasionen, Kriegen und Verwüstungen des 11. Jahrhunderts kannte Armenien das Massenphänomen der Auswanderung. Es waren oft die

2. Historical and social background

As book printing arrived in Europe around the year 1450 Armenia was experiencing one of the harshest periods of its history. The 15th and 16th centuries are known as the "Dark Age" of Armenia. The country was almost completely under foreign oppression and became the scene of warring conflicts that laid waste to the region. In the early 16th century one part of the country came under Iranian and the other part under Ottoman rule - a condition that lasted for over three hundred years.

In this situation the Armenian Church with its head, the catholicos in Ejmiadzin, was the only remaining national institution. The catholicos and his clergy alone were able to represent national interests and thus make possible the survival of the people and their culture. The clergy gave its attention to preserving the national Christian culture in a hostile environment. In the oppressed country cultural renewal could be achieved only through education, through passing down national, religious and intellectual traditions and through keeping historic traditions alive.

The book assumed a central importance in this respect. But the scriptoria deteriorated, libraries were destroyed and there was a great lack of written religious books. When the news arrived in Armenia of Gutenberg's invention the church leaders hoped to use this method of reproducing words and knowledge as a means for achieving their aim. In the case of Armenia the clergy, generally part of society's conservative forces, became the bearers of a phenomenal social modernisation and cultural renaissance. Until the end of the 17th century all initiatives in Armenian book printing were taken by the clergy, often directly by the head of the Armenian Apostolic Church, the catholicos in Ejmiadzin.

But there was another class without whom the undertaking of book printing for the benefit of Armenian society would have been doomed to fail: the Armenian merchant class in the European and Asian trading metropolises. Ever since the invasions, wars and devastation of the 11th century Armenia experienced a phenomenon of mass emigration. Often the most mobile elements of society were the

mobilsten Elemente der Gesellschaft, die den katastrophalen Lebensbedingungen in der Heimat entfliehen wollten und von denen einige später welt- und sprachgewandte Vermittler im Orient-Handel wurden. Seit dem Mittelalter, teilweise noch in byzantinische Zeit zurückreichend, lassen sich armenische Kolonien z. B. in Venedig, Livorno, Amsterdam oder Marseille nachweisen. Durch die Kaufmannschaft, dieses im physischen wie geistigen Sinne bewegliche Element der armenischen Gesellschaft, kam das von der Entwicklung abgeschnittene Armenien in Kontakt mit der europäischen Kultur. Es waren armenische Kaufleute, die weniger von Profitgier als vom Wunsch nach Bewahrung der armenischen Kultur gelenkt, die ersten Mäzene, Auftraggeber, Vermittler und Kunden der armenischen Buchdrucker wurden.

3. Europa als Wiege des armenischen Buchdrucks

Schon 1512, rund 60 Jahre nach Gutenberg, schlug in Venedig die Geburtsstunde des armenischen Buchdrucks. Es sollten über hundertachtzig Jahre vergehen, bis armenische Druckereien dauerhaft im Orient Fuß faßten und gar 260 Jahre, bis der Buchdruck 1772 auf armenischem Boden selbst angekommen war.

Die Gründung einer Druckerei in Armenien erwies sich im 16. und 17. Jahrhundert als unmöglich: Die Situation des Landes war durch ständige Kriege instabil und unsicher, durch die wirtschaftliche Zurückgebliebenheit der Region fehlte jede technische Infrastruktur. Überdies stellte die große räumliche Entfernung von Europa die Drucker vor große Nachschubprobleme bei der nötigen Ausrüstung und beim Papier. Zu jener Zeit bot allein Europa die notwendigen Voraussetzungen für den Buchdruck. Die Pioniere der Zunft orientierten sich also nach Europa und hier zuerst nach Venedig. Die Lagunenstadt hatte mehrere entscheidende Vorteile zu bieten. Es existierte dort seit dem 13. Jahrhundert eine armenische Kolonie, die einen Anlaufpunkt für die Neuankömmlinge bot, deren Mitglieder sich vor Ort auskannten und als Mäzene auftraten. Venedig galt mit über 200 Druckereien im ausgehenden 15. Jahrhundert als *das* Zentrum des europäischen Buchdrucks. Hier war die katholische Zensur vergleichsweise milde, was Drukker aus aller Herren Länder anzog: Neben italienischen gab es u. a. deutsche, französische, serbische, griechische, jüdische Werkstätten.[1]

ones to flee from the catastrophic living conditions in their homeland. Later some of them became sophisticated and multi-lingual mediators in Eastern trade. There were Armenian colonies for instance in Venice, Livorno, Amsterdam or Marseille since the Middle Ages, some going back to the Byzantine age. The merchants, the physically and intellectually mobile elements of Armenian society, allowed isolated Armenia to come in contact with European culture. Those Armenian merchants who were motivated less by greed for profits than by the desire to preserve Armenian culture became the first patrons, commissioners, mediators and clients of Armenian book printers.

3. Europe as the cradle of Armenian book printing

As early as 1512, roughly 60 years after Gutenberg, Armenian book printing was born in Venice. It would be over 180 years before Armenian printing presses gained a permanent footing in the East and a full 260 years before book printing would finally arrive on Armenian soil in 1772.

In the 16th and 17th centuries establishing a printing press in Armenia was impossible. The country's situation was unstable and unsafe because of constant wars. The economic retardation of the region meant that there was no technical infrastructure whatsoever. Furthermore because of the country's great distance from Europe the printers were faced with major supply problems for equipment and paper. At that time Europe alone offered the necessary prerequisites for book printing. The trade's pioneers hence were oriented towards Europe and initially towards Venice. The lagoon city had a number of decisive advantages to offer. There had been an Armenian colony there since the 13th century that offered new arrivals a refuge and whose members were familiar with the local territory and acted as patrons. With more than 200 presses in the final years of the 15th century, Venice was the centre of European book printing. Catholic censorship here was comparatively mild, a fact that attracted printers from all nations. In addition to Italian presses there were, for example, German, French, Serb, Greek and Jewish presses.[1]

Bevor sich Konstantinopel ab Ende des 17. Jahrhunderts allmählich zum Zentrum des armenischen Buchgewerbes entwickelte, waren es europäische Städte wie Venedig, Amsterdam, Livorno und Marseille, die den ersten armenischen Druckern Arbeitsmöglichkeiten boten.

Neben Venedig gebührt wohl Amsterdam ein Ehrenplatz in der armenischen Buchdruck- und Geistesgeschichte, als der Stadt, in der in den Jahren 1666 bis 1668 die erste armenische Bibel gedruckt wurde.

Before Constantinople gradually developed into the centre of the Armenian book trade beginning in the late 17th century, the first Armenian printers were offered the opportunity to work in European cities such as Venice, Amsterdam, Livorno and Marseille.

Besides Venice, Amsterdam as well deserves a place of honour in Armenian book printing and spiritual history as the city in which the first Armenian Bible was printed in the years 1666–68.

4. Der armenische Buchdruck im Orient

Es waren Juden (seit 1493 in Konstantinopel), Armenier (seit 1567 in Konstantinopel, seit 1638 in Persien) und Griechen (seit 1627 in Konstantinopel), die als erste im Orient lebende Völker dort die Gutenbergsche Erfindung nutzten.

Den beiden ersten armenischen Bestrebungen, den Buchdruck näher an das armenische Heimatland zu bringen, war noch kein dauerhafter Erfolg beschieden: 1567 existierte in Konstantinopel für zwei Jahre die Druckerei des Abgar Toxatec'i. 1638 druckten Armenier in Nor Jowġa/Isfahan das erste Buch im Iran. Erst im 18. Jahrhundert verlagerte sich das Zentrum des armenischen Buchdrucks endgültig von Europa in den Orient.

In Europa steckten die armenischen Drucker in immer größeren Schwierigkeiten. Die Buchproduktion wurde aufgrund schlechter Absatzmöglichkeiten zunehmend unrentabler. Viele Drucker überschuldeten sich, ihre Werkstätten wurden gepfändet und geschlossen. Das Mäzenatentum der armenischen Kaufleute in Europa reichte allein nicht mehr aus: Die Druckereien mußten näher an ihre Käufer kommen.

Erste Station und Hochburg des armenischen Buchdrucks für die nächsten 200 Jahre wurde Konstantinopel. In der osmanischen Hauptstadt lebten um 1700 bereits ca. 40 000 Armenier, deren geistiges und politisches Zentrum das armenische Patriarchat von Konstantinopel bildete. Die Stadt mit ihrer kosmopolitischen Bevölkerung und ihrer Lage zwischen Orient und Okzident bot den armenischen Druckereien viele Vorteile: Sie lag einerseits nahe genug an Europa, um die Beschaffung des notwendigen technischen Gerätes, des Papiers und der Druckfarbe zu gewährleisten, andererseits nahe genug am armenischen Kernland, um die Transportwege zu den po-

4. Armenian book printing in the East

The first peoples living in the East to make use of Gutenberg's invention were the Jews (since 1493 in Constantinople), Armenians (since 1567 in Constantinople and since 1638 in Iran) and Greeks (since 1627 in Constantinople).

The two first Armenian efforts to take book printing closer to the Armenian homeland did not meet with permanent success. From 1567 the printing press of Abgar Toxatec'i existed in Constantinople for two years. In 1638 Armenians in Nor Jowġa, Isfahan printed the very first book in Iran. Not until the 18th century did the centre of Armenian printing permanently move from Europe to the East.

In Europe the Armenian printers worked under ever-greater difficulties. Owing to the poor sales potential book production became increasingly unprofitable. Many printers went into debt; their presses were seized and closed. The patronage of Armenian merchants alone in Europe was no longer enough: the presses had to move nearer to their buyers.

For the next 200 years the first station and stronghold of Armenian book printing was Constantinople. Around 1700 the Ottoman capital city was already the home of approximately 40,000 Armenians, whose spiritual and political centre was the Armenian patriarchate of Constantinople. The city, with its cosmopolitan population and its geographical position between the Orient and Occident, offered the Armenian printing presses many advantages. On the one hand it was close enough to Europe to make procurement of the necessary technical equipment, paper and printing ink possible, on the other hand it was close enough to the Armenian

tentiellen Käufern wesentlich zu verkürzen. Die armenische Kolonie in Konstantinopel war unvergleichlich größer als die jeder europäischen Stadt und unter den Konstantinopler Armeniern befanden sich genug reiche Kaufleute und Bankiers, die als Mäzene der Drucker auftreten konnten. Das armenische Patriarchat hatte ebenfalls Bedarf an Büchern für seine Kirchen und Schulen. In Konstantinopel konnten die armenischen Drucker, so paradox es klingt, freier arbeiten als im christlichen Europa. Die alten Zentren des armenischen Buchdrucks lagen, mit Ausnahme Amsterdams, alle im Einflußbereich des Papstes und damit der katholischen Zensur. Im 17. Jahrhundert ging Rom zu einer immer offensiveren Missionspolitik gegenber den orientalischen Christen über, wovon die Gründung der Sacra Congregatio de Propaganda Fide (SCPF) 1622 Zeugnis ablegte. Nun verschärfte sich die katholische Zensur derart, das den nicht-katholischen armenischen Druckereien die Arbeit fast unmöglich wurde. In Konstantinopel hingegen lag die Aufsicht über den armenischen Buchdruck nicht beim osmanischen Staat, sondern beim armenischen Patriarchat. Das sollte bis zum osmanischen Pressegesetz von 1866 so bleiben. Diese relative Freiheit war ein weiterer wichtiger Grund für die Konzentration des armenischen Druck- und Verlagswesens in der osmanischen Hauptstadt.[2] Im Laufe des 18. Jahrhunderts existierten dort ca. 20 armenische Druckereien. Die Vorherrschaft Europas auf dem Sektor war gebrochen: Im 18. Jahrhundert erschienen bereits ca. 300 armenische Titel in Konstantinopel gegenüber 270 Titeln in Venedig.

homeland to shorten significantly the transport routes to potential buyers. The Armenian colony in Constantinople was incomparably larger than in any other European city and among the Constantinople Armenians were enough rich merchants and bankers to serve as the printers' patrons. The Armenian patriarchate also demanded books for its churches and schools. Paradoxical as it may seem, Armenian printers were able to work more freely in Constantinople than in Christian Europe. The former centres of Armenian book printing, with the exception of Amsterdam, all lay within the sphere of influence of the Pope and hence Catholic censorship. In the 17th century Rome began an increasingly offensive missionary policy towards Eastern Christians, as evidenced by the founding of the Sacra Congregatio de Propaganda Fide (SCPF) in 1622. Catholic censorship now became so strict that work became almost impossible for the non-Catholic Armenian presses. In Constantinople the Ottoman state did not monitor Armenian book printing, but rather the Armenian patriarchate. This remained the case until the Ottoman Press Act of 1866. This relative freedom was another important reason for Armenian printing to concentrate in the Ottoman capital.[2] Over the course of the 18th century there were approximately 20 Armenian printing presses in the city. Europe's dominance over the sector had been broken: in the 18th century approximately 300 Armenian titles were published in Constantinople compared with 270 in Venice.

5. Technische Herausforderungen

Die ersten armenischen Drucker kamen ohne größere finanzielle Mittel und ohne Erfahrung in der neuen Technik nach Europa. Das machte die Eröffnung einer eigenen Werkstatt zunächst unmöglich und zwang dazu, bestehende einheimische Druckereien zu nutzen. Die Herstellung der 38 armenischen Drucktypen besorgten, nach handgezeichneten Vorlagen, erfahrene Schriftgießer in Venedig und Amsterdam. Die Typen der Druckerei „Sowrb Ejmiacin ew Sowrb Sargis Zôravar" in Amsterdam z. B. goß kein geringerer als Christoffel van Dijk vom Hause Elzevier. Das für den Druckprozeß benötigte Papier zu beziehen erwies sich in Europa und später auch in Konstantinopel als unproblema-

5. Technical challenges

The first Armenian printers arrived in Europe without major funds and without experience in the new technique. This made it impossible for them to open their own presses at first and forced them to use existing native printing presses. Experienced type founders in Venice and Amsterdam produced the 38 Armenian types after hand-drawn originals. The types of the press "Sowrb Ejmiacin ew Sowrb Sargis Zôravar" in Amsterdam, for example, were cast by no less a craftsman than Christoffel van Dijk from the house of Elzevier. Purchasing the paper required for the printing process proved unproblematic in Europe and later in Constantinople as well – but not in remote regions of Armenia. The first printing

Abb. 1:
Nahapêt Agowlec'i
Seidenhändler und Buchdrucker

Ill. 1:
Nahapêt Agowlec'i
Silk trader and printer

tisch - nicht jedoch in abgelegenen Gegenden Armeniens. Die 1772 gegründete erste Druckerei in Armenien sollte mit diesem Problem lange zu kämpfen haben.

Transport und Vertrieb der Bücher zu den Lesern in Armenien und anderen Ländern des Orients zu sichern oblag den armenischen Kaufleuten in Europa. Die Drucker machten sich deren Vertriebswege zu nutze, um die Bücher per Schiff z. B. nach Smyrna zu bringen. Von dort aus brachten sie mobile Händler in die armenischen Siedlungsgebiete.[3]

In den 1730er Jahren entstanden in Konstantinopel armenische Buchhandlungen. Die Buchhändler professionalisierten nicht nur den Vertrieb, sondern erlangten bald Einfluß auf die Verlagsprogramme - nicht wenige Publikationen entstanden von nun an auf den Rat oder auf Bestellung von Buchhändlern.[4]

press founded in Armenia in 1772 would long be confronted by this problem.

Ensuring the transport and sale of the books to readers in Armenia and other Eastern countries was the responsibility of the Armenian merchants in Europe. The printers took advantage of their sales routes to transport the books, for instance by ship to Smyrna. From there mobile traders carried them to Armenian settlements.[3]

In the 1730s Armenian booksellers settled in Constantinople. The booksellers not only made sales more professional, but also soon gained influence over the publishing programs - from now on it was not uncommon for publications to be produced on the advice or the order of booksellers.[4]

6. Menschliche Herausforderungen

Die Pioniere armenischen Buchdrucks galten immer ein wenig als Märtyrer und Idealisten – sie lebten in der Fremde nicht selten in großer materieller Not und waren Gläubigern und Zensoren ausgeliefert. Einige der frühen Drucker waren zuvor Schreiber von Handschriften gewesen und wendeten ihr Handwerk nun beim Druck von Büchern an. Alle jedoch konnten als gebildete Personen gelten. Ihr Beruf umfaßte schließlich wesentlich mehr als nur die Abwicklung des technischen Druckverfahrens: Sie waren zugleich Verleger. Ihnen oblag meist die Auswahl der zu druckenden Handschrift und ihre inhaltliche Vorbereitung, sie waren Herausgeber, Redakteur und Korrektor, Setzer, Drucker und Besitzer der Werkstatt in einem. Die dazu notwendige Bildung hatten zur Zeit des armenischen Frühdrucks fast nur Priester, die ihre Ausbildung an den Klosteruniversitäten erhielten. Die Ausbildung umfaßte Theologie, Philosophie, Geschichte, Musik und Naturwissenschaften, aber auch das Kopieren, Binden und Illuminieren von Büchern, manchmal sogar die Herstellung von Papier. So verwundert es nicht, daß die ersten Drucker-Verleger fast ausnahmslos Angehörige des niederen oder höheren Klerus waren. Zwei der herausragenden Gestalten des frühen armenischen Buchdrucks, T'ômas Vanandec'i und Oskan Erewanc'i bekleideten gar das Amt eines Bischofs.

Ausnahmen bildeten hier lediglich Gaspar Šêhrimanean, Eremia K'êomiwrčean, Nahapêt Agowlec'i (Abb. 1) und Simêon Georgi.[5]

Erst im 18. Jahrhundert trat, vor allem in Konstantinopel, eine neue Generation von weltlichen Drucker-Verlegern auf den Plan, deren Ambitionen zunehmend auf künstlerisch-literarischem Gebiet lagen und die den Buchdruck als Handwerk und Geschäft betrieben.

Ihnen standen gleichwohl stets gebildete Personen für die Auswahl und das Lektorieren der Manuskripte zur Seite. Oftmals waren es Geistliche wie der Konstantinopler Patriarch Yovhannês Kolot, der eng mit dem Drucker Grigor Marzvanec'i zusammenarbeitete, oder aber Gelehrte wie Paġtasar Dpir, der über 50 Jahre die Werke der Druckerei des Astowacatowr (Dpir) Kostandnowpolsec'i in Konstantinopel betreute.[6]

6. Human challenges

The pioneers of Armenian book printing were always considered somewhat as martyrs and idealists; in foreign lands they often lived in great poverty and were at the mercy of creditors and censors. Some of the early printers had previously been scribes and now applied their craft to the printing of books. But all of them could be considered educated persons. Their occupation consisted of far more than handling the technical process of printing: at the same time they were publishers. They were usually responsible for selecting the manuscripts to be printed and preparing their content, they were editors and proof-readers, typesetters, printers and owners of the press all in one person. The learning required for this in the days of early Armenian printing was possessed almost only by priests, who acquired their education at the monastic universities. Studies there encompassed theology, philosophy, history, music and natural sciences, as well as the copying, binding and illumination of books, sometimes even the manufacture of paper. Hence it is not surprising that the first printer-publishers were almost without exception membersof the lower or higher clergy. Two of the outstanding figures of early Armenian book printing, T'ômas Vanandec'i and Oskan Erewanc'i, were even bishops.

Exceptions to this were Gaspar Šêhrimanean, Eremia K'êomiwrčean, Nahapêt Agowlec'i (Ill. 1) and Simêon Georgi.[5]

Not until the 18th century did a new generation of secular printer-publishers appear on the scene – primarily in Constantinople – whose ambitions increasingly lay in art and literature and who pursued book printing as a craft and a business.

Nonetheless educated persons always assisted these printers in selecting and editing the manuscripts. These were often clergy such as the Constantinople Patriarch Yovhannês Kolot, who worked closely with the printer Grigor Marzvanec'i, or scholars such as Paġtasar Dpir, who supervised the works of the press of Astowacatowr (Dpir) Kostandnowpolsec'i in Constantinople for more than 50 years.[6]

7. Gestalt und Inhalt der Drucke

Höchstes drucktechnisches Niveau erreichten die Amsterdamer armenischen Drucke des 17. Jahrhunderts und die venezianischen Drucke des 17./18. Jahrhunderts. Den Konstantinopler Werkstätten fiel es anfangs nicht leicht, damit zu konkurrieren – so berichten Kolophone vom Ende des 17. und Anfang des 18. Jahrhunderts vom Fehlen großer Lettern, weswegen das gesamte Buch klein gesetzt werden mußte, oder beklagen die Grobheit des Drucks. Doch gerade die besten Drucke von Grigor Marzvanec'i und Astowacatowr Dpir zeugen davon, daß man schon in der Mitte des 18. Jahrhunderts und aus eigener Kraft den Anschluß an das drucktechnische Niveau Europas geschafft hatte. Das hier ausgestellte *Yaysmawowrk'* (Synaxarion – [34]) von 1730 aus der Werkstatt Marzvanec'i ist eine typographische Meisterleistung. Die armenischen Drucke aus Nor J̌owġa/Isfahan, Madras, Kalkutta oder Nor Nachitschewan (Rostow am Don) hingegen blieben bis zum Ende des 18. Jahrhunderts, dem hier untersuchten Zeitraum, sehr bescheiden in Aussehen und drucktechnischem Stand und zeugen außerdem von den permanenten Schwierigkeiten, gutes Papier zu bekommen.

Die künstlerische Gestaltung der armenischen Frühdrucke orientierte sich am Aussehen der traditionellen armenischen Handschriften und entsprach damit dem Geschmack des Publikums. Charakteristisch sind Schmuckinitialen in Tier-, Menschen- oder Pflanzengestalt, verzierte Kopfleisten, Seitenumrahmungen, Randverzierungen, Vignetten, Zierbuchstaben und Kanonbögen. War bei Meßbüchern oder Hymnarien die Angabe von Musiknoten vonnöten, setzte man die traditionellen armenischen Tonschriftzeichen (Xazen), in etwa mit den Neumen vergleichbar, über die Wörter. Ansonsten unterschied sich das frühe armenische Buch nicht von den zeitgenössisch europäischen. Die eingefügten Holz- oder Kupferschnitte der meist religiösen Bücher waren Werke europäischer Künstler, die in vielen Büchern wiederverwendet wurden. Die 160 Holzschnitte des ersten armenischen Bibeldrucks zum Beispiel stammen aus der Werkstatt des holländischen Meisters Christophel van Sichem. Das manchmal eigentümlich anmutende Nebeneinander von Elementen des traditionellen armenischen Handschriftenstils mit gänzlich europäischen Illustrationen in einem Buch änderte sich erst mit dem Ansiedlung der Werkstätten im Orient. Die Drucker

7. Form and content of the printed works

Armenian printing in Amsterdam in the 17th century and Venice in the 17th and 18th centuries attained the highest levels of technical perfection. The Constantinople presses did not find it easy at first to compete with them. Hence colophons from the late 17th and early 18th centuries report of the lack of capital letters, so that an entire book had to be set in lower case, or complained of the roughness of the print. But the best books printed by Grigor Marzvanec'i and Astowacatowr Dpir prove that even in the mid-18th century they had attained European standards in printing, entirely through their own ability. The *Yaysmawowrk'* (Synaxarion – [34]) exhibited here of 1730 from the press of Marzvanec'i is a typographical masterpiece. The Armenian prints from Nor J̌owġa, Isfahan, Madras, Calcutta or Nor Nakhichevan (Rostov-on-Don) by contrast remained very modest in appearance and technical printing standards until the end of the 18th century, the time period examined here, and also reveal the constant difficulties printers had in acquiring good paper.

The artistic layout of the early Armenian editions was based on the appearance of traditional Armenian manuscripts and hence suited the taste of the readers. It is characterised by ornamental initials in animal, human or plant form, decorated headpieces, side frames, margin ornaments, vignettes, ornamental letters and arched canon tables. If missals or hymnals required the use of musical notation, the traditional Armenian tonal signs (Xazen), somewhat comparable to neumes, were set above the words. In other respects early Armenian books did not differ from contemporary European books. The woodcuts or copperplate engravings of the primarily religious books were the works of European artists and were reused in many books. The 160 woodcuts in the first printed Armenian Bible, for example, originate from the workshop of the Dutch master Christophel van Sichem. The sometimes oddly singular blend in one book of elements from traditional Armenian manuscript style with entirely European illustrations did not change until the presses moved to the East. There the printers turned to Armenian artists whose woodcuts or copperplate engravings now decorated their books. Some of the works exhibited here from Constantinople presses, in particular the abovementioned *Yaysmawowrk'* [34] from the Marzvanec'i

griffen dort auf armenische Künstler zurück, deren Holzschnitte oder Kupferstiche nun ihre Bücher zierten. Einige der hier ausgestellten Werke aus Konstantinopler Werkstätten, ganz besonders das erwähnte *Yaysmawowrk'* [34] aus der Marzvanec'i-Druckerei, oder auch das *Girk harc'manc'* ('Buch der Fragen' - [35]) des Grigor Tat'ewac'i aus der Werkstatt des Astowacatowr Dpir demonstrieren diese neue Einheitlichkeit in der buchkünstlerischen Gestaltung.

Vom Fortleben der Handschriftentraditionen im frühen armenischen Buchdruck zeugen auch die meist am Ende des Buches befindlichen Kolophone (armenisch: *Yišatakaranner, wörtlich*: 'Erinnerungsschriften'), die die sachlichen Informationen des Titelblattes ergänzten. Informative, ausführliche Kolophone stellten bereits ein Charakteristikum armenischer Handschriften dar. Doch auch die Kolophone der frühen Drucke sprechen von den historischen und gesellschaftlichen Zeitumständen, vom Leben und den Gefühlen des Druckers und empfehlen Gott dessen Seele. Erst mit Beginn des 19. Jahrhunderts verschwindet das Kolophon aus den armenischen Drucken, um einem sachlichen, von barockem Ballast befreiten Titelblatt nach europäischem Vorbild Platz zu machen. Zur selben Zeit kam auch die obligate Nennung der jeweils amtierenden höchsten Würdenträger der armenischen Kirche, des Katholikos und der Patriarchen von Konstantinopel oder Jerusalem, auf dem Titelblatt außer Gebrauch.[7]

Bis zum Ende des 17. Jahrhunderts blieb die Vorherrschaft des religiösen Buches ungebrochen. Psalter, Bibeln, Breviere, Meßbücher, Heiligenviten und Kalender dominierten die Buchproduktion - jene Bücher also, die der Klerus als Hauptauftraggeber der Drucker am dringendsten benötigte. Der Rest setzte sich aus klassischen armenischen historischen Werken, Handelshandbüchern, Lehrbüchern für Sprachen, Mathematik, geographischen Werken, Wörterbüchern, medizinischen oder astrologischen Texten und Unterhaltungsliteratur zusammen.[8] Diese Aufteilung widerspiegelt sehr genau die Bedürfnisse der Auftraggeber und Leser, mehrheitlich Kleriker oder Kaufleute. Erst im 19. Jahrhundert, als das Buch ein Mittel zur Bildung und Erbauung breiterer Kreise der armenischen Bevölkerung wurde, ändert sich diese inhaltliche Gewichtung grundlegend. Damit einher ging der Vormarsch des Neuarmenischen (Ašxarhabar) und die allmähliche Zurückdrängung des klassischen Armenisch (Grabar)

printing press, or the *Girk harc'manc'* ('Book of Questions' - [35]) of Grigor Tat'ewac'i from the press of Astowacatowr Dpir, demonstrate this new uniformity in artistic book design.

The colophons usually found at the end of the book (Armenian: *Yišatakaranner*, literally: 'memorial writings'; memoranda), which supplemented the factual information on the title page, also provide evidence of the continuation of manuscript traditions in early Armenian book printing. Informative, detailed colophons were already a characteristic of Armenian hand-written works. But the colophons of the early printed works also speak of the historical and social circumstances of the times, of the lives and the emotions of the printers and commend their souls to God. Not until the early 19th century does the colophon disappear from Armenian books to make room for an informative title page freed from Baroque ballast, after the European model. At the same time the obligatory citation of the incumbent highest dignitary of the Armenian Church, the catholicos and the patriarchs of Constantinople or Jerusalem, was no longer used on the title page.[7]

Until the end of the 17th century the dominance of religious books remained unbroken. Psalters, bibles, breviaries, missals, lives of the saints and calendars dominated book production - hence, i. e. books that the clergy, as the printers' primary customers, needed most. The rest consisted of classical Armenian histories, trade manuals, language textbooks, mathematical and geographical works, dictionaries, medical or astrological texts and popular fiction.[8] These categories very precisely reflect the demands of the clients and readers, the majority of whom were clergy or merchants. Not until the 19th century, when they became a means for educating and edifying broader circles of the Armenian population, did this balance of subject-matter fundamentally change. This was accompanied by the predominance of Modern Armenian (Ašxarhabar) and the gradual decline of Old Armenian (Grabar) in the printed book. The literate laity wanted to read books in the language they understood and also have their religion made accessible to them in this language. In

im gedruckten Buch. Die lesenden Laien wollten Bücher in der ihnen verständlichen Sprache lesen und auch die Religion in dieser Sprache nahegebracht bekommen. 1675 erscheint in Marseille der erste Druck in Neuarmenisch, 1687 der zweite in der Druckerei des Nahapêt Agowlec'i in Venedig. In diesem Psalmenkommentar sind die Psalmen in Grabar, die Kommentare jedoch in Neuarmenisch verfaßt. Insgesamt blieb die Anzahl der Ašxarhabar-Titel in der armenischen Frühdruckzeit jedoch sehr gering: Im 17. Jahrhundert sind es gerade 3, im 18. Jahrhundert 20 Bücher. Erst in der zweiten Hälfte des 19. Jahrhunderts hatte sich das moderne Armenisch im Buchdruck durchgesetzt.

Bis weit ins 17. Jahrhundert erreichten armenische Bücher nur geringe Auflagenhöhen. Schätzungen sprechen von 200 bis 500 Exemplaren pro Auflage. Erst die sehr langlebige und produktive Druckerei Sowrb Ejmiacin ew Sowrb Sargis Zôrawar in Amsterdam, Marseille und Konstantinopel erreichte mit ihren Drucken Auflagen von 1000 bis 3000 Exemplaren.[9]

1675 the first printed work in Modern Armenian appeared in Marseille, in 1687 the second was printed by the press of Nahapêt Agowlec'i in Venice. In this psalm commentary the psalms are written in Grabar, but the commentary in Modern Armenian. On the whole, however, the number of titles in Ašxarhabar in the early period of Armenian printing remained very low: in the 17th century there were merely three and in the 18th century 20 books in Ašxarhabar. Modern Armenian did not assert itself in book printing until the second half of the 19th century.

Until far into the 17th century Armenian books were only printed in small editions. Estimates speak of 200 to 500 copies per edition. Only the very long-lasting and productive press of Sowrb Ejmiacin ew Sowrb Sargis Zôrawar in Amsterdam, Marseille and Constantinople reached editions of 1,000 to 3,000 copies with its works.[9]

8. Chronik des armenischen Buchdrucks 1512–1800

8.1. Das 16. Jahrhundert

Die Identität des ersten armenischen Druckers Yakob Meġapart und seine Beweggründe, in den Jahren 1511/12 mit dem *Owrbatagirk'* ('Freitagbuch') in Venedig die neue Gutenbergsche Drucktechnik für die Armenier zu nutzen, liegen bis heute im Dunkeln. Yakob Meġaparts fünf armenische Titel entstanden zwischen 1511/12 und 1513 in einer venezianischen Werkstatt mit dem Zeichen D.I.Z.A. – drei von ihnen könnte man wohl als „mittelalterliche" Bücher bezeichnen, die mit Zaubersprüchen, Traumdeutungen und populären Ratschlägen Kaufleute auf ihren langen Reisen unterhalten sollten.

Dem *Owrbat'agirk'* von 1511 oder 1512, einer Sammlung von Gebeten und Beschwörungsformeln gegen Dämonen, folgten *Aġt'ark* 1511/12, ein volkstümliches Astrologie- und Medizinbuch, *Parzatowmar* 1513 [36], ein vereinfachter Kalender mit Traumdeutungen, *Patarakatetr* 1513, ein Meßbuch, und schließlich 1513 das *Taġaran*, eine Sammlung vorwiegend religiöser Poesie u.a. von Nersês Šnorhali und Grigor Narekac'i.[10]

Um dem Geschmack seines Leserschaft zu ent-

8. Chronicle of Armenian book printing 1512–1800

8.1. The 16th century

The identity of the first Armenian printer, Yakob Meġapart, and his motives for using the new Gutenberg printing technique for the Armenians in Venice in 1511/12 with the *Owrbatagirk'* ('Friday Book'), are still obscure. Yakob Meġapart's five Armenian books originated between 1511/12 and 1513 in a Venetian press with the mark D.I.Z.A. – three of them could be described as "mediæval" books, intended to entertain merchants on their long journeys with magic spells, dream interpretations and popular advice.

The *Owrbat'agirk'* of 1511 or 1512, a collection of prayers and incantations against demons, was followed by the *Aġt'ark* of 1511/12, a vernacular astrology and medical book, *Parzatowmar* in 1513 [36], a simplified calendar with dream interpretations, *Patarakatetr* in 1513, a missal, and finally in 1513 by the *Taġaran*, a collection of primarily religious poetry by writers such as Nersês Šnorhali and Grigor Narekac'i.[10]

In order to meet the tastes of his readership Yakob

sprechen, näherte Yakob seine Drucke äußerlich so weit als möglich einer armenischen Handschrift an. Im Kolophon spricht er sogar von „schreiben" statt von drucken.

Bis in die 1880er Jahre hielt man Abgar Toxatec'i für den ersten Drucker und sein Psalmenbuch von 1565 für das erste gedruckte armenische Buch. Die Entdeckung der wahren Chronologie und die Beschreibung der armenischen Erstdrucke 1883 durch Garegin Zarbhanalean und Grigor Govrigean in Nummer 10/1889 der Zeitschrift *Handês amsoreay* rief in gebildeten armenischen Kreisen keine einhellige Begeisterung hervor.[11] Fast schämte man sich des bescheidenen Yakob Meġapart und seiner volkstümlichen Bücher. Leo[12] bezeichnete sie gar als „dunkle Werke", als „Dummheiten und Betrügereien"[13] und hätte wohl, wie viele andere auch, lieber ein Psalmenbuch als armenischen Jungferndruck gesehen.

Nach Yakobs venezianischen Büchern stand die armenische Druckerpresse für 50 Jahre still. Abgar Toxatec'i, der zweite armenische Drucker, sah sich 1565 jedoch in der Nachfolge Yakobs: Im Kolophon seines Psalters ist von *nor gir* (neuen Buchstaben) die Rede. Abgars Wirken ist wesentlich besser dokumentiert als das von Yakob, war seine Tätigkeit als Buchdrucker doch eng mit politisch-diplomatischen Aktivitäten der armenischen Kirche verbunden. Im 16. Jahrhundert intensivierte der Klerus seine Bestrebungen, mit dem christlichen Europa in Kontakt zu treten, um Armeniens Unabhängigkeit von türkischer und persischer Fremdherrschaft zu erlangen. 1562 schickte Katholikos Mik'ayêl Sebastac'i den Gelehrten Abgar Toxatec'i in dieser Mission nach Europa. Blieb die Mission auch politisch ergebnislos, so war ihr doch in anderer Hinsicht Erfolg beschieden: Bei seinem freundlichen Empfang durch Papst Pius IV. erhielt Abgar die Erlaubnis zum Druck armenischer Bücher. 1565 ließ er in Venedig zwei Arten neuer armenischer Lettern schneiden und druckte dort zwei Titel: einen einblättrigen Kalender *Xarnayp'nt'owr towmar* und *Saġmos*, ein Psalmenbuch.

Im selben Jahr starb jedoch Papst Pius IV. Sein Nachfolger, Pius V. der ehemalige Großinquisitor, verschärfte katholische Zensur und Inquisition derart, daß an den Druck von armenisch-apostolischen Büchern im katholischen Einflußbereich nicht mehr zu denken war. Abgar wich nach Konstantinopel aus. Mit Unterstützung des Patriarchen Yakob I. richtete er 1567 die erste selbständige armenische Druckerei ein. Aus dieser Werkstatt kamen von

made his printed books appear as similar as possible to Armenian manuscripts. In the colophon he even speaks of "writing" rather than printing.

Until the 1880s Abgar Toxatec'i was considered the first printer and his book of psalms of 1565 the first Armenian printed book. The discovery of the true chronology and the description of the first Armenian printed editions in 1883 by Garegin Zarbhanalean and Grigor Govrigean in issue 10/1889 of the journal *Handês amsoreay* did not elicit unanimous enthusiasm among educated Armenians.[11] They seemed almost ashamed of modest Yakob Meġapart and his popular books. Leo[12] even described them as "dark works", as "follies and deceits"[13] and would rather, like many others, have seen a book of psalms as the maiden Armenian printing.

After Yakob's Venetian books the Armenian printing press stood still for 50 years. In 1565 Abgar Toxatec'i, the second Armenian printer, considered himself the successor of Yakob: in the colophon of his Psalter he mentions *nor gir* (new letters). Abgar's work is far better documented that Yakob's, since his work as a book printer was closely tied to the political and diplomatic activities of the Armenian Church. In the 16th century the clergy intensified its efforts to come into contact with Christian Europe in order to attain Armenia's independence from Turkish and Iranian foreign domination. In 1562 the catholicos Mik'ayêl Sebastac'i sent the scholar Abgar Toxatec'i to Europe on this mission. Although the mission remained politically ineffective, it was successful in another respect: during his friendly reception by Pope Pius IV, Abgar was granted permission to print Armenian books. In 1565 he had two kinds of Modern Armenian type cut in Venice and printed two titles there: a single-paged calendar *Xarnayp'nt'owr towmar* and *Saġmos*, a book of psalms.

That same year, however, Pope Pius IV died. His successor, Pius V, the former Grand Inquisitor, intensified Catholic censorship and the Inquisition to such an extent that printing Armenian Apostolic books within the Catholic sphere of influence was impossible. Abgar moved to Constantinople. With the support of Patriarch Yakob I he set up the first independent Armenian printing press in 1567. Six titles originated in this workshop between

1567–69 sechs Titel. Außer dem ersten, einer armenischen Grammatik für Kinder *P'ok'r k'erakanowt'iwn kam aybbenaran*, waren sie ausschließlich religiösen Inhalts.[14]

Nach dem Ende von Abgars Druckerei vergingen über 100 Jahre bis sein Werk in Konstantinopel durch Eremia K'êomiwrčean fortgesetzt wurde.

Abgars Spuren reichen jedoch bis ins nächste Jahrhundert: Sein Sohn Sultanšah wurde vom Papst katholisch getauft und nannte sich nach seiner Priesterweihe Bartolomeo Abagaro. Er blieb in Rom und fungierte von 1584 bis 1623 als Abt des 1579 dort gegründeten armenisch-katholischen Klosters, Übersetzer beim Papst und päpstlicher Berater in armenischen Angelegenheiten. Er trat aber auch in die Fußstapfen seines Vaters und betreute die sechs armenischen Editionen der vatikanischen Druckerei von 1584 bis 1623, dem Zeitpunkt der Gründung der SCPF und ihrer Druckerei.[15]

Der armenische Priester Yovhannês Terznc'i und sein Sohn Xač'atowr druckten 1584 gemeinsam mit Bartolomeo Abagaro zwei Titel in der vatikanischen Druckerei: *Tomar grigorean* ('Gregorianischer Kalender' – [37]) und *Dawanowt'iwn owġġap'arowt'ean hromêakan* ('Glaubensbekenntnis der Hl. Römischen Kirche'). Der Druck der armenischen Bibel jedoch, der dringendste Wunsch der armenischen Kirchenführung wie auch Yovhannês Ternzc'is, wurde von Rom für häretisch erachtet und verhindert. Mit dem Druck eines Psalters 1587 in Venedig endeten die verlegerischen Unternehmungen von Yovhannês Ternzc'i.

Mit ihm ging die früheste Phase des armenischen Buchdruckes zu Ende, in der insgesamt 17 armenische Titel die Druckerpresse verließen.[16]

8.2. Das 17. Jahrhundert

In der ersten Hälfte des 17. Jahrhunderts nahm der armenische Buchdruck noch keine kontinuierliche Entwicklung: Die Unternehmungen waren vereinzelt und kurzlebig. Das sollte sich erst 1660 mit der Gründung der Druckerei des Bischofs Oskan Erewanc'i in Amsterdam ändern.

Rom

Im 17. Jahrhundert flankierte der Vatikan seine Bestrebungen, die armenische Kirche zur Union mit Rom zu bewegen, durch verstärkte verlegerische Aktivitäten. Insgesamt erschienen ca. 30 armenische Titel in Rom, hauptsächlich missionarisch-propa-

1567 and 1569. With the exception of the first, an Armenian grammar for children called *P'ok'r k'erakanowt'iwn kam aybbenaran*, all had religious content.[14]

After Abgar's printing press ceased operation over 100 years passed before his work was continued in Constantinople by Eremia K'êomiwrčean.

Yet Abgar's mark lasted well into the next century: his son Sultanšah was christened a Catholic by the Pope and after his ordination to the priesthood called himself Bartolomeo Abagaro. He remained in Rome and was from 1584 until 1623 the abbot of the Armenian Catholic monastery founded there in 1579, a translator for the Pope and papal advisor in Armenian affairs. However, he also followed in his father's footsteps and supervised the six Armenian editions of the Vatican press from 1584 until 1623, the time of the founding of the SCPF and its printing press.[15]

In 1584 the Armenian priest Yovhannês Terznc'i and his son Xač'atowr printed two titles in collaboration with Bartolomeo Abagaro at the Vatican press: *Tomar grigorean* ('Gregorian Calendar' – [37]) and *Dawanowt'iwn owġġap'arowt'ean hromêakan* ('Creed of the Holy Roman Church'). The printing of the Armenian Bible, however, the most urgent concern of the Armenian church leaders as well as of Yovhannês Ternzc'i, was considered heretical by Rome and prevented. With the printing of a Psalter in 1587 in Venice the publishing undertakings of Yovhannês Ternzc'i came to an end.

With him the earliest phase of Armenian book printing ended, during which a total of 17 Armenian titles left the printing presses.[16]

8.2. The 17th century

In the first half of the 17th century Armenian book printing did not undergo any continuous development: the undertakings were isolated and short-lived. This did not change until 1660 with the founding of the printing press of Bishop Oskan Erewanc'i in Amsterdam.

Rome

In the 17th century the Vatican stepped up its efforts to influence the Armenian Church to unite with Rome through intensified publishing activities. A total of approximately 30 Armenian titles appeared in Rome, chiefly of missionary-propagandistic con-

gandistischen Inhalts. Die 1622 gegründete SCPF mit der 1627 gegründeten, nach Papst Urban VII. benannten Missionsdruckerei publizierte davon den Löwenanteil. Von bleibendem Wert sind hiervon die exzellente Armenischgrammatik des Missionars und Armenologen Clemens Galanos von 1645, das Grabar-Handbuch (*Ztowt'iwn haykapanowt'ean – Puritas linguae armenicae*) des Yovhannês Holov von 1674, und das Lateinisch-Armenisch-Wörterbuch (*Paṙgirk' latinac'owoc' ew hayoc'*) des Astowactowr Nersesovič' von 1695. Die Missionsdruckerei der SCPF existierte bis 1796 und brachte über 44 armenische Titel hervor.[17]

Lvov
Aus der 1616 in Lvov vom armenischen Bischof der Stadt, Yovhannês K'armatenenc', gegründeten Druckerei gingen in den drei Jahren ihres Bestehens drei bescheiden ausgestattete Titel hervor: Ein Psalter (*Saġmosaran*, 1616), ein Medizinbuch (*Bžškaran*, 1616) und ein Gebetbuch (*Aġot'agirk'*, 1618). Letzteres weist eine Besonderheit aus: Es ist nicht nur das erste gedruckte Buch in Armeno-kiptschakisch, der Umgangssprache der Armenier in Lvov und Umgebung, sondern auch das erste in einem armenischen Dialekt gedruckte geistliche Buch überhaupt.[18]

Nor Jowġa/Isfahan (Persien)
1605 siedelte der persische Schah Abbas die von ihm verschleppte Bevölkerung der armenischen Stadt Jowġa in einem Vorort seiner Hauptstadt Isfahan an und stattete sie mit vielfältigen Privilegien aus. In den dreißiger Jahren des 17. Jahrhunderts bereits stand das neue Jowġa (Nor Jowġa) wie die Deportierten ihre neue Heimat in Erinnerung an die alte nannten, in voller wirtschaftlicher und kultureller Blüte. Die Stadt hatte sich zu einem der wichtigsten Handelszentren des Orients entwickelt und verfügte, vor allem dank der Initiative ihres Bischofs, über Schulen, Bibliotheken und eine Universität. Bischof Xač'atowr Kesarac'i, ein gebildeter, europaerfahrener Mann, betrieb seit 1636 auch das von seiten der armenischen Kirchenführung in Etschmiadzin geförderte Projekt der Gründung einer Druckerei. Die Geschichte dieser Druckerei, der ersten in Persien, zeugt vom Enthusiasmus der Mönche des „Heiligen-Erlöser-Klosters" der Stadt. Sie erfanden, nach vagen Erzählungen von Europareisenden, den Buchdruck quasi zum zweiten Mal. Alles, vom Typenmaterial bis zur technischen Ausrüstung und zum Papier,

tent. The SCPF founded in 1622 and the Mission Printing Press founded in 1627 and named after Pope Urban VII published the lion's share. Of these the excellent Armenian grammar by the missionary and Armenian linguist Clemens Galanos of 1645, the Grabar manual (*Ztowt'iwn haykapanowt'ean – Puritas linguae armenicae*) by Yovhannês Holov of 1674, and the Latin-Armenian dictionary (*Paṙgirk' latinac'owoc' ew hayoc'*) by Astowactowr Nersesovič' of 1695 are of enduring value. The mission press of the SCPF existed until 1796 and published over 44 Armenian titles.[17]

Lvov
The printing press established in 1616 in Lvov by the Armenian bishop of the city, Yovhannês K'armatenenc', brought out three modestly produced titles in the three years of its existence: a Psalter (*Saġmosaran*, 1616), a medical book (*Bžškaran*, 1616) and a prayer book (*Aġot'agirk'*, 1618). The latter is unique not only in that it is the first printed book in Armeno-Kipchak, the colloquial language of the Armenians in Lvov and its surroundings, but also the first religious book ever printed in an Armenian dialect.[18]

Nor Jowġa, Isfahan (Iran)
In 1605 after expelling the population of the Armenian city Jowġa, the Iranian Shah Abbas settled them in a suburb of his capital city of Isfahan and equippgranted them manifold privileges. In the 1630s the new Jowġa (Nor Jowġa), as the deportees called their new home in memory of the old, was already in its economic and cultural heyday. The city had developed to become one of the most important trade centres of the East and, thanks chiefly to the initiative of its bishops, possessed schools, libraries and a university. Bishop Xač'atowr Kesarac'i, an educated man, with experience of Europe, began operating a printing press in 1636, a project also promoted by the Armenian church leaders in Ejmiadzin. The history of this printing press, the first in Iran, reveals the enthusiasm of the monks of the city's "Holy Redeemer Monastery." According to vague tales told by European travellers they invented book printing more or less for the second time. Everything, from the type material to the technical equipment to the paper, had to be manufactured locally and without outside help. If,

mußte vor Ort und aus eigenen Kräften hergestellt werden. Mutet das Ergebnis, vom typographischen Standpunkt aus, auch bescheiden an, so wird der äußere Eindruck doch durch die Hochachtung vor der Leistung des Bischofs und seiner Mitstreiter wettgemacht.

Zwischen 1638 und 1647 druckte man im „Heiligen-Erlöser-Kloster" von Nor Jowġa insgesamt fünf Titel: erwähntes Psalmenbuch (*Saġmos i Dawit'*, 1638), ein Meßbuch (*Xorhrdatetrak*, 1641), ein *Haranc' vark'* ('Vitae Patrum', 1641 – [38]), ein Buch der Gottesdienstordnung (*Girk' žamarkargowt'ean*, 1642) und einen Kalender (*Girk' towmarac'*, 1647). Den Druck des letzten Titels besorgte nach dem Tod von Xač'atowr Kesarac'i bereits dessen Schüler Yovhannês Jowġayec'i. Von 1687 bis 1688 lebte die Druckerei noch einmal kurz auf und brachte vier Titel hervor.[19]

Venedig

Im 17. Jahrhundert unternahm die armenische Kirchenführung verschiedene Vorstöße in Rom, um den Druck der armenischen Bibel zu erreichen. Einer davon ist mit dem Namen Yovhannês Ankiwrac'i, Dolmetscher Venedigs in Smyrna, verknüpft. Yovhannês hielt sich von 1637 bis 1641 in Rom auf und arbeitete an einer mit Rom abgestimmten Fassung der armenischen Bibel mit. Als das Projekt jedoch auf der Stelle trat, wich er 1642 nach Venedig aus um, sozusagen vorbereitend, erst einmal ein Psalmenbuch und *Yisows ordi* von Nerses Šnorhali in der griechischen Druckerei „Salicata" zu drucken. Es sollte schließlich aber nicht ihm, sondern Oskan Erewanc'i in Amsterdam vorbehalten sein, über hundert Jahre armenischer Bemühungen um den Druck des „Buches der Bücher" mit Erfolg zu krönen.

Zwei reiche armenische Kaufleute initiierten in den Jahren 1686/87 in Venedig ambitionierte Druckprojekte: Gaspar Šêhrimanean aus Nor Jowġa und Nahapêt Agowlec'i aus Agowlis. Da beide der katholischen Kirche nahestanden, legte ihnen die römische Zensur auch keine Steine in den Weg.

Gaspar Šêhrimanean war schon zuvor als Mäzen des armenischen Buchdrucks in Erscheinung getreten. Jetzt gründete er seine eigene Druckerei und publizierte, mit Hilfe zweier gelehrter armenisch-katholischer Kleriker, Yovhannês Holov und T'adêos Hamazaspean, drei Werke: ein Meßbuch (*Xorhrdatetr srbazan pataragi*), ein dreibändiges Lektionar (*Čašoc' girk'* – [39]) und ein Werk von Yov-

from a typographical point of view, the result is modest, the outward impression is outweighed by great admiration for the accomplishments of the bishops and his helpers.

Between 1638 and 1647 the "Holy Redeemer Monastery" of Nor Jowġa printed a total of five titles: the above-mentioned book of psalms (*Saġmos i Dawit'*, 1638), a missal (*Xorhrdatetrak*, 1641), *Haranc' vark'* ('Vitae Patrum', 1641 – [38]), a book on the order of service (*Girk' žamarkargowt'ean*, 1642) and a calendar (*Girk' towmarac'*, 1647). The latter was printed after the death of Xač'atowr Kesarac'i by his pupil Yovhannês Jowġayec'i. From 1687 until 1688 the printing press had a brief revival and published four titles.[19]

Venice

In the 17th century the Armenian church leaders made various attempts in Rome to publish the Armenian Bible. One of these is linked with the name of Yovhannês Ankiwrac'i, Venice's interpreter in Smyrna. Yovhannês resided in Rome from 1637 until 1641 and collaborated on a version of the Armenian Bible with Rome. However, when the project came to a standstill he moved in 1642 to Venice, to print, as it were in preparation, first a book of psalms and *Yisows ordi* by Nerses Šnorhali in the Greek press "Salicata." But in the end it was not he, but Oskan Erewanc'i in Amsterdam who was destined to crown with success over one hundred years of Armenian efforts to print the "Book of Books".

In the years 1686/87, two rich Armenian merchants initiated ambitious printing projects in Venice: Gaspar Šêhrimanean from Nor Jowġa and Nahapêt Agowlec'i from Agowlis. Since both were close to the Catholic Church the Roman censors put no obstacles in their way.

Gaspar Šêhrimanean had already appeared as a patron of Armenian book printing. He now founded his own printing press and published, with the aid of two learned Armenian Catholic clergymen, Yovhannês Holov and T'adêos Hamazaspean, three works: a missal (*Xorhrdatetr srbazan pataragi*), a three-volume lectionary (*Čašoc' girk'* – [39]) and a work by Yovhannês Holov (*Xokowm k'ristoneakan* –

hannês Holov (*Xokowm k'ristoneakan* - Christliche Meditation). Besonders die prächtige Ausstattung des hier gezeigten Lektionars von 1686 wird heute noch bewundert.

Nahapêt Agowlec'i, reicher Seidenhändler und seit 1675 in Venedig ansäßig galt als einer der großzügigsten Gönner der dortigen armenischen Kolonie. Durch Pater Yovhannês Holov kam er in Kontakt mit dem Druckwesen. Zuerst finanzierte Nahapêt die Drucklegung von dessen Werken bei italienischen Werkstätten, schließlich gründete er 1686 seine eigene Druckerei. Er produzierte drei Titel, wovon der letzte, eine von Yovhannês Holov edierte aufwendig ausgestattete Psalmensammlung mit Kommentar in Neuarmenisch, besonders interessant ist.

In der zweiten Hälfte des 17. Jahrhunderts entdeckten vier venezianische Drucker das armenische Buch als Einnahmequelle:

Der erste war Giovanni Battista Povis, der 1660 in seiner Werkstatt mit Hilfe zweier junger Armenier „Jesus der Sohn" (*Yisows ordi*) von Nerses Šnorhali und einen Psalter druckte. Er scheint dabei das Typenmaterial von Yovhannês Ankiwrac'i wieder verwendet zu haben.[20]

Die armenischen Aktivitäten von Michelangelo Barboni währten von 1680 bis 1690 und brachten 12 Werke hervor. Als Spiritus Rector seiner Arbeit taucht einmal mehr der umtriebige Pater Yovhannês Holov auf, der durch seine guten Beziehungen auch gleich die erforderlichen Mäzene einwarb. Es handelt sich bis auf zwei Ausnahmen um religiöse Literatur. Interessant ist ein Armenisch-Italienisches Wörterbuch (*Bargirk' Taliani*), das komplett, also auch im italienischen Teil, mit armenischen Lettern gedruckt wurde.

Giacomo Moretti druckte mit der finanziellen Hilfe armenischer Kaufleute zwei armenische Titel: 1685 einen Psalter und 1686 gemeinsam mit Nahapêt Agowlec'i *Yisows ordi* von Nerses Šnorhali.

Der weitaus erfolgreichste Venezianer in diesem Geschäft war aber Antonio Bortoli. Er und seine Nachfolger druckten seit 1694 bis zum Ende des 18. Jahrhunderts armenische Bücher. Zeitweise hielt die Familie sogar das Monopol auf den armenischen Buchdruck in Venedig. Anfangs verlegte er vor allem leicht verkäufliche Bücher wie Psalter und Kalender. Im 17. Jahrhundert erschienen erst vier armenische Titel bei Bortoli.

'Christian Meditation'). In particular the splendid design of the 1686 lectionary (exhibited here) is still admired today.

Nahapêt Agowlec'i, a rich silk trader living in Venice since 1675, was considered one of the most generous benefactors of the Armenian colony there. He came into contact with printing through Father Yovhannês Holov. First Nahapêt funded the printing of his works at Italian presses, until he founded his own in 1686. He produced three titles, the last of which - a lavishly produced collection of psalms with commentaries in Modern Armenian edited by Yovhannês Holov - is particularly interesting.

In the second half of the 17th century four Venetian printers discovered Armenian books as a source of income:

The first was Giovanni Battista Povis, who printed "Jesus the Son" (*Yisows ordi*) by Nerses Šnorhali and a Psalter in his shop in 1660 with the help of two young Armenians. He appears to have reused the type material of Yovhannês Ankiwrac'i.[20]

The Armenian activities of Michelangelo Barboni lasted from 1680 until 1690 and produced 12 works. The itinerant Father Yovhannês Holov appears once again as the *spiritus rector* of his work and also acquired the necessary patrons through his good connections. All of the works were of a religious nature with the exception of two. An Armenian-Italian dictionary (*Bargirk' Taliani*) entirely printed with Armenian type, even in the Italian section, of particular interest.

With the financial assistance of Armenian merchants Giacomo Moretti printed two Armenian titles: a Psalter in 1685 and in 1686, together with Nahapêt Agowlec'i, *Yisows ordi* by Nerses Šnorhali.

Yet by far the most successful Venetian in this business was Antonio Bortoli. He and his successors printed Armenian books from 1694 until the end of the 18th century. For a time the family even held the monopoly in Armenian book printing in Venice. Initially he mainly published easily sold books such as Psalters and calendars. In the 17th century Bortoli produced only four Armenian titles.

Amsterdam

Die Druckerei

„Sowrb Ejmiacin ew Sowrb Sargis Zôravar"

Die Gründung dieser Druckerei durch Bischof Oskan Erewanc'i 1658 in Amsterdam läutete ein neues Zeitalter im armenischen Buchdruck ein. Zum ersten Mal existierte eine armenische Druckerei kontinuierlich über einen Zeitraum von achtundzwanzig Jahren, zum ersten Mal erreichten armenische Drucke Auflagen von bis zu 3000 Exemplaren und ein solch hohes typographisches und editorisch-wissenschaftliches Niveau.

Hinter der Gründung des Unternehmens standen die deprimierenden Erfahrungen der armenischen Kirchenführung mit ihren Bemühungen, in Rom oder im katholischen Einflußbereich den Druck der armenischen Bibel zu erreichen. Trotz weitgehender armenischer Zugeständnisse konnte sich die Kurie nicht dazu entschließen, den Armeniern ihre „häretische" Bibelversion in die Hand zu geben. Der Mangel an Bibeln wurde jedoch immer drückender, und so entschloß sich der Katholikos in Etschmiadzin, das Projekt unabhängig von Rom und im protestantischen Amsterdam in Angriff zu nehmen. 1656 ließ er dort eine Druckerei einrichten und suchte nach einem geeigneten Mann für ihre Leitung. Die Wahl fiel auf Bischof Oskan Erewanc'i aus Nor Jowġa, einen der führenden armenischen Intellektuellen seiner Zeit. Da er sich bereits mit einer Bibeledition aus verschiedenen Handschriftenversionen beschäftigt hatte, galt er als ausgezeichnet qualifiziert für seine Aufgabe.

1664 traf Oskan in Amsterdam ein und druckte im selben Jahr ein Hymnarium (*Šaraknoc'* – [40]) mit Notenzeichen und Illustrationen. Dann machte er sich an den Druck der Bibel. Druckbeginn war der 11. März 1666 – zweieinhalb Jahre später, Ende 1668 lag das Ergebnis vor. Es sollte die „Königin der alten armenischen Drucke"[21] werden und Vorbild für alle Nachfolger – was Typographie (es wurden allein 159 Stiche verwandt) und editorische Sorgfalt betraf. Die Oskansche Bibel enthält eine Konkordanz zur lateinische *Vulgata*.

In Amsterdam erschienen noch dreizehn weitere Titel der Druckerei: neben religiösen auch eine Fibel für Kinder und Erwachsene (*Girk' aybowbenic'*, 1666), die „Geographie" von Movsês Xorenac'i (*Girk' ašxarhac'*, 1668) und das Geschichtsbuch (*Girk' patmowt'eanc'*, 1669) des zeitgenössischen Historikers Arak'êl Davrižec'i.

Amsterdam

The printing press

"Sowrb Ejmiacin ew Sowrb Sargis Zôravar"

The establishment of this printing press in 1658 by Bishop Oskan Erewanc'i in Amsterdam rang in a new age for Armenian book printing. For the first time an Armenian printing press existed continuously for a period of 28 years, and for the first time Armenian editions reached 3,000 copies and attained a high typographical and scholarly editorial level.

The enterprise was founded because of the disheartening experiences of the Armenian church leaders in their efforts to attain achieve the printing of the Armenian Bible in Rome or within the Catholic sphere of influence. In spite of far-reaching Armenian concessions, the Curia was unable to make a decision on allowing the Armenians their "heretical" version of the Bible. The lack of bibles became ever more pressing, however, until the catholicos in Ejmiadzin decided to start the project independently of Rome and in Protestant Amsterdam. In 1656 he had a printing press set up there and sought a suitable man to run it. The choice was Bishop Oskan Erewanc'i from Nor Jowġa, one of the leading Armenian intellectuals of his day. Since he had already been working on an edition of the Bible from various hand-written versions he was considered excellently qualified for the task.

In 1664 Oskan arrived in Amsterdam and that same year printed a hymnal (*Šaraknoc'* – [40]) with notes and illustrations. Then he began work on the Bible. Printing began on 11 March 1666 and two and a half years later, in late 1668, the work was completed. It was to become the "queen of old Armenian printed books"[21] and serve as the example for all to follow with regard to typography (159 engravings alone were used) and editorial care. Oskan's Bible contains a concordance to the Latin *Vulgata*.

The printing press in Amsterdam published 13 more titles; not only religious books but also a primer for children and adults (*Girk' aybowbenic'*, 1666), a "Geography" by Movsês Xorenac'i (*Girk' ašxarhac'*, 1668) and a history book (*Girk' patmowt'eanc'*, 1669) by the contemporary historian Arak'êl Davrižec'i.

1669 begann die Odyssee der Oskanschen Druckerei. Er und seine Mitarbeiter verließen Amsterdam. Die Gründe dafür sind nicht ganz klar, da es nicht an der Zensur gelegen haben kann, vermuten manche Autoren, daß der Steuerdruck schuld war.[22] Die Druckerei blieb drei Jahre in Livorno, doch hier fanden vor der katholischen Zensur nur drei Titel Gnade. 1672 zog Oskan weiter nach Marseille, dort erschienen bis 1686 siebzehn Titel. Darunter 1675 der erste ganz in Neuarmenisch gedruckte Titel: ein mathematisch-kalkulatorisches Werk (*Arhêst hamarogowt'ean*). 1674 starb Oskan. Des ersten Druckers der armenischen Bibel wurde noch lange in den Kolophonen seiner Nachfolger gedacht. Oskans wissenschaftlich gründliche Editionen setzten Maßstäbe und wurden bis weit ins 18. Jahrhundert bei Neuausgaben zu Grunde gelegt. Oskans Mitarbeiter traten sein Vermächtnis an - sein Cousin Soġomon Levonean führte das Unternehmen fort, sein Kompagnon T'adêos Hamazaspean druckte in Venedig weiter, und Matt'êos Vanandec'i, wurde Begründer der Vanandec'i-Druckerei.[23]

Die Druckerei Vanandec'i

Matt'êos Vanandec'i, 14 Jahre lang Mitarbeiter von Oskan, gründete 1685 in Amsterdam seine eigene Werkstatt. Bis 1692 erscheinen bei Matt'êos zwei Titel - ein Hymnarium (*Šaraknoc'*) und eine Gebetsordnung (*Kargaworowt'iwn hasarakay aġot'ic'*) in jeweils zwei Auflagen. Ab 1695 entwickelte sich aus dieser Werkstatt ein Familienunternehmen der Vanandec'i-Familie - Matt'êos' Cousin Erzbischof T'ômas Vanandec'i und dessen Neffen Ġowkas und Mik'ayêl stießen hinzu. Die Blütezeit der Werkstatt begann. War Matt'êos die handwerkliche Seele des Geschäfts, so gelten die Brüder Ġowkas und Mik'ayêl, Absolventen des Urban-Kollegiums der SCPF in Rom, als die intellektuellen Köpfe und Erzbischof T'ômas als dessen Leiter. Das erste gemeinsame Werk, die erste Druckausgabe von Movsês Xorenac'is Geschichtswerk *Azgabanowt'iwn tôhmin yabet'ean* (1695) ist gleichzeitig eines der wissenschaftlich bedeutendsten Werke der Druckerei.

Ihm sollten in den folgenden 10 Jahren 14 weitere Werke folgen: neben religiösen wie Psaltern, Hymnarien und einem neuen Bibeldruck von 1698 befanden sich darunter aber auch erstmals gleichberechtigt wissenschaftliche Publikationen, meist aus der Feder von Ġowkas oder Mik'ayêl Vanandec'i. Ġowkas erstellte außerdem die erste gedruckte arme-

The Oskan press began an odyssey in 1669. He and his co-workers left Amsterdam for reasons that are not quite clear. Since it could not have been because of censorship, some authors assume that the cause was the burden of taxation.[22] The printing press stayed three years in Livorno, but only three titles were spared by the Catholic censors. In 1672 Oskan moved on to Marseille, where 17 titles were published up to 1686, including the first book printed entirely in Modern Armenian in 1675: an arithmetical work (*Arhêst hamarogowt'ean*). Oskan died in 1674. The first printer of the Armenian Bible was long memorialized in the colophons of his successors. Oskan's scientifically thorough editions set standards and served as the basis for new editions until long into the 18th century. Oskan's co-workers took over his legacy - his cousin Soġomon Levonean continued the enterprise, his associate Tadêos Hamazaspean continued to print in Venice and Matt'êos Vanandec'i founded the Vanandec'i print ing press. [23]

The Vanandec'i Printing Press

Matt'êos Vanandec'i, who had worked with Oskan for 14 years, founded his own press in Amsterdam in the year 1685. Until 1692 two titles were published by Matt'êos - a hymnal (*Šaraknoc'*) and an order of prayer (*Kargaworowt'iwn hasarakay aġot'ic'*), each in two editions. Beginning in 1695 this shop developed into a family enterprise of the Vanandec'i family - Matt'êos's cousin the archbishop T'ômas Vanandec'i and his nephews Ġowkas and Mik'ayêl joined their ranks. The press's golden age began. Whilst Matt'êos was the technical spirit of the business, the brothers Ġowkas and Mik'ayêl, graduates of the Urban College of the SCPF in Rome, were the intellectual brains and archbishop T'ômas their supervisor. Their first joint work, the first printed edition of Movsês Xorenac'is's historical *Azgabanowt'iwn tôhmin yabet'ean* (1695) is also one of the most significant scholarly works of the press.

It was to be followed over the next 10 years by 14 further works. In addition to religious books such as Psalters, hymnals and a new Bible of 1698, these included for the first time equally important scholarly publications, usually from the pen of Ġowkas or Mik'ayêl Vanandec'i. Ġowkas also produced the first printed Armenian map in 1695. From 1705 it

nische Karte von 1695. Seit 1705 scheint Ġowkas das Unternehmen allein geführt zu haben. Bis zur Schließung im Jahre 1718 erscheinen nochmals 10 Titel, darunter ein Psalter (*Girk' sağmosac'* – [41]) von 1714 und der typographisch bestechende und wissenschaftlich bedeutende *Thesaurus linguae armenicae* [42] des deutschen Armenologen Johann Joachim Schröder. Die Vanandec'i-Familie stand in Kontakt mit der geistigen Elite ihrer Zeit, z. B. mit Gottfried Wilhelm Leibniz. Ġowkas Vanandec'i führte Johann Joachim Schröder in die Feinheiten der armenischen Sprache ein und war nicht nur als Drucker an der Entstehung von dessen *Thesaurus* beteiligt. 1718 schloß wahrscheinlich die holländische Steuerbehörde die Vanandec'i-Druckerei und besiegelte damit das Ende eines Unternehmens, mit dessen Namen nicht nur typographisch exzellente Drucke verbunden waren, sondern auch die erstmalige Hinwendung des armenischen Druckwesens zum wissenschaftlichen Buch. Mit der Schließung der Vanandec'i-Druckerei endete gleichzeitig die fast 60-jährige Geschichte des armenischen Buchdrucks in Amsterdam.[24]

Konstantinopel

Im 17. Jahrhundert durchlebten die Armenier der osmanischen Hauptstadt unruhige Zeiten. Es tobten Kämpfe innerhalb der Gemeinschaft, in deren Folge der Patriarchenstuhl zum Zankapfel und eine kontinuierliche Führung der Gemeinschaft unmöglich wurde. Überdies verschärften sich die Auseinandersetzungen mit der katholischen Kirche, deren Missionierungsversuche auf erbitterten Widerstand stießen. So lag im allgemeinen Chaos auch der Buchdruck darnieder. Erst 1677 faßte die Gutenbergsche Erfindung wieder Fuß in der armenischen Gemeinschaft.

Der Politiker, Schriftsteller und Humanist Eremia K'êomiwrčean richtete, mit Unterstützung des erfahrenen Druckers T'adêos Hamazaspean, ein Atelier ein und publizierte im gleichen Jahr zwei Titel: *Yisows ordi* von Nerses Šnorhali und ein eigenes Werk über die heiligen Stätten in Jerusalem (*Teġeac' tnôrinakanac' Teařn meroy Yisowsi K'ristosi*), die er auf einer Reise 1665 besucht hatte.

1695 taucht die Druckerei „Sowrb Ejmiacin ew Sowrb Sargis Zôravar" in Konstantinopel wieder auf. Zwischen 1696 und 1718 wird die Druckerei unter einem neuem Besitzer in der Stadt aktiv. Bei den Auseinandersetzungen zwischen armenisch-apostolischen und katholischen Christen schlägt sich die

appears that Ġowkas managed the business on his own. Until its closing in the year 1718 another 10 titles appeared, including a Psalter (*Girk' sağmosac'* – [41]) of 1714 and the typographically captivating and philologically significant *Thesaurus linguae armenicae* – [42]) by the German Armenian linguist Johann Joachim Schröder. The Vanandec'i family was in contact with the intellectual elite of their time, such as Gottfried Wilhelm Leibniz. Ġowkas Vanandec'i introduced Johann Joachim Schröder to the nuances of the Armenian language and was involved in the creation of his *thesaurus* as more than just a printer. In 1718 the Vanandec'i printing press was closed, probably by the Dutch tax authorities, thus marking the end of an enterprise whose name was linked not only with typographically excellent printing, but also the first reorientation of Armenian printers towards scholarly books. The closing of the Vanandec'i printing press also ended the nearly 60-year history of Armenian book printing in Amsterdam.[24]

Constantinople

The Armenians in the Ottoman capital lived through restless times in the 17th century. Conflict raged within the community, leading to the chair of the patriarch becoming a bone of contention, so that continuous leadership of the community became impossible. In addition the clashes with the Catholic Church intensified as its attempts at missionary work met with bitter resistance. In the general chaos book printing also languished. Not until 1677 did Gutenberg's invention find a footing again in the Armenian community.

The politician, writer and humanist Eremia K'êomiwrčean, with the support of the experienced printer T'adêos Hamazaspean, set up a printing studio and that same year published two titles: *Yisows ordi* by Nerses Šnorhali and his own work on the holy sites in Jerusalem (*Teġeac' tnôrinakanac' Teařn meroy Yisowsi K'ristosi*), which he had visited on a journey in 1665.

In 1695 the printing press "Sowrb Ejmiacin ew Sowrb Sargis Zôravar" re-emerged in Constantinople. Between 1696 and 1718 the press became active once again in the city under new ownership. In the conflicts between the Armenian Apostolic

Druckerei auf die Seite Letzterer und druckt die Schriften katholischer Missionare und Priester. Um der Verfolgung durch das armenisch-apostolische Patriarchat zu entgehen, nennen viele dieser Schriften als Druckort Marseille, Livorno oder Amsterdam, obwohl sie in Konstantinopel gedruckt wurden. Von 1696 bis 1701 fungiert der armenisch-katholische Bischof der Stadt als Herausgeber von 15 Titeln. 1701 nimmt die Katholikenverfolgung gewalttätigere Formen an, was die Arbeit der Druckerei erschwert und völlig in die Illegalität drängt. Insgesamt brachte die Druckerei in ihren Konstantinopler Jahren 32 meist religiöse Titel hervor. Raymond Kévorkian gibt jedoch zu bedenken, daß aufgrund falscher Druckortangaben nicht alle Drucke identifizierbar seien. Bemerkenswert sind vier Titel, die Mxit'ar Sebastac'i, vor seinem erzwungenen Weggang aus Konstantinopel, zwischen 1700 und 1701 dort publizierte.[25]

8.3 Das 18. Jahrhundert

Im 18. Jahrhundert blühte der armenische Buchdruck weiter auf. Konstantinopel wurde sein neues Zentrum, aber auch in Smyrna, Indien, Rußland und endlich auch in Etschmiadzin, also in Armenien selbst, entstanden Werkstätten. Venedig behauptete aber weiter seine Rolle als eines der armenischen Buchdruckzentren.

Venedig

Seit dem 18. Jahrhundert sollte Venedigs Name in der armenischen Geistesgeschichte mit dem des Mönches Mxit'ar Sebastac'i (Mechithar aus Sebaste 1676–1749 - Abb. *I) verbunden sein. Der von ihm 1701 gegründete armenisch-katholische Mechitharistenorden fand 1717 eine dauerhafte Heimstatt auf der Venedig vorgelagerten Insel San Lazzaro. Mxit'ar bediente sich von Anfang an des Buchdrucks. Sein editorisches Programm umfaßte die Herausgabe der Klassiker der armenischen Geschichtsschreibung und Literatur, religiöser Werke, sowie eigener theologischer und philologischer Arbeiten. Von 1715 bis 1789 druckte die Druckerei Bortoli den Großteil der Werke der gelehrten Ordensangehörigen: insgesamt ca. 100 armenische Titel. Zu den wissenschaftlich und kulturgeschichtlich herausragenden, typographisch immer exzellenten Publikationen des Ordens vor der Gründung der eigenen Druckerei gehören: Mxit'ars erste Grammatik des Westarmenischen (*Dowṙn k'erakanowt'ean ašxarhabar lezowin hayoc'*,

and Catholic Christians, it took the side of the latter and printed writings of Catholic missionaries and priests. To escape persecution by the Armenian Apostolic patriarchate many of these writings cite the printing locations as Marseille, Livorno or Amsterdam, although they were printed in Constantinople. Between 1696 and 1701 the Armenian Catholic bishop of the city functioned as the editor of 15 titles. In 1701 persecution of Catholics took on more violent forms, hindering the work of the printing press and forcing it into complete illegality. The press published a total of 32 mostly religious titles in its years in Constantinople. Raymond Kévorkian notes, however, that owing to the false imprint, not all editions are identifiable. Mxit'ar Sebastac'i published four remarkable titles in the city between 1700 and 1701 before his enforced departure from Constantinople.[25]

8.3. The 18th century

Armenian book printing revived once again in the 18th century. Constantinople became its new centre, but presses arose also in Smyrna, India, Russia and eventually also in Ejmiadzin, i. e. in Armenia itself. However, Venice again asserted its role as one of the centres of Armenian book printing.

Venice

Since the 18th century the name of Venice in Armenian spiritual history would be linked with that of the monk Mxit'ar Sebastac'i (Mechitar of Sebaste 1676–1749 - Ill. *I). The Armenian Catholic Mechitarist order founded by him in 1701 found a permanent home in 1717 on the island of San Lazzaro in the Venetian lagoon. Mxit'ar used book printing from the very beginning. His editorial program encompassed the publication of classics of Armenian history and literature, religious works as well as his own theological and philological works. The press of Antonio Bortoli in particular printed the majority of the works of the learned members of the order from 1715 until 1789: approximately 100 Armenian titles. The publications of the order before the founding of its own printing press were always typographically excellent, and among them are works that stand out also for their importance in the history of scholarship and culture: Mxit'ars first grammar in West Armenian (*Dowṙn k'erakanowt'ean*

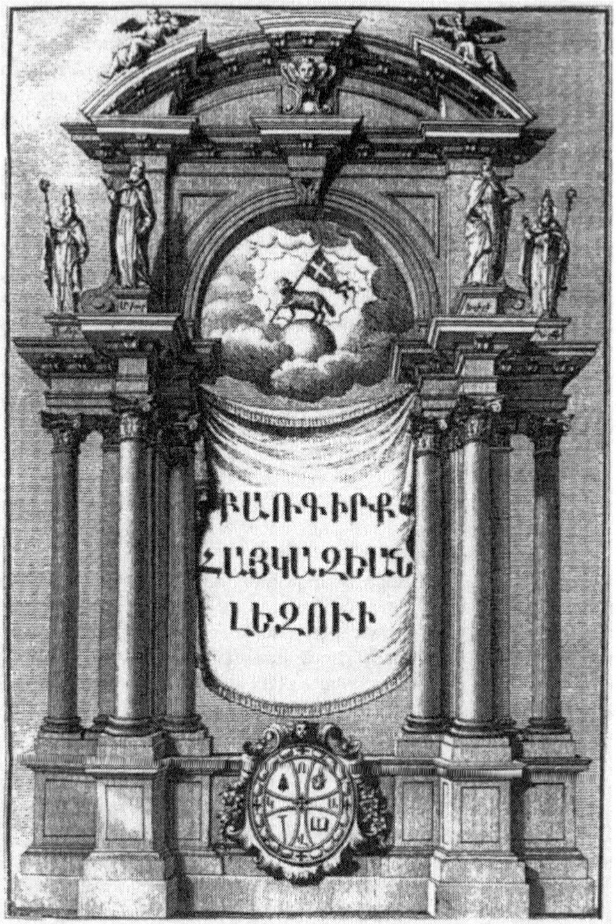

Abb./Ill. 2:
Bařgirk' haykazean lezowi

1727), sein Bibeldruck (*Astowacašownč' girk'*, 1735 - 43), sein monumentales zweibändiges armenisches Wörterbuch (*Bařgirk' haykazean lezowi*, 1749, 1769 [Abb. 2]) sowie Mik'ayêl Č'amč'eans Grammatik (*K'erakanowt'iwn haykazean lezowi*, 1779) und Geschichte (*Patmowt'iwn hayoc'*, 1784). Den praktischeren Bedürfnissen von armenischen Händlern und Studenten in Italien diente Gabriêl Awetik'eans *Kerakanowt'iwn t'ôsk'anean lezowi* ('Grammatik der toskanischen Sprache', 1792), deren Erläuterungen auch in türkisch mit armenischen Buchstaben abgefaßt waren (Abb. 3). Mxit'ar meisterte den Vertrieb besser als seine Vorgänger im Druckerei- und Ver-

ašxarhabar lezowin hayoc', 1727), his printing of the Bible (*Astowacašownč' girk'*, 1735 - 43), his monumental two-volume Armenian dictionary (*Bařgirk' haykazean lezowi*, 1749, 1769 [Ill. 2]) as well as Mik'ayêl Č'amč'ean's grammar (*K'erakanowt'iwn haykazean lezowi*, 1779) and history (*Patmowt'iwn hayoc'*, 1784). Gabriêl Awetik'eans *Kerakanowt'iwn t'ôsk'anean lezowi* ('Grammar of the Tuscan language', 1792) met the practical needs of the Armenian traders and students in Italy. Its explanations were written in Turkish but making use of the Armenian letters (Ill. 3). Mxit'ar mastered the process of distribution better than his predecessors in the print-

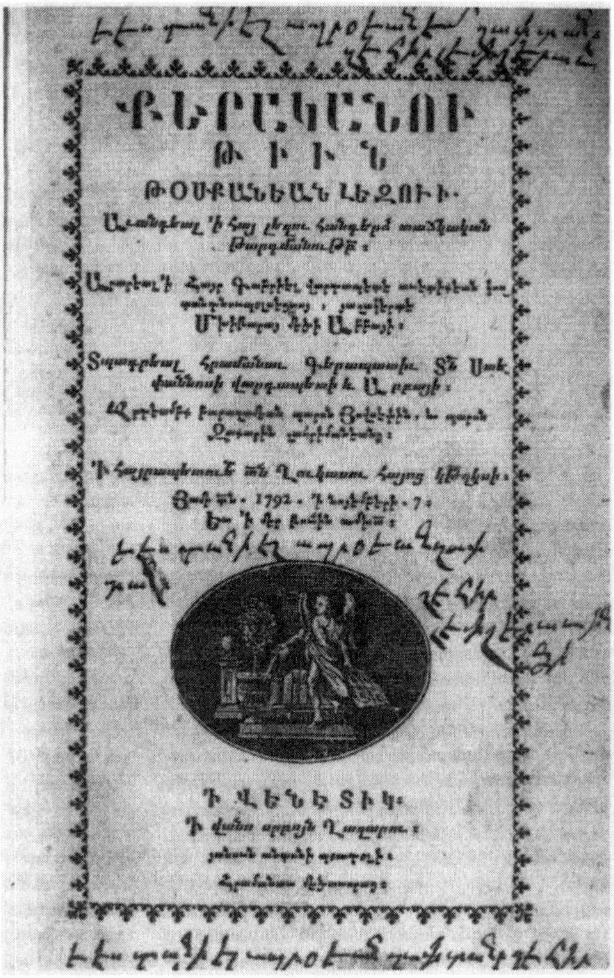
ՔԵՐԱԿԱՆՈՒ
ԹԻՒՆ
ԹՈՒՐՔԱՆԵԱՆ ԼԵԶՈՒԻ·
1792
Ի ՎԵՆԵՏԻԿ·

Abb./Ill. 3:
K'erakanowt'iwn tôsk'anean lezowi

lagsgeschäft. Dank der guten Beziehungen seiner Mönche, meist Söhne Konstantinopler Kaufleute, und eines Netzes armenischer Buchhändler, vor allem in den armenischen Provinzen des Osmanischen Reiches, gestaltete sich der Verkauf der Bücher profitabel. So profitabel, daß die Familie Bortoli ihr Privileg zum Druck armenischer Bücher in Venedig mit Klauen und Zähnen verteidigte. Deshalb gelang es den gelehrten Mönchen erst 1789, ihre eigene Druckerei auf der Kloster-Insel San Lazzaro zu gründen. Sie führten damit das Ende des armeni-

ing and publishing business. Thanks to the good connections of his monks, most of them sons of Constantinople merchants, and a network of Armenian booksellers, primarily in the Armenian provinces of the Ottoman Empire, the sale of books was profitable. It was so profitable that the Bortoli family fought tooth and nail for her privilege of printing Armenian books in Venice. This is the reason that the learned monks were not able to found their own printing press on the monastery island of San Lazzaro until 1789. When they did so they brought Arme-

Abb. 4: Blick in die Druckerei des Mechitharistenordens in Wien (1910)

Ill. 4: View of the printing press of the Mechitarist order at Vienna (1910)

schen Buchdrucks in venezianischen Werkstätten herbei. Die neu gegründete Druckerei brachte bis zum Ende des Jahrhunderts bereits über dreißig Titel heraus. Unter ihnen wichtige Klassikerausgaben von Mxit'ar Goš, Ġazar P'arpec'i, Grigor Narekac'i und Movsês Xorenac'i. Aber auch bedeutende wissenschaftliche Leistungen von Ordensangehörigen wie die des Geographen-Historikers Ġowkas Inčičean konnten nun in Eigenregie erscheinen.

Bereits seit 1776 existierte die Druckerei des Mechitharistenordens in Triest. Bis zur Übersiedlung dieses Zweiges des Ordens nach Wien 35 Jahre später (Abb. 4) druckte sie 70 Titel.[26]

Das goldene Zeitalter beider Mechitharistenkongregationen und ihrer Druckereien brach aber erst im 19. Jahrhundert an. Sie verlegten die meisten armenologischen Werke, Autoren waren Mönche des Ordens, und die Anzahl ihrer Publikationen überstieg die aller anderen Druckereien.[27]

Etschmiadzin (Armenien)

Die Einrichtung der ersten Druckerei in Armenien geht auf die Initiative des Katholikos Simêon Erewanc'i (1763-1780 Amtszeit) zurück. Nach mehreren fehlgeschlagenen Versuchen, eine Druckereiausrüstung aus Konstantinopel oder Amsterdam überführen zu lassen, griff Simêon 1771 zur Selbsthilfe: Das Typenmaterial goß der ortsansässige Goldschmied Yarowt'iwn, Korrektoren und Lektoren waren Mönche des Klosters, oft der Katholikos selbst. 1772 verließ der erste, noch unvollendete

nian book printing in Venetian printing houses to an end. The newly established printing press published over 30 titles even before the end of the century, among them important editions of classics by Mxit'ar Goš, Ġazar P'arpec'i, Grigor Narekac'i and Movsês Xorenac'i. But significant scholarly accomplishments of members of the order such as the geographical historian Ġowkas Inčičean could also now be produced by the order itself.

As early as 1776 the Mechitarist order had a printing press in Trieste. Until this branch moved to Vienna 35 years later (Ill. 4) it printed 70 titles.[26]

The golden age of both Mechitarist congregations and their printing presses, however, did not begin until the 19th century. They published most of the books on the Armenian language, written by the monks of the order, and the number of publications exceeded that of all other printing presses.[27]

Ejmiadzin (Armenia)

The establishment of the first printing press in Armenia was initiated by the catholicos Simêon Erewanc'i (in office from 1763–1780). After a number of failed attempts to import printing equipment from Constantinople or Amsterdam, Simêon resorted to self-help in 1771. The type material was cast by the local goldsmith Yarowt'iwn, monks from the monastery, and often the catholicos himself, served as proofreaders and editors. In 1772 the first, albeit uncompleted, edition, a prayer book from the

Druck, ein Gebetbuch aus der Feder des Katholikos (*Zbosaran hogewor*), die nach Gregor dem Erleuchter benannte Druckerei („Tparan Sowrb Grigor Lowsaworič'"). Auch der permanente Papiermangel konnte schließlich aus eigener Kraft behoben werden: 1776 ging in Etschmiadzin eine Papierfabrik in Betrieb. Doch Kriege, Invasionen und Zerstörungen behinderten immer wieder die Arbeit und brachten sie 1794 vorerst völlig zum Erliegen. Im seit 1800 tobenden russisch-persischen Krieg wurden Druckerei und Papierfabrik geplündert. Bis zu dieser Zeit waren 13 Titel in Etschmiadzin gedruckt worden. Hervorzuheben sind hiervon ein zweibändiger Festkalender (*Tônac'oyc'*, 1774-75), der im Gegensatz zu den vom Mechitharistenorden herausgegebenen rein armenisch-apostolisch ist, 1787 die armenische Übersetzung von Flavius Josephus *Der jüdische Krieg* und fünf theologische Werke aus der Feder des Katholikos Simêon Erewanc'i. Der Bedarf an gedruckten Büchern wurde aber durch die eigene Druckerei in Etschmiadzin nicht gedeckt und man bezog weiterhin einen Großteil der benötigten Literatur aus armenischen Druckereien in Rußland und Konstantinopel. Erst 1818 nahm die Druckerei von Etschmiadzin die Arbeit wieder auf.[28]

Rußland

1781 erschien in Sankt Petersburg das erste armenische Buch, eine Fibel (*Aybbenaran*), in der Druckerei des aus Nor Jowġa stammenden Kaufmanns Grigor Xaldareanc'. Das Unternehmen brachte bis 1788 16 Titel hervor - neben dringend benötigten religiösen Büchern und populären Klassikern wie *Yisows ordi* (1785) von Nerses Šnorhali, das Geschichtswerk (*Patmowt'iwn Vardananc'*, 1787) von Eġišê, ein armenisch-russisches Wörterbuch von Grigor Xaldareanc' und ein Lehrbuch des Ostarmenischen, „Schlüssel des Wissens" (*Banali gitowt'ean*, 1788), von der zeitgenössischen Autorin Kleopatra Sarafean. Nach dem Tod ihres Gründers Xaldareanc' 1787 übernahm die armenische Kirchenführung in Etschmiadzin die Werkstatt und überführte sie in Städte mit starkem armenischem Bevölkerungsanteil - 1789 erst nach Nor Nachitschewan (von nun an „Tparan S. Xač' Vank'i") und 1796 dann nach Astrachan („Tparan Argowt'eanc'"/„Tparan S. Ejmiacni"), wo sie bis 1837 bestand.[29] Insgesamt produzierte die Druckerei von 1781 bis 1837 57 Werke. Da sie vor allem für den Katholikos arbeitete waren diese naturgemäß meist religiöser Natur. Außerdem verlegte man mittelalterliche armenische Klassiker

pen of the catholicos (*Zbosaran hogewor*) left the press, which was named after St. Gregory the Illuminator ("Tparan Sowrb Grigor Lowsaworič'"). They were even able to solve the problem of the permanent lack of paper on their own: a paper factory began operation in Ejmiadzin in 1776. But wars, invasions and destruction repeatedly impeded the work and in 1794 brought it to a complete standstill for a time. In the Russo-Iranian war that raged from 1800 onwards the printing press and paper factory were pillaged. Until this time 13 titles had been printed in Ejmiadzin. The most notable of these are a two-volume feast calendar (*Tônac'oyc'*, 1774-75), which is purely Armenian Apostolic in contrast to those produced by the Mechitarist order, the Armenian translation of Flavius Josephus's *The History of the Jewish War* (1787) and five theological works from the pen of the catholicos Simêon Erewanc'i. The printing press in Ejmiadzin could not, however, meet the demand for printed books and a large part of the literature which was needed continued to be bought from Armenian printing presses in Russia and Constantinople. The printing press of Ejmiadzin did not resume its work until 1818.[28]

Russia

In 1781 the first Armenian book was published in Saint Petersburg, a primer (*Aybbenaran*), by the printing press of the merchant Grigor Xaldareanc' who came from Nor Jowġa. Until 1788 the enterprise produced 16 titles: besides the urgently needed religious books and popular classics such as *Yisows ordi* (1785) by Nerses Šnorhali, the historical work (*Patmowt'iwn Vardananc'*, 1787) by Eġišê, an Armenian-Russian dictionary by Grigor Xaldareanc' and an East Armenian textbook, "Key of Knowledge" (*Banali gitowt'ean*, 1788), by the contemporary female author Kleopatra Sarafean. After the death of its founder Xaldareanc' in 1787 the Armenian church leaders in Ejmiadzin took over the shop and moved it to cities with large Armenian populations – first in 1789 to Nor Nakhichevan (then called "Tparan S. Xač' Vank'i") and then in 1796 to Astrakhan ("Tparan Argowt'eanc'"/ "Tparan S. Ejmiacni"), where it remained until 1837.[29] Between 1781 and 1837 the printing press produced a total of 57 works. Since it worked chiefly for the catholicos these were, of course, mostly of a religious nature. The press also published classical mediæval Armenian authors such as Step'an Ôrbelean (1790) and

wie Step'an Ôrbelean (1790) und Yovhannês Erznkac'i (1792), Kalender, ein Medizinbuch (*Bžškaran hamarôt*, 1793) von Y. K'alant'arean und die armenische Übersetzung von François Fénélons *Les aventures de Télémaque* (1794/95).

Indien

Die armenische Kolonie in Indien, mit ihren Zentren in Madras und Kalkutta, geht hauptsächlich auf Auswanderer aus Nor Jowġa in Persien zurück. In der ersten Hälfte des 18. Jahrhunderts machte die innere Schwäche der Safawiden-Dynastie die Situation der Armenier in Persien unsicher. Etliche entschlossen sich zur Auswanderung und fanden in Indien eine neue Heimat.

Es waren Kaufleute und Handwerker, die in der zweiten Hälfte des 18. Jahrhunderts den Wohlstand der armenischen Gemeinden Indiens begründeten und ihre Aktivitäten bald auf kulturelle und politische Felder ausdehnten. 1772 gründete der Kaufmann Šahamir Šahamirean in Madras unter dem Namen seines Sohnes Yakob die erste armenische Druckerei Indiens. Šahamir Šahamireans Name ist eng mit frühen bürgerlich-aufklärerischen Bestrebungen zur Befreiung Armeniens verbunden. So nimmt es nicht wunder, daß seine Druckerei als erste armenische Druckerei mit politischen Schriften hervortrat: *Nor tetrak or koč'i yordorak* von Movsês Bagramean ('Ermahnung', 1772) und *Orogayt' p'ařac'* ('Die Falle des Ruhms', 1773) von Šahamirean selbst, in dem er die Schaffung eines unabhängigen republikanischen Armeniens propagiert. Daneben entstanden eine Fibel *Aybbenaran* (1772), der Erstdruck eines Geschichtswerks aus dem 9. Jahrhundert von Mesrop Erêc' *Patmowt'iwn mnacordac' hayoc' ew vrac'* (1775) [44], eine Geschichte der Taten des zeitgenössischen persischen Schah Nadir (*Patmowt'iwn varowc'n ew gorcoc' Natr Šah t'agaworin Parsic'*, 1780), die Übersetzung eines Gunst- und Schutzbriefes der Zarin Katharina an die Armenier in Nor Nachitschewan im russischen Reich (1781) und eine Verfassung der armenischen Gemeinde von Madras *Tetrak or koč'i nšawak* (1783) wieder von Šahamir Šahamirean.

Der Priester Yarowt'iwn Šmavonean (Širazec'i) gründete 1789 die zweite armenische Druckerei in Madras. Sie bestand bis 1810 und brachte insgesamt 24 Titel hervor. Wichtige Werke aus seiner Werkstatt sind u.a. *K'erakanowt'iwn* ('Grammatik in zwei Bänden', 1791) von Paġtasar Dpir, *Grkoyk' erkrač'ap'akan* ('Geometrie-Büchlein', 1792) von Yakob

Yovhannês Erznkac'i (1792), calendars, a medical book (*Bžškaran hamarôt*, 1793) by Y. K'alant'arean and the Armenian translation of François Fénélon's *Les aventures de Télémaque* (1794/95).

India

The Armenian colony in India, with its centres in Madras and Calcutta, originated chiefly from immigrants from Nor Jowġa in Iran. In the first half of the 18th century the inner weakness of the Safavid dynasty made the situation of Armenians in Iran unsafe. Many of them decided to emigrate and found their new home in India.

In the second half of the 18th century merchants and craftsmen established the prosperity of the Armenian communities in India and soon extended their activities to cultural and political spheres. In 1772 the merchant Šahamir Šahamirean founded India's first Armenian printing press in Madras under the name of his son Yakob. Šahamir Šahamirean's name is linked closely with early civil-enlightenment efforts for the liberation of Armenia. Hence it is not surprising that his printing press was the first Armenian printing press to produce political writings: *Nor tetrak or koč'i yordorak* by Movsês Bagramean ('Admonition', 1772) and *Orogayt' p'ařac'* ('The Fall of Fame', 1773) written by Šahamirean himself in which he propagates the creation of an independent Armenian republic. He also printed the primer *Aybbenaran* (1772), the first edition of a 9th-century historical work by Mesrop Erêc' *Patmowt'iwn mnacordac' hayoc' ew vrac'* (1775) [44], a history of the deeds of the contemporary Iranian Šah Nadir (*Patmowt'iwn varowc'n ew gorcoc' Natr Šah t'agaworin Parsic'*, 1780), the translation of a Letter of Favour and Protection by Tsarina Catherine to the Armenians in Nor Nakhichevan in the Russian empire (1781) and a constitution of the Armenian community of Madras *Tetrak or koč'i nšawak* (1783) again by Šahamir Šahamirean.

The priest Yarowt'iwn Šmavonean (Širazec'i) founded the second Armenian printing press in Madras in 1789. It existed until 1810 and produced 24 titles. Important works from his press include *K'erakanowt'iwn* (2-volume grammar, 1791) by Paġtasar Dpir, *Grkoyk' erkrač'ap'akan* (geometry booklet, 1792) by Yakob T'aġean and *Oġb Hayasta-*

T'aġean, *Oġb Hayastaneac'* ('Klage um Armenien', 1791), eine patriotische Schrift des zeitgenössischen Autors T'adêos Sogineanc'. Die Bedeutung Šmavoneans und seiner Druckerei macht jedoch vor allem aus, daß er mit *Azdarar* ('Der Anzeiger') von 1794 bis 1796 die erste armenische Zeitung herausgab und druckte.

1792 eröffnete in Kalkutta ein anderer Priester, Yovsêp' Step'anean, die erste armenische Druckerei am Ort. Sie bestand allerdings nur zwei Jahre und brachte insgesamt fünf Titel hervor - u.a. die zeitgenössische Geschichte des Abraham Kretac'i (*Patmowt'iwn anc'icn iwroc' ew Natr-Šahin parsic'*, 1796).

Konstantinopel
Mit der Wahl von Yovhannês Kolot zum armenischen Patriarchen endete 1715 eine Periode der politischen Zwistigkeiten und der Lähmung in der armenischen Gemeinschaft Konstantinopels. Die Amtszeit des gebildeten und tatkräftigen Patriarchen brachte Kontinuität und geistiges Aufblühen - kurz, die notwendigen Bedingungen für das Gedeihen des Buchdrucks. Die harten Auseinandersetzungen zwischen apostolischen Armeniern und katholischen Missionaren und ihren armenischen Anhängern gingen unterdes weiter. Auch die Buchdrucker ergriffen Partei und setzten das Buch als Mittel in der Auseinandersetzung ein.

Die Druckerei Marzvanec'i
Grigor Marzvanec'i gilt als Vorreiter des neuen aufblühenden Druck- und Verlagswesens im Konstantinopel des 18. Jahrhunderts - ihm folgte eine ganze Generation nach. Seine Werkstatt existierte von ca. 1694 bis 1734 und brachte 14 Titel hervor.[30] Mit seinem Namen ist die Veröffentlichung von inhaltlich wichtigen, typographisch teilweise herausragenden Titeln verbunden.

1698 erschien sein Erstlingswerk - ein Gesangbuch. 1706 legte Marzvanec'i bereits sein Meisterstück vor: das *Yaysmawowrk'*. Dafür goß er mehr als zweitausend verschiedene Formen von Bildern, Kanonbögen, Initialen, Blockschriften und Buchstaben. Dieses Synaxarion, das Ergebnis zwölfjähriger Mühen, ist eines der schönsten Beispiele armenischer Buchdruckkunst. Der zweite Druck des Werkes von 1730 wird hier gezeigt [34].

Zu Marzvanec'is großen Verdiensten gehört der Erstdruck wichtiger nationaler Literaturdenkmäler: auf Bestellung des Katholikos druckte Marzvanec'i

neac' ('Lamentation for Armenia', 1791), a patriotic text by the contemporary author T'adêos Sogineanc'. The importance of Šmavonean and his printing press, however, lies chiefly in his editing and printing the first Armenian newspaper, *Azdarar* ('The Advertiser') from 1794 until 1796.

In 1792 another priest, Yovsêp' Step'anean, opened the first Armenian printing press in Calcutta. It existed, however, for only two years and produced a total of five titles - including the contemporary history of Abraham Kretac'i (*Patmowt'iwn anc'icn iwroc' ew Natr-Šahin parsic'*, 1796).

Constantinople
The election of Yovhannês Kolot as Armenian patriarch in 1715 ended a period of political disputes and the paralysis in the Armenian community of Constantinople. The term of office of the educated and energetic patriarch brought continuity and intellectual revival - in short those conditions needed for book printing to thrive. The harsh conflicts between Apostolic Armenians and Catholic missionaries and their Armenian followers continued nonetheless. The book printers also took sides and employed the book as a means in the conflict.

The Marzvanec'i printing press
Grigor Marzvanec'i is considered a pioneer of the newly revived printing and publishing world of Constantinople in the 18th century - and he was followed by an entire generation. His press existed from about 1694 until 1734 and produced 14 titles.[30] His name is linked with the publication of titles of important content and some of typographical excellence.

His first work appeared in 1698 - a hymnbook. Marzvanec'i produced his masterpiece as early as 1706: the *Yaysmawowrk'*. To do so he cast two thousand different shapes of images, arched canon-tables, initials, block types and letters. This Synaxarion, the result of twelve years of work, is one of the most beautiful examples of Armenian book printing art. The second printing dated 1730 is shown here [34].

Among Marzvanec'i's great merits is the first printing of important national monuments of literature: on the order of the catholicos he printed

1710 die *Geschichte* des Agat'angeġos. Auf Kosten des Patriarchen Kolot und von ihm herausgegeben erschien 1719 die *Geschichte* des Zenob Asori (Glak) aus dem 10. Jahrhundert.

Erwähnenswert sind ebenfalls Drucke von Werken der Kirchenväter Johannes Chrysostomos (Yovhan Oskeberan) 1717, 1734, und Grigor Narekac'i (*Girk' aġot'ic'*, 1726).

Zu den Werken, die direkt in der Auseinandersetzung mit der katholischen Fraktion stehen, gehören: *Krt'owt'iwn hawatoy* ('Erziehung zum Glauben', 1713) von Yovhannês Mrgowz sowie zwei Werke von Grigor Tat'ewac'i: *Girk' harc'manc'* ('Buch der Fragen', 1720 - dieser Druck blieb jedoch unvollendet) und *Nkadowmn čšmartowt'ean* ('Bemerkungen zur Wahrheit', 1713).

Ab 1734 verlieren sich die Spuren des Grigor Marzvanec'i und seiner Druckerei.

the *History* of the Agat'angeġos in 1710. In 1719 Patriarch Kolot financed and edited the *History* of Zenob Asori (Glak) from the 10th century.

Also notable are editions of works by the church fathers Johannes Chrysostomos (Yovhan Oskeberan) of 1717 and 1734 and Grigor Narekac'i (*Girk' aġot'ic'*, 1726).

Those works that are directly involved in the conflict with the Catholic faction include: *Krt'owt'iwn hawatoy* ('Training in Faith', 1713) by Yovhannês Mrgowz as well as two works by Grigor Tat'ewac'i: *Girk' harc'manc'* ('Book of Questions', 1720 - although this printing remained unfinished) and *Nkadowmn čšmartowt'ean* ('Notes on Truth', 1713).

From 1734 we lose track of Grigor Marzvanec'i and his printing press.

Die Druckerei des Astowacatowr Dpir
und seiner Nachfolger

Diese langlebigste armenische Druckerei Konstantinopels bestand unter den Familien Astowacatowr und Arapean mit wechselnden Namen insgesamt 150 Jahre - von 1699 bis in die 1850er Jahre. Der Gründer Astowacatowr Dpir soll die Druckerei bis zu seinem Tode um 1750 geleitet haben, die dann auf seinen Sohn Yovhannês überging. 1776 übernahm die Arapean-Familie das Geschäft und führte es erfolgreich weiter.[31]

Ein Sarakan-Druck (Hymnarium) stand 1699 am Anfang der Tätigkeit des Astowacatowr Dpir. Der Schwerpunkt seiner Arbeit sollte auch später auf dem Gebiet des religiösen Buches liegen. Bei Astowacatowr erschienen, meist in mehreren Auflagen und Ausgaben, Gebetbücher (*Žamagirk'*, 1701, *Maštoc'*, 1704, 1714), Synaxarien (*Yaysmawowrk'*, 1706-08), Gesangbücher (*Taġaran*, 1701, 1740 - 45), Kalendarien (*Tônac'oyc'*, 1703) und Meßbücher (*Čašoc'*, 1722). Doch Astowcatowr bediente nicht nur den Bedarf der Kirche, sondern trug auch dem steigenden Interesse des Publikums an unterhaltsamer und lehrreicher Literatur Rechnung: 1721 erschien z.B. „Die Geschichte des Kaisers Pontianos" (*Girk' patmowt'ean Kaysern P'onc'ianosi*), ein volkstümliches Lesebuch mittelalterlicher Geschichten, 1731 eine zeitgenössische „Geschichte der heiligen und großen Gottesstadt Jerusalem" (*Girk' patmowt'ean srboy ew meci k'aġak's Erowsaġêmi*), von Yovhannês Hanna für Pilger geschrie-

The printing press of Astowacatowr Dpir
and his successors

This longest-lived Armenian printing press in Constantinople existed under the Astowacatowr and Arapean families with changing names for a total of 150 years - from 1699 until the 1850s. The founder, Astowacatowr Dpir, is said to have run the printing press until his death around 1750, when it passed to his son Yovhannês. In 1776 the Arapean family took over the business and managed it successfully thereafter.[31]

Astowacatowr Dpir's work began with the printing of a Sharakan (hymnal) in 1699, and his later work also focussed on religious books. Astowacatowr published, usually in a number of issues and editions, prayer-books (*Žamagirk'*, 1701, *Maštoc'*, 1704, 1714), Synaxaria (*Yaysmawowrk'*, 1706-08), hymnbooks (*Taġaran*, 1701, 1740 - 45), calendars (*Tônac'oyc'*, 1703) and missals (*Čašoc'*, 1722). Astowcatowr not only supplied the church, but also satisfied the growing interest of the public in entertaining and instructive literature: for example in 1721 he produced "The History of Emperor Pontianos" (*Girk' patmowt'ean Kaysern P'onc'ianosi*), a popular reading book of mediæval stories, in 1731 a contemporary "History of the Holy and Great City of God Jerusalem" (*Girk' patmowt'ean srboy ew meci k'aġak's Erowsaġêmi*), written by Yovhannês Hanna for pilgrims, and *Patmowt'iwn pġnje k'aġak'in* ('History of the City of Copper', 1731), a well-loved storybook.

ben, und *Patmowt'iwn pġnje k'aġak'in* ('Geschichte der kupfernen Stadt', 1731), ein beliebtes Geschichtenbuch.

Auch Klassiker wie der volkstümliche „Narek" (Erstdruck des *Matean oġbergowt'ean,* 1701) von Grigor Narekac'i, der drei Neuauflagen erreichte, und Dawit' Anyaġt's *Girk' saġmanac'* ('Psalmenbuch', 1731) sowie Literatur in der Auseinandersetzung mit der katholische Kirche wie *Dawanowt'iwn hawatoy* ('Bekenntnis des Glaubens', 1713–14) von Yovhannês Mrgowz und das hier gezeigte *Girk' harc'manc'* ('Buch der Fragen', 1729 – [35]) von Grigor Tatewac'i standen auf dem Programm.

Typographisch erreichte die Werkstatt noch zu Zeiten ihres Gründers ein sehr hohes Niveau.

Bis 1776 führte Astowactowrs Sohn Yovhannês die Druckerei unter dem Namen seines Vaters weiter. In dieser Zeit geschah wenig Spektakuläres. Yovhannês druckte größtenteils Neuauflagen religiöser Bücher. Der aufwendige und gelungene Erstdruck (zwei Titelblätter und 220 illustrierte Seiten) von Eġišês *Vardananc' patmowt'iwn* von 1764 „sichert ihm jedoch einen Platz in der armenischen Druckgeschichte".[32]

Ab 1776 ging die große Werkstatt in die Hände von Yovhannês Apowč'exc'i Arapean und seines Sohnes Poġos über. Nun begann die Ära der Arapean-Dynastie, die bedeutende Schriftsetzer und Drucker hervorbrachte. Nach dem Tode von Yovhannês Arapean um 1810 führte sein Sohn Poġos Arapean (1742–1835), der auch ein berühmter Schriftgießer war, das Unternehmen erfolgreich allein weiter. 1820 eröffnete er in Ortaköy/Konstantinopel eine neue große Druckerei in einem zweistöckigen Steinhaus. Poġos Arapeans Name spielt auch in der türkischen Druckgeschichte eine wichtige Rolle: Er schuf die türkischen Nesih- und Tal'iklettern, nach ihm auch Araboğlu-Lettern genannt.[33]

1816 wurde Poġos Arapean zum Direktor der Druckerei des Sultans ernannt. Dort druckte er 1831 die erste türkische Zeitung.[34]

Poġos Arapean und seine drei Söhne blieben in der 1. Hälfte des 19. Jahrhunderts die beherrschenden Gestalten des armenischen Druckwesens in Konstantinopel: Die Werkstätten der Arapean-Familie brachten bis ca. 1850 über 150 armenische Titel hervor. Überwog bis zum Ende des 18. Jahrhunderts noch das religiöse Buch, so brachte das neue Jahrhundert nicht nur eine größere Anzahl von Titeln (ca. 120), sondern auch eine größere Themenvielfalt

The programme also included classics such as the popular "Narek" (first printing of *Matean oġbergowt'ean* 1701) by Grigor Narekac'i, which reached three new editions, and *Girk' saġmanac'* ('Book of Psalms', 1731) by Dawit' Anyaġt', as well as literature from the conflict with the Catholic Church such as *Dawanowt'iwn hawatoy* ('Profession of Faith', 1713–14) by Yovhannês Mrgowz and the *Girk' harc'manc'* ('Book of Questions', 1729 – [35]), shown here, by Grigor Tatewac'i.

The workshop attained very high typographical standards right from the time of its founder.

Astowactowr's son Yovhannês ran the printing press under his father's name until 1776. During this period he did not produce any spectacular works. Yovhannês primarily printed new editions of religious books. The lavish and successful first edition (two title pages and 220 illustrated pages) of *Eġišês Vardananc' patmowt'iwn* in 1764 "nevertheless secures his place in the history of Armenian printing".[32]

From 1776 the large printing-shop passed into the hands of Yovhannês Apowč'exc'i Arapean and his son Poġos. This began the era of the Arapean dynasty, which produced significant typesetters and printers. Following the death of Yovhannês Arapean around 1810 his son Poġos Arapean (1742–1835), also a famous type founder, successfully continued the enterprise on his own. In 1820 he opened a new large printing press in a two-story stone house in Ortaköy, Constantinople. Poġos Arapean's name is also important in the history of Turkish printing: he created the Turkish Nesih and Tal'ik types, also called Araboğlu type after him.[33]

In 1816 Poġos Arapean was appointed director of the printing press of the sultan, where he printed the first Turkish newspaper in 1831.[34]

Poġos Arapean and his three sons remained the dominating figures of Armenian printing in the first half of the 19th century in Constantinople: the presses of the Arapean family produced over 150 Armenian titles until about 1850. Although religious books dominated until the end of the 18th century, the new century brought not only a larger number of books (approximately 120), but also a greater variety of subject matter with the addition of gram-

– Grammatik, Wörterbücher, Literatur, Politik und Geschichte traten hinzu.

Im 18. Jahrhundert arbeiteten über zwanzig weitere armenische Druckereien in der Stadt, deren Bedeutung jedoch nicht mit denen von Marzvanec'i oder Astowacatowr/Arapean zu vergleichen ist. Es handelt sich dabei u.a. um die Unternehmen von Sargis Dpir und seinem Sohn Martiros (1701–58), Č'nč'in Yovhannês (1746–52), Parsêġ und Yakob Sebastac'iner (1736–40), Parsêġ Sebastac'i (1755–77), Gabriêl Sebastac'i Parsêġean (1745–50), Abraham T'rkac'i (1733–46), Yovhannês und Yakob (1766–69), Step'anos Petrosean (1770–92), „Mayr tpratown" (1792–98).[35]

Smyrna

Smyrna (heute Izmir) wurde die zweite Heimstatt des armenischen Buchdrucks im Osmanischen Reich. 1759 eröffnete hier Mahtesi Markos eine Werkstatt, die bis 1763 bestand und drei Titel veröffentlichte. Davon verdient einer besondere Beachtung: Es ist der Erstdruck des um 445 entstandenen Werkes des Eznik aus Koġb *Girk' ęnddimowt'eanc'* ('Wider die Irrlehren', 1762/63), von dem bis zu diesem Zeitpunkt nur noch eine einzige handschriftliche Version existierte.[36]

9. Armenisch in europäischen Drucken

Bereits im 15. Jahrhundert tauchen armenische Lettern in Drucken von Europäern auf. In der deutschen Ausgabe vom 21. Juni 1486 der *Peregrinatio in terram sanctam* des Mainzer Domherren Bernhard von Breydenbach finden sich die ersten jemals gedruckten armenischen Buchstaben [63].[37] Es handelt sich um ein kleines armenisches Alphabet, das nach handgezeichneten Vorlagen durch einen deutschen Holzschnitzer ausgeführt wurde. Daß die Buchstaben nur auf den zweiten Blick als armenische zu erkennen sind, schmälert nicht die Bedeutung dieser Premiere des Armenischen im Buchdruck.

Ab dem 16. Jahrhundert waren es Missionare und Orientalisten, die ihren Publikationen größere oder kleinere Textpassagen in armenischen Lettern beifügten. Die wichtigsten Titel seien hier genannt:

Der französische Gelehrte Guillaume Postel druckte in seinem 1538 in Paris erschienenen *Linguarum duodecim characteribus differentium alphabetum* ... auch eine Textprobe des Armenischen (ein

mars, dictionaries, literature, politics and history books.

In the 18th century more than twenty other Armenian printing presses operated in the city, yet their importance is not comparable to that of Marzvanec'i or Astowacatowr and Arapean. These included the enterprises of Sargis Dpir and his son Martiros (1701–58), Č'nč'in Yovhannês (1746–52), Parsêġ and Hakob Sebastac'iner (1736–40), Parsêġ Sebastac'i (1755–77), Gabriêl Sebastac'i Parsêġean (1745–50), Abraham T'rkac'i (1733–46), Yovhannês and Yakob (1766–69), Step'anos Petrosean (1770–92) and "Mayr tpratown" (1792–98).[35]

Smyrna

Smyrna (now Izmir) became the second home of Armenian book printing in the Ottoman Empire. In 1759 Mahtesi Markos opened a printing press here that existed until 1763 and published three titles. One of these deserves particular attention: the first printing of the work originally written around 445 by Eznik of Koġb *Girk' ęnddimowt'eanc'* ('Against False Teaching', 1762/63), which existed only as one single handwritten version until this time.[36]

9. Armenian in European printing

As early as the 15th century Armenian letters appear in European printed books. The German edition of 21 June 1486 of the *Peregrinatio in terram sanctam* by the canon of Mainz Bernhard von Breydenbach contains the first Armenian letters ever printed [63].[37] It is a small Armenian alphabet made by a German woodcutter after a hand painted original. The fact that the letters can only be recognised as Armenian at second glance does not diminish the significance of this premiere appearance of Armenian in book printing.

From the 16th century missionaries and students of Eastern languages inserted larger or smaller passages in Armenian type in their publications. The most important titles are cited here.

In his *Linguarum duodecim characteribus differentium alphabetum* ... (Paris, 1538) the French scholar Guillaume Postel printed a sample of Armenian (the Lord's Prayer) and an alphabet. Postel, a pioneer

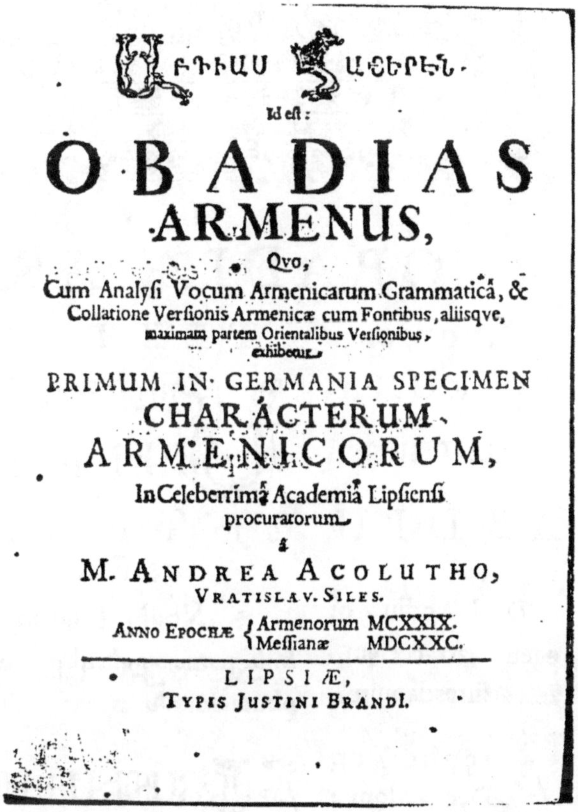

ԱԲԴԻԱՍ ՄԱՐԳԱՐԷՆ.
Id est:
OBADIAS
ARMENUS,
Qvo,
Cum Analysi Vocum Armenicarum Grammaticâ, & Collatione Versionis Armenicæ cum Fontibus, aliisqve, maximam partem Orientalibus Versionibus, exhibetur,
PRIMUM IN GERMANIA SPECIMEN
CHARACTERUM
ARMENICORUM,
In Celeberrimâ Academiâ Lipsiensi procuratorum,
à
M. ANDREA ACOLUTHO,
VRATISLAV. SILES.
ANNO EPOCHÆ { Armenorum MCXXIX. Messianæ MDCXXC.
LIPSIÆ,
TYPIS JUSTINI BRANDI.

Abb./Ill. 5a

Vaterunser) und ein Alphabet ab. Außerdem gibt Postel, ein Vorreiter der Orientalistik, auch einige Erklärungen zum Armenischen. Die armenischen Passagen sind in Holzschnitt ausgeführt.

Teseus Ambrosius, einer der frühen Orientalisten, nahm ein Jahr später, in seine 1539 in Padua erschienene Sammlung orientalischer Sprachen *Introductio in chaldaicum linguam, Syriacam, atque Armeniacam, et decem alias linguas* ... ebenfalls das Armenische auf. Seine über dreißig Seiten umfassende Untersuchung der armenischen Grammatik anhand von Textproben aus den Evangelien wurde bereits mit beweglichen Lettern gedruckt.

In zwei 1583 in Berlin erschienenen Drucken des Leonhard Thurneysser zum Thurm sind armenische,

Orientalist, also gave some explanations on Armenian. The Armenian passages are cut on wood.

A year later Teseus Ambrosius, another early Orientalist, also included Armenian in his collection of oriental languages *Introductio in chaldaicam linguam, Syriacam, atque Armeniacam, et decem alias linguas* ..., published in 1539 in Pavia. His over thirty-page study of Armenian grammar based on sample texts from the Gospels was already printed with movable type.

Two prints by Leonhard Thurneysser zum Thurm produced in 1583 in Berlin contain Armenian texts

I. N. J.

OBADIÆ ARMENI

LECTIO.	TEXTUS.	VERSIO.
MARCHA-REUTTIUN	ՄԱՐԳԱՐԷՈՒԹԻՒՆ	PROPHETIA
ABDIU.	ԱԲԴԻՈՒ :	OBADIÆ.
	verſ. 1.	
Deſil Abdiu, or egeu jarracccham zels Aſuresdanujn.	✲ Տեսիլ Աբդիու որ եղև յառաջքան զելս առ ըեստամնոյս :	Viſio Obadiæ, qvæ fuit ante Aſcenſûs in Aſſyriam.
AISBES ASE Der zedom: Lur luvav i Derne: Eu baſcharumn arracheaz i hettanuſs: Aricch, eu jarizzucch ivr nuza i baderazm.	ԱՅՍՊԷՍ ԱՍԷ Տէր դեղօմ. լուր լուաւ 'ի Տէ. և պաշտօնումն առաքեաց 'ի հեթանոսս : Արիք. և յարիցուք իվը նոյ 'ի պատերազմ :	HOC MODO dicit Dominus ad Edom: Rumorem audivit à Domino, & Obſidionem miſit gentibus: Surgite, & ſurgemus adverſus illos in bellum.
	V. 2.	
Aha Sagavavor edu zchez jazchs, eu anarcheal es tu jujgi.	✲ Ահա սակաւաւոր ետու զքեզ յազգս. և անարգեալ ես դու յոյժ :	Ecce parvum reddidi te in gentibus, & contemtus es tu valde.
	A	verſ. 3.

Abb./Ill. 5b

in Holzschnitt ausgeführte Texte enthalten. In *Onomastico und interpretatio* sowie *Magna alchymia* wurden die armenischen Passagen aus der Bibel, der Medizin und Astrologie jedoch so sehr der deutschen gotischen Schrift angepaßt, daß sie nur mühsam lesbar sind.

Die Arbeiten des Missionars und Armenologen Francesco Rivola waren bereits von großem Wert für die junge Wissenschaft. Rivola, Dozent für Armenisch am Ambrosianischen Kolleg in Mailand, publizierte 1621 sein Wörterbuch *Dictionarium armeno-latinum*[38] und 1624 seine *Grammatica armena*. Beide Werke bezeugen Rivolas umfassende Kenntnis des Armenischen, die er wahrscheinlich dem Unterricht des Bartolomeo Abagaro verdankte.

Auch zwei Deutsche, Martin Kempe und Andreas Acoluth, verwendeten in ihren Werken armenische Lettern.

Kempes *Dissertatio de statu Armeniae* von 1665 enthält nur wenige, ungelenk und in Holzschnitt ausgeführte armenische Lettern. Sein Buch zeugt zwar vom zeitgenössischen Interesse für das armenische Thema, ist aber für die Armenologie ohne Bedeutung.

Anders verhält es sich da mit Andreas Acoluth. Sein Werk *Abdias hayeren, id est Obadias Armenus* (Abb. 5) von 1680 gilt als Beginn der deutschen wissenschaftlichen Beschäftigung mit Armenien. Die armenischen Texte sind mit beweglichen, von Acoluth in Leipzig mit Hilfe des armenischen Priesters Grigorenc' angefertigten Lettern gedruckt.

Im 17. und 18. Jahrhundert erschienen insgesamt 60 europäische Titel mit armenischen Passagen.[39]

in woodcuts. In *Onomastico und interpretatio* and the *Magna alchymia* the Armenian passages from the Bible, from medicine and astrology were, however, so adapted to the German Gothic script that they are very difficult to read.

The works of the missionary and Armenian linguist Francesco Rivola were already of great value to this young branch of scholarship. Rivola, lecturer for Armenian at the Ambrosian College in Milan, published his dictionary *Dictionarium armeno-latinum*[38] in 1621 and in 1624 his *Grammatica armena*. Both works provide evidence of Rivola's extensive knowledge of Armenian, which he probably owed to the instruction of Bartolomeo Abagaro.

Two Germans, Martin Kempe and Andreas Acoluth, also used Armenian type in their works.

Kempe's *Dissertatio de statu Armeniae* of 1665 contains only a few clumsy woodcut Armenian letters. His book reveals the contemporary interest in Armenia, but is insignificant for Armenian studies.

Not so with Andreas Acoluth. His work *Abdias hayeren, id est Obadias Armenus* (Ill. 5) of 1680 is considered the beginning of German scholarly concern with Armenia. The Armenian texts are printed with movable type created by Acoluth in Leipzig with the help of the Armenian priest Grigorenc'.

In the 17th and 18th centuries a total of 60 European books were printed with passages in Armenian.[39]

10. Entwicklungen im 19. Jahrhundert

Das 19. Jahrhundert sollte die Blütezeit des armenischen Buchdruckes bringen. Das Druck- und Verlagswesen erreichten einen Aufschwung wie er weder davor noch danach wieder erreicht wurde. Die Branche befreite sich von den Traditionen der Vergangenheit und modernisierte sich radikal – auf technisch-editorischem wie typographischem Gebiet. Druckerei und Verlag spezialisierten und trennten sich mehr und mehr. Der Vertrieb nahm professionelle Formen an. Armenische Bücher zeigten sich in neuem, modernen Stil, mit einfachem Titelblatt, ohne Kolophone und die noch aus der Handschriftenzeit stammenden Abbreviaturen. Das Buch

10. Developments in the 19th century

The 19th century was the golden age of Armenian book printing. Printing and publishing attained a pinnacle that was never reached either before or after. The industry freed itself from the traditions of the past and radically modernised – in both the technical/editorial and typographical domains. Printing presses and publishers specialised and became more and more distinct from each other. Distribution adopted professional methods. Armenian books appeared in a new, modern style, with a simple title page, without the colophons and abbreviations left over from the manuscript era. The book became the general property of broad classes of the

wurde Allgemeingut breiter Schichten der armenischen Bevölkerung - die Auflagen schossen in die Höhe und die Themenpalette verbreiterte sich. Der Aufschwung des armenischen Bildungswesens und die damit verbundene Gründung von Bildungsvereinen und Schulen taten ein Übriges zur Verbreitung des gedruckten Buches. Schließlich trat auch das moderne Armenisch im 19. Jahrhundert seinen Siegeszug im Buch an. Zentren des Buchdrucks blieben Venedig und Konstantinopel, Tiflis und Wien traten hinzu.

NINEL OSKANYANS Bibliographie des armenischen Buches von 1512-1800 zählt 1 154 Drucke aus dieser Zeit. In der ersten Hälfte des 19. Jahrhunderts erschienen bereits mehr armenische Bcher als in den drei Jahrhunderten zuvor.

Armenian population - the numbers of copies printed shot up and the array of subject matter widened. The upsurge in the Armenian educational systems and the connected establishment of educational associations and schools what remained to disseminate the printed book. Finally in the 19th century Modern Armenian made its triumphant entry into the printed book. Venice and Constantinople remained the centres of book printing, followed by Tiflis and Vienna.

NINEL OSKANYAN's bibliography of Armenian books from 1512 to 1800 enumerates 1154 printed works from this period. In the first half of the 19th century more Armenian books were published than in the previous three centuries.

11. Exkurs: Armenische Pressegeschichte (1794-1920)

Die Geschichte der armenischen Presse begann 1794 im indischen Madras. Seit Mitte des 19. Jahrhunderts nahm das Pressewesen einen großen Aufschwung und erreichte in den 1880er Jahren bis 1915 seine Blütezeit. Gerade die Armenier in ihrer besonderen Diasporasituation bedienten sich eifrig dieses Mediums für Information und interne Verständigung. Von 1794 bis 1920, dem hier untersuchten „vorsowjetischen" Zeitraum, wurden weltweit ca. 2000 armenische Periodika gedruckt[40] - in Konstantinopel, Tiflis, Smyrna, Kalkutta, Singapur, Moskau, Erevan, Wan, Paris - kurz überall, wo Armenier lebten.

11. A brief excursion in the history of the Armenian press (1794-1920)

Armenian press history began in 1794 in the Indian city of Madras. The press made a huge upturn in the mid-19th century and reached its highest level in the 1880s, which lasted until 1915. The Armenians in particular, in their special situation as a Diaspora, keenly made use of this medium for information and internal communication. From 1794 until 1920, in the "pre-Soviet" era examined here, approximately 2,000 Armenian periodicals were printed around the globe[40] - in Constantinople, Tiflis, Smyrna, Calcutta, Singapore, Moscow, Erevan, Van, Paris - in brief everywhere that Armenians lived.

11.1. Die Anfänge des armenischen Journalismus

Der Herausgeber der ersten armenischen Zeitschrift *Azdarar* ('Der Anzeiger', 1794 in Madras), der Priester Yarowt'iwn Šmavonean, hatte sich an den englischen Blättern in Indien ein Vorbild genommen. *Azdarar*, von dem innerhalb von zwei Jahren 18 Nummern erschienen, erreichte, trotz einer Auflage von nur 200-300 Exemplaren, armenische Leser in der ganzen Welt. Šmavonean und seinem 28köpfigen Redaktionskomitee ging es um Bildung und Aufklärung, um die Stärkung des nationalen Bewußtseins und darum, das verstreute armenische Volk in Kontakt mit fortschrittlichen Entwicklungen in Europa zu bringen. Damit ist bereits das Pro-

11.1. The beginnings of Armenian journalism

The publisher of the first Armenian journal *Azdarar* ('The Advertiser', Madras, 1794), the priest Yarowt'iwn Šmavonean, took as a model the English papers in India. *Azdarar*, which appeared in 18 issues within two years, reached Armenian readers all over the world in spite of its circulation of only 200-300 copies. The aims of Šmavonean and his 28-member editorial committee were education and enlightenment; to strengthen national awareness and to bring the scattered Armenian people into contact with progressive developments in Europe. This already sketches the programme pursued by the Armenian press in its early stages. Often national

gramm umrissen, das die armenische Presse in ihrer Frühphase verfolgte. Herausgeber und Finanziers dieser Zeitschriften und Zeitungen waren dann auch oft nationale Bildungsvereine.

Die nächsten drei armenischen Zeitschriften sind mit dem Namen des Mechitharistenpaters Ġowkas Inčičean verbunden. 1799-1803 gab er das Jahrbuch *Taregrowt'iwn* in Venedig heraus und war damit der erste, der die neuwestarmenische Sprache in seiner Zeitschrift verwendete. 1803-20 setzte Inčičean seine journalistische Arbeit mit einem Jahrbuch allgemeinen Inhalts - von Politik bis Astrologie - fort. *Eġanak Biwzandean* ('Byzantinische Zeitschrift') wurde in Venedig gedruckt, in Konstantinopel aber geschrieben und vertrieben. 1807 gab derselbe umtriebige Mechitharistenpater mit *Yišatakaran* ('Erinnerungsschrift') wiederum eine politisch-zeitgeschichtliche Zeitschrift heraus, aus der ab 1808 *Ditak biwzandean* ('Byzantinischer Beobachter') mit 14tägiger Erscheinungsweise wurde. Von 1812-16 trat der Konstantinopler Bildungsverein „Aršarowneac'" als Herausgeber der Zeitschrift in Erscheinung. Sein Credo war es, das Volk durch Zeitschriften „zu unterhalten, zu bilden und zu belehren".[41] Um einen wirklich großen Leserkreis zu erreichen ging man dazu über, in der neuarmenischen Volkssprache zu schreiben.

Weitere Zeitschriften erschienen an der armenischen Peripherie: 1815 das armenisch-russische Wochenblatt *Arevelean Canowc'manc'* ('Östlicher Anzeiger') in Astrachan und 1820-23 *Očanasp'iwrean* ('Hilfsbringer') in Bombay von dem gleichnamigen Bildungsverein in Steindruck hergestellt, 1820-23 in Kalkutta *Hayeli Kalkat'ean* ('Spiegel Kalkuttas') vom Bildungsverein Imastaxndrean, dessen Ziel die Verbreitung des Lese- und Lerneifers durch Buch- und Zeitschriftendruck war.

1832 faßt mit *Lroy gir meci têrowt'eann Ôsmanean* ('Nachrichtenschrift des großen Osmanischen Reiches')[42] die armenische Presse dort Fuß, wo bis 1915 das Zentrum des armenischen Journalismus liegen wird - in Konstantinopel. Die Redaktion dieses osmanischen Staatsanzeigers hatten armenische Beamte des Außenministeriums inne.

Zwei Zeitschriften aus Konstantinopel und Smyrna läuteten 1840 eine neue Qualität im armenischen Pressewesen ein - den persönlichen Journalismus mit einer starken Herausgeberpersönlichkeit, die maßgeblich Stil und Meinungen ihres Blattes prägt. Xač'atowr Oskaneans *Aztarar Biwzandean* ('Byzantinischer Anzeiger') in Konstantinopel und *Aršaloys*

educational associations were the publishers and funders of these journals.

The next three Armenian journals are linked with the name of the Mechitarist father Ġowkas Inčičean. From 1799 to 1803 he published the annual *Taregrowt'iwn* in Venice and was the first to use the Modern West Armenian language in his journal. From 1803 to 1820 Inčičean continued his journalistic work with an annual of general content - ranging from politics to astrology. *Eġanak Biwzandean* ('Byzantine Magazine') was printed in Venice, but written and distributed in Constantinople. In 1807 the same itinerant Mechitarist father published again a contemporary political magazine called *Yišatakaran* ('Memorial'), which from 1808 became the bi-monthly *Ditak biwzandean* ('Byzantine Observer'). From 1812-16 the Constantinople educational association "Aršarowneac'" appeared as the publisher of the magazine. Its credo was "to entertain, to educate and to instruct" the people through magazines.[41] In order to reach a really large readership the journal was printed in the Modern Armenian vernacular.

More magazines appeared on the Armenian periphery: in 1815 the Armenian-Russian weekly *Arevelean Canowc'manc'* ('Eastern Advertiser') in Astrakhan and from 1820-23 *Očanasp'iwrean* ('Helper') in Bombay produced lithographically by the educational association of the same name, from 1820-23 in Calcutta *Hayeli Kalkat'ean* ('Mirror of Calcutta') by the educational association Imastaxndrean, whose objective was to spread the zeal for reading and learning through printing books and magazines.

In 1832 with *Lroy gir meci têrowt'eann Ôsmanean* ('Newspaper of the Great Ottoman Empire')[42] the Armenian press found its footing in the place that would be the centre of Armenian journalism until 1915 - Constantinople. This Ottoman state paper was edited by Armenian civil servants from the foreign office.

In 1840 two magazines from Constantinople and Smyrna introduced a new level of quality to the Armenian press - personal journalism with a strong personality as publisher, which decisively characterised the style and the opinions of their papers. These were Xač'atowr Oskanean's *Aztarar Biwzandean* ('Byzantine Advertiser') in Constantinople und

Araratean ('Ararat-Morgenröte') von Ġowkas Baġtasarean und später Yovhannês Svačean in Smyrna. *Aršaloys Araratean* hatte überregionalen Charakter und ist mit 47 Erscheinungsjahren die erste kontinuierlich erscheinende armenische Zeitschrift.

11.2. Aufschwung der armenischen Presse in der Mitte des 19. Jahrhunderts

Mehr Freiheiten für die Armenier des Osmanischen Reiches durch die Verfassung von 1856, die Entstehung einer neuen armenischen Intelligenzia, das nationale Erwachen und die höhere Bildung breiterer armenischer Bevölkerungsschichten führten ab Mitte des 19. Jahrhunderts zu einem Aufschwung der armenischen Presse.[43] Die Auflagen stiegen auf durchschnittlich 500-1200 Exemplare.[44] Moderne Zeitungen mit Glossen, Feuilleton, Theaterkritiken und aktueller Berichterstattung wurden immer mehr zum „täglichen Bedarf". Zeitungen und Zeitschriften dienten (vor der Gründung politischer Parteien ab 1881) zunehmend als Plattform des Meinungsstreits innerhalb einer Gemeinschaft in Umwälzung - Konservative polemisierten gegen Reformer, Freigeister gegen Kleriker, der Mittelstand gegen die Oberschicht. Hier sollen nur die wichtigsten Publikationen genannt werden.

Von 1843 bis heute erscheint *Bazmavêp* ('Der Polyhistor'), die wissenschaftlich-philologische Zeitschrift der Mechitharisten in Venedig. 1846 hält mit *Kavkas* ('Der Kaukasus') die armenische Presse auch im Kaukasus Einzug. Seit 1855 hat auch Paris seinen Platz in der armenischen Pressegeschichte: Die Blätter *Arevelk'* ('Der Osten'; 1855/56) und *Arevmowtk'* ('Der Westen'; 1859-65) des revolutionären Demokraten Step'an Oskanean wollten die Armenier mit dem fortschrittlichen Geist Europas konfrontieren. Oskanean bekämpfte konservativere Strömungen wie sie z. B. die in Paris 1855-58 (1859-65 in Theodossia) vom Mechitharistenpater Gabriel Aywasean herausgegebene Zeitschrift *Maseac' aġavni* ('Taube vom Ararat') verkörperte. Von 1852-1908 erschien unter dem Herausgeber K. S. Iwt'iwčean in Konstantinopel die liberal-gemäßigte Zeitung *Masis* [46], eine der namhaftesten armenischen Zeitungen ihrer Zeit. *Masis* schuf die moderne westarmenische Zeitungssprache und war durch die Qualität ihres Journalismus beispielgebend.[45] Seit der Mitte des 19. Jahrhunderts rückte Tiflis allmählich zum zweiten Zentrum des armenischen Journalismus neben Konstantinopel auf. Freiere Lebensbedingungen der Armenier in Russisch-Armenien und eine starke

Aršaloys Araratean ('Ararat Dawn') by Ġowkas Baġtasarean and later Yovhannês Svačean in Smyrna. *Aršaloys Araratean* was of supra-regional character and, with 47 years of publication, was the first continually published Armenian magazine.

11.2. Progress of the Armenian press in the mid-19th century

The mid-19th century saw more liberties for the Armenians in the Ottoman Empire granted by the 1856 constitution, the rise of a new Armenian intelligentsia, national awakening and the better education of more classes of the Armenian population. All these factors led to a progress of the Armenian press.[43] The numbers of copies grew to an average of 500-1200.[44] Modern newspapers with commentaries, arts sections, theatre reviews and up-to-date reporting increasingly became an "everyday necessity". Newspapers and magazines increasingly served (before the establishment of political parties from 1881) as platforms for the differences of opinion within a community in the throes of revolution - conservatives campaigned against reformers, free thinkers against clerics, the middle class against the upper class. Here we will only name the most important publications.

Bazmavêp ('The Polyhistor'), the academic-philological journal of the Mechitarists in Venice has been published from 1843 until today. In 1846 the Armenian press entered the Caucasus with *Kavkas* ('The Caucasus'). Since 1855 Paris also has had its place in Armenian press history: the papers *Arevelk'* ('The East'; 1855/56) and *Arevmowtk'* ('The West'; 1859-65) of the revolutionary democrat Step'an Oskanean aimed to confront Armenians with the progressive spirit of Europe. Oskanean battled against more conservative trends as embodied for example in the magazine published in Paris from 1855 to 1858 (from 1859-65 in Theodossia) by the Mechitarist father Gabriel Aywasean called *Maseac' aġavni* ('Dove of Ararat'). From 1852 until 1908 publisher K. S. Iwt'iwčean in Constantinople brought out the moderate liberal newspaper *Masis* [46], one of the most noteworthy Armenian newspapers of its time. *Masis* created the Modern West Armenian newspaper language and the quality of its journalism was exemplary.[45] Since the mid-19th century Tiflis gradually rose to become the second centre of Armenian journalism after Constantinople. The freer living conditions of the Armenians in Russian Armenia and the greater industrialisation of the Caucasus

Industrialisierung des Kaukasus waren hier begünstigende Faktoren. 1858-86 erschien in Tiflis *Meġow Hayastani* ('Biene Armeniens'), ein populäres, konservatives Wochenblatt für den Mittelstand mit einer Auflage von 480 Exemplaren.

Die Monatsschrift *Krownk hayoc' ašxarhi* ('Kranich der armenischen Welt'), später *Hayoc' ašxarh* ('Armenische Welt') wurde zwischen 1860 und 1879 nacheinander in Tiflis, Schuschi, Gandzak, Baku und Erevan publiziert und scharte bedeutende Intellektuelle um sich.

Eine der prägendsten, zugleich auch die auflagenstärkste armenische Zeitung der Zeit (mit 2500 Exemplaren), war jedoch die von 1872-1920 in Tiflis erscheinende liberal-nationale *Mšak* ('Der Kultivator'). Mit Herausgeber Grigor Arcrowni stand einer der herausragendsten armenischen Publizisten an der Spitze dieser ersten ostarmenischen Tageszeitung, deren Wirkung auf die öffentliche Meinung enorm war.[46] Zur fortschrittlichen Fraktion zählte die Zeitschrift *Meġow* ('Die Biene') aus Konstantinopel (1856-74) mit ihrer Kritik gegen Kleriker und Amiras (die armenischen Notabeln). Ständiger Mitarbeiter und späterer Herausgeber war der Meistersatiriker Yakob Paronean. Derselbe zeichnete von 1874-77 für die satirische Wochenzeitung *T'atron* ('Das Theater') verantwortlich, was ihn öfters in Konflikte mit der osmanischen Zensur brachte. 1858 gründete Step'anos Nazareanc' in Moskau mit *Hiwsisap'ayl* ('Nordlicht'), die „richtungsgebende fortschrittliche Monatsschrift",[47] die Einfluß auf das ganze armenische Volk ausübte. Ebensolche überregionale Ausstrahlung hatte die Monatsschrift *Arevelean Mamowl* ('Die Östliche Presse') des Matt'êos Mamowrean aus Smyrna (1871-1909, N.F. 1919-21). Zur selben Kategorie der führenden Zeitungen ist *Hayrenik'* ('Vaterland'; 1870-1909) aus Konstantinopel zu zählen. Ihr Chefredakteur, der Schriftsteller Arp'iar Arp'iarean, machte aus ihr eine der maßgeblichen armenischen Zeitungen, an der auch bedeutende Literaten mitwirkten. Den Redakteuren schwebte ein Journalismus französischer Prägung vor, mit starkem Engagement für soziale und nationale Themen.

were favourable factors here. From 1858 until 1886 *Meġow Hayastani* ('Armenia's Bee') was published in Tiflis, a popular, conservative weekly for the middle class with a circulation of 480.

The monthly *Krownk hayoc' ašxarhi* ('Crane of the Armenian World'), later called *Hayoc' ašxarh* ('Armenian World') was published consecutively between 1860 and 1879 in Tiflis, Shushi, Gandzha, Baku and Erevan and gathered notable intellectuals.

One of the most influential as well as highly circulated Armenian newspapers of the time (2,500 copies), was however the liberal national *Mšak* ('The Cultivator') published from 1872 until 1920 in Tiflis. In the publisher Grigor Arcrowni, one of the most outstanding Armenian publicists headed this first East Armenian daily newspaper, which had enormous influence on public opinion.[46] The progressive faction included the magazine *Meġow* ('The Bee') from Constantinople (1856-74) with its criticism of clerics and Amiras (the Armenian notables). The master satirist Yakob Paronean was its regular contributor and later publisher. He was also responsible from 1874 until 1877 for the satirical weekly *T'atron* ('The Theatre'), which often brought him into conflicts with the Ottoman censors. In 1858 Step'anos Nazareanc' founded *Hiwsisap'ayl* ('Northern Light') in Moscow, the "trend-setting progressive monthly",[47] which influenced the entire Armenian people. The monthly paper *Arevelean Mamowl* ('The Eastern Press') of Matt'êos Mamowrean from Smyrna (1871-1909, N.F. 1919-21) had the same national charisma. Among the same category of leading newspapers is *Hayrenik'* ('Fatherland'; 1870-1909) from Constantinople. Its editor-in-chief, the author Arp'iar Arp'iarean, transformed it into one of the authoritative Armenian newspapers, which also employed notable literary figures. The editors had French-style journalism in mind, with great commitment to social and national topics.

11.3. Religiöse und Klosterzeitschriften als besondere Periodika

Eine gesonderte Kategorie bilden die religiösen und Klosterzeitschriften. Von 1855-64 gab der spätere Patriarch Xrimean Hayrik erst in Konstantinopel,

11.3. Religious and monastic journals as a special category of periodicals

The religious and monastic journals are a special category. From 1855 until 1864 the later patriarch Xrimean Hayrik published *Arciw Vaspurakani*

dann im Waner Kloster Warag *Arciw Vaspurakani* ('Adler von Waspurakan') heraus. Der engagierte Geistliche nutzte das Forum seiner Zeitschrift, um auf die drückende Lage der Armenier in den Provinzen aufmerksam zu machen. Von 1868–1920 existierte *Ararat* als Zentralorgan des Katholikossats von Etschmiadzin, die mit 4000 Exemplaren auflagenstärkste armenische Zeitschrift. *Sion* ('Zion'), die Monatsschrift des Jerusalemer armenischen Patriarchats, erschien von 1866–77 und von 1927 bis heute. *Yoys* ('Hoffnung'), die Zeitung des Klosters Armaš, bestand von 1864–78. Alle diese Zeitschriften hatten über ihren religiösen Charakter hinaus ein breites, oft wissenschaftlich anspruchsvolles Themenspektrum.

('Eagle of Vaspurakan') first in Constantinople, then in the Warag monastery in Van. This dedicated clergyman used the forum of his magazine to draw attention to the serious situation of Armenians in the provinces. From 1868 until 1920 *Ararat* was the official organ of the catholicos of Ejmiadzin, the most highly circulated Armenian magazine with 4,000 copies. *Sion* ('Zion'), the monthly journal of the Armenian patriarchate in Jerusalem, was published from 1866 to 1877 and from 1927 until today. *Yoys* ('Hope'), the newspaper of the Armaš monastery, existed from 1864 until 1878. All of these magazines covered a broad, often academically sophisticated spectrum of topics going beyond their religious character.

11.4. Die Blütezeit des armenischen Journalismus (1880 bis 1915)

Die Blütezeit des armenischen Journalismus fällt in die Zeit zwischen 1880 und 1915. Erstmals werden durchschnittliche Auflagenhöhen von 2000–3000, in der Spitze sogar von bis zu 7000 Exemplaren erreicht.[48] Die Gründe für den Aufschwung sind vielfältig. Mit den im Berliner Vertrag von 1878 geweckten Hoffnungen auf Reformen in den armenischen Provinzen des Osmanischen Reiches politisierte sich die Gesellschaft, was sich in der Presse niederschlug. Durch Gründung armenischer politischer Parteien entwickelte sich ab 1885 eine starke Parteipresse. Ab 1905 verbesserte sich die Lage der Armenier im Russischen Reich, die armenische Presse im Osmanischen Reich konnte sich in der kurzen Zeitspanne von der jungtürkischen Revolution 1909 bis zum Völkermord 1915 frei entfalten. Das brachte fast eine Verdreifachung der Zahl der Periodika mit sich.[49] Von 1918–21 erlebte die armenische Presse noch einmal einen Boom im alliiert besetzten Konstantinopel, im Kaukasus, in Frankreich und in den USA. Die großen Hoffnungen auf Freiheit und einen eigenen Staat nach dem Ende des Krieges spiegeln sich in der Tatsache wider, daß 1919, nach einem großen Einbruch in den Jahren 1915/16, wieder 173 armenische Periodika erschienen.[50]

Von 1884 bis 1912 existierte *Arevelk'* ('Der Osten') als national-liberale Tageszeitung in Konstantinopel mit herausragendem Feuilleton. Die konservative, dem Patriarchat nahestehende Tageszeitung *Biwzandion* ('Byzanz') wurde von 1896–1918 von Biwzand Keč'ean in Konstantinopel herausgegeben.

11.4. The heyday of Armenian journalism between 1880 and 1915

The heyday of Armenian journalism was in the period between 1880 and 1915. For the first time average circulation figures of 2,000–3,000, even of up to 7,000 copies, were attained.[48] The reasons for the upturn are diverse. The hopes for reforms in the Armenian provinces of the Ottoman Empire awakened by the Treaty of Berlin of 1878 politicised society and this was reflected in the press. A strong party press developed from 1885, owing to the establishment of Armenian political parties. From 1905 the situation of Armenians in the Russian Empire improved, and the Armenian press in the Ottoman Empire was able to develop freely in the short period between the revolution of the Young Turks in 1909 until the genocide of 1915. This resulted in the number of periodicals nearly tripling.[49] From 1918 to 1921 the Armenian press experienced yet another boom in Allied-occupied Constantinople, in the Caucasus, in France and in the USA. The great hopes for freedom and an independent state after the end of the war are reflected in the year 1919, after a major collapse in 1915/16, in the reappearance of 173 Armenian periodicals.[50]

Arevelk' ('The East'), a liberal national daily newspaper in Constantinople with an outstanding arts section existed from 1884 until 1912. The conservative, patriarchate-affiliated daily *Biwzandion* ('Byzantium') was published from 1896 to 1918 by Biwzand Keč'ean in Constantinople.

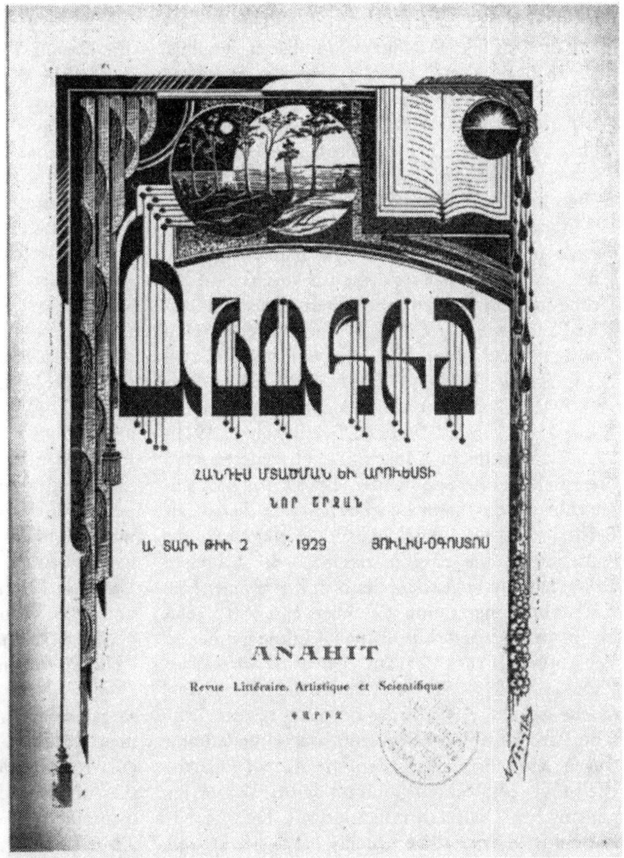

Abb./Ill. 6

In Tiflis erkämpfte sich die neue liberale Wochenzeitung *Arjagank'* ('Das Echo'; 1892–98) unter Abgar Yovhanniseany ihren Platz neben *Mšak*. Als konservativer Konkurrent erstand ebenfalls in Tiflis *Nor Dar* ('Neues Jahrhundert'; 1884–1908) von Spandar Spandarean. Seit 1908 existiert die Konstantinopler neutrale Tageszeitung *Žamanak* ('Die Zeit') ununterbrochen und die 1914 gegründete Konstantinopler Abendzeitung *Verjin Lowr* ('Letzte Nachrichten') erschien immerhin bis 1954. 1885 begann mit der in Marseille gedruckten Zeitschrift *Armenia*, dem Zentralorgan der ältesten armenischen Partei Armenakan (gegründet 1881), die Ära der blühenden armenischen Parteienpresse. 1887 folgte mit *Hnč'ak* ('Die Glocke') das Organ der Hnč'ak-Partei, gedruckt

In Tiflis the new liberal weekly *Arjagank'* ('The Echo'; 1892–98) under Abgar Yovhanniseany fought for its position next to *Mšak*. Its conservative rival in Tiflis was *Nor Dar* ('New Century'; 1884–1908) published by Spandar Spandarean. The neutral Constantinople daily *Zamanak* ('Time') has existed uninterrupted since 1908 and the Constantinople evening newspaper *Verjin Lowr* ('Final News') founded in 1914 was published until 1954. In 1885, with the magazine *Armenia* printed in Marseille as the voice of the oldest Armenian party Armenakan (established 1881), the era of the blossoming Armenian political party press commenced. In 1887 it was followed by *Hnč'ak* ('The Bell'), the organ of the Hnč'ak Party, which was printed in London, Geneva

in London, Genf und Paris. *Drošak* ('Die Fahne'), Zentralorgan der Daschnakzutiun-Partei, erschien von 1890-1914 in Genf. Darüber hinaus gingen zahlreiche Zeitungsneugründungen auf das Konto der Parteien: *Jaraj* (1909, Erserum), *Horizon* (1904, Tiflis), *Yowsapêr* (1914, Kairo), *Asparez* (1908, Fresno), *Azatamart* (1909, Konstantinopel) u. a. gehörten z. B. zur Daschnakzutiun-Partei.

Mit dem Aufschwung des armenischen Pressewesens im hier untersuchten Zeitraum ging auch eine Verbreiterung des Themenspektrums und die Gründung von Spartenzeitschriften einher. Literarische Blätter wie *Caġik* ('Die Blume'; 1886-1911) in Konstantinopel unter Mitarbeit von Aršak C'opanean; *Anahit* (1898-1911, N.F. 1929-47) in Paris von Aršak C'opanean (Abb. 6), sowie *Šant'* ('Der Blitz'; 1911-15) und *Ostan* ('Die Hochburg', 1911-12, 1919), beide in Konstantinopel, zeugten vom literarischen Interesse breiter Bevölkerungsschichten. Die wissenschaftlichen Zeitschriften dieser Zeit liefern uns heute unschätzbare Quellentexte zur Armenologie wie *Handês amsoreay*, die führende armenisch-philologische Zeitschrift der Wiener Mechitharistenkongregation (Wochenzeitschrift; 1886 bis heute), *Azgagrakan Hantês* ('Ethnographische Zeitschrift', 1896-1911) aus Tiflis, *Banasêr* ('Der Philologe', 1899-1907) aus Paris und *Nor Dproc'* ('Neue Schule'; 1908-15), eine pädagogische Zeitschrift aus Tiflis. Dem Bedürfnis nach Unterhaltung trugen satirische Zeitschriften wie *Kavroš* ('Gavroche'; 1908-22) Rechnung, mit oft derben Witzen im armenischen Dialekt Konstantinopels. Die Jugendzeitschrift *Aġbiwr* ('Die Quelle', 1893-1919) und *Taraz* ('Die Tracht', 1890-1919), beide aus Tiflis, sprachen ebenfalls spezielle Leserschichten an.

Der Völkermord an Armeniern im Osmanischen Reich 1915/16 brachte auch die Aktivitäten der armenischen Presse dort zum Erliegen. Im kaukasischen Armenien bedeutete die Sowjetisierung 1922 zwar nicht das Ende der armenischen Presse, wohl aber das Ende des freien Journalismus. Eine freie armenische Presse gab es bis zur Gründung der zweiten unabhängigen Republik Armenien 1991 nur noch in den Zentren der Diaspora, vor allem in Frankreich und in den USA.

and Paris. *Drošak* ('The Flag'), the official organ of the Dashnaktsutyun Party, was published from 1890 until 1914 in Geneva. In addition a number of new papers were founded by the parties: *Jaraj* (1909, Erzurum), *Horizon* (1904, Tiflis), *Yowsapêr* (1914, Cairo), *Asparez* (1908, Fresno), *Azatamart* (1909, Constantinople) and others belonged to the Dashnaktsutyun Party.

The upsurge of the Armenian presses in the period described here was accompanied by a widened spectrum of topics and the founding of special interest magazines. Literary journals such as *Caġik* ('The Flower'; 1886-1911) in Constantinople with the collaboration of Aršak C'opanean; *Anahit* (1898-1911, N.F. 1929-47) in Paris by Aršak C'opanean (Ill. 6) as well as *Šant'* ('Lightning'; 1911-15) and *Ostan* ('The Stronghold'; 1911-12, 1919), both in Constantinople, revealed the literary interests of the broader public. The academic journals of this period offer us today inestimable sources for Armenian studies: for example, *Handês amsoreay*, the leading Armenian philological magazine of the Viennese Mechitarist congregation (weekly magazine; 1886 to today), *Azgagrakan Hantês* ('Ethnographical Journal'; 1896-1911) from Tiflis, *Banastêr* ('The Philologist'; 1899-1907) from Paris and *Nor Dproc'* ('New School'; 1908-15), a pedagogical magazine from Tiflis. The demand for entertainment was filled by satirical magazines such as *Kavroš* ('Gavroche'; 1908-22), with often earthy humour in the Armenian dialect of Constantinople. The youth magazine *Aġbiwr* ('The Source', 1893-1919) and *Taraz* ('The National Costume'; 1890-1919), both from Tiflis, also addressed special readerships.

The genocide of Armenians in the Ottoman Empire in 1915/16 brought the activities of the Armenian press there to a complete standstill. Sovietisation of Caucasian Armenia in 1922 meant not the end of the Armenian press, but the end of free journalism. Until the founding of the second independent Republic of Armenia in 1991 there was a free Armenian press only in the centres of the Diaspora, primarily in France and in the USA.

[1] Vgl. IŠXANEAN 1981, 25; s. auch *Lexikon des Buchwesens*, hrsg. von JOACHIM KIRCHNER. Stuttgart 1953, 824 f.

[2] Vgl. TUĞLACI 1991, 112 f.

[3] Vgl. KÉVORKIAN 1986, 11.

[4] Vgl. KORKOTYAN 1964, 48.

[5] Vgl. KÉVORKIAN 1986, 16.

[6] Vgl. KORKOTYAN 1964, 47.

[7] Vgl. ebenda, 25.

[8] Vgl. KÉVORKIAN 1996, 89.

[9] Vgl. IŠXANEAN 1981, 66; s. auch KÉVORKIAN 1986, 8 f.

[10] Vgl. KÉVORKIAN 1986, 24 f.

[11] Vgl. OWRBATAGIRK'/TAĠARAN 1975, 10; s. auch Ter Xač'atowrean 1966, 3 f.

[12] Mit wirklichem Namen Arak'ēl Babaxanean (1860–1932), armenischer Historiker und Schriftsteller.

[13] LEVONYAN 1958, 56.

[14] Vgl. IŠXANEAN 1981, 37 f., LEVONYAN 1958, 64 f. Zu Abgars Wirken s. auch ZARBHANALEAN 1895, 37 f.

[15] Vgl. KÉVORKIAN 1986, 153 f., s. auch ORENGO 1999, 257 f.

[16] Vgl. OSKANYAN 1988, 1 f.

[17] Vgl. ibid., 857.

[18] Vgl. IŠXANEAN 1981, 49.

[19] Vgl. OSKANYAN 1988, 106 f. Darunter der Erstdruck des *Girk' harc'manc'* von Grigor Tat'ewac'i, vgl. ibid., 786.

[20] Vgl. KÉVORKIAN 1986, 141.

[21] Vgl. IŠXANEAN 1981, 61.

[22] Vgl. ibid., 63; s. auch KÉVORKIAN 1986, 40.

[23] Vgl. KÉVORKIAN 1986, 58 f.

[24] Vgl. ibid., 69 f.

[25] Vgl. KÉVORKIAN 1981, 401-419.

[26] Darunter waren 25 Drucke in Türkisch mit armenischen Lettern, vgl. IŠXANEAN 1981, 87.

[27] Vgl. ZEKIYAN 1999, 269 f.; s. auch SARGISEAN 1905, 42.

[28] Vgl. IŠXANEAN 1981, 96 f.

[29] Vgl. DAVT'YAN 1967, 524.

[30] Vgl. Korkotyan 1964, 32.

[31] Vgl. T'ĒODIK 1912, 56-65. Nach T'ēodik' firmierte die Werkstatt unter folgenden, wechselnden Namen: „Č'nč'in Yovhannēs" (1746-76), „Yovhannēs ew Poġos Astowacatowrean" (1777-90), „Poġos Yohannisean" (1799-1819). Letzterer änderte seinen Namen und arbeitete als „Poġos Arapean (Apowč'exc'i)" von 1820 bis 1835. Es folgten seine Söhne unter: „Tparan Eric' Ordwoc' Poġosi Arapean" (1836-53), und deren Söhne „Arapean Eġbark'" (1855). Bis zum Ende des 19. Jahrhunderts wirkten deren Söhne Yarowt'iwn und Xač'ik Arapean als Schriftgießer. T'ēodik' ist außerdem der Ansicht, daß es sich bei Astowacatowr und Arapean um ein und dieselbe Familie handelt.

[32] Vgl. KORKOTYAN 1964, 58.

[33] Vgl. TUĞLACI 1991, 51.

[34] Vgl. ibid. Es handelt sich um ein Amtsblatt der osmanischen Regierung mit dem Titel *Takvim-i Vekayi*. Die armenische Version erschien unter dem Titel *Lro gir meci tērowt'eanin ōsmanean*.

[35] Vgl. IŠXANEAN 1981, 79; s. auch OSKANYAN 1988, 857.

[36] Vgl. IŠXANEAN 1981, 82.

[37] Diese Erkenntnis verdanken wir GEWORG ABGARJANS

[1] Cf. IŠXANEAN 1981, 25; cf. Lexikon des Buchwesens, ed. by JOACHIM KIRCHNER. Stuttgart 1953, 824 sq.

[2] Cf. TUĞLACI 1991, 112 sq.

[3] Cf. KÉVORKIAN 1986, 11.

[4] Cf. KORKOTYAN 1964, 48.

[5] Cf. KÉVORKIAN 1986, 16.

[6] Cf. KORKOTYAN 1964, 47.

[7] Cf. ibid., 25.

[8] Cf. KÉVORKIAN 1996, 89.

[9] Cf. IŠXANEAN 1981, 66; cf. KÉVORKIAN 1986, 8 sq.

[10] Cf. KÉVORKIAN 1986, 24 sq.

[11] Cf. OWRBATAGIRK'/TAĠARAN 1975, 10; cf. Ter Xač'atowrean 1966, 3 sq.
3 sq.

[12] Whose real name was Arak'ēl Babaxanean (1860-1932), Armenian historian and author.

[13] LEVONYAN 1958, 56.

[14] Cf. IŠXANEAN 1981, 37 sq., LEVONYAN 1958, 64 sq. On Abgar's work cf. ZARBHANALEAN 1895, 37 sq.

[15] Vgl. KÉVORKIAN 1986, 153 sq., cf. ORENGO 1999, 257 sq.

[16] Cf. OSKANYAN 1988, 1 sq.

[17] Cf. ibid., 857.

[18] Cf. IŠXANEAN 1981, 49.

[19] Cf. OSKANYAN 1988, 106 sq. Among the printed titles was the first edition of *Girk' harc'manc'* by Grigor Tat'ewac'i, cf. ibid., 786.

[20] Cf. KÉVORKIAN 1986, 141.

[21] Cf. IŠXANEAN 1981, 61.

[22] Cf. ibid., 63; cf. KÉVORKIAN 1986, 40.

[23] Cf. KÉVORKIAN 1986, 58 sq.

[24] Cf. ibid., 69 sq.

[25] Cf. KÉVORKIAN 1981, 401-419.

[26] Including 25 in Turkish with Armenian type, cf. IŠXANEAN 1981, 87.

[27] Cf. ZEKIYAN 1999, 269 sq.; cf. SARGISEAN 1905, 42.

[28] Cf. IŠXANEAN 1981, 96 sq.

[29] Cf. DAVT'YAN 1967, 524.

[30] Cf. Korkotyan 1964, 32.

[31] Cf. T'ĒODIK: *Tip ow tar.* Konstantinopel 1912, 56-65. After T'ēodik' the press worked under the following, changing succession of names: "Č'nč'in Yovhannēs" (1746-76), "Yovhannēs ew Poġos Astowacatowrean" (1777-90), "Poġos Yohannisean" (1799-1819). The latter changed his name and worked as "Poġos Arapean (Apowč'exc'i)" from 1820 until 1835. His sons followed him as: "Tparan Eric' Ordwoc' Poġosi Arapean" (1836-53), and his sons "Arapean Eġbark'" (1855). Until the end of the 19th century their sons Yarowt'iwn and Xač'ik Arapean worked as type founders. T'ēodik' also believes that Astowacatowr and Arapean are one and the same family.

[32] Cf. KORKOTYAN 1964, 58.

[33] Cf. TUĞLACI 1991, 51.

[34] Ibid. This is an official notice of the Ottoman government entitled *Takvim-i Vekayi*. The Armenian version was published as *Lro gir meci terowt'eanin ōsmanean*.

[35] Cf. IŠXANEAN 1981, 79; cf. OSKANYAN 1988, 857.

[36] Cf. IŠXANEAN 1981, 82.

Artikel *Hayoc' tpagir aybowbenę hingharîwr tarekanę* in: Hayrenk'i jayn, 4.1986, 5-6. Siehe auch den Beitrag ROPER, Arabischer Frühdruck in Europa, im vorliegenden Band.

[38] Es wurde 1633 in Paris neu aufgelegt.

[39] Vgl. OSKANYAN 1988, 779. Zu europäischen Drucken mit armenischen Passagen s. auch KÉVORKIAN 1986, S. 171 ff.; NERSESSIAN 1980, 147 ff.

[40] *Haykakan* 1990, Band 1-4. Als Bibliographie zum Thema armenische Presse wurde verwendet: *Hay parberakan mamowli matenagitowt'yown (1794-1967)*, (red.) A. KIRAKOSYAN. Erevan 1970.

[41] FROUNDJIAN 1960, 83.

[42] Vgl. auch Anm. 34. Die armenische Ausgabe erschien mit der Nr. 12 des *Takvim-i Vekayi* in Türkisch mit armenischen Buchstaben und in umgangssprachlichem Armenisch. Sie existierte bis 1850. Vgl. auch LEVONYAN 1934, XX.

[43] FROUNDJIAN 1960, 95.

[44] Ebenda, 151.

[44] POTOWREAN 1909, 119-144.

[45] Ebenda, 226-238; FROUNDJIAN 1960, 105, 228 f.

[46] FROUNDJIAN 1960, 102.

[48] Ebenda, 151.

[49] 1900 erschienen 53 armenische Zeitungen und Zeitschriften. 1914 waren es 137, vgl. ebenda 115.

[50] Ebenda, 154.

[37] This is known thanks to GEWORG ABGARJANS's article *Hayoc' tpagir aybowbenę hingharîwr tarekanę* in: Hayrenk'i jayn, 4.1986, 5-6. See the essay by ROPER, Early Arabic Printing in Europe, in this volume.

[38] It was issued again in Paris in 1633.

[39] Vgl. OSKANYAN 1988, 779. On European printed books with Armenian passages cf. KÉVORKIAN 1986, S. 171 sqq.; NERSESSIAN 1980, 147 sqq.

[40] *Haykakan* 1990, Band 1-4. The bibliography on the subject of the Armenian press used was: *Hay parberakan mamowli matenagitowt'yown (1794-1967)*, (ed.) A. KIRAKOSYAN. Erevan 1970.

[41] FROUNDJIAN 1960, 83.

[42] Cf. note 34. The Armenian edition appeared in No. 12 of *Takvimi-i Vekayi* in Turkish with Armenian letters and in vernacular Armenian. It existed until 1850. Cf. LEVONYAN 1934, XX.

[43] FROUNDJIAN 1960, 95.

[44] Ibid., 151.

[44] POTOWREAN 1909, 119-144.

[46] FROUNDJIAN 1960, 102.

[48] Ibid., 151.

[49] In 1900 53 Armenian newspapers and magazines were published. In 1914 there were 137, cf. ibid. 115.

[50] Ibid., 154.

[27]

Edward Breath and the Typography of Syriac*

J. F. Coakley

The Syriac script, arguably the most beautiful of all the Middle Eastern scripts of antiquity, has a somewhat complicated printing history. This is a consequence of the fact that Syriac writing, starting from a single early form, was subsequently cultivated and developed in two different ecclesiastical traditions. There are thus three forms of the script in all: the oldest (known as *estrangela*), the West Syrian, and the East Syrian.[1] European printing with Syriac type (Bibles, patristic editions, lexica, grammars), from its beginning in 1539 and for the next three hundred years, was almost all done in the West Syrian character. The *estrangela* script, although not favored for texts, was also cut several times during these centuries and used in titles and headings.[2] The East Syrian script, however, has had a printing history rather apart from the other two, and it is this which will be the particular concern of the present article.

J. F. Coakley is Senior Lecturer in the Department of Near Eastern Languages and Civilizations, and on the staff of the Manuscript Department at Houghton Library.

The East Syrian script is the form of writing historically associated with the Assyrian Church of the East (less correctly known as the Nestorian church) and its Catholic counterpart the Chaldean church.[3] Scholars in Europe were relatively unfamiliar with these churches. A Syriac grammar printed in Rome in 1596 showed an East Syrian alphabet[4] (figure 1), but aside from this one appearance in an academic book, it was in religious publications that the script eventually came into print. Until the nineteenth century these were few, and before 1840 only three working founts of the type had ever been produced.[5]

1 Some confusion can result from the various other names attached to these scripts. The West Syrian script is properly called *serto*, but is also known as "Jacobite" or "Maronite"; the East Syrian, as "Nestorian" or "Chaldean". For these ecclesiastical names, see n. 3 below. They are best avoided in printing contexts. Some further confusion is caused when the East Syrian script is not distinguished from *estrangela*, as, e.g., in the discussion of Syriac in T. B. Reed, *History of the Old English Letter Foundries*, ed. A. F. Johnson (London: Faber and Faber, 1952), 59–61.

2 It is since ca. 1850 that *estrangela* has predominated over *serto* as the type of choice for the edition of ancient texts. For more on these two forms of Syriac type see my article "Some Syriac Types at Oxford and Cambridge," *Matrix* 10 (1990): 181–92.

3 On these churches and their nomenclature, see the convenient artices in K. Parry et al., eds., *A Dictionary of Eastern Christianity* (Oxford: Blackwell, 1997, forthcoming). Reference may also be made to my study *The Church of the East and the Church of England* (Oxford: Clarendon Press, 1992): 11–18.

4 G. Amira, *Grammatica Syriaca, sive Chaldaica* (Rome, 1596), 2–3, on which see R. Smitskamp, *Philologia Orientalis* (Leiden: Brill, 1992), 164–65.

5 I exclude the East Syrian types of G. Bodoni, which were very probably never used for printing Syriac. Bodoni's inventory shows four founts called "Caldeo" of 78 characters each (H. C. Brooks, *Compeniosa bibliografia di Edizioni Bodoniane* [Florence, 1927], 329). Two are shown in his *Oratio dominica in CLV. linguas* (Parma, 1806), X, XI, and also in H. C. Brooks, ed., *Saggio di caratteri di Giambatista Bodoni sinora non pubblicati* (Florence, 1929), 5–6. However, the texts printed in these two books are in Western Aramaic (a language often called "Chaldean"). There are also quite a few misshapen letters which would have been unacceptable to readers of Syriac.

* The text size of this article has been adjusted to fit the text area of this volume.

Figure 1. Table of Syriac alphabets, showing the East Syrian letters in the column "Nestorianus" (G. Amira, Grammatica Syriaca, 1596). This is the first showing of this script in print. Houghton Library.

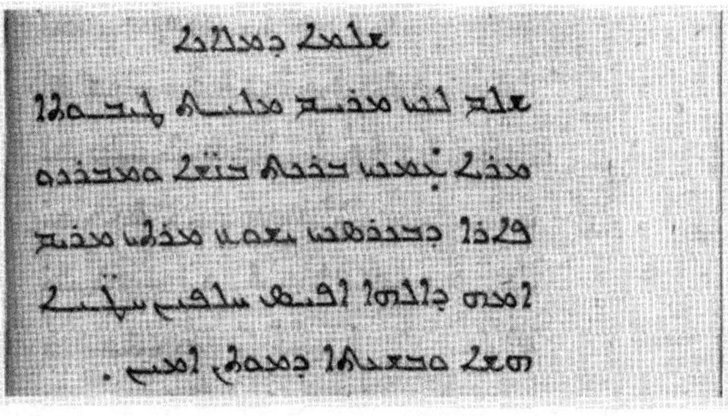

Figure 2. The first East Syrian type of the Propaganda Press (Alphabetum Chaldaicum, *1634*). *Houghton Library.*

The first two founts came from the Propaganda Press in Rome. In 1633 a Syriac translation of the *Doctrina Christiana* of St. Robert Bellarmine was printed in the East Syrian character.[6] The type correctly reproduces the cursive nature of the script, including two or more different forms of some letters depending on whether they join to other letters on the right or left. The letters themselves, round and humanistic (figure 2), are elegant in their own way but they lack the contrast of thick and thin pen-strokes that is distinctive in the traditional handwriting. The loose fit of the letters also made the type unsuitable for a long text, and it seems to have been set aside.[7] When the Propaganda Press came to print a missal for the Chaldean church in 1767, it used a new type (figure 3) which owed nothing to the earlier design. At first sight this type looks crude and (unless it is the fault of consistently poor presswork) unskilfully cut, and because the letters have generally only a single form irrespective of whether they connect to other letters or not, they do not join smoothly.[8] However, compared to the earlier type the script is squarer, darker, and closer-fitting, and approaches more nearly the traditional handwriting of a copyist of manuscripts. It also represented a considerable advance in sophistication in having the vowel points cast on to the letters. The third type was cut by the foundry of Richard Watts for an edition of the Four Gospels published by the British and Foreign Bible Society in 1829. A project of the missionary traveller Joseph Wolff, the book was intended for circulation among the Syrian Christians in Persia and Kurdistan.[9] Thomas Pell Platt,

6 Smitskamp, *Philologia Orientalis*, 163.

7 It was used in a specimen of 1634 (*Alphabetum Chaldaicum*, 6 leaves; Smitskamp, *Philologia Orientalis*, 174) and in a subsequent edition of Bellarmine's catechism in 1665. One might have expected to see it in volume 3 of J. S. Assemani's *Bibliotheca Orientalis* (Propaganda Press, 1728) dealing with the Church of the East, but it does not appear. It was still on hand, however, in 1797 to print the alphabet in the Propaganda Press specimen of that date (*Alphabetum Syro-Chaldaicum*, 30 pp; specif. p. 19).

8 The missal type may be the one mentioned in David Stoddard's reference to "one or two small Papal tracts, published a few years since at Constantinople, with miserable type prepared under the supervision of the Jesuits in that city" (*Grammar of the Modern Syriac Language* (n.44 below), 5—although I have never been able to identify these publications. Certainly the Mekhitarist Press in Venice had some of the type, and it appears in their polyglot edition of *Preces S. Nersis Clajensis* (1823 ed.: "Caldaice", 347–77). At some point a smaller size was added. Both sizes may be seen in J. Guriel, *Doctrinae Christianae rudimenta in vernaculam Chaldaeorum linguam Urmiensis provinciae translata* (Propaganda Press, 1861).

9 See T. H. Darlow and H. F. Moule, *Historical catalogue of the printed editions of Holy Scripture in the library of the British and Foreign Bible Society* (London: Bible House, 1903–11), 2: 1543; Coakley, *Church of the East*, 19–20.

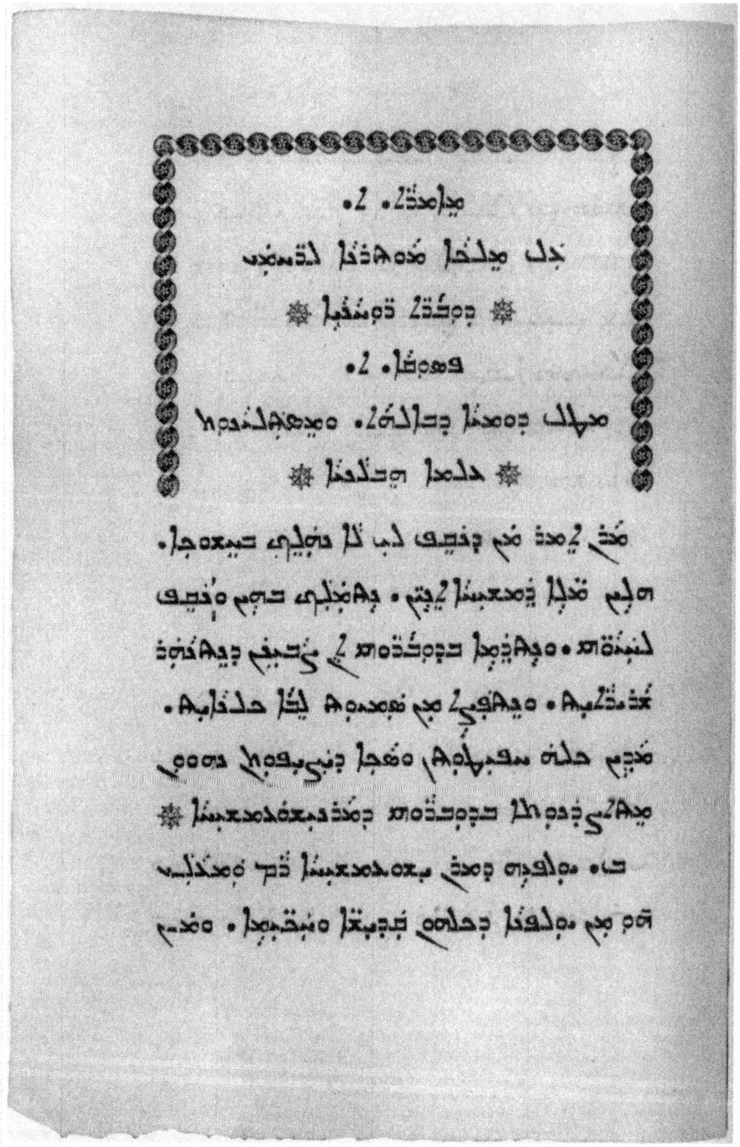

Figure 3. The Propaganda's second type (Thomas à Kempis, Imitatio Christi *in ancient Syriac, 1857). Andover-Harvard Theological Library.*

the editor of the text, also directed the preparation of the new type.[10] It was simpler (at least for the typefounder) than the Propaganda type, being made up of unpointed letters and separate vowel points that had to be assembled by the compositor as he set the lines of text.

The fourth East Syrian type, which appeared in 1843, brings us to the Nestorian mission (as it was called) of the American Board of Commissioners for Foreign Missions and its printer, Edward Breath. Breath did not design this particular type, but in the same year he began to design and produce types for his own printing office, eventually making, before his early death, *thirteen* working East Syrian founts. Aesthetically, every one of these types was at least creditable, and in sequence they show steady progress in dealing with the technical problems posed by the cursive vocalized Syriac script. A study of Breath's work ought to be worthwhile.[11] Harvard collections, moreover, furnish the sources for such a study. There is an almost complete inventory of Breath's printing,[12] and in the archives of the American Board there is his correspondence along with that of his colleagues.[13] The two sources produce different kinds of evidence which need to be mutually controlled, but put together they form an adequate basis for an account of Breath's typographical career.

Edward Breath was born in New York in 1808 and moved with his family to Illinois in 1819.[14] There he was apprenticed to a printer, subsequently working in the office of the New York *Evening Post* before returning to Alton, Illinois, sometime in or before 1831. (A Presbyterian church pamphlet of that year printed in Alton bears Breath's name.)[15] The *Alton Spectator* began publication in 1832, and Breath seems to have been both its printer and its editor. Such a position was an indication of ability on the part of the young man, especially as he had received "only a common English education" (as he said of himself).[16] Later he was printer

[10] Platt, "An account of all the translations circulated by the Society" (12 manuscript vols. in the archives of the Bible Society in the Cambridge University Library), vol. 7. The manuscript of 1640 on which the edition, and perhaps the type, were based, is now Bible Society MS 447. See M. R. Falivene and A. F. Jesson, *Historical Catalogue of Manuscripts of Bible House Library* (London: British and Foreign Bible Society, 1982), 214.

[11] Breath's work is, of course, mentioned in R. Anderson, *History of the Missions of the American Board of Commissioners for Foreign Missions to the Oriental Churches* (2 vols., Boston, 1872), 2: 316, and P. Kawerau, *Amerika und die orientalischen Kirchen*, Arbeiten zur Kirchengeschichte, 31 (Berlin, 1958), 278–80, 379–80. Both these books depend on notices in the ABCFM magazine *Missionary Herald* which do not always get the printing history right. Also regrettably, in Anderson's list of missionaries (2: 498) Breath's name appears as Edwin, a mistake followed by Kawerau, and by me in my earlier article (n. 2 above).

[12] There are two collections at Harvard. The ABCFM Library's own holdings came to Harvard officially in 1944. These consisted, more or less, of the 60 items listed by the Board's librarian Mary A. Walker in Kawerau, *Amerika und die orientalischen Kirchen*, 639–41. At Harvard they received call numbers beginning "Miss". Most of these books are now at Houghton, but items which were editions of any parts of the Scriptures were subsequently transferred to the library of Andover-Newton Seminary. They retain their Miss numbers there. The second collection is at the Andover-Harvard Library of the Divinity School. These items come from the library of the old Andover Seminary, which acquired them from the estate of Isaac H. Hall in 1900. This collection is slightly smaller but contains some items not found among the Miss books.

[13] On the deposit of these papers at Houghton see Mary A. Walker, "The Archives of the American Board for Foreign Missions," *Harvard Library Bulletin* 6 (1951): 52–68. The Board was incorporated into the United Church Board for World Ministries in 1961. I am grateful to the Rev. David Y. Hirano for permission to use and quote from the ABCFM papers in this article. References to these papers are by their Houghton call numbers, beginning "ABC".

[14] The information in this paragraph comes chiefly from the papers pertaining to Breath's application to serve with the American Board in 1839 (see nn. 16, 18 below). Some further data are provided by Justin Perkins in Breath's obituary notice in *Missionary Herald* (see n. 53).

[15] Cecil K. Byrd, *A Bibliography of Illinois Imprints 1814–58* (Chicago: University of Chicago Press, 1966), 39 (no. 121).

[16] Breath to W. J. Armstrong (an official of the Board), 1 August 1839, in ABC 6 vol. 14, no. 105.

of the *Alton Observer,* an anti-slavery weekly whose publisher, Elijah P. Lovejoy, was killed by a mob in a notorious incident in 1837.[17] Breath moved to Galena, Illinois, where he "became pious" (that is, he made a Christian profession) in January 1838. The local Presbyterian congregation offered to sponsor him to train for the ministry, but after consulting other friends Breath decided to offer himself instead to the American Board as a missionary printer.

Breath's application (1 August 1839) was supported by warm recommendations from his former business associates, one of whom called him "a good practical printer—as good, perhaps, as can be found West of the Alleghanies."[18] He met the Committee of the Board sometime at the end of 1839 and was accepted. He was at first earmarked for assignment to Beirut, where it was planned to print in Arabic using newly-manufactured types. Then another man came forward who knew some Arabic, and Breath was asked instead to go to the Nestorian mission, the ABCFM's work with the Church of the East in Urmia, Persia.[19]

The Nestorian mission had felt the want of a press since its foundation in 1833. There was no printed literature—in fact, little or no writing at all—in the local dialect of modern Syriac; and even in ancient Syriac, the language of the Bible and liturgy, the only available printed books in the East Syrian character were the Bible Society edition of the Four Gospels and one lithographed spelling book. The head of the mission, the Rev. Justin Perkins, naturally had an eye to filling the literary void, and at his instance the ABCFM had ordered a press and a fount of the Bible Society/Watts type in 1836. The cargo got as far as Trebizond, but the press proved to be impossible to transport over land to Persia. The type remained in Trebizond with an agent, and the press was shipped back to Constantinople and sold. At that moment it hardly mattered, since the Board could not afford to add a printer to the mission staff in Persia. Breath, however, now had to take a new press with him, and he prudently bought one in dismantled form for assembly on arrival.

He also had to hope that the English type would be in order and serve the purpose. It so happened that while he was waiting to take ship for the east in the spring and summer of 1840, Breath was supporting himself in New York. In the same place the inventor Sidney E. Morse was just developing the new process which he called cerography, in which a letterpress printing surface was produced from an engraving on wax.[20] Morse had begun to supply the ABCFM with printing plates for maps made by this process.[21] It occurred to someone at the Board that cerography might be a way of printing Syriac by having a native scribe engrave the wax, so dispensing with type altogether. "Perhaps Mr. Morse will be willing to give you a few lessons," wrote Rufus Anderson the Board secretary to Breath.[22] Although the process was then still a trade secret, Morse must have acceded to the request, and when Breath departed he took with him a stock of supplies for cerography.

[17] According to Perkins, "he stood by Mr. Lovejoy's side"; but that may be an exaggeration of his part in the affair. In the report of the subsequent trials, his name is only once and incidentally mentioned (John F. Trow, *Alton Trials* [New York, 1838], 35). However, one of Breath's references (see the next note) came from W. S. Gilman, Lovejoy's chief supporter.

[18] Horace H. Houghton to Armstrong, 5 August 1839, in ABC 6 vol. 14, no. 107. Other testimonials are nos. 106–110 in this volume.

[19] ABC 1.1 vol. 12 (1839–40), no. 479; vol. 13 (1840), no. 12.

[20] David Woodward, *The All-American Map* (Chicago: University of Chicago Press, 1977), 16–23.

[21] ABC 1.1 vol. 12 (1839–40), nos. 273, 285, 414, 514; ABC 10 vol. 29 (1838–43), nos. 384–9. Morse's earliest maps for the ABCFM are those published in J. Tracy et al., *History of American Missions to the Heathen* (Worcester, Mass., 1840).

[22] ABC 1.1 vol. 13, no. 44 (27 March 1840).

Breath arrived in Persia, via Smyrna and Trebizond, in November 1840. The press, he reported, had been "a source of *wonderment* on the road, some pronouncing it a steam engine, and others a machine for making cannon." It was at once set up in Perkins's cellar. The type, which had been found intact in Trebizond, likewise arrived safely with Breath. The first pull from it was taken on 21 November, the Lord's Prayer in ancient Syriac. Perkins wrote in his journal, "The 'Press' is now the *Lion* here. Numbers call daily to visit it. The Nestorians are greatly delighted with it, alike as a curiosity, and as holding out a pledge of important aid and benefit to their people."[23] To Anderson he wrote on 28 December that Breath "appears to be a very intelligent man—& admirably fitted for his department."[24]

The first book to be undertaken by the press was the East Syrian liturgical Psalter, an ambitious work printed in red and black. Along with this text in ancient Syriac, one was produced in the modern language, consisting of extracts from the Bible, the Lord's Prayer with short commentary, and Ten Commandments. This smaller book was finished first, on 13 March 1841, to the "mute astonishment and rapture" of the two local priests who were Perkins's assitants, at seeing their spoken language in print[25] (figure 4). The Psalter was issued later in the year.

In both these books the type from England was used satisfactorily. Only minor adaptations had been necessary. Most noticeably, a tilde was improvised to go under the letters *gamal* and *kap* when needed in the modern language; and whereas in the Four Gospels there had been only one *e* vowel, ܒܹ, now the long *a* vowel was used upside-down below the line to distinguish long *e*, ܒܴ. The type was "suited to the tastes of the Nestorians," Breath wrote to Anderson on 26 December, and (at least while cerography remained promising) there was no need to think of commissioning a new fount. All the same, the type gave Breath some anxiety about its future use. It was not simply that it was unpointed. The extra labor of setting points separately was not a prohibitive cost in the mission field as it might have been at home. (Breath had at that time a workforce of six local men, paid $5 per month each.) There were other technical reasons too for preferring an unpointed type, as we shall see, although Breath probably did not yet appreciate these at the beginning of his career. However, the Watts typeface had a particular disadvantage. In order to allow the points to fit closely, the type was cast on only a pica or small-pica body,[26] just covering the x-height, the ascenders and descenders being then on rather long kerns. Not surprisingly, these were liable to break, and it was uncomfortable to be dependent on resupply from London. (Even without the problem of the kerns, such resupply would have to happen every three or four years, Breath reckoned, as the type wore out.) Not only so, but at the same time that the type was small in its body, it appeared large and loose-fitting on the page. The boldness was not unattractive, but the Psalter

[23] ABC 16.8.7 vol. 2, no. 139, p. 3. A slightly touched-up version appears in J. Perkins, *A Residence of Eight Years in Persia among the Nestorians* (Andover, Mass., 1843), 444. The volumes of correspondence ABC 16.8.7 vols. 2–3 (1838–44), 5–6 (1847–59), 7–8 (1860–70), and ABC 16.8.1 vol. 3 (1844–6) are the sources for the narrative in the rest of this article unless otherwise specified.

[24] ABC 16.8.7 vol. 2, no. 74.

[25] Perkins, *Residence*, 456.

[26] So it is shown in the Watts specimens of 1851 and 1856 resp. In the ca. 1932 specimen of William Clowes it is shown as 11-point. (These specimens are in the St. Bride Printing Library, London.)

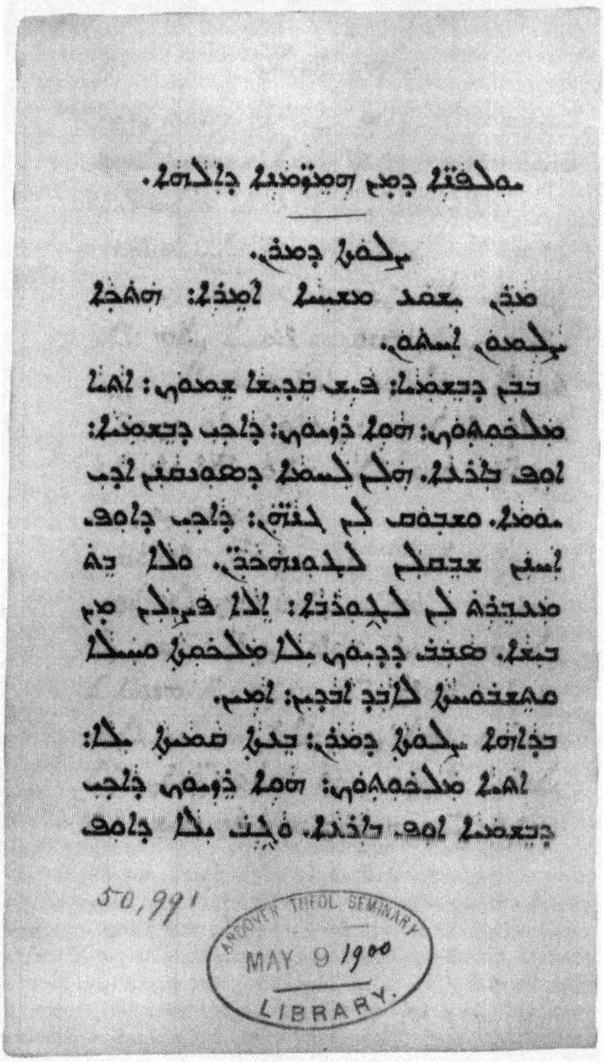

*Figure 4. Watts's type of 1829, as used by Edward Breath in Urmia (*Lessons from the Words of God*, 1841). This is the first printed book in modern Syriac. Andover-Harvard Theological Library.*

alone required 196 quarto pages; and if more extensive parts of the Bible were to be undertaken some smaller type would certainly have to be used.

Circumstances, in the mean time, conspired against the intended experiments with cerography. On his outward journey Breath had suffered the loss of one pack animal, and it was carrying some of the requisite supplies. What he could not replace in Persia was bismuth,[27] and so a wait ensued while Breath requested

[27] "Bismuth enters largely into the composition from which the plates are cast" (Breath to Anderson, 26 December; ABC 16.8.7 vol. 3, no. 130)—a fact conjectured by Woodward (*All American Map*, 22) but not otherwise attested.

50 lbs. of the metal to be sent. It was uncertain that the process would after all work when the supplies came, and so when the opportunity to get a new fount of Syriac did present itself, Breath took it. At the end of 1841, the ABCFM's printer and typefounder in Smyrna, Homan Hallock, returned to the United States and was attempting with some help from the Board to set up as a punch-cutter on his own. Breath thought it might cost no more to commission Hallock to cut a set of punches, even for a pointed type, than to buy new unpointed type from London. To be sure, on his own Hallock could not be expected to make the punches and matrices: the scheme of letters plus points was too complicated, and without manuscripts he would not have a sufficiently good feel for the appearance of the script.[28] Perkins, however, was just then on furlough and offered to supervise his work (with help from the bishop Mar Yohannan who was accompanying him), and so the new type was put in hand.

The project began promisingly. Perkins boarded with Hallock's family for several weeks in mid-1842 while they worked together on the type. Breath sent some specimens of Syriac writing to help them. Still, the matrices were not finished when Mr. and Mrs. Perkins reembarked for Persia in April 1843, and when in September the Urmia missionaries did receive a sample of printing from the new type, it looked to them problematic. Perhaps this sample was the same setting of the Lord's Prayer that appeared in an article on "Oriental Types" in a later issue of the ABCFM magazine *Missionary Herald.*[29] In this specimen a number of vowel points are missing, a fact suggesting that the matrices did not include all the necessary combinations of letter plus point. Hallock supposed that this defect could be made up by casting new types from the existing matrices and filing off unwanted points. With the type, punches and matrices, when they arrived at the end of 1843, were a type mold and some files.

The tools did not, however, suffice to repair the defects. In a trial, the first form of a duodecimo book in modern Syriac turned up eighty-three deficiencies in the type, of which only twenty could be supplied by casting from the matrices. To salvage something from this disaster, the letters were then cast unpointed in a mold of small-pica size (or thereabouts; it was probably homemade), so that the old Watts points could be used with them. With the type thus fitted up, Breath and his workmen produced a pocket edition of the Gospel of Matthew in modern Syriac. This book looks well enough (figure 5), and the type certainly does not disgrace its designer, but the missionaries pronounced it a failure. Considered purely as a script, Hallock's type is leaner and less formal than the Watts type, and evidently neither Breath nor the local adherents of the mission thought these qualities made for any improvement. Nor was the type more economical: as adapted without points it saved little or no space over the Watts type, and it was just as laborious to compose. In its original form the type with points was smaller, great primer in size, but it seems no one thought this advantage was worth the trouble of sending the punches back to Hallock for him to strike the necessary extra matrices. Nothing more was seen of Hallock's Syriac, and when three years later the punches and matrices were stolen from Breath's room, he reported the matter without much regret.

[28] There were at this date perhaps no Syriac manuscripts in the United States at all. Harvard's first acquisition (Houghton Library MS Syriac 1, a West Syrian manuscript) came in 1863.

[29] 40 (May 1844), 170–72, showing three of Hallock's types. The author of the accompanying notice, Edward Robinson, did not mention the chief new feature of Hallock's Syriac, that it had the points cast on.

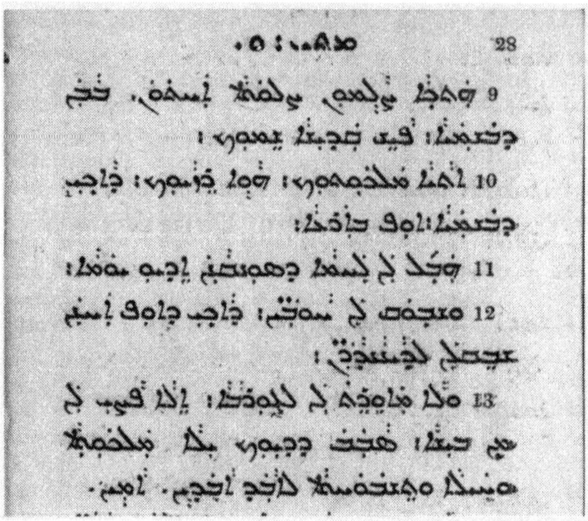

Figure 5. Homan Hallock's pointed type (Gospel of Matthew, 1843). Trask Library, Andover-Newton Seminary.

It was, however, just the rejection of this type, with the presence to hand of the punchcutter's files sent by Hallock, that set the stage for Breath's own debut as a designer and founder of type. It is unfortunate that we have no account by Breath of how he began. The actual casting of types from a hand-mold is relatively simple, but the cutting of punches and the striking and justification of matrices are skilled and precise operations. Breath gave nothing away when he later wrote that "I never saw punches made, or the tools for making them until I was compelled to make them and use them myself."[30] A. H. Wright, Breath's colleague who also had some responsibility at the press, mentions in a letter that Breath had one assistant. This must have been Ismial, who, according to a biographical sketch published later,

> was a type-founder, and cast most of the type used during his life. He could also cut punches very well; and he made a type-mould that answered a very good purpose, compelled by the necessities of the case. He also "fitted" matrices; that is, filed, straightened, and thus adjusted, to the type-mould, the pieces of copper into which the steel-lettered punch is driven. He was never at a loss, and in any country would have passed for a man of rare ingenuity.[31]

Still, we should like to know much more: who made the drawings, how they obtained materials, and how they attained the necessary accuracy, for example in the depth of the strikes, with their basic and improvised tools. How ever they did it, the first two founts took them only three or four months, and by the beginning of 1846 two more founts had been added to their production.[32]

30 Breath to Edward Salisbury, 27 February 1851 (n. 43 below).

31 "Ismial [sic] the Printer", by Breath, in *Nestorian Biography: Being Sketches of Pious Nestorians Who Have Died at Oroomiah, Persia* (Boston, 1857), 62–64.

32 All the external information about Breath's first three types depends on two letters: Wright to Anderson, 14 April 1845; and Perkins to Anderson, 14 November 1845 (ABC 16.8.1 vol. 3, nos. 171, 177 resp.).

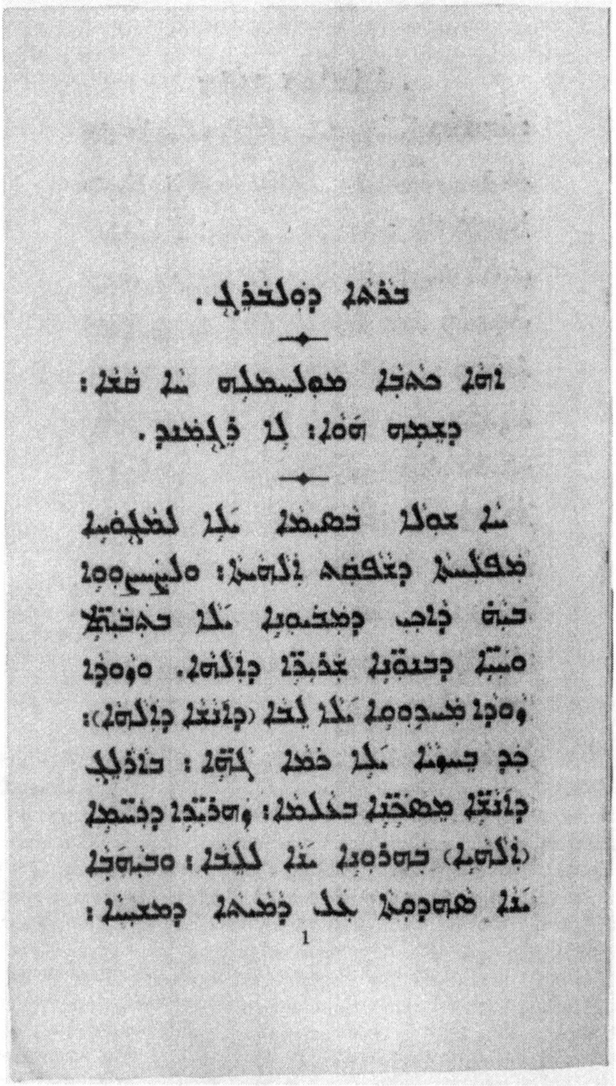

Figure 6. Type 2 (The Dairyman's Daughter, *1844*). *Houghton Library.*

The first two types, according to Wright, "resemble each other, the difference being that in one the stroke is larger and the letter more open." Both founts were praised in a general way by Wright and Perkins, but the smaller one is not said to have been used for any book, and, as far as I can discover, no piece of printing survives to show what it looked like. (We thus have no illustration of type 1.) Type 2—"a still better success," as Perkins put it—is the one that appears by itself in three books of 1844–45. These were the pious story of *The Dairyman's*

Daughter, translated into modern Syriac by Perkins (and printed at the expense of the American Tract Society) (figure 6), an edition of the Four Gospels (printed at the expense of the American Bible Society), and a combined catechism and hymnbook.[33]

Type 3 was finished in the spring or summer of 1845, in time to be put into service for the press's most ambitious work so far: the New Testament in parallel columns of ancient and modern Syriac. Printing began with type 2 for the ancient text, and type 3 for the modern. Type 3, just slightly lighter and narrower in set than type 2, was suited to print the modern Syriac column of the New Testament, since the translation took more words than the original and required a smaller type to keep it in step. The shapes of the letters show a few slight refinements, e.g. sharper serifs on *lamad* and *gamal,* and a *waw* which is more nearly circular.

Type 4 appears not long into the New Testament (in signature 14 out of 105) as a replacement for type 2. Although the changeover is hardly perceptible to the ordinary reader, there are again small refinements to be seen in most of the letters. These chiefly carry over and sharpen up further the changes already seen in type 3. The letter *lamad* makes a more acute angle than in either of the previous types (figure 7).

Perkins, who was as much amazed as anyone about the local production of types, wrote to Anderson (14 November 1845):

> Little [did] Mr. Breath, or the rest of our mission, imagine [that] fonts of type would ever be made to spring up [from the] Plain of Oroomiah, almost with the rapidity [-]ness of *mushrooms,* under his then en[tirely un-]practised hand, when he so strongly urged [the im-]portance of Mr. Hallock's engaging in [the work] for us, under the unavoidable disadvanta[ges of dis-]tance from the people who use the languag[e, and in] the absence of some of the *best* models, while I was [in Amer-]ica.[34]

Figure 7. (opposite page) Types 3, 4, 5 (end of the letter to the Romans; The New Testament in ancient and modern Syriac, 1840). Andover Harvard Theological Library.

It was certainly marvellous that the types should spring up so quickly—and this was written probably even before type 4 appeared—but even more extraordinary is the quality of their design. The contrast of thick and thin strokes is consistent, and the letters fit closely and agreeably. By comparison with the Watts type every letter comes closer to manuscript writing. Indeed, even by comparison with Breath's subsequent work, which was almost all done under the necessity of making the type smaller, these first types are striking. They appear rather like private-press types next to the more industrial ones to come.

Breath's first types followed for the most part the scheme of the Watts type. The letters were, of course, unpointed and required separate vowel points. Breath also made most of the same economies as in that type in dealing with the cursive Syriac letters. In the Watts type there were no separate final forms for most of the letters (excluding *kap, mem* and *nun,* which have special and unavoidable forms). Only *yod* and *lamad* had one extra final form each; otherwise, there was a separate finishing-stroke character which could be added on the left of the other letters when they were in final position in a word. Breath followed the same expedient, only deleting the extra *yod* and *lamad.* Less agreeably, the initial forms

33 Each year the press aimed to do some printing at the expense of these two societies, both of whom gave annual grants for the purpose, besides what had to be charged to the Board.

34 ABC 16.8.1 vol. 3, no.177. The bracketed words and spaces represent text lost from a corner of the page which has been torn away.

of some letters had also been eliminated in the Watts type. There were the correct two forms of some letters (*bet, dalat, gamal, he, zayn, ṭet, mem, nun, semkat, qop, resh, taw*), one with a stroke protruding on the right for connection to a preceding letter; but others (*ḥet, yod, kap, lamad, ʿayin, pe, ṣade, shin*) had only one form, squared off on the right, for use with or without a connecting letter. Breath must have recognized that this was over-economizing, and he made separate initial forms of the letters *kap, lamad, ʿayin,* and *pe* (although still not *ḥet, yod, ṣade,* or *shin*). In the Watts fount the letter *waw* had all four possible forms, following a mistaken belief that it was correct for *waw* to join onto certain following letters. Breath retained, and used, all these forms. He likewise retained the three forms of *alap,* one for use only after *lamad*. The Watts type included an alternative form of *taw* (even though Platt had practically discontinued using it part-way through the Gospels), and two different forms of *taw-alap* ligature. These too Breath kept in his founts. Types 2, 3 and 4 were now on a long primer body (approximately), slightly smaller than the Watts type. The points began by being cast on a minion (again, approximately) body, but they added so much to the depth of each line that they must have been re-cast on smaller bodies (about nonpareil) for the New Testament, so making space for two more lines on each quarto page.

Type 3 was used on its own with the smaller points to print another short text, a catechism, in 1846; but it was still too large for a text of any length. As the New Testament was in the press at the end of 1845, Breath began work on a smaller type that would meet the requirement for economy of space. He wrote to Anderson on 20 January 1846 to ask for a diamond-size mold, that is, even smaller than nonpareil, presumably to cast points for this type. The type itself (type 5) was soon ready, well before the New Testament was finished (the printing was suspended for a time for want of ink, which had to be imported). The edition had not so far included the traditional subscriptions to the individual books, but the new small type was finished in time for these to be printed for the Pauline epistles. Since these subscriptions (e.g., "Here ends the letter to the Romans, which was written from Corinth") were not part of the inspired text, it is surprising to see them in the edition at all, and it must be that Breath wanted a chance to display the type.

Even so, he cannot have been satisfied with it, and nothing else appeared in this type. In February 1847 Breath was reported still at work on a small type for printing the Old Testament. It was this project, the completion of the Scriptures in modern Syriac, which excited the missionaries. It had run into difficulties, however, with the committees in America, both of the ABCFM and of the American Bible Society. The missionaries insisted that in order for a translation from the Hebrew text to be acceptable among the local Christians it would have to be accompanied by the old Syriac version (the so-called Peshitta) in a parallel column. The committee members, however, disparaged the ancient version, and permission for the two-column arrangement was refused.[35] So the matter stood when Breath's type (type 6) was finished. A proof was set up from Genesis 4 in modern Syriac (figure 8), but it was not clear on what conditions the printing could go ahead.

[35] For the ABS: "Languages of the Near East, 1831–1860", essay no. 16, Part IV–F, §8: unpublished typescript in the archives of the American Bible Society. I am grateful to Dr. Mary F. Cordato for the chance to consult this. For the ABCFM: Piet Dirksen, "The Urmia Edition of the Peshitta: the Story behind the Text," *Textus* 18 (1995): 157–67, specif. 163.

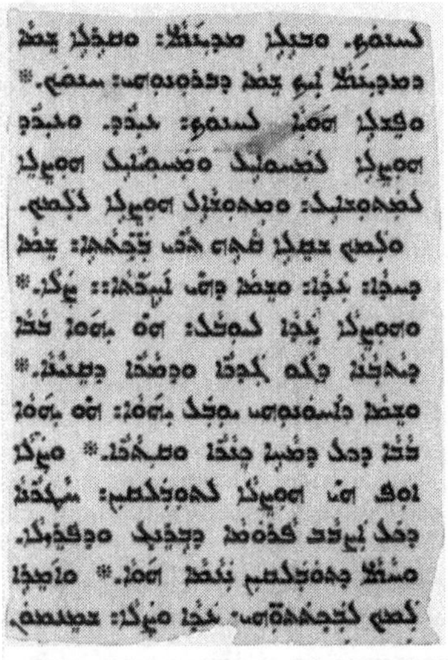

Figure 8. Type 6 (part of Genesis 4). Houghton Library.

From Breath's two small types of 1846–47 it is clear that, technically, punches and matrices at this size were difficult for him. Type 5 includes a few badly shaped letters, particularly some forms of *mem* and *alap*. *Semkat*, with its two counters, is too large. In type 6, however, proportions are good. As may be seen from the illustration (the only surviving scrap of setting from this type)[36] the letters have an even and comfortable appearance, although the serifs on some letters have become larger and spikier in proportion to the letters themselves in consequence of the smaller size. (The resulting horned shape of *qop* is particularly clear.) The lines of text are 6.2 mm apart, only just more than great primer set solid. This was Breath's finest technical achievement so far.

Breath was a single man. When Perkins was in America in 1841 Breath had written to thank him for his "willingness to serve me in *that particular*, and hope you may be successful."[37] *That particular* we may take to mean the finding of a wife; but whatever Perkins may have done for his colleague, it did not bring the desired result, and now five years later Breath wished to look for himself. In requesting leave to return home he was too embarrassed to state that this was his aim, but Anderson thought he rightly understood it. After a delicate exchange of letters, the leave was granted, and Breath departed in March 1847. He brought with him to the United States copies of the New Testament just issued, and he explained to Anderson his plan for the next refinement in Syriac typography. To produce a type any smaller than type 6 would require the points to be cast on the letters. Matrices for such a type necessitated step punches that could accommodate the points and produce a pointed matrix in one strike.[38] These punches would also have to be closer work than Breath had yet succeeded in doing.

[36] ABC 16.8.7 vol. 5, no. 93.

[37] ABC 16.8.7 vol. 3, no. 132.

[38] P. Gaskell, *A New Introduction to Bibliography* (Oxford: Clarendon Press, 1972), 31.

Therefore, while in the United States he would find a craftsman to produce the punches, and then he would make the matrices and type himself in Persia.

Within a few months Breath found a punchcutter who had lost his position when his employer's typefoundry burned down and was therefore available to do the Syriac punches. Breath told Anderson (1 September 1847) that they would cost about $1 apiece, or less than $100 for an entire set. They were evidently ready by the middle of 1848. Breath's other errand took longer, but he was married to Miss Sarah Ann Young on 13 June 1849. The punches, and probably also the matrices (if he had occupied some of his time before the wedding by striking the Syriac matrices as he planned), were with Mr. and Mrs. Breath when they arrived in Urmia in mid-October.

In June 1848 the American Bible Society had relented and given permission for the edition of the Old Testament in parallel columns. Perkins, eager to begin the printing, had to wait patiently first for Breath to return and then for him to cast the type. (In Breath's absence the press had operated at a reduced level, and it had also suffered by the sudden death of the best printer, Ismial.[39] The most significant production of these months was a bulky edition of *Pilgrim's Progress* in modern Syriac, using type 3.) Printing of the Old Testament began at last in the summer of 1850, and it occupied more than two years. Perkins wrote on 18 March 1851:

> The aching head and smarting eyes of him who has so indefatigably toiled over the type, as also of those who are still toiling over the revision of the copy and the correction of the proofs, by day and by night, are cheered by the prospect, now not distant, when the Nestorians shall have the matchless boon of the Bible, in so attractive a garb, in both their classical and vernacular tongues.[40]

The pages that issued from the press were dense and black (or anyhow gray, the press being evidently not powerful enough for a good impression over such a large printing surface): the new type (type 7), only english in size including the points, wasted no space when set solid (figure 9). It needed to be so, since even with this crowded layout the Old Testament in ancient and modern Syriac made a heavy large quarto volume of 1051 pages.[41]

While the Old Testament was in the press, Breath received a request from the American Oriental Society for some of his Syriac type. David T. Stoddard, one of Breath's colleagues, had been elected to the Society in 1848 and he had promised to prepare a grammar of modern Syriac. For this book and for future use he suggested to the Corresponding Secretary, Professor Edward E. Salisbury of Yale, that the Mission might supply them with some type. Salisbury asked for a hundred pounds of type with points cast on. In answer (27 February 1851) Breath first declared the inexpediency of supplying type at all, owing to the shortage of type metal and the difficulty of transporting such a heavy cargo. A set of matrices would do as well as type, and this he offered. The matrices would, however, be unpointed. As Breath explained:

> We could not send you a set of matrices with the points attached to the letters short of some months labor, and then there would be many deficiencies unless we had before us the work you are about to print; and you would find your set again defi-

39 *Nestorian Biography*, 64.

40 ABC 16.8.7 vol. 5, no. 194, p. 8.

41 In this book, incidentally, the Mission's orthography of modern Syriac achieved its settled form. See H. L. Murre–van den Berg, "From a Spoken to a Written Language: the introduction and development of Literary Urmia Aramaic" (Ph.D. diss., Leiden University, 1995), 165.

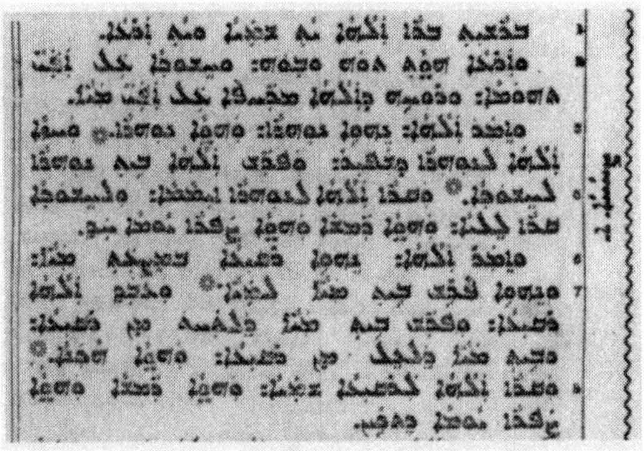

Figure 9. Type 7 (beginning of Genesis; the Old Testament in ancient and modern Syriac, 1852). Andover-Harvard Theological Library.

> cient should you attempt to print anything else. The ancient language calls for forms that are not at all required in the modern, and the modern some that are not used in the ancient. There are forms used only in single words. For example, you would have no occasion for ܦ̮ except in a "snake story"...[42]... I have still to make an occasional matrix for the Old Testament, although it is about one fourth completed; the form newly made not having been called for in the previous part of the book.

The matrices he was sending would be free of charge, he said: they were, like all his work, "awkward", and "I confess I am ashamed of them."[43]

What Breath sent to Salisbury was, it appears, a set of matrices at least partly struck from the punches (without points) of type 7. (We number it here as 7a.) Type was cast by the Rogers foundry of Boston, and Stoddard's grammar printed in New Haven both separately and as part of the *Journal of the American Oriental Society*[44] (figure 10). According to a note at the end, a certain S. S. Kilburn at the foundry recut "several letters and points" and made "some important additions to the font." The additions can be fairly easily identified: there are separate initial forms for *ḥet, ṭet, yod, ṣade, shin*, against Breath's practice. There is a (poorly drawn) ligature for *lamad-alap* which is certainly not Breath's work. (A very ungainly medial *ṭet* also appears in the table on p. 9 but fortunately not again.) The alternative *taw* (ܬ) reappears, after having been eliminated by Breath in type 7.[45] Certain other letters (*taw, pe, qop, lamad* at least) that are slightly different from type 7 are probably the ones recut by Kilburn, although they might in principle be Breath's alterations. Regrettably, after all the labor which went into the preparation of this quite satisfactory type, it was hardly ever used again by the American Oriental Society, and no other academic printing in the East Syrian character was ever done in the United States.[46]

42 The next phrase seems to read "or ܦ unless you were treating of rice"; but I regret I cannot make sense of this. The word for "snakes" here must be modern Syriac ܚܘܘܬܐ (so spelled in Numbers 21.6, though later in the Old Testament it is ܚܘܘܵܬܐ).

43 This one letter from Breath, and others from Stoddard, to Edward Salisbury are preserved in the archives of the American Oriental Society in Sterling Memorial Library, Yale University.

44 *Journal of the American Oriental Society* 5 (1855): 1–180h, separately printed as D. Stoddard, *Grammar of the modern Syriac language, as spoken in Oroomiah, Persia*, and in Koordistan (New Haven, 1855), with the same pagination.

45 It is curious to see Stoddard's assertion that the form ܬ is used only for *taw* in initial position (*Grammar*, 9) at the same time as Breath was printing it in all positions.

46 See *Journal of the American Oriental Society* 6 (1860): 574; 8 (1866): 183–212. The type does also appear in the New York-printed editions of Scripture of 1864, 1874 and 1893 (see n. 56 below) in titles and headings.

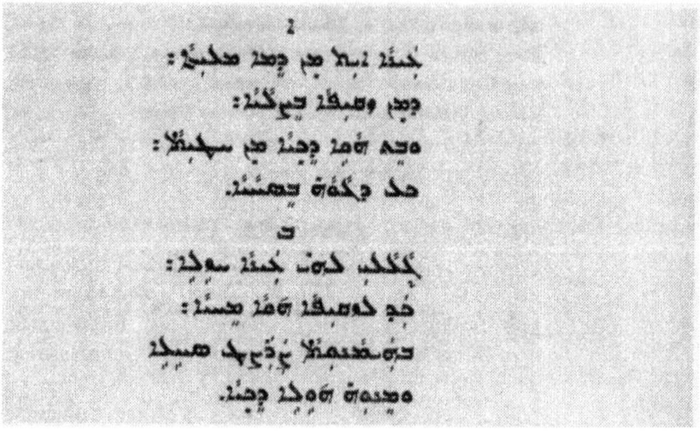

Figure 10. Type 7a (William Cowper's hymn "There is a fountain filled with blood" in modern Syriac; D. Stoddard, Grammar of the Modern Syriac Language, *1855). Houghton Library.*

*Figure 11. (opposite page) Types 8, 9 (*Green Pastures for the Lord's Flock, *a book of daily devotions, 1855). Houghton Library.*

To return to Breath's own printing office: the Old-Testament type (type 7) was for a time in daily use. A periodical just begun by the missionaries entitled *Rays of Light* (incidentally, the first regular periodical publication in Persia in any language)[47] used it from its second issue. So did the next sizable book to come from the press, another Protestant classic, Richard Baxter's *The Saints' Everlasting Rest,* translated by Perkins and issued in 1854. For this job the type was agreeably leaded; but already by March 1853 Breath was reported to have produced a new fount of type, and the Old-Testament type passed into disuse. Part of the reason was the scarcity of type metal. It was usual to melt one type when a new one came into use, and the larger size of a pointed fount made it even more necessary to use old metal. However, Breath was probably also dissatsified with the cutting of the letters by his hired craftsman. Certain characters in type 7, notably *alap* and *nun,* have a thinner stroke than the rest, and others like *lamad* and *mem* are muddy. These deficiencies were submerged in the technical achievement of producing a pointed type, but they will certainly have become obtrusive in time. In any case, the new type 8 displaces it in publications from 1854 on.

This fount demonstrates what Breath's letter to Salisbury had earlier implied, that he had now attained the skill to produce pointed matrices himself. It is also a sign of technical command that Breath allowed this fount (and all his subsequent ones) the luxury of separate final forms for the letters *bet, ḥet, lamad, semkat, ʿayin, pe, qop, shin.* (One might wish that he had supplied some more initial forms too, especially *yod* and *ḥet,* which are not correct with initial up-strokes.) On the whole type 8, although very bold (the ratio of base-line width to x-height is .35), is pleasing (figure 11). The letters are well shaped, except for *ṭet* (which is disproportionately wide), initial *lamad* (still muddy) and *mem* (where the counter is not in the middle). With type 8 we also see the full maturity of the mission's typographical conventions. Most noticeably, the old practice of joining *waw* on the left to certain other letters is now abandoned. The alternative *taw* appears only very rarely and its corresponding *taw-alap* ligature seemingly not at all. The other *taw-alap* ligature is also

[47] See G. Yonan, *Journalismus bei den Assyrern* (Augsburg: Zentralverband der Assyrischen Vereinigungen in Deutschland und Mitteleuropa, 1985), 22–23.

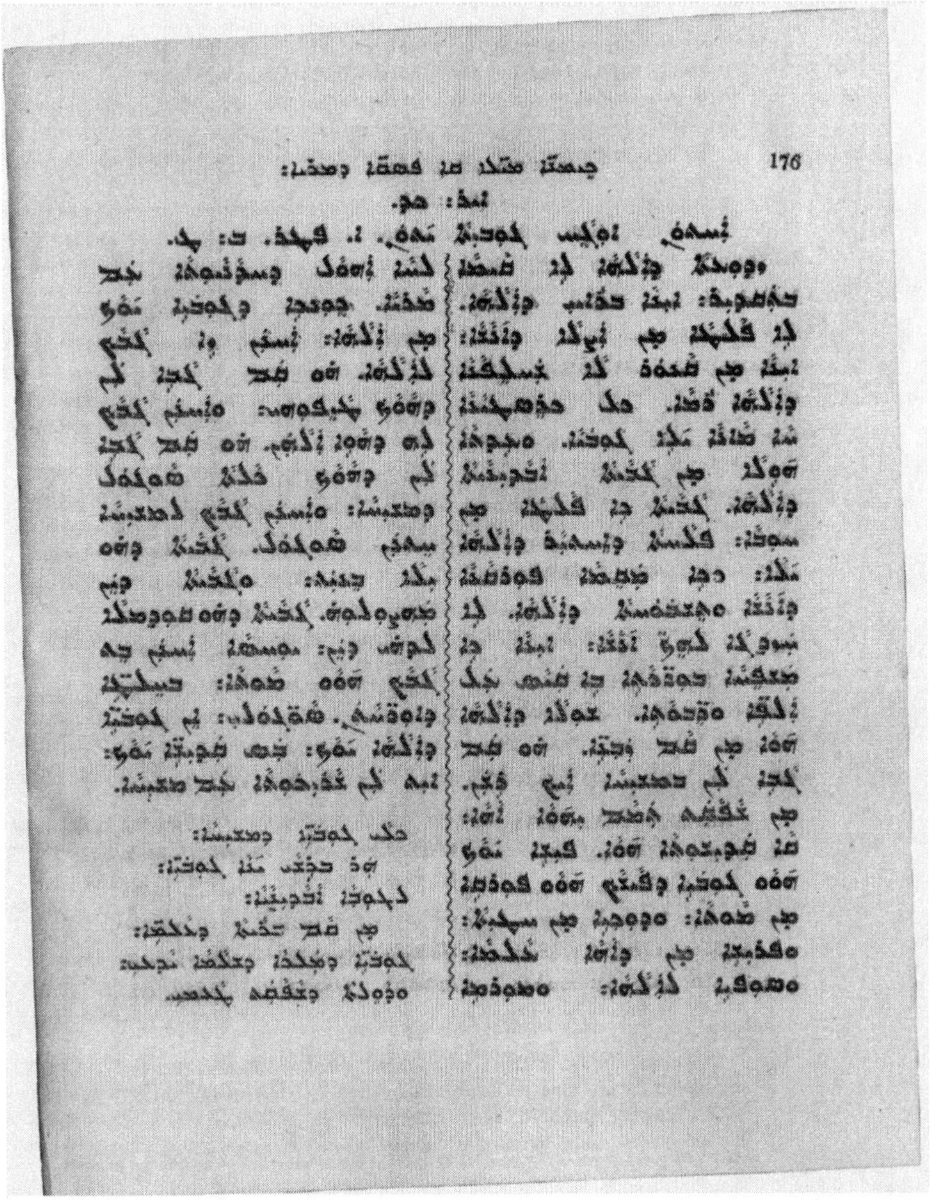
176

used less frequently than in the early books of the press. Unlike all the previous types, this one remained in use by the press well after Breath's day, although most often in headings and for emphasis, rather than for continuous text.[48]

We must imagine that it was for this purpose, the easy reading of continuous text, that Breath was still in search of the perfect typeface. His next essay, a light-face character (type 9), was suggested no doubt by the fact that in English light-face types are easier to read than bold ones. This type appeared first in 1855 in an arithmetic textbook, where it was particularly well suited not to overpower the light-face (Western) figures. The fount had again the alternative *taw* and in this book the compositor used it freely, although in subsequent books it is rare. Recalling that Hallock's type was also a light-face and of approximately the same body-size, it is instructive to see how much improvement had come from Breath's twelve years' education in Syriac punchcutting. The leanness of the type was, however, exaggerated by its too wide set, and some other letters, especially the over-wide final *mem* and several other letters like *he* which seem slightly too large, are obtrusive. The effect was evidently not to everyone's taste. Perkins commented (17 November 1855):

> A new and valuable font of type, of quite a *small size,* prepared by Mr. Breath, was used in printing the Arithmetic; which of course contributes to the economy of this department, though not on the whole more acceptable to the native eye, naturally partial to the larger type, which corresponds more nearly to the bold stroke of the Nestorian Pen.[49]

The type continued in use for about a year, always alongside type 8.

After 1855, four more Syriac types are encountered in the Mission publications. All of them must be the work of Edward Breath, although we have no information about them beyond what is provided by the books in which they appear. Breath did not usually mention the typefounding side of his activity (as opposed to the printing of books) in his correspondence anyway, and to Perkins the appearance of new types must have become such an everyday occurrence that he did not think to record it either.

In 1858 the Mission published a Syriac translation of C. G. Barth's *History of the Church of Christ* (a work "well adapted to check the progress of Popery").[50] The text of this book was set in yet another new type (10), Breath's last and most successful attempt at a type for continuous reading. The success of the type lies not so much in any innovations in the design of the letters but in the even ensemble of the whole fount and the absence of any obtrusive individual sorts. The degree of boldness also seems to have been aimed at moderation, the ratio of base-line width to x-height being .30, which was more than in type 9 but less than in type 8.

In the same book, Barth's *Church History,* there was another new type, a large unpointed display type on the title page (type 11, figure 12). Breath's earliest books, after the fashion of Syriac manuscripts generally, had had no title pages; but they were soon introduced. Several of the more pretentious books had

[48] Some type was later lent to the Anglican mission in Urmia and appears in their printed missal of 1892. See my "The Archbishop of Canterbury's Assyrian Mission Press: A Bibliography," *Journal of Semitic Studies* 30 (1985): 35–73, specif. 42, 49.

[49] ABC 16.8.7 vol. 5, no. 215, p. 2.

[50] *Report of the American Board of Commissioners for Foreign Missions... 1857* (Boston, 1857), 88. The Syriac version was made from the English translation of 1839; German original 1835.

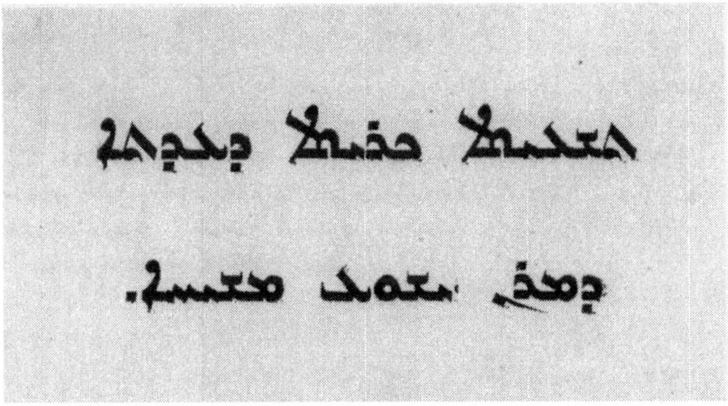

Figure 12. Type 11 (C. G. Barth, History of the Christian Church, *1856). Houghton Library.*

freehand-written titles—in a curly script evidently intended to imitate Western ornamental typography—reproduced from wood engraving or perhaps by cerography. The new display fount, decidedly plain, fixed a different style and gave subsequent mission-press title pages a characteristic and rather more earnest look. (One might have wished for the titles at least to be printed in red, but the press had never printed in two colors since the Psalter of 1841. It is almost as if they identified rubrication with the idea of a fixed liturgy—always a bugbear of Evangelical missionaries.)

In 1858 the Mission published an edition of the Old Testament in modern Syriac with cross-references in the margins. The text is in type 10, with the references (bare biblical chapter and verse numbers) in an unpointed type smaller than anything hitherto seen (figure 13). This type (12) must have been a special production by Breath for this volume. The limited evidence indicates that it is a straightforward reduction of type 10. The New Testament followed in the same format in 1860.

Breath told Perkins in the summer of 1859 that he was ready to return to the United States with his family. He considered that with sufficient printed copies of the Bible to last for years to come—and, though he did not say it, with a good stock of Syriac types—the press would have only the routine printing of school books and the like to do, which the local printers could manage without him. Anderson, however, pressed him to stay,[51] and he complied—though it was not to be for long.

The small type 13, Breath's last design, must have been made at about this time. It looks like a further reduction of type 12, with the addition of points and including all the extra final and initial forms of types 8–10. To make a fount of such sophistication on a type body of only long-primer size including points, must count as a *tour de force* of punchcutting. The type came into use only after Breath's death,[52] first in 1862 or 3 in *Rays of Light,* then in biblical commentaries where it was found useful to separate the commentary in small type from the biblical text, then in all kinds of subsequent publications. Just a few letters are odd: ʿ*ayin* is curiously narrow and upright, and *semkat* is still too large. However,

[51] Anderson to Breath, ABC 2.1.1 vol. 25, pp. 400–1 (22 August 1859); Breath to Anderson, ABC 16.8.7 vol. 5, no. 121 (7 December 1859).

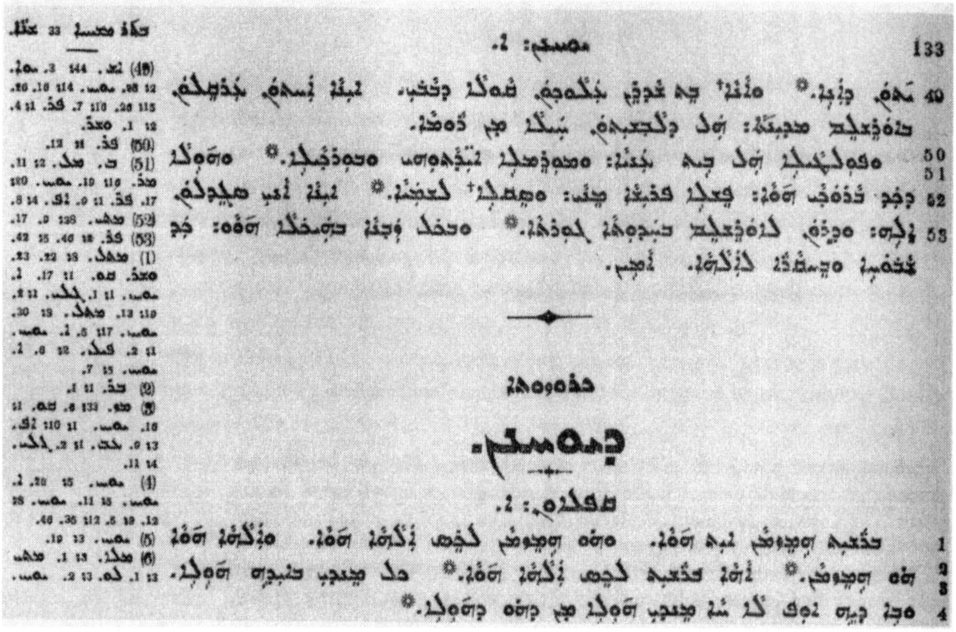

Figure 13. Types 10, 12 (part of John 1; the New Testament in modern Syriac with references, 1860). Andover-Harvard Theological Library.

the script is remarkably clear and readable. It is a worthy type to stand as Breath's last production (figure 14).

Edward Breath died suddenly of cholera on 18 November 1861. His wife returned with their three surviving children (three others having earlier died) to the United States. Breath was an eirenical and respected member of the mission staff, and his death was mourned by his colleagues most sincerely. Tributes (which were not limited to Breath's accomplishments in printing) were published in the *Missionary Herald*. Here may be quoted just the part of Perkins's which touches on the subject of this article.

> With wonderful tact and talent he has cut and constructed our beautiful fonts of Syriac type, on the spot, from year to year, with a hand before unpracticed in that art, but which has astonished us by his rare and complete success. He has thus saved thousands of dollars to the American Board. Through his press he has issued for the Nestorians more than 80,000 volumes, including several editions of the Scriptures in Modern Syriac, thus giving to that hungering people a precious Christian literature of about 16,000,000 pages, in a language never before printed.[53]

[52] A single, all too uninformative, reference to this type is found in a letter of one of the missionaries, Samuel Rhea, to Anderson (30 April 1863): "I send you a few specimen lines of the small type we are now using in printing notes on the Gospel of Matthew. We have not used this type, which was cast since Mr. Breath's death by Iwas, our ingenious type-maker, for any book, only occasionally printing a column or two in the monthly paper." This might suggest some uncertainty in identifying the type as Breath's. Yet Rhea does not say that Iwas "cut" the type, only that he "cast" it. Moreover, for it to have been made in the space of a year by a local "type-maker" who cannot have had long experience and whose name is otherwise never mentioned in any correspondence or printed report, would be unbelievable. In spite of the silence of the sources during Breath's lifetime, I think that at least the punches, if not all the matrices, must be his work.

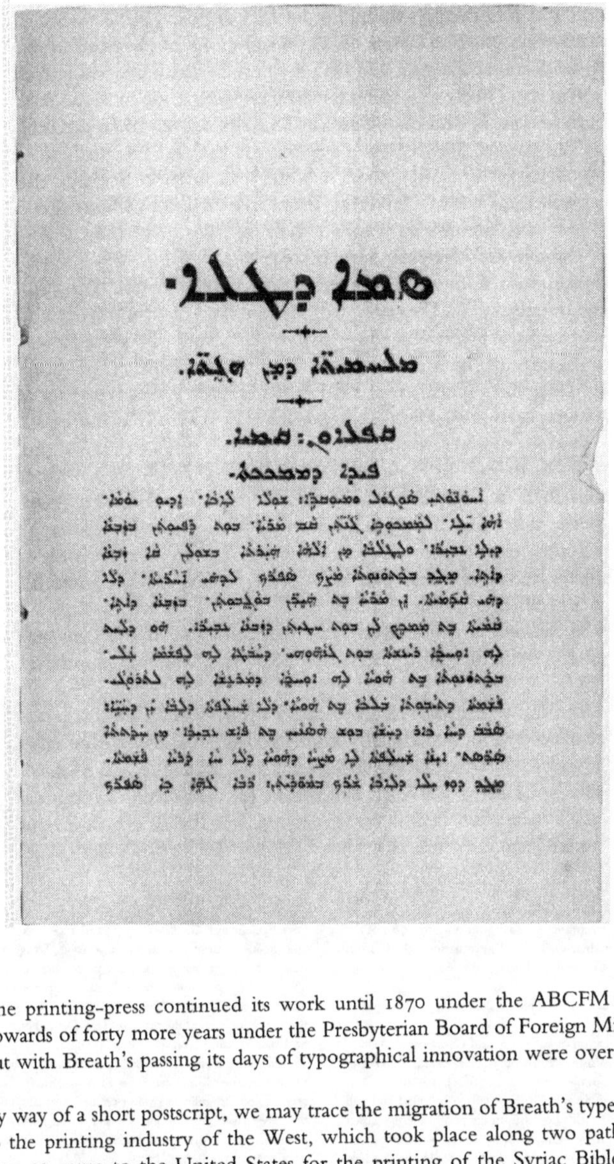

Figure 14. Type 13 (Richard Baxter, The Reformed Pastor, *1864). Houghton Library.*

The printing-press continued its work until 1870 under the ABCFM and for upwards of forty more years under the Presbyterian Board of Foreign Missions,[54] but with Breath's passing its days of typographical innovation were over.

By way of a short postscript, we may trace the migration of Breath's type-designs to the printing industry of the West, which took place along two paths. First, type 13 came to the United States for the printing of the Syriac Bible by the American Bible Society. The project began in 1862 in response to a request from

53 *Missionary Herald* 58 (April 1862): 111; for the whole obituary, pp. 110–12. There is also an obituary in Syriac in *Rays of Light* 11:11 (November 1861): 80–3

54 For the transfer of the Mission to the Presbyterian Board see my *Church of the East*, 72. There is as yet no history of the Mission, still less of the press, in the years after 1870.

the Mission, just after Breath's death, for the ABS to print a pocket edition of the New Testament in modern Syriac. A. H. Wright, one of the Mission staff, was in the United States at the time and read the proofs. The book was published in 1864. It seems most likely that matrices and type were made in New York from the punches of type 13 sent from Persia.[55] This edition was often reprinted, and editions of the classical Syriac New Testament (1874), and eventually the whole Bible in modern Syriac (1893), were published, all in New York, in the same type.[56] In 1898 the Oxford University Press ordered a fount from the Farmer foundry, who had presumably cast the type in 1862, and used it for A. J. Maclean's *Dictionary of Vernacular Syriac* in 1901.[57]

The second path followed by Breath's type designs to the West leads via Leipzig and the firm of W. Drugulin. In 1885 the Vincentian scholar Paul Bedjan (1838–1920) began a publishing career that would eventually place to his credit thirty-six volumes of Syriac texts in the East Syrian character, all printed by Drugulin.[58] Drugulin's specimen of 1879 shows no East Syrian types, so it might be that the ones used in Bedjan's books were laid in especially at his order.[59] The two types used for running text are obviously Breath's types 10 and 13, or rather, careful copies of them.[60] In these copies the size of Breath's types was retained exactly, and there are otherwise only minute variations from his design, for example in the larger size, the slight moderation of the bowed top of *bet* and the spike at the upper right corner of *he*; and in the smaller size, the widening of *ʿayn*. Drugulin later recut the final *nun* in a bolder round shape, presumably to strengthen it against breaking, but that is the only letter which is not almost exactly as Breath drew it. Drugulin also supplied these two founts to other printers, among them the Cambridge University Press, which acquired the larger size in 1887.[61]

A look at Syriac type design in this century would go beyond this article, but such a look would show that Breath's influence has been strong even where his types have not been copied exactly. In recent years literature and journalism in modern Eastern Syriac (or Assyrian, as it is now usually called) have proliferated, especially with the advent of desktop typesetting, and Breath's work is now seen by more readers than ever. It is right that its history should be a matter of record.

55 This is my hypothesis based, again, on inspection of the print rather than on archival information which, from both the ABCFM and the ABS sides, is curiously wanting.

56 On these see Darlow and Moule, *Historical Catalogue*, 2: 1547, 1555.

57 "Some Syriac types at Oxford and Cambridge," 188.

58 See J.-M. Vosté, "Paul Bedjan, le Lazariste persan," *Orientalia Christiana Periodica* 11 (1945): 45–102.

59 Bedjan came from a Christian village in Persia and will have seen Breath's books from his youth. He explained later that his publications were aimed at breaking the Protestant monopoly in religious books in modern Syriac. See J. Legerer, "Paul Bedjan, ein chaldäischer Sprachgelehrter," *Die Kultur* 13 (1912): 200–8, specif. p. 202. In his narrative, all Bedjan says about Drugulin is that "diese Firma hat die besten chaldäischen Typen." Vosté (see the previous note) is no more informative.

60 The types are shown as "Tertia" and "Cicero" in size in the 1929 specimen of the printers Haag-Drugulin (in the St. Bride Printing Library).

61 "Some Syriac Types," 186–87. A look at some books printed by the Dominican Press in Mosul shows what seems to be Drugulin's version of Breath's small type. If this press was also among Drugulin's customers, it would make the journey of Breath's design a round trip back to the Middle East.

Name Index

Abagaro, Bartolomeo (Sultanshah T'oxat'c'i) xxii, 508, 515–516, 535
'Abbās I Pasha, viceroy of Egypt 5
'Abbās I, Shah 517
'Abd Allāh, prince 410
'Abd Allāh Ibn 'Abbās 18–19
'Abd Allāh al-Tarjumān al-Mayūrqī 461
'Abd al-Ḥafīẓ 'Alī 435, 437
'Abd al-Hamīd, Sayyid 291
'Abd al-Khāliq al-Mahdī 289
'Abd al-Latīf, Sayyid 290
'Abd al-Nūr, Yūsuf 290
'Abd al-Raḥmān III al-Nāṣir, Umayyad Caliph of Córdoba 148, 198
'Abd al-Raḥmān al-Ṣāliḥī al-Dimashqi 120
'Abd al-Ra'ūf al-Sinkilī 181
'Abd al-Wāḥid al-Ṭūbī 289
'Abd al-Wāḥid b. Mawlānā Marvdashī 116
Abdi Çelebi 54
'Abduh, Muḥammad 433, 437
Abdülhamid I, Sultan 157, 158, 227, 358, 359
Abdülhamid II, Sultan 159, 212, 338, 340, 473
Abdullah Bey 473
Abdullah, Şeyh 412
Abdurrahman Efendi 361
Abdulrazak, Fawzi 5, 399
Abedi, Mehdi 302
'Abīda al-Salmānī 15
Abou-el-Haj, Rifaat Ali 151
Abraham ben Moses Yathom 215–16, 235
Abraham ben Shalom ha-Levi 216, 218, 220
Abū al-'Alā al-Ma'arrī 13, 100
Abū al-'Aynayn Muḥammad 290
Abū Bakr Muḥammad b. 'Alī at-Tājirī al-Ishbīlī 353
Abū al-Barakāt al-Baghdādī 9
Abū Dharr al-Harawī 111
Abū Dulaf al-Khazrajī 189, 192–3, 197, 198
Abū al-Fidā 473
Abū Ḥayyān al-Tawḥīdī 14–15, 17, 18
Abū Ibrāhīm, Aghlabid Emir 88
Abū al-Ghāzī Bahādur Khān 473
Abū al-Ghāzī Būrāshughli 361
Abū al-Qāsim al-Samarqandī 371
Abū al-Su'ūd, Şeyhülislam 206
Abū Muḥammad Ibn al-Hasan 14
Abū Nu'aym al-Iṣfahānī 15
Abū Qilāba 15
Abū Tāhā, 'Ali 291
Abū Tammām 17–18, 100
Abū 'Ubayd al-Qāsim b. Sallām 98
Abū Zāyid, 'Alī Husnī 289
Acoluth, Andreas 535
Adam, P. 80
'Adud al-Dīn al-Ījī 371, 372
Aesop 465
'Affāṣ, Bihnām Faḍīl 392
al-Afghāni, Jamāl ad-Dīn 431–2
Agâh Efendi 459
Agowlec'i, Nahapêt 511, 514, 518, 519
Ahmad, Qādī 5
Ahmad Ef. Şeyhzade 117
Aḥmad Khān, Sayyid 172
Ahmed III, Sultan 153, 202, 203, 206–7, 307, 357, 359, 412
al-Akhḍarī, 'Abd al-Raḥmān b. Muḥammad 372
Akimushkin, O. 118, 120
al-Akwa, Muhammad 313–14
Albin, Michael W. 3–6, 391
Albukher, Shmuel 239
Alexandratos, Gerasimos 475
Âli, Mustafa 47
Ali Bey (Albertus Bobovius) 461
Ali Çelebi 50–52, 55, 56
Ali, Derviş 117
Aliye, Fatma 466
Almosnino, Moshe 240
Alonzo, Alfonse Antun 496
Altınay, Ahmed Refik 203
Alvarès, D. Lévi 473
Amaraji, Yitzhak Bechor 243
Ambrosius, Teseus 533
'Amira, 'Abd Allāh 290
Amram, Nathan ben Ḥayyim 220
Anderson, Benedict 301
Anderson, Rufus 550–51, 556, 558, 559–60, 565

al-Anja, 'Abd al-Qādir Efendi 283
Anyagt', Dawit' 531
Ankiwrac'i, Yovhannês 518, 519
Antonius, George 389
Apkar 410
Appian 314
Arabajian, Mihran B. 468, 479
Arapean, Pogos 531
Arapean, Yovhannês Apowč'exc'i 531
Arcrowni, Grigor 539
Arrian 464
Aristotle 464
Arkoun, Muhammad 121
Arnold, T.W. 69
Arshag II, King 470
al-Artājī, Abū 'Abd Allāh M. b. Ḥāmid b. Mufarraj b. Ghiyāth 99
Asaf, Milad 290
Asaf, Yusuf Faris 291
Ashkeloni, Yosef ben Yitzhak 233
Ashkenazi, Avrahim 247
Ashkenazi, Bezalel Halevi 241, 242
Ashkenazi, Hayyim Ze'ev 243
Ashkenazi, Jonah ben Jacob 215
Ashkenazi, Sa'adi Halevi 242–3
Ashkenazi, Ya'akov 247
Ashkenazi, Yehuda Shmuel 247
ha-Ashkenazi, Yonah 234–5, 246
Asori, Zenob 530
al-'Asqalānī, Ibn Ḥajar 15, 92, 95
Atif, Patinakizade Mehmed 473
al-'Attār, Hasan 428, 432
'Attiya, Murqus 289
Aurelius, Marcus 461
Avakian, H.A. 407–20
Avicenna 127, 149
Awetik'eans, Gabriêl 524
Ayache, G. 303
Ayalon, Ami 277–97, 493–504
Ayash, Moshe Ya'akov 243
Ayman Fu'ād Sayyid 116
Aywasean, Gabriel 538
al-A'zamī, Nu'mān 291
Azharī, Muḥammad 183
Aziz Efendi 467
Azoviv, David Avraham 240
Azulai, Ḥayyim Joseph David 220

al-Bābi al-Halabī, Ahmad 289
al-Bābī al-Halabī, Mustafa 435
Bacon, Francis 4
Badr, slave of prince 'Abd Allāh 4
al-Bagdadi, Nadia 403
Bagramean, Movsês 528
Bagtasarean, Gowkas 538
Bahran, Muhammad bin Yahya 304
al-Bajūrī, Ibrāhīm b. Muhammad 372, 428
Bak, Nissan 495
Bak, Yisrael 495
Bakhkhash, Jamil 291
Balentz, Bedros 463
Balzac, Honoré 468
Banasun, Vincent 289
Banshi, Muhammad 291
Barboni, Michelangelo 519
Barelvī, Sayyid Aḥmad 173
Barki, Mordechai ben Yitzhak 247
Barth, C.G. 564
Bat-Sheva, Avraham 240
Bat-Sheva, Matiya 240
Baxter, Richard 562
Baydas, Khalīl 499
Bayezid II, Sultan 146
Baysal, Jale 365
Bedjan, Paul 568
Bedreddin, Hasan 473
Behar, Nissim 237
Behcet, Mustafa 475
Behic Efendi, Mehmed Emin 158–9
Beit-Arié, Malachi xvi, 33–46
Bek, Salim 291
Belīgh, Seyyid Ismā'īl 204
Bellarmino, Cardinal 463
Benayahu, M. 268
Ben Cheikh, Abdelkader 390, 395
Ben Cheneb, M. 303
Ben Na'eh, Yaron xxii, 225–75
Ben Simeon, Raphael Aaron 220
Ben Ya'akov, Yonah (Yonah ha-Ashkenazi) 234–5, 246
Ben Yisrael, Menashe 245
Benjamin, Walter 302
Berger, Lutz 404
Berkes, Niyazi 211, 338
Bernardini, Michele 114
Berquin, Arnaud 466, 476
Beshiktashlian, Mgrdich 470
Beyatlı, Yahya Kemal 203
Béziès, Charles 290
Bhabha, Homi K. 310

Birgivi / Birkawī, Muhammad b. Pīr 'Alī 155, 163, 360–61, 367, 371
Birnbaum, Eleazar 393
al-Bīrūnī, Abū Rayhān 19
Bishr al-Ḥāfī 15
Blair, Sheila 118
Bobovius, Albertus 461
Bobtchev, S. 479
Bobzin, Hartmut 404
Bochter, E. 354
Bogos, Arapoğlu 236
Bonaparte, Napoléon 166, 421–2, 461, 477
Borkenau, Franz 423
Bortoli, Antonio 519, 523, 525
Bosworth, C.E. 192–4
Boyarin, Jonathan 309
Breath, Edward 549–54 *passim*, 556, 558–62 *passim*, 564–8 *passim*
von Breydenbach, Bernhard 532
Brockelmann, Carl 3, 5
Browne, W.F. 169, 187
al-Bukhārī, Muhammad 9
Bukht-Naṣar (Nebukadnezar) 208
Bulliet, Richard W. xxiii, 189–200
Bunyan, John 468–9
Būrāshughli, Abū al-Ghāzī 361
Busbecq, Ogier Ghiselin 148, 161
al-Bustānī, Būtrus 288, 290
al-Bustānī, Sulaymān 464

Caillol, Henri 478
Calfa, Ambroise 458, 466, 467
Calfayan, Khoren 470
Čamč'eans, Mik'ayêl 524
Campe, Joachim Heinrich 466
Canfelias, Yom Tov 241
Cantemir, Demetrius 475
Carmona, Elia 471
Carrère, P. 65
Carter, Thomas Francis 148, 299, 407, 412, 413
Castro, Yitzhak ben Avraham 236
Cavaliere, Shlomo 239
Cayol, Henri 478
Celal-zade, Muhyi al-Din 117
Çemsir, Hafız Salih 119
Cevdet, Abdullah 470
Cevdet Pasha, Ahmed 161, 466, 472, 477
Chamchian, Michael 473
Chardin, Jean 113, 114, 116, 118, 120, 122
Chartier, Roger 402, 403
Chateaubriand, François-René 476, 477
Chauvin, V. 413
Cherezli, Salomon Israel 463
Chilingirian, Krikor 476
Chingiz Khan 208
Chrysostomos, Johannes 530
Chuli, Ya'akov 228
Churchill, William 459
Ciakciak, Emmanuel 466
Coakley, James F. xxiii, 545
Cole, Juan 402
Constantinides, Alexander 470, 473
Contes, G.P. 470
C'opanean, Aršak 542
Copernicus, Nicolas 4

al-Dabbāgh, 'Abd al-'Azīz 435
Dadian, Artin Pasha 478
Dadian, Mgrdich 468
Dāmād Ibrāhīm Pasha 202
Dāmullā Mirzā 'Abd al Raḥmān A'lām Mullā 119
Dāmullā Raḥīm-Jān 119
Danon, Avraham 245
Dapontes 475
al-Dārānī, Abū Sulaymān 14
al-Darini, Muhammad 290
Darnton, Robert 4
Darwīsh, Shaykh 437
Da'ūd, Yūsuf 291
Davrižec'i, Arak'êl 520
Dāwūd al-Tā'ī 14, 15–16
De Châteauvieux, Frédéric Lullin 477
De Cremone, Raimondi 409
Dedeyan, Dikran H. 477, 478
De Guignes 473
Demeerseman, André 5, 186, 187, 301, 302, 307–8, 404
De Mollenville, Herbelo 149
Denon, Vivant 422
Depasta, Anthony 463
Depasta, Nicholas 463
Derman, Uğur 119
Déroche, François 113–23
De Sacy, Sylvestre 461
De St Pierre, Bernardin 457
De Saussure, César 147
De Strata, Filippo 143, 319
De Toulon, Astruc ben Ya'akov 238
Diehl, Katharine Smith 6

van Dijk, Christoffel 509
Dikran Serafim Efendi 463
Di Marsigli, Conte 147
al-Dīnawarī, Abū Bakr 99
Dodge, Bayard 114
D'Ohsson, Ignace Mouradgea 147, 322
Donado, Giovanni 147–8
Dpir, Astowacatowr 530–31
Dpir, Martiros 532
Dpir, Pagtasar 511–12
Dpir, Sargis 532
Dpir, Yovhannês 530–31
Drugulin, W. 568
Drumev, Vasil 458
Du Marc, Edouard 290
Dumas, Alexandre 459, 467, 468, 470, 476, 477, 478
Duruy, Victor 473
Du Terrail, Ponson 468
Dwight, Henry Otis 471

Ebener, Khawaja 289
Ebied, R.Y. 97
Ebüzziya Tevfik 471
Edib, Halide 467
Eĝisê 527
Eickelman, Dale 300
Eisenstein, Elizabeth xxiv–vi, 4–5, 143, 144, 390, 391, 395, 397–403, 405, 406
Elnekave, Yosef ben Avrahim 238
Emmanuel, I.S. 229, 243, 262
Endress, Gerhard 391
Epictetus, 464
Erêc, Mesrop 528
Erewanc'i, Oskan 511, 516, 518, 520–21
Erewanc'i, Simêon 526–7
Erpenius, Thomas 409
Esad Efendi, Es-Seyid Mustafa 324, 326
Euclid 148, 149
Evliya Çelebi 321, 341–2
Eznik Koġbac'i 532

Fabian, Johannes 309
Fahmi, Mustafa 289
Falcon, Samuel 241
Faraji, Daniel 243
Faraji, Eliahu 243
Faris, Ibrahim Efendi 286, 289
Fāris al-Shidyāq 399, 403, 458, 461, 462, 472, 473
Fawāz, Iliyās 282, 290
Fawāz, Khalīl 290
Fawāz, Nakhla 290
Fawzi, Ibrahim 289
Febvre, Lucien 391, 399, 406
Fénélon, François 340, 458, 465, 471, 528
Ferera, Isaac 471
Féval, Paul 480
Findley, Carter Vaughn 395
Fischer, Michael M.J. 302
Fleischer, Cornell H. 47–63
Fox, M.V. 8
Fraenkel, Carlos 193
Franco, Avraham 235
Franco, Shlomo ben David 234
Franklin, Benjamin 461
French, Geoffrey 390
Fresco, David 480

Gabbay, Avraham ben Yedidia 234, 241, 245
Gabbay, Yehezkel 459
Gacek, Adam 103–112
Gaillard, L. 65
Galanos, Clemens 517
Galland, Antoine 149, 150, 409, 411
al-Garbi, El-Hajj Mehmed 149
Gdoura, Wahid 6, 392
Gedaliah, Don Yehuda (Ibn Gedalya) 238
Geiss, A. 410
Gengis Khan 208
Georgi, Simêon 511
Gharzūzi, Jurji 290
al-Ghazālī, Abū Ḥāmid 173
al-Ghazzī, Badr al-Dīn 104, 105, 106, 107–9, 110, 111
Ghush, Antun 290
Gibb, H. 206
Glass, Dagmar 394, 397
Göçek, Fatma Müge 151
Gökalp, Ziya 467
Goldsmith, Oliver 465
Gonzalez-Quijano, Yves 401, 402
Goš, Mxit'ar 526
Govrigean, Grigor 515
Graf, Georg 5
Graham, William 171, 181
Gran, Peter 4
Granjon, Robert 409
Gregorius XIII, Pope 409
Grohmann, A. 69

Gutenberg, Johannes xxiv, xxvi, 175, 227, 278, 297, 301, 334, 404, 506, 507, 508, 522

Habermas, Jürgen 402
Hacohen, Avraham ben Shmuel 232
Hacohen, Moshe 240
al-Ḥāfī, Bishr 15
Hafız Ahmed Efendi, Sahhaf 325, 331
Hafız Hasan Efendi, Sahhaf 331
Hafız Salih Çemsir 119
Hager, Abraham 241
Hájjī Khalīfah (Kâtib Çelebi) 15–17, 20, 150, 159, 473
Hakohen, Michael 220
al-Halabī, Ahmad al-Bābi 289
al-Ḥalabī, Ibrāhîm b. Muḥammad 372
al-Halabī, Mahmūd 289
al-Halabī, Mustafa al-Bābī 435
Halevy, Bessalel 460
Hallock, Homan 553–4, 556, 564
al-Hamadhānī, 'Abd al-Raḥmān b. 'Īsá 100
Hamawi, Dimitri 291
al-Ḥamawī, 'Īsá 291
Hamazaspean, T'adêos 518, 521, 522
Hamdullah, Şeyh 117
von Hammer Purgstall, Joseph 410, 461
Ḥammūda, Maḥmūd 'Abbās 390
Hananya, Jurji Habib 496–9 *passim*
Hanebutt-Benz, Eva 394
Hanna, 'Awad 289
Hanna, Yovhannês 530
Ḥaqqī, Ismā'īl 374, 375
Ḥaqqī, Muḥammad 182
al-Ḥarīrī, Abū Muḥammad al-Qāsim 98, 99
Hārūn al-Rashīd 473
Ḥasan al-Ḍiyā'ī 117
Hashim, Muhammad 291
Hayachini, Abraham 234
Hayguni, Armenag 475
Hayreddin Bey 52–3, 55
Ḥayyim Vital 215
Hazan, Avraham 239
Hazan, David 246
Hazan, Israel Moses 220
Hazan, Soloman 220
Hazan, Yehuda 246
Hekim, Shmuel 247
Hekim, Yitzhak ben Siman Tov 232, 247
Hekim, Yosef 232
Helitz, Shmuel 232
Helvacıoğlu 58, 59
Herder, Johann Gottfried 422
Herodotus 465
Herrera, Joseph Israel 478
Ḥikmat Allāh Maḥmūd, Mīrzā 119
al-Ḥillī, Ṣafī al-Dīn 189, 193–4, 197
Hilmî, Ahmed 473
Hindīya, Amīn 277–8, 289
Hippocrates 18, 19
Hirsh, R. 414, 418
Hisarian, Hovhannes 456, 458, 460
Hitti, Philip K. 180, 389
Holov, Yovhannés 517, 518–19
Homer 464
Hourani, Albert 391
Hugo, Victor 468, 476, 477
Hülâgü Khan 208, 424
Hunwick, John Owen 3
Hürmüzian, Edward 466
Hüsam al-Din Halife 117
Ḥusayn al-Jazā'irī 117
Husayn, Tāhā 295–6
Hüseyin Çelebi 51–2, 53
Hüseyin, El-Hac 329
Husnī, 'Alī 289
Hussein, M.A. xvii

Ibn al-'Abbār 410
Ibn Abī al-Su'ūd, Aḥmad ibn Ismā'īl 16
Ibn Abū al-Ḥawārī, Ahmad 15–16
Ibn al-'Adīm, Kamāl al-Dīn 98
Ibn al-'Alā', Abū 'Amr 14
Ibn 'Arabī, Muhyiddīn 13, 373
Ibn Asbāt, Yūsuf 14
Ibn Badīs, al-Mu'izz 5
Ibn Durustūyah, 'Abd Allāh ibn Ja'far 105
Ibn Gedalya 238
Ibn Habib, Ya'akov 238
Ibn Ḥajar al-'Asqalānī 15, 92, 95
Ibn Ḥanbal, Ahmad 13–14, 15
Ibn al-Iflīlī, Abū al-Qāsim Ibrāhīm b. Muḥammad 109
Ibn 'Īsá, Yūnus 15
Ibn Jamā'a, Badr al-Dīn 16–17, 104, 105, 106, 109, 111
Ibn al- Jawālīqī, Abu Mansūr Mawhūb 99–100
Ibn Junayd, Yaḥyá Maḥmūd 393
Ibn Kemāl (Kemāl Pāshā-zāde) 106
Ibn Khaldūn, 'Abd al-Rahman b. Muhammad 19–20, 173, 180, 206, 353, 472, 473

Ibn Khallād al-Rāmahurmuzī, 104, 110, 111
Ibn Khallikān, Abū-l 'Abbas Ahmad 9
Ibn al-Khashshāb 100
Ibn Lev, Yosef 233
Ibn Mas'ūd, Abdullāh 15
Ibn al-Nadīm, Abū'l-Faraj Muhammad b. Ishāq al-Warrāq 5, 20, 114, 122
Ibn al-Naḥḥās 100
Ibn Nahmias, David xxii, 231
Ibn Qayyim al-Jawzīya 13
Ibn Raslan, Ahmad 303–4
Ibn Riḍwān, 'Alī 12
Ibn Sīnā 127, 149
Ibn Sīrīn, Muhammad 18–19
Ibn al-Waḥid, Muhammad 115
Ibn Zunbul, Ahmad b. 'Alī 352
Ibnir, Khawaja 289
Ibrahim Bey 281
Ibrāhīm Efendi 176
Ibrāhīm Ḥaqqī-i Endurunu 373
Ibrāhīm al-Ḥarbī 117
Ibrâhîm Pasha, viceroy of Egypt 293, 373
Ibscher, Hugo 69, 80
al-Idrīsī, Muhammad 149
al-'Idwī, Hasan 429, 437
al-Ījī, 'Adud al-Dīn 371, 372
Iliyās, Khawājā 282
Imber, Colin 206
Inčičean, Ġowkas 526, 537
Innis, Harold xv, 399, 406
al-Ishbīlī, Abū Ḅakr Muḥammad b. 'Alī at-Tājirī 353
al-'Ishshī, Ahmad 289
Isidorides-Skylisses, John 476
Iskender, bookseller 463
Ismā'īl, Khedive of Egypt 5
Ismā'īl, Shah 467
Ismail Efendi, es-Seyyid el-Hac 324, 327, 330
Ismail Efendi Halife 117
Israelije, David 242
Istanli, Murad (Baron Henry Edward John Stanley) 461
'Iyāḍ, Qāḍī 104, 109, 110

al-Jabartī, 'Abd al-Rahmān 461
Ja'far Kātib Khātūnābādi, Mirzā 'Alī b. Muẓaffar 116
al-Jahil, Jirjis 290
al-Jāḥiẓ, Abū 'Uthmān 'Amr b. Bahr 17, 18
Jahon, Yitzhak 242
al-Jalakh, Habīb 290
Jalāl al-Din Rūmī 120
Jamal, Muhammad 291
James, David 115
al-Jamil, As'ad 290
al-Jawharī, Ismā'īl ibn Hāmid 205
Jawīsh, Fathullāh As'ad 290
Jawīsh, Sulaymān 286
al-Jazā'irī, Ḥusayn 117
al-Jazā'irī, Ṭāhir ibn Sạlih 106
Johns, Anthony H. 181
Josephus, Flavius 527
Jowgayec'i, Yovhannês 518
Jubran, Hanna 291
Julius II, Pope 314

Kal'ai, Hayyim Leon 242
Kal'ai, Judah 241–2
K'alant'arean, Y. 528
Kaldy-Nagy, Gy. 413
Kamil, Hasan 289
Kāmil, Muhammad 'Alī 289
Kâmil Pasha, Yusuf 458, 465, 466, 467, 471
Kant, Immanuel 422
Karabacek, Josef 189, 197
Karahisari el-Hac Ali Rıza Efendi 326
K'armatenec', Yovhannês 517
Kasap, Teodor 465, 470, 478
al-Kāshifī, 'Alī b. Husayn 373–4
Kashti, David ben Eliahu 233
Kasım, son of Helvacıoğlu 58–63
Kaspariants, Minas 465
Kâtib Çelebi (Hájjī Khalīfah) 15–17, 20, 150, 159, 473
Kavafian, Hovsep 474
Kazancızade, Ahmad Ef. 117
Keçicizade, Macid Pasha 479
Kélékian, Diran 471
Kemal, Namık 431–2, 471, 478
Kemāl Pāshā-zāde 106
Kemaleddin Efendi, Sahhaf es-Seyyid Mehmed 327, 329, 331
Kempe, Martin 535
Kempis, Thomas à 463
K'êomiwrčean, Eremia 511, 516, 522
Kerem, Âşık 467
Kesarac'i, Xač'atowr 517, 518
Kethuda, Mahmud 54
al-Khafash, Sālih 279, 291
Khalid, Adeeb 302, 309

Khalidov, A. 118, 120
Khān, Sayyid Aḥmad 172
Khapsoulas, John 462
al-Khashaf, As'ad 290
al-Khashshāb, 'Umar 289
al-Khaṭīb al-Baghdādī 104, 105, 107–8
al-Khaṭīb al-Tabrīzī 100
Khātūnābādi, Mirzā 'Alī b. Muẓaffar Ja'far Kātib 116
Khayr al-Dīn al-Tūnisī 431, 472
al-Khuri, Amin 290, 291
al-Khuri, Khalil 290
Khuri, Shukrallah Nasrallah 291
Kilburn, S.S. 561
Kilpatrick, Hilary 481
Kimhi, David 232
Kieffer, Daniel 461
Kolot, Yovhannės 511, 529, 530
Kreiser, Klaus 394, 403
Kretac'i, Abraham 529
al-Kubba, Sayyid Muhyī al-Dīn 283
Kumarian, Krikor 464
Kunt, Metin 60

al-Labābidī, Misbāh 291
Labīb, Klaudios xxiii
Lamartine, Alphonse 476
al-Lamtī, Ahmad b. Mubārak 435
Lane, Edward 281
al-Laqānī, Ibrāhīm b. Ibrāhīm 371
Lasfu, Martin 496
Leibniz, Gottfried Wilhelm 522
Lermina, Jules 470
Levey, Martin 5
ha-Levi, Abraham ben Shalom 216, 218, 220
Lévi-Provençal, E. 303
Levonean, Sogomon 521
Levtzion, Nehemia 172
Long, Albert 469
Loria, Jacques 480, 481
Louis XV, King 165
Lovejoy, Elijah P. 550
Lucian 464
Luftī Paşa 207
Lutfi, Agop 465

al-Ma'arrī, Abū al-'Alā 13, 100
MacKay, P.A. 98, 101
Maclean, A.J. 568
McLuhan, Marshall 3, 342, 399, 406
Maḥbūb b. Ṣadr al-Sharī'a 116
al-Mahdī, 'Abd al-Khāliq 289
al-Mahdī, Muhammad al-'Abbāsī 437
Mahdi, Muhsin 127–41, 308, 396
Mahmūd, apprentice of Ali Çelebi 51–7 *passim*, 63
Mahmūd II, Sultan 160, 212, 322, 366, 461
Maimonides xvi
Maliji, Muhammad 289
Mallouf, Nassif 476
Mamourian, Matteos (Matt'êos Mamowrean) 476, 539
al-Manṣūr 353
Maragos, Osta 246
Marçais, Georges 65, 88
Marcel, J.J. 426
Mar'ī, Jurjī 291
Marker, Gary 398
Markos, Mahtesi 532
al-Marrūdhī, Abū Bakr 13
Martin, Henri-Jean 391, 399
Marzolph, Ulrich 397
Marzvanec'i, Grigor 511–12, 529–30
Masābikī, Mīkhā'īl 479
Masābikī, Niqūla 426
Masābikī, Yūsuf 426
Maspéro 473
al-Masrī, Muhammad 291
Maštoc', Mesrop 505
Matar, Elias 467
Matra, James Mario 158
Matza, David ben Aharon 240
Mavrocordato, Nicolas 460
Maydani, Salim 291
Medhurst, Walter Henry 177–8
de Medina, Judah 240
de Medina, Moshe 240
de Medina, Samuel 242
Megapart, Yakob 514–15
Meghamiz, Zeki 473
Mehmed, Ottoman Prince 49
Mehmed Said Efendi 202, 411
Mehmed II Fatih, Ottoman Sultan 327
Melamed, Ephraim 248
Ménage, Victor 60
Meninski, Mesgnien 353
Meo, Boulus (Bulus) 501
Merquam, Henri 466
Messick, Brinkley 299–317, 395
Metaxas, Nicodemus 410

Mez, A. 17
Michaud, Joseph 427, 462
Midhat Efendi, Ahmed 465, 466–7, 469, 470, 471, 472, 474, 478
Midhat Ibnül Ahmed 479
Mikhailovski, Nikola 480
Minorsky, V. 5
al-Minyawī, Muhammad Imbābī 289
Misailidis, Evangelinos 479
al-Miskawayh, Abū 'Alī Aḥmad 18
Mitchell, Timothy 406
Mitri, Najib 289
Mizrahi, Eliya 233
Mizrahi, Faraj Ḥayyim 220
Moda'i, Nissim Ḥayyim 247
Molcho, Yosef 242
Montesquieu, Charles de Secondat, baron de 460
Moretti, Giacomo 519
Morse, Sidney E. 550
Moses Israel 216
Moses Yeshua Tuviana 218
Moshe ben El'azar 232
Moshe ben Shmuel Fisilino 231
Mourkidès, L. 480
Mrgowz, Yovhannês 530, 531
al-Mu'ayyad, Ṣādiq 472
Mubārak, 'Alī 430
Muhammad IV, Sultan of Morocco 5
Muhammad Alī Pasha xviii, 5, 166, 220, 278, 426
Muḥammad Azharī 183
Muhyiddin Çelebi 49
Münif Pasha 160, 458
Murad II, Sultan 49
Murad III, Sultan 148
Musābikī, Niqūla 426
Musābikī, Yūsuf 426
Mushahwar, Bandali 503
Mustafa, Sahhaf el-Hac 326, 330
Mustafa Âli 47
Mustafa Efendi, Hoca 467
Müteferrika, Ibrahim xxv, 6, 143, 145, 147, 152–4 *passim,* 156–7, 158, 159, 161, 165, 171, 175, 178, 181, 182, 202, 203, 205–6, 207–8, 210–13, 322–3, 325–6, 327, 329, 334, 341–2, 403, 411, 412, 417

Nādir Shah 528
al-Naharī, Abdallāh 291
Nahman, Avraham ben David 241
Nahman, Mordechai 241–2
Naḥman Sa'dun 218
Nahmias, Samuel ben David 231
al-Nakha'ī, Ibrāhīm b. Yazīd 111
Namık Kemal 431–2, 471, 478
Naon, Avram 471
Napoléon Bonaparte 166, 421–2, 461, 477
Narekac'i, Grigor 514, 526, 530, 531
al-Nasafī, 'Umar b. Muḥammad 371
Na'san, Muhammad Sa'id 291
Nāṣir-i Khusrow 354
Nasīr al-Dīn al-Tūsī 148
Nasr, Salim 290
Nasrallah, Joseph 5
Nawfal Efendi, Ni'matullāh 472
Nazareanc' Step'anos 539
Nazif, Süleyman 470
Nazım, Hüseyin 480
Nebukadnezar (Bukht-Naṣar) 208
Needham, Joseph 5
Nersesovič', Astowactowr 517
Nesimi 54, 56–7
Nicolaîdes, Demetrios 480
Niebuhr, Carsten 300–302
Nuri, Celal 160
Nusayr, 'Âyida Ibrâhīm 369, 392

Öljeytü, Il-Khan 115, 121
Omont, H. 307, 413, 414
Ong, Walter J. 309, 310
Ôrbelean, Step'an 527
Oskanean, Xač'atowr 537
Oskanyan, Ninel 536
Osman, Kayiszade Hafiz 119, 120–21

de Paganino, Alessandro 127, 128
Palachi, Hayyim 243, 247
Pardo, Raphael Hayyim 235
Pardoe, Julia 455
Paronean, Yakob 539
P'arpec'i, Gazar 526
Parsêgean, Gabriêl Sebastac'i 532
Patroklos, I. 478
Paulus V, Pope 409
Peçevi, Ibrahim 150, 159, 359
Pedersen, Johannes 5, 302, 390
Pehlivanian, Meliné xxii, 505–44
Pellico, Silvio 479
Perkins, Justin 469, 550, 551, 553, 555–6, 559, 560, 562, 564, 565, 566
Petersen, Theodore C. xvii, 65–88

Petrosean, Step'anos 532
Pfander, K.G. 461
Piccolos, Nicolas 456
Piferno, Nissim Hayyim 236
Pius IV, Pope 515
Pius V, Pope 515
Platt, Thomas Pell 547
Poinssot, Louis 65, 88
Poli, Yaakov 247
Pontrimoli, Avraham 247
Pontrimoli, Raphael Haim 247
Postel, Guillame 532
Poujoulat, J.J. François 462
Povis, Giovanni Battista 519
Proudfoot, Ian 165–88, 405
Pushkin, Alexandr 499

Qabawat, Iskander 291
Qabil, 'Umar 289
al-Qābisī, Abū al-Ḥasan 111
Qādī Ahmad 5
Qâḍîzâdeh Istanbulû Aḥmad b. Muḥammad Amîn 361, 367
Qâḍîzâdeh Mehmed 361
al-Qalāl, Aḥmad Muḥammad 392
Qalfaz, Nakhla 290, 291
al-Qalqashandī, Ahmad 105–6
al-Qastamūnī, 'Alī Ḥāfiz 374
Quiring-Zoche, Rosemarie 116
al-Qullusī, Abū Bakr 410
Qutb, Sayyid 296

Racine, Jean 472
Raḍwān, Abū al-Futūḥ 5
Rāgıb Mehmed Paşa 118, 135
Rahma, Mikhā'īl 291
Rakīm, Efendi 169
al-Rāmahurmuzī, Ibn Khallād 104, 110, 111
Ramazan b. Ismail 117, 118
Rashīd al-Dīn 118–19
al-Rashīd, Hārūn 473
Rashīd, Muḥammad 358
Raşid Mehmed Efendi 158
Râsih, Osman 465
Recaîzade Mahmud Ekrem 478–9
Recep Halife 117
Refi, Hafiz 465
Reichmuth, Stefan 201–13
Rendu, Ambroise 466
Rezvan, E. 118, 120
Rhasis, Georges 464
Ricaut, Paul 146–7
Richardson, Brian 145
Richebourg, Émile 469
Richmond, Leigh 469
Riḍwān, Abū al-Futūḥ 5
Rifaat Ali Abou-el-Haj 151
al-Rifā'ī, 'Abdallāh 291
al-Rifā'ī, Muhammad Sa'id 289
Rivola, Francesco 535
Roberts, C.H. xvii
Robertson, William 465, 472
Robinson, Francis 171–3, 299–300, 302, 400
Roditi, Benzion Binyamin 247
Roditi, Yehoshu'a Moses 247
Roper, Geoffrey 389–406
Rosenthal, Franz 7–29
Rosenthal, M. 249, 252, 260, 261, 263, 265
Rosenzweig, Fischel 290
Rossi, Binyamin ben Moshe 235
Rossi, Ettore 305
Rowland-Smith, Diana 215–21
Roy, Rammohan 172
Rozanes, Avraham 235, 241
Rubir, Khalil 290
Rūmī, Jalāl al-Din 120
Rushdī Bāshā, 'Abd al-Raḥmān 429
Rüstem Paşa 58, 59, 61

Saba, Hanna 289
Ṣābāt, Khalīl 302, 305, 390
Sabev, Orlin (Orhan Salih) xxiv, xxv, 143–63, 319–32
Sabih, Muhammad 'Ali 289
Sabri, Muhammad 290
de Sacy, Sylvestre 461
Sadir, Ibrahim 286, 290
Ṣādiq, Ibn Muḥammad Ḥusayn Muḥammad 119
Ṣadr-i Dhiyā 119
Sadrā, Mullā 135
Sadullah Efendi, Sahhaf Ibrahim 325–6, 330
Ṣafī al-Dīn al-Ḥillī 189, 193–4, 197
Šahamirean, Šahamir 528
Šahamirean, Yakob 528
Said Efendi, Yirmisekiz Mehmed 202, 411
Said Çelebi 152, 153, 161
Sa'īd Pasha, viceroy of Egypt 5
Sa'īd, Būlus 291, 501–2, 503
Sa'id, Wadi 291, 501–2, 503
Salāh al-Dīn al-Ayyūbī (Saladin) 432

Salih, Muhammad 289
Salih, Orhan (Orlin Sabev) xxiv, xxv, 143–63, 319–32
Salisbury, Edward E. 560, 562
al-Salmānī, ʻAbīda 15
Salmon Ibn Yeruham 8
al-Samʻānī, ʻAbd al-Karīm 104
al-Samarqandī, Abū al-Qāsim 371
Samartsides, Christophoros 480
al-Samhūdī, Nūr al-Dīn Abū al-Ḥasan ʻAlī 104, 105
Sami Pasha, Abdurrahman 471
Sami, Şemseddin 466, 472, 473
Sand, George 468
al-Sanūsī, Muhammad b. ʻAlī 435
al-Sanūsī, Muhammad b. Yūsuf 372
Sarafean, Kleopatra 527
Sardar, Ziauddin 396
Sarkīs, Khalīl 288, 290, 472
Sarkīs, Rizqallāh 291
al-Sasī, Muhammad 289
Sayyid Aḥmad Khān 172
al-Sayyid, Jīhān Maḥmūd 393
Schaefer, Karl xxiii
Schiller, Friedrich 422
Schimmel, Annemarie 181
von Schlechta-Wssehrd, Ottocar 461, 472
Schleifer, Abdullah 401
von Schmid, Christoph 466, 479
Schröder, Johann Joachim 522
Schulze, Reinhard 345–88, 398, 421–55
Sebastacʻi, Mikʻayêl 515
Sebastacʻi, Mxitʻar 523–4
Sebastacʻi, Parsêg 532
Sebastacʻiner, Hakob 532
Sebastacʻiner, Parsêg 532
Segneri, Paolo 464
Šêhrimanean, Gaspar 511, 518
Seignobos, Charles 347
Selim, Prince 49
Selim I, Sultan 146
Selim III, Sultan 157, 158, 212
Senefelder, Alois 177, 183, 301, 366
Senior, Ben 247
Şevket Efendi, Mehmed 326
Sezgin, Fuat 3, 5
al-Shaʻbī, Abū al-Qāsim 19
Sharaf, Mahmud 289
Shadīd, Bishāra 478
al-Shahīd al-Thānī al-ʻĀmilī 104, 105, 106, 109
Shahin, Jirjis 290
al-Shahrazūrī, Ibn al-Salāḥ 104, 109, 110, 111
al-Shākir, Shākir 291
Shaul, Hayyim Yitzhak 247
al-Shawkānī, Muhammad 313–14
Shayt, Yusuf Jirjis 285, 289
al-Shidyāq, Fāris 399, 403, 458, 461, 462, 472, 473
Shifāʻī, ʻUmar 350
Shihāb, ʻAbd al-Ghanī 289
Shimon, Moshe 240
Shimon, Shlomo 240
Shuʻba b. al-Ḥajjāj 15
van Sichem, Christophel 512
Sid, Yosef ben Yitzhak 238
al-Sīrāfī, Abū Saʻīd 14–15
Skeat, T.C. xvii
Skouphos, N. 477
Skovgaard-Petersen, Jakob 400
Slaveikov, P.R. 476
Šmavonean, Yarowtʻiwn (Širazecʻi) 528–9, 536
Šnorhali, Nersês 514, 518, 519, 522, 527
Sogineancʻ Tʻadêos 529
Soloman al-Gazi 215
Soloman, Joel Moses 220
Soncino, Gershom ben Moses 215, 232, 239
Soncino, Gershom ben Eliezer 215, 232, 239
Soncino, Moshe 239
Soullides, Nikolaki 470
Spandarean, Spandar 541
Stamatiades, Alexander 470
Stamenes, N. 480
Stanley, Henry Edward John (Murad Istanli) 461
Stepʻanean, Yovsêpʻ 529
Stoddard, David T. 560
Strauss, Johann 397, 455–92
Suavi, Ali 461, 464
Subhi, Abdüllatif 472
Sue, Eugène 459, 462, 468, 470, 476–7, 480
Sufayr, Musa 291
Sufayr, Yusuf 291
Sufyān al-Thawrī 14, 15
al-Sufyānī, Abū'l-Abbās Ahmed ibn Muhammed 5
Sukkar, Muhammad 289
Süleyman Çelebi 466
Süleyman Pasha 473
Süleyman Penah Efendi 157–9
Süleyman, Şahabeddin 470

Süleyman I Kanuni, Sultan 48, 50, 55–6, 60, 61, 206, 432
al-Ṣūlī, Abū Bakr Muhammad 105
Sultanshah T'oxat'c'i (Bartolomeo Abagaro) xxii, 508, 515–516, 535
al-Suyūṭī, Jalāl al-Dīn 350
Svačean, Yovhannês 538
Sylvestre de Sacy 461
Szyliowicz, J.S. 333–43, 398

Tağean, Yakob 528
al-Ṭahṭāwī, Rifā'a Rāfi' 354, 428, 432, 464–5, 471, 473
al-Tā'ī, Dāwūd 14, 15–16
Taitazak, Shlomo 239
Taitazak, Yosef 239
al-Taji, Muhammad 291
Tajir, Fathallah 282, 290
al-Ṭanāḥī, Maḥmūd Muḥammad 392
al-Tarabishi, Muhammad Khalifa 289
al-Tarjumān al-Mayūrqī, 'Abd Allāh 461
Tarrazi, Mitri 291
Ṭāshkandī, 'Abbās ibn Ṣāliḥ 393
Ṭāshköprüzādeh, Aḥmad ibn Muṣṭafā 20
Tat'ewac'i, Grigor 513, 530, 531
al-Tawḥīdī, Abū Ḥayyān 14–15, 17, 18
al-Ṭayālisī, Abū al-Walīd 108
Teghtabanian, P. 476
Terzian, Thomas 470
Terznc'i, Xač'atowr 516
Terznc'i, Yovhannês 516
Tevfik, Ebüzziya 471
Thevet, André 146
Thököly, Imre 152
Thomas à Kempis 463
Thurneyesser zum Thurm, Leonhard 533
al-Tibi, Rashid 291
Tilkian, Vichen 475
al-Tirmidhī, Abū 'Īsá Muḥammad 374
Toledano, Eliezer 238
Tolstoy, Leo 499
T'oxat'c'i, Abgar (Sultanshah) xxii, 508, 515–516, 535
Tozlian, Arrakel 463
Tsakyroglou, Michael 471
Tsankov, Dragan 478
al-Tūkhī, Ahmad 429
Tuqtamishoglu, 'Abd al-'Azīz 360
al-Tūnisī, Khayr al-Dīn 431, 472
al-Tūsī, Nasīr al-Dīn 148

Tzarfati, Yaakov 239

Ubicini, A. 465, 466, 478
'Ulaysh, Muhammad 429, 432
Urban VII, Pope 517
Ütüdjian, Garabed S. 478, 479

Vajda, G. 8, 97, 101
Valensi, Ya'akov 246
Vanandec'i, Ğowkas 521–2
Vanandec'i, Matt'êos 521
Vanandec'i, Mik'ayêl 521
Vanandec'i, T'ômas 511, 521
Vankulu Mehmed Efendi 156, 157
Vartan Pasha 457, 458, 459, 460, 469–70, 475
Vasıf Efendi 158
Vehbī, Seyyid 206
Vendotis, George 465
Verne, Jules 340, 468
Voll, John Obert 172
Voltaire 340
Voukas, Vasilaki 464

al-Wadī-Ashī, Aḥmad b. Muḥammad 116
Wahbi, Mustafa 429
al-Wajīh al-Naḥwī 13
Wāsif, Aḥmad 358
Watson, William J. 156, 411
Watt, W. Montgomery 171
Watts, Richard 547
Wells, Charles 461
Wertheim, Shimshon 236
White, Charles 143, 159, 462
Wilde, Oscar 319
Williams, Henry G. 462
Williams, Raymond 144
Witkam, Jan Just 89–102
Wolff, Joseph 547
Wright, A.H. 554–5, 568

Xaldareanc', Grigor 527
Xenos, Stephanos 458
Xorenac'i, Movsês 520, 521

Ya'abetz, Shlomo 232–3, 239, 244
Ya'abetz, Yosef 232–3, 239–40, 244
Ya'ari, Abraham 218, 229, 236, 243, 246, 248, 250, 251, 271
Yahya Kemal Beyatlı 203
Yakob I, Patriarch 515

Yalman, A.E. 339
Yamut, Muhammad 'Umar 291
Yani, 'Abduh 291
Yāqūt al-Hamawī 17–18, 117
Yatom, Avraham ben Moshe 215–16, 235
Yazıcıoğlu Mehmed 155
al-Yāzijī, Nāsīf 282
Yehuda ben Yosef Sasson 231
Yeremian, Hovhannes 464
Yesaian, Emmanuel 470
Yohannan, Mar 553
Yosef ben 'Ayad Kabzi 231
Young, Edward 464
Young, M.J.L. 97
Young, Sarah Ann 560
Yovhannês, Č'nč'in 532
Yovhanniseany, Abgar 541
Yusuf, Fawzi 502–3

Zabara, Ahmad Muhammad 314–15
Zabara, Muhammad 313–14
al-Zabīdī, Muhammad Murtada 117, 429
Zaccone, Pierre 470
Zadik, Abraham 215
Zahhar, Lutfallah 290
Zaid Aga 411
Zand, Aziz 287–8, 289
Zarbhanalean, Garegin 515
al-Zarkashī, Badr al-Dīn 18
Zayd Ibn Thābit 103
Zaydān, Jurjī 287–8, 471, 473, 476
al-Zayn, Ahmad 'Arif 291
Zohrab, Krikor 471
Zohrabian, Hovhannes 461

For Product Safety Concerns and Information please contact our EU
representative GPSR@taylorandfrancis.com
Taylor & Francis Verlag GmbH, Kaufingerstraße 24, 80331 München, Germany

www.ingramcontent.com/pod-product-compliance
Lightning Source LLC
Chambersburg PA
CBHW080402300426
44113CB00015B/2378
* 9 7 8 1 0 3 2 9 1 8 2 8 0 *